The Complete Reference™

Networking
Third Edition

Bobbi Sandberg

New York Chicago San Francisco
Athens London Madrid
Mexico City Milan New Delhi
Singapore Sydney Toronto

Cataloging-in-Publication Data is on file with the Library of Congress

Networking: The Complete Reference, Third Edition

1 2 3 4 5 6 7 8 9 0   DOC DOC   1 0 9 8 7 6 5

ISBN   978-0-07-182764-5
MHID   0-07-182764-1

Sponsoring Editor
Roger Stewart

Editorial Supervisor
Patty Mon

Project Manager
Asheesh Ratra, MPS Limited

Acquisitions Coordinator
Amanda Russell

Technical Editors
Randall Nollan
Dwight Spivey
Van Aguirre

Copy Editor
Kim Wimpsett

Proofreader
Lisa McCoy

Indexer
Jack Lewis

Production Supervisor
James Kussow

Composition
MPS Limited

Illustration
MPS Limited

Art Director, Cover
Jeff Weeks

Cover Designer
Jeff Weeks

Great thanks and humble appreciation to
all of those who helped with this book.
And to my kids and their kids, and ever
and always to Sandy.

About the Author

Bobbi Sandberg is a small business consultant and retired CPA who has been a trainer, instructor, and teacher of all things computer in the Pacific Northwest for more than 40 years. She has "played" with computers since they occupied entire rooms and required perforated paper tape and punch cards. Today, she teaches hardware and software classes, solves hardware and software issues for a number of clients, and keeps networks functional on a regular basis. Bobbi is the author or coauthor of several computer books, including *QuickBooks 2015: The Small Business Guide*, *Quicken 2015: The Official Guide*, *Quicken 2014: The Official Guide*, *Microsoft Office 2013 QuickSteps*, and *Computing for Seniors QuickSteps*.

About the Technical Editors

Randal Nollan has been working with technology since the late 1970s when he wrote his first program on pink punch cards. Randal joined the U.S. Navy in 1980 as an Aviation Ordnanceman and retired in 2001. During that time, he maintained the dBase III vaccination database for the squadron corpsman and was always in the thick of maintaining the token ring network, computers, and terminals they had at the time. He graduated from Skagit Valley College CIS (networking) and MIT (programming) in 2003. He worked in Internet tech support from 2003 to 2005 and has since been working in computer repair for a local telephone company on Whidbey Island, Washington. In his spare time, he enjoys the outdoors by fishing, crabbing, bicycling, camping, and hunting. Indoor fun includes playing with anything tech related, remodeling his home, and making wine from any fruit that lands on his doorstep; some time he may even stop working and drink it.

Dwight Spivey is the author of more than 20 books on computers and technology and has happily lent his expertise as a technical editor to several more titles. Dwight is happily married to Cindy, and they reside on the Gulf Coast of Alabama along with their four children. He studies theology, draws comic strips, and roots for the Auburn Tigers in his ever-decreasing spare time.

Van Aguirre is an information technology specialist who has broad experience in the field. Since the late 1990s, he has developed and taught courses in networking and multimedia technology, computing security, computer crime forensics, IT risk management, IT business continuity, and disaster recovery planning. Working with other IT professionals, he has planned and managed the implementation of evolving technologies, including virtualization, mobile, and cloud computing to support institutional business and strategic initiatives. As a project manager in educational technology, Van has established and promoted successful apprenticeship programs in IT desk service management for college students, integrating LEAN principles and ITIL processes to supplement technical skills.

Contents

Acknowledgments

This book, like most others, is the end product of a lot of hard work by many people. All of the people involved deserve great thanks. A special thank-you to the following:

- Roger Stewart, acquisitions editor at McGraw-Hill Education, for his support, understanding, and always available ear. He and his team are unbeatable.

- Two other members of the team, Patty Mon and Amanda Russell. Patty is the finest editorial supervisor around. She is beyond helpful, always considerate and thoughtful, and just "there" for any questions. She is a gem. The generous, organized, and always on "top" of any concern or issue, editorial coordinator Amanda Russell. Amanda either has the answer at hand or finds out quickly and reliably. These few descriptive words are only the tip of the iceberg when discussing their talent, professionalism, and always generous spirits.

- The technical editors, Randy Nollan and Dwight Spivey, for the support, suggestions, and ideas. These skilled and proficient gentlemen made the process fun. And a special thank-you to Van Aguirre for his hard work at the beginning of the project.

- Asheesh Ratra and his team at MPS Limited, who deserve great thanks and appreciation for their hard work and expertise. It was a pleasure and honor working with them!

Introduction

This book is designed as a thorough, practical planning guide and underpinning of knowledge for IT networking professionals around the world, including students of IT networking courses, beginning network administrators, and those seeking work in the IT networking field.

Benefit to You, the Reader

After reading this book, you will be able to set up an effective network. The book teaches everything, including methodology, analysis, case examples, tips, and all the technical supporting details needed to suit an IT audience's requirements, so it will benefit everyone from beginners to those who are intermediate-level practitioners.

What This Book Covers

This book covers the details as well as the big picture for networking, including both physical and virtual networks. It discusses how to evaluate the various networking options and explains how to manage network security and troubleshooting.

Organization

This book is logically organized into six parts. Within each part, the chapters start with basic concepts and procedures, most of which involve specific networking tasks, and then work their way up to more advanced topics.

It is not necessary to read this book from beginning to end. Skip around as desired. The following sections summarize the book's organization and contents.

Part I: Network Basics

This part of the book introduces networking concepts and explains both the OSI and TCP/IP models.

- **Chapter 1**: What Is a Network?
- **Chapter 2**: The OSI Reference Model

Part II: Network Hardware

This part of the book discusses the various hardware items used in a computer network. It also explains some basics when designing a network.

- **Chapter 3**: Network Interface Adapters
- **Chapter 4**: Network Interface Adapters and Connection Devices
- **Chapter 5**: Cabling a Network
- **Chapter 6**: Wireless LANs
- **Chapter 7**: Wide Area Networks
- **Chapter 8**: Server Technologies
- **Chapter 9**: Designing a Network

Part III: Network Protocols

This part of the book explains the various rules and protocols for networks.

- **Chapter 10**: Ethernet Basics
- **Chapter 11**: 100Base Ethernet and Gigabit Ethernet
- **Chapter 12**: Networking Protocols

Part IV: Network Systems

This part of the book discusses the various network operating systems.

- **Chapter 13**: TCP/IP
- **Chapter 14**: Other TCP/IP Protocols
- **Chapter 15**: The Domain Name System
- **Chapter 16**: Internet Services

Part V: Network Operating Services

In this part of the book, you will learn a bit more about the basics of some of the other services available, including cloud networking. In Chapter 23, you will learn some of the basics needed to secure your network.

- **Chapter 17**: Windows
- **Chapter 18**: Active Directory
- **Chapter 19**: Linux
- **Chapter 20**: Unix
- **Chapter 21**: Other Network Operating Systems and Networking in the Cloud

Part VI: Network Services

From clients to security to the all-important backup, this section covers some of the day-to-day operations in networking.

- **Chapter 22**: Network Clients
- **Chapter 23**: Network Security Basics

Conventions

All how-to books—especially computer books—have certain conventions for communicating information. Here's a brief summary of the conventions used throughout this book.

Menu Commands

Windows and most other operating systems make commands accessible on the menu bar at the top of the application window. Throughout this book, you are told which menu commands to choose to open a window or dialog or to complete a task. The following format is used to indicate menu commands: Menu | Submenu (if applicable) | Command.

Keystrokes

Keystrokes are the keys you must press to complete a task. There are two kinds of keystrokes:

- **Keyboard shortcuts**   Combinations of keys you press to complete a task more quickly. For example, the shortcut for "clicking" a Cancel button may be to press the ESC key. When you are to press a key, you will see the name of the key in small caps, like this: ESC. If you must press two or more keys simultaneously, they are separated with a hyphen, like this: CTRL-P.

- **Literal text**   Text you must type in exactly as it appears in the book. Although this book doesn't contain many instances of literal text, there are a few. Literal text to be typed is in boldface type, like this: Type **help** at the prompt.

- **Monospace font**   Text that you see at the command line. It looks like this:

```
Nslookup - nameserver
```

PART

I

Network Basics

CHAPTER 1

What Is a Network?

At its core, a network is simply two (or more) connected computers. Computers can be connected with cables or telephone lines, or they can connect wirelessly with radio waves, fiber-optic lines, or even infrared signals. When computers are able to communicate, they can work together in a variety of ways: by sharing their resources with each other, by distributing the workload of a particular task, or by exchanging messages. Today, the most widely used network is the Internet. This book examines in detail how computers on a network communicate; what functions they perform; and how to go about building, operating, and maintaining them.

The original model for collaborative computing was to have a single large computer connected to a series of terminals, each of which would service a different user. This was called *time sharing* because the computer divided its processor clock cycles among the terminals. Using this arrangement, the terminals were simply communications devices; they accepted input from users through a keyboard and sent it to the computer. When the computer returned a result, the terminal displayed it on a screen or printed it on paper. These terminals were sometimes called *dumb* terminals because they didn't perform any calculations on their own. The terminals communicated with the main computer, never with each other.

As time passed and technology progressed, engineers began to connect computers so that they could communicate. At the same time, computers were becoming smaller and less expensive, giving rise to mini- and microcomputers. The first computer networks used individual links, such as telephone connections, to connect two systems. There are a number of computer networking types and several methods of creating these types, which will be covered in this chapter.

Local Area Network

Soon after the first IBM PCs hit the market in the 1980s and rapidly became accepted as a business tool, the advantages of connecting these small computers became obvious. Rather than supplying every computer with its own printer, a network of computers could share a single printer. When one user needed to give a file to another user, a network eliminated the need to swap floppy disks. The problem, however, was that connecting a dozen computers in an office with individual point-to-point links between all of them was not practical. The eventual solution to this problem was the local area network (LAN).

A LAN is a group of computers connected by a shared medium, usually a cable. By sharing a single cable, each computer requires only one connection and can conceivably communicate with any other computer on the network. A LAN is limited to a local area by the electrical properties of the cables used to construct them and by the relatively small number of computers that can share a single network medium. LANs are generally restricted to operation within a single building or, at most, a campus of adjacent buildings.

Some technologies, such as fiber optics, have extended the range of LANs to several kilometers, but it isn't possible to use a LAN to connect computers in distant cities, for example. That is the province of the wide area network (WAN), as discussed later in this chapter.

In most cases, a LAN is a baseband, packet-switching network. An understanding of the terms *baseband* and *packet switching*, which are examined in the following sections, is necessary to understand how data networks operate because these terms define how computers transmit data over the network medium.

Baseband vs. Broadband

A baseband network is one in which the cable or other network medium can carry only a single signal at any one time. A broadband network, on the other hand, can carry multiple signals simultaneously, using a discrete part of the cable's bandwidth for each signal. As an example of a broadband network, consider the cable television service you probably have in your home. Although only one cable runs to your TV, it supplies you with dozens of channels of programming at the same time. If you have more than one television connected to the cable service, the installer probably used a splitter (a coaxial fitting with one connector for the incoming signals and two connectors for outgoing signals) to run the single cable entering your house to two different rooms. The fact that the TVs can be tuned to different programs at the same time while connected to the same cable proves that the cable is providing a separate signal for each channel at all times. A baseband network uses pulses applied directly to the network medium to create a single signal that carries binary data in encoded form. Compared to broadband technologies, baseband networks span relatively short distances because they are subject to degradation caused by electrical interference and other factors. The effective maximum length of a baseband network cable segment diminishes as its transmission rate increases. This is why local area networking protocols such as Ethernet have strict guidelines for cable installations.

NOTE A *cable segment* is an unbroken network cable that connects two nodes.

Packet Switching vs. Circuit Switching

LANs are called packet-switching networks because their computers divide their data into small, discrete units called *packets* before transmitting it. There is also a similar technique called *cell switching*, which differs from packet switching only in that cells are always a consistent, uniform size, whereas the size of packets is variable. Most LAN technologies, such as Ethernet, Token Ring, and Fiber Distributed Data Interface (FDDI), use packet switching. Asynchronous Transfer Mode (ATM) is the cell-switching LAN protocol that is most commonly used.

Understanding Packets

E-mail may be the easiest way to understand packets. Each message is divided by the sending service into a specific number of bytes, often between 1,000 and 1,500. Then each packet is sent using the most efficient route. For example, if you are sending an e-mail to your company's home office from your vacation cabin, each packet will probably travel along a different route. This is more efficient, and if any one piece of equipment is not working properly in the network while a message is being transferred, the packet that would use that piece of equipment can be routed around the problem area and sent on another route. When the message reaches its destination, the packets are reassembled for delivery of the entire message.

Segmenting the data in this way is necessary because the computers on a LAN share a single cable, and a computer transmitting a single unbroken stream of data would monopolize the network for too long. If you were to examine the data being transmitted over a packet-switching network, you would see the packets generated by several different systems intermixed on the cable. The receiving system, therefore, must have a mechanism for reassembling the packets into the correct order and recognizing the absence of packets that may have been lost or damaged in transit.

The opposite of packet switching is circuit switching, in which one system establishes a dedicated communication channel to another system before any data is transmitted. In the data networking industry, circuit switching is used for certain types of wide area networking technologies, such as Integrated Services Digital Network (ISDN) and frame relay. The classic example of a circuit-switching network is the public telephone system. When you place a call to another person, a physical circuit is established between your telephone and theirs. This circuit remains active for the entire duration of the call, and no one else can use it, even when it is not carrying any data (that is, when no one is talking).

In the early days of the telephone system, every phone was connected to a central office with a dedicated cable, and operators using switchboards manually connected a circuit between the two phones for every call. While today the process is automated and the telephone system transmits many signals over a single cable, the underlying principle is the same.

LANs were originally designed to connect a small number of computers into what later came to be called a *workgroup*. Rather than investing a huge amount of money into a large, mainframe computer and the support system needed to run it, business owners came to realize that they could purchase a few computers, cable them together, and perform most of the computing tasks they needed. As the capabilities of personal computers and applications grew, so did the networks, and the technology used to build them progressed as well.

Cables and Topologies

Most LANs are built around copper cables that use standard electrical currents to relay their signals. Originally, most LANs consisted of computers connected with coaxial cables, but eventually, the twisted-pair cabling used for telephone systems became more popular. Another alternative is fiber-optic cable, which doesn't use electrical signals at all but instead uses pulses of light to encode binary data. Other types of network infrastructures eliminate cables entirely and transmit signals using what is known as unbounded media, such as radio waves, infrared, and microwaves.

NOTE For more information about the various types of cables used in data networking, see Chapter 5.

LANs connect computers using various types of cabling patterns called *topologies* (see Figure 1-1), which depend on the type of cable used and the protocols running on the computers. The most common topologies are as follows:

- **Bus**   A bus topology takes the form of a cable that runs from one computer to the next one in a daisy-chain fashion, much like a string of Christmas tree lights. All of the signals transmitted by the computers on the network travel along the bus in both directions to all of the other computers. The two ends of the bus must be terminated with electrical resistors that nullify the voltages reaching them so that the signals do not reflect in the other direction. The primary drawback of the bus topology is that, like the string of Christmas lights it resembles, a fault in the cable anywhere along its length splits the network in two and prevents systems on opposite sides of the break from communicating. In addition, the lack of termination at either half can prevent computers that are still connected from communicating properly. As with Christmas lights, finding a single faulty connection in a large bus network can be troublesome and time consuming. Most coaxial cable networks, such as the original Ethernet LANs, use a bus topology.

- **Star (hub and spoke)**   A star topology uses a separate cable for each computer that runs to a central cabling nexus called a *hub* or *concentrator*. The hub propagates the signals entering through any one of its ports out through all of the other ports so that the signals transmitted by each computer reach all the other computers. Hubs also amplify the signals as they process them, enabling them to travel longer distances without degrading. A star network is more fault tolerant than a bus because a break in a cable affects only the device to which that cable is connected, not the entire network. Most of the networking protocols that call for twisted-pair cable, such as 10Base-T and 100Base-T Ethernet, use the star topology.

- **Star bus**   A star bus topology is one method for expanding the size of a LAN beyond a single star. In this topology, a number of star networks are joined together using a separate bus cable segment to connect their hubs. Each computer can still communicate with any other computer on the network because each of the hubs transmits its incoming traffic out through the bus port as well as the other star ports. Designed to expand 10Base-T Ethernet networks, the star bus is rarely seen today because of the speed limitations of coaxial bus networks, which can function as a bottleneck that degrades the performance of faster star network technologies such as Fast Ethernet.

- **Ring**   This topology is similar to a bus topology, except these topologies transmit in one direction only from station to station. A ring topology often uses separate physical ports and wires to send and receive data. A ring topology is functionally equivalent to a bus topology with the two ends connected so that signals travel from one computer to the next in an endless circular fashion. However, the communications ring is only a logical construct, not a physical one. The physical network is actually cabled using a star topology, and a special hub called a *multistation access unit* (MSAU) implements the logical ring by taking each incoming signal and transmitting it out through the next downstream port only (instead of through all of the other ports, like a star hub). Each computer, upon receiving an incoming signal, processes it (if necessary) and sends it right back to the hub for transmission to the next station on the ring. Because of this arrangement, systems that transmit signals onto the network must also remove the signals after they have traversed the entire ring. Networks configured in a ring topology can use several different types of cable. Token Ring networks, for example, use twisted-pair cables, while FDDI networks use the ring topology with fiber-optic cable.

- **Daisy chains**   These topologies are the simplest form as one device is connected to another through serial ports. Think of a computer hooked to a printer and the printer, in turn, being hooked to a laptop.

- **Hierarchical star**   The hierarchical star topology is the most common method for expanding a star network beyond the capacity of its original hub. When a hub's ports are all filled and you have more computers to connect to the network, you can connect the original hub to a second hub using a cable plugged into a special port designated for this purpose. Traffic arriving at either hub is then propagated to the other hub as well as to the connected computers. The number of hubs that a single LAN can support is dependent on the protocol it uses.

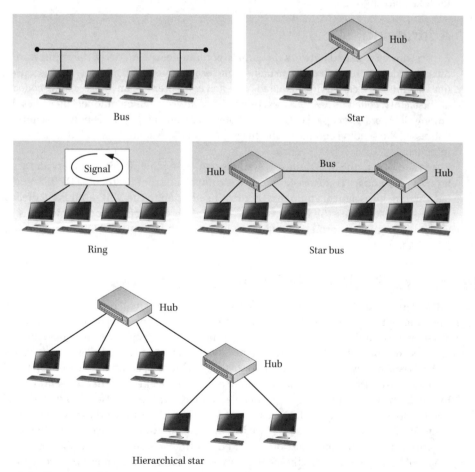

Figure 1-1   Common cable topographies

The topologies discussed here are *physical* topologies, which differ from *logical* topologies that are discussed in later chapters. Physical topologies refer to the placement of cables and other components of the network. Logical topologies refer to the flow of data on the network.

Media Access Control

When multiple computers are connected to the same baseband network medium, there must be a media access control (MAC) mechanism that arbitrates access to the network to prevent systems from transmitting data at the same time. A MAC mechanism is a fundamental part of all local area networking protocols that use a shared network medium. The two most common MAC mechanisms are Carrier Sense Multiple Access with Collision Detection (CSMA/CD), which is used by Ethernet networks, and token passing, which is used by Token Ring, FDDI, and other protocols. These two mechanisms are fundamentally different, but they accomplish the same task by providing each system on the network with an equal opportunity to transmit its data. (For more information about these MAC mechanisms, see Chapter 10 for CSMA/CD and Chapter 12 for token passing.)

Addressing

For systems on a shared network medium to communicate effectively, they must have some means of identifying each other, usually some form of numerical address. In most cases, the network interface card (NIC) installed into each computer has an address hard-coded into it at the factory, called its *MAC address* or *hardware address,* which uniquely identifies that card among all others. Every packet that each computer transmits over the network contains the address of the sending computer and the address of the system for which the packet is intended.

In addition to the MAC address, systems may have other addresses operating at other layers. For example, Transmission Control Protocol/Internet Protocol (TCP/IP) requires that each system be assigned a unique IP address in addition to the MAC address it already possesses. Systems use the various addresses for different types of communications. (See Chapter 3 for more information on MAC addressing and Chapter 13 for more information on IP addressing.)

Repeaters, Bridges, Switches, and Routers

LANs were originally designed to support only a relatively small number of computers—30 for thin Ethernet networks and 100 for thick Ethernet—but the needs of businesses quickly outgrew these limitations. To support larger installations, engineers developed products that enabled administrators to connect two or more LANs into what is known as an *internetwork,* which is essentially a network of networks that enables the computers on one network to communicate with those on another. Don't confuse the generic term *internetwork* with the Internet. The Internet is an example of an extremely large internetwork, but any installation that consists of two or more LANs connected is also an internetwork. This terminology is confusing because it is so often misused. Sometimes what users mean when they refer to a network is actually an internetwork, and at other times, what may seem to be an internetwork is actually a single LAN. Strictly speaking, a LAN or a network segment is a group of computers that share a network cable so that a broadcast message transmitted by one system reaches all of the other systems, even if that segment is actually composed of many pieces of cable. For example, on a typical 10Base-T Ethernet LAN, all of the computers are connected to a hub using individual lengths of cable. Regardless of that fact, this arrangement is still an example of a network segment or LAN. Individual LANs can be connected using several different types of devices, some of which simply extend the LAN while another creates an internetwork. These devices are as follows:

- **Repeaters**   A repeater is a purely electrical device that extends the maximum distance a LAN cable can span by amplifying the signals passing through it. The hubs used on star networks are sometimes called *multiport repeaters* because they have signal amplification capabilities integrated into the unit. Stand-alone repeaters are also available for use on coaxial networks to extend them over longer distances. Using a repeater to expand a network segment does not divide it into two LANs or create an internetwork.

- **Bridges**   A bridge provides the amplification function of a repeater, along with the ability to selectively filter packets based on their addresses. Packets that originate on one side of the bridge are propagated to the other side only if they are addressed to a system that exists there. Because bridges do not prevent broadcast messages from being propagated across the connected cable segments, they, too, do not create multiple LANs or transform a network into an internetwork.

- **Switches**   Switches are revolutionary devices that in many cases eliminate the shared network medium entirely. A switch is essentially a multiport repeater, like a hub, except that instead of operating at a purely electrical level, the switch reads the destination address in each incoming packet and transmits it out only through the port to which the destination system is connected.

- **Routers**   A router is a device that connects two LANs to form an internetwork. Like a bridge, a router forwards only the traffic that is destined for the connected segment, but unlike repeaters and bridges, routers do not forward broadcast messages. Routers can also connect different types of networks (such as Ethernet and Token Ring), whereas bridges and repeaters can connect only segments of the same type.

Wide Area Networks

Internetworking enables an organization to build a network infrastructure of almost unlimited size. In addition to connecting multiple LANs in the same building or campus, an internetwork can connect LANs at distant locations through the use of wide area network links. A WAN is a collection of LANs, some or all of which are connected using point-to-point links that span relatively long distances. A typical WAN connection consists of two routers, one at each LAN site, connected using a long-distance link such as a leased telephone line. Any computer on one of the LANs can communicate with the other LAN by directing its traffic to the local router, which relays it over the WAN link to the other site.

WAN links differ from LANs in that they do not use a shared network medium and they can span much longer distances. Because the link connects only two systems, there is no need for media access control or a shared network medium. An organization with offices located throughout the world can build an internetwork that provides users with instantaneous access to network resources at any location. The WAN links themselves can use technologies ranging from telephone lines to public data networks to satellite systems. Unlike a LAN, which is nearly always privately owned and operated, an outside service provider (such as a telephone company) is nearly always involved in a WAN connection because private organizations don't usually own the technologies needed to carry signals over such long distances. Generally speaking, WAN connections can be slower and more expensive than LANs, and sometimes much more so. As a result, one of the goals of the network administrator is to maximize the efficiency of WAN traffic by eliminating unnecessary communications and choosing the best type of link for the application. See Chapter 7 for more information on WAN technologies.

There are also wireless LAN/WAN networks and metropolitan area networks (MANs). A MAN has three features that differentiate it from both a LAN and a WAN:

- A MAN's size is usually between that of a LAN and a WAN. Typically, it covers between 3 and 30 miles (5 to 50 km). A MAN can encompass several buildings, a company campus, or a small town.

- As with WANs, MANs are normally owned by a group or a network provider.

- MANs are often used as a way to provide shared access to one or more WANs.

Protocols and Standards

Communications between computers on a network are defined by protocols, standardized methods that the software programs on the computers have in common. These protocols define every part of the communications process, from the signals transmitted over network cables to the query languages that enable applications on different machines to exchange messages. Networked computers run a series of protocols, called a *protocol stack,* that spans from the application user interface at the top to the physical network interface at the bottom. The stack is traditionally split into seven layers. The Open Systems Interconnection (OSI) reference model defines the functions of each layer and how the layers work together to provide network communications. Chapter 2 covers the OSI reference model in detail.

Early networking products tended to be proprietary solutions created by a single manufacturer, but as time passed, interoperability became a greater priority, and organizations were formed to develop and ratify networking protocol standards. Most of these bodies are responsible for large numbers of technical and manufacturing standards in many different disciplines. Today, most of the protocols in common use are standardized by these bodies, some of which are as follows:

- **Institute of Electrical and Electronic Engineers (IEEE)**   A U.S.-based society responsible for the publication of the IEEE 802 working group, which includes the standards that define the protocols commonly known as Ethernet and Token Ring, as well as many others.

- **International Organization for Standardization (ISO)**   A worldwide federation of standards bodies from more than 100 countries, responsible for the publication of the OSI reference model document.

- **Internet Engineering Task Force (IETF)**   An ad hoc group of contributors and consultants who collaborate to develop and publish standards for Internet technologies, including the TCP/IP protocols.

Clients and Servers

Local area networking is based on the client-server principle, in which the processes needed to accomplish a particular task are divided between computers functioning as clients and servers. This is in direct contrast to the mainframe model, in which the central computer did all of the processing and simply transmitted the results to a user at a remote terminal. A server is a computer running a process that provides a service to other computers when they request it. A client is the computer running a program that requests the service from a server.

For example, a LAN-based database application stores its data on a server, which stands by, waiting for clients to request information from it. Users at workstation computers run a database client program in which they generate queries that request specific information in the database and transmit those queries to the server. The server responds to the queries with the requested information and transmits it to the workstations, which format it for display to the users. In this case, the workstations are responsible for providing a user interface and translating the user input into a query language understood by the server. They are also responsible for taking the raw data from the server and displaying it in a comprehensible form to the user. The server may have to service dozens or hundreds of clients, so it is still a powerful computer. By offloading some of the application's functions to the workstations, however, its processing burden is nowhere near what it would be on a mainframe system.

Operating Systems and Applications

Clients and servers are actually software components, although some people associate them with specific hardware elements. This confusion is because some network operating systems require that a computer be dedicated to the role of server and that other computers function solely as clients. This is a client-server operating system, as opposed to a peer-to-peer operating system, in which every computer can function as both a client and a server. The most basic client-server functionality provided by a network operating system (NOS) is the ability to share file system drives and printers, and this is what usually defines the client and server roles. At its core, a NOS makes services available to its network clients. The system can provide the following:

- Printer services, including managing devices, print jobs, who is using what asset, and what assets are not available to the network
- Managing user access to files and other resources, such as the Internet
- System monitoring, including providing network security
- Making network administration utilities available to network administrators

Apart from the internal functions of network operating systems, many LAN applications and network services also operate using the client-server paradigm. Internet applications, such as the

World Wide Web, consist of servers and clients, as do administrative services such as the Domain Name System (DNS).

Most of today's desktop operating systems are capable of providing some of the services traditionally ascribed to NOSs since many small-office/home-office (SOHO) LAN implementations take advantage of the fact. Understanding this may help clarify the distinction between LANs that are truly client-server, relying on network operating systems, and those network configurations that leverage powerful computers with today's operating systems. These operating systems are not limited to computers, but can include cell phones, tablets, and other products that are not considered to be "computers."

CHAPTER 2

The OSI Reference Model

Network communications take place on many levels and can be difficult to understand, even for the knowledgeable network administrator. The Open Systems Interconnection (OSI) reference model is a theoretical construction that separates network communications into seven distinct layers, as shown in Figure 2-1. Each computer on the network uses a series of protocols to perform the functions assigned to each layer. The layers collectively form what is known as the *protocol stack* or *networking stack*. At the top of the stack is the application that makes a request for a resource located elsewhere on the network, and at the bottom is the physical medium that actually connects the computers and forms the network, such as a cable.

| 1. Application |
| 2. Presentation |
| 3. Session |
| 4. Transport |
| 5. Network |
| 6. Data link |
| 7. Physical |

Figure 2-1 The OSI reference model with its seven layers

The OSI reference model was developed in two separate projects by the International Organization for Standardization (ISO) and the Comité Consultatif International Téléphonique et Télégraphique (Consultative Committee for International Telephone and Telegraphy, or CCITT), which is now known as the Telecommunications Standardization Sector of the International Telecommunications Union (ITU-T). Each of these two bodies developed its own seven-layer model, but the two projects were combined in 1983, resulting in a document called "The Basic Reference Model for Open Systems Interconnection" that was published by the ISO as ISO 7498 and by the ITU-T as X.200.

The OSI stack was originally conceived as the model for the creation of a protocol suite that would conform exactly to the seven layers. This suite never materialized in a commercial form, however, and the model has since been used as a teaching, reference, and communications tool. Networking professionals, educators, and authors frequently refer to protocols, devices, or applications as operating at a particular layer of the OSI model because using this model breaks a complex process into manageable units that provide a common frame of reference. Many of the chapters in this book use the layers of the model to help define networking concepts. However, it is important to understand that none of the protocol stacks in common use today conforms exactly to the layers of the OSI model. In many cases, protocols have functions that overlap two or more layers, such as Ethernet, which is

OSI	TCP/IP
Application	Application
Presentation	
Session	Transport
Transport	
Network	Internet
Data link	
Physical	Link

Figure 2-2   The OSI reference model and the TCP/IP protocol stack

considered a data link layer protocol but which also defines elements of the physical layer.

The primary reason why real protocol stacks differ from the OSI model is that many of the protocols used today (including Ethernet) were conceived before the OSI model documents were published. In fact, the TCP/IP protocols have their own layered model, which is similar to the OSI model in several ways but uses only four layers (see Figure 2-2). In addition, developers are usually more concerned with practical functionality than with conforming to a preexisting model. The seven-layer model was designed to separate the functions of the protocol stack in such a way as to make it possible for separate development teams to work on the individual layers, thus streamlining the development process. However, if a single protocol can easily provide the functions that are defined as belonging in separate layers of the model, why divide it into two separate protocols just for the sake of conformity?

Communications Between the Layers

Networking is the process of sending messages from one place to another, and the protocol stack illustrated in the OSI model defines the basic components needed to transmit messages to their destinations. The communication process is complex because the applications that generate the messages have varying requirements. Some message exchanges consist of brief requests and replies that have to be exchanged as quickly as possible and with a minimum amount of overhead. Other network transactions, such as program file transfers, involve the transmission of larger amounts of data that must reach the destination in perfect condition, without alteration of a single bit. Still other transmissions, such as streaming audio or video, consist of huge amounts of data that can survive the loss of an occasional bit, byte, or packet, but that must reach the destination in a timely manner.

The networking process also includes a number of conversions that ultimately take the application programming interface (API) calls generated by applications and transform them into electrical charges, pulses of light, or other types of signals that can be transmitted across the network medium. Finally, the networking protocols must see to it that the transmissions reach the appropriate destinations in a timely manner. Just as you package a letter by placing it in an envelope and writing an address on it, the networking protocols package the data generated by an application and address it to another computer on the network.

Data Encapsulation

To satisfy all of the requirements just described, the protocols operating at the various layers work together to supply a unified quality of service. Each layer provides a service to the layers directly above and below it. Outgoing traffic travels down through the stack to the network physical medium, acquiring the control information needed to make the trip to the destination system as it goes. This control information takes the form of headers (and in one case a footer) that surround the data received from the layer above, in a process called data encapsulation. The headers and footer are composed of individual fields that contain control information (necessary/required by the system to deliver) used to get the packet to its destination. In a sense, the headers and footer form the envelope that carries the message received from the layer above.

In a typical transaction, shown in Figure 2-3, an application layer protocol (which also includes presentation and session layer functions) generates a message that is passed down to a transport layer protocol. The protocol at the transport layer has its own packet structure, called a protocol data unit (PDU), which includes specialized header fields and a data field that carries the payload. In this case, the payload is the data received from the application layer protocol. By packaging the data in its own PDU, the transport layer encapsulates the application layer data and then passes it down to the next layer.

The network layer protocol then receives the PDU from the transport layer and encapsulates it within its own PDU by adding a header and using the entire transport layer PDU (including the application layer data) as its payload. The same process occurs again when the network layer passes its PDU to the data link layer protocol, which adds a header and footer. To a data link layer protocol, the data within the frame is treated as payload only, just as postal employees have no idea what is inside the envelopes they process. The only system that reads the information in the payload is the computer possessing the destination address. That computer then either passes the network layer protocol data contained in the payload up through its protocol stack or uses that data to determine what the next destination of the packet should be. In the same way, the protocols operating at the other layers are conscious of their own header information but are unaware of what data is being carried in the payload.

Once it is encapsulated by the data link layer protocol, the completed packet (now called a frame) is then ready to be converted to the appropriate type of signal used by the network

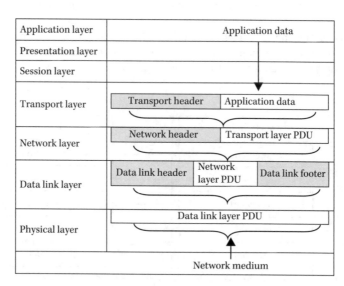

Figure 2-3   The application layer data is encapsulated for transmission by the protocols at the lower layers in the stack.

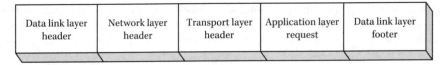

Data link layer header	Network layer header	Transport layer header	Application layer request	Data link layer footer

Figure 2-4   An encapsulated frame, ready for transmission

medium. Thus, the final packet, as transmitted over the network, consists of the original application layer data plus several headers applied by the protocols at the succeeding layers, as shown in Figure 2-4.

NOTE   Each layer must translate data into its specific format before sending it on. Therefore, each layer creates its own PDU to transmit to the next layer. As each layer receives data, the PDU of the previous layer is read, and a new PDU is created using that layer's protocol. Remember, a PDU is a complete message (or packet) that includes the protocol of the sending layer. At the physical layer, you end up with a message that consists of all the data that has been encapsulated with the headers and/or footers from each of the previous layers.

Horizontal Communications

For two computers to communicate over a network, the protocols used at each layer of the OSI model in the transmitting system must be duplicated at the receiving system. When the packet arrives at its destination, the process by which the headers are applied at the source is repeated in reverse. The packet travels up through the protocol stack, and each successive header is stripped off by the appropriate protocol and processed. In essence, the protocols operating at the various layers communicate horizontally with their counterparts in the other system, as shown in Figure 2-5.

The horizontal connections between the various layers are logical; there is no direct communication between them. The information included in each protocol header by the transmitting system is a message that is carried to the same protocol in the destination system.

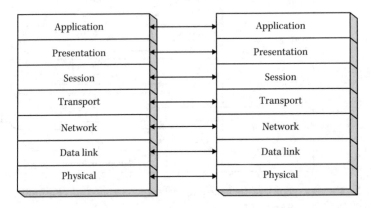

Figure 2-5   Each layer has logical connections with its counterpart in other systems.

Vertical Communications

The headers applied by the various protocols implement the specific functions carried out by those protocols. In addition to communicating horizontally with the same protocol in the other system, the header information enables each layer to communicate with the layers above and below it, as shown in Figure 2-6. For example, when a system receives a packet and passes it up through the protocol stack, the data link layer protocol header includes a field that identifies which network layer protocol the system should use to process the packet. The network layer protocol header in turn specifies one of the transport layer protocols, and the transport layer protocol identifies the application for which the data is ultimately destined. This vertical communication makes it possible for a computer to support multiple protocols at each of the layers simultaneously. As long as a packet has the correct information in its headers, it can be routed on the appropriate path through the stack to the intended destination.

Encapsulation Terminology

One of the most confusing aspects of the data encapsulation process is the terminology used to describe the PDUs generated by each layer. The term *packet* specifically refers to the complete unit transmitted over the network medium, although it also has become a generic term for the data unit at any stage in the process. Most data link layer protocols are said to work with frames because they include both a header and a footer that surround the data from the network layer protocol. The term *frame* refers to a PDU of variable size, depending on the amount of data enclosed. A data link layer protocol that uses PDUs of a uniform size, such as Asynchronous Transfer Mode (ATM), is said to deal in *cells*.

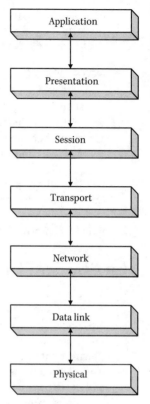

Figure 2-6 Each layer in the OSI model communicates with the layer above and below it.

    When transport layer data is encapsulated by a network layer protocol, such as the Internet Protocol (IP) or Internetwork Packet Exchange (IPX), the resulting PDU is called a *datagram*. During the course of its transmission, a datagram might be split into fragments, each of which is sometimes incorrectly called a *datagram*. The terminology at the transport layer is more protocol-specific than at the lower layers. TCP/IP, for example, has two transport layer protocols. The first, called the User Datagram Protocol (UDP), also refers to the PDUs it creates as datagrams, although these are not synonymous with the datagrams produced at the network layer.

    When the UDP protocol at the transport layer is encapsulated by the IP protocol at the network layer, the result is a datagram packaged within another datagram. The difference between UDP and the Transmission Control Protocol (TCP), which also operates at the transport layer, is that UDP datagrams are self-contained units that were designed to contain the entirety of the data generated by the application layer protocol. Therefore, UDP is traditionally used to transmit small amounts of data, while TCP, on the other hand, is used to transmit larger amounts of application layer data that usually do not fit into a single packet. As a result, each of the PDUs produced by the TCP protocol is called a *segment,* and the collection of segments that carry the entirety of the application layer protocol data is called a *sequence*. The PDU produced by an application layer protocol is typically called a *message*. The session and presentation layers are usually not associated with individual protocols. Their functions are incorporated into other elements of the protocol stack, and they do not have their own headers or PDUs. All of these terms are frequently confused, and it is not surprising to see even authoritative documents use them incorrectly.

NOTE While TCP is often used to transmit data packets today, there are instances where UDP is suitable. For example, UDP is used when newer data will replace previous data, such as in video streaming or gaming. As another example of the need for newer data, consider weather information that must be updated quickly during inclement weather. Also, since TCP is a connection-oriented, streaming protocol, UDP is the preferred way to *multicast* (send data across a network to several users at the same time).

The following sections examine each of the seven layers of the OSI reference model in turn, the functions that are associated with each, and the protocols that are most commonly used at those layers. As you proceed through this book, you will learn more about each of the individual protocols and their relationships to the other elements of the protocol stack.

The Physical Layer

The physical layer of the OSI model defines the actual medium that carries data from one computer to another. The two most common types of physical layer used in data networking are copper-based electrical cable and fiber-optic cable. A number of wireless physical layer implementations use radio waves, infrared or laser light, microwaves, and other technologies. The physical layer includes the type of technology used to carry the data, the type of equipment used to implement that technology, the specifications of how the equipment should be installed, and the nature of the signals used to encode the data for transmission.

For example, for many years, the most popular physical layer standards used for local area networking was 10Base-T Ethernet. Ethernet is primarily thought of as a data link layer protocol. However, as with most protocols functioning at the data link layer, Ethernet includes specific physical layer implementations, and the standards for the protocol define the elements of the physical layer as well. 10Base-T referred to the type of cable used to form a particular type of Ethernet network. The Ethernet standard defined 10Base-T as an unshielded twisted-pair cable (UTP) containing four pairs of copper wires enclosed in a single sheath. Today, Ethernet is found at much faster speeds such as 100Base-T running at 100 megabits per second, or 1000Base-T, which runs at 1 gigabit per second.

NOTE The physical layer uses the binary data supplied by the data link layer protocol to encode the data into pulses of light, electrical voltages, or other impulses suitable for transmission over the network medium.

However, the construction of the cable itself is not the only physical layer element involved. The standards used to build an Ethernet network also define how to install the cable, including maximum segment lengths and distances from power sources. The standards specify what kind of connectors you use to join the cable, the type of network interface card (NIC) to install in the computer, and the type of hub you use to join the computers into a network topology. Finally, the standard specifies how the NIC should encode the data generated by the computer into electrical impulses that can be transmitted over the cable.

Thus, you can see that the physical layer encompasses much more than a type of cable. However, you generally don't have to know the details about every element of the physical layer standard. When you buy Ethernet NICs, cables, and hubs, they are already constructed to the Ethernet specifications and designed to use the proper signaling scheme. Installing the equipment, however, can be more complicated.

Physical Layer Specifications

While it is relatively easy to learn enough about a LAN technology to purchase the appropriate equipment, installing the cable (or other medium) is much more difficult because you must be aware of all the specifications that affect the process. For example, the Ethernet standards published by the IEEE 802.3 working group specify the basic wiring configuration guidelines that pertain to the protocol's media access control (MAC) and collision detection mechanisms. These rules specify elements such as the maximum length of a cable segment, the distance between workstations, and the number of repeaters permitted on a network. These guidelines are common knowledge to Ethernet network administrators, but these rules alone are not sufficient to perform a large cable installation. In addition, there are local building codes to consider, which might have a great effect on a cable installation. For these reasons, large physical layer installations should, in most cases, be performed by professionals who are familiar with all of the standards that apply to the particular technology involved. See Chapter 4 for more information on network cabling and cable installation.

NOTE The latest revision to the IEEE 802.3 "Standard for Ethernet" was published in September 2012. It was amended to "address new markets, bandwidth speeds, and media types" according to the IEEE web site at http://standards.ieee.org.

NOTE Collision detection is when one device (or node) on a network determines that data has "collided." This is similar to two people coming through a revolving door at the same time, but in that case, one person can see the other person and stops. If one node hears a distorted version of its own transmission, that node understands that a collision has occurred and, just like the person who stops to allow the other to go through the revolving door, that node will stop the transmission and wait for silence on the network to send its data.

Physical Layer Signaling

The primary operative component of a physical layer installation is the transceiver found in NICs, repeating hubs, and other devices. The transceiver, as the name implies, is responsible for transmitting and receiving signals over the network medium. On networks using copper cable, the transceiver is an electrical device that takes the binary data it receives from the data link layer protocol and converts it into signals of various voltages. Unlike all of the other layers in the protocol stack, the physical layer is not concerned in any way with the meaning of the data being transmitted. The transceiver simply converts zeros and ones into voltages, pulses of light, radio waves, or some other type of signal, but it is completely oblivious to packets, frames, addresses, and even the system receiving the signal.

The signals generated by a transceiver can be either analog or digital. Most data networks use digital signals, but some of the wireless technologies use analog radio transmissions to carry data. Analog signals transition between two values gradually, forming the sine wave pattern shown in

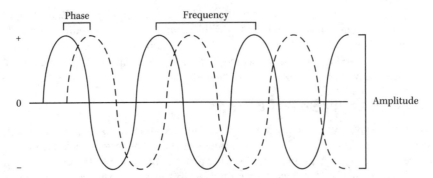

Figure 2-7　Analog signals form wave patterns.

Figure 2-7, while digital value transitions are immediate and absolute. The values of an analog signal can be determined by variations in amplitude, frequency, phase, or a combination of these elements, as in amplitude modulated (AM) or frequency modulated (FM) radio signals or in analog phase loop lock (PLL) circuits.

The use of digital signals is much more common in data networking, however. All of the standard copper and fiber-optic media use various forms of digital signaling. The signaling scheme is determined by the data link layer protocol being used. All Ethernet networks, for example, use the Manchester encoding scheme, whether they are running over twisted-pair, coaxial, or fiber-optic cable. Digital signals transition between values almost instantaneously, producing the square wave shown in Figure 2-8. Depending on the network medium, the values can represent electrical voltages, the presence or absence of a beam of light, or any other appropriate attribute of the medium. In most cases, the signal is produced with transitions between a positive voltage and a negative voltage, although some use a zero value as well. Given a stable voltage within circuit specifications, the transitions create the signal.

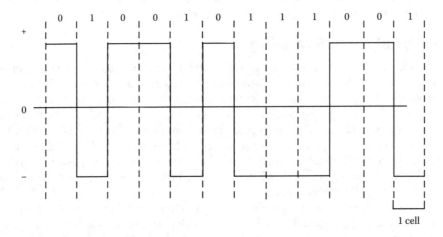

Figure 2-8　Polar encoding

NOTE Digital signals are susceptible to voltage degradation; a digital circuit designed for a 5-volt application will most likely behave erroneously if voltage attenuation results in signals of 3 volts, meaning the circuit will now not be able to distinguish whether there was a transition event since the signal is below the design threshold.

Figure 2-8 illustrates a simple signaling scheme called *polar signaling*. In this scheme, the signal is broken up into units of time called *cells,* and the voltage of each cell denotes its binary value. A positive voltage is a zero, and a negative voltage is a one. This signaling code would seem to be a simple and logical method for transmitting binary information, but it has one crucial flaw, and that is timing. When the binary code consists of two or more consecutive zeros or ones, there is no voltage transition for the duration of two or more cells. Unless the two communicating systems have clocks that are precisely synchronized, it is impossible to tell for certain whether a voltage that remains continuous for a period of time represents two, three, or more cells with the same value. Remember that these communications occur at incredibly high rates of speed, so the timing intervals involved are extremely small.

Some systems can use this type of signal because they have an external timing signal that keeps the communicating systems synchronized. However, many data networks run over a baseband medium that permits the transmission of only one signal at a time. As a result, these networks use a different type of signaling scheme, one that is *self-timing*. In other words, the data signal itself contains a timing signal that enables the receiving system to correctly interpret the values and convert them into binary data.

The *Manchester encoding* scheme used on Ethernet networks is a self-timing signal by virtue of the fact that every cell has a value transition at its midpoint. This delineates the boundaries of the cells to the receiving system. The binary values are specified by the direction of the value transition; a positive-to-negative transition indicates a value of zero, and a negative-to-positive transition indicates a value of one (see Figure 2-9). The value transitions at the beginnings of the cells have no function other than to set the voltage to the appropriate value for the midcell transition.

Token Ring networks use a different encoding scheme called *Differential Manchester,* which also has a value transition at the midpoint of each cell. However, in this scheme, the direction of

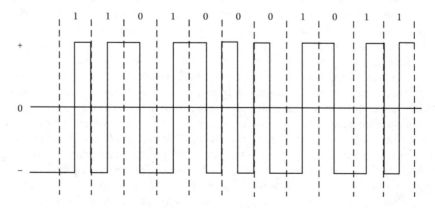

Figure 2-9   The Manchester encoding scheme

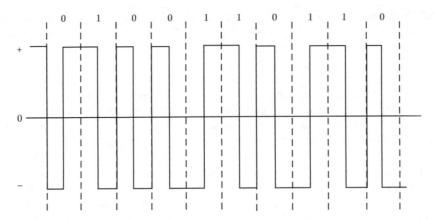

Figure 2-10   The Differential Manchester encoding scheme

the transition is irrelevant; it exists only to provide a timing signal. The value of each cell is determined by the presence or absence of a transition at the beginning of the cell. If the transition exists, the value of the cell is zero; if there is no transition, the value of the cell is one (see Figure 2-10). As with the midpoint transition, the direction of the transition is irrelevant.

The Data Link Layer

The data link layer protocol provides the interface between the physical network and the protocol stack on the computer. A data link layer protocol typically consists of three elements:

- The format for the frame that encapsulates the network layer protocol data
- The mechanism that regulates access to the shared network medium
- The guidelines used to construct the network's physical layer

The header and footer applied to the network layer protocol data by the data link layer protocol are the outermost on the packet as it is transmitted across the network. This frame is, in essence, the envelope that carries the packet to its next destination and, therefore, provides the basic addressing information needed to get it there. In addition, data link layer protocols usually include an error-detection facility and an indicator that specifies the network layer protocol that the receiving system should use to process the data included in the packet.

On most LANs, multiple systems access a single shared baseband network medium. This means that only one computer can transmit data at any one time. If two or more systems transmit simultaneously, a collision occurs, and the data is lost. The data link layer protocol is responsible for controlling access to the shared medium and preventing an excess of collisions.

When speaking of the data link layer, the terms *protocol* and *topology* are often confused, but they are not synonymous. Ethernet is sometimes called a topology when the topology actually refers to the way in which the computers on the network are cabled together. Some forms of Ethernet use a bus topology, in which each of the computers is cabled to the next one in a daisy-chain fashion, while the star topology, in which each computer is cabled to a central hub, is more prevalent today. A ring topology is a bus with the ends joined together, and a mesh topology is one in which each computer has a cable connection to every other computer on the network. These last two types are mainly theoretical; LANs today do not use them. Token Ring networks use a logical ring, but the computers are actually cabled using a star topology. This confusion is understandable since most data link layer protocols include elements of the physical layer in their specifications. It is necessary for the data link layer protocol to be intimately related to the physical layer because media access control mechanisms are highly dependent on the size of the frames being transmitted and the lengths of the cable segments.

Addressing

The data link layer protocol header contains the address of the computer sending the packet and the computer that is to receive it. The addresses used at this layer are the hardware (or MAC) addresses that in most cases are hard-coded into the network interface of each computer and router by the manufacturer. On Ethernet and Token Ring networks, the addresses are 6 bytes long, the first 3 bytes of which are assigned to the manufacturer by the Institute of Electrical and Electronic Engineers (IEEE), and the second 3 bytes of which are assigned by the manufacturer. Some older protocols used addresses assigned by the network administrator, but the factory-assigned addresses are more efficient, insofar as they ensure that no duplication can occur.

The data link layer protocol does the following:

- Provides packet addressing services
- Packages the network layer data for transmission
- Arbitrates network access
- Checks transmitted packets for errors

Data link layer protocols are not concerned with the delivery of the packet to its ultimate destination, unless that destination is on the same LAN as the source. When a packet passes through several networks on the way to its destination, the data link layer protocol is responsible only for getting the packet to the router on the local network that provides access to the next network on its journey. Thus, the destination address in a data link layer protocol header always references a device on the local network, even if the ultimate destination of the message is a computer on a network miles away.

The data link layer protocols used on LANs rely on a shared network medium. Every packet is transmitted to all of the computers on the network segment, and only the system with the address specified as the destination reads the packet into its memory buffers and processes it. The other systems simply discard the packet without taking any further action.

Media Access Control

Media access control is the process by which the data link layer protocol arbitrates access to the network medium. In order for the network to function efficiently, each of the workstations sharing the cable or other medium must have an opportunity to transmit its data on a regular basis. This is why the data to be transmitted is split into packets in the first place. If computers transmitted all of their data in a continuous stream, they could conceivably monopolize the network for extended periods of time.

Two basic forms of media access control are used on most of today's LANs. The token passing method, used by Token Ring and FDDI systems, uses a special frame called a token that is passed from one workstation to another. Only the system in possession of the token is allowed to transmit its data. A workstation, on receiving the token, transmits its data and then releases the token to the next workstation. Since there is only one token on the network at any time (assuming that the network is functioning properly), it isn't possible for two systems to transmit at the same time.

The other method, used on Ethernet networks, is called Carrier Sense Multiple Access with Collision Detection (CSMA/CD). In this method, when a workstation has data to send, it listens to the network cable and transmits if the network is not in use. On CSMA/CD networks, it is possible (and even expected) for workstations to transmit at the same time, resulting in packet collisions. To compensate for this, each system has a mechanism that enables it to detect collisions when they occur and retransmit the data that was lost.

Both of these MAC mechanisms rely on the physical layer specifications for the network to function properly. For example, an Ethernet system can detect collisions only if they occur while the workstation is still transmitting a packet. If a network segment is too long, a collision may occur after the last bit of data has left the transmitting system and thus may go undetected. The data in that packet is then lost, and its absence can be detected only by the upper layer protocols in the system that are the ultimate destinations of the message. This process takes a relatively long time and significantly reduces the efficiency of the network. Thus, while the OSI reference model might create a neat division between the physical and data link layers, in the real world, the functionality of the two is more closely intertwined.

Protocol Indicator

Most data link layer protocol implementations are designed to support the use of multiple network layer protocols at the same time. This means there are several possible paths through the protocol stack on each computer. To use multiple protocols at the network layer, the data link layer protocol header must include a code that specifies the network layer protocol that was used to generate the payload in the packet. This requirement is so that the receiving system can pass the data enclosed in the frame up to the appropriate network layer process.

Error Detection

Most data link layer protocols are unlike all of the upper layer protocols in that they include a footer that follows the payload field in addition to the header that precedes it. This footer contains a *frame check sequence* (FCS) field that the receiving system uses to detect any errors that have occurred during the transmission. To do this, the system transmitting the packet computes a cyclical redundancy check (CRC) value on the entire frame and includes it in the FCS field. When the packet reaches its next destination, the receiving system performs the same computation and compares its results with the value in the FCS field. If the values do not match, the packet is assumed to have been damaged in transit and is silently discarded.

The receiving system takes no action to have discarded packets retransmitted; this is left up to the protocols operating at the upper layers of the OSI model. This error-detection process occurs at each hop in the packet's journey to its destination. Some upper-layer protocols have their own mechanisms for end-to-end error detection.

The Network Layer

The network layer protocol is the primary end-to-end carrier for messages generated by the application layer. This means that, unlike the data link layer protocol, which is concerned only with getting the packet to its next destination on the local network, the network layer protocol is responsible for the packet's entire journey from the source system to its ultimate destination. A network layer protocol accepts data from the transport layer and packages it into a datagram by adding its own header. Like a data link layer protocol header, the header at the network layer contains the address of the destination system, but this address identifies the packet's final destination. Thus, the destination addresses in the data link layer and network layer protocol headers may actually refer to two different computers. The network layer protocol datagram is essentially an envelope within the data link layer envelope, and while the data link layer envelope is opened by every system that processes the packet, the network layer envelope remains sealed until the packet reaches its final destination.

The network layer protocol provides

- End-to-end addressing
- Internet routing services
- Packet fragmentation and reassembly
- Error checking

Routing

Network layer protocols use different types of addressing systems to identify the ultimate destination of a packet. The most popular network layer protocol, the Internet Protocol (IP), provides its own 32-bit address space that identifies both the network on which the destination system resides and the system itself.

An address by which individual networks can be uniquely identified is vital to the performance of the network layer protocol's primary function, which is routing. When a packet travels through a large corporate internetwork or the Internet, it is passed from router to router until it reaches the network on which the destination system is located. Properly designed networks have more than one possible route to a particular destination, for fault-tolerance reasons, and the Internet has millions of possible routes. Each router is responsible for determining the next router that the packet should use to take the most efficient path to its destination. Because data link layer protocols are completely ignorant of conditions outside of the local network, it is left up to the network layer protocol to choose an appropriate route with an eye on the end-to-end journey of the packet, not just the next interim hop.

The network layer defines two types of computers that can be involved in a packet transmission: end systems and intermediate systems. An end system is either the computer generating and transmitting the packet or the computer that is the ultimate recipient of the packet. An intermediate system is a router or switch that connects two or more networks and forwards packets on the way to their destinations. On end systems, all seven layers of the protocol stack are involved in either the creation or the reception of the packet. On intermediate systems, packets arrive and travel up through the stack only as high as the network layer. The network layer protocol chooses a route for the packet and sends it back down to a data link layer protocol for packaging and transmission at the physical layer.

NOTE On intermediate systems, packets travel no higher than the network layer.

When an intermediate system receives a packet, the data link layer protocol checks it for errors and for the correct hardware address and then strips off the data link header and footer and passes it up to the network layer protocol identified by the Ethernet-type field or its equivalent. At this point, the packet consists of a datagram—that is, a network layer protocol header and a payload that was generated by the transport layer protocol on the source system. The network layer protocol then reads the destination address in the header and determines what the packet's next destination should be. If the destination is a workstation on a local network, the intermediate system transmits the packet directly to that workstation. If the destination is on a distant network, the intermediate system consults its routing table to select the router that provides the most efficient path to that destination.

The compilation and storage of routing information in a reference table is a separate network layer process that is performed either manually by an administrator or automatically by specialized network layer protocols that routers use to exchange information about the networks to which they are connected. Once it has determined the next destination for the packet, the network layer protocol passes the information down to the data link layer protocol with the datagram so that it can be packaged in a new frame and transmitted. When the IP protocol is running at the network layer, an additional process is required in which the IP address of the next destination is converted into a hardware address that the data link layer protocol can use.

Fragmenting

Because routers can connect networks that use different data link layer protocols, it is sometimes necessary for intermediate systems to split datagrams into fragments to transmit them. If, for example, a workstation on a Token Ring network generates a packet containing 4,500 bytes of data, an intermediate system that joins the Token Ring network to an Ethernet network must split the data into fragments between 64 and 1,518 bytes because 1,518 bytes is the largest amount of data that an Ethernet frame can carry.

Depending on the data link layer protocols used by the various intermediate networks, the fragments of a datagram may be fragmented themselves. Datagrams or fragments that are fragmented by intermediate systems are not reassembled until they reach their final destinations.

Connection-Oriented and Connectionless Protocols

There are two types of end-to-end protocols that operate at the network and transport layers: connection-oriented and connectionless. The type of protocol used helps to determine what other functions are performed at each layer. A *connection-oriented* protocol is one in which a logical connection between the source and the destination system is established before any upper-layer data is transmitted. Once the connection is established, the source system transmits the data, and the destination system acknowledges its receipt. A failure to receive the appropriate acknowledgments serves as a signal to the sender that packets have to be retransmitted. When the data transmission is completed successfully, the systems terminate the connection. By using this type of protocol, the sending system is certain that the data has arrived at the destination successfully. The cost of this guaranteed service is the additional network traffic generated by the connection establishment, acknowledgment, and termination messages, as well as a substantially larger protocol header on each data packet.

A *connectionless protocol* simply packages data and transmits it to the destination address without checking to see whether the destination system is available and without expecting packet acknowledgments. In most cases, connectionless protocols are used when a protocol higher up in the networking stack provides connection-oriented services, such as guaranteed delivery. These additional services can also include flow control (a mechanism for regulating the speed at which data is transmitted over the network), error detection, and error correction.

Most of the LAN protocols operating at the network layer, such as IP and IPX, are connectionless. In both cases, various protocols are available at the transport layer to provide both connectionless and connection-oriented services. If you are running a connection-oriented protocol at one layer, there is usually no reason to use one at another layer. The object of the protocol stack is to provide only the services that an application needs, and no more.

The Transport Layer

Once you reach the transport layer, the process of getting packets from their source to their destination is no longer a concern. The transport layer protocols and all the layers above them rely completely on the network and data link layers for addressing and transmission services. As discussed earlier, packets being processed by intermediate systems travel only as high as the network layer, so the transport-layer protocols operate on only the two end systems. The transport layer PDU consists of a header and the data it has received from the application layer above, which is encapsulated into a datagram by the network layer below.

The transport layer provides different levels of service depending on the needs of the application:

- Packet acknowledgment
- Guaranteed delivery
- Flow control
- End-to-end error checking

One of the main functions of the transport layer protocol is to identify the upper-layer processes that generated the message at the source system and that will receive the message at the destination system. The transport layer protocols in the TCP/IP suite, for example, use port numbers in their headers to identify upper-layer services.

Protocol Service Combinations

Data link and network layer protocols operate together interchangeably; you can use almost any data link layer protocol with any network layer protocol. However, transport layer protocols are closely related to a particular network layer protocol and cannot be interchanged. The combination of a network layer protocol and a transport layer protocol provides a complementary set of services suitable for a specific application. As at the network layer, transport layer protocols can be connection oriented (CO) or connectionless (CL). The OSI model

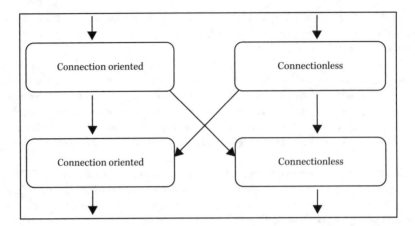

Figure 2-11   Any configuration of connection-oriented and connectionless protocols can be used.

document defines four possible combinations of CO and CL protocols at these two layers, depending on the services required, as shown in Figure 2-11. The process of selecting a combination of protocols for a particular task is called *mapping* a transport layer service onto a network layer service.

The selection of a protocol at the transport layer is based on the needs of the application generating the message and the services already provided by the protocols at the lower layers. The OSI document defines five theoretical classes of transport layer protocol, as shown here:

- **TP0**   This class does not provide any additional functionality beyond fragmenting and reassembly functions. This class determines the size of the smallest PDU required by any of the underlying networks and segments as needed.

- **TP1**   This class performs the functions of TP0 plus providing the capability to correct errors that have been detected by the protocols operating at the lower layers.

- **TP2**   This class provides fragmentation and reassembly functions, multiplexing, and demultiplexing and includes codes that identify the process that generated the packet and that will process it at the destination, thus enabling the traffic from multiple applications to be carried over a single network medium.

- **TP3**   This class offers error recovery, segmentation, reassembly, multiplexing, and demultiplexing. It combines the services provided by TP1 and TP2.

- **TP4**   This class provides complete connection-oriented service, including error detection and correction, flow control, and other services. It assumes the use of a connectionless protocol at the lower layers that provides none of these services.

This classification of transport layer services is another place where the theoretical constructs of the OSI model differ substantially from reality. No protocol suite in common use has five different transport layer protocols conforming to these classes. Most of the suites, like TCP/IP, have two protocols that basically conform to the TP0 and TP4 classes, providing connectionless and connection-oriented services, respectively.

Transport Layer Protocol Functions

The UDP protocol is a connectionless service that, together with IP at the network layer, provides minimal services for brief transactions that do not need the services of a connection-oriented protocol. Domain Name System (DNS) transactions, for example, generally consist of short messages that can fit into a single packet, so no flow control is needed. A typical transaction consists of a request and a reply, with the reply functioning as an acknowledgment, so no other guaranteed delivery mechanism is needed. UDP does have an optional error-detection mechanism in the form of a checksum computation performed on both the source and destination systems. Because the UDP protocol provides a minimum of additional services, its header is only 8 bytes long, providing little additional control overhead to the packet.

TCP, on the other hand, is a connection-oriented protocol that provides a full range of services but at the cost of much higher overhead. The TCP header is 20 bytes long, and the protocol also generates a large number of additional packets solely for control procedures, such as connection establishment, termination, and packet acknowledgment.

Segmentation and Reassembly

Connection-oriented transport layer protocols are designed to carry large amounts of data, but the data must be split into segments to fit into individual packets. The segmentation of the data and the numbering of the segments are critical elements in the transmission process and also make functions such as error recovery possible. The routing process performed at the network layer is dynamic; in the course of a transmission, it is possible for the segments to take different routes to the destination and arrive in a different order from that in which they were sent. It is the numbering of the segments that makes it possible for the receiving system to reassemble them into their original order. This numbering also makes it possible for the receiving system to notify the sender that specific packets have been lost or corrupted. As a result, the sender can retransmit only the missing segments and not have to repeat the entire transmission.

Flow Control

One of the functions commonly provided by connection-oriented transport layer protocols is flow control, which is a mechanism by which the system receiving the data can notify the sender that it must decrease its transmission rate or risk overwhelming the receiver and losing data. The TCP header, for example, includes a Window field in which the receiver specifies the number of bytes it can receive from the sender. If this value decreases in succeeding packets, the sender knows that it has to slow down its transmission rate. When the value begins to rise again, the sender can increase its speed.

Error Detection and Recovery

The OSI model document defines two forms of error recovery that can be performed by connection-oriented transport layer protocols. One is a response to *signaled errors* detected by other protocols in the stack. In this mechanism, the transport layer protocol does not have to detect the transmission errors themselves. Instead, it receives notification from a protocol at the network or data link layer that an error has occurred and that specific packets have been lost or corrupted. The transport layer protocol only has to send a message back to the source system listing the packets and requesting their retransmission.

The more commonly implemented form of error recovery at the transport layer is a complete process of error detection and correction that is used to cope with *unsignaled errors,* which are errors that have not yet been detected by other means. Even though most data link layer protocols have their own error-detection and correction mechanisms, they function only over the individual hops between two systems. A transport layer error-detection mechanism provides error checking between the two end systems and includes the capability to recover from the errors by informing the sender which packets have to be resent. To do this, the checksum included in the transport layer protocol header is computed only on the fields that are not modified during the journey to the destination. Fields that routinely change are omitted from the calculation.

The Session Layer

When you reach the session layer, the boundaries between the layers and their functions start to become more obscure. There are no discrete protocols that operate exclusively at the session layer. Rather, the session layer functionality is incorporated into other protocols, with functions that fall into the provinces of the presentation and application layers as well. Network Basic Input/Output System (NetBIOS) and NetBIOS Extended User Interface (NetBEUI) are two of the best examples of these protocols. The session layer provides mechanisms by which the message dialog between computers is established, maintained, and terminated. For specific examples that may further clarify, see the ISO 8327 standard that defines session layer protocols and is assumed to be used by various IOS 8823 standard protocols in the presentation layer.

The boundary to the session layer is also the point at which all concern for the transmission of data between two systems is transcended. Questions of packet acknowledgment, error detection, and flow control are all left behind at this point because everything that can be done has been done by the protocols at the transport layer and below.

The session layer is also not inherently concerned with security and the network logon process, as the name seems to imply. Rather, the primary functions of this layer concern the exchange of messages between the two connected end systems, called a *dialog.* There are also numerous other functions provided at this layer, which really serves as a multipurpose "toolkit" for application developers.

The services provided by the session layer are widely misunderstood, and even at the time of the OSI model's development, there was some question concerning whether they should be allotted a layer of their own. In fact, 22 different services are provided by the session layer, grouped into subsets such as the Kernel Function Unit, the Basic Activity Subset, and the Basic Synchronization Subset. Most of these services are of interest only to application developers, and some are even duplicated as a result of a compromise that occurred when the two committees creating OSI model standards were combined.

Communications between the layers of the OSI reference model are facilitated through the use of *service request primitives,* which are the tools in the toolkit. Each layer provides services to the layer immediately above it. A process at a given layer takes advantage of a service provided by the layer below by issuing a command using the appropriate service request primitive, plus any additional parameters that may be required. Thus, an application layer process issues a request for a network resource using a primitive provided by the presentation layer. The request is then passed down through the layers, with each layer using the proper primitive provided by the layer below, until the message is ready for transmission over the network. Once the packet arrives at its destination, it is decoded into *indication primitives* that are passed upward through the layers of the stack to the receiving application process.

The two most important services attributed to the session layer are dialog control and dialog separation. Dialog control is the means by which two systems initiate a dialog, exchange messages, and finally end the dialog while ensuring that each system has received the messages intended for it. While this may seem to be a simple task, consider the fact that one system might transmit a message to the other and then receive a message without knowing for certain when the response was generated. Is the other system responding to the message just sent or was its response transmitted before that message was received? This sort of *collision case* can cause serious problems, especially when one of the systems is attempting to terminate the dialog or create a checkpoint. *Dialog separation* is the process of inserting a reference marker called a *checkpoint* into the data stream passing between the two systems so that the status of the two machines can be assessed at the same point in time.

Dialog Control

When two end systems initiate a session layer dialog, they choose one of two modes that controls the way they will exchange messages for the duration of the session: either *two-way alternate (TWA)* or *two-way simultaneous (TWS) mode*. Each session connection is uniquely identified by a 196-byte value consisting of the following four elements:

- Initiator SS-USER reference
- Responder SS-USER reference
- Common reference
- Additional reference

Once made, the choice of mode is irrevocable; the connection must be severed and reestablished in order to switch to the other mode.

In TWA mode, only one of the systems can transmit messages at any one time. Permission to transmit is arbitrated by the possession of a *data token*. Each system, at the conclusion of a transmission, sends the token to the other system using the S-TOKEN-GIVE primitive. On receipt of the token, the other system can transmit its message.

The use of TWS mode complicates the communication process enormously. As the name implies, in a TWS mode connection, there is no token, and both systems can transmit messages at the same time.

NOTE Remember that the references to tokens and connections at the session layer have nothing to do with the similarly named elements in lower-layer protocols. A session layer token is not the equivalent of the token frame used by the Token Ring protocol, nor is a session layer connection the equivalent of a transport layer connection such as that used by TCP. It is possible for end systems to terminate the session layer connection while leaving the transport layer connection open for further communication.

The use of the token prevents problems resulting from crossed messages and provides a mechanism for the orderly termination of the connection between the systems. An orderly termination begins with one system signaling its desire to terminate the connection and transmitting the token. The other system, on receiving the token, transmits any data remaining in its buffers and uses the S-RELEASE primitive to acknowledge the termination request. On receiving the S-RELEASE primitive, the original system knows that it has received all of the data pending from the other system and can then use the S-DISCONNECT primitive to terminate the connection.

There is also a negotiated release feature that enables one system to refuse the release request of another, which can be used in cases in which a collision occurs because both systems have issued a release request at the same time, and a release token that prevents the occurrence of these collisions in the first place by enabling only one system at a time to request a release.

All of these mechanisms are "tools" in the kit that the session layer provides to application developers; they are not automatic processes working behind the scenes. When designing an application, the developer must make an explicit decision to use the S-TOKEN-GIVE primitive instead of S-TOKEN-PLEASE, for example, or to use a negotiated release instead of an orderly termination.

Dialog Separation

Applications create checkpoints in order to save their current status to disk in case of a system failure. This was a much more common occurrence at the time that the OSI model was developed than it is now. As with the dialog control processes discussed earlier, *checkpointing* is a procedure that must be explicitly implemented by an application developer as needed.

When the application involves communication between two systems connected by a network, the checkpoint must save the status of both systems at the same point in the data stream. Performing any activity at precisely the same moment on two different computers is nearly impossible. The systems might be performing thousands of activities per second, and their timing is nowhere near as precise as would be needed to execute a specific task simultaneously. In addition, the problem again arises of messages that may be in transit at the time the checkpoint is created. As a result, dialog separation is performed by saving a checkpoint at a particular point in the data stream passing between the two systems, rather than at a particular moment in time.

When the connection uses TWA mode, the checkpointing process is relatively simple. One system creates a checkpoint and issues a primitive called S-SYNC-MINOR. The other system, on receiving this primitive, creates its own checkpoint, secure in the knowledge that no data is left in transit at the time of synchronization. This is called a *minor synchronization* because it works with data flowing in only one direction at a time and requires only a single exchange of control messages.

It is still possible to perform a minor synchronization in TWS mode using a special token that prevents both systems from issuing the S-SYNC-MINOR primitive at the same time. If it was possible to switch from TWS to TWA mode in midconnection, the use of an additional token would not be necessary, but mode switching is not possible. This is something that many people think is a major shortcoming in the session layer specification.

In most cases, systems using TWS mode communications must perform a *major synchronization,* which accounts not only for traffic that can be running in both directions but also for expedited traffic. A primitive called S-EXPEDITED enables one system to transmit to the other using what amounts to a high-speed pipeline that is separate from the normal communications channel. To perform a major synchronization, the system in possession of yet another token called the *major/activity token* issues a primitive called S-SYNC-MAJOR and then stops transmitting until it receives a response. However, the system issuing this primitive cannot create its checkpoint yet, as in a minor synchronization, because there may be traffic from the other system currently in transit.

On receiving the primitive, the other system is able to create its own checkpoint because all of the data in transit has been received, including expedited data, which has to have arrived before the primitive. The receiving system then transmits a confirmation response over the normal channel and transmits a special PREPARE message over the expedited channel. The system that initiated the synchronization procedure receives the PREPARE message first and then the confirmation, at which time it can create its own checkpoint.

The Presentation Layer

Unlike the session layer, which provides many different functions, the presentation layer has only one. In fact, most of the time, the presentation layer functions primarily as a *pass-through service,* meaning that it receives primitives from the application layer and issues duplicate primitives to the session layer below using the Presentation Service Access Point (PSAP) and the Session Service Access Point (SSAP). All of the discussion in the previous sections about applications utilizing session layer services actually involves the use of the pass-through service at the presentation layer because it is impossible for a process at any layer of the OSI model to communicate directly with any layer other than the one immediately above or beneath it. The presentation layer negotiates the use of a transfer syntax that is supported by both of the connected devices so the end systems of different types can communicate.

While the basic functions of the primitives are not changed as they are passed down through the presentation layer, they can undergo a crucial translation process that is the primary function of the layer. Applications generate requests for network resources using their own native syntax, but the syntax of the application at the destination system receiving the request may be different in several ways. The systems might also implement encryption and/or compression on the data to be transmitted over the network.

This translation process occurs in two phases, one of which runs at the presentation layer on each system. Each computer maintains an *abstract syntax,* which is the native syntax for the application running on that system, and a *transfer syntax,* which is a common syntax used to transmit the data over the network. The presentation layer on the system sending a message converts the data from the abstract syntax to the transfer syntax and then passes it down to the session layer. When the message arrives at the destination system, the presentation layer converts the data from the transfer syntax to the abstract syntax of the application receiving the message. The transfer syntax chosen for each abstract syntax is based on a negotiation that occurs when a presentation layer connection is established between two systems. Depending on the application's requirements and the nature of the connection between the systems, the transfer context may provide data encryption, data compression, or a simple translation.

NOTE The presentation layer connection is not synonymous with the connections that occur at the lower layers, nor is there direct communication between the presentation layers of the two systems. Messages travel down through the protocol stack to the physical medium and up through the stack on the receiver to the presentation layer there.

The syntax negotiation process begins when one system uses the P-CONNECT primitive to transmit a set of presentation contexts, which are pairs of associated abstract contexts and transfer contexts supported by that system. Each presentation context is numbered using a unique odd-numbered integer called a *presentation context identifier*. With this message, one system is essentially informing the other of its presentation layer capabilities. The message may contain multiple transfer contexts for each abstract context to give the receiving system a choice.

Once the other system receives the P-CONNECT message, it passes the presentation contexts up to the application-layer processes, which decide which of the transfer contexts supported by each abstract context they want to use. The receiver then returns a list of contexts to the sender with either a single transfer context or an error message specified for each abstract context. On receipt by the original sender, this list becomes the defined context set. Error messages indicate that the receiving system does not support any of the transfer contexts specified for a specific abstract context. Once the negotiation process is completed, the systems can propose new presentation contexts for addition to the defined context set or remove contexts from the set using a primitive called P-ALTER-CONTEXT.

The Application Layer

As the top layer in the protocol stack, the application layer is the ultimate source and destination for all messages transmitted over the network. All of the processes discussed in the previous sections are triggered by an application that requests access to a resource located on a network system. Application-layer processes are not necessarily synonymous with the applications themselves, however. For example, if you use a word processor to open a document stored on a network server, you are redirecting a local function to the network. The word processor itself does not provide the application layer process needed to access the file. In most cases, it is an element of the operating system that distinguishes between requests for files on the local drive and those on the network. Other applications, however, are designed specifically for accessing network resources. When you run a dedicated FTP client, for example, the application itself is inseparable from the application layer protocol it uses to communicate with the network. The application layer protocol is the interface between the application running on the computer that is requesting the services of the network and the protocol stack that converts that request into the transmitted signals.

Some of the other protocols that are closely tied to the applications that use them are as follows:

- **DHCP**   Dynamic Host Configuration Protocol
- **TFTP**   Trivial File Transfer Protocol
- **DNS**   Domain Name System
- **NFS**   Network File System
- **RIP**   Routing Information Protocol
- **BGP**   Border Gateway Protocol

NOTE These protocols are somewhat different from applications that are designed for the users, such as word processors or spreadsheets. These protocols are primarily designed to be used by the systems.

In between these two extremes are numerous application types that access network resources in different ways and for different reasons. The tools that make that access possible are located in the application layer. Some applications use protocols that are dedicated to specific types of network requests, such as the Simple Mail Transport Protocol (SMTP) and Post Office Protocol (POP3) both used for e-mail, the Simple Network Management Protocol (SNMP) used for remote network administration, and the Hypertext Transfer Protocol (HTTP) used for World Wide Web communications.

As you have seen in this chapter, the bottom four layers of the OSI reference model perform functions that are easily differentiated, while the functions of the session, presentation, and application layers tend to bleed together. Many of the application layer protocols listed here contain functions that rightly belong at the presentation or session layers, but it is important not to let the OSI model assert itself too forcibly into your perception of data networking. The model is a tool for understanding how networks function, not a guide for the creation of networking technologies.

Part I

PART

II

Network Hardware

CHAPTER 3

Network Interface Adapters

Every computer that participates on a network must have an interface to that network, using either a cable or some form of wireless signal that enables it to transmit data to the other devices on the network. The most common form of wired network interface is part of the mainboard and connects to a network cable, typically referred to as a *network interface card* (or *controller*), or NIC for short (see Figure 3-1). Also called a *network interface adapter,* this is normally an Ethernet connection and is used by small and medium-sized businesses as well as home network configurations.

Figure 3-1   A typical Ethernet network card (photo provided by Dsimic at English Wikipedia under the GNU Free Documentation License)

NIC Functions

The network interface adapter, in combination with the network adapter driver, implements the data link layer protocol used on the computer, usually Ethernet, as well as part of the physical layer. The NIC also provides the link between the network layer protocol, which is implemented completely in the operating system, and the network medium, which is usually a cable connected to the NIC. If you use an Ethernet NIC, your connection is made with an Ethernet cable with an RJ-45 connection. The RJ-45 connector looks like a telephone connection (RJ-11) but is larger.

The NIC and its driver perform the basic functions needed for the computer to access the network. The process of transmitting data consists of the following steps (which, naturally, are reversed during packet reception):

1. **Data transfer**   The data stored in the computer's memory is transferred to the NIC across the system bus using one of the following technologies: *direct memory access* (DMA), shared memory, or programmed I/O.

2. **Data buffering**   The rate at which the PC processes data is different from the transmission rate of the network. The NIC includes memory buffers that it uses to store data so it can process an entire frame at once.

NOTE *Bandwidth* is the term used to indicate speed capabilities of the physical devices used when interacting with a network. Basic Ethernet, for example, has a bandwidth of 10 Mbps, so using an Internet connection faster than that would be largely wasted speed. Fast Ethernet reaches 100 Mbps, usually adequate for home computer connections. Gigabit Ethernet can reach 1 Gbps, and 10 Gigabit Ethernet is 10 Gbps. Even wireless connections are limited by bandwidth. Wireless 802.11b is 11 Mbps, and Wireless-G 802.11g has a top speed of 54 Mbps. Wireless-N 802.11 can reach 300 Mbps.

---

3. **Frame construction**   The NIC receives data that has been packaged by the network layer protocol and encapsulates it in a frame that consists of its own data link layer protocol header and footer. Depending on the size of the packet and the data link layer protocol used, the NIC may also have to split the data into segments of the appropriate size for transmission over the network. For incoming traffic, the NIC reads the information in the data link layer frame, verifies that the packet has been transmitted without error, and determines whether the packet should be passed up to the next layer in the networking stack. If so, the NIC strips off the data link layer frame and passes the enclosed data to the network layer protocol.

4. **Media access control**   The NIC is responsible for arbitrating the system's access to the shared network medium, using an appropriate *media access control* (MAC) mechanism. This is necessary to prevent multiple systems on the network from transmitting at the same time and losing data because of a packet collision. The MAC mechanism is the single most defining element of a data link layer protocol. (The MAC mechanism is not needed for incoming traffic.)

5. **Parallel/serial conversion**   The system bus connecting the NIC to the computer's main memory array transmits data 16 or 32 bits at a time in parallel fashion, while the NIC transmits and receives data from the network serially—that is, one bit at a time.

The NIC is responsible for taking the parallel data transmission that it receives over the system bus into its buffers and converting it to a serial bit stream for transmission out over the network medium. For incoming data from the network, the process is reversed.

6. **Data encoding/decoding**   The data generated by the computer in binary form must be encoded in a matter suitable for the network medium before it can be transmitted, and in the same way, incoming signals must be decoded on receipt. This and the following step are the physical layer processes implemented by the NIC. For a copper cable, the data is encoded into electrical impulses; for fiber-optic cable, the data is encoded into pulses of light. Other media may use radio waves, infrared light, or other technologies. The encoding scheme is determined by the data link layer protocol being used.

7. **Data transmission/reception**   The NIC takes the data it has encoded, amplifies the signal to the appropriate amplitude, and transmits it over the network medium. This process is entirely physical and depends wholly on the nature of the signal used on the network medium.

The NIC also provides the data link layer hardware (or MAC) address that is used to identify the system on the local network. Most data link layer protocols rely on addresses that are hard-coded into the NIC by the manufacturer. In actuality, the MAC address identifies a particular network interface, not necessarily the whole system. In the case of a computer with two NICs installed and connected to two different networks, each NIC has its own MAC address that identifies it on the network to which it is attached.

Some older protocols, such as ARCnet, required the network administrator to set the hardware address manually on each NIC. If systems with duplicate addresses were on the network, communications problems resulted. Today, MAC addresses are assigned in two parts, much like IP addresses and domain names. The Institute of Electrical and Electronic Engineers (IEEE) maintains a registry of NIC manufacturers and assigns 3-byte address codes called *organizationally unique identifiers* (OUIs) to them as needed.

NIC Features

In addition to the basic functionality described thus far, NICs can have a variety of other features, depending on the manufacturer, protocol, price point, and the type of computer in which the device is to be used. Some of these features are discussed in the following sections.

Full Duplex

Most of the data link layer protocols that use twisted-pair cable separate the transmitted and received signals onto different wire pairs. Even when this is the case, however, the NIC typically operates in half-duplex mode, meaning that at any given time, it can be transmitting or receiving data, but not both simultaneously. NICs that operate in full-duplex mode can transmit and receive at the same time, effectively doubling the throughput of the network (see Figure 3-2).

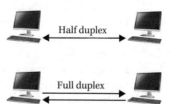

Figure 3-2   Full-duplex systems can transfer data in both directions at the same time, while half-duplex systems transfer information in one direction at a time.

When a NIC is operating in full-duplex mode, it can transmit and receive data at any time, eliminating the need for a media access control mechanism. This also eliminates collisions, which increases the overall efficiency of the network. Running a full-duplex network requires more than just NICs that support this feature, however. The hub, switch, router, or other device to which each computer connects must also support full-duplex operation.

Bus Mastering

Normally, when data is transmitted between the computer's memory and an expansion card over the system bus, the processor functions as the middle man, reading data from the source and transmitting it to the destination. This utilizes processor clock cycles that could otherwise be running applications or performing other important tasks. An expansion card capable of *bus mastering* has a chipset that arbitrates the card's access to the bus, eliminating the need for the system processor's involvement in the transfer of data to and from memory. Bus mastering NICs enable the computer to operate more efficiently because they conserve the processor clock cycles that would otherwise be expended in data transfers.

Parallel Tasking

Parallel Tasking is a feature that was developed by 3Com Corporation and subsequently implemented by other NIC manufacturers, using different names. The term describes a process by which the NIC can begin to transmit a packet over the network while the data is still being transferred to the NIC over the system bus. A NIC without this capability must wait until an entire packet is stored in its buffers before it can transmit. Today, many NICs feature Parallel Tasking II, which improves bus mastering communications over the Peripheral Component Interconnect (PCI) bus. Previously, a PCI NIC could transfer only 64 bytes at a time during a single bus master operation, which required dozens of operations to transfer each packet. Parallel Tasking II enables the NIC to stream up to an entire Ethernet packet's worth of data (1,518 bytes) during a single bus master operation.

Wake-on-LAN or Wake-on-Wireless-LAN

Today's industry standard, Wake-on-LAN (WoL) is a feature that enables a computer to "wake" from a very low power state. WoL is an enhancement built into network interface adapters and computer motherboards that enables an administrator to turn a computer on from a remote location. Once turned on, the administrator can perform any necessary maintenance tasks. For this feature to function, both the computer's motherboard and the NIC must have a three-pin remote wake-up connector, which is connected with a cable. When the computer is turned off, it actually switches to a low-power sleep state instead of being completely powered off. While in this state, the NIC continuously monitors the network for a special wake-up packet that can be delivered to it by a desktop management application running on an administrator's computer.

When the NIC receives the packet, it signals the motherboard, which in turn switches the power supply back into its full power state, effectively turning on the computer. Once the computer is up and running, the administrator can take control of the system using whatever tools are available.

Selecting a NIC

When your mainboard does not have an acceptable NIC or you simply want to upgrade the built-in card, you need to consider several factors:

- The data link layer protocol used by the network
- The transmission speed of the network
- The type of interface that connects the NIC to the network
- The type of system bus into which you will install the NIC
- The hardware resources the NIC requires
- The electric power the NIC requires
- The role of the computer using the NIC (server versus workstation and home versus office)
- Appropriate driver availability

NOTE The most common network interface cards are a PCI, ISA, or PCMCIA card. The kind you choose largely depends on the computer you will be installing the card in and what type of interface that computer offers. A PCI card goes into a PCI slot of your computer and operates at a fast speed. This is the most common choice for most users. An ISA card that connects to a computer's motherboard can be less expensive than a PCI card but may also be less reliable. PCMCIA cards are placed in an appropriate slot in laptops.

The following sections examine these criteria and how they can affect the performance of the NIC and your network.

Protocol

The data link layer protocol is the single most defining characteristic of a network interface adapter. The most popular protocol used at the data link layer is Ethernet, but NICs are also available that support Token Ring, FDDI, ATM, and others, as well as variations on these protocols.

All of the computers on the network must, of course, be using the same data link layer protocol, and the selection of that protocol should be a decision made long before you're ready to purchase NICs. This is because all of the other network hardware, such as cables, hubs, and other devices, are also protocol specific. The NIC you select must also support the type of cable or other medium the network uses, as well as the transmission speed of the network. You can also select Ethernet NICs that support the use of unshielded twisted-pair (UTP), two types of coaxial, or fiber-optic cable, as well as various types of wireless transmissions. These are all aspects of the network configuration that you must consider before making NIC purchases.

Transmission Speed

Some data link layer protocols can run at different speeds, and the capability of a NIC to support these speeds can be an important part of selecting the correct product for your network. In some protocols, an increase in speed has been fully assimilated into the technology, while in others, the faster version is still an optional feature. Fast Ethernet (running at 100 Mbps) has, for all practical purposes, replaced traditional 10 Mbps Ethernet. Some of the Fast Ethernet NICs manufactured today are combination devices that support both 10 and 100 Mbps operation, making it possible to gradually upgrade an older Ethernet network. When the connection is established between the NIC and the hub, the devices negotiate the highest possible speed they have in common.

Network Interface

The type of cable (or other medium) that forms the fabric of the network determines the network interface used on the NIC. The network cable type is typically selected at the same time as the data link layer protocol, and the NICs you purchase must support that medium. Some data link layer protocols support different types of cables, and NICs are available for each one, while other protocols are designed to use only one type of cable.

Today, you can choose to install a NIC that uses the Ethernet cable with an RJ-45 connector. The PCI or PCI Express cards require that you open the computer to install the cards. You can also purchase Universal Serial Bus (USB) devices that simply connect to your computer at a USB port.

Ethernet also supports the use of fiber-optic cable in that it carries data coded into light pulses rather than into electric voltages. The components on a fiber-optic NIC are therefore substantially different in form (if not function) from those on a copper-based Ethernet NIC, including the network interface, which is usually a straight-tip (ST) connector. Fast Ethernet can use fiber-optic cable to run at 100 Mbps over far longer distances than any copper medium. Because of these technological differences, fiber-optic Fast Ethernet NICs are not usually combined with other technologies. Fiber-optic network hardware is often more expensive than comparable copper-based products.

Bus Interface

The network interface adapter enables a network system to transmit data from its main memory array to an outside destination, just like a parallel or serial port does. The data travels from the memory to the network adapter across the system bus, in the same manner as with any other expansion card, like a graphics or audio adapter. The type of bus the NIC uses to communicate with the computer can affect the performance of the network connection, but the selection of a bus type for the NIC is unique to each computer. PCI is the bus type used in virtually all of the desktop computers sold today. Laptops and other portables use the PC Card bus (formerly known as the Personal Computer Memory Card International Association, or PCMCIA bus). Older systems used various other types of expansion buses, such as VESA Local Bus (VLB), Micro Channel Architecture (MCA), or Extended Industry Standard Architecture (EISA). USB adapters require no internal installation. You simply plug the adapter into a computer's USB port, plug the network cable into the adapter, and install the appropriate driver for the new device. No external power connection is needed; the adapter derives power from the bus. This makes for an extremely simple installation, but the performance of a USB network adapter can be inferior to other NICs.

Table 3-1 lists the characteristics of these buses and their respective bus speed.

Bottlenecks

The bus type selection can affect network performance if the selected bus is slow enough to cause a bottleneck in the network. In networking, a *bottleneck* occurs when one element of a network connection runs at a significantly slower speed than all of the others. This can cause the entire

Bus Type	Bus Width	Bus Speed	Bandwidth
ISA	16 bit	4 MHz	8 Mbps
PCI	32 bit	33 MHz	133 Mbps
PCI-X 66	64 bit	66 MHz	533 Mbps
PCIe 1.0 x1	1 bit	2.5 GHz	250 Mbps
PCIe 2.0 x16	16 bit	5 GHz	8,000 Mbps
PCIe 3.0 x16	16 bit	8 GHz	16,000 Mbps

Table 3-1   PC Bus Types, Widths, Speed, and Bandwidth

network to slow down to the speed of its weakest component, resulting in wasted bandwidth and needless expense. As an exaggerated example, consider a network that consists of modern PCs with the fast processors, connected by a Fast Ethernet network running at 100 Mbps. All of the workstations on the network have NICs that use the PCI bus except for the main database server, which has an old ISA NIC. The result of this is that the ISA NIC will probably be the slowest component in all of the workstation/server connections and will be a bottleneck that prevents the rest of the equipment from achieving its full potential.

The process of identifying actual bottlenecks is rarely this clean-cut. Just because a network protocol runs at 100 Mbps doesn't mean that data is continuously traveling over the cable at that speed, and the raw speed of a particular bus type is not indicative of that actual throughput rate for the data generated by the system. However, it is a good idea to use common sense when purchasing NICs and to try to maximize the performance of your network.

ISA or PCI?

If you have to deal with the older bus types, you may encounter Industry Standard Architecture (ISA) cards. The choice for most desktop systems manufactured after about 1995 was between ISA and PCI. For a traditional Ethernet network running at 10 Mbps or a Token Ring network running at 4 or 16 Mbps, an ISA NIC was more than sufficient. In fact, ISA NICs can be perfectly serviceable on 100 Mbps networks as well, at least for workstations, because the average network user does not require anything approaching 100 Mbps of bandwidth on a continuous basis. The main reason for the ISA NIC being the bottleneck in the scenario described earlier is that it is installed in the server. A server PC that is handling data requests generated by dozens or hundreds of workstations simultaneously naturally requires more bandwidth than any single workstation. In a server, therefore, the use of the fastest bus available is always recommended.

However, there is another element to the bus type decision that you must consider, and that is the availability of expansion bus slots in your computers. Obviously, to install a network interface card into a PC, it must have a free bus slot. Legacy PCs have varying numbers of PCI and ISA slots, and the hardware configuration of the machine determines how many of those slots (if any) are free. Many older "full-featured computers" have peripheral devices installed that occupy many of the bus slots. Because it is possible for a card to occupy a slot without protruding through the back of the computer, simply looking at the outside of a system is not sufficient to determine how many free slots there are. You must open the machine to check for free slots and to determine which types of slots are available. If no slots are available, an external network adapter using the USB port may be your only recourse.

Administrators of large networks often purchase workstations that do not have all the state-of-the-art features found in many home systems, which may leave more slots free for additional components such as a NIC. In addition, PCs targeted at the corporate market are more likely to have peripheral devices such as audio and video adapters integrated into the motherboard, which also can leave more free slots. However, an office computer may also use a slimline or low-profile case design that reduces the number of slots to minimize the computer's footprint.

Even in legacy systems, the selection of the bus type for the NIC should be based on the network bandwidth requirements of the user and not on the type of bus slot the computer has free. However, you may have no other choice than to put an ISA NIC in a computer that could benefit from a PCI card but has only an ISA slot free.

Integrated Adapters

As mentioned earlier, many PCs have peripheral devices integrated into the motherboard. One of these devices may be the network interface adapter. Because an integrated network adapter is not a separate card, it cannot rightfully be called a NIC, but it does perform the same function as a network adapter that is installed into the system's expansion bus. Although they reduce the distance the signals have to travel to reach the adapter and avoid the electrical interference that occurs during a bus transfer, the problem with integrated network adapters is that they are not upgradable. A system that has an integrated network adapter is under no obligation to use it. You can nearly always disable the adapter by going through the system BIOS, by manipulating a switch or jumper on the motherboard, or simply by installing a NIC into a bus slot. You might find a deal on workstations with the wrong type of integrated network adapter that is good enough to be worth buying NICs for the computers as well.

Fiber-Optic NICs

The first considerations for choosing a fiber-optic network card are network type and transmission rate. Consider the bandwidth needs of the server or workstation, along with the physical medium used for transmission to determine the transmission rate of the card you purchase. Since Ethernet offers speeds that vary between 10 Mbps, 10/100 Mbps, 1000 Mbps, and even 10 Gbps, it is usually best to choose a card that works with the lowest component in the network. For example, if your network uses a 100 Mbps cable, using a 1000 Mbps card will still only result in 100 Mbps.

Also, pay attention to the bus type. Servers and workstations typically use some form of the PCI bus, such as the Peripheral Component Interconnect Express (PCIe) card. Today, most PCs no longer support the ISA connector, so when you purchase network cards for your PC, do not buy the outdated ISA network card. Instead, choose a current PCI card.

Remember, you must also consider the connector type used by the NIC. The network card needs to be connected with the network, so it must have a fiber-optic connector to link with other computer network equipment.

Portable Systems

Network interface adapters for laptops and other portable systems take the form of PC CardBus NICs or USB-connected adapters. As such, consider the speed of the network with which you will be connecting, as well as the price and reliability of the device you choose.

Hardware Resource Requirements

In addition to a bus slot or an available USB port, a computer must have the appropriate hardware resources free to support a NIC. A network interface adapter requires a free *interrupt request line* (IRQ) and usually either an I/O port address, a memory address, or both. When evaluating NICs, you must take into account both the resource requirements of the NIC and the resources available on the computer. On a PC with a lot of peripheral devices already installed, most of the IRQs may already be in use, and adding a NIC may be difficult. This is because a NIC may be able to use only a select few of the system's IRQs, and if all of those IRQs are occupied, the card cannot function. Two devices configured to use the same resource will sometimes conflict, causing both to malfunction. In some cases, however, it's possible for two devices to share an IRQ. To free up one of the IRQs usable by the NIC, you may have to configure another device to use a different IRQ. Thus, you have to consider not only the number of available IRQs on the computer but also which ones are available. The same is true for the other resources required by the card.

Many older NICs supported only two or three IRQs and other resources, and configuring the devices in the computer was a manual trial-and-error process. System administrators could spend hours trying different combinations of hardware settings for the components in a single computer before finding one that enabled all of the devices to function simultaneously. Today, however, NICs are generally more flexible and support a wider range of resource settings. In addition, the BIOS and the operating system of a modern PC have features that simplify the process of configuring peripheral devices to work together.

Plug-and-play, when it functions properly, eliminates the need to worry about hardware resource configuration for peripheral devices. When a system has a BIOS, an operating system, and hardware that all support the plug-and-play standard, the computer assigns hardware resources to each device dynamically when the system starts. When plug-and-play is not supported for a particular device such as a NIC, operating systems (such as Microsoft Windows) provide tools that can identify the free resources in the machine and indicate whether the NIC's current configuration conflicts with any other devices in the system.

Thus, when selecting NICs, you should be conscious of the hardware resources in use on the computers that will use them. When using NICs and computers of recent manufacture, this is rarely a problem. However, a computer with a lot of installed peripherals may be unable to support an additional card without removing one of the existing components. In other cases, you may have to reconfigure other devices to support the addition of a NIC. Most NIC manufacturers publish specification sheets (often available on their web sites) that list the hardware resources their NICs can use. By comparing this information to the current configuration of a PC, you can determine whether the computer has the resources to support the NIC.

Power Requirements

The power supplies in today's computers usually provide more than enough voltage to support a full load of expansion cards and other internal peripherals. However, if you're running a system with a large number of internal devices, you may want to compare the power load incurred by these devices with the voltage furnished by the computer's power supply before you install a NIC. Because the power drain of mechanical drives varies depending on how often and how heavily they're used, a system putting out insufficient power to support its hardware load may experience intermittent problems that are difficult to diagnose. What may seem to be a faulty drive may, in fact, be the effect of an insufficient power supply for the hardware.

Server vs. Workstation NICs

The NICs in servers and workstations perform the same basic functions, and yet there are cards on the market that are targeted specifically for use in servers. Some of these NICs use protocols, such as Gigabit Ethernet, that are intended primarily for servers because their cost and capabilities make them impractical for use in desktop workstations. Others, however, are NICs that use standard protocols but that contain additional features to make them more useful in servers. Naturally, these extra features drive the price of the NIC up considerably, and it is up to you to decide whether they are worth the extra expense.

Today, server NICs are more sophisticated and perform many functions. Advances such as flexible LANs on motherboard (LOMs) and smart NICs can use their own onboard processors to provide functionalities such as encryption/decryption, firewall, TCP/IP offload engine (TOE), iSCSI, and remote direct memory address. Understanding these contemporary NIC technologies is critical in the advent of virtualization and cloud computing.

CHAPTER 4

Network Interface Adapters and Connection Devices

Originally, LANs consisted of nothing more than computers and cables, but as the technology evolved, more equipment was required. As the early coaxial cable networks grew to span longer distances, devices called *repeaters* were added to boost the signals. Later, when the dominant medium for Ethernet networks shifted from coaxial to unshielded twisted-pair (UTP) cable, hubs became an essential network component. As networks grew from tools for localized workgroups to companywide resources, components such as bridges, switches, and routers were developed in order to create larger networks. Using these devices makes it possible to build networks that span longer distances, support more computers, and provide increased bandwidth for each system on the network. This chapter examines the functions of these devices and how you can integrate them into your network infrastructure.

Today, a wide variety of devices are used in networking. Many of the following items are considered *legacy* devices, in that they are no longer used in networks built today. However, you may still encounter them in older systems.

Repeaters

As a signal travels over a cable, the natural resistance of the medium causes it to gradually weaken until it is no longer viable. The longer the cable, the weaker the signal gets. This weakening is called *attenuation,* and it is a problem that affects all types of cable to some degree. The effect of attenuation is dependent on the type of cable. Copper cable, for example, is much more prone to attenuation than fiber-optic cable. This is one reason why fiber-optic cable segments can be much longer than copper ones.

When building a LAN, the standard for the data link layer protocol you intend to use contains specifications for the types of cable you can use and the guidelines for installing them. These guidelines include, among other things, the minimum and maximum lengths for the cables connecting the computers. The cable's attenuation rate is one of the most important factors affecting the maximum cable length. When you have to run a cable across a longer distance than is specified in the standard, you can use a repeater to amplify the signal, enabling it to travel greater distances without attenuating to the point of being unreadable by the destination system.

In its simplest form, a repeater is an electrical device used on a copper-based network that receives a signal through one cable connection, amplifies it, and transmits it out through another connection.

Repeaters were first used in data networking to expand the length of coaxial cable segments on Ethernet networks. On a coaxial network, such as a thin or thick Ethernet LAN, a stand-alone repeater enables you to extend the maximum bus length past 185 meters (for thin Ethernet) or 500 meters (for thick Ethernet). This type of repeater is simply a small box with two BNC connectors on it and a power cable. Using T connectors and terminators, you connect two cable segments to the repeater and the repeater to a power source. Signals entering either one of the two connectors are immediately amplified and transmitted out through the other connector. On most networks today, it is rare to see a stand-alone repeater because this function is built into another device, such as a hub or a switch.

Because its function is purely electrical, this type of repeater functioned at the network's physical layer only. The repeater cannot read the contents of the packets traveling over the network or even know that they are packets. The device simply amplified the incoming electrical signals and passed them on. Repeaters are also incapable of performing any sort of filtration on the data traveling over the network. As a result, two cable segments joined by a repeater form a single collision domain and therefore a single network.

Hubs

A hub is a device that functions as the cabling nexus for a network that uses the star topology. Each computer has its own cable that connects to the central hub. The responsibility of the hub is to see to it that traffic arriving over any of its ports is propagated out through the other ports. Depending on the network medium, a hub might use electrical circuitry, optical components, or other technologies to disseminate the incoming signal out among the outgoing ports. A fiber-optic hub, for example, actually uses mirrors to split the light impulses.

The hub itself is a box, either freestanding or rack-mounted, with a number of ports to which the cables connect. The ports can be the standard RJ-45 connectors used by twisted-pair networks, ST connectors for fiber-optic cable, or any other type of connector used on a star network. In many cases, hubs also have one or more LEDs for each port that light up to indicate when a device is connected to it, when traffic is passing through the port, or when a collision occurs.

The term *hub* or *concentrator* is used primarily in reference to Ethernet networks; the equivalent device on a Token Ring network is called a *multistation access unit* (MAU). Other protocols typically use one or the other of these terms, depending on the media access control (MAC) mechanism the protocol uses. The internal functions of hubs and MAUs are very different, but they serve the same basic purpose: to connect a collection of computers and other devices into a single collision domain.

Passive Hubs

Unlike stand-alone repeaters, which were all essentially the same, many different types of hubs exist with different capabilities. At its simplest, a hub supplies cable connections by passing all the signals entering the device through any port out through all the other ports. This is known as a *passive* hub because it operates only at the physical layer, has no intelligence, and does not amplify or modify the signal in any way. This type of hub was at one time used on ARCnet networks, but it is almost never used on networks today.

Repeating, Active, and Intelligent Hubs

The hubs used on Ethernet networks propagated received signals through any of their ports out through all of the other ports in the device simultaneously. This creates a shared network medium and joins the networked computers into a single collision and broadcast domain, just as if they were connected to the same cable, as on a coaxial Ethernet network. Ethernet hubs also supply repeating functionality by amplifying the incoming signals as they propagate them to the other ports. In fact, Ethernet hubs were sometimes referred to as *multipoint* repeaters. Unlike a passive hub, a repeating (or active) hub requires a power source to boost the signal. The device still operates at the physical layer, however, because it deals only with the raw signals traveling over the cables.

Some hubs go beyond repeating and can repair and retime the signals to synchronize the transmissions through the outgoing ports. These hubs use a technique called *store and forward,* which involves reading the contents of the packets to retransmit them over individual ports as needed. A hub with these capabilities can lower the network performance for the systems connected to it because of processing delays. At the same time, packet loss is diminished, and the number of collisions is reduced.

An Ethernet hub connects all of your computers into a single collision domain, which is not a problem on a small network. Larger networks consist of multiple network segments connected by other types of devices, such as bridges, switches, or routers. Because an Ethernet hub also functions as a repeater, each of the cables connecting the hub to a computer can be the maximum length allowed by the protocol standard. For Ethernet running on UTP cable, the maximum length is 100 meters.

Using multiple hubs on a single LAN is possible by connecting them together to form a hierarchical star network, as shown in Figure 4-1. When you do this using standard repeating hubs, all the computers remain in the same collision domain, and you must observe the configuration guidelines for the data link layer protocol used on the network. Just as with the

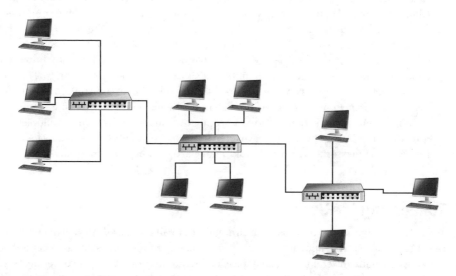

Figure 4-1   This star network uses multiple hubs to expand the collision domain.

stand-alone repeaters discussed earlier in this chapter, the path between any two machines on a 10 Mbps Ethernet network cannot include more than four repeaters (hubs). Fast Ethernet networks typically support only two hubs.

Intelligent hubs are units that have some form of integrated management capability. A basic repeating hub is essentially an electrical device that propagates incoming packets to all available ports without discrimination. Intelligent hubs do the same thing, but they also monitor the operation of each port. The management capabilities vary widely between products, but many intelligent hubs use the Simple Network Management Protocol (SNMP) to send information to a centralized network management console. Other devices might use a terminal directly connected to the hub or an HTML interface easily accessed from the Internet from anywhere on the network.

The object of the management capability is to provide the network administrator with a centralized source of information about the hubs and the systems connected to them. This eliminates the need for the staff supporting a large network to go running to each wiring closet looking for the hub or system causing a problem. The management console typically displays a graphical model of the network and alerts the administrator when a problem or failure occurs on any system connected to the hub.

On smaller networks, this capability isn't needed, but when you're managing an enterprise network with hundreds or thousands of nodes, a technology that can tell you exactly which one of the hub ports is malfunctioning can be helpful. The degree of intelligence built into a hub varies greatly with the product. Most devices have sufficient intelligence to go beyond the definition of a hub and provide bridging, switching, or routing functions.

Collision Domains and Broadcast Domains

A collision domain is a group of computers connected by a network so that if any two computers transmit at the same time, a collision between the transmitted packets occurs, causing the data in the packets to be damaged. This is in contrast to a *broadcast domain,* which is a group of computers networked together in such a way that if one computer generates a broadcast transmission, all of the other computers in the group receive it. These two concepts are the tests used to define the functionality of network connection devices (such as repeaters, hubs, bridges, switches, and routers) and are used repeatedly in this chapter. Other factors besides attenuation limit the maximum distance a network signal can travel. On an Ethernet network, for example, the first bit of a packet being transmitted by one computer must reach all the other computers on the local network before the last bit is transmitted. Therefore, you cannot extend a network segment without limit by adding multiple repeaters. A 10 Mbps Ethernet network can have up to five cable segments connected by four repeaters. Fast Ethernet networks are more limited, allowing a maximum of only two repeaters.

Token Ring MAUs

Token Ring networks use hubs as well, although they call them *multistation access units*. While the MAU, to all external appearances, performs the same function as an Ethernet hub, its internal workings are quite different. Instead of passing incoming traffic to all the other ports at one time, like in an Ethernet hub, the MAU transmits an incoming packet out through each port in turn, one at a time. After transmitting a packet to a workstation, the MAU waits until that packet returns through the same port before it transmits it out the next port. This implements the logical ring topology from which the protocol gets its name.

MAUs contain switches that enable specific ports to be excluded from the ring in the event of a failure of some kind. This prevents a malfunctioning workstation from disturbing the functionality of the entire ring. MAUs also have ring-in and ring-out ports that you can use to enlarge the ring network by connecting several MAUs.

NOTE See Chapter 12 for more information on network protocols.

Hub Configurations

Hubs are available in a wide variety of sizes and with many different features, ranging from small, simple devices designed to service a handful of computers to huge rack-mounted affairs for large, enterprise networks. Hub designs fall into three categories, as follows:

- Stand-alone hubs
- Stackable hubs
- Modular hubs

A *stand-alone hub* is a usually a small box about the size of a paperback book that has anywhere from 4 to 16 ports in it. As the name implies, the device is freestanding, has its own power source, and can easily fit on or under a desk. Four- or five-port hubs can work for home networks or for providing quick, ad hoc expansions to a larger network. Larger units can support more connections and often have LEDs that indicate the presence of a link pulse signal on the connected cable and, possibly, the occurrence of a collision on the network.

Despite the name, a stand-alone hub usually has some mechanism for connecting with other hubs to expand the network within the same collision domain. The following sections examine how the most common mechanisms are used for this purpose.

The Uplink Port

The cables used on a twisted-pair network are wired *straight through,* meaning that each of the eight pins on the RJ-45 connector on one end of the cable is wired to the corresponding pin on the other end. UTP networks use separate wire pairs within the cable for transmitting and receiving data. For a UTP connection between two computers to function, however, the transmit contacts on each system must be connected to the receive contacts on the other. Therefore, a crossover must exist somewhere in the connection, and traditionally this occurs in the hub, as shown in Figure 4-2. The pins in each of a hub's ports are connected to those of every other port using crossover circuits that transpose the transport data (TD) and receive data (RD) signals. Without this crossover circuit, the transmit contacts on the two systems are connected, as are the receive contacts, preventing any communication from taking place.

NOTE See more information on cabling in Chapter 5.

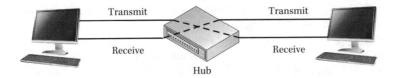

Figure 4-2 Hubs that contain crossover circuits allow cables to be wired straight through.

Many hubs have a port that bypasses the crossover circuit, which you can use to connect to another hub. This port is typically labeled *uplink* and may or may not have a switch that enables you to specify whether the port should be crossed over or wired straight through. If you have more than one hub on your system, you connect them using the uplink port on one hub only and a standard port on the other. If you connect two hubs using the uplink ports on both devices, the two crossovers would cancel each other out, and the connection between a computer attached to one hub and a computer attached to the other would be the equivalent of a straight-through connection. If a hub does not have an uplink port, you can still connect it to another hub using a standard port and a *crossover cable,* which is a cable that has the transmit pins on each end wired directly to the receive pins on the other end. You typically use the uplink port to connect hubs when they're located some distance away from each other and you want to use the same cable medium throughout the network. When you are evaluating hubs, being aware of just how many hub ports are available for workstation connections is important. A device advertised as an eight-port hub may have seven standard ports and one uplink port, leaving only seven connections for computers. No matter what the size of the network, purchasing hubs with a few ports more than you need right now, for expansion purposes, is always a good idea.

When you have several 10Base-T Ethernet hubs connected in a hierarchical star topology using their uplink ports, each length of cable is a separate segment. Because the Ethernet guidelines allow the path from one system to another to travel across only five segments, connected by four repeaters, you are limited to four hubs on any particular LAN.

As you expand this type of network further, you may run into another Ethernet limitation not yet mentioned. The bus connecting the hubs is called a *mixing segment* because it has more than two devices connected to it. A segment that connects only two devices, such as the UTP cable connecting hubs through the uplink port, is called a *link segment.* Of the five segments permitted on a 10BaseT LAN, only three of these can be mixing segments. This guideline, stating that you can connect up to five segments using four repeaters and that no more than three of the segments can be mixing segments, is known as the Ethernet 5-4-3 rule.

Stackable Hubs

As you move up the scale of hub size and complexity, you find units called *stackable hubs* that provide greater expandability. As the name implies, these hubs have cases designed to stack one on top of the other, but this is not the only difference. Unlike stand-alone hubs, which can be located in different rooms or floors and still connected together, stackable hubs are typically located in a data center or wiring closet and are connected together with short cables.

When you connect stackable hubs, they form what is functionally a single larger hub. The cables connecting the units do not form separate segments, so you can have more than four hubs interconnected. In addition, these devices can share their capabilities. A single intelligent hub unit can manage its own ports, as well as those of all the other units in the array.

Stackable hubs have their own power supplies and can function independently, thus providing a much more expandable environment than stand-alone hubs. You can start with a single unit, without incurring the major expense of a chassis (like that used by modular hubs), and connect additional units as the network grows.

Modular Hubs

Modular hubs are designed to support the larger networks and provide the greatest amount of expandability and flexibility. A modular hub consists of a chassis that is nearly always mounted in a standard 19-inch equipment rack and contains several slots into which you plug individual communications modules. The chassis provides a common power source for all the modules, as well as a back-plane that enables them to communicate with each other. The modules contain the ports to which you connect the computer cables. When you plug multiple modules into the chassis, they become, in effect, a single large hub.

Bridges

A bridge is another device used to connect LAN cable segments, but unlike hubs, bridges operate at the data link layer of the OSI model and are selective about the packets that pass through them. Repeaters and hubs are designed to propagate all the network traffic they receive to all of the connected cable segments. A bridge has two or more network interfaces (complete with their own MAC addresses) with their ports connected to different cable segments and operating in *promiscuous* mode.

NOTE If a computer is in promiscuous mode, it could mean the network or that computer has been accessed illegally.

Promiscuous mode means that the interfaces receive all of the packets transmitted on the connected segments. As each packet enters the bridge, the device reads its destination address in the data link layer protocol header and, if the packet is destined for a system on another segment, forwards the packet to that segment. If the packet is destined for a system on the segment from which it arrived, the bridge discards the packet because it has already reached its destination. This process is called *packet filtering*. Packet filtering is one of the fundamental principles used by network connection devices to regulate network traffic. In this case, the packet filtering is occurring at the data link layer, but it can also occur at the network and transport layers.

Just the ability to read the contents of a packet header elevates a bridge above the level of a hub or repeater, both of which deal only with individual signals. However, as with a hub or repeater, the bridge makes no changes in the packet whatsoever and is completely unaware of the contents within the data link layer frame. In Chapter 2, the protocol operating at the Open Systems Interconnection (OSI) model's data link layer was compared to a postal system, in which each packet is a piece of mail and the data link layer frame functions as the envelope containing the data generated by the upper layers. To extend that analogy, the bridge is able to read the addresses on the packet envelopes, but it cannot read the letters inside. As a result, you don't have to consider the protocols running at the network layer and above at all when evaluating or installing bridges.

By using packet filtering, the bridge reduces the amount of excess traffic on the network by not propagating packets needlessly. Broadcast messages are forwarded to all of the connected segments, however, making it possible to use protocols that rely on broadcasts without manual system configuration. Unlike a repeater or hub, however, a bridge does not relay data to the connected segments until it has received the entire packet. (Remember, hubs and repeaters work with signals, while bridges work with packets.) Because of this, two systems on bridged segments can transmit simultaneously without incurring a collision. Thus, a bridge connects network segments in such a way as to keep them in the same broadcast domain but in different collision domains. The segments are still considered to be part of the same LAN, however.

If, for example, you have a LAN that is experiencing diminished performance because of high levels of traffic, you can split it into two segments by inserting a bridge at the midpoint. This will keep the local traffic generated on each segment local and still permit broadcasts and other traffic intended for the other segment to pass through. On an Ethernet network, reducing traffic in this way also reduces the number of collisions, which further increases the network's efficiency. Bridges also provide the same repeating functions as a hub, enabling you to extend the cable length accordingly.

Bridges have mainly been replaced by routers and switches, which are covered later in this chapter. Today, bridges are used primarily in wireless configurations. See Chapter 6 for information about wireless LANs.

The Spanning Tree Protocol

To address the problem of endless loops and broadcast storms on networks with redundant bridging, the Digital Equipment Corporation devised the *spanning tree algorithm* (STA), which preserves the fault tolerance provided by the additional bridges, while preventing the endless loops. STA was later revised by the Institute of Electrical and Electronic Engineers (IEEE) and standardized as the 802.1d specification.

The algorithm works by selecting one bridge for each network segment that has multiple bridges available. This designated bridge takes care of all the packet filtering and forwarding tasks for the segment. The others remain idle but stand ready to take over should the designated bridge fail.

During this selection process, each bridge is assigned a unique identifier (using one of the bridge's MAC addresses, plus a priority value), as is each individual port on each bridge (using the port's MAC address). Each port is also associated with a path cost, which specifies the cost of transmitting a packet onto the LAN using that port. Path costs typically can be specified by an administrator when a reason exists to prefer one port over another, or they can be left to default values.

Once all the components have been identified, the bridge with the lowest identifier becomes the *root bridge* for the entire network. Each of the other bridges then determines which of its ports can reach the root bridge with the lowest cost (called the *root path cost*) and designates it as the root port for that bridge.

(continued)

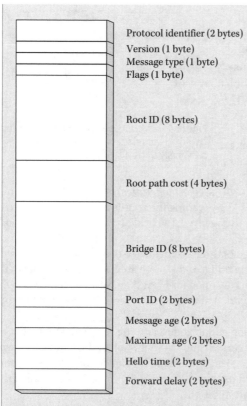

Protocol identifier (2 bytes)

Version (1 byte)

Message type (1 byte)

Flags (1 byte)

Root ID (8 bytes)

Root path cost (4 bytes)

Bridge ID (8 bytes)

Port ID (2 bytes)

Message age (2 bytes)

Maximum age (2 bytes)

Hello time (2 bytes)

Forward delay (2 bytes)

Figure 4-3   The format of the data message used when computing the spanning tree protocol algorithm

Finally, for each network segment, a designated bridge is selected, as well as a *designated* port on that bridge. Only the designated port on the designated bridge is permitted to filter and forward the packets for that network segment. The other (redundant) bridges on that segment remain operative—in case the designated bridge should fail—but are inactive until they are needed. Now that only one bridge is operating on each segment, packets can be forwarded without loops forming.

To perform these calculations, bridges must exchange messages among themselves, using a message format defined in the 802.1d standard (see Figure 4-3). These messages are called *bridge protocol data units* (BPDUs).

For each criterion, a lower value is better than a higher one. If a bridge receives a BPDU message with better values than those in its own messages, it stops transmitting BPDUs over the port through which it arrived—in effect relinquishing its duties to the bridge better suited for the job. The bridge also uses the values in that incoming BPDU to recalculate the fields of the messages it will send through the other ports.

NOTE The spanning tree algorithm must complete before the bridges begin forwarding any network traffic.

Once the spanning tree algorithm has designated a bridge for each network segment, it must also continue to monitor the network so that the process can begin again when a bridge fails or goes offline. All of the bridges on the network store the BPDUs they've received from the other bridges and track their ages. Once a message exceeds the maximum allowable age, it is discarded and the spanning tree message exchanges begin again.

Today, a variation of STP called *Rapid Spanning Tree Protocol* (RSTP) is recommended and has been added as IEEE 802.1w, which has become the standard. The convergence time for legacy STP (IEEE 802.1d), which is the gap when network bridges and switches are not forwarding any traffic, is about 30 to 50 seconds. In modern networks, this convergence time gap issue is unacceptable. RSTP (IEEE 802.1w) addresses the problem. This new standard enables root ports and designated ports to forward traffic in a few seconds.

Transparent Bridging

To filter the packets reaching it effectively, a bridge has to know which systems are located on which network segments so it can determine which packets to forward and which to discard. The bridge stores this information in an address table that is internal to the unit. Originally, network administrators had to create the address table for a bridge manually, but today's bridges compile the address table automatically, a process called *transparent bridging*.

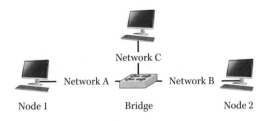

Figure 4-4   A transparent bridge forwards packets based on address tables it compiles from previously transmitted packets.

As soon as a transparent bridge (also known as a *learning bridge*) is connected to the network segments, it begins to compile its address table. By reading the source addresses in the arriving packets and noting the interface over which they arrived, the bridge can build a table of node addresses for each segment connected to it.

To illustrate, picture a network composed of three segments (A, B, and C), all connected to a local bridge, as shown in Figure 4-4. When the bridge is first activated, it receives a packet from Node 1 over the interface to Network A that is destined for Node 2 on Network B. Because the bridge now knows Node 1 is located on Network A, it creates an entry in its table for Network A that contains Node 1's MAC address.

At this time, the bridge has no information about Node 2 and the segment on which it's located, so it transmits its packet out to Networks B and C—that is, all of the connected segments except the one from which the packet arrived. This is the default behavior of a bridge whenever it receives a packet destined for a system not in its tables. It transmits the packet over all of the other segments to ensure that it reaches its destination.

Once Node 2 receives the packet, it transmits a reply to Node 1. Because Node 2 is located on Network B, its reply packet arrives at the bridge over a different interface. Now the bridge can add an entry to its table for Network B containing Node 2's address. On examining the packet, the bridge looks for the destination address in its tables and discovers that the address belongs to Node l, on Network A. The bridge then transmits the packet over the interface to Node A only.

From this point on, when any other system on Network A transmits a packet to Node l, the bridge knows to discard it because there is no need to pass it along to the other segments. However, the bridge still uses those packets to add the transmitting stations to its address table for Network A.

Eventually, the bridge will have address table entries for all the nodes on the network, and it can direct all of the incoming packets to the appropriate outgoing ports.

Bridge Loops

When the segments of a network are connected using bridges, the failure or malfunction of a bridge can be catastrophic. For this reason, administrators often connect network segments with redundant bridges to ensure that every node can access the entire network, even if a bridge should fail.

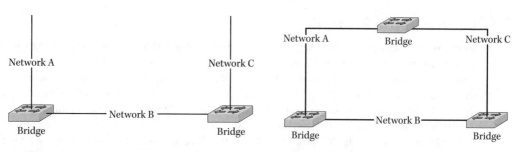

Figure 4-5 When each segment is connected to the others using one bridge, a single point of failure is created.

Figure 4-6 Connecting each segment to two bridges provides fault tolerance.

In Figure 4-5, three segments are connected by two bridges. If one of the bridges fails, one of the segments is cut off from the rest of the network. To remedy this problem and to provide fault tolerance, you can add a third bridge connecting the two end segments, as shown in Figure 4-6. This way, each system always has two possible paths to the other segments.

Installing redundant bridges can be a good idea, but it also produces what can be a serious problem. When a computer (Node 1) is located on a segment connected to two bridges, as shown in Figure 4-7, both of the bridges will receive the first packet the system transmits and add the machine's address to their tables for that segment, Network A. Both bridges will then transmit the same packet onto the other segment, Network B. As a result, each bridge will then receive the packet forwarded by the other bridge. The packet headers will still show the address of Node 1 as the source, but both bridges will have received the packet over the Network B interface. As a result, the bridges may (or may not) modify their address tables to show Node 1 as being on Network B, not A. If this occurs, any subsequent transmissions from Node 2 on Network B that are directed to Node 1 will be dropped because the bridges think Node 1 is on Network B, when it is, in fact, on A.

The result of this occurrence is lost data (because the bridges are improperly dropping frames) and degraded network performance. Eventually, the incorrect entries in the bridges' address tables will expire or be modified, but in the interim, Node 1 is cut off from the systems on the other network segments.

If this problem isn't bad enough, what happens when Node 1 transmits a broadcast message is worse. Both of the bridges forward the packet to Network B, where it is received by the other bridge, which forwards it again. Because bridges always forward broadcast packets without filtering them, multiple copies of the same message circulate endlessly between the two segments, constantly being forwarded by both bridges. This is called a *broadcast storm,* and it can effectively prevent all other traffic on the network from reaching its destination.

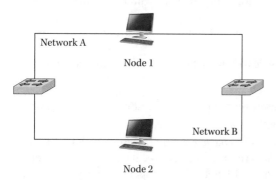

Figure 4-7 Redundant bridges provide fault tolerance, but they can also create bridging loops and broadcast storms.

Source Route Bridging

Source route bridging is an alternative to transparent bridging that was developed by IBM for use on multisegment Token Ring networks and is standardized in IEEE 802.5. On a network that uses transparent bridging, the path a packet takes to a destination on another segment is determined by the designated bridges selected by the spanning tree algorithm. In *source route bridging*, the path to the destination system is determined by the workstation and contained in each individual packet.

To discover the possible routes through the network to a given destination, a Token Ring system transmits an *All Rings Broadcast* (ARB) frame that all the bridges forward to all connected rings. As each bridge processes the frame, it adds its route designator (RD), identifying the bridge and port, to the packet. By reading the list of RDs, bridges prevent loops by not sending the packet to the same bridge twice.

If more than one route exists to the destination system, multiple ARBs will arrive there, containing information about the various routes they took. The destination system then transmits a reply to each of the ARBs it receives, using the list of RDs to route the packet back to the sender.

When the original sender of the ARBs receives the responses, it selects one of the routes to the destination as the best one, based on one or more of the following criteria:

- The amount of time required for the explorer frame to return to the sender
- The number of hops between the source and the destination
- The size of the frame the system can use

After selecting one of the routes, the system generates its data packets and includes the routing information in the Token Ring frame header.

The format for the ARB packet and for a data packet containing routing information is the same as a standard IEEE 802.5 frame, except that the first bit of the source address field, called the *routing information indicator* (RII) bit, is set to a value of 1, indicating that the packet contains routing information. The routing information itself, which is nothing more than a list of the bridges the packet will use when traveling through the network, is carried through the *routing information field* (RIF) that appears as part of the information field, just after the frame's source address field.

The RIF consists of a 2-byte routing control section and a number of 2-byte route designator sections.

Broadcast indicators (3 bits) specify the type of routing to be used by the frame, according to the following values:

- **Nonbroadcast** Indicates that the packet contains a specific route to the destination in the route designator sections of the RIF field.
- **100: All routes broadcast** Indicates that the packet should be routed through all the bridges on the network (without traversing the same bridge twice) and that each bridge should add a route designator section to the RIF field identifying the bridge and the port onto which it is being forwarded.
- **110: Single route broadcast** Indicates that the packet should be routed only through the bridges designated by the spanning tree algorithm and that each bridge should add a

route designator section to the RIF field identifying the bridge and the port onto which it is being forwarded.

- **Length (5 bits)**   Indicates the total length of the RIF field, from 2 to 30 bytes.

- **Direction bit (1 bit)**   Specifies the direction in which the packet is traveling. The value of this bit indicates whether the transmitting node should read the route designator sections in the RIF field from left to right (0) or from right to left (1).

- **Largest frame (3 bits)**   Indicates the largest frame size that can be accommodated by the route, called the *maximum transfer unit* (MTU). Initially set by the transmitting system, a bridge lowers this value if it forwards the packet onto a segment that supports only smaller frames. The permitted values are as follows:

  - 000 indicates a MAC MTU of 552 bytes

  - 001 indicates a MAC MTU of 1,064 bytes

  - 010 indicates a MAC MTU of 2,088 bytes

  - 011 indicates a MAC MTU of 4,136 bytes

  - 100 indicates a MAC MTU of 8,232 bytes

  - Unused (4 bits)

The IBM standard for source route bridging originally specified a maximum of 8 route designator sections in a single packet, but the IEEE 802.5 standard allows up to 14. Each workstation must maintain its own routing information to each of the systems with which it communicates. This can result in a large number of ARB frames being processed by a destination system before it even sees the first byte of application data.

Bridging Ethernet and Token Ring Networks

Generally speaking, Ethernet networks use transparent bridging, and Token Ring networks use source route bridging. So, what happens when you want to connect an Ethernet segment to a Token Ring using a bridge? The answer is complicated because the task presents a number of significant obstacles.

Some of the fundamental incompatibilities of the two data link layer protocols are as follows:

- **Bit ordering**   Ethernet systems consider the first bit of a MAC address to be the low-order bit, while Token Ring systems treat the first bit as the high-order bit.

- **MTU sizes**   Ethernet frames have a maximum transfer unit size of 1,500 bytes, while Token Ring frames can be much larger. Bridges are not capable of fragmenting packets for transfer over a segment with a lower MTU and then reassembling them at the destination, like routers are. A too-large packet arriving at a bridge to a segment with a smaller MTU can only be discarded.

- **Exclusive Token Ring features**   Token Ring networks use frame status bits, priority indicators, and other features that have no equivalent in Ethernet.

In addition, the two bridging methods have their own incompatibilities. Transparent bridges neither understand the special function of the ARB messages used in source route bridging nor can they make use of the RIF field in Token Ring packets. Conversely, source route bridges do not understand the spanning tree algorithm messages generated by transparent bridges, and they do not know what to do when they receive frames with no routing information.

Two primary methods exist for overcoming these incompatibilities, neither of which is an ideal solution:

- Translational bridging
- Source route transparent bridging

Translational Bridging

In *translational bridging,* a special bridge translates the data link layer frames between the Ethernet and Token Ring formats. No standard at all exists for this process, so the methods used by individual product manufacturers can vary widely. Some compromise is needed in the translation process because no way exists to implement all the features fully in each of the protocols and to bridge those features to its counterpart. Some of the techniques used in various translational bridges to overcome the incompatibilities are described in the following paragraphs.

One of the basic functions of the bridge is to map the fields of the Ethernet frame onto the Token Ring frame and vice versa. The bridge reverses the bit order of the source and destination addresses for the packets passing between the segments and may or may not take action based on the values of a Token Ring packet's frame status, priority, reservation, and monitor bits. Bridges may simply discard these bits when translating from Token Ring to Ethernet and set redetermined values for them when translating from Ethernet to Token Ring.

To deal with the different MTU sizes of the network segments, a translation bridge can set the largest frame value in the Token Ring packet's RIF field to the MTU for the Ethernet network (1,500 bytes). As long as the Token Ring implementations on the workstations read this field and adjust their frame sizes accordingly, no problem should occur, but any frames larger than the MTU on the Ethernet segments will be dropped by the bridge connecting the two networks.

The biggest difference between the two types of bridging is that, on Ethernet networks, the routing information is stored in the bridges, while on Token Ring networks, it's stored at the workstations. For the translational bridge to support both network types, it must appear as a transparent bridge to the Ethernet side and a source route bridge to the Token Ring side.

To the Token Ring network, the translational bridge has a ring number and bridge number, just like a standard source route bridge. The ring number, however, represents the entire Ethernet domain, not just the segment connected to the bridge. As packets from the Token Ring network pass through the bridge, the information from their RIF fields is removed and cached in the bridge. From that point on, standard transparent bridging gets the packets to their destinations on the Ethernet network.

When a packet generated by an Ethernet workstation is destined for a system on the Token Ring network, the translational bridge looks up the system in its cache of RIF information and adds an RIF field to the packet containing a route to the network, if possible. If no route is available in the cache or if the packet is a broadcast or multicast, the bridge transmits it as a single-route broadcast.

Source Route Transparent Bridging

IBM has also come up with a proposed standard that combines the two primary bridging technologies, called *source route transparent* (SRT) bridging. This technology is standardized in Appendix C of the IEEE 802.1d document. SRT bridges can forward packets originating on either source route bridging or transparent bridging networks, using a spanning tree algorithm common to both. The standard spanning tree algorithm used by Token Ring networks for single-route broadcast messages is incompatible with the algorithm used by Ethernet, as defined in the 802.1d specification. This appendix reconciles the two.

SRT bridges use the value of the RIF bit to determine whether a packet contains RIF information and, consequently, whether it should use source route or transparent bridging. The mixing of the two technologies is not perfect, however, and network administrators may find it easier to connect Ethernet and Token Ring segments with a switch or a router rather than either a translational or SRT bridge.

Routers

In the previous sections, you learned how repeaters, hubs, and bridges can connect network segments at the physical and data link layers of the OSI model, creating a larger LAN with a single collision domain. The next step up in the network expansion process is to connect two completely separate LANs at the network layer. This is the job of a router. Routers are more selective than bridges in the traffic they pass between the networks, and they are capable of intelligently selecting the most efficient path to a specific destination. Because they function at the network layer, routers can also connect dissimilar networks. You can, for example, connect an Ethernet network to a Token Ring network because packets entering a router are stripped of their data link layer protocol headers as they pass up the protocol stack to the network layer. This leaves a protocol data unit (PDU) encapsulated using whatever network layer protocol is running on the computer. After processing, the router then encapsulates the PDU in a new data link layer header using whatever protocol is running on the other network to which the router is connected.

Routers are used for both homes and business networks. If, for example, you use your home computer to dial into your system at work and access resources on the office network, your work computer is functioning as a router. In the same way, if you share an Internet connection with systems on a LAN, the machine connected to the Internet is a router. A router, therefore, can be either a hardware or a software entity, and it can range from the simple to the extraordinarily complex.

Routers are protocol specific; they must support the network layer protocol used by each packet. By far, the most common network layer protocol in use today is the Internet Protocol (IP), which is the basis for the Internet and for most private networks.

A computer that is connected to two or more networks is said to be a *multihomed system*. Most Windows systems today function as routers as well. Whether wired or wireless, network routers work at the network layer of the OSI model.

Most of the routers used on large networks, though, are stand-alone devices that are essentially computers dedicated to routing functions. Routers come in various sizes, from small units that connect a workgroup network to a backbone to large, modular, rack-mounted devices. However, while routers vary in their capabilities, such as the number of networks to which they connect, the protocols they support, and the amount of traffic they can handle, their basic functions are essentially the same.

Router Applications

Although the primary function of a router is to connect networks and pass traffic between them, routers can fulfill several different roles in network designs. The type of router used for a specific function determines its size, cost, and capabilities. The simplest type of routing architecture is when a LAN must be connected to another LAN some distance away, using a wide area network (WAN) connection. A branch office for a large corporation, for example, might have a WAN connection to the corporate headquarters in another city (see Figure 4-8).

To make communications between the networks in the two offices possible, each must connect its LAN to a router, and the two routers are linked by the WAN connection.

The WAN connection may take the form of a leased telephone line, an Integrated Services for Digital Network (ISDN) connection, or a digital subscriber line (DSL) connection. The technology used to connect the two networks is irrelevant, as long as the routers in both offices are connected. Routers are required in this example because the LAN and WAN technologies are fundamentally incompatible. You can't run an Ethernet connection between two cities, nor can you use leased telephone lines to connect each workstation to the file server in the next room.

In a slightly more complicated arrangement, a site with a larger network may have several LANs, each of which is connected to a backbone network using a router. Here, routers are needed because one single LAN may be unable to support the number of workstations required. In addition, the individual LANs may be located in other parts of a building or in separate buildings on the same campus and may require a different type of network to connect them. Connections between campus buildings, for example, require a network medium that is suitable for outdoor use, such as fiber-optic cable, while the LANs in each building can use more inexpensive copper cabling. Routers are available that can connect these different network types, no matter what protocols they use.

These two examples of router use are often combined. A large corporate network using a backbone to connect multiple LANs will almost certainly want to be connected to the Internet. This means that another router is needed to support some type of WAN connection to an Internet service provider (ISP). Users anywhere on the corporate network can then access Internet services.

Both of these scenarios use routers to connect a relatively small number of networks, and they are dwarfed by the Internet, which is a routed network composed of thousands of networks all over the world. To make it possible for packets to travel across this maze of routers with reasonable efficiency, a hierarchy of routers leads from smaller, local ISPs to regional providers, which in turn get their service from large national services (see Figure 4-9). Traffic originating from a system using a small ISP travels up through this virtual tree to one of the main backbones, across the upper levels of the network, and back down again to the destination.

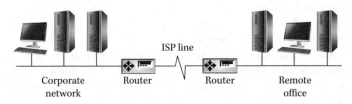

Figure 4-8   Wired and wireless routers enable the use of wide area connections to join two LANs.

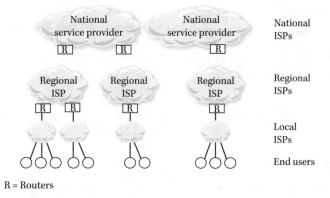

Figure 4-9   A hierarchy of routers helps you forward traffic to any location using the Internet.

You can see the route that packets take from your computer through the Internet to a specific destination by using the Traceroute utility. The Windows command is tracert. This command-line utility takes the IP address or DNS name you specify and uses Internet Control Message Protocol (ICMP) messages to display the names and addresses of all the intermediate routers on the path to the destination. A typical Traceroute display generated by a Windows 8 system appears in Figure 4-10.

Router Functions

The basic function of a router is to evaluate each packet arriving on one of the networks to which it is connected and send it on to its destination through another network. The goal is for the router to select the network that provides the best path to the destination for each packet. A packet can pass through several different routers on the way to its destination. Each router on a packet's path is referred to as a *hop*, and the object is to get the packet where it's going with the smallest number of hops. On a private network, a packet may need three or four (or more) hops to get to its destination. On the Internet, a packet can easily pass through 20 or more routers along its path.

```
C:\>traceert google.com

Tracing route to google.com [173.194.33.39] over a maximum of 30 hops

1    <1 ms <1 ms <1 ms  192.168.2.1
2     8 ms   7 ms   7 ms  wtcds 1-66-165-30-2.whidbeyteldsl.net  [66.165.30.2]
3    11 ms   7 ms   7 ms  209.166.68.85
4     8 ms   8 ms   8 ms  g1-46-seaigr1-evpe1-iv4f.sea.fibercloud.net  [216.145.7.117]
5     8 ms   8 ms   8 ms  216-145-7-30/.sea.fibercloud.net [216.145.7.30]
6    16 ms  10 ms   9 ms  six.sea01.google.com [206.81.80.17]
7     7 ms   8 ms   9 ms  66.249.94.214
8     9 ms   8 ms   8 ms  209.85.253.26
9     9 ms   8 ms   9 ms  sea09s02-im-f7.1e100.net [173.194.33.39]

Trace complete
```

Figure 4-10   A typical Traceroute in Windows 8.

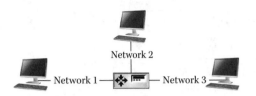

Figure 4-11   Routers have direct knowledge about the networks to which they are connected.

A router, by definition, is connected to two or more networks. The router has direct knowledge about those networks for the protocols that it supports. If, for example, a workstation on Network 1 (see Figure 4-11) transmits a packet to a system on Network 2, the router connecting Networks 1, 2, and 3 can directly determine which of the two networks (2 or 3) contains the destination system and forward the packet appropriately.

Routing Tables

The router forwards packets by maintaining a list of networks and hosts, called a *routing table*. For computers to communicate over a network, each machine must have its own address. In addition to identifying the specific computer, however, its address must identify the network on which it's located. On TCP/IP networks, for example, the standard 32-bit IP address consists of a network identifier and a host identifier. A routing table consists of entries that contain the network identifier for each connected network (or in some cases the network and host identifiers for specific computers). When the router receives a packet addressed to a workstation on Network 3, it looks at the network identifier in the packet's destination address, compares it to the routing table, and forwards it to the network with the same identifier.

This is a rather simple task, as long as the router is connected to all of the LANs on the network. When a network is larger and uses multiple routers, however, no single router has direct knowledge of all the LANs. In Figure 4-12, Router A is connected to Networks 1, 2, and 3 as before and has the identifiers for those networks in its routing table, but it has no direct knowledge of Network 4, which is connected using another router.

How then does Router A know where to send packets that are addressed to a workstation on a distant network? The answer is that routers maintain information in their routing tables about other networks besides those to which they are directly attached. A routing table may contain information about many different networks all over the enterprise. On a private network, it is not uncommon for every router to have entries for all of the connected networks. On the Internet, however, there are so many networks and so many routers that no single routing table can contain all of them and function efficiently. Thus, a router connected to the Internet sends packets to another router that it thinks has better information about the network to which the packet is ultimately destined.

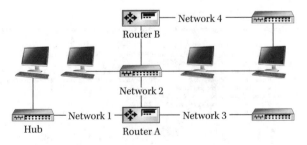

Figure 4-12   Router A has no direct knowledge of Network 4 because it is connected to a different router.

Windows Routing Tables

Every computer on a TCP/IP network has a routing table, even if it is connected to only one network. At the very least, the routing table identifies the system's default gateway and instructs it how to handle traffic sent to the local network and the loopback network address (127.0.0.0). A typical routing table for a Windows system appears in Figure 4-13.

To display the routing table in a Windows or a Linux system, type *route* at a command prompt. You can also use *netstat – rn* in Windows, Linux, Unix, or Mac OS.

The entries in the table run horizontally. The function of the information in each column is as follows:

- **Network address** Specifies the network address for which routing information is to be provided. While most entries have network addresses in this field, it's also possible to supply routing information for a specific host address. This is called a *host route*.

- **Netmask** Specifies the subnet mask used to determine which bits of the network address function as the network identifier.

- **Gateway** Specifies the IP address of the gateway (router) the system should use to send packets to the network address. When the entry is for a network to which the system is directly attached, this field contains the address of the system's network interface.

- **Interface** Specifies the IP address of the network interface the system should use to send traffic to the gateway address.

- **Metric** Specifies the distance between the system and the destination network, usually in terms of the number of hops needed for traffic to reach the network address.

NOTE TCP/IP and Internet terminology often use the term *gateway* synonymously with *router*. In general networking parlance, a gateway is an application layer interface between networks that involves some form of high-level protocol translation, such as an e-mail gateway or a gateway between a LAN and a mainframe. When a Windows system refers to its "default gateway," however, it is referring to a standard router, operating at the network layer.

Routing Table Parsing

Whether a system is functioning as a router or not, the responsibility of a network layer protocol like IP is to determine where each packet should be transmitted next. The IP header in each packet contains the address of the system that is to be its ultimate destination, but before passing

Network Destination	Netmask	Gateway	Interface	Metric
0.0.0.0	.0.0.0.0	192.168.2.1	192.168.2.5	20
127.0.0.0	255.0.0.0	On-link	127.0.0.1	306
127.0.0.1	255.255.255.255	On-link	127.0.0.1	306

Figure 4-13   A typical routing table in a Windows system

each packet down to the data link layer protocol, IP uses the routing table to determine what the data link layer destination address should be for the packet's next hop. This is because a data link layer protocol like Ethernet can address a packet only to a system on the local network, which may or may not be its final destination. To make this determination, IP reads the destination address for each packet it processes from the IP header and searches for a matching entry in the routing table, using the following procedure:

1. IP first scans the routing table, looking for a host route that exactly matches the destination IP address in the packet. If one exists, the packet is transmitted to the gateway specified in the routing table entry.

2. If no matching host route exists, IP uses the subnet mask to determine the network address for the packet and scans the routing table for an entry that matches that address. If IP finds a match, the packet is transmitted either to the specified gateway (if the system is not directly connected to the destination network) or out the specified network interface (if the destination is on the local network).

3. If no matching network address is in the routing table, IP scans for a default (or 0.0.0.0) route and transmits the packet to the specified gateway.

4. If no default route is in the table, IP returns a destination unreachable message to the source of the packet (either the application that generated it or the system that transmitted it).

Static and Dynamic Routing

The next logical question concerning the routing process is, how do the entries get into the routing table? A system can generate entries for the default gateway, the local network, and the broadcast and multicast addresses because it possesses all of the information needed to create them. For networks to which the router is not directly connected, however, routing table entries must be created by an outside process. The two basic methods for creating entries in the routing table are called *static routing*, which is the manual creation of entries, and *dynamic routing*, which uses an external protocol to gather information about the network.

On a relatively small, stable network, static routing is a practical alternative because you have to create the entries in your routers' tables only once. Manually configuring the routing table on workstations isn't necessary because they typically have only one network interface and can access the entire network through one default gateway. Routers, however, have multiple network interfaces and usually have access to multiple gateways. They must, therefore, know which route to use when trying to transmit to a specific network.

To create static entries in a computer's routing table, you use a program supplied with the operating system. The standard tool for this on Unix and Windows systems is a character-based utility called *route* (in Unix) or *route.exe* (in Windows). To create a new entry in the routing table on a Windows computer, for example, you use a command like the following:

ROUTE ADD 192 . 168.5.0 MASK 255.255.255 . 0   192 .168.2.1 METRIC 2

This command informs the system that to reach a network with the address 192.168.5.0, the system must send packets to a gateway (router) with the address 192.168.2.1, and that the destination network is two hops away.

In some cases, graphical utilities are available that can perform the same task. For example, the Windows 2012 Server system with its Routing and Remote Access Server service running enables you to create static routes.

Static routes created this way remain in the routing table until you manually change or remove them, and this can be a problem. If a gateway specified in a static route should fail, the system continues to send packets to it, to no avail. You must either repair the gateway or modify the static routes that reference it throughout the network before the systems can function normally again.

On larger networks, static routing becomes increasingly impractical, not only because of the sheer number of routing table entries involved, but also because network conditions can change too often and too quickly for administrators to keep the routing tables on every system current. Instead, these networks use dynamic routing, in which specialized routing protocols share information about the other routers in the network and modify the routing tables accordingly. Once configured, dynamic routing needs little or no maintenance from network administrators because the protocols can create, modify, or remove routing table entries as needed to accommodate changing network conditions. The Internet is totally dependent on dynamic routing because it is constantly mutating, and no manual process could possibly keep up with the changes.

Selecting the Most Efficient Route

Many networks, even relatively small ones, are designed with multiple routers that provide redundant paths to a given destination. Thus, while creating a network that consists of several LANs joined in a series by routers would be possible, most use something approaching a mesh topology instead, as shown in Figure 4-14. This way, if any one router should fail, all of the systems can still send traffic to any other system on any network.

When a network is designed in this way, another important part of the routing process is selecting the best path to a given destination. The use of dynamic routing on the network typically results in all possible routes to a given network being entered in the routing tables, each of which includes a metric that specifies how many hops are required to reach that network. Most of the time, the efficiency of a particular route is measured by the metric value because each hop involves processing by another router, which introduces a slight delay. When a router has to forward a packet to a network represented by multiple entries in the routing table, it chooses the one with the lower metric.

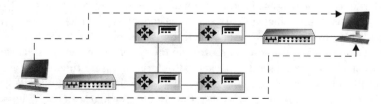

Figure 4-14 By interconnecting routers, packets from one computer can travel to a destination computer on another network on a different route.

Discarding Packets

The goal of a router is to transmit packets to their destinations using the path that incurs the smallest number of hops. Routers also track the number of hops that packets take on the way to their destinations for another reason. When a malfunction or misconfiguration occurs in one or more routers, it is possible for packets to get caught in a router loop and be passed endlessly from one router to another.

To prevent this, the IP header contains a *Time to Live* (TTL) field that the source system gives a certain numerical value when a packet is created. This value is 128 on many systems and cannot start higher than 255. As a packet travels through the network, each router that processes it decrements the value of this field by 1. If, for any reason, the packet passes through routers enough times to bring the value of this field down to 0, the last router removes it from the network and discards it. The router then returns an ICMP Time to Live Exceeded in Transit message to the source system to inform it of the problem.

Packet Fragmentation

Routers can connect networks of vastly different types, and the process of transferring datagrams from one data link layer protocol to another can require more than simply stripping off one header and applying a new one. The biggest problem that can occur during this translation process is when one protocol supports frames that are larger than the other protocol.

If, for example, a router connects a Token Ring network to an Ethernet one, it may have to accept 4,500-byte datagrams from one network and then transmit them over a network that can carry only 1,500-byte datagrams. Routers determine the maximum transfer unit of a particular network by querying the interface to that network. To make this possible, the router has to break up the datagram into fragments of the appropriate size and then encapsulate each fragment in the correct data link layer protocol frame. This fragmentation process may occur several times during a packet's journey from the source to its destination, depending on the number and types of networks involved.

For example, a packet originating on a Token Ring network may be divided into 1,500-byte fragments to accommodate a route through an Ethernet network, and then each of those fragments may themselves be divided into 576-byte fragments for transmission over the Internet. Note, however, that while routers fragment packets, they never defragment them. Even if the 576-byte datagrams are passed to an Ethernet network as they approach their destination, the router does not reassemble them into 1,500-byte datagrams. All reassembly is performed at the network layer of the final destination system.

Routing and ICMP

The Internet Control Message Protocol provides several important functions to routers and the systems that use them. Chief among these is the capability of routers to use ICMP messages to provide routing information to other routers. Routers send ICMP redirect messages to source systems when they know of a better route than the system is currently using. For example, a workstation on Network A sends a packet to Router A that is destined for a computer on Network B, and Router A determines that the next hop should be to Router B, which is on the same network as the transmitting workstation, Router A will use an ICMP message to inform the workstation that it should use Router B to access Network B instead (see Figure 4-15). The workstation then modifies the entry in its routing table accordingly.

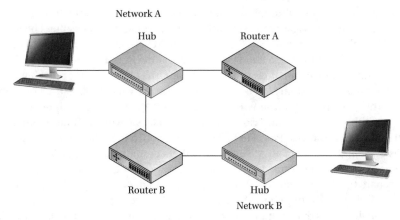

Figure 4-15   ICMP redirect messages provide simple routing information to transmitting systems.

Routers also generate ICMP Destination Unreachable messages of various types when they are unable to forward packets. If a router receives a packet that is destined for a workstation on a locally attached network and it can't deliver the packet because the workstation is offline, the router generates a Host Unreachable message and transmits it to the system that originated the packet. If the router is unable to forward the packet to another router that provides access to the destination, it generates a Network Unreachable message instead. Network layer protocols provide end-to-end communications, meaning it is usually the end systems that are involved in a dialog. ICMP is therefore a mechanism that enables intermediate systems (routers) to communicate with a source end system (the transmitter) in the event that the packets can't reach the destination end system.

Other ICMP packets, called Router Solicitation and Advertisement messages, can enable workstations to discover the routers on the local network. A host system generates a Router Solicitation message and transmits it as either a broadcast or a multicast to the All Routers on This Subnet address (2240.02). Routers receiving the message respond with Router Advertisement messages that the host system uses to update its routing table. The routers then generate periodic updates to inform the host of their continued operational status. Most systems can update their routing tables with information from ICMP Router Advertisement messages. Support for these messages in hardware router implementations varies from product to product.

The ICIVIP Redirect and Router Solicitation/Advertisement messages do not constitute a routing protocol per se because they do not provide systems with information about the comparative efficiency of various routes. Routing table entries created or modified as a result of these messages are still considered to be static routes.

Routing Protocols

Routers that support dynamic routing use specialized protocols to exchange information about themselves with other routers on the network. Dynamic routing doesn't alter the actual routing process; it's just a different method of creating entries in the routing table. There are two types of routing protocols: interior gateway protocols and exterior gateway protocols. Private networks typically use only *interior gateway protocols* because they have a relatively small number of routers and it is practical for all of them to exchange messages with each other.

On the Internet, the situation is different. Having every one of the Internet's thousands of routers exchange messages with every other router would be impossible. The amount of traffic involved would be enormous, and the routers would have little time to do anything else. Instead, as is usual with the Internet, a two-level system was devised that splits the gigantic network into discrete units called *autonomous systems* or *administrative domains* or just *domains*.

An autonomous system (AS) is usually a private network administered by a single authority, such as those run by corporations, educational institutions, and government agencies. The routers within an AS use an interior gateway protocol, such as the Routing Information Protocol (RIP) or the Open Shortest Path First (OSPF) protocol, to exchange routing information among themselves. At the edges of an AS are routers that communicate with the other autonomous systems on the Internet, using an exterior gateway protocol, the most common of which on the Internet are the Border Gateway Protocol (BC-P) and the Exterior Gateway Protocol (EGP).

By splitting the routing chores into a two-level hierarchy, packets traveling across the Internet pass through routers that contain only the information needed to get them to the right AS. Once the packets arrive at the edge of the AS in which the destination system is located, the routers there contain more specific information about the networks within the AS. The concept is much like the way that IP addresses and domain names are assigned on the Internet. Outside entities track only the various network addresses or domains. The individual administrators of each network are responsible for maintaining the host addresses and hostnames within the network or domain.

See Chapter 12 for more information on routing protocols.

Switches

The traditional network configuration uses multiple LANs connected by routers to form a network that is larger than would be possible with a single LAN. This is necessary because each LAN is based on a network medium that is shared by multiple computers, and there is a limit to the number of systems that can share the medium before the network is overwhelmed by traffic. Routers segregate the traffic on the individual LANs, forwarding only those packets addressed to systems on other LANs.

Routers have been around for decades, but today switches have revolutionized network design and made it possible to create LANs of almost unlimited size. A switch is essentially a multiport bridging device in which each port is a separate network segment. Similar in appearance to a hub, a switch receives incoming traffic through its ports. Unlike a hub, which forwards the traffic out through all of its other ports, a switch forwards the traffic only to the single port needed to reach the destination (see Figure 4-16). If, for example, you have a small network with each computer connected to a port in the same switching hub, each system has what amounts to a dedicated, full-bandwidth connection to every other system. No shared network medium exists, and consequently, there are no collisions or traffic congestion. As an added bonus, you also get increased security because, without a shared medium, an unauthorized workstation cannot monitor and capture the traffic not intended for it.

Switches operate at layer 2 of the OSI reference model, the data link layer, so consequently, they are used to create a single large network instead of a series of smaller networks connected by routers. This also means that switches can support any network layer protocol. Like transparent bridges, switches can learn the topology of a network and perform functions such as forwarding and packet filtering. Many switches are also capable of full-duplex communications and automatic speed adjustment. In the traditional arrangement for a larger

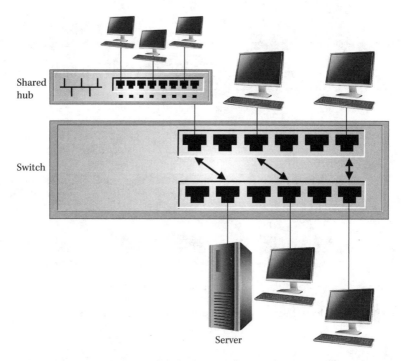

Shared hub

Switch

Server

Figure 4-16   Switches repeat incoming traffic, but only to the specific port for which the packet is intended.

network, multiple LANs are connected to a backbone network with routers. The backbone network is a shared-medium LAN like all of the others, however, and must therefore carry all of the network traffic generated by the horizontal networks. This is why the backbone network traditionally uses a faster protocol. On a switched network, workstations are connected to individual workgroup switches, which in turn are connected to a single, high-performance switch, thus enabling any system on the network to open a dedicated connection to any other system (see Figure 4-17). This arrangement can be expanded further to include an intermediate layer of departmental switches. Servers accessed by all users can then be connected directly to a departmental switch or to the top-level switch for better performance.

Replacing hubs with switches is an excellent way to improve the performance of a network without changing protocols or modifying individual workstations. Even a legacy Ethernet network exhibits a dramatic improvement when each workstation is given a full ten Mbps of bandwidth. Today, switches are available for nearly all networks, both wired and wireless.

Switch Types

There are two basic types of switching: cut-through switching and store-and-forward switching. A *cut-through switch* reads only the MAC address of an incoming packet, looks up the address in its forwarding table, and immediately begins to transmit it out through the port providing access to the destination. The switch forwards the packet without any additional processing, such as error checking, and before it has even received the entire packet. This type of switch is relatively inexpensive and more commonly used at the workgroup or department level, where the lack of

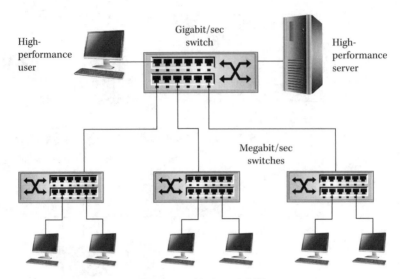

Figure 4-17   Today, hierarchies of switches replace both hubs and routers.

error checking will not affect the performance of the entire network. The immediate forwarding of incoming packets reduces the latency (that is, the delay) that results from error checking and other processing. If the destination port is in use, however, the switch buffers incoming data in memory, incurring a latency delay anyway, without the added benefit of error checking.

A *store-and-forward switch,* as the name implies, stores an entire incoming packet in buffer memory before forwarding it out the destination port. While in memory, the switch checks the packet for errors and other conditions. The switch immediately discards any packets with errors; those without errors are forwarded out through the correct port. These switching methods are not necessarily exclusive of each other. Some switches can work in cut-through mode until a preset error threshold is reached, and then switch to store-and-forward operation. Once the errors drop below the threshold, the switch reverts to cut-through mode.

Switches implement these functions using one of three hardware configurations. *Matrix switching,* also called *crossbar switching,* uses a grid of input and output connections, such as that shown in Figure 4-18. Data entering through any port's input can be forwarded to any port for output. Because this solution is

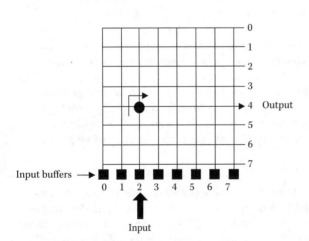

Figure 4-18   Matrix switching uses a grid of input and output circuits.

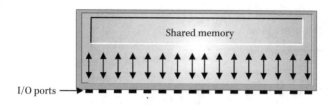

Figure 4-19   Shared memory switching

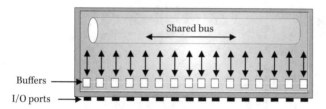

Figure 4-20   Bus-architecture switching

hardware based, there is no CPU or software involvement in the switching process. In cases where data can't be forwarded immediately, the switch buffers it until the output port is unblocked.

In a *shared memory switch,* all incoming data is stored in a memory buffer that is shared by all of the switch's ports and then forwarded to an output port (see Figure 4-19). A more commonly used technology (shown in Figure 4-20), called *bus-architecture switching,* forwards all traffic across a common bus, using time-division multiplexing to ensure that each port has equal access to the bus. In this model, each port has its own individual buffer and is controlled by an application-specific integrated circuit

(ASIC). Today, switches are available for any size network, from inexpensive workgroup switches designed for small office networks to stackable and modular units used in the largest networks.

Routing vs. Switching

The question of whether to route or switch on a network is a difficult one. Switching is faster and cheaper than routing, but it raises some problems in most network configurations. By using switches, you eliminate subnets and create a single flat network segment that hosts all of your computers. Any two systems can communicate using a dedicated link that is essentially a temporary two-node network. The problems arise when workstations generate broadcast messages. Because a switched network forms a single broadcast domain, broadcast messages are propagated throughout the whole network, and every system must process them, which can waste enormous amounts of bandwidth.

One of the advantages of creating multiple LANs and connecting them with routers is that broadcasts are limited to the individual networks. Routers also provide security by limiting transmissions to a single subnet. To avoid the wasted bandwidth caused by broadcasts, it has become necessary to implement certain routing concepts on switched networks. This has led to a number of new technologies that integrate routing and switching to varying degrees. Some of these technologies are examined in the following sections.

Virtual LANs

A *virtual LAN* (VLAN) is a group of systems on a switched network that functions as a subnet and communicates with other VLANs through routers. The physical network is still switched, however; the VLANs exist as an overlay to the switching fabric, as shown in Figure 4-21. Network administrators create VLANs by specifying the MAC port or IP addresses of the systems that are to be part of each subnet. Messages that are broadcast on a VLAN are limited to the subnet, just as in a routed network. Because VLANs are independent of the physical network, the systems in a

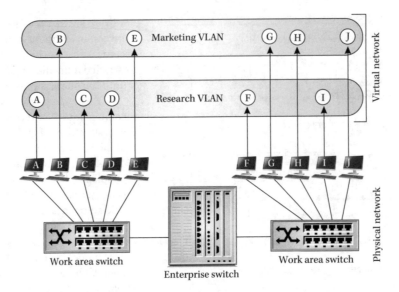

Figure 4-21   VLANs are pseudo-subnets of switched workstations, connected by routers.

particular subnet can be located anywhere, and a single system can even be a member of more than one VLAN.

Despite the fact that all the computers are connected by switches, routers are still necessary for systems in different VLANs to communicate. VLANs that are based solely on layer 2 technology, such as those that use port configuration or MAC addresses to define the member systems, must have a port dedicated to a router connection. In this type of VLAN, the network administrator either selects certain switch ports to designate the members of a VLAN or creates a list of the workstations' MAC addresses.

Because of the additional processing involved, routing is slower than switching. This particular arrangement is sometimes referred to as "switch where you can, route where you must" because routing is used for communication only between VLANs; all communication within a VLAN is switched. This is an efficient arrangement as long as the majority of the network traffic (70 to 80 percent) is between systems in the same V/LAN. Communication speed within a VLAN is maximized at the expense of the inter-VLAN communication. When too much traffic occurs between systems in different subnets, the routing slows down the process too much, and the speed of the switches is largely wasted.

Layer 3 Switching

Layer 3 switches are similar to routers and often support the same routing protocols. Layer 3 switches also use VLANs but mix routing and switching functions to make communication between VLANs more efficient. This technology is known by several different names, depending on the vendor of the equipment. The essence of the concept is described as "route once, switch afterward." A router is still required to establish connections between systems in different VLANs, but once the connection has been established, subsequent traffic travels over the layer 2 switching fabric, which is much faster.

Most of the hardware devices called layer 3 switches combine the functions of a switch and a router into one unit. The device is capable of performing all of a router's standard functions but is also able to transmit data using high-speed switches, all at a substantially lower cost than a standard router. Layer 3 switches are optimized for use on LAN and metropolitan area network (MAN) connections, not WANs. By replacing the routers that connect workgroup or department networks to the backbone with layer 3 switches, you retain all of the router functionality, while increasing the overall speed at which data is forwarded.

Multiple-Layer Switching

As Gigabit Ethernet becomes the norm, newer switches can prioritize network traffic by using information from other OSI layers in either hardware or software configurations. For example, *layer 4 switching* is a way to allow better quality of service (QoS) with better management across several servers. Routers have used OSI layer 4 information for prioritizing network traffic for many years. Since today global applications need rapid dissemination of session information, layer 4 switches can make intelligent decisions for forwarding frames, based on TCP/UDP port information and the IP destination/source addresses. This type of switching can do the following:

- Examine the direction of client requests at the layer 4 switch
- Process multiple requests across any available server
- Measure both availability and responsiveness of each server
- Establish policy controls for traffic management

For more information about modern server technologies, see Chapter 8.

Part II

CHAPTER

5

Cabling a Network

Although there are networks that use radio transmissions and other wireless technologies to transmit data, the vast majority of today's networks use some form of cable as the network medium. Most of the cables used for data networking use a copper conductor to carry electrical signals, but *fiber-optic,* a spun glass cable that carries pulses of light, is an increasingly popular alternative.

Cabling issues have, in recent years, become separated from the typical network administrator's training and experience. Many veteran administrators have never installed (or *pulled*) cable themselves and are less than familiar with the technology that forms the basis for the network. In many cases, the use of twisted-pair cable has resulted in telephone system contractors being responsible for the network cabling. Network consultants typically outsource all but the smallest cabling jobs to outside companies.

Network cabling is, in many cases, structurally integrated in the building or other structures within the whole network site. Therefore, cable installation, replacement, or upgrade oftentimes entails planning beyond the information technology department's operational control. Even what may seemingly appear to be a simple cable segment replacement project can turn out to be logistically complicated.

However, although the cabling represents only a small part of a network's total cost (as little as 6 percent), it has been estimated to be responsible for as much as 75 percent of network downtime. The cabling is also usually the longest-lived element of a network. You may replace servers and other components more than once before you replace the cable. For these reasons, spending a bit extra on good-quality cable, properly installed, is a worthwhile investment. This chapter examines the types of cables used for networks, their composition, and the connectors they use.

Cable Properties

Data link layer protocols are associated with specific cable types and include guidelines for the installation of the cable, such as maximum segment lengths. In most cases, you have a choice as to what kind of cable you want to use with the protocol, while in others you do not. Part of the process of evaluating and selecting a protocol involves examining the cable types and their suitability for your network site. For example, a connection between two adjacent buildings is better served by fiber-optic than copper, so with that requirement in mind, you should proceed to evaluate the data link layer protocols that support the use of fiber-optic cable.

Your cable installation may also be governed, in part, by the layout of the site and the local building codes. Cables generally are available in both nonplenum and plenum types. A *plenum* is an air space within a building, created by the components of the building themselves, that is designed to provide ventilation, such as a space between floors or walls. Buildings that use plenums to move air usually do not have a ducted ventilation system. In most communities, to run cable through a plenum, you must use a plenum-rated cable that does not give off toxic gases when it burns because the air in the plenum is distributed throughout the building. The outer covering of a plenum cable is usually some sort of Teflon product, while nonplenum cables have a polyvinyl chloride (PVC) sheath, which does produce toxic gases when it burns. Not surprisingly, plenum cable costs more than nonplenum, and it is also less flexible, making it more difficult to install. However, it is important to use the correct type of cable in any installation. If you violate the building codes, the local authorities can force you to replace the offending cable and possibly make you pay fines as well. Because of always increasing insurance costs, some companies will use specific plenum cables to lower their liability in case of fire because the use of plenum cable can result in less physical damage should there be a fire.

Cost is certainly an element that should affect your cable selection process, not only of the cable itself but also of the ancillary components such as connectors and mounting hardware, the network interface cards (NICs) for the computers, and the labor required for the cable installation. The qualities of fiber-optic cable might make it seem an ideal choice for your network, but when you see the costs of purchasing, installing, and maintaining it, your opinion may change.

Finally, the quality of the cable is an important part of the evaluation and selection process. When you walk into your local computer center to buy a prefabricated cable, you won't have much of a selection, except for cable length and possibly color. Vendors that provide a full cable selection, however (many of whom sell online or by mail order), have a variety of cable types that differ in their construction, their capabilities, and, of course, their prices.

Depending on the cable type, a good vendor may have both bulk cable and prefabricated cables. Bulk cable (that is, unfinished cable without connectors) should be available in various grades, in both plenum and nonplenum types. The grade of the cable can depend on several features, including the following:

- **Conductor gauge** The gauge is the diameter of the actual conductor within a cable, which in the case of copper cables is measured using the American Wire Gauge (AWG) scale. The lower the AWG rating, the thicker the conductor. A 24 AWG cable, therefore, is thinner than a 22 AWG cable. A thicker conductor provides better conductivity and more resistance against attenuation.

- **Category rating** Some types of cables are assigned ratings by a standards body, like the Electronic Industries Alliance/Telecommunications Industry Association (EIA/TIA). Twisted-pair cable, for example, is given a category rating that defines its capabilities. Most of the twisted-pair cable found today is Category 5e or Category 6, known as *Cat 5e* or *Cat 6*. Newer installations may use Cat 6a, which has improved performance at frequencies up to 500 MHz.

- **Shielded or unshielded**   Some cables are available with casings that provide different levels of shielding against electromagnetic interference. The shielding usually takes the form of foil or copper braid, the latter of which provides better protection. Twisted-pair cabling, for example, is available in shielded and unshielded varieties. For a typical network environment, unshielded twisted-pair provides sufficient protection against interference because the twisting of the wire pairs itself is a preventative measure.

- **Solid or stranded conductor**   A cable with a solid metal conductor provides better protection against attenuation, which means it can span longer distances. However, the solid conductor hampers the flexibility of the cable. If flexed or bent repeatedly, the conductor inside the cable can break. Solid conductor cables, therefore, are intended for permanent cable runs that will not be moved, such as those inside walls or ceilings. (Note that the cable can be flexed around corners and other obstacles during the installation; it is repeated flexing that can damage it.) Cables with conductors composed of multiple copper strands can be flexed repeatedly without breaking but are subject to greater amounts of attenuation. Stranded cables, therefore, should be used for shorter runs that are likely to be moved, such as for patch cables running from wall plates to computers.

NOTE Attenuation refers to the tendency of signals to weaken as they travel along a cable because of the resistance inherent in the medium. The longer a cable, the more the signals *attenuate* before reaching the other end. Attenuation is one of the primary factors that limits the size of a data network. Different types of cable have different attenuation rates, with copper cable being far more susceptible to the effect than fiber-optic cable.

These features naturally affect the price of the cable. A lower gauge is more expensive than a higher one, a higher category is more expensive than a lower, shielded is more expensive than unshielded, and solid is more expensive than stranded. This is not to say, however, that the more expensive product is preferable in every situation. In addition to the cable, a good vendor should have all of the equipment you need to attach the appropriate connectors, including the connector components and the tools for attaching them.

Prefabricated cables have the connectors already attached and should be available in various lengths and colors, using cable with the features already listed, and with various grades of connectors. The highest-quality prefabricated cables, for example, usually have a rubber boot around the connector that seals it to the cable end, prevents it from loosening or pulling out, protects the connector pins from bending, and reduces signal interference between the wires (called *crosstalk*). On lower-cost cables, the connector is simply attached to the end, without any extra protection.

Cabling Standards

Prior to 1991, the cabling used for networks was specified by the manufacturers of individual networking products. This resulted in the incompatibilities that are common in proprietary systems, and the need was recognized for a standard to define a cabling system that could support a multitude of different networking technologies. To address this need, the American National Standards Institute (ANSI), the Electronic Industry Association, and the Telecommunications Industry Association, along with a consortium of telecommunications companies, developed the ANSI/EIA/TIA-568-1991 Commercial Building Telecommunications Cabling Standard. This document was revised in 1995 and was known as ANSI/TIA/EIA-T568-A. An additional wiring standard, the T568-B, was adopted in 2001. The primary difference between the two is that two of the wiring pairs are swapped. Each standard defines the pinout (or order of connection) for the eight-pin connector plugs. See "Connector Pinouts" later in this chapter for more information.

Both of these standards were superseded by the current TIA/EIA-568-C standard.

TIA/EIA-568

The 568 standard defines a structured cabling system for voice and data communications in office environments that has a usable life span of at least ten years, supports products of multiple technology vendors, and uses any of the following cable types for various applications. The current standard (TIA/EIA-568-C) defines the general requirements with subsections that focus on cabling systems. Additional standards, such as TIA-569-A and TIA-570-A, address commercial and residential cabling.

The documents also include specifications for installing the cable within the building space. Toward this end, the building is divided into the following subsystems:

- **Building entrance**   The location at which the building's internal cabling interfaces with outside cabling. This is also referred to as the *demarcation point,* where the external provider network ends and connects with the customer's on-premise wiring.

- **Equipment room**   The location of equipment that can provide the same functions as that in a telecommunications closet but that may be more complex.

- **Telecommunications closet**   The location of localized telecommunications equipment, such as the interface between the horizontal cabling and the backbone.

- **Backbone cabling**   The cabling that connects the building's various equipment rooms, telecommunications closets, and the building entrance, as well as connections between buildings in a campus network environment.

- **Horizontal cabling**   The cabling and other hardware used to connect the telecommunications closet to the work area.

  The wirings are usually run through wireways, conduits, or ceiling spaces of each floor and can either be plenum cabling or internal wiring (IW).

- **Work area**   The components used to connect the telecommunications outlet to the workstation.

Thus, the cable installation for a modern building might look something like the diagram shown in Figure 5-1. The connections to external telephone and other services arrive at the building entrance and lead to the equipment room, which contains the network servers and other equipment. A backbone network connects the equipment room to various telecommunications closets throughout the building, which contain network interface equipment, such as switches, bridges, routers, or hubs. From the telecommunications closets, the horizontal cabling branches out into the work areas, terminating at wall plates. The work area then consists of the patch cables that connect the computers and other equipment to the wall plates.

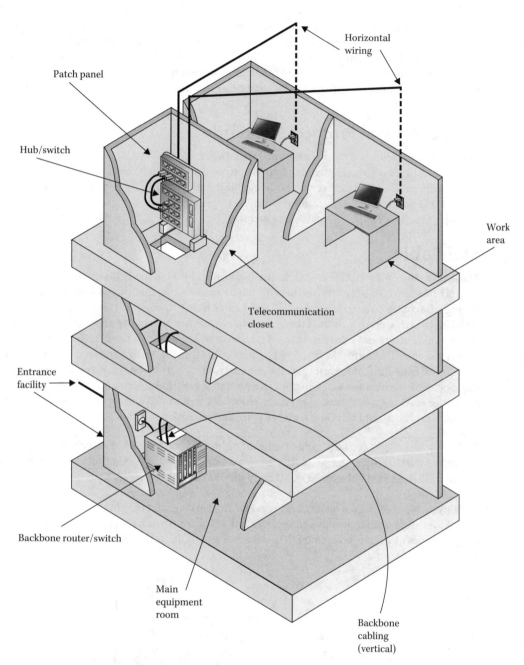

Figure 5-1 A generic building cabling system as defined by TIA/EIA T-568

This is, of course, a simplified and generalized plan. The T568 standard, in coordination with other TIA/EIA standards, provides guidelines for the types of cabling within and between these subsystems that you can use to create a wiring plan customized to your site and your equipment.

Contractors you hire to perform an office cable installation should be familiar with these standards and should be willing to certify in writing that their work conforms to the guidelines they contain.

Data Link Layer Protocol Standards

The protocols traditionally associated with the data link layer of the OSI reference model, such as Ethernet and Token Ring, also overlap into the physical layer in that they contain specifications for the network cabling. Thus, Ethernet and Token Ring standards, like those produced by the IEEE 802 working group, can also be said to be cabling standards. However, these documents do not go as deeply into the details of the cable properties and enterprise cable system design as T568.

Coaxial Cable

The first commercially viable network technologies introduced in the 1970s used coaxial cable as the network medium. Coaxial cable is named for the two conductors that share the same axis running through the cable's center. Many types of copper cable have two separate conductors, such as a standard electrical cord. In most of these, the two conductors run side by side within an insulating sheath that protects and separates them. A coaxial cable, on the other hand, is round, with a copper core at its center that forms the first conductor. It is this core that carries the actual signals. A layer of dielectric foam insulation surrounds the core, separating it from the second conductor, which is made of braided wire mesh and functions as a ground. As with any electrical cable, the signal conductor and the ground must always be separated or a short will occur, producing noise on the cable. This entire assembly is then enclosed within an insulating sheath (see Figure 5-2).

NOTE Coaxial cables can have either a solid or a stranded copper core, and their designations reflect the difference. The suffix /U indicates a solid core, while A/U indicates a stranded core. Thin Ethernet used either an RC-58-U or an RG-58A/U cable.

Several types of coaxial cables were used for networking, and they had different properties, even if they were similar in appearance. Data link layer protocols called for specific types of cable, the properties of which determined the guidelines and limitations for the cable installation.

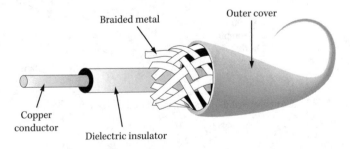

Figure 5-2   A cross-section of a coaxial cable

Today, *coax cable* is primarily used for connecting televisions to cable boxes or satellite receivers. It also may be used to connect a computer's cable modem to an Internet service provider (ISP). In the early days of computer networks, the cable was connected with a special connector called a *BNC*. The actual meaning of the bayonet-style connecter's name is shrouded in mystery, with most technicians divided between British Naval Connector and Bayonet Neill-Concelman.

Thick Ethernet

RG-8/U cable was usually referred to as *thick Ethernet trunk cable* because that was its primary use. The RG-8/U cable used for thick Ethernet networks had the least amount of attenuation of the coaxial cables, due in no small part to it being much thicker than the other types. This is why a thick Ethernet network could have cable segments up to 500 meters long, while thin Ethernet was limited to 185 meters.

At .405 inches in diameter, RG-8/U was similar in size to a garden hose but much heavier and less flexible, which made it difficult to bend around corners. For these reasons, the cable was typically installed along the floor of the site. By contrast, the RC-58A/U cable used by thin Ethernet was thinner, lighter, and flexible enough to run directly to the NIC.

Thick Ethernet cable was usually yellow and was marked every 2.5 meters for the taps to which the workstations connect. To connect a workstation to the cable, you applied what was known as a vampire tap. A *vampire* tap is a clamp that you connected to the cable after drilling a hole in the sheath. The clamp had metal "fangs" that penetrated into the core to send and receive signals. The vampire tap also included the transceiver (external to the computer on a thick Ethernet network), which connected to the NIC with a cable with connectors at both ends.

As a result of the inconvenience caused by its expense and rigidity, and despite its better performance than its successor, thin Ethernet, thick Ethernet is rarely seen today, even on legacy networks.

Thin Ethernet

The main advantage of the RG-58 cable used for thin Ethernet networks over RG-8 was its relative flexibility, which simplifies the installation process and makes it possible to run the cable directly to the computer, rather than using a separate AUI cable. Compared to twisted-pair, however, thin Ethernet is still ungainly and difficult to conceal because every workstation must have two cables connected to its NIC using a T fitting. Instead of neat wall plates with modular jacks for patch cables, an internal thin Ethernet installation had two thick, semirigid cables protruding from the wall for every computer.

As a result of this installation method, the bus was actually broken into separate lengths of cable that connect each computer to the next, unlike a thick Ethernet bus, which ideally was one long cable segment pierced with taps along its length. This made a big difference in the functionality of the network because if one of the two connections to each computer was broken for any reason, the bus was severed. When this happened, network communications failed between systems on different sides of the break, and the loss of termination on one end of each fragment jeopardized all of the network's traffic.

RG-58 cable used BNC connectors to connect to the T and to connect the T to the NIC in the computer. Even at the height of its popularity, thin Ethernet cable was typically purchased in bulk, and the connectors were attached by the installer or administrator; prefabricated cables were relatively rare. The process of attaching a BNC connector involved stripping the insulation off the cable end to expose both the copper core and the ground. The connector is then applied as separate components (a socket that the cable threads through and a post that slips over the core). Finally, the socket is compressed so it grips the cable and holds the post in place, using a plierslike tool called a *crimper*.

Cable Television

Just because coaxial cable is no longer used for networks does not mean that it has totally outlived its usefulness. Antennas, radios, and particularly the cable television industry still use it extensively. The cable delivering TV service to your home is RG-59 75-ohm coaxial, used in this case for broadband rather than baseband transmission (meaning that the single cable carries multiple, discrete signals simultaneously). This cable is also similar in appearance to thin Ethernet, but it has different properties and uses different connectors. The E connector used for cable TV connections screws into the jack, while BNC connectors use a bayonet lock coupling.

Many cable TV providers use this same coaxial cable to supply Internet access to subscribers, as well as television signals. In these installations, the coaxial cable connects to a device typically referred to as a *cable modem*, which then is connected to a computer using a 10Base-T Ethernet cable.

Twisted-Pair Cable

Twisted-pair cable is the current standard for networks. When compared to coaxial, it is easier to install, is suitable for many different applications, and provides far better performance. Perhaps the biggest advantage of twisted-pair cable, however, is that it is already used in countless telephone system installations throughout the world.

This means that many contractors are familiar with the installation procedures and that in a newly constructed office it is possible to install the cables at the same time as the telephone cables. In fact, many private homes now being built include twisted-pair network cabling as part of the basic service infrastructure.

Unlike coaxial cable, which has only one signal-carrying conductor and one ground, the twisted-pair cable used in most data networks has four pairs of insulated copper wires within a single sheath. Each wire pair is twisted with a different number of twists per inch to avoid electromagnetic interference from the other pairs and from outside sources (see Figure 5-3).

Each pair of wires in a twisted-pair cable is color coded, using colors defined in the TIA/EIA-T568-A or B standard, as shown in Table 5-1. In each pair, the solid-colored wire carries the signals, while the striped wire acts as a ground.

Unshielded Twisted-Pair

The outer sheathing of a twisted-pair cable can be either relatively thin, as in *unshielded twisted-pair* (UTP) cable, or thick, as in *shielded twisted-pair* (STP). UTP cable is the more commonly used of the two; most Ethernet networks are more than adequately served by UTP cable. The UTP cable uses 22 or 24 AWG copper conductors and has an impedance of 100 ohms. The insulation can be plenum rated or nonplenum.

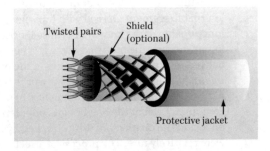

Figure 5-3   A cross-section of a twisted-pair cable

T-568A Pair Number	Description	T-568B Pair Number	Description
Pair 1	Solid blue or white with blue stripe	Pair 1	Solid blue or white with blue stripe
Pair 2	Solid orange or white with orange stripe	Pair 2	Solid green or white with green stripe
Pair 3	Solid green or white with green stripe	Pair 3	Solid orange or white with orange strip
Pair 4	Solid brown or white with brown stripe	Pair 4	Solid brown or white with brown stripe

Table 5-1   Color Codes for TIA/EIA T-568

Beyond these specifications, the TIA/EIA-T568 standard defines levels of performance for UTP cable that are referred to as *categories*. A higher category rating means that a cable is more efficient and able to transmit data at greater speeds. The major difference between the different cable categories is the tightness of each wire pair's twisting, commonly referred to as *twist per inch*. Table 5-2 lists some of the categories defined by the T568 standard, the speed ratings, the maximum run length, the network applications, and the maximum frequency for each category.

Category 3 cable was traditionally used for telephone system installations and was also suitable for 10Base-T Ethernet networks, which run at 10 Mbps. Category 3 was not suitable for the 100 Mbps speed used by Fast Ethernet, except in the case of 100Base-T4, which was specifically designed to run on Category 3 cable. 100BaseT4 was able to function only on this cable because it used all four of the wire pairs to carry data, while the standard technologies of the time used only two pairs.

Category 4 cable provided a marginal increase in performance over Category 3 and was, for a time, used in Token Ring networks. Since its ratification in 1995, however, most of the UTP cable installed for computer networks (and telephone networks as well) was Category 5. Category 5

Category	Common Name	Speed	Max Length	Network Application	Max Frequency
Cat 1	Analog telephone				0 MHz
Cat 3		4 Mbps		10Base-T	16 MHz
Cat 5	Fast Ethernet	100 Mbps	100m (328 feet)	100Base-T	100 MHz
Cat 5e	Gigabit Ethernet	1 Gbps	100m (328 feet)	1GBase-T	250 MHz
Cat 6	10 Gigabit Ethernet	10 Gbps	50m (164 feet)	10GBase-T	250 MHz
Cat 6a	10 Gigabit Ethernet	10 Gbps	100m (328 feet)	10GBase-T	500 MHz
Cat 7	Gigabit Ethernet	10 Gbps	100m (328 feet)	1000Base-TX	600 MHz
Cat 7a	Gigabit Ethernet	10 Gbps	100m (328 feet)	10GBase-T	1000 MHz

Table 5-2   Cable Category Specifications

UTP cable (often known simply as Cat 5) provided a substantial performance increase, supporting transmissions at up to 100 MHz.

Category 5e

While Category 5 cable was sufficient for use on 100 Mbps networks such as Fast Ethernet, technology continued to advance, and with Gigabit Ethernet products becoming available, running at 1 Gbps (1,000 Mbps), it was necessary to accommodate the higher speeds.

UTP cable ratings have continued to advance as well. However, the process by which the TIA/EIA standards are defined and ratified is much slower than the pace of technology, and many high-performance cable products arrived on the market that exceeded the Category 5 specifications to varying degrees. In 1999, after a surprisingly accelerated development period of less than two years, the TIA/ETA ratified the Category 5e (or Enhanced Category 5) standard.

The Category 5e standard was revised more than 14 times during its development because there was a great deal of conflict among the concerned parties as to how far the standard should go. Category 5e was intended primarily to support the IEEE 802.3ab Gigabit Ethernet standard, also known as 1000Base-T, which is a version of the 1,000 Mbps networking technology designed to run on the standard 100-meter copper cable segments also used by Fast Ethernet. As you can see in Table 5-2, the Category 5e standard calls for a maximum frequency rating of only 100 MHz, the same as that of Category 5 cable. However, Gigabit Ethernet uses frequencies up to 125 MHz, and Asynchronous Transfer Mode (ATM) networks, which were also expected to use this cable, could run at frequencies of up to 155 MHz. As a result, there was a good deal of criticism leveled at the 5e standard, saying that it didn't go far enough to ensure adequate performance of Gigabit Ethernet networks.

It's important to understand that the TIA/EIA UTP cable standards consist of many different performance requirements, but the frequency rating is the one that is most commonly used to judge the transmission quality of the cable. In fact, the Category 5e standard is basically the Category 5 standard with slightly elevated requirements for some of its testing parameters, such as *near end crosstalk* (NEXT), the attenuation-to-crosstalk ratio (ACR), return loss, and differential impedance.

Cat 6 and 6a

Cat 6 was established in 2001. This standard for Gigabit Ethernet is backward compatible with the Cat 3, 5, and 5e standards. This cable features higher specifications for suppression of both system noise and crosstalk issues. It was specifically designed to be interoperable, meaning cable meeting this standard must work with products manufactured by most vendors.

Because Cat 6 cables contain larger copper conductors, the size is a bit larger than the earlier Category 5 and 5e cables. The diameter of Cat 6 ranges from .021 inch to .25 inch (5.3mm to 5.8mm). Since Cat 5 and 5e cables fall in the range from 0.19 inch to 0.22 inch (4.8mm to 5.5mm), the physical size can make a difference in an installation.

Crosstalk is reduced in Cat 6 by making each pair a twist of .5 inch or less, while the larger conductor size provides less signal loss (attenuation) over the length of the cable.

Augmented Category 6 (Cat 6a) cable improves the bandwidth of Cat 6. However, because it is available in STP format, it must have specialized connectors to ground the cable and is therefore more expensive than Cat 6.

Cat 7

Cat 7 (originally known as Class F) is backward compatible with both Cat 5 and Cat 6. It is a twisted-pair cable that was designed as a standard for Gigabit Ethernet. It has additional shielding that helps to reduce both crosstalk and system noise. Because of this additional shielding, Cat 7 cable is bulkier and more difficult to bend. As with Cat 6a, each layer must be grounded or its through-put performance declines to nearly that of Cat 6.

NOTE Remember, when upgrading cabling, all of the network components must be rated at the same category. This means you will not have a Cat 6 network if some of the connectors or other components are rated at Cat 5.

Currently, as technology advances, so do new standards. Cat 7a is currently available for some applications, primarily multiple applications across a single cable. Cat 8 and beyond are in the works.

Connector Pinouts

Twisted-pair cables use RJ-45 modular connectors at both ends (see Figure 5-4). An RJ-45 (RJ is the acronym for *registered jack*) is an eight-pin version of the four-pin (or sometimes six-pin) RJ-11 connector used on standard satin telephone cables. The pinouts for the connector, which are also defined in the TIA/ElA-T568-A and B standards, are shown in Figure 5-5.

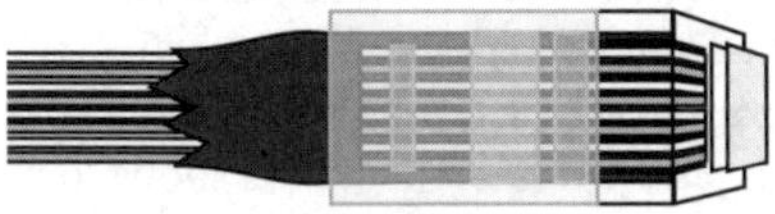

The USOC standard (as shown in Figure 5-6) was the traditional pinout originated for voice communications in the United States, but this configuration is not suitable for data. This is because while pins 3 and 6 do connect to a single-wire

Figure 5-4   An RJ-45 connector

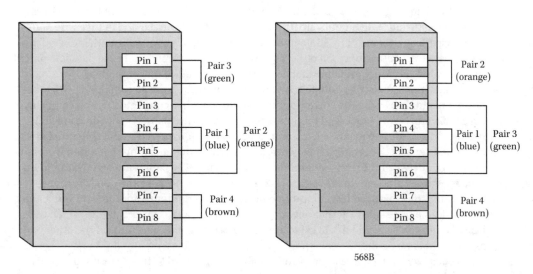

Figure 5-5   The 568 A and 568 B pinouts

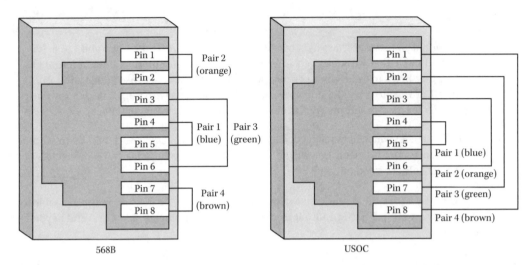

Figure 5-6   The 568B and USOC pinouts

pair, pins 1 and 2 are connected to separate pairs. AT&T discovered this shortcoming when it began doing research into computer networks that would run over the existing telecommunications infrastructure. In 1985, AT&T published its own standard, called 258A, which defined a new pinout in which the proper pins used the same wire pairs.

The TIA/EIA, which was established in 1985 after the breakup of AT&T, then published the 258A standard as an adjunct to TIA/EIA-T568-A in 1995, giving it the name T568-B (as shown on the left in Figure 5-6). Thus, while the pinout now known as 568B would seem to be newer than 568A, it is actually older. Pinout 568B began to be used widely in the United States before the TIA/EIA-T568-A standard was even published.

As you can see in Figure 5-6, the USOC standard uses a different layout for the wire pairs, while the 568A and 568B pinouts are identical except that the green and orange wire pairs are transposed. Thus, the two TIA/EIA standards are functionally identical; neither one offers a performance advantage over the other, as long as both ends of the cable use the same pinout. Prefabricated cables are available that conform to either one of these standards.

In most cases, twisted-pair cable is wired straight through, meaning that each of the pins on one connector is wired to its corresponding pin on the other connector, as shown in Figure 5-7. On a typical network, however, computers use separate wire pairs for transmitting and receiving data. For two machines to communicate, the transmitted signal generated at each computer must be delivered to the receive pins on the other, meaning that a signal crossover must occur between the transmit and receive wire pairs. The cables are wired straight through (that is, without the crossover) on a normal Ethernet LAN because the hub is responsible for performing the crossover. If you want to connect one computer to another without a hub to form a simple two-node Ethernet network, you must use a crossover cable, in which the transmit pins on each end of the cable are connected to the receive pins on the other end, as shown in Figure 5-8.

Because each pin on a straight-through cable is connected to the corresponding pin at the other end, it doesn't matter what colors the wires are, as long as the pairs are properly oriented. So, when purchasing prefabricated cables, either the 568A or 568B pinouts will function properly.

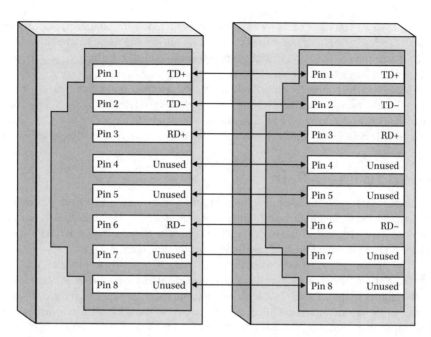

Figure 5-7   UTP straight-through wiring

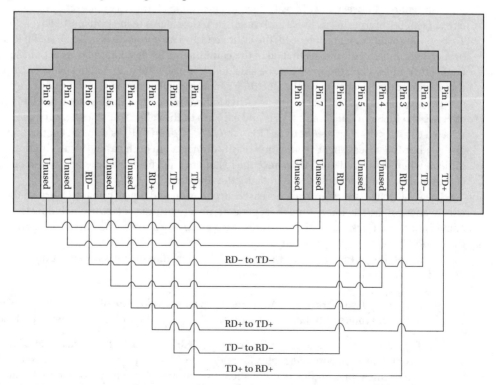

Figure 5-8   UTP crossover wiring

The time when you must make a conscious decision to use one standard or the other is when you install bulk cable (or have it installed). You must connect the same colors on each end of the cable to the same pins so you get a straight-through connection. Selecting one standard and sticking to it is the best way to avoid confusion that can result in nonfunctioning connections.

Attaching the connectors to a cable requires a crimper tool, much like the one used for coaxial cable, except that the process is complicated by having eight conductors to deal with instead of only two. A network administrator who is not handy with a crimper can easily purchase twisted-pair cables with connectors attached in a wide variety of grades, lengths, and colors.

Shielded Twisted-Pair

Shielded twisted-pair is 150-ohm cable containing additional shielding that protects signals against the electromagnetic interference (EMI) produced by electric motors, power lines, and other sources. Originally used in Token Ring networks, STP is also intended for installations where UTP cable would provide insufficient protection against interference.

The shielding in STP cable is not just an additional layer of inert insulation, as many people believe. Rather, the wires within the cable are encased in a metallic sheath that is as conductive as the copper in the wires. This sheath, when properly grounded, converts ambient noise into a current, just like an antenna. This current is carried to the wires within, where it creates an equal and opposite current flowing in the twisted pairs. The opposite currents cancel each other out, eliminating noise that injects disturbance to the signals passing over the wires.

This balance between the opposite currents is delicate. If they are not exactly equal, the current can be interpreted as noise and can disturb the signals being transmitted over the cable. To keep the shield currents balanced, the entire end-to-end connection must be shielded and properly grounded. This means that all of the components involved in the connection, such as connectors and wall plates, must also be shielded. It is also vital to install the cable correctly so that it is grounded properly and the shielding is not ripped or otherwise disturbed at any point.

The shielding in an STP cable can be either foil or braided metal. The metal braid is a more effective shield, but it adds weight, size, and expense to the cable. Foil-shielded cable, sometimes referred to as *screened twisted-pair* (ScTP) or *foil twisted-pair* (FTP), is thinner, lighter, and cheaper but is also less effective and more easily damaged. In both cases, the installation is difficult when compared to UTP because the installers must be careful not to flex and bend the cable too much, or they could risk damaging the shielding.

The cable may also suffer from increased attenuation and other problems because the effectiveness of the shielding is highly dependent on a multitude of factors, including the composition and thickness of the shielding, the type and location of the EMI in the area, and the nature of the grounding structure.

The properties of the STP cable itself were defined by IBM during the development of the Token Ring protocol:

- **Type 1A**   Two pairs of 22 AWC wires, each pair wrapped in foil, with a shield layer (foil or braid) around both pairs, and an outer sheath of either PVC or plenum-rated material

- **Type 2A**   Two pairs of 22 AWG wires, each pair wrapped in foil, with a shield layer (foil or braid) around both pairs, plus four additional pairs of 22 AWG wires for voice communications, within an outer sheath of either PVC or plenum-rated material

- **Type 6A**   Two pairs of 22 AWG wires, with a shield layer (foil or braid) around both pairs, and an outer sheath of either PVC or plenum-rated material

- **Type 9A**   Two pairs of 26 AWG wires, with a shield layer (foil or braid) around both pairs, and an outer sheath of either PVC or plenum-rated material

Fiber-Optic Cable

Fiber-optic cable is completely different from all of the other cables covered thus far in this chapter because it is not based on electrical signals transmitted through copper conductors. Instead, fiber-optic cable uses pulses of light (photons) to transmit the binary signals generated by computers. Because fiber-optic cable uses light instead of electricity, nearly all of the problems inherent in copper cable, such as electromagnetic interference, crosstalk, and the need for grounding, are completely eliminated. In addition, attenuation is reduced enormously, enabling fiber-optic links to span much greater distances than copper—up to 120 kilometers in some cases.

Fiber-optic cable is ideal for use in network backbones, especially for connections between buildings, because it is immune to moisture and other outdoor conditions. Fiber cable is also inherently more secure than copper because it does not radiate detectable electromagnetic energy like copper, and it is extremely difficult to tap.

The drawbacks of fiber optic mainly center around its installation and maintenance costs, which are usually thought of as being much higher than those for copper media. What used to be a great difference, however, has come closer to evening out in recent years. The fiber-optic medium is at this point only slightly more expensive than UTP. Even so, the use of fiber does present some problems, such as in the installation process. Pulling the cable is basically the same as with copper, but attaching the connectors requires completely different tools and techniques—you can essentially throw everything you may have learned about electric wiring out the window.

Fiber optics has been around for a long time; even the early 10 Mbps Ethernet standards supported its use, calling it FOIRL, and later 10BaseF. Fiber optics came into its own, however, as a high-speed network technology, and today virtually all of the data link layer protocols currently in use support it in some form.

Fiber-Optic Cable Construction

A fiber-optic cable consists of a core made of glass or plastic and a cladding that surrounds the core; then it has a plastic spacer layer, a layer of Kevlar fiber for protection, and an outer sheath of Teflon or PVC, as shown in Figure 5-9. The relationship between the core and the cladding enables fiber-optic cable to carry signals long distances. The transparent qualities of the core are slightly greater than those of the cladding, which makes the inside surface of the cladding reflective. As the light pulses travel through the core, they reflect back and forth off the cladding. This reflection enables you to bend the cable around corners and still have the signals pass through it without obstruction.

There are two main types of fiber-optic cable, called *singlemode* and *multimode,* that differ in several ways. The most important difference is in the thickness of the core and the cladding. Singlemode fiber is typically rated at 8.3/125 microns and

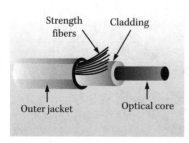

Figure 5-9   Cross-section of a fiber-optic cable

multimode fiber at 62.5/125 microns. These measurements refer to the thickness of the core and the thickness of the cladding and the core together. Light travels down the relatively thin core of singlemode cable without reflecting off the cladding as much as in multimode fiber's thicker core. The signal carried by a singlemode cable is generated by a laser and consists of only a single wavelength, while multimode signals are generated by a light-emitting diode (LED) and carry multiple wavelengths. Together, these qualities enable singlemode cable to operate at higher bandwidths than multimode and traverse distances up to 50 times longer.

However, singlemode cable is often more expensive and has a relatively high bend radius compared to multimode, which makes it more difficult to work with. Most fiber-optic LANs use multimode cable, which, although inferior in performance to singlemode, is still vastly superior to copper.

Multimode cables are often used for local network installations when extreme distance is not an issue. Since singlemode cables transmit laser light, it travels in only one direction so that the wavelength it uses is compatible with the laser light detector at the receiving end. This type of fiber-optic cable is used primarily where data speed and distance are paramount.

Fiber-optic cables are available in a variety of configurations because the cable can be used for many different applications. Simplex cables contain a single fiber strand, while duplex cables contain two strands running side by side in a single sheath. Breakout cables can contain as many as 24 fiber strands in a single sheath, which you can divide to serve various uses at each end. Because fiber-optic cable is immune to copper cable problems such as EMI and crosstalk, it's possible to bundle large numbers of strands together without twisting them or worrying about signal degradation, as with UTP cable.

Fiber-Optic Connectors

The original connector used on fiber-optic cables was called a *straight tip* (ST) connector. It was a barrel-shaped connector with a bayonet locking system, as shown in Figure 5-10. It was replaced by the SC type (which stands for *subscriber connector, standard connector,* or *Siemon connector*), which many consider now to be the traditional connector. The SC has a square body and locks by simply pushing it into the socket. Figure 5-10 shows the ST and SC connectors.

Today, connectors with smaller form factors are replacing the traditional fiber-optic connectors. These smaller connectors reduce the footprint of the network by allowing more connectors to be installed in each faceplate. One of the most common of these small connectors is the LC (which stands for *local connector* or *Lucent connector*). The LC is a duplex connector that is designed for two fiber-optic cables.

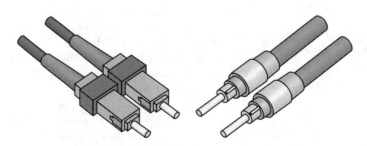

Figure 5-10   Fiber-optic connectors SC (left) and ST (right)

Using fiber-optic cable imparts a freedom to the network designer that could never be realized with copper media. Because fiber optic permits segment lengths much greater than UTP, having telecommunications closets containing switches or hubs scattered about a large installation is no longer necessary. Instead, horizontal cable runs can extend all the way from wall plates down to a central equipment room that contains all of the network's patch panels, hubs, switches, routers, and other such devices. This is known as a *collapsed backbone*. Rather than traveling constantly to remote areas of the installation, the majority of the infrastructure maintenance can be performed at this one location. For more information about network design, see Chapter 9.

Part II

CHAPTER

6

Wireless LANs

Until recently, computer networks were thought of as using cables for their communications medium, but there have also been wireless networking solutions available for many years. Wireless networking products typically use some form of radio or light waves; these are called *unbounded* media (as opposed to *bounded* media, which refers to cabled networks). These media enable users with properly equipped computers to interact with other networked computers, just as if they were connected to them with cables. Wireless networking products long had a reputation for poor performance and unreliability. It is only in the last ten or twelve years that these technologies have developed to the point at which they are serious tools for business users.

In many cases, users have come to expect connectivity in nearly every setting, whether it be in the grocery store, on a commuter train, or in a restaurant line. Whether it be with a cell phone, a tablet, or a laptop, we expect to be able to download e-mail and access both the Internet and our company's network in an instant. Most telephone service providers now enable users to access all of these services in any location. One of the advantages of cellular-based data networking is its range. Users can access the Internet and other networks from any place supported by the cellular network.

Wireless Networks

Wireless networks, or *wireless local area networks (WLANs),* connect devices with radio waves rather than cables. The ability to connect servers, printers, scanning devices, and workstations without dragging cabling through walls is the biggest advantage of wireless networking.

NOTE Wide area networks are also wireless and are introduced in Chapter 7.

The main difference between a traditional, cabled network and a wireless network is the way the data is transmitted. Wireless networks use a transmitter called a *wireless access point* (WAP) that has been wired into an Internet connection to create a *hotspot* for the connection. Access to the wireless network then depends on several things:

- **Distance from a WAP**   The closer one is to an access point, the better the signal.

- **Transmission strength of the wireless card**   Wireless fidelity (WiFi) cards have varying degrees of transmitting capabilities. Normally, lower-cost cards have less power than more expensive cards and therefore must be closer to the access point.

- **Existing interference**   Microwave devices, cordless phones, computers, and even Bluetooth devices can interfere with a WiFi network.

- **Current traffic on the network, including the number of current users**   Depending on the IEEE 802.11 standard of a WAP and what the current users are doing, more than 20 users accessing a specific WAP can cause the connection to degrade. This is especially true if users are using file-sharing software or peer-to-peer applications such as Skype.

- **Local environment characteristics**   Be sure to note how physical obstructions or barriers such as walls, placement of devices, and other such issues will affect your network. In a small-office environment, there are many cases of poorly designed wireless installations due to lack of understanding of the effects of physical obstructions and the choice between lower and higher frequencies to mitigate these limitations.

NOTE See "The IEEE 802.11 Standards" section later in this chapter for more information.

Advantages and Disadvantages of Wireless Networks

While wireless networks are certainly useful and have their advantages, they have some definite disadvantages when compared with wired (cabled) networks. Table 6-1 discusses some of the advantages and disadvantages.

Types of Wireless Networks

There are many types of wireless, such as WiFi, Bluetooth, satellite services, and others, in use today. *Bluetooth,* named for a tenth-century Danish king, provides short-range wireless communications between devices such as cellular phones, keyboards, or printers at a very low cost. Bluetooth uses radio frequency signals, which are not limited to line-of-sight transmissions. Often, keyboards or mice are available with Bluetooth technology to use with a cell phone, laptop, or tablet.

The most widely used technology today is *WiFi.* This technology has better connection speeds and, if configured properly, is more secure than a Bluetooth connection. Table 6-2 shows some of the differences between the two.

Wireless Applications

The most immediate application for wireless local area networking is the situation where it is impractical or impossible to install a cabled network. In some cases, the construction of a building may prevent the installation of network cables, while in others, cosmetic concerns

Type of Network	Wired	Wireless
Security against attacks	A wired network is much more secure than a wireless network. Wired networks require direct access to your ISP's network or to your wired router.	Invaders can easily obtain access or intercept your data, even from a location just outside your window. Just as you can obtain a radio station from distant locations, others can conceivably gain access to a wireless network.
Control	Wired networks can be controlled with passwords, physical layout, and layers of security.	While wireless networks can be password protected, there is often at least one point at which the network is vulnerable to outside access. Non-company-owned devices can subject the network to malware. When non-company-owned devices are used, this use opens other avenues of potential attack by outside attackers.
Physical characteristics	Ethernet cables and other devices are available and inexpensive. Cables are often unsightly and require space to install and maintain. Loose cables can cause network failure and can be a hazard to "navigation" within the workplace.	Wireless connections allow users to utilize devices throughout an office, building, or other locations. The lack of cables can make the workplace appear cleaner.
Speed	Wired connections, such as Gigabit Ethernet, can connect at higher speeds than wireless networks.	By their nature, wireless networks are slower, and the outside sources can affect transmitted signals.
Reliability	Wired devices have been in use for many years and are very reliable. The signals transmitted over cabling are seldom subject to bandwidth fluctuations and interference.	Since radio waves are used in wireless networks, they are subject to interferences and dropped connections because of distance or range issues.

Table 6-1   Advantages and Disadvantages of Wireless Networks vs. Wired Networks

may be the problem. For example, a kiosk containing a computer that provides information to guests might be a worthwhile addition to a luxury hotel, but not at the expense of running unsightly cables across the floor or walls of a meticulously decorated lobby. The same might be the case for a small two- or three-node network in a private home, where installing cables inside walls would be difficult and using external cables would be unacceptable in appearance.

Another application for wireless LANs is to support mobile client computers. These mobile clients can range from laptop-equipped technical support personnel for a corporate internetwork to roving customer service representatives with specialized handheld devices, such as rental car and baggage check workers in airports. With today's handheld computers and a wireless LAN

	Bluetooth	WiFi
Frequency	2.4 GHz	2.4 to 5 GHz
Standard	IEEE 802.15	IEEE 802.11
Authority	Bluetooth SIG	IEE, WECA
Power usage	Low	High
Bit rate	2.1 Mbps	600 Mbps
Range	5 to 30 meters	Typically 32 meters indoors/95 meters outdoors. Antennas increase the range.
Usability	Simple to use; can connect up to seven devices at one time	Requires hardware and software configuration
Uses	Mobile phones, office peripherals	Tablets, notebook and desktop computers, television, and newer mobile devices
Requirements	Bluetooth adapter for each device	Wireless adapter on each device; wireless router or other wireless access

Table 6-2 Bluetooth vs. WiFi

protocol that is reliable and reasonably fast, the possibilities for its use are endless. Here are some examples:

- Hospitals can store patient records in a database and permit doctors and nurses to continually update them by entering new information into a mobile computer.

- Workers in retail stores can dynamically update inventory figures by scanning the items on the shelves.

- A traveling salesperson can walk into the home office with a laptop in hand, and as soon as the computer is within range of the wireless network, it connects to the LAN, downloads new e-mail, and synchronizes the user's files with copies stored on a network server.

The IEEE 802.11 Standards

In 1997, the IEEE published the first version of a standard that defined the physical and data link layer specifications for a wireless networking protocol that would meet the following requirements:

- The protocol would support stations that are fixed, portable, or mobile, within a local area. The difference between portable and mobile is that a portable station can access the network from various fixed locations, while a mobile station can access the network while it is actually in motion.

- The protocol would provide wireless connectivity to automatic machinery, equipment, or stations that require rapid deployment—that is, rapid establishment of communications.

- The protocol would be deployable on a global basis.

This document (as of the writing of this chapter) is now known as IEEE 802.11, 2012 edition, "Wireless LAN Medium Access Control (MAC) and Physical Layer (PHY) Specifications." Because 802.11 was developed by the same IEEE 802 committee responsible for the 802.3 (Ethernet) and 802.5 (Token Ring) protocols, it fits into the same physical and data link layer stack arrangement. The data link layer is divided into the logical link control (LLC) and media access control (MAC) sublayers. The 802.11 documents define the physical layer and MAC sublayer specifications for the wireless LAN protocol, and the systems use the standard LLC sublayer defined in IEEE 802.2. From the network layer up, the systems can use any standard set of protocols, such as TCP/IP or IPX.

NOTE For more information on LLC, see Chapter 10.

Despite the inclusion of 802.11 in the same company as Ethernet and Token Ring, the use of wireless media calls for certain fundamental changes in the way you think about a local area network and its use. Some of these changes are as follows:

- **Unbounded media**   A wireless network does not have readily observable connections to the network or boundaries beyond which network communication ceases.
- **Dynamic topology**   Unlike cabled networks, in which the LAN topology is meticulously planned out before the installation and remains static until deliberate changes are made, the topology of a wireless LAN changes frequently, if not continuously.
- **Unprotected media**   The stations on a wireless network are not protected from outside signals as cabled networks are. On a cabled network, outside interference can affect signal quality, but there is no way for the signals from two separate but adjacent networks to be confused. On a wireless network, roving stations can conceivably wander into a different network's operational perimeter, compromising security.
- **Unreliable media**   Unlike a cabled network, a protocol cannot work under the assumption that every station on the network receives every packet and can communicate with every other station.
- **Asymmetric media**   The propagation of data to all of the stations on a wireless network does not necessarily occur at the same rate. There can be differences in the transmission rates of individual stations that change as the device moves or the environment in which it is operating changes.

As a result of these changes, the traditional elements of a data link layer LAN protocol (the MAC mechanism, the frame format, and the physical layer specifications) have to be designed with different operational criteria in mind.

The Physical Layer

The 802.11 physical layer defines two possible topologies and three types of wireless media, operating at four possible speeds.

Physical Layer Topologies

As you learned in Chapter 1, the term *topology* usually refers to the way in which the computers on a network are connected. A bus topology, for example, means that each computer is connected to the next one, in daisy-chain fashion, while in a star topology, each computer is connected to a central hub. These examples apply to cabled networks, however. Wireless networks don't have a concrete topology like cabled ones do. Unbounded media devices, by definition, enable wireless network devices to transmit signals to all of the other devices on the network simultaneously. However, this does not equate to a mesh topology, as described in Chapter 1. Although each device theoretically can transmit signals to all of the other wireless devices on the network at any time, this does not necessarily mean that it will. Mobility is an integral part of the wireless network design, and a wireless LAN protocol must be able to compensate for systems that enter and leave the area in which the medium can operate. The result is that the topologies used by wireless networks are basic rules that they use to communicate, and not static arrangements of devices at specific locations. IEEE 802.11 supports two types of wireless network topologies: the ad hoc topology and the infrastructure topology.

The fundamental building block of an 802.11 wireless LAN is the basic service set (BSS). A BSS is a geographical area in which properly equipped wireless stations can communicate. The configuration and area of the BSS are dependent on the type of wireless medium being used and the nature of the environment in which it's being used, among other things. A network using a radio frequency–based medium might have a BSS that is roughly spherical, for example, while an infrared network would deal more in straight lines. The boundaries of the BSS can be affected by environmental conditions, architectural elements of the site, and many other factors, but when a station moves within the basic service set's sphere of influence, it can communicate with other stations in the same BSS. When it moves outside of the BSS, communication ceases.

The simplest type of BSS consists of two or more wireless computers or other devices that have come within transmission range of each other, as shown in Figure 6-1. The process by which the devices enter into a BSS is called *association*. Each wireless device has an operational range dictated by its equipment, and as the two devices approach each other, the area of overlap between their ranges becomes the BSS. This arrangement, in which all of the network devices in

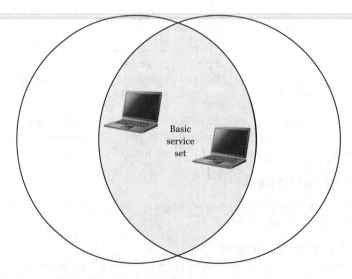

Figure 6-1   A basic service set can be as simple as two wireless stations within communication range of each other.

the BSS are mobile or portable, is called an *ad hoc topology* or an *independent BSS* (IBSS). The term *ad hoc topology* refers to the fact that a network of this type may often come together without prior planning and exist only as long as the devices need to communicate. This type of topology operates as a peer-to-peer network because every device in the BSS can communicate with every other device. An example might be transmitting a file to your printer or diagram to a colleague's tablet. Multiple ad hoc networks can be created to transfer data between several devices. By their nature, ad hoc networks are temporary. While Figure 6-1 depicts the BSS as roughly ovular and the convergence of the communicating devices as being caused by their physically approaching each other, the actual shape of the BSS is likely to be far less regular and more ephemeral. The ranges of the devices can change instantaneously because of many different factors, and the BSS can grow, shrink, or even disappear entirely at a moment's notice.

While an ad hoc network uses basic service sets that are transient and constantly mutable, it's also possible to build a wireless network with basic service sets that are more permanent. This is the basis of a network that uses an infrastructure topology. An infrastructure network consists of at least one wireless access point (AP), which is either a stand-alone device or a wireless-equipped computer that is also connected to a standard bounded network using a cable. The access point has an operational range that is relatively fixed (when compared to an IBSS) and functions as the base station for a BSS. Any mobile station that moves within the AP's sphere of influence is associated into the BSS and becomes able to communicate with the cabled network (see Figure 6-2). Note

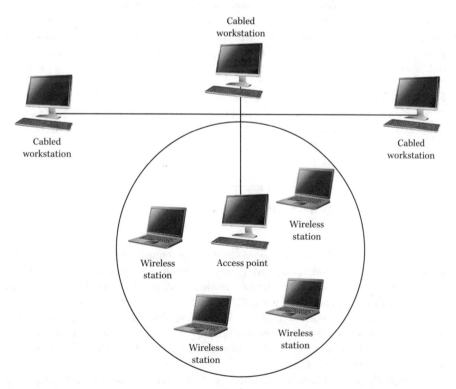

Figure 6-2   An access point enables wireless stations to access resources on a cabled network.

that this is more of a client-server arrangement than a peer-to-peer one. The AP enables multiple wireless stations to communicate with the systems on the cabled network but not with each other. However, the use of an AP does not prevent mobile stations from communicating with each other independently of the AP.

It is because the AP is permanently connected to the cabled network and not mobile that this type of network is said to use an infrastructure topology. This arrangement is typically used for corporate installations that have a permanent cabled network that also must support wireless devices that access resources on the cabled network. An infrastructure network can have any number of access points and therefore any number of basic service sets. The architectural element that connects basic service sets together is called a *distribution system* (DS). Together, the basic service sets and the DS that connects them are called the *extended services set* (ESS). In practice, the DS is typically a cabled network using IEEE 802.3 (Ethernet) or another standard data link layer protocol, but the network can conceivably use a wireless distribution system (WDS). Technically, the AP in a network of this type is also called a *portal* because it provides access to a network using another data link layer protocol. It's possible for the DS to function solely as a means of connecting APs and not provide access to resources on a cabled network. Whether the media used to form the BSS and the DS are the same or different (the standard takes no stance either way), 802.11 logically separates the wireless medium from the distribution system medium.

The basic service sets connected by a distribution system can be physically configured in almost any way. The basic service sets can be widely distant from each other to provide wireless network connectivity in specific remote areas, or they can overlap to provide a large area of contiguous wireless connectivity. It's also possible for an infrastructure BSS to be concurrent with an IBSS. The 802.11 standard makes no distinction between the two topologies because both must present the same appearance to the LLC sublayer operating at the upper half of the data link layer.

Physical Layer Media

The original IEEE 802.11 standard defined three physical layer media, two that used radio frequency (RF) signals and one that used infrared light signals. A wireless LAN could use any one of the three media, all of which interface with the same MAC layer. These three media were as follows:

- Frequency-hopping spread spectrum (FHSS)
- Direct-sequence spread spectrum (DSSS)
- Infrared

The two RF media both used spread spectrum communication, which is a common form of radio transmission used in many wireless applications. Invented during the 1940s, spread spectrum technology takes an existing narrowband radio signal and divides it among a range of frequencies in any one of several ways. The result is a signal that utilizes more bandwidth but is louder and easier for a receiver to detect. At the same time, the signal is difficult to intercept because attempts to locate it by scanning through the frequency bands turn up only isolated fragments. It is also difficult to jam because you would have to block a wider range of frequencies for the jamming to be effective.

The 802.11 RF media operate in the 2.4 GHz frequency band, occupying the 83 MHz of bandwidth between 2.400 and 2.483 GHz. These frequencies are unlicensed in most countries, although there are varying limitations on the signal strength imposed by different governments.

The difference between the various types of spread spectrum communications lies in the method by which the signals are distributed among the frequencies. *Frequency-hopping spread spectrum,* for example, used a predetermined code or algorithm to dictate frequency shifts that occur continually, in discrete increments, over a wide band of frequencies. The 802.11 FHSS implementation called for seventy nine 1 MHz channels, although some countries imposed smaller limits. Obviously, the receiving device must be equipped with the same algorithm in order to read the signal properly. The rate at which the frequency changes (that is, the amount of time that the signal remains at each frequency before hopping to the next one) is independent of the bit rate of the data transmission. If the frequency-hopping rate is faster than the signal's bit rate, the technology is called a *fast hop system.* If the frequency-hopping rate is slower than the bit rate, you have a *slow hop system.* The 802.11 FHSS implementation ran at 1 Mbps, with an optional 2 Mbps rate.

In *direct-sequence spread spectrum* communications, the signal to be transmitted is modulated by a digital code called a *chip* or *clapping code,* which has a bit rate larger than that of the data signal. The chipping code is a redundant bit pattern that essentially turns each bit in the data signal into several bits that are actually transmitted. The longer the chipping code, the more the original data signal is enlarged. This enlargement of the signal makes it easier for the receiver to recover the transmitted data if some bits are damaged. The more the signal is enlarged, the less significance attributed to each bit. Like with FHSS, a receiver that doesn't possess the chipping code used by the transmitter can't interpret the DSSS signal, seeing it as just noise. The DSSS implementation in the original 802.11 document supported 1 and 2 Mbps transmission rates. IEEE 802.11b expanded this capability by adding transmission rates of 5.5 and 11 Mbps. Only DSSS supported these faster rates, which is the primary reason why it was the most commonly used 802.11 physical layer specification.

Later amendments have improved on the transmission rates, as shown in Table 6-3.

Infrared communications use frequencies in the 850 to 950 nanometer range, just below the visible light spectrum. This medium is rarely implemented on wireless LANs because of its limited range. Unlike most infrared media, the IEEE 802.11 infrared implementation does not require direct line-of-sight communications; an infrared network can function using diffuse or reflected signals. However, the range of communications is limited when compared to FHSS and DSSS, about 10 to 20 meters, and can function properly only in an indoor environment with surfaces that provide adequate signal diffusion or reflection. This makes infrared unsuitable for mobile devices and places more constraints on the physical location of the wireless device than either FHSS or DHSS. Like FHSS, the 802.11 infrared medium supported a 1 Mbps transmission rate and an optional rate of 2 Mbps.

Orthogonal Frequency Division Multiplexing was approved in 1999. This protocol increases throughput to 54 Mbps, and in 2003 this process was approved for the 2.4 GHz band. This method is often used for wideband transmission popular for DSL Internet access, 4G mobile communication, and digital television. Its main advantage is the use of multiple, narrow band carriers rather than one wide band carrier to transport data. It is efficient and works well even when receiving interference from a narrow band. However, OFDM is sensitive to *frequency offset,* an intentional shift of broadcast frequencies done to eliminate or lessen interference from other radio transmitters.

Since 1999 there have been several amendments to the IEEE 802.11 standard, as shown in Table 6-3.

802.11 Protocol	Approval Date	Bandwidth (MHz)	Frequency (GHz)	Media	Estimated Range (Indoors) in Feet	Estimated Range (Outdoors) in Feet
Original	June 1997	20	2.4	DSSS and FHSS	70	330
a	September 1999	20	5	OFDM	115	500
b	September 1999	20	2.4	DSSS	115	500
g	June 2003	20	2.4	OFDM and DSSS	125	500
n	October 2009	20 to 40	2.4 to 5	OFDM	250	850
ac	December 2013	20 to 160	Up to 866.7	OFDM		
af	February 2014	54 to 790		OFDM		

Table 6-3 802.11 Standards and Current Amendments

NOTE Table 6-3 shows information as of the writing of this chapter.

Physical Layer Frames

Instead of a relatively simple signaling scheme such as the Manchester and Differential Manchester techniques used by Ethernet and Token Ring, respectively, the media operating at the 802.11 physical layer have their own frame formats that encapsulate the frames generated at the data link layer. This is necessary to support the complex nature of the media.

The Frequency-Hopping Spread Spectrum Frame

The FHSS frame consists of the following fields:

- **Preamble (10 bytes)**   Contains 80 bits of alternating zeros and ones that the receiving system uses to detect the signal and synchronize timing.
- **Start of Frame Delimiter (2 bytes)**   Indicates the beginning of the frame.
- **Length (12 bits)**   Specifies the size of the data field.
- **Signaling (4 bits)**   Contains one bit that specifies whether the system is using the 1 or 2 Mbps transmission rate. The other three bits are reserved for future use. No matter which transmission rate the system is using, the preamble and header fields are always transmitted at 1 Mbps. Only the data field is transmitted at 2 Mbps.
- **CRC (2 bytes)**   Contains a cyclic redundancy check value, used by the receiving system to test for transmission errors.
- **Data (0 to 4,095 bytes)**   Contains the data link layer frame to be transmitted to the receiving system.

The Direct-Sequence Spread Spectrum Frame

The DSSS frame is illustrated in Figure 6-3 and consists of the following fields:

- **Preamble (16 bytes)**   Contains 128 bits that the receiving system uses to adjust itself to the incoming signal

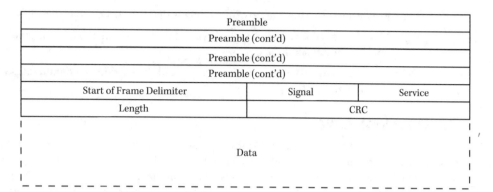

Preamble		
Preamble (cont'd)		
Preamble (cont'd)		
Preamble (cont'd)		
Start of Frame Delimiter	Signal	Service
Length	CRC	

Data

Figure 6-3   The DSSS frame format

- **Start of Frame Delimiter (SFD) (2 bytes)**   Indicates the beginning of the frame
- **Signal (1 byte)**   Specifies the transmission rate used by the system
- **Service (1 byte)**   Contains the hexadecimal value 00, indicating that the system complies with the IEEE 802.11 standard
- **Length (2 bytes)**   Specifies the size of the data field
- **CRC (2 bytes)**   Contains a cyclic redundancy check value, used by the receiving system to test for transmission errors
- **Data (variable)**   Contains the data link layer frame to be transmitted to the receiving system

The Infrared Frame

The frame used for infrared transmissions consists of the following fields:

- **Synchronization (SYNC) (57 to 73 slots)**   Used by the receiving system to synchronize timing and, optionally, to estimate the signal-to-noise ratio and perform other preparatory functions
- **Start of Frame Delimiter (SFD) (4 slots)**   Indicates the beginning of the frame
- **Data Rate (3 slots)**   Specifies the transmission rate used by the system
- **DC Level Adjustment (DCLA) (32 slots)**   Used by the receiver to stabilize the DC level after the transmission of the preceding fields
- **Length (2 bytes)**   Specifies the size of the data field
- **CRC (2 bytes)**   Contains a cyclic redundancy check value, used by the receiving system to test for transmission errors
- **Data (0 to 2,500 bytes)**   Contains the data link layer frame to be transmitted to the receiving system

The Orthogonal Frequency Division Multiplexing Frame

The OFDM frame has four regions:

- **Short Preamble**   This section consists of 10 short symbols that have been assigned to subcarriers (-24 through 24).

- **Long Preamble**   This includes two long symbols that have been assigned to all subcarriers.
- **Signal Field**   This contains one OFDM symbol that is assigned to all subcarriers. The signal field is not scrambled.
- **Data/Service Field**   This region is scrambled and the encoding and data rates vary, along with the modulation.

The Data Link Layer

Like with IEEE 802.3 (Ethernet) and 802.5 (Token Ring), the 802.11 document defines only half of the functionality found at the data link layer. Like the other IEEE 802 protocols, the LLC sublayer forms the upper half of the data link layer and is defined in the IEEE 802.2 standard. The 802.11 document defines the MAC sublayer functionality, which consists of a connectionless transport service that carries LLC data to a destination on the network in the form of MAC service data units (MSDUs). Like other data link layer protocols, this service is defined by a frame format (actually several frame formats, in this case) and a media access control mechanism. The MAC sublayer also provides security services, such as authentication and encryption, and reordering of MSDUs.

Data Link Layer Frames

The 802.11 standard defines three basic types of frames at the MAC layer, which are as follows:

- **Data frames**   Used to transmit upper layer data between stations
- **Control frames**   Used to regulate access to the network medium and to acknowledge transmitted data frames
- **Management frames**   Used to exchange network management information to perform network functions such as association and authentication

Figure 6-4 shows the general MAC frame format. The functions of the frame fields are as follows:

- **Frame Control (2 bytes)**   Contains 11 subfields that enable various protocol functions. The subfields are as follows:
  - **Protocol Version (2 bits)**   This specifies the version of the 802.11 standard being used.
  - **Type (2 bits)**   This specifies whether the packet contains a management frame (00), a control frame (01), or a data frame (10).
  - **Subtype (4 bits)**   This identifies the specific function of the frame.
  - **To DS (1 bit)**   A value of 1 in this field indicates that the frame is being transmitted to the distribution system (DS) via an access point (AP).
  - **From DS (1 bit)**   A value of 1 in this field indicates that the frame is being received from the DS.
  - **More Frag (1 bit)**   A value of 1 indicates that the packet contains a fragment of a frame and that there are more fragments still to be transmitted. When fragmenting frames at the MAC layer, an 802.11 system must receive an acknowledgment for each fragment before transmitting the next one.

- **Retry (1 bit)**   A value of 1 indicates that the packet contains a fragment of a frame that is being retransmitted after a failure to receive an acknowledgment. The receiving system uses this field to recognize duplicate packets.

- **Pwr Mgt (1 bit)**   A value of 0 indicates that the station is operating in active mode; a value of 1 indicates that the station is operating in power-save mode. APs buffer packets for stations operating in power-save mode until they change to active mode or explicitly request that the buffered packets be transmitted.

- **More Data (1 bit)**   A value of 1 indicates that an AP has more packets for the station that are buffered and awaiting transmission.

- **WEP (1 bit)**   A value of 1 indicates that the Frame Body field has been encrypted using the Wired Equivalent Privacy (WEP) algorithm, which is the security element of the 802.11 standard. WEP can be used only in management frames used to perform authentications.

- **Order (1 bit)**   A value of 1 indicates that the packet contains a data frame (or fragment) that is being transmitted using the Strictly Ordered service class, which is designed to support protocols that cannot process reordered frames.

- **Duration/ID (2 bytes)**   In control frames used for power-save polling, this field contains the association identity (AID) of the station transmitting the frame. In all other frame types, the field indicates the amount of time (in microseconds) needed to transmit a frame and its short interframe space (SIFS) interval.

- **Address 1 (6 bytes)**   This contains an address that identifies the recipient of the frame, using one of the five addresses defined in 802.11 MAC sublayer communications, depending on the values of the To DS and From DS fields.

- **Address 2 (6 bytes)**   This contains one of the five addresses used in 802.11 MAC sublayer communications, depending on the values of the To DS and From DS fields.

- **Address 3 (6 bytes)**   This contains one of the five addresses used in 802.11 MAC sublayer communications, depending on the values of the To DS and From DS fields.

- **Sequence Control (2 bytes)**   This contains two fields used to associate the fragments of a particular sequence and assemble them into the right order at the destination system:

  - **Fragment Number (4 bits)**   Contains a value that identifies a particular fragment in a sequence.

  - **Sequence Number (12 bits)**   Contains a value that uniquely identifies the sequence of fragments that make up a data set.

- **Address 4 (6 bytes)**   This contains one of the five addresses used in 802.11 MAC sublayer communications, depending on the values of the To DS and From DS fields. It is not present in control and management frames and some data frames.

- **Frame Body (0 to 2,312 bytes)**   This contains the actual information being transmitted to the receiving station.

- **Frame Check Sequence (4 bytes)**   This contains a cyclic redundancy check (CRC) value used by the receiving system to verify that the frame was transmitted without errors.

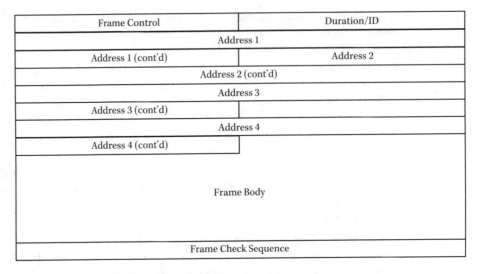

Figure 6-4   The IEEE 802.11 MAC sublayer frame format

The four address fields in the MAC frame identify different types of systems depending on the type of frame being transmitted and its destination in relation to the DS. The five different types of addresses are as follows:

- **Source address (SA)**   An IEEE MAC individual address that identifies the system that generated the information carried in the Frame Body field.

- **Destination address (DA)**   An IEEE MAC individual or group address that identifies the final recipient of an MSDU.

- **Transmitter address (TA)**   An IEEE MAC individual address that identifies the system that transmitted the information in the Frame Body field on the current wireless medium (typically an AP).

- **Receiver address (RA)**   An IEEE MAC individual or group address that identifies the immediate recipient of the information in the Frame Body field on the current wireless medium (typically an AP).

- **Basic service set ID (BSSID)**   An IEEE MAC address that identifies a particular BSS. On an infrastructure network, the BSSID is the MAC address of the station functioning as the AP of the BSS. On an ad hoc network (IBSS), the BSSID is a randomly generated value generated during the creation of the IBSS.

Media Access Control

As with all data link layer protocols that use a shared network medium, the media access control mechanism is one of the protocol's primary defining elements. IEEE 802.11 defines the use of a MAC mechanism called Carrier Sense Multiple Access with Collision Avoidance (CSMA/CA), which is a variation of the Carrier Sense Multiple Access with Collision Detection (CSMA/CD) mechanism used by Ethernet.

The basic functional characteristics of wireless networks have a profound effect on the MAC mechanisms they can use. For example, the Ethernet CSMA/CD mechanism and the token-passing method used by Token Ring and FDDI networks both require every device on the network to receive every transmitted packet. An Ethernet system that doesn't receive every packet can't detect collisions reliably. In addition, the Ethernet collision detection mechanism requires full-duplex communications (because the indication that a collision has occurred is simultaneous transmit and receive signals), which is impractical in a wireless environment. If a token-passing system fails to receive a packet, the problem is even more severe because the packet cannot then be passed on to the rest of the network, and network communication stops entirely. One of the characteristics of the wireless networks defined in 802.11, however, is that stations can repeatedly enter and leave the BSS because of their mobility and the vagaries of the wireless medium. Therefore, the MAC mechanism on a wireless network must be able to accommodate this behavior.

The CSMA part of the CSMA/CD mechanism is the same as that of an Ethernet network. A computer with data to transmit listens to the network medium and, if it is free, begins transmitting its data. If the network is busy, the computer backs off for a randomly selected interval and begins the listening process again. Also like Ethernet, the CSMA part of the process can result in collisions. The difference in CSMA/CA is that systems attempt to avoid collisions in the first place by reserving bandwidth in advance. This is done by specifying a value in the Duration/ID field or using specialized control messages called *request-to-send* (RTS) and *clear-to-send* (CTS).

The carrier sense part of the transmission process occurs on two levels, the physical and the virtual. The physical carrier sense mechanism is specific to the physical layer medium the network is using and is equivalent to the carrier sense performed by Ethernet systems. The virtual carrier sense mechanism, called a *network allocation vector* (NAV), involves the transmission of an RTS frame by the system with data to transmit and a response from the intended recipient in the form of a CTS frame. Both of these frames have a value in the Duration/ID field that specifies the amount of time needed for the sender to transmit the forthcoming data frame and receive an acknowledgment (ACK) frame in return. This message exchange essentially reserves the network medium for the life of this particular transaction, which is where the collision avoidance part of the mechanism comes in. Since both the RTS and CTS messages contain the Duration/ID value, any other system on the network receiving either one of the two observes the reservation and refrains from trying to transmit its own data during that time interval. This way, a station that is capable of receiving transmissions from one computer but not the other can still observe the CSMA/CA process.

In addition, the RTS/CTS exchange enables a station to more easily determine whether communication with the intended recipient is possible. If the sender of an RTS frame fails to receive a CTS frame from the recipient in return, it retransmits the RTS frame repeatedly until a preestablished timeout is reached. Retransmitting the brief RTS message is much quicker than retransmitting large data frames, which shortens the entire process.

To detect collisions, IEEE 802.11 uses a positive acknowledgment system at the MAC sublayer. Each data frame that a station transmits must be followed by an ACK frame from the recipient, which is generated after a CRC check of the incoming data. If the frame's CRC check fails, the recipient considers the packet to have been corrupted by a collision (or other phenomenon) and silently discards it. The station that transmitted the original data frame then retransmits it as many times as needed to receive an ACK, up to a predetermined limit. Note that the failure of the sender to receive an ACK frame could be because of the corruption or nondelivery of the original data frame or the nondelivery of an ACK frame that the recipient did send in return. The 802.11 protocol does not distinguish between the two.

NOTE For additional information about current 802.11 standards, see Chapters 12 and 24.

CHAPTER

7

Wide Area Networks

The physical and data link layer protocols used to build local area networks (LANs) are quite efficient over relatively short distances. Even for campus connections between buildings, fiber-optic solutions enable you to use a LAN protocol such as Ethernet throughout your whole internetwork. However, when you want to make a connection over a long distance, you move into an entirely different world of data communications called *wide area networking*. A *wide area network* (WAN) is a communications link that spans a long distance and connects two or more LANs.

WAN connections make it possible to connect networks in different cities or countries, enabling users to access resources at remote locations. Many companies use WAN links between office locations to exchange e-mail, groupware, and database information, or even just to access files and printers on remote servers. Banks and airlines, for example, use WAN s because they must be in continual communication with all of their branch offices to keep their databases updated, but WAN connections can also function on a much smaller scale, such as a system that periodically dials in to a remote network to send and retrieve the latest e-mail messages.

Today, with the increased use of cloud technology, WAN visualization and optimization are becoming more common. See Chapter 26 for more information about these two areas.

A WAN connection requires a router or a bridge at each end to provide the interface to the individual LANs, as shown in Figure 7-1. This reduces the amount of traffic that passes across the link. Remote link bridges connect LANs running the same data link layer protocol at different locations using an analog or digital WAN link. The bridges prevent unnecessary traffic from traversing the link by filtering packets according to their data link layer MAC addresses. However, bridges do pass broadcast traffic across the WAN link. Depending on the speed of the intended link and applications, this may be a huge waste of bandwidth. It's possible to make a good case that using remote link bridges to connect networks at two sites is technically not a WAN because you are actually joining the two sites into a single network, instead creating an internetwork. However, whether the final result is a network or an internetwork, the technologies used to join the two sites are the same and are commonly called *WAN links*.

If the WAN link is intended only for highly specific uses, such as e-mail access, data link layer bridges can be wasteful because they provide less control over the traffic that is permitted to pass

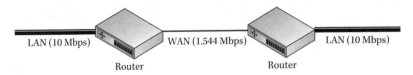

Figure 7-1   Routers or bridges connect WAN links to LANs.

over the link. Routers, on the other hand, keep the two LANs completely separate. In fact, the WAN link is a network in itself that connects only two systems, namely, the routers at each end of the connection. Routers pass no broadcasts over the WAN link (except in exceptional cases, such as when you use DHCP or BOOTP relay agents). Therefore, administrators can exercise greater control over the traffic passing between the LANs. Routers also enable you to use different data link layer protocols on each of the LANs because they operate at the network layer of the Open Systems Interconnection (OSI) model.

While bridges are always separate units, the routers used to connect two networks with a WAN link can take the form of either a computer or a dedicated hardware device. When a remote user connects to a host PC with a connection and accesses other systems on the network, the host PC is functioning as a router. Most sites use dedicated routers. The router or bridge located at each terminus of the WAN link is connected to the local LAN and to whatever hardware is used to make the physical layer connection to the WAN.

Introduction to Telecommunications

When you enter the world of wide area networking, you experience a major paradigm shift from the local area networking world. When you design, build, and maintain a LAN, you are working with equipment that you (or your organization) owns and controls completely. Once you pay for the equipment itself, the network and its bandwidth are yours to do with as you please. When you connect networks using WAN links, however, you almost never own all of the technology used to make the connections. Unless your organization has the means to run its own long-distance fiber-optic cables or launch its own satellite (and we're talking millions, if not billions, of dollars needed to do this in most cases), you have to deal with a third-party telecommunications service provider that makes it possible for you to send your data signals over long distances.

The need to rely on an outside service provider for WAN communications can enormously complicate the process of designing, installing, and maintaining the network. LAN technicians are often tinkerers by trade. When problems with the network occur, they have their own procedures for investigating, diagnosing, and resolving them, knowing that the cause is somewhere nearby if they can only find it. Problems with WAN connections can conceivably be caused by the equipment located at one of the connected sites, but it's more likely for the trouble to be somewhere in the service provider's network infrastructure. A heavy equipment operator a thousand miles away in Akron, Ohio, can sever a trunk cable while digging a trench, causing your WAN link to go down. Solar flares on the surface of the sun 93 million miles away can disturb satellite communications, causing your WAN link to go down. In either case, there is nothing you can do about it except call your service provider and complain. Because of this reliance on outside parties, many network administrators maintain backup WAN links that use a different technology or service provider for critical connections.

Telecommunications is a separate networking discipline unto itself that is at least as complicated as data networking, if not more so. (If you think that local area networking has a lot of cryptic acronyms, wait until you start studying telecommunications.) A large organization relies at least as much on telecommunications technology as on its data networking technology. If the computer network goes down, people complain loudly; if the phone system goes down, people quickly begin to panic. In many large organizations, the people who manage the telecommunications infrastructure are different from those who administer the data network. However, it is in the area of WAN communications that these two disciplines come together. It isn't common to find technical people who are equally adept at data networking and telecommunications; most technicians tend to specialize in one or the other. However, a LAN administrator has to know something about telecommunications if the organization has offices at multiple locations that are to be connected using WANs.

All data networking is about bandwidth, or the ability to transmit signals between systems at a given rate of speed. On a LAN, when you want to increase the bandwidth available to users, you can upgrade to a faster protocol or add network connection components such as bridges, switches, and routers. After the initial outlay for the new equipment and its installation, the network has more bandwidth, forever. In the world of telecommunications, bandwidth costs money, often lots of it. If you want to increase the speed of a WAN link between two networks, not only do you have to purchase new equipment, but you probably also have to pay additional fees to your service provider. Depending on the technology you've chosen and your service provider, you may have to pay a fee to have the equipment installed, a fee to set up the new service, and permanent monthly subscriber fees based on the amount of bandwidth you want. Combined, these fees can be substantial, and they're ongoing; you continue to pay as long as you use the service.

The result of this expense is that WAN bandwidth is far more expensive than LAN bandwidth. In nearly every case, your LANs will run at speeds far exceeding those of your WAN connections, as shown in Table 7-1.

WAN Utilization

WAN technologies vary in the way they're structured, the way you pay for them, and the way you use them. The costs of specific technologies depend on your location.

Selecting a WAN Technology

The selection of a WAN connection for a specific purpose is generally a trade-off between speed and expense. Because your WAN links will almost certainly run more slowly than the networks that they connect, and cost more as well, it's important to determine just how much bandwidth you need and when you need it as you design your network.

It usually is not practical to use a WAN link in the same way you would use a LAN connection. You might have to limit the amount of traffic that passes over the link in ways other than just using routers at each end. One way is to schedule certain tasks that require WAN communications to run at off-peak hours. For example, database replication tasks can easily monopolize a WAN link for extended periods of time, delaying normal user activities. Many applications that require periodic data replication, including directory services such as Active Directory, enable you to specify when these activities should take place. Active Directory, for example, enables you to split

Item	LAN (Found in Home or Office)	WAN (Crosses National and Metropolitan Boundaries)
Area	Covers a small geographic area (100 meters or less) Normally needs no leased telecommunication lines	Covers a broad geographic area (more than 100 meters) Uses leased telecommunication lines because of large geographic area
Bandwidth	High bandwidth	Low bandwidth
Components	Usually hubs, repeaters, bridges, switches	Routers, multilayer switches, ATM, frame relay switches
Connection types	Can be interconnected to other LANs by both telephone wire and wirelessly using radio waves	Often uses public networks, specifically telephone systems; can also use leased lines or satellites
Connectivity devices	Often Ethernet and Token Ring	Often frame relay, MPLS, ATM
Cost of adding devices	Usually quite inexpensive	Can be expensive in isolated areas; however, if using a public network, devices can be added using software for little cost
OSU Layer	Often layer 1 and layer 2 devices	Often layer 3 devices
Ownership	Usually owned by a single entity	Usually not owned by anyone, such as the Internet; usually has joint ownership and management over wide geographic areas
Speed	Usually high, such as 1000 Mbps	Often slower, such as 150 Mbps
Transmission issues	Usually experiences few errors transmitting data and usually has a high data transfer rate	Compared to LANs, more data-transmitting errors and usually lower data transfer rates than LANs

Table 7-1   LANs vs. WANs

your internetwork into units called *sites* and regulate the time and frequency of the replication that occurs between domain controllers at different sites.

Before you select a WAN technology, you should consider the applications for which it will be used. Different functions require different amounts of bandwidth and different types as well. E-mail, for example, not only requires relatively little bandwidth but also is intermittent in its traffic. High-end applications, such as full-motion video, not only require enormous amounts of bandwidth but also require that the bandwidth be continuously available to avoid dropouts in service. The needs of most organizations fall somewhere between these two extremes, but it is important to remember that the continuity of the bandwidth can sometimes be as important as the transmission rate.

NOTE   While the transmission rates shown in Table 7-2 indicate the maximum rated throughput, these rates are not usually reflected in reality because of a variety of reasons.

Table 7-2 lists some of the technologies used for WAN connections and their transmission speeds. The sections following the table examine some of the technologies that are most

Connection Type	Transmission Rate
X.25	64 Kbps
ISDN	Up to 128 Kbps
T-1	1.544 Mbps
T-3	44.736 Mbps
Frame relay	56 Kbps to 1.54 Mbps
DSL	Up to 51.84 Mbps
SONET	51.8 Mbps to 2.5 Gbps
ATM	25.6 Mbps to 622 Mbps

Table 7-2   WAN Technologies and Their Transmission Rates

commonly used for WAN connectivity. These technologies, for a variety of reasons, usually do not necessarily reflect the actual throughput realized by applications using them. In the real world, the throughput is generally lower.

PSTN (POTS) Connections

A WAN connection does not necessarily require a major investment in hardware and installation fees. Many network connections are formed using a *public switched telephone network* (PSTN) or *plain old telephone service* (POTS). A standard asynchronous modem that connects telephone lines to connect your computer to a network (such as that of an ISP) is technically a wide area link, and for some purposes, this is all that is needed. For example, an employee working at home or on the road can dial in to a server at the office and connect to the LAN to access e-mail and other network resources. In the same way, a small LAN connection may be sufficient for a small branch office to connect to the corporate headquarters for the same purposes.

The maximum possible connection speed is 56 Kbps (for digital-to-analog traffic only; analog-to-digital traffic is limited to 31.2 Kbps). Analog modem communications are also dependent on the quality of the lines involved. Many telephone companies still certify their lines for voice communications only, and do not perform repairs to improve the quality of data connections.

Using these public carrier lines usually costs much less than trying to establish a private line. When using public lines, many share the costs, and the lines are, by their nature, more reliable than trying to create a private infrastructure. The issues involved in any WAN are the same: delay time, quality of the link, and available bandwidth. The larger the geographic area, the more these issues come into play.

In most cases, a LAN to WAN connection uses a computer as a router, although many use stand-alone devices that perform the same function. The most basic arrangement uses a computer, tablet, or smart phone for remote network access. The remote computer can be running an e-mail client, a web browser, or another application designed to access network resources, or simply access the file system on the network's servers. This simple arrangement is best suited to users who want to connect to their office computers while at home or traveling.

A computer can also host multiple connections. When a user on one LAN performs an operation that requires access to the other LAN, the server automatically dials in to a server on the other network, establishes the connection, and begins routing traffic. When the link remains idle for a preset time, the connection terminates. There are also stand-alone routers that perform in the same way, enabling users to connect to a remote LAN or the Internet as needed. This arrangement provides WAN access to users without them having to establish the connection manually.

Today, the world's largest WAN, the Internet, actually uses PSTN lines for much of its infrastructure, so this technology will not soon be obsolete. Obviously, the chief drawback to using the PSTN for other WAN connections is the limited bandwidth, but the low cost of the hardware and services required make these connections compelling, and many network administrators make use of them in interesting and creative ways. In earlier dial-up connections, some networks used inverse multiplexing to combine two small bandwidth channels into a larger channel. Inverse multiplexing is the process of combining bandwidth of multiple connections into a single conduit. See the sections "Frame Relay" and "ATM" for more information about how inverse multiplexing is used today.

Leased Lines

A leased line is a dedicated, permanent connection between two sites that runs through the telephone network. The line is said to be *dedicated* because the connection is active 24 hours a day and does not compete for bandwidth with any other processes. The line is *permanent* because there are no telephone numbers or dialing involved in the connection, nor is it possible to connect to a different location without modifying the hardware installation. While this book is naturally more interested in leased lines as WAN technologies, it's important to understand that they are also a vital element of the voice telecommunications network infrastructure. When a large organization installs its own private branch exchange (PBX) to handle its telephone traffic, the switchboard is typically connected to one or more T-1 lines, which are split into individual channels with enough bandwidth to handle a single voice-grade connection (56 to 64 Kbps). Each of these channels becomes a standard voice "telephone line," which is allocated by the PBX to users' telephones as needed.

You install a leased line by contacting a telephone service provider, either local or long distance, and agreeing to a contract that specifies a line granting a certain amount of bandwidth between two locations, for a specified cost. The price typically involves an installation fee, hardware costs, and a monthly subscription fee, and it depends on both the bandwidth of the line and the distance between the two sites being connected. The advantages of a leased line are that the connection delivers the specified bandwidth at all times and that the line is as inherently secure as any telephone line because it is private. While the service functions as a dedicated line between the two connected sites, there is not really a dedicated physical connection, such as a separate wire running the entire distance. The service provider installs a dedicated line between each of the two sites and the provider's nearest *point of presence* (POP), but from there, the connection uses the provider's standard switching facilities to make the connection. The provider guarantees that its facilities can provide a specific bandwidth and quality of service.

From the LAN side, the line usually connects to a router and on the WAN side, a hub. This type of connection can become very expensive over time. The performance of the service is based on the percentage of error-free seconds per day, and its availability is computed in terms of the time that the service is functioning at full capacity during a specific period, also expressed as a percentage. If the provider fails to meet the guarantees specified in the contract, the customer receives a financial remuneration in the form of service credits. A leased-line contract typically quantifies the quality of service using two criteria: service performance and availability.

Leased-Line Types

Leased lines can be analog or digital, but digital lines are more common. An analog line is simply a normal telephone line that is continuously open. When used for a WAN connection, modems are required at both ends to convert the digital signals of the data network to analog form for transmission and back to digital at the other end. In some cases, the line may have a greater service quality than a standard PSTN line.

Digital leased lines are more common because no analog-to-digital conversion is required for data network connections, and the signal quality of a digital line is usually superior to that of an analog line, whether leased or dial-up. Digital leased lines are based on a hierarchy of digital signal (D5) speeds used to classify the speeds of carrier links. These levels take different forms in different parts of the world. In North America, the D5 levels are used to create the T-carrier (for "trunk-carrier") service. Europe and most of the rest of the world uses the E-carrier service, which is standardized by the Telecommunications sector of the International Telecommunications Union (ITU-T), except for Japan, which has its own J-carrier service. Each of these services names the various levels by replacing the DS prefix with that of the particular carrier. For example, the DS-l level is known as a T-1 in North America, an E-1 in Europe, and a J-1 in Japan.

The only exception to this is the DS-0 level, which represents a standard 64 Kbps voice-grade channel and is known by this name throughout the world. As you go beyond the DS-l service, bandwidth levels rise steeply, as do the costs. In North America, many networks use multiple T-1 lines for both voice and data. T-3s are used mainly by ISPs and other service providers with high-bandwidth needs. See Table 7-3 for an explanation of the various "T" lines in North America.

While it's possible to install a leased line using any of the service levels listed for your geographical location, you are not limited to the amounts of bandwidth provided by these services. Because the bandwidth of each service is based on multiples of 64 Kbps, you can split a digital link into individual 64 Kbps channels and use each one for voice or data traffic. Service providers frequently take advantage of this capability to offer leased lines that consist of any

DS Level	Line Type	Requirements	Equivalency	Speed	Usage
DS-1	T-1	Normal copper telephone lines	24 phone lines	187,500 bytes per second	Small businesses
DS-3	T-3	Fiber-optic lines	28 T-1 lines	5,592 million bytes per second	Medium and large businesses
DS-4	T-4	Fiber-optic lines	6 T-3 lines	34,272 million bytes per second	Major companies that provide data and voice transmission services

Table 7-3   "T" Line Types in North America

number of these 64 Kbps channels that the subscriber needs, combined into a single data pipe. This is called *fractional* T-1 service.

Leased-Line Hardware

A T-l line requires two twisted pairs of wires, and originally the line was *conditioned,* meaning that a repeater was installed 3,000 feet from each endpoint and every 6,000 feet in between. Later, a signaling scheme called *high-bit-rate digital subscriber line* (HDSL) made it possible to transmit digital signals at T-l speeds over longer distances without the need for repeating hardware.

The hardware that was required at each end of a digital leased line was called a *channel service unit/data service unit* (CSU/DSU), which was actually two devices that are usually combined into a single unit. The CSU provided the terminus for the digital link and kept the connection active even when the connected bridge, router, private branch exchange (PBX), or other device wasn't actually using it. The CSU also provided testing and diagnostic functions for the line. The DSU was the device that converts the signals it received from the bridge, router, or PBX to the bipolar digital signals carried by the line.

In appearance, a CSU/DSU looked something like a modem, and as a result, they were sometimes incorrectly called digital modems. (Since a modem, by definition, is a device that converts between analog and digital signals, the term *digital modem* was actually something of an oxymoron. However, just about any device used to connect a computer or network to a telephone or Internet service has been incorrectly called a modem, including ISDN and cable network equipment.)

The CSU/DSU was connected to the leased line on one side using an RJ connector and to a device (or devices) on the other side that provided the interface to the local network (see Figure 7-2), using a V.35 or RS-232 connector. This interface can be a bridge or a router for data networking or a PBX for voice services. The line can be either *unchanneled,* meaning that it is used as a single data pipe, or *channeled,* meaning that a multiplexor is located in between the CSU/DSU and the interface to break up the line into separate channels for multiple uses.

Digital leased lines use time division multiplexing (TDM) to create the individual channels in which the entire data stream is divided into time segments that are allocated to each channel in turn. Each time division is dedicated to a particular channel, whether it is used or not. Thus, when one of the 64 Kbps voice lines that are part of a T-1 was idle, that bandwidth was wasted, no matter how busy the other channels were.

Leased-Line Applications

T-1s and other leased lines are used for many different purposes. T-1s are commonly used to provide telephone services to large organizations. On the WAN front, organizations with offices in several

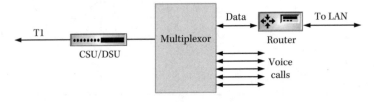

Figure 7-2   The CSU/DSU provides the interface between a LAN and a leased line.

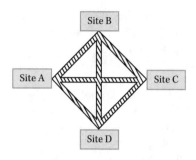

Figure 7-3   A private WAN that uses leased lines requires a separate connection between every two sites.

locations can use leased lines to build a *private network* for both voice and data traffic. With such a network in place, users can access network resources in any of the sites at will, and telephone calls can be transferred to users in the different offices. The problem with building a network in this manner is that it requires a true mesh topology of leased lines—that is, a separate leased line connecting each office to every other office—to be reliable. An organization with four sites, for example, would need six leased lines, as shown in Figure 7-3, and eight sites would require twenty-eight leased lines! It would be possible for the sites to be connected in series, using seven links to connect eight sites, but then the failure of any one link or router would split the network in two.

Today, most organizations use a less expensive technology to create WAN links between their various offices. One alternative to a private network would be to use leased lines at each site to connect to a public carrier network using a technology such as frame relay or ATM to provide the required bandwidth. Each site would require only a single, relatively short-distance leased line to a local service provider, instead of a separate line to each site. For more information on this alternative, see "Packet-Switching Services" later in this chapter. The most common application for T-1 lines in WANs today, however, is to use them to connect a private network to an ISP in order to provide Internet access to its users and to host Internet services, such as web and e-mail servers.

T-1s are well-suited for providing Internet access to corporate networks because services such as e-mail have to be connected around the clock. ISPs also usually have a local point of presence, so the leased line does not have to span a tremendously long distance and is not too terribly expensive. A single T-1 connection to the Internet can serve the needs of hundreds of average users simultaneously.

ISDN

Integrated service digital network (ISDN) and *digital subscriber line* (DSL) are both services that utilize the existing copper POTS cable at an installation to carry data at much higher transmission rates. In both cases, the site must be relatively close to the telephone company's nearest point of presence (POP), a location containing telephone switching equipment. Basic rate ISDN, for example, requires a location no farther than 18,000 feet (3.4 miles) from the POP; DSL distances vary with the data rate. ISDN and DSL are sometimes called *last-mile technologies* because they are designed to get data from the user site to the POP at high speed.

The copper cable running from the POP to the individual user site is traditionally the weakest link in the phone system. Once a signal reaches the POP, it moves through the telephone company's switches at high speed. By eliminating the bottlenecks at both ends of the link, traffic can maintain that speed from end to end. While these technologies have been marketed in the United States primarily as Internet connectivity solutions for home users, they both are usable for office-to-office WAN connections.

ISDN was a digital point-to-point telephone system that had been around for many years but that was not adopted as widely in the United States as its proponents had hoped. Originally, ISDN was designed to completely replace the current phone system with all-digital service, but it then became positioned as an alternative technology for home users who required high-bandwidth network connections and for links between business networks. In this country, ISDN technology garnered a reputation for being overly complicated, difficult to install, and not particularly reliable, and to some extent, this reputation was justified. At one time, inquiries to most local phone companies about ISDN service would be met only with puzzlement, and horror stories from consumers about installation difficulties were common.

ISDN was a digital service that provided a good deal more bandwidth than standard telephone service, but unlike a leased line, it was not permanent. ISDN devices dialed a number to establish a connection, like a standard telephone, meaning that users connected to different sites as needed. For this reason, ISDN was known as a circuit-switching service because it created a temporary point-to-point circuit between two sites. For the home or business user connecting to the Internet, this meant they could change ISPs without any modifications to the ISDN service by the telephone company. For organizations using ISDN for WAN connections between offices, this meant they could connect to different office networks when they needed access to their resources.

ISDN Services

There are two main types of ISDN service, which are based on units of bandwidth called *B channels*, running at 64 Kbps, and *D channels*, running at 16 or 64 Kbps. B channels carry voice and data traffic, and D channels carry control traffic only. The service types are as follows:

- **Basic Rate Interface (BRI)**   Also called 2B+D, because it consists of two 64 Kbps B channels and one 16 Kbps D channel. BRI was targeted primarily at home users for connections to business networks or the Internet.

- **Primary Rate Interface (PRI)**   Consists of up to 23 B channels and one 64 Kbps D channel, for a total bandwidth equivalent to a T-1 leased line. PR1 was aimed more at the business community, as an alternative to leased lines that provided the same bandwidth and signal quality with greater flexibility.

One of the primary advantages of ISDN was the ability to combine the bandwidth of multiple channels as needed, using inverse multiplexing. Each B channel has its own separate ten-digit number. For the home user, one of the B channels of the BRI service carried voice traffic while the other B channel was used for data, or both B channels could be combined to form a single 128 Kbps connection to the Internet or to a private network.

The PR1 service combines any number of the B channels in any combination to form connections of various bandwidths. In addition, the ISDN service supports bandwidth-on-demand, which can supplement a connection with additional B channels to support a temporary increase in bandwidth requirements. Depending on the equipment used, it's possible to add bandwidth according to a predetermined schedule of usage needs or to dynamically augment a connection when the traffic rises above a particular level. For bandwidth needs that fluctuated, an ISDN connection was often far more economical than a leased line because you pay only for the channels that are currently in use. With a leased line, you must pay whether it's being used or not.

ISDN Communications

The ISDN B channels carry user traffic only, whether in the form of voice or data. The D channel is responsible for carrying all of the control traffic needed to establish and terminate connections between sites. The traffic on these channels consists of protocols that span the bottom three layers of the DST reference model. The physical layer establishes a circuit-switched connection between the user equipment and the telephone company's switching office that operates at 64 Kbps and also provides diagnostic functions such as loopback testing and signal monitoring. This layer is also responsible for the multiplexing that enables devices to share the same channel.

At the data link layer, bridges and PBXs using an ISDN connection employ the *Link Access Procedure for D Channel* (LAPD) protocol, as defined by the International Telecommunications Union (ITU-T) documents Q.920 through Q.923, to provide frame-relay and frame-switching services. This protocol (which is similar to the LAP-B protocol used by X.25) uses the address information provided by the ISDN equipment to create virtual paths through the switching fabric of the telephone company's network to the intended destination. The end result is a private network connection much like that of a leased line.

The network layer is responsible for the establishment, maintenance, and termination of connections between ISDN devices. Unlike leased lines and similar technologies, which maintain a permanently open connection, ISDN must use a handshake procedure to establish a connection between two points. The process of establishing an ISDN connection involves messages exchanged between three entities: the caller, the switch (at the POP), and the receiver. As usual, network layer messages are encapsulated within data link layer protocol frames. The connection procedure is as follows:

1. The caller transmits a SETUP message to the switch.

2. If the SETUP message is acceptable, the switch returns a CALL PROC (call proceeding) message to the caller and forwards the SETUP message to the receiver.

3. If the receiver accepts the SETUP message, it rings the phone (either literally or figuratively) and sends an ALERTING message back to the switch, which forwards it to the caller.

4. When the receiver answers the call (again, either literally or figuratively), it sends a CONNECT message to the switch, which forwards it to the caller.

5. The caller then sends a CONNECT ACK (connection acknowledgment) message to the switch, which forwards it to the receiver. The connection is now established.

ISDN Hardware

ISDN does not require any modifications to the standard copper POTS wiring. As long as your site is within 18,000 feet of a POP, you can convert an existing telephone line to ISDN just by adding the appropriate hardware at each end. The telephone company uses special data-encoding schemes (called 2BIQ in North America and 4B3T in Europe) to provide higher data transmission rates over the standard cable. All ISDN installations needed a device called a *Network Termination 1* (NT1) connected to the telephone line at each end. The service from the telephone company provides what is known as a U interface operating over one twisted pair of wires. The NT1 connects to the U interface and converts the signals to the four-wire S/T interface used by ISDN terminal equipment (that is, the devices that use the connection).

Devices that connect directly to the S/T interface, such as ISDN telephones and ISDN fax machines, were referred to as *terminal equipment 1* (TE1). Devices that were not ISDN capable, such as standard analog phones and fax machines, as well as computers, were called *terminal equipment 2* (TE2). To connect a TE2 device to the S/T interface, you needed an intervening *terminal adapter* (TA). You could connect up to seven devices to an NT1, both TE1 and TE2.

In North America, it was up to the consumer to provide the NT1, which was available in several forms as a commercial product. In Europe and Japan, where ISDN was much more prevalent, the NT1 was owned and provided by the telephone company; users only needed to provide the terminal equipment. For the BRI service, a separate NT1 is required if you are going to use more than one type of terminal equipment, such as a terminal adapter for a computer and an ISDN telephone. If the service was going to be used only for data networking, as was often the case in the United States, there were single devices available that combined the NT1 with a terminal adapter. These combination devices often took the form of an expansion card for a PC, or a separate device. Once again, the units that are often called *ISDN modems* were technically not modems at all because they did not convert signals between analog and digital formats.

DSL

A *digital subscriber line* (DSL) is a collective term for a group of related technologies that provide a WAN service that is somewhat similar to ISDN but at much higher speeds. Like ISDN, DSL uses standard POTS wiring to transmit data from a user site to a telephone company POP using a private point-to-point connection. From there, signals travel through the telephone company's standard switching equipment to another DSL connection at the destination. Also like ISDN, the distance between the site and the POP is limited; the faster the transmission rate, the shorter the operable distance.

The transmission rates for DSL services vary greatly, and many of the services function *asymmetrically,* meaning they have different upload and download speeds. This speed variance occurs because the bundle of wires at the POP is more susceptible to a type of interference called *near-end crosstalk* when data is arriving from the user site than when it is being transmitted out to the user site. The increased signal loss rate resulting from the crosstalk requires that the transmission rate be lower when traveling in that direction.

Standard telephone communications use only a small amount of the bandwidth provided by the POTS cable. DSL works by utilizing frequencies above the standard telephone bandwidth (300 to 3,200 Hz) and by using advanced signal encoding methods to transmit data at higher rates of speed. Some of the DSL services use only frequencies that are out of the range of standard voice communications, which makes it possible for the line to be used for normal voice traffic while it is carrying digital data.

DSL is still the most common Internet access solution. However, the higher-speed services like high-bit-rate digital subscriber line (HDSL) have been deployed heavily by local telephone carriers. Asymmetrical operation is not much of a problem for services such as asymmetrical digital subscriber line (ADSL), which were used for Internet access, because the average Internet users download far more data than they upload. For WAN connections, however, symmetrical services like HDSL are standard for some time. DSL differs from ISDN in that it uses permanent connections; it has dial-up service, no numbers assigned to the connections, and no session-establishment procedures. The connection is continuously active and private, much like that of a leased line.

As an Internet access solution, DSL grew quickly because of its relatively low prices and high transmission rates and has all but eclipsed ISDN in this market. DSL and cable connections are now the two biggest competing technologies in the end-user, high-speed Internet connection market.

Acronym	Type	Maximum Download Speed	Maximum Upload Speed	Lines Required	Maximum Link Length
ADSL	Asymmetrical digital subscriber line	8.448 Mbps	800 Kbps	1	5,500 meters (18,000 feet)
HDSL	High bit-rate digital subscriber line	1.544 Mbps	1.54 Mbps	2	3,650 meters (12,000 feet)
RADSL	Rate adaptive digital subscriber line	8.448 Mbps	1.5444 Mbps	1	5,500 meters (18,000 feet)
SDSL	Symmetrical digital subscriber line	2.3333 Mbps	2.3333 Mbps	1	6,700 meters (22,000 feet)
VDSL	Very high bit-rate digital subscriber line	52 Mbps	16 Mbps	1	1,200 meters (4,000 feet)

Table 7-4   DSL Types and Properties

The various DSL services have abbreviations with different first letters, which is why the technology is sometimes called XDSL, with the X acting as a placeholder. Table 7-4 shows these services and their properties.

The hardware required for a DSL connection is a standard POTS line and a DSL "modem" at both ends of the link. For services that provide simultaneous voice and data traffic, a POTS splitter is needed to separate the lower frequencies used by voice traffic from the higher frequencies used by the DSL service. In addition, the telephone line cannot use *loading coils,* inductors that extend the range of the POTS line at the expense of the higher frequencies that DSL uses to transmit data. As shown in Table 7-4, most DSL connections are asymmetrical, although there are some symmetrical variations that deliver the same speed both uploading and downloading.

As telephone companies have upgraded their T1 and T3 lines to fiber-optic lines, so have DSL speeds increased. However, data rate still depends on the distance to the central telephone office. And, in many cases, line noise is a factor that reduces line speed.

NOTE   As cable television has grown, so have its services. Many cable companies now offer high-speed Internet access in addition to television and Voice over Internet Protocol (VoIP) services. See Chapter 23 for more information about VoIP and cable connections.

Switching Services

Each WAN involves moving information through up to thousands of individual networks. This happens by way of several switching (routing) technologies. *Switching* entails moving data, including e-mails, large documents, and all of the myriad types of information being transmitted throughout the world. Each item is sent in intermediate steps, rather than information following a direct line from the origination point to the destination.

Packet-Switching Services

Each message is broken down into small packets to be sent through the network. A *packet-switching service* transmits data between two points by routing packets through the switching network owned by a carrier such as AT&T, Sprint, or another telephone company. The end result is a high-bandwidth connection similar in performance to a leased line, but the advantage of this type of service is that a single WAN connection at a network site can provide access to multiple remote sites simply by using different routes through the network. Today, packet-switching networks transmit everything from a voice telephone call to digital television reception.

The packet-switching service consists of a network of high-speed connections that is sometimes referred to as the *cloud*. Once data arrives at the cloud, the service can route it to a specific destination at high speeds. It is up to the consumers to get their data to the nearest POP connected to the cloud, after which all switching is performed by the carrier. Therefore, an organization setting up WAN connections between remote sites installs a link to an *edge switch* at a local POP using whatever technology provides suitable performance. This local link can take the form of a leased line, ISDN, or DSL.

Once the data arrives at the edge switch, it is transmitted through the cloud to an edge switch at another POP, where it is routed to a private link connecting the cloud to the destination site (see Figure 7-4).

For example, an organization with eight offices scattered around the country would need 28 leased lines to interconnect all of the sites, some of which may have to span long distances. In this arrangement, the organization does all of its own switching. Using a packet-switching service instead requires one leased line connecting each site to the service's local POP. Eight leased lines are far cheaper than 28, especially when they span relatively short distances. To get the data where it's going, the carrier programs *virtual circuits* (VCs) from the POP used by each site to each of the seven other POPs. Thus, there are still 28 routes connecting each location to every other location, but the service maintains them, and the client pays only for the bandwidth used.

Unlike a leased line, however, a packet-switching service shares its network among many users. The link between two sites is not permanently assigned a specific bandwidth. In some instances, this can be a drawback, because your links are competing with those of other clients for the same bandwidth. However, you can now contract for a specific bandwidth over a frame-relay network, and ATM is built around a quality of service (QoS) feature that allocates bandwidth for certain types of traffic. In addition, these technologies enable you to alter the bandwidth allotted to your links. Unlike a leased line with a specific bandwidth that you can't exceed and that you pay for whether you're using it or not, you contract with a packet-switching service to provide a certain amount of bandwidth, which you can exceed during periods of heavy traffic (possibly with an additional charge) and which you can increase as your network grows.

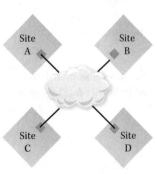

Figure 7-4 Packet-switching networks use a network cloud to route data between remote sites.

As the packet-switching network becomes more crowded, the entire network slows down. Think about a highway system. The more cars using the highway, the more traffic slows. Since this medium of transportation is shared, there is no guarantee for the time of arrival at the packet's destination. Each packet may use a different circuit, and the message is not connected until it arrives at its destination.

Circuit-Switching Services

This service is a temporary connection, such as ISDN or a dial-up connection. Because the connection is dedicated, information can be transmitted rapidly. However, unless the bandwidth is being used, that bandwidth is wasted. Today, narrowband ISDN and switched T1 connections still use circuit-switched technologies.

Frame Relay

Frame-relay networks provide the high-speed transmission of leased lines with greater flexibility and lower costs. Frame-relay service operates at the data link layer of the OSI reference model and runs at bandwidths from 56 Kbps to 44.736 Mbps (T-3 speed). You negotiate a *committed information rate* (CIR) with a carrier that guarantees you a specific amount of bandwidth, even though you are sharing the network medium with other users. It is possible to exceed the CIR, however, during periods of heavy use, called *bursts*. A burst can be a momentary increase in traffic or a temporary increase of longer duration. Usually, bursts up to a certain bandwidth or duration carry no extra charge, but eventually, additional charges will accrue.

The contract with the service provider also includes a *committed burst information rate* (CBIR), which specifies the maximum bandwidth that is guaranteed to be available during bursts. If you exceed the CBIR, there is a chance that data will be lost. The additional bandwidth provided during a burst may be "borrowed" from your other virtual circuits that aren't operating at full capacity or even from other clients' circuits. One of the primary advantages of frame relay is that the carrier can dynamically allocate bandwidth to its client connections as needed. In many cases, it is the leased line to the carrier's nearest POP that is the factor limiting bandwidth.

Frame-Relay Hardware

Each site connected to a frame-relay cloud must have a *frame-relay access device* (FRAD), which functions as the interface between the local network and the leased line (or other connection) to the cloud (see Figure 7-5). The FRAD is something like a router, in that it operates at the network layer. The FRAD accepts packets from the LAN that are destined for other networks, strips off the data link layer protocol header, and packages the datagrams in frames for transmission through the cloud. In the same way, the FRAD processes frames arriving through the cloud and packages them for transmission over the LAN. The difference between a FRAD and a standard router, however, is that the FRAD takes no part in the routing of packets through the cloud; it simply forwards all the packets from the LAN to the edge switch at the carrier's POP.

The only other hardware element involved in a frame-relay installation is the connection to the nearest POP. In frame relay, the leased line is the most commonly used type of connection. When selecting a carrier, it is important to consider the locations of their POPs in relation to the sites you want to connect because the cost of the leased lines (which is not usually included in the frame-relay contract) depends on their length. The large long-distance carriers usually have the most POPS, scattered over the widest areas, but it is also possible to use different carriers for your sites and create frame-relay links between them.

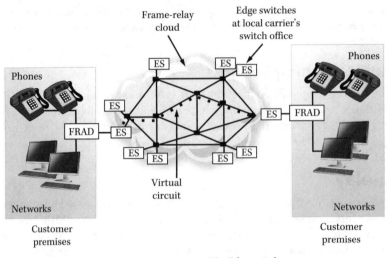

Figure 7-5 and its labels: Frame-relay cloud, Edge switches at local carrier's switch office, Phones, Phones, ES, ES, ES, ES, ES, ES, ES, ES, ES, ES, FRAD, FRAD, Virtual circuit, Networks, Networks, Customer premises, Customer premises

ES = Edge switch
FRAD = Frame-relay access device

Figure 7-5 Frame-relay connections use a FRAD to connect a LAN to the cloud.

When installing leased lines, it is important to take into account the number of virtual circuits that will run from the FRAD to your various sites. Unlike the private network composed of separate leased lines to every site, the single leased-line connection between the FRAD and the carrier's edge server will carry all of the WAN data to and from the local network. Multiple VCs will be running from the edge server through the cloud to the other sites, and the leased line from the FRAD will essentially multiplex the traffic from all of those VCs to the LAN, as shown in Figure 7-6. Thus, if you are connecting eight remote sites together with frame-relay WAN links, the leased line at each location should be capable of handling the combined bandwidth of all seven VCs to the other locations.

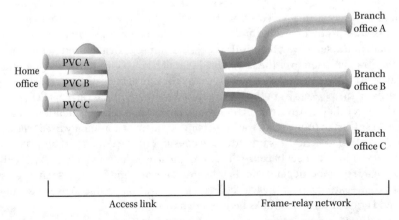

Figure 7-6 labels: Branch office A, Branch office B, Branch office C, Home office, PVC A, PVC B, PVC C, Access link, Frame-relay network

Figure 7-6 The connection from the FRAD to the cloud carries data for all of the virtual circuits.

In most cases, the actual traffic moving across a WAN link does not utilize all of the bandwidth allotted to it at all times. Therefore, it may be possible to create a serviceable WAN by contracting for VCs that have T-l speeds between all eight offices and using T-l leased lines to connect all of the sites to the cloud. Be aware, however, that the leased lines are the only elements of the WAN that are not flexible in their bandwidth. If you find that your WAN traffic exceeds the capacity of the leased line, the only recourse is to augment its bandwidth by installing another connection. This does not necessarily mean installing another T-1, however. You can augment the bandwidth connecting the FRAD to the edge server by adding a fractional T-1 or even a dial-up connection that activates during periods of high traffic.

Virtual Circuits

The virtual circuits that are the basis for frame-relay communications come in two types: *permanent virtual circuits* (PVCs) and *switched virtual circuits* (SVCs). PVCs are routes through the carrier's cloud that are used for the WAN connections between client sites. Unlike standard internetwork routing, PVCs are not dynamic. The frame-relay carrier creates a route through its cloud for a connection between sites, assigns it a unique 10-bit number called a *data link connection identifier* (DLCI), and programs it into its switches. Programming a FRAD consists of providing it with the DLCIs for all of the PVCS leading to other FRADS. DLCIs are locally significant only; each FRAD has its own DLCI for a particular virtual circuit. Frames passing between two sites always take the same route through the cloud and use the DLCI as a data link layer address. This is one of the reasons why frame relay is so fast; there is no need to dynamically route the packets through the cloud or establish a new connection before transmitting data.

Each PVC can have its own CIR and CBIR, and despite the description of the VC as permanent, the carrier can modify the route within a matter of hours if one of the sites moves. It is also possible to have the carrier create a PVC for temporary use, such as for a meeting in which a special videoconferencing session is required. Although it was originally created for data transfers, you can also use frame relay to carry other types of traffic, such as voice or video. To set up a voice call or a videoconference between two sites, there has to be a virtual circuit between them. This is easy if the communications are between two of an organization's own sites, which are already connected by a PVC; but conferencing with a client or other outside user requires a call to the carrier to set up a new PVC.

Frame-Relay Messaging

Frame relay uses two protocols at the data link layer: LAPD for control traffic and *Link Access Procedure for Frame-mode Bearer Services* (LAPF) for the transfer of user data. The LAPD protocol, the same one used by ISDN (ITL-T Q921), is used to establish VCs and prepare for the transmission of data. LAPF is used to carry data and for other processes, such as multiplexing and demultiplexing, error detection, and flow control.

Figure 7-7 shows the format of the frame used to carry data across a frame-relay cloud. The functions of the fields are as follows:

- **Flag, 1 byte**   Contains the binary value 01111110 (or 7E in hexadecimal form) that serves as a delimiter for the frame.

- **Link Info, 2 bytes**   Contains the frame's address and control fields, as follows:

    - **Upper DLCI, 6 bits**   Contains the first 6 bits of the 10-bit DLCI identifying the virtual circuit that the frame will use to reach its destination.

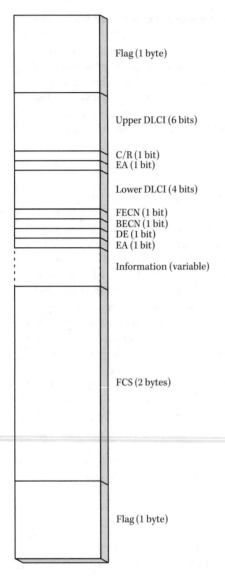

Flag (1 byte)

Upper DLCI (6 bits)

C/R (1 bit)
EA (1 bit)

Lower DLCI (4 bits)

FECN (1 bit)
BECN (1 bit)
DE (1 bit)
EA (1 bit)

Information (variable)

FCS (2 bytes)

Flag (1 byte)

Figure 7-7   The frame-relay frame format

- **Command/Response (C/R), 1 bit**   Undefined.

- **Extended Address (EA), 1 bit**   Indicates whether the current byte contains the last bit of the DLCI. The eighth bit of every byte in the Link Info field is an EA bit. When the frames use standard 10-bit DLCIs, the value of this bit will always be 0.

- **Lower DLCI, 4 bits**   Contains the last 4 bits of the 10-bit DLCI identifying the virtual circuit that the frame will use to reach its destination.

- **Forward Explicit Congestion Notification (FECN), 1 bit**   Indicates that network congestion was encountered in the direction from source to destination.

- **Backward Explicit Congestion Notification (BECN), 1 bit**   Indicates that network congestion was encountered in the direction from destination to source.

- **Discard Eligibility (DE), 1 bit**   Indicates that a frame is of lesser importance than the other frames being transmitted and that it can be discarded in the event of network congestion.

- **Extended Address (EA), 1 bit**   Indicates whether the current byte contains the last bit of the DLCI. When the frames use standard 10-bit DLCIs, the value of this bit will always be l. The EA field is intended to support the future expansion of frame-relay clouds in which DLCIs longer than 10 bits are needed.

- **Information, variable**   Contains a protocol data unit (PDU) generated by a network layer protocol, such as an IP datagram. The frame-relay protocols do not modify the contents of this field in any way.

- **Frame Check Sequence (FCS), 2 bytes**   Contains a value computed by the source FRAD that is checked at each switch during the frame's journey through the cloud. Frames in which this value does not match the newly computed value are silently discarded. Detection of the missing frame and retransmission are left to the upper-layer protocols at the end systems.

- **Flag, 1 byte**   Contains the binary value 01111110 (or 7E in hexadecimal form) that serves as a delimiter for the frame.

ATM

Asynchronous Transfer Mode (ATM) has long been the holy grail of the networking industry. Once known as the ultimate networking technology, ATM is designed to carry voice, data, and video over various network media, using a high-speed, cell-switched, connection-oriented, full-duplex, point-to-point protocol.

Instead of using variable-length frames like Ethernet, frame relay, and other protocols, all ATM traffic is broken down into 53-byte cells. This makes it easier to regulate and meter the bandwidth passing over a connection because by using data structures of a predetermined size, network traffic becomes more readily quantifiable, predictable, and manageable. With ATM, it's possible to guarantee that a certain quantity of data will be delivered within a given time. This makes the technology more suitable for a unified voice/data/video network than a nondeterministic protocol like Ethernet, no matter how fast it runs. In addition, ATM has quality of service (Q0S) features built into the protocol that enable administrators to reserve a certain amount of bandwidth for a specific application.

ATM is both a LAN and WAN protocol and is a radical departure from the other lower-layer protocols examined in this book. All ATM communication is point-to-point. There are no broadcasts, which means that switching, and not routing, is an integral part of this technology. ATM can also be deployed on public networks, as well as private ones. Public carriers can provide ATM services that enable clients to connect LANs at remote locations. On private networks, ATM implementations at various speeds can run throughout the network, from the backbone to the desktop. Thus, the same cells generated by a workstation can travel to a switch that connects the LAN to an ATM carrier service, through the carrier's ATM cloud, and then to a workstation on the destination network. At no point do the cells have to reach higher than the data link layer of an intermediate system, and transmission speeds through the cloud can reach as high as 2.46 Gbps.

While not yet totally realized, a large part of this potential has come to pass. ATM is being used as a high-speed backbone protocol and for WAN connections, but the 25.6 Mbps ATM LAN solution intended for desktop use has been eclipsed by Fast Ethernet, which runs at 100 Mbps and is far more familiar to the majority of network administrators. Many enterprise backbones run over ATM, largely because administrators find that its Q05 capabilities and support for voice, data, and video make it a better performer than traditional LAN protocols.

You can use an ATM packet-switching service for your WAN links in roughly the same way as you would use frame relay, by installing a router at your sites and connecting them to the carrier's POPs using leased lines. This process transmits the LAN data to the POP first and then repackages it into cells. It's also possible, however, to install an ATM switch at each remote site, either as part of an ATM backbone or as a separate device providing an interface to the carrier's network. This way, the LAN data is converted to ATM cells at each site before it is transmitted over the WAN. Like frame relay, ATM supports both PVCs and SVCs, but ATM was designed from the beginning to support voice and video using SVCs, while in frame relay, PVCs and SVCs were a later addition. ATM has an advantage over frame relay because of its greater speed and manageability.

Many of the familiar concepts of other protocols, such as media access control and variable-length frames, are not applicable to ATM. Because ATM does not share bandwidth among systems, there is no need for a MAC mechanism such as CSMA/CD or token passing. Switches provide a dedicated connection to every device on the ATM network. Because all ATM transmissions are composed of fixed-length cells, the switching process is simpler and predictable. All ATM switching is hardware based because there is no need for software-managed flow control and other such technologies. References to ATM systems and devices refer to switches and routers, as well as actual computers. The bandwidth delivered by an ATM network is also readily quantifiable,

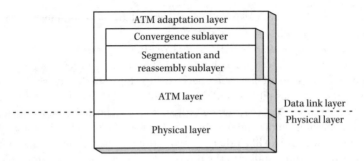

Figure 7-8 ATM architecture

making it easier to designate the appropriate amount of bandwidth for a specific application. On an Ethernet network, for example, it may be necessary to provide much more bandwidth than is actually needed to ensure good performance from a videoconferencing application. This is because you must account for the bandwidth required for videoconferencing on top of the maximum bandwidth used by all other applications combined. The network, therefore, is designed to accommodate the peak traffic condition that occurs only a small fraction of the time. On an ATM network, bandwidth can be more precisely calculated.

Like Ethernet and Token Ring, ATM encompasses the physical and data link layers of the OSI reference model but is itself divided into three layers (see Figure 7-8), which are as follows:

- Physical layer
- ATM layer
- ATM adaptation layer

The following sections examine the functions performed at each of these layers.

The Physical Layer

The ATM standards do not specify precise physical layer technologies as most other data link layer protocols do. This media independence is one of the guiding design principles behind the technology. ATM can run at various speeds over Synchronous Optical Network (SONET) and D5-3 connections and locally over multimode fiber-optic and shielded twisted-pair (STP) cable, among others. Speeds range from 25.6 Mbps for desktop connections to 2.46 Gbps, although the most common implementations run at 155 or 625 Mbps.

The higher speeds are commonly used for backbones and WAN connections.

NOTE SONET is a fiber-optic standard that defines a series of optical carrier (OC) services ranging from OC-1, operating at 51.84 Mbps, to OC-192 operating at 9,952 Mbps.

The ATM physical layer is divided into two sublayers, called the *physical medium dependent* (PMD) sublayer and the *transmission convergence* (TC) sublayer. The PMD sublayer defines the actual medium used by the network, including the type of cable and other hardware, such as connectors, and the signaling scheme used. This sublayer is also responsible for maintaining the synchronization of all the clocks in the network systems, which it does by continuously transmitting and receiving clock bits from the other systems.

The TC sublayer is responsible for the following four functions:

- **Cell delineation**   Maintains the boundaries between cells, enabling systems to isolate cells within a bit stream

- **Header error control (HEC) sequence generation and verification**   Ensures the validity of the data in the cells by checking the error-control code in the cell headers

- **Cell rate decoupling**   Inserts or removes idle cells to synchronize the transmission rate to the capacity of the receiving system

- **Transmission frame adaptation**   Packages cells into the appropriate frame for transmission over a particular network medium

The ATM Layer

The ATM layer specifies the format of the cell, constructs the header, implements the error-control mechanism, and creates and destroys virtual circuits. There are two versions of the cell header, one for the *User Network Interface* (UNI), which is used for communications between user systems or between user systems and switches, and the *Network-to-Network Interface* (NNI), which is used for communications between switches.

In each case, the 53 bytes of the cell are divided into a 5-byte header and a 48-byte payload. Compared to an Ethernet header, which is 18 bytes, the ATM header seems quite small, but remember that an Ethernet frame can carry up to 1,500 bytes of data. Thus, for a full-sized Ethernet frame, the header is less than 2 percent of the packet, while an ATM header is almost 10 percent of the cell. This makes ATM considerably less efficient than Ethernet, as far as the amount of control data transmitted across the wire is concerned.

Figure 7-9 shows the format of the ATM cell. The functions of the fields are as follows:

- **Generic flow control (GFC), 4 bits**   Provides local functions in the UNI cell that are not currently used and are not included in the NXI cell.

- **Virtual path identifier (VPI), 8 bits**   Specifies the next destination of the cell on its path through the ATM network to its destination.

- **Virtual channel identifier (VCI), 16 bits**   Specifies the channel within the virtual path that the cell will use on its path through the ATM network to its destination.

- **Payload type indicator (PTI), 3 bits**   Specifies the nature of the data carried in the cell's payload, using the following bit values:
  - **Bit 1**   Specifies whether the cell contains user data or control data.
  - **Bit 2**   When the cell contains user data, specifies whether congestion is present on the network.
  - **Bit 3**   When the cell contains user data, specifies whether the payload contains the last segment of an AAL-5 PDU.

- **Cell loss priority (CLP), 1 bit**   Specifies a priority for the cell, which is used when a network is forced to discard cells because of congestion. A value of 0 indicates a high

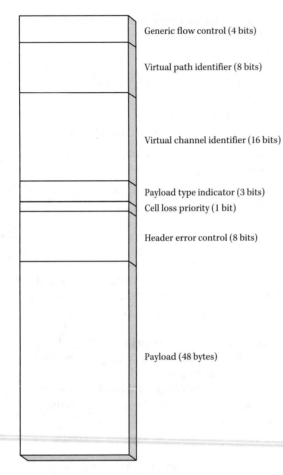

Generic flow control (4 bits)

Virtual path identifier (8 bits)

Virtual channel identifier (16 bits)

Payload type indicator (3 bits)

Cell loss priority (1 bit)

Header error control (8 bits)

Payload (48 bytes)

Figure 7-9 The ATM cell format

priority for the cell, while a value of 1 indicates that the cell may be discarded.

- **Header error control (EC), 8 bits** Contains a code computed on the preceding four bits of the header, which is used to detect multiple-bit header errors and correct single-bit errors. This feature detects errors in the ATM header only; there is no error control of the payload at this layer.

- **Payload, 48 bytes** Contains the user, network, or management data to be transported in the cell.

Virtual Circuits

A connection between two ATM systems takes the form of a *virtual circuit*. Like frame relay, ATM uses two types of virtual circuits: *permanent virtual circuits* (PVCs), which network administrators manually create and which are always available, and *switched virtual circuits* (SVCs), which systems dynamically create as needed and then terminate after use.

Establishing a virtual circuit through the network to a destination enables the transmission of cells through that circuit without extensive processing by intermediate systems along the way. A virtual circuit is composed of a *virtual path* (VP) and a *virtual channel* (VC). A virtual path is a logical connection between two systems that is composed of multiple virtual circuits, much as a cable between two points can contain multiple wires, each carrying a separate signal. Once a VP is established between two points, creating an additional VC for a new connection within that VP is a relatively simple matter.

In addition, managing the VP is an easy way of modifying the properties of all of the VCs it contains. When a switch fails, for example, the VP can be rerouted to use another path, and all of its VCs are rerouted with it. Every ATM cell header contains a virtual path identifier and a virtual channel identifier, which specify the VP that the cell is using and the VC within that VP.

ATM Addressing

ATM networks have their own addresses for each device, in addition to any upper-layer addresses they might possess. The addresses are 20 bytes long and hierarchical, much like telephone numbers, enabling them to support extremely large networks. Unlike protocols that share network bandwidth, it isn't necessary to include source and destination addresses in each cell because ATM transmissions use dedicated point-to-point links. Instead, the addresses are used by the ATM switches to establish the VPIs and VCIs for a connection.

The ATM Adaptation Layer

The primary function of the *ATM adaptation layer* (AAL) is to prepare the data received from the network layer protocol for transmission and segment it into 48-byte units that the ATM layer will package as cells by applying the header. The AAL consists of two sublayers, called the *convergence sublayer* (CS) and the *segmentation and reassembly sublayer* (SAR). The CS prepares the network-layer data for segmentation by applying various fields that are specific to the type of service that will transmit the data, creating convergence sublayer protocol data units (CS-PDUs). The SAR then splits the CS-PDUs into segments of the appropriate size for packaging in cells.

Several AAL protocols are available at this sublayer, which provide different types of service to support various applications. The AAL protocols are as follows:

- **AAL-1**   A connection-oriented service intended for applications that require circuit emulation, such as voice and videoconferencing. This service requires clock synchronization, so a network medium that supports clocking, such as SONET, is required. For this service, the CS sublayer adds Sequence Number (SN) and Sequence Number Protection (SNP) fields to the data that enable the receiving system to assemble the cells in the proper order.

- **AAL-3/4**   Supports both connection-oriented and connectionless data transfers with cell-by-cell error checking and multiplexing. The CS creates a PDU by adding a beginning/ending tag to the data as a header and a length field as a footer. After the SAR layer splits the CS-PDU into cell-sized segments, it adds a CRC value to each segment for error-detection purposes.

- **AAL-5**   Also called *Simple and Efficient Adaptation Layer* (SEAL), AAL-5 provides both connection-oriented and connectionless services and is most commonly used for LAN traffic. The CS takes a block of network layer data up to 64KB in size and adds a variable-length pad and an 8-byte trailer to it. The pad ensures that the data block falls on a cell boundary, and the trailer includes a block length field and a CRC value for the entire PDU. The SAR splits the PDU into 48-byte segments for packaging into cells. The third bit of the PTI field in the ATM header is then set to a value of 0 for all of the segments of the data block except the last one, in which it is set to 1.

ATM Support

One problem is the cost and complexity of installing and supporting an ATM network. While a competent Ethernet LAN administrator should be able to install the components of a Gigabit Ethernet backbone with little trouble, an ATM backbone is a completely different story. ATM networks are a hybrid of telecommunications and data networking technologies. These are two separate types of networks, but in the case of ATM, both can use the same cables and switches. An ATM backbone, therefore, may be connected not only to data networking components such as routers, switches, and servers, but also to PBXs and other telecommunications devices.

SONET

Synchronous Optical Network (SONET) carries data over fiber-optic cables used today by many long-distance carriers. It was originally designed to transmit many information types, including voice, video, and data. This system, along with *Synchronous Digital Hierarchy* (SDH), is used throughout the world to transmit information.

SONET works at the physical layer, and its protocols specify a consistent method of multiplexing many small signals into one larger (and faster) transmission. Several characteristics make this technology attractive:

- Built-in support for maintenance and management
- The ability to carry nearly all higher-level protocols
- Definition of clear standards between various products

This technology provides standards for line rates up to 9.953 Gbps. Because some have experienced line rates approaching 20 Gbps, SONET has been called the foundation for the physical layer of broadband ISDN. ATM can run as a layer on top of both SONET and other technologies.

CHAPTER

8

Server Technologies

All of the computers on a local area network contain roughly the same components, such as a microprocessor, memory modules, mass storage devices, keyboards, video adapters, and other input/output mechanisms. However, you can still divide the computers into two basic categories: servers and client workstations. At one time, it was easy to differentiate between servers and clients because servers functioned only as servers and clients only as clients. Servers in earlier days were essentially computers with more of everything: faster processors, more memory, and larger hard drives, for example. Now that many computers can function as both servers and clients simultaneously, the boundary between the server and client functions has been obscured somewhat. Recent years have seen great developments in the features and technologies that make a server different from a workstation. From application servers to web servers, each machine offers different services and has different features. This chapter examines some of these features and technologies and explains how they can enhance the performance of your network.

Purchasing a Server

When building a local area network (LAN), you can purchase virtually any computer and use it as a server. The primary attributes that make a computer a server are determined by the network operating system's hardware requirements. For example, the Windows 2012 Server requirements call for 256MB of memory, but you can actually run the operating system on a standard workstation computer with as little as 128MB. It won't run as well, but it will run. When shopping for computers, you'll see that some products are specifically designed to be servers and not just because of the operating system installed on them or the amount of memory or disk space they contain. For a small network consisting of only a handful of nodes, it may not be practical for you to spend the extra money on a computer designed to be a server. Instead, you can purchase a high-end workstation with sufficient resources to run the server operating system and use that. When you do need the features of a real server, it's important to understand how a server can differ from a workstation and which features you need for your network.

When you look at the description of a server computer in a catalog or on a web site, it may seem at first as though you're paying more money for less. Servers often do not come with monitors, and they generally do not include the high-performance video adapters and audio systems you find in nearly every home or office computer package.

The video adapter in a server is in many cases integrated into the computer's motherboard and includes sufficient memory to power a display at a variety of resolutions. However, the video subsystem in a server usually does not include the 3-D accelerator and other components found on a separate adapter card used in a workstation for more video-intensive tasks, such as game-playing and multimedia applications. A video adapter in a server also tends not to use the Accelerated Graphics Port (AGP) for its interface to the computer because AGP uses system memory for some of its functions, and in a server, you want as much system memory as possible to be devoted to your server applications.

As for audio, most servers include no audio adapter at all or, at most, a rudimentary one that is also integrated into the motherboard. Speakers are usually not included. The only purpose for having any audio capabilities in a server is to provide audible feedback alerting the administrator of particular system conditions. However, since servers are often kept in a locked closet or data center, even this basic audio capability usually isn't necessary.

NOTE Although servers generally do not come equipped with high-end video and audio adapters, there is usually no reason why you can't add them later and use the computer for tasks more traditionally associated with client workstations.

The question then remains, what do you get when you purchase a server for more money than you would spend on a workstation with the same processor and a comparable amount of memory and disk space? The following list examines the ways in which the basic components in a server differ from their counterparts in a workstation:

- **Case**   A server case can be larger than that of a workstation in order to provide room for greater expansion. Server cases are usually either freestanding towers or specially designed to be mounted in a standard 19-inch equipment rack. Expandability is an important quality in a server, and the cases typically have a large number and variety of bays to support the installation of additional drives.

  Since a server doesn't usually take up space on a user's desk, maintaining a small footprint is not a concern, and server cases tend not to have their components shoehorned into them in the interest of saving space. The result is that there is more room to work inside the case and easier access to the components. A server case might also have greater physical security than a standard computer case, such as a key-lockable cover that prevents any access to the server controls and drives.

- **Power supply**   To support the greater number of drives and other devices frequently found in a server, the power supply is typically more robust. The power supply usually also has more internal power connectors available to attach to installed devices. In some cases, a server's power supply might have its own internal surge protection circuitry. Some servers also have redundant power supplies, providing fault tolerance in the event of a power supply failure.

- **Fans**   The possibility of having many more drives and multiple processors in a server means that the computer can potentially generate a lot more heat than a workstation. Server cases typically have multiple fans in them, aside from the one in the power supply.

A well-designed case will also have a carefully planned ventilation path that blows the cooler air from the outside directly across the components that most need to be kept cool. In some cases, servers use a sealed case design in which all of the air entering the case runs through a filter, enabling the server to function in an industrial environment without contaminating the internal components with dust and other particles. Some high-end servers designed for mission-critical applications also have hot-swappable modular fan assemblies, meaning that should a fan fail, it's possible to replace the unit without shutting down the server.

- **Processor**   Servers use the same model processors as workstations, and given the computer industry's dedication to aggressively marketing the newest and fastest processors to home users, you may find that a server's processor is not any faster than a workstation's. In fact, because servers are designed with an emphasis on expandability and because they cost more, they tend to have longer lives than workstations, meaning that they might have a processor that is slower than the "latest and greatest." Where servers do differ from workstation in this area is that they often have more than one processor. For more information, see "Using Multiple Processors" later in this chapter.

- **Memory**   Servers are typically capable of supporting more memory than workstations, sometimes a lot more. Examining the inside of the server and a workstation, you may not see any difference because a server may have the same number of memory slots as a workstation and use the same basic type of memory modules. The server will support modules containing more memory, however, in a greater variety of configurations.

In addition to these differences in a server's basic components, there are other more advanced technologies that can have an even greater impact on the computer's performance, as discussed in the following sections.

Using Multiple Processors

Even though the processor designs used in computers today are continually being enhanced and upgraded to run at ever faster speeds, servers often require more processing power than any single processor can provide. This is because a server application such as a database engine may have to service requests from dozens or even hundreds of users at the same time. To increase the processing power available to the application, you can add more processors. You can multiply the processing power of a server in two ways: by installing multiple processors into the computer or by connecting multiple computers using a hardware or software product that joins them into a cluster or a *system area network* (SAN).

Parallel Processing

The use of multiple processors in a single computer is not a new idea, although it has become common in the PC industry only in the last few years. The two biggest advantages of using multiple processors are economy and expandability. When a processor manufacturer releases a new product, its price compared to the previous models is always disproportionately high for the performance increase it provides. As each new processor is superseded by the next model, the price drops quickly. By purchasing a server with multiple processors in it, you can realize nearly the same processing power as the latest chip on the market for much less money. Multiple processor support can also extend the life of a server by enabling the owner to upgrade it as needed. You can buy a single-processor server containing a motherboard that supports up to four processors for only slightly more than a computer with a standard single processor motherboard. Later, as the burden on the server is increased by the addition of more users or applications, you can buy additional processors and install them into the empty motherboard sockets.

The method by which a computer makes use of multiple processors is known as *parallel processing*. This consists of distributing computing tasks among the available processors so that they are all continuously active. There are various methods in which computers with multiple processors can implement parallel processing. Supercomputer systems, for example, can combine the capabilities of hundreds of processors to perform complex tasks that require enormous numbers of computations, such as weather forecasting. In most cases, these supercomputers use a technique called *massively parallel processing* (MPP), in which the processors are grouped into nodes and connected by a high-speed switch. In this arrangement, each node has its own memory array and its own bus connecting the processors to the memory. There is no sharing of resources between nodes, and communication between them is restricted to a dedicated messaging system.

Symmetric Multiprocessing

The servers with multiple processors used on LANs today employ a different method, called *symmetrical multiprocessing* (SMP). In an SMP system, the processors share a single memory array, input/output (I/O) system, and interrupts, as shown in Figure 8-1. Processing tasks are distributed evenly between all of the processors, so it isn't possible for one processor to be overloaded while another sits idle. This is in contrast to another system, called *asymmetrical multiprocessing*, in which tasks are assigned to each processor individually and the workload may not be balanced.

Sharing a single memory array eliminates the need for the messaging system found in MPP. The processors in an SMP computer can communicate and synchronize their activities more quickly than most other parallel processing technologies.

It is important to note that having multiple processors in a computer is not considered to be a fault-tolerance mechanism. If one of the processors should fail while the system is running, the coherency of the cached operating system and application information are likely to be affected, eventually causing a crash. Failure or removal of a processor while the computer is shut down, however, will not have a deleterious effect since the operating system detects the number of available processors during the startup sequence and configures itself accordingly.

Hardware and Software Requirements

To use multiple processors in a LAN server, SMP must be supported by the processors themselves, the computer's motherboard, the operating system, and the applications running on the server. If you install an operating system or an application that doesn't support SMP on a server with multiple processors, the software functions in the normal manner using only one of the processors.

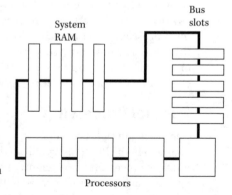

Figure 8-1   SMP computers have a single memory array and I/O bus, which are shared by all of the processors.

Most of the operating systems intended for use on servers support SMP. Most of the Unix operating systems support SMP, including Linux versions as well as Mac. In some cases, such as FreeBSD, you have to substitute a multiprocessor kernel for the standard one supplied with the operating system. Interestingly, although it is not considered a server application, Adobe Photoshop also supports SMP, making it possible for graphic designers working with large image files and complex functions to take advantage of a computer with multiple processors.

Server Clustering

A *cluster* is a group of servers that are connected by cables and that function as a single entity. To a client on the network, the cluster appears to be a single server, even though it consists of two or more computers. Clustering can provide the same advantage as having multiple processors in a single server since it is possible to divide the server's workload between the processors in the various computers that make up the cluster. However, clustering can also provide fault tolerance in ways that SMP cannot.

The computers that make up a cluster are connected programmatically as well as physically. In some cases, operating systems provide direct support for clustering, while in others, a separate application is required.

Clustering can provide two basic advantages over a single server: load balancing and fault tolerance. Load balancing is the process by which the tasks assigned to the server are distributed evenly among the computers in the cluster. This concept can work in different ways, depending on the application involved. For example, a cluster of web servers can balance its load by sending each of the incoming requests from web browser clients to a different server. When you connect to a hugely popular Internet web site, you can be sure that all of its thousands of concurrent users are not being served by a single computer. Instead, the site uses a *server farm* that consists of many identically configured computers. Each time you connect to the site with your web browser, you are probably accessing a different server. A clustered terminal server works in the same way; each new client connecting to the server is directed to the computer that is currently carrying the lightest load. Other applications that split the processing into threads can distribute those threads equally among the computers in the cluster.

This load balancing capability greatly enhances the expandability of the server. If you reach a point where the server is overburdened by the application traffic it must handle, you can simply add another computer to the cluster, and the workload will automatically be balanced among the available systems, thus reducing the load on each one. You can also upgrade the server by installing additional processors to SMP computers in the cluster or by replacing a computer with one that is faster and more capable.

Load balancing also provides fault tolerance. If one of the computers in the cluster should fail, the others continue to function with the load redistributed between them. However, it's also possible to construct a cluster with more extensive failover capabilities. A failover cluster is one on which connected computers are configured so that when one fails, the other takes over all of its functions. This type of cluster is better suited to database and e-mail servers that must be continuously available. E-commerce is one of the few technologies that can require both load balancing and failover technologies in one cluster.

In today's clustering products, a group of computers can be clustered in a failover configuration without leaving some of the machines idle. If one of the computers fails, its applications are migrated to another computer in the cluster, which takes over its functions, as shown in Figure 8-2. (For this to occur, all of the computers in the cluster must have access to the applications and data used by the other computers.)

System Area Networks

A *system area network* (or SAN, not to be confused with a storage area network, also abbreviated SAN) is essentially a dedicated, switched network that connects a group of computers that are in the same administrative domain and located relatively close to each other. The network achieves greater transmission speeds by implementing a reliable transport service (much like the Transmission Control Protocol [TCP]) in hardware instead of software. The SAN hardware consists of network interface adapter cards that use Fibre Channel connections to a central switch. A SAN network interface adapter makes individual transport endpoints (much like the ports used in a TCP software implementation) available to the connected computers. These endpoints are memory-based registers

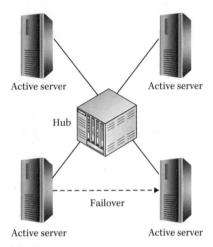

Figure 8-2   In a server cluster, all of the servers are active, with functions ready to fail over to other servers.

that are shared by the SAN network adapter and the computer's processor. The processor can therefore pass the incoming traffic directed at a particular endpoint immediately to the appropriate application running on the computer. In a sense, a SAN operates much like a distributed memory array, rather than a standard networking technology.

Cluster Networking Hardware

There are two areas in which the use of server clustering can affect the hardware used to construct a network: the network connections themselves and the server's mass storage hardware. The computers in a cluster use standard network connections to communicate with each other. In fact, it is possible to build a server cluster with no additional networking hardware other than each computer's normal connection to the enterprise network. In a failover configuration, the servers in the cluster communicate by exchanging signals at regular intervals called *heartbeats*. These heartbeats serve as an indication to each computer that the other computers in the cluster are up and running properly. If a computer fails to transmit a predetermined number of consecutive heartbeats, the other computers in the cluster assume that it has failed and take action to assume its functions. This same heartbeat method also functions at the application level. If a single application fails on one of the computers in the cluster, the cluster service attempts to restart it on the same computer. If this should fail, the service then migrates the application to another computer in the cluster.

The heartbeats can be exchanged over the normal network connection, but if the cluster is on a shared network with other systems, the additional traffic generated by the heartbeats can be a problem. In addition, the network connection provides a single point of failure. If a cable break or a failure in a hub or other network component should occur, the heartbeats can fail to reach all of the computers in the cluster, resulting in a condition in which both computers attempt to take on the functions of the other.

To address these problems, it's a good idea to build a separate, private network that is dedicated to the computers in the cluster. Ethernet is typically the protocol of choice for this arrangement, with Gigabit Ethernet an option for installations that can benefit from greater speeds. Not only does this private network ensure that the heartbeats generated by each computer reach the others in a timely fashion, it also provides a backup for the intracluster communications. Later in this chapter, you will see how this separate network can also be used with a higher-speed protocol such as Fibre Channel to connect the servers to external drive arrays and other storage devices. This is called a *storage area network*.

Cluster Storage Hardware

One of the elements that complicate the implementation of a clustering solution in a failover configuration is that each of the computers in the cluster requires access to the applications and data running on the other computers. There are three ways to accomplish this, which have come to define the three basic hardware configurations you can use in a computer that is part of a cluster. These three hardware configurations are as follows:

- **Shared disk**   In a shared disk configuration, the computers in the cluster are all connected to the same disk array using a common I/O bus so that all of the computers can access the same applications and data simultaneously. The disk array typically uses some form of SCSI, Fibre Channel, or serial storage architecture (SSA) to connect to the computers. Because this arrangement makes it possible for two computers to update files on the shared drives at the same time, an additional software component called a *distributed lock manager* is needed to prevent files from being corrupted and new data from being overwritten.

- **Shared nothing**   A shared nothing configuration is one in which there is no simultaneous access of the same data stores by different computers in the cluster. The redundant connection is so that if one computer should fail and its applications fail over to another computer, the substitute can immediately access the same data stores as the original system and continue where it left off.

- **Mirrored disk**   In a mirrored disk configuration, each computer maintains its own storage drives, and data is replicated between the computers on a regular basis.

Using Hierarchical Storage Management

Hierarchical storage management (HSM) is a technique for storing data on a variety of device types in order to minimize storage costs while providing easy accessibility. As a general rule, the cheaper the medium, the slower its access time. By installing various types of drives in a server, you can minimize your storage costs by putting the most frequently used files on hard drives, occasionally used files on optical discs, and seldom used files on magnetic tape.

The problem with this arrangement is keeping track of which files are stored on which device, and this is where HSM provides a solution. HSM is a software product that automatically migrates files between the various media, depending on how often they're accessed. A typical HSM installation consists of a server with one or more hard drives and an optical disc jukebox or magnetic tape, or both. These devices enable you to maintain large amounts of storage and still access it without human intervention. This is known as *nearline storage*.

When a file on a hard drive goes a certain number of days without being accessed, the HSM software migrates it to the secondary medium, such as an optical disc. After copying the file to the optical disc, the software creates a tiny key file in its place on the hard drive. The key file specifies the location of the actual file and provides a placeholder for network users. If the file goes even longer without being accessed, HSM migrates it to a tertiary medium (such as tape) and updates the key file. To a user on the network, the files that have been migrated to other media appear to still be on the hard drive. When the user attempts to access the file, HSM reads the contents of the key file, loads the appropriate disk or tape into the drive, reads the file, and supplies it to the user. The only sign to the user that the file is not stored on the hard drive is the additional time it takes for HSM to supply the file. Everything else is completely invisible. If the user modifies the file, HSM migrates it back to the hard drive, where it remains until it reaches the migration interval once again.

HSM software products are usually highly configurable, enabling you to use various combinations of media and specify whatever migration intervals you want. An HSM installation is not cheap, but for a network that must store vast amounts of data while keeping it all available at a few minutes' notice, HSM is a viable solution.

Fibre Channel Networking

The development of new network storage technologies, such as network attached storage (NAS) and storage area networks (SANs), that call for storage hardware external to the server has resulted in the need for a means to transmit large amounts of data between relatively distant devices at high speeds.

Fibre Channel was conceived in 1988 as a high-speed networking technology that its advocates hoped would be the successor to Fast Ethernet and Fiber Distributed Data Interface (FDDI) on backbone networks that required large amounts of bandwidth. Ratified in a series of American National Standards Institute (ANSI) standards in 1994, Fibre Channel never found acceptance as a general local area networking protocol, although Gigabit Ethernet, an extension of the Ethernet standard using the Fibre Channel physical layer options, did. Instead, Fibre Channel has become the protocol of choice for high-end network storage technologies and has particularly become associated with SANs. A Fibre Channel connection can transfer data at the rate of 32 Gbps.

NOTE The unusual spelling of *fibre* is deliberate and intended to distinguish the term *Fibre Channel* from *fiber optic*.

Unlike devices that connect storage devices and servers using a bus, Fibre Channel is essentially a separate network that can connect various types of storage devices with the servers on a network. Fibre Channel uses standard networking hardware components, such as cables, hubs, and ports, to form the network medium, and the connected nodes transmit and receive data using any one of several services, providing various levels of performance. Fibre Channel differs from standard networking protocols such as the Internet Protocol (IP) in that much of its "intelligence" is implemented in hardware, rather than in software running on a host computer.

The Fibre Channel protocol stack consists of five layers that perform the functions attributed to the physical and data link layers of the Open Systems Interconnection (OSI) reference model. These layers are as follows:

- **FC-0**   This layer defines the physical components that make up the Fibre Channel network, including the cables, connectors, transmitters, and receivers, as well as their properties.

- **FC-1**   This layer defines the encoding scheme used to transmit the data over the network, as well as the timing signals and error detection mechanism. Fibre Channel uses an encoding scheme called 8B/10B, in which 10 bits are used to represent 8 bits of data, thus yielding a 25 percent overhead.

- **FC-2**   This layer defines the structure of the frame in which the data to be transmitted is encapsulated and the sequence of the data transfer.

- **FC-3**   This layer defines additional services such as the striping of data across multiple signal lines to increase bandwidth and the use of multiple ports with a single alias address.

- **FC-4**   This layer maps the Fibre Channel network to the upper-layer protocols running over it. While it's possible to map Fibre Channel to standard networking protocols, such as IP, the Fibre Channel Protocol (FCP) is the protocol used to adapt the standard parallel SCSI commands to the serial SCSI-3 communications used by storage devices on a Fibre Channel network.

The Fibre Channel Physical Layer

Fibre Channel supports both fiber-optic and copper cables, with fiber optic providing greater segment lengths.

The three physical layer cable options are as follows:

- **Singlemode fiber optic**   Nine-micron singlemode fiber-optic cable, using standard SC connectors, with a maximum cable length of 10,000 meters

- **Multimode fiber optic**   Fifty- or 62.5-micron multimode fiber-optic cable with SC connectors, with a maximum cable length of 500 meters

- **Shielded twisted-pair (STP)**   Type 1 STP cable with DB-9 connectors, with a maximum cable length of 30 meters

Using any of these cable types, you can build a Fibre Channel network with any one of the three following topologies:

- **Point-to-point**   The point-to-point topology links a Fibre Channel host bus adapter installed into a computer to a single external storage device or subsystem.

- **Loop**   The loop topology, also called a *continuous arbitrated loop,* can contain an unlimited number of nodes, although only 127 can be active at any one time. You can connect the nodes to each other using a physical loop, or you can implement the loop logically using a hub and a physical star topology, as in a Token Ring network. Traffic travels only one direction on the loop, unlike SSA and FDDI, which have redundant loops that permit bidirectional communications. Therefore, in the case of a physical loop, a cable break or node failure can take down the whole loop, while the hub in a logical loop can remove the malfunctioning node and continue operating. Each of the nodes in a Fibre Channel loop acts as a repeater, which prevents signal degradation due to attenuation, but a loop is still a shared network with multiple devices utilizing the same bandwidth, which can limit the performance of each device.

- **Fabric**   The fabric topology consists of nodes connected to switches with point-to-point connections. Just as on an Ethernet network, switching enables each device to use the full bandwidth of the network technology in its transmissions. Fibre Channel uses nonblocking switches, which enable multiple devices to send traffic through the switch simultaneously. A switched Fibre Channel network has the benefit of almost unlimited expandability while maintaining excellent performance.

Fibre Channel Communications

Communications over a Fibre Channel network are broken down into three hierarchical structures. The highest-level structure is called an *exchange,* which is a bidirectional, application-oriented communication between two nodes on the network. In the context of a storage operation, an exchange would be the process of reading from or writing to a file. A single device can maintain multiple exchanges simultaneously, with communications running in both directions, if needed.

An exchange consists of unidirectional transmissions between ports called *sequences,* which in the context of a read or write operation are the individual blocks transmitted over the network. Each sequence must be completed before the next one can begin. Sequences are composed of *frames,* and the frame is the smallest protocol data unit transmitted over a Fibre Channel network. Fibre Channel frames are constructed much like the frames used in other networking protocols, such as Ethernet and IP. The frame consists of discrete fields that contain addressing and error detection information, as well as the actual data to be transmitted. In the storage context, a frame is the equivalent of a SCSI command.

Fibre Channel provides three classes of service, with different resource requirements and levels of performance provided by each. These service classes are as follows:

- **Class 1**   Class 1 is a reliable, connection-oriented, circuit-switched service in which two ports on the network reserve a path through the network switches to establish a connection for as long as they need it. The result is the functional equivalent of a point-to-point connection that can remain open for any length of time, even permanently. Because a virtual circuit exists between the two nodes, frames are always transmitted and received in the same order, eliminating the additional processing required to reorder the packets, as on an IP network. The Class 1 service tends to waste bandwidth when the connection is not in use all of the time, but for applications that require a connection with the ultimate in reliability and performance, the expenditure can be worthwhile.

- **Class 2**   Class 2 is a connectionless service that provides the same reliability as Class 1 through the use of message delivery and nondelivery notifications. Since Class 2 is not a circuit-switched service, frames may arrive at the destination port in the wrong order. However, it is the port in the receiving node that reorders the frames, not the processor inside the server or storage subsystem containing the port. By placing the responsibility for ordered delivery of frames on the port rather than on the switch, as in the Class 1 service, the switches are better able to provide the maximum amount of bandwidth to all of the nodes on the network. The Class 2 service can therefore provide performance and reliability that is nearly that of the Class 1 service, with greater overall efficiency. Most storage network implementations use Class 2 rather than Class 1 for this reason.

- **Class 3**   Class 3 is an unreliable connectionless service that does not provide notification of delivery and nondelivery like Class 2. Removing the processing overhead required to implement the notifications reduces port latency and therefore greatly increases the efficiency of the network. This is particularly true in the case of a loop network, which uses a shared medium. In the case of a storage network, the FCP protocol provides frame acknowledgment and reordering services, making it unnecessary to implement them in the network hardware.

NOTE There is also an extension to the Class I service called Intermix, which enables other processes to utilize the unused bandwidth of a Class I connection for the transmission of Class 2 and Class 3 traffic. In this arrangement, however, the Class I traffic maintains absolute priority over the connection, which can cause the nodes to buffer or discard Class 2 and 3 frames, if necessary.

Network Storage Subsystems

In the original client-server network design, the server was a computer constructed very much like a client, except with more storage capacity, more memory, a faster processor, and so on. As the years have passed and data storage requirements have increased at an exponential level, it has become unwieldy for a personal computer to contain enough space and power for the many drives used in modern storage arrays. Moving the storage management tasks away from the server and into a dedicated device also reduces the processing burden on the server. Today, with server clusters and other advanced server technologies becoming more popular, there is a drive toward storage arrays with greater capabilities.

One of the solutions is to integrate the standard storage I/O architecture with the networking architecture used for other communications between systems. Combining I/O and networking makes it possible to locate the servers and the storage arrays virtually anywhere, build a more flexible and expandable storage solution, and enable any server on the network to work with any storage device. There are two technologies that are leading the way in this new area of development: network attached storage and storage area networks. These technologies are not mutually exclusive; in fact, the future network is likely to encompass both to some degree.

Network Attached Storage

Network attached storage is a term that is generally applied to a stand-alone storage subsystem that connects to a network and contains everything needed for clients and servers to access the data stored there. An NAS device, sometimes called a *network storage appliance,* is not just a box with a power supply and an I/O bus with hard drives installed in it. The unit also has a self-contained file system and a stripped-down, proprietary operating system that is optimized for the task of serving files. The NAS appliance is essentially a stand-alone file server that can be accessed by any computer on the network. For a network that has servers dedicated primarily to file-serving tasks, NAS appliances can reduce costs and simplify the deployment and ongoing management processes. Because the appliance is a complete turnkey solution, there is no need to integrate separate hardware and operating system products or be concerned about compatibility issues.

NAS appliances can connect to networks in different ways, and it is here that the definition of the technology becomes confusing. An NAS server is a device that can respond to file access requests generated by any other computer on the network, including clients and servers. The device typically uses a standard file system protocol like the Network File System (NFS) or the Common Internet File System (CIFS) for its application layer communications. There are two distinct methods for deploying an NAS server, however. You can connect the appliance directly to the LAN, using a standard Ethernet connection, enabling clients and servers alike to access its file system directly, or you can build a dedicated storage network, using Ethernet or Fibre Channel, enabling your servers to access the NAS and share files with network clients.

The latter solution places an additional burden on the servers, but it also moves the I/O traffic from the LAN to a dedicated storage network, thus reducing network traffic congestion. Which option you choose largely depends on the type of data to be stored on the NAS server. If you use the NAS to store users' own work files, for example, it can be advantageous to connect the device to the LAN and let users access their files directly. However, if the NAS server contains databases or e-mail stores, a separate application server is required to process the data and supply it to clients. In this case, you may benefit more by creating a dedicated storage network that enables the application server to access the NAS server without flooding the client network with I/O traffic.

Storage Area Networks

A *storage area network* is simply a separate network with an enterprise that is used to connect storage devices and the computers that use them. In practice, SANs are usually associated with Fibre Channel networks, but actually you can use any type of network for this purpose, including SSA or Ethernet (usually Gigabit Ethernet). The reasons for building an SAN have been repeated throughout this chapter. Server technologies such as clustering and remote disk arrays require high-bandwidth connections, and using the same data network as the client computers for this purpose could easily result in massive amounts of traffic. In addition, the bandwidth requirements of a storage I/O network far exceed those of a typical data network. Constructing a separate SAN using Fibre Channel or Gigabit Ethernet is far cheaper than equipping all of the computers on your network with ultra-high-speed network interface adapters.

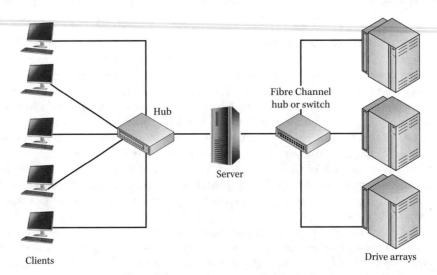

Figure 8-3   A complex SAN using a Fibre Channel loop or fabric network

In a typical enterprise network containing an SAN, the servers have interfaces to both the data network (the LAN) and the storage network (the SAN). The LAN, therefore, is completely ordinary, containing client and server computers, and the storage devices are connected only to the SAN. Where the servers store their data is of no consequence to the clients, which do not even have to know of the SAN's existence.

A typical SAN using Fibre Channel to connect servers to the storage devices can take many forms. The simplest possible SAN consists of a single server connected to a drive array using a point-to-point Fibre Channel connection. The server accesses the data stored on the array, which would typically use RAID to provide added performance and fault tolerance. One of the primary differences between an SAN and an NAS device is that SANs provide block-level access to data, while NAS appliances provide file-level access.

A more complicated SAN would consist of several servers and several storage arrays, all connected to the same network, as shown in Figure 8-3. If the SAN uses Fibre Channel for its communications, the network's topology can take the form of a loop or a fabric, depending on whether the devices are all connected to a hub or a switch. This enables the servers to communicate with each other and with all of the storage devices on the SAN. The storage devices can be drive arrays using RAID, NAS servers, or any other technology that may evolve, as long as it supports Fibre Channel or whatever networking protocol the SAN uses.

Part II

CHAPTER

9

Designing a Network

Planning is an essential part of any network deployment, and the design of the network is a crucial element of the planning process. Depending on its size and location, the process of designing your network can be simple or extremely complex. This chapter examines some of the concepts involved in designing networks that range from small home networks to large enterprise internetworks.

A network design can encompass decisions made at many levels. At a minimum, the design should include what hardware you intend to purchase, how much it costs, where you're going to locate it at your site, and how you're going to connect it all. For a home or small-business network, this can be as easy as taking a few computers, choosing a network interface card (NIC) for each one, and buying some cables and a hub and/or a wireless router. You can make all of the other decisions involved in setting up and configuring the network as you proceed. For a large enterprise internetwork, the design process is considerably more complicated. As you've learned, an internetwork is a collection of LANs that have been connected so that each computer can communicate with any other computer on any of the LANs. You can design each LAN separately, using standard hardware already mentioned, but then you must consider how you are going to connect the LANs into an internetwork and regulate the communications between them. You also have to consider all of the services that you must provide to your users and how you intend to provide them. This means the network design might include software products and configurations, outside services provided by third parties, and operating procedures, as well as a hardware list and a network diagram.

In addition to purely technical issues, designing a large internetwork involves a number of important business decisions. Generally, the early phases of the internetwork design process tend to proceed as follows:

1. Identify the business needs that the network is intended to satisfy.
2. Create an ideal network design that satisfies all of the previously defined needs.
3. Estimate the cost of building the network as designed.
4. Determine whether the benefits of building the network rationalize the expense.
5. Revise the network design to bring the expense in line with the benefits.

This is a high-level overview of the network design process as a business decision, and while economic issues may not be the primary concern of the people involved in the technical side of the process, the cost of the project will certainly have a profound effect on the design. This chapter is more involved with the technical side of the design process than with the business side, but having some idea of the budget allotted for the network and the cost of implementing the technologies you select can streamline the whole design and approval process considerably.

Reasoning the Need

The first step in designing a network is always to list the reasons for building it in the first place. For a home or small-business network, the list is often short and simple, containing items such as the desire to share one printer among several computers and to access the Internet using a single connection. In most cases, the economic decision is equally simple. Weigh the price of a few cables and a hub or a wireless router against the cost of supplying each computer with its own printer or Internet connection, and the conclusion is obvious.

For a large internetwork installation, the list of requirements is usually much longer, and the decision-making process is far more complex. Some of the questions that you should ask yourself as you're first conceiving the network are as follows:

- What business needs will the network satisfy?
- What services do you expect the network to provide now and in the future?
- What applications must the network run now and in the future?
- What are the different types of users you expect the network to support now?
- What types of users (and how many of them) do you expect the network to support in the future?
- What level of service do you expect the network to provide in terms of speed, availability, and security?
- What environmental factors at the site can possibly affect the network?
- What is the geographic layout of the business? Are there remote offices to connect?
- What network maintenance skills and resources are available to the organization?

By answering questions like these, you should be able to come up with a basic, high-level concept of the type of network you need. This concept should include a sketch of the network indicating the number of levels in the hierarchy. For example, a network at a single site might consist of a number of LANs connected by a backbone, while a network encompassing multiple sites might consist of several LANs, connected by a backbone at each location, all of which are then connected by WAN links. This plan may also include decisions regarding the network media and protocols to use, a routing strategy, and other technical elements.

NOTE Depending on the environment in which a *backbone* exists, it can have two meanings. The first is the physical connection such as fiber or Gigabit Ethernet, and the second is a transmission method such as frame relay through the cloud.

Seeking Approval

The next step is to start making generic technology and equipment selections in order to develop an estimate of the costs of building and maintaining the network. For example, you might at this point decide that you are going to build an internetwork consisting of ten LANs, connected by a fiber-optic backbone and using a T-1 line for access to the Internet. With this information, you can start to figure out the general costs of purchasing and installing the necessary equipment.

With a rough cost estimate in hand, it's generally time to decide whether building the network as conceived is economically feasible. In many cases, this requires an evaluation by nontechnical people, so a layperson's summary of the project and its cost is usually in order. At this point, some of the following questions may be considered:

- Does the network design satisfy all of the business needs listed earlier?
- Do the business needs that the network will satisfy justify the cost expenditures?
- Can the costs of the network be reduced while still providing a minimum standard of performance?
- How will reducing the quality of the network (in regard to elements such as speed, reliability, and/or security) affect the business needs it is able to satisfy?
- Can the network be reconceived to lower the initial costs while still providing sufficient capability for expansion in the future?

This review process may involve individuals at several management layers, each with their own concerns. In many cases, business and economic factors force a redesign of the network plan at this point, either to better address business needs not considered earlier or to reduce costs. Usually, it's better for these modifications to occur now, while the network design plan is still in its preliminary stages. Once the elements of the plan are developed in greater detail, it will become more difficult and inefficient to drastically change them.

When the economic and business factors of the network design have been reconciled with the technical factors, you can begin to flesh out the plan in detail. The following sections examine some of the specific elements that should be included in your network design plan.

Designing a Home or Small-Office Network

A network for a home or small office typically consists of a single LAN connecting anywhere from 2 to 16 computers. The LAN might also have additional network devices attached to it, such as a network printer or a router providing a connection to the Internet or another office. For this kind of network, the design process consists mostly of selecting products that are suitable for your users' needs and for the physical layout of the site.

Selecting Computers

Virtually all the computers on the market today can be connected to a network, so compatibility in this area is not usually a concern. However, for the sake of convenience, it's easier to design, build, and maintain a small network in which all of the computers use the same platform. If most of your users are accustomed to using Windows PCs, then make the network all Windows PCs. If most are comfortable with Macintosh, Linux, or Unix systems, then use those. It's not impossible to connect computers running different platforms to the same network by any means, but if you're planning a small network and you want to have as easy a time of it as possible, stick to one platform.

Standardizing on a single platform may be difficult in some situations, however. For a home network, for example, you may have kids who use Macs in school and adults who use PCs at work. In a small-business environment, you are more likely to be able to impose one platform on your employees, unless they have special requirements such as different types of machines. If you do feel compelled to mix platforms, you must be careful to select products that are compatible with every type of computer you plan to use. Generally, it is not too difficult to configure different types of computers to access shared network resources such as printers and Internet connections. However, file sharing can be a problem because the computers may use different file formats. The other important consideration when selecting the computers to be connected to a network is whether they have the resources needed for networking. For the most part, this just means you must determine what type of network interface adapter the computer uses. If any of the machines to be included in the network do not have appropriate adapters, you can purchase a network interface card and either install the adapter in a free PCI slot or purchase a Universal Serial Bus (USB) network interface adapter.

Selecting a Networking Protocol

The protocol your network uses at the data link layer of the OSI reference model is the single most defining element of the network design. The data link layer protocol determines, among other things, what network medium you will use, what networking hardware you will buy, how you will connect the computers, and how fast the network can transfer data. The most common choices in data link layer protocols are Ethernet for LANs or point-to-point (PPP) for larger networks.

Choosing a Network Medium

The Ethernet protocol supports a variety of network media, but when installing a new network today, the choice for a bounded (cabled) network comes down to unshielded twisted-pair (UTP) or fiber-optic cable. The other alternative is a wireless (unbounded) medium. UTP cable is perfectly suitable for most home and small-business networks. To use UTP, you have to purchase an Ethernet hub (unless you are networking only two computers), and each of your network devices must be connected to the hub using a cable no more than 100 meters long. Category 5 UTP is sufficient for networks running at speeds up to 100 Mbps. For speeds up to 1,000 Mbps (1 Gbps), use either Category 5e or Category 6 UTP cables. Cat 5e transmits at 100 MHz and Cat 6 transmits at 250 MHz. Both have a maximum length of 100 meters when being used for 1 Gbps networking. The difference is if the Cat 6 is used in a 10 Gbps network, and then it gets cut down to between 37 and 55 meters, depending on the crosstalk environment.

If you are in a situation where the locations of your computers call for longer segments, however, or the network must operate in an environment with extreme amounts of electromagnetic interference (EMI) present, you can opt to use fiber-optic cable. Fiber-optic cable is immune to EMI and supports longer segments, but it is also more expensive than UTP and more difficult to install.

For a small network, the ease of installation is often a major factor in the selection of a network medium. An Ethernet network using UTP is the simplest type of cabled network to install. UTP Ethernet NICs, hubs, and prefabricated cables are available in almost any computer store; all you have to do is use the cables to connect the computers to the hub. (If your computers do not have a NIC, you will have to install the adapters before making the connection.)

The same is not true for fiber-optic cables, which are generally purchased as components (bulk cable, connectors, and so on) from professional suppliers. Unless you are willing to spend a good deal of money, time, and effort on learning about fiber-optic cabling, you are not going to install it yourself.

It's possible to install UTP cable from components also, and this is usually how professional, internal installations are performed. An internal cable installation is one in which the cables are installed inside wall cavities and drop ceilings. The only elements of the installation that are visible to the network user are the wall plates to which their computers are attached. This type of installation is neater than an external one that uses prefabricated cables that are usually left exposed, but it requires more expertise to perform correctly, as well as additional tools and access to internal wall cavities. For a small-business network in a traditionally designed office space, a small-scale internal installation is feasible, but homeowners are less likely to want to drill holes in their walls, floors, and ceilings for the installation of cables, despite a greater concern for the installation's cosmetic appearance.

For network installations where cables are impractical or undesirable, you can also elect to install a wireless LAN. There are many products now on the market at competitive prices, and for home users wanting to network their computers without leaving cables exposed or performing a major cable installation, this solution can be ideal.

Choosing a Network Speed

Another consideration when designing an Ethernet LAN is the speed at which the network will run. East Ethernet runs at 100 Mbps, and Gigabit Ethernet runs at 1,000 Mbps. You can find many Ethernet NICs that support either speed. The NIC autodetects the speed of the hub to which it's attached and configures itself accordingly.

Designing an Internetwork

The design elements discussed thus far apply to large internetworks as well as to small, single-segment LANs. Even the largest internetwork consists of individual LANs that require the same components as a stand-alone LAN, such as computers, NICs, cables, hubs, and switches. For a large internetwork with more varied requirements, you can design each LAN separately, selecting protocols and hardware that best suit the physical environment and the requirements of the users, or you can create a uniform design suitable for all of the LANs. Once you get beyond the individual LANs, however, you face the problem of connecting them to form the internetwork. The following sections examine the technologies you can use to do this.

Segments and Backbones

The traditional configuration for a private internetwork is to have a series of LANs (called *network segments* or sometimes *horizontal networks*) connected using another, separate network called a *backbone*. A backbone is nothing more than a network that connects other networks, forming an internetwork. The individual segments can be networks that service workgroups, departments, floors of a building, or even whole buildings. Each of the segments is then connected to a

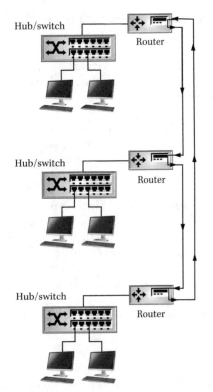

Hub/switch

Router

Hub/switch

Router

Hub/switch

Router

Figure 9-1   An example of multiple LANs, connected by a backbone

backbone network, using a router or a switch, as shown in Figure 9-l. This enables a workstation on any of the networks to communicate with any other workstation. The term *backbone* can refer to a LAN that connects other LANs (usually in the same building or campus) or to a network of wide area links that connect networks or internetworks at remote locations.

One of the most common configurations for a large internetwork that encompasses an entire building with multiple floors is to have a separate LAN connecting all of the network devices on each floor (which is the origin of the term *horizontal network*) and a backbone network running vertically between the floors, connecting all of the LANs. Of course, the configuration you use must depend on the building in which the internetwork is installed. If your entire organization is housed in an enormous building with only two floors, you will probably have to create several LANs on each floor and connect them with a backbone that runs throughout the building.

When two computers on the same LAN communicate with each other, the traffic stays on that local network. However, when the communicating computers are on different LANs, the traffic goes through the router connecting the source computer to the backbone and then to the LAN on which the destination computer is located. It is also common practice to connect network resources required by all of the internetwork's users directly to the backbone, instead of to one of the horizontal networks. For example, if you have a single e-mail server for your entire organization, connecting it to one of the horizontal networks forces all of the e-mail client traffic from the entire internetwork to travel to that segment, possibly overburdening it. Connecting the server to the backbone network enables the traffic from all of the horizontal segments to reach it equitably. Because the backbone is shared by the horizontal networks, it carries all of the internetwork traffic generated by each of the computers on every LAN. This can be a great deal of traffic, and for this reason, the backbone typically runs at a higher speed than the horizontal networks. Backbones may also have to traverse greater distances than horizontal networks, so it is common for them to use fiber-optic cable, which can span much longer distances than copper.

When the concept of the backbone network originated, the typical departmental LAN was relatively slow, running 10 Mbps Ethernet. The first backbones were thick Ethernet trunks, selected because the RG-8 coaxial cable could be installed in segments up to 500 meters long. These backbones ran at the same speed as the horizontal networks, however. To support all of the internetwork traffic, a distributed backbone running at a higher speed was needed. This led to the use of data link layer protocols like Fiber Distributed Data Interface (FDDI). FDDI ran at 100 Mbps, which was faster than anything else at the time, and it used fiber-optic cable, which can span much greater distances than thick Ethernet.

Once Fast Ethernet products arrived on the market, the situation changed by an order of magnitude; 100 Mbps horizontal networks became common, and an even faster backbone technology was needed to keep up with the traffic load they generate. This led to the development of protocols like Asynchronous Transfer Mode (ATM), running at speeds up to 655 Mbps, and Gigabit Ethernet, at 1,000 Mbps.

Distributed and Collapsed Backbones

There are two basic types of backbone LANs in general use: the *distributed backbone* and the *collapsed backbone*. In a distributed backbone, the backbone takes the form of a separate cable segment that runs throughout the enterprise and is connected to each of the horizontal networks using a router or switch. In a collapsed backbone, the hub on each of the horizontal networks is connected to a centrally located modular router or switch (see Figure 9-2). This router or switch functions as the backbone for the entire internetwork by passing traffic between the horizontal networks. This type of backbone uses no additional cable segment because the central router/switch has individual modules for each network, connected by a backplane. The *backplane* is an internal communications bus that takes the place of the backbone cable segment in a distributed backbone network.

The advantage of a collapsed backbone is that internetwork traffic has to pass through only one router on the way to its destination, unlike a distributed backbone, which has separate routers connecting each network to the backbone. The disadvantage of a collapsed backbone is that the hub on each network must connect to the central router with one cable segment. Depending on the layout of the site and the location of the router, this distance may be too long for copper cable.

Because a collapsed backbone does not use a separate cable segment to connect the horizontal networks, it does not need its own protocol. Today's technology has made the collapsed backbone a practical solution.

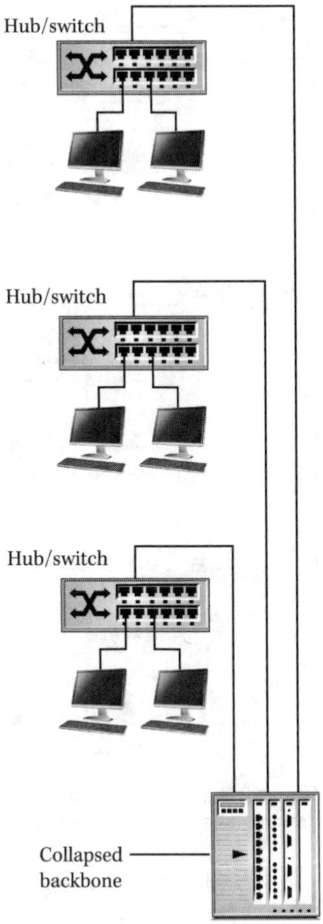

While this may be an ideal solution for a new network being constructed today, there are thousands of existing networks that still use 10 Mbps Ethernet or other relatively slow protocols on their horizontal networks and can't easily adapt to the collapsed backbone concept. Some or all of the horizontal networks might be using older media, such as Category 3 UTP or even thin Ethernet, and can't support the long cable runs to a central router. The horizontal networks might even be in separate buildings on a campus, in which case a collapsed backbone would require each building to have a cable run to the location of the router. In cases like these, a distributed backbone is necessary.

Figure 9-2   A single router or switch connects all of the LANs in a collapsed backbone.

Backbone Fault Tolerance

Because it provides all internetwork communications, the backbone network is a vitally important part of the overall design. A horizontal network that can't access the backbone is isolated. Computers on that LAN can communicate with each other but not with the computers on other LANs, which can cut them off from vital network services. To ensure continuous access

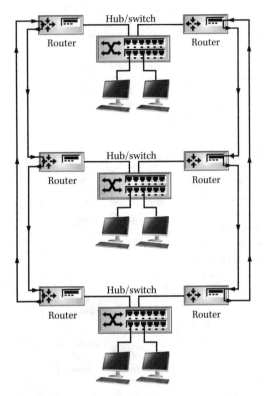

to the backbone, some internetworks design redundant elements into the plan for fault-tolerance purposes. You can, for example, use two routers on each LAN, both of which connect to the backbone network hub so that if one router fails, the other provides continued access to the rest of the network. Some designs go so far as to include two separate distributed backbone networks.

This plan also calls for two routers on each horizontal network, but in this case, the routers are connected to two different backbone networks, as shown in Figure 9-3. This way, the internetwork can continue to function despite the failure of a router, a backbone hub, or any backbone cable segment. Another benefit of this design is the ability to balance the internetwork traffic load among the two backbones. By configuring half of the computers to use one backbone and half the other (by varying their default gateway addresses), you split the internetwork traffic between the two. This can make the use of Ethernet on both the horizontal and backbone networks a practical proposition, even on a highly trafficked network. With a single backbone connecting Ethernet LANs, you may find that you need to use Gigabit Ethernet or another high-speed protocol to support the internetwork traffic.

Figure 9-3 Redundant backbones can provide both load balancing and fault tolerance.

Selecting a Backbone LAN Protocol

The protocol that you use on the backbone connecting your horizontal networks should depend on the amount of traffic it has to carry and the distance it has to span. In some organizations, most of the network communications are limited to the individual horizontal LANs. If, for example, your company consists of several departments that are largely autonomous, each with their own servers on a separate horizontal LAN, all of the intradepartmental traffic remains on the horizontal network and never reaches the backbone. In a case like this, you can probably use the same technology on the backbone as the horizontal LANs, such as Ethernet throughout. If, on the other hand, your company consists of departments that all rely on the same resources to do their work, such as a central database, it makes sense to connect the database servers directly to the backbone. When you do this, however, the backbone must be able to support the traffic generated by all of the horizontal networks combined. If the horizontal networks are running Fast Ethernet, the backbone should usually use a faster technology, such as Gigabit Ethernet, in order to keep up.

The distance that the backbone LAN must span and the environment in which it's used can also affect the protocol selection. If your site is large enough that the backbone cable runs are likely to exceed the 100-meter limit for unshielded twisted-pair cable, you should consider using fiber-optic cable. Fiber optic is also the preferred solution if you have to connect horizontal LANs that are located in different buildings on the same campus. Fiber optic is more expensive to purchase and install than UTP, but it is interoperable with copper cable in most cases. For example, you can purchase Fast Ethernet hubs and routers that support both cable types so that you can use UTP on your horizontal networks and fiber optic on the backbone.

Connecting to Remote Networks

In addition to connecting LANs at the same site, many internetworks use a backbone to connect to remote networks. In some cases, the organization consists of multiple offices in different cities or countries that must communicate with each other. If each office has its own internetwork, connecting the offices with WAN links forms another backbone that adds a third level to the network hierarchy and creates a single, enterprise internetwork. However, even an organization with one internetwork at a single location is likely to need a WAN connection to an Internet service provider so that users can access e-mail and other Internet services.

The technology you select for your WAN connections depends on factors such as the amount of bandwidth your network needs, when it needs it, and, as always, your budget. You can use anything from dial-on-demand telephone connections to high-speed leased lines to flexible bandwidth solutions, such as frame relay.

Selecting a WAN Topology

Another factor in selecting a WAN technology is the topology you will use to connect your various sites. WAN topologies are more flexible than those on LANs, which are dictated by the data link and physical layer protocols you elect to use. You can use WAN links to build an internetwork in many different ways. For example, the full mesh topology, when used on a WAN, consists of a separate, dedicated link (such as a leased line) between each two sites in your organization. If you have five offices in different cities, each office has four separate WAN links connecting it to the other offices, for a total of ten links (see Figure 9-4). If you have eight offices, a total of 28 separate WAN links are required. This arrangement provides the greatest amount of fault tolerance since a single link failure affects only the two sites involved, as well as the most efficient network, since each site can communicate directly with each of the other sites. However, this solution can also be expensive as well as wasteful, unless your network generates sufficient WAN traffic between each pair of sites to fill all of these links most of the time.

A full mesh topology, consisting of individual links between the sites, assumes the use of dedicated, point-to-point WAN connections such as leased lines. However, there are alternatives to this type of link that can provide what amounts to a full mesh topology at much less expense. Frame relay uses a single leased line at each site to connect to a service provider's network, called the *cloud*. With all of the sites connected to the same cloud (using access points local to each location), each site can establish a virtual circuit to every other site as needed.

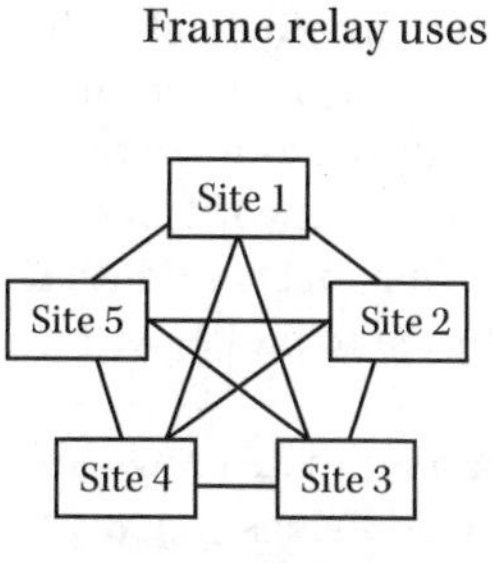

At the other end of the spectrum from the full mesh topology is the star topology, which designates one site as the main office (or hub) and consists of a separate, dedicated connection between the hub and each of the other branch sites. This topology uses the fewest number of WAN links to connect all of the sites, providing the greatest economy, and enables the main office to communicate directly with each of the branch sites. However, when two of the branch sites have to communicate, they must do so by going through the

Figure 9-4   The full mesh WAN topology

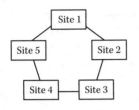

Figure 9-5   The ring
WAN topology

hub. Whether the star topology is suitable for your network depends on whether the branch sites frequently need to communicate with each other.

A *ring* topology has each site connected to two other sites, as shown in Figure 9-5. This topology uses only one link more than a star, but it provides a greater degree of fault tolerance. If any one link fails, it is still possible for any two sites to communicate by sending traffic around the ring in the other direction. By contrast, a link failure in a star internetwork disconnects one of the sites from the others completely. The disadvantage of the ring is the delay introduced by the need for traffic to pass through multiple sites in order to reach its destination, in most cases. A site on a star internetwork is never more than two hops from any other site, while ring sites may have to pass through several hops.

Each of these topologies represents an extreme example of a network communication technique, but none of them has to be followed absolutely in every case. You can, for example, create a partial mesh topology by eliminating some of the links from the full mesh design. Not all of your sites may require a dedicated link to every other site, so you can eliminate the extraneous links, thus reducing the cost of the network. When a site has to communicate with another site to which it does not have a direct connection, it can go through one of its connected sites instead. In the same way, you can build more fault tolerance into a star network by having two hub sites instead of one and connecting each of the other sites to both hubs. This requires twice as many links as a standard star topology but still fewer than a full mesh.

Planning Internet Access

Connecting a network to the Internet is usually far less complicated than connecting multiple sites with WAN links. Even if your internetwork consists of several sites, it is more common to equip each one with its own Internet connection, rather than connect one site and have the other sites access the Internet through the intersite WAN. The WAN technology you use to connect each site to the Internet should once again depend on the bandwidth you require and your budget.

Locating Equipment

Designing the individual LANs that make up the internetwork is similar to designing a single, stand-alone LAN, except you must work the backbone connections into the design. Large internetworks are more likely to use internal bulk cable installations for the network segments, rather than the prefabricated, external cables commonly used for home and small-business networks. In an internal installation, cables run inside walls and ceilings and terminate at wall plates and patch panels. This type of installation is much more complicated than an external one where the cables are left exposed. Therefore, this installation is frequently outsourced to a contractor who specializes in on-premises wiring. For these reasons, a detailed network plan showing the route of each cable and the location of each wall plate and patch panel is essential. You don't want to have to call the contractor in after the installation is finished to pull additional cables.

Designing such a network and creating the plan are tasks that require an intimate knowledge of the building in which the network is to be located. As with a home or small-business LAN, you must decide where all of the computers and other network devices are going to be located and then work out how you are going to run the cables that connect them to the hub. For an internetwork design, you also have to decide where you're going to put the router that connects each LAN to the backbone (in the case of a distributed backbone network) or how you're going to connect each LAN to the main router/switch (in the case of a collapsed backbone network).

Wiring Closets

In the classic example of a multifloored office building with a horizontal network on each floor and a distributed backbone connecting them vertically, it is common practice to have a telecommunications room, often called a *wiring closet*, on each floor. This closet can serve as the location for the patch panel where all of the cable runs for the floor terminate, as well as the hub that connects all of the devices on the floor into a LAN and the router that connects the LAN to the backbone network. It's also possible to install workgroup or even enterprise servers in these closets. To facilitate the backbone cabling, the best arrangement is for the wiring closets on each floor to be on top of each other, with a chase or wiring conduit running vertically through them and connecting all of the closets in the building.

To some people, the term *wiring closet* might invoke visions of hubs and routers shoved into a dark little space along with mops and buckets, but this should definitely not be the case. Wiring closets may already exist, even in a building not already cabled for a data network, to support telephone equipment and other building services. The closet may indeed be a small space, but it should be well lit and have room enough to work in, if necessary. The room is called a closet because there is typically no room (or need) for desks and workstations inside. Most of the routers, servers, and other networking equipment available today can be equipped with remote administration capabilities, which minimizes the need to actually open the closet to physically access the equipment. Unlike an equipment storage closet, a wiring or server closet must also maintain an appropriate environment for the equipment inside. A space that is not heated in the winter nor air conditioned in the summer can greatly shorten the life of delicate electronics. Wiring closets must also be kept locked, of course, to protect the valuable equipment from theft and "experimentation" by unauthorized personnel.

Data Centers

Wiring closets are eminently suitable for distributed backbone networks because this type of network requires that a relatively large amount of expensive equipment be scattered throughout the building. Another organizational option, better suited for a collapsed backbone network, is to have a single data center containing all of the networking equipment for the entire enterprise. In this context, a data center is really just a larger, more elaborate wiring closet. Typically, a data center is a secured room or suite that has been outfitted to support large amounts of electronic equipment. This usually includes special air conditioning, extra power lines, power conditioning and backup, additional fixtures such as a modular floor with a wiring space beneath it, and extra security to prevent unauthorized access.

The center typically contains the network's enterprise servers and the routers that join the LANs together and provide Internet and WAN access. If the building housing the network is not too large, you can place all of the hubs for the individual LANs in the data center as well. This means that every wall plate in the building to which a computer is connected has a cable connecting it to a hub in the data center. This arrangement is feasible only if the length of the cable runs are less than 100 meters, assuming that the horizontal networks are using UTP cable. If the distance between any of your wall plate locations and the data center exceeds 100 meters, you must either use fiber-optic cable (which supports longer segments) or place the hubs at the location of each LAN. If you choose to do the latter, you only have to find a relatively secure place for each hub.

When the hubs are distributed around the building, you need only one cable run from each hub to the data center. If you use centralized hubs, each of your cable runs extends all the way from the computer to the data center. Not only can this use much more cable, but the sheer bulk of the cables might exceed the size of the wiring spaces available in the building. However, the advantage of having centralized hubs is that network support personnel can easily service them and monitor their status, and connecting them to the hub or switch that joins the LANs into an internetwork is simply a matter of running a cable across the room.

Typically, the equipment in a data center is mounted in racks, which can extend from floor to ceiling. Virtually all manufacturers of servers, hubs, routers, and other network devices intended for large enterprise networks to have products designed to bolt into these standard-sized racks, which makes it easier to organize and access the equipment in the data center.

Finalizing the Design

As you flesh out the network design in detail, you can begin to select specific vendors, products, and contractors. This process can include shopping for the best hardware prices in catalogs and on web sites, evaluating software products, interviewing and obtaining estimates from cable installation contractors, and investigating service providers for WAN technologies. This is the most critical part of the design process, for several reasons. First, this is the point at which you'll be able to determine the actual cost of building the network, not just an estimate. Second, it is at this phase that you must make sure all the components you select are actually capable of performing as your preliminary plan expects them to. If, for example, you discover that the router model with all of the features you need is no longer available, you may have to modify the plan to use a different type of router or to implement the feature you need in another way. Third, the concrete information you develop at this stage enables you to create a deployment schedule. A network design plan can *never* have too much detail. Documenting your network as completely as possible, both before, during, and after construction, can only help you to maintain and repair it later. The planning process for a large network can be long and complicated, but it is rare for any of the time spent to be wasted.

Network Protocols

10   Ethernet Basics

Ethernet is the data link layer protocol used by the vast majority of the local area networks operating today. Since the 1990s, the Ethernet standards have been revised and updated to support many different types of network media and to provide dramatic speed increases over the original protocol. Because all of the Ethernet variants operate using the same basic principles and because the high-speed Ethernet technologies were designed with backward compatibility in mind, upgrading a standard network is usually relatively easy. This is in marked contrast to other high-speed technologies such as Fiber Distributed Data Interface (FDDI) and Asynchronous Transfer Mode (ATM), for which upgrades can require extensive infrastructure modifications, such as new cabling, as well as training and acclimation for the personnel supporting the new technology.

This chapter examines the fundamental Ethernet mechanisms and how they provide a unified interface between the physical layer of the Open Systems Interconnection (OSI) reference model and multiple protocols operating at the network layer. Then you'll learn how newer technologies such as Fast Ethernet and Gigabit Ethernet improve on the older standards and provide sufficient bandwidth for the needs of virtually any network application. Finally, there will be a discussion of upgrade strategies and real-world troubleshooting techniques to help you improve the performance of your own network.

Ethernet Defined

The Ethernet protocol provides a unified interface to the network medium that enables an operating system to transmit and receive multiple network layer protocols simultaneously. Like most of the data link layer protocols used on LANs, Ethernet is, in technical terms, connectionless and unreliable. Ethernet makes its best effort to transmit data to the appointed destination, but no mechanism exists to guarantee a successful delivery. Instead, services such as guaranteed delivery are left up to the protocols operating at the higher layers of the OSI model, depending on whether the data warrants it.

NOTE In this context, the term *unreliable* means only that the protocol lacks a means of acknowledging that packets have been successfully received.

As defined by the Ethernet standards, the protocol consists of three essential components:

- A series of physical layer guidelines that specify the cable types, wiring restrictions, and signaling methods for Ethernet networks

- A frame format that defines the order and functions of the bits transmitted in an Ethernet packet

- A media access control (MAC) mechanism called Carrier Sense Multiple Access with Collision Detection (CSMA/CD) that enables all of the computers on the LAN equal access to the network medium.

From a product perspective, the Ethernet protocol consists of the network interface adapters installed in the network's computers usually in the form of network interface cards (NICs), the network adapter drivers the operating system uses to communicate with the network adapters, and the hubs and cables you use to connect the computers. When you purchase network adapters and hubs, you must be sure they all support the same Ethernet standards for them to be able to work together optimally.

Ethernet Standards

When Ethernet was first designed in the 1970s, it carried data over a baseband connection using coaxial cable running at 10 Mbps and a signaling system called Manchester encoding. This eventually came to be known as *thick Ethernet* because the cable itself was approximately 1 centimeter wide, about the thickness of a garden hose (indeed, its color and rigidity led to its being referred to as the "frozen yellow garden hose" by whimsical network administrators). The first Ethernet standard, which was titled "The Ethernet, a Local Area Network: Data Link Layer and Physical Layer Specifications," was published in 1980 by a consortium of companies that included DEC, Intel, and Xerox, giving rise to the acronym DIX, thus, the document became known as the DIX Ethernet standard.

Ethernet II

The DIX 2.0 standard, commonly known as DIX Ethernet II, was published in 1982 and expanded the physical layer options to include a thinner type of coaxial cable, which came to be called *thin Ethernet, ThinNet,* or *cheapernet* because it was less expensive than the original thick coaxial cable.

IEEE 802.3

During this time, a desire arose to build an international standard around the Ethernet protocol. In 1980, a working group was formed by a standards-making body called the Institute of Electrical and Electronics Engineers (IEEE), under the supervision of their Local and Metropolitan Area Networks (LAN/MAN) Standards Committee, for the purpose of developing an "Ethernet-like" standard. This committee is known by the number 802, and the working group was given the designation IEEE 802.3. The resulting standard, published in 1985, was called the "IEEE 802.3 Carrier Sense Multiple Access with Collision Detection (CSMA/CD) Access Method and Physical Layer Specifications." The term *Ethernet* was (and still is) scrupulously avoided by the IEEE 802.3

group because they wanted to avoid creating any impression that the standard was based on a commercial product that had been registered as a trademark by Xerox. However, with a few minor differences, this document essentially defines an Ethernet network under another name, and to this day, the products conforming to the IEEE 802.3 standard are called by the name Ethernet.

NOTE The IEEE Standards are available for downloading at http://standards.ieee.org/about/get/802/802.3.html.

DIX Ethernet and IEEE 802.3 Differences

While the DIX Ethernet II standard treated the data link layer as a single entity, the IEEE standards divide the layer into two sublayers, called *logical link control* (LLC) and *media access control* (MAC). The LLC sublayer isolates the functions that occur beneath it from those above it and is defined by a separate standard: IEEE 802.2. The IEEE committee uses the same abstraction layer with the network types defined by other 802 standards, such as the 802.5 Token Ring network. The use of the LLC sublayer with the 802.3 protocol also led to a small but important change in the protocol's frame format, as described in the "The Ethernet Frame" section later in this chapter. The MAC sublayer defines the mechanism by which Ethernet systems arbitrate access to the network medium, as discussed in the forthcoming section "CSMA/CD."

By 1990, the IEEE 802.3 standard had been developed further and now included other physical layer options that made coaxial cable all but obsolete, such as the twisted-pair cable commonly used in telephone installations and fiber-optic cable. Because it is easy to work with, inexpensive, and reliable, twisted-pair (or 10Base-T) Ethernet quickly became the most popular medium for this protocol. Most of the Ethernet networks installed today use twisted-pair cable, which continues to be supported by the new, higher-speed standards. Fiber-optic technology enables network connections to span much longer distances than copper and is immune from electromagnetic interference.

Table 10-1 lists the primary differences between the IEEE 802.3 standard and the DIX Ethernet II standard.

IEEE Shorthand Identifiers

The IEEE is also responsible for the shorthand identifiers that are often used when referring to specific physical layer Ethernet implementations, such as 100Base-T for a Fast Ethernet network. In this identifier, the 100 refers to the speed of the network, which is 100 Mbps. All of the Ethernet identifiers begin with 10, 100, or 1000.

	IEEE 802.3	DIX Ethernet II
Physical Layer Options	Coaxial, UTP, fiber optic	Coaxial only
Bits 13 to 14 of the Frame Header	Length of the date field	Ethertype
External Transceiver Test	SQE test	Collision presence test (heartbeat)

Table 10-1 Differences Between the IEEE 802.3 Standards and the Old DIX Ethernet II Standards

Identifier	Common Name	Network Type
10Base5	Thick Ethernet	10 Mbps bus network using RG-8 coaxial cable in segments up to 500 meters long
10Base2	Thin Ethernet	10 Mbps bus network using RG-58 coaxial cable in segments up to 185 meters long
10Base-T	Twisted-pair Ethernet	10 Mbps star network using twisted-pair cable
10Base-F	Fiber-optic Ethernet	Generic term for three types of 10 Mbps fiber-optic networks: 10Base-FB, 10Base-FP, and 10Base-FL
100Base-T	Fast Ethernet	Generic term for all of the Fast Ethernet physical layer options, including twisted-pair and fiber-optic cables
100Base-X	Fast Ethernet	Generic term for the 100Base-TX and 100Base-FX standards, both of which use the same 4B/5B block-encoding method
100Base-T4	Fast Ethernet	100 Mbps network using all four of the pairs in a Category 3 twisted-pair cable
1000Base-T	Gigabit Ethernet	1,000 Mbps network using four of the wire pairs in a Category 5 twisted-pair cable

Table 10-2 IEEE Shorthand Identifiers for Ethernet Networks

The *Base* refers to the fact that the network uses baseband transmissions. As explained in Chapter 1, a baseband network is one in which the network medium carries only one signal at a time, as opposed to a broadband network, which can carry many signals simultaneously. All of the Ethernet variants are baseband, except for one broadband version, which is rarely, if ever, used.

The *T* in 100Base-T specifies the type of medium the network uses. For example, the *T* in 100Base-T stands for twisted-pair cable. Table 10-2 explains some of the Ethernet identifiers. For a complete list, go to http://standards.ieee.org/about/get/802/802.3.html and enter the specific standard.

NOTE Beginning with the 10Base-T specification, the IEEE began including a hyphen after the *Base* designator to prevent people from pronouncing 10Base-T as "ten bassett."

CSMA/CD

Today, many of the issues with collisions on an Ethernet network have been eliminated with shared, full-duplex, point-to-point channels between the node originating transmission and the receiver. However, since CSMA/CD is supported for backward compatibility, IEEE 802.3 still defines the specification.

Like any MAC method, CSMA/CD enabled the computers on the network to share a single baseband medium without data loss. There are no priorities on an Ethernet network as far as media access is concerned; the protocol was designed so that every node has equal access rights to the network medium. Figure 10-1 illustrates the process by which CSMA/CD arbitrates access to the network medium on an Ethernet network. While obsolete in today's Ethernet

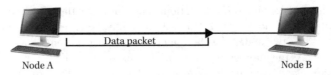

Figure 10-1   If Node B begins to transmit data before the transmission from Node A reaches it, a collision will occur.

networks, it is supported for compatibility with earlier networks, so you need to understand the process.

When a node on an Ethernet network wants to transmit data, it first monitors the network medium to see whether it is currently in use. This is the *carrier sense* phase of the process. If the node detects traffic on the network, it pauses for a short interval and then listens to the network again. Once the network is clear, any of the nodes on the network may use it to transmit their data. This is the *multiple access* phase. This mechanism in itself arbitrates access to the medium, but it is not without fault.

It is entirely possible for two (or more) systems to detect a clear network and then transmit their data at nearly the same moment. This results in what the 802.3 standard calls a *signal quality error* (SQE) or, as the condition is more commonly known, a *packet collision*. Collisions occur when one system begins transmitting its data and another system performs its carrier sense during the brief interval before the first bit in the transmitted packet reaches it. This interval is known as the *contention time* (or *slot time*) because each of the systems involved believes it has begun to transmit first. Every node on the network is, therefore, always in one of three possible states: transmission, contention, or idle.

When packets from two different nodes collide, an abnormal condition is created on the cable that travels on toward both systems. On a coaxial network, the voltage level spikes to the point at which it is the same or greater than the combined levels of the two transmitters (+/−0.85V). On a twisted-pair or fiber-optic network, the anomaly takes the form of signal activity on both the transmit and receive circuits at the same time.

When each transmitting system detects the abnormality, it recognizes that a collision has taken place, immediately stops sending data, and begins taking action to correct the problem. This is the *collision detection* phase of the process. Because the packets that collided are considered to be corrupted, both the systems involved transmit a *jam pattern* that fills the entire network cable with voltage, informing the other systems on the network of the collision and preventing them from initiating their own transmissions.

The jam pattern is a sequence of 32 bits that can have any value, as long as it does not equal the value of the cyclic redundancy check (CRC) calculation in the damaged packet's frame check sequence (FCS) field. A system receiving an Ethernet packet uses the FCS field to determine whether the data in the packet has been received without error. As long as the jam pattern differs from the correct CRC value, all receiving nodes will discard the packet. In most cases, network adapters simply transmit 32 bits with the value 1. The odds of this also being the value of the CRC for the packet are 1 in 232 (in other words, not likely).

After transmitting the jam pattern, the nodes involved in the collision both reschedule their transmissions using a randomized delay interval they calculate with an algorithm that uses their MAC addresses as a unique factor. This process is called *backing off*. Because both nodes perform their own independent backoff calculations, the chances of them both retransmitting at the same time are substantially diminished. This is a possibility, however, and if another collision occurs between the same two nodes, they both increase the possible length of their delay intervals and back off again. As the number of possible values for the backoff interval increases, the probability of the systems again selecting the same interval diminishes. The Ethernet specifications call this process *truncated binary exponential backoff* (or *truncated BEB*). An Ethernet system will attempt to transmit a packet as many as 16 times (reported as an "excessive collision error"), and if a collision results each time, the packet is discarded.

Collisions

Every system on an Ethernet network uses the CSMA/CD MAC mechanism for every packet it transmits, so the entire process obviously occurs quickly. Most of the collisions that occur on a typical Ethernet network are resolved in microseconds (millionths of a second). The most important thing to understand when it comes to Ethernet media arbitration is that packet collisions are natural and expected occurrences on this type of network, and they do not necessarily signify a problem. If you use a protocol analyzer or other network monitoring tool to analyze the traffic on an Ethernet network, you will see that a certain number of collisions always occur.

NOTE The type of packet collision described here is normal and expected, but there is a different type, called a *late collision*, that signifies a serious network problem. The difference between the two types of collisions is that normal collisions are detectable and late collisions are not. See the next section, "Late Collisions," for more information.

Normal packet collisions become a problem only when there are too many of them and significant network delays begin to accumulate. The combination of the backoff intervals and the retransmission of the packets themselves (sometimes more than once) incurs delays that are multiplied by the number of packets transmitted by each computer and by the number of computers on the network.

The fundamental fault of the CSMA/CD mechanism was that the more traffic there was on the network, the more collisions there were likely to be. The utilization of a network is based on the number of systems connected to it and the amount of data they send and receive over the network. When expressed as a percentage, the network utilization represents the proportion of the time the network is actually in use—that is, the amount of time that data is actually in transit. On an average Ethernet network, the utilization was likely to be somewhere in the 30 to 40 percent range. When the utilization increases to approximately 80 percent, the number of collisions increases to the point at which the performance of the network noticeably degrades. In the most extreme case, known as a *collapse,* the network is so heavily trafficked, it is almost perpetually in a state of contention, waiting for collisions to be resolved. This condition can conceivably be caused by the coincidental occurrence of repeated collisions, but it is more likely to result from a malfunctioning network interface that is continuously transmitting bad frames without pausing for carrier sense or collision detection. An adapter in this state is said to be *jabbering.*

NOTE Data link layer protocols that use a token-passing media access control mechanism, such as Token Ring and FDDI, are not subject to performance degradation caused by high-network traffic levels. This is because these protocols use a mechanism that makes it impossible for more than one system on the network to transmit at any one time. On networks like these, collisions are not normal occurrences and signify a serious problem. For more information on token passing, see Chapter 12.

Late Collisions

The physical layer specifications for the Ethernet protocol are designed so that the first 64 bytes of every packet transmission completely fill the entire aggregate length of cable in the collision domain. Thus, by the time a node has transmitted the first 64 bytes of a packet, every other node on the network has received at least the first bit of that packet. At this point, the other nodes will not transmit their own data because their carrier sense mechanism has detected traffic on the network.

It is essential for the first bit of each transmitted packet to arrive at every node on the network before the last bit leaves the sender. This is because the transmitting system can detect a collision only while it is still transmitting data. (Remember, on a twisted-pair or fiber-optic network, it is the presence of signals on the transmit and receive wires at the same time that indicates a collision.) Once the last bit has left the sending node, the sender considers the transmission to have completed successfully and erases the packet from the network adapter's memory buffer. It is because of this collision detection mechanism that every packet transmitted on an Ethernet network must be at least 64 bytes in length, even if the sending system has to pad it with useless (0) bits to reach that length.

If a collision should occur after the last bit has left the sending node, it is called a *late collision*, or sometimes an *out-of-window collision*. (To distinguish between the two types of collisions, the normally occurring type was sometimes called an *early collision*.) Because the sending system has no way of detecting a late collision, it considers the packet to have been transmitted successfully, even though the data has actually been destroyed. Any data lost as a result of a late transmission cannot be retransmitted by a data link layer process. It is up to the protocols operating at higher layers of the OSI model to detect the data loss and to use their own mechanisms to force a retransmission. This process can take up to 100 times longer than an Ethernet retransmission, which is one reason why this type of collision is a problem.

Late collisions result from several different causes. If a network interface adapter should malfunction and transmit a packet less than 64 bytes long (called a *runt*), the last bit could leave the sender before the packet has fully propagated around the Internet. In other cases, the adapter's carrier sense mechanism might fail, causing it to transmit at the wrong time. In both instances, you should replace the malfunctioning adapter. Another possible cause of late collisions is a network that does not fall within the Ethernet cabling guidelines.

Physical Layer Guidelines

The Ethernet specifications define not only the types of cable you can use with the protocol, but also the installation guidelines for the cable, such as the maximum length of cable segments and the number of hubs or repeaters permitted. As explained earlier, the configuration of the physical layer medium is a crucial element of the CSMA/CD media access control mechanism. If the

Designation	10Base5 (Thick Ethernet)	10Base2 (Thin Ethernet)	10Base-T (Twisted Pair)	10Base-FL (Fiber Optic)
Maximum Segment Length (Meters)	500 meters	185 meters	100 meters	1,000/2,000
Maximum Nodes per Cable Segment	100	30	2	2
Cable Type	RG-8 coaxial	RG-58 coaxial	Category 3 and 5 unshielded twisted pair	62.5/125 multimode fiber optic
Connector Type	N	BNC	RJ-45	ST

Table 10-3 Physical Layer Options for 10 Mbps Ethernet

overall distance between two systems on the network is too long or there are too many repeaters, diminished performance can result, which is quite difficult to diagnose and troubleshoot.

Tables 10-3 and 10-4 display the cabling guidelines, which vary for each of the media to compensate for the performance characteristics of the different cable types.

10Base-5 (Thick Ethernet)

Thick Ethernet, or *ThickNet*, used RG-8 coaxial cable in a bus topology to connect up to 100 nodes to a single segment no more than 500 meters long. Because it can span long distances and is well shielded, thick Ethernet was commonly used for backbone networks in the early days of Ethernet. However, RG-8 cable, like all of the coaxial cables used in Ethernet networks, cannot support transmission rates faster than 10 Mbps, which limits its utility as a backbone medium. As soon as a faster alternative was available (such as FDDI), most network administrators abandoned thick Ethernet. However, although it is hardly ever used anymore, the components of a thick Ethernet network are a good illustration of the various components involved in the physical layer of an Ethernet network.

Designation	100Base-T (TX) (Uses Two of the Four Twisted Pairs in the Cable)	100Base T4 (Uses Four of the Four Twisted Pairs in the Cable)	100Base-FX	1000Base-T	10GBase-T
Maximum Segment Length (Meters)	100	100	2,000	100	300
Cable Type	Cat 5 UTP	Cat 5 UTP	Fiber optic	Cat 5 UTP	Cat 6, 6a, or 7 UTP
Connector Type	RJ-45	RJ-45	MT-RJ	RJ-45	SFP (small form-factor pluggable transceiver)

Table 10-4 Physical Layer Options for Today's Ethernet Types

The coaxial cable segment on a thick Ethernet network should, whenever possible, be a single unbroken length of cable, or at least be pieced together from the same spool or cable lot using N connectors on each cable end and an N barrel connector between them. There should be as few breaks as possible in the cable, and if you must use cable from different lots, the individual pieces should be 23.4, 70.2, or 117 meters long to minimize the signal reflections that may occur. Both ends of the bus must be terminated with a 50-ohm resistor built into an N terminator, and the cable should be grounded at one (and only one) end using a grounding connector attached to the N terminator.

NOTE For more information on RG-8 and all of the cables used to build Ethernet networks, see Chapter 4.

Unlike all of the other Ethernet physical layer options, the thick Ethernet cable did not run directly to the network interface card in the PC. This is because the coaxial cable itself was large, heavy, and comparatively inflexible. Instead, the NIC is connected to the RG-8 trunk cable with another cable, called the *attachment unit interface* (AUI) cable. The AUI cable has 15-pin D-shell connectors at both ends, one of which plugs directly into the NIC, and the other into a *medium attachment unit* (MAU), also known as a transceiver. The MAU connects to the coaxial cable using a device called the *medium dependent interface* (MDI), which clamps to the cable and makes an electrical connection through holes cut into the insulating sheath. Because of the fanglike appearance of the connector, this device is commonly referred to as a *vampire tap*.

NOTE Do not confuse the MAUs used on thick Ethernet networks with the multistation access units (MAUs) used as hubs on Token Ring networks. The maximum of 100 nodes on a thick Ethernet cable segment (and 30 nodes on a ThinNet segment) is based on the number of MAUs present on the network. Because repeaters include their own MAUs, they count toward the maximum.

NOTE If for no other reason, the DIX Ethernet standard should be fondly remembered for using more sensible names for many of Ethernet's technical concepts, such as *collision* rather than *signal quality error*. The DIX Ethernet name for the medium attachment unit is the *transceiver* (because it both transmits and receives), and its name for the attachment unit interface cable is *transceiver cable*.

Each standard AUI cable on a thick Ethernet network could be up to 50 meters long, which provided for an added degree of flexibility in the installation. Standard AUI cables were the same thickness as the thick Ethernet coaxial and similarly hard to work with. There were also thinner and more flexible "office-grade" AUI cables, but these were limited to a maximum length of 12.5 meters.

The 500-meter maximum length for the thick Ethernet cable made it possible to connect systems at comparatively long distances and provided excellent protection against interference and attenuation. Unfortunately, the cable was difficult to work with and even harder to hide. Today, sites that require long cable segments or better insulation are apt to use fiber optic.

10Base-2 (Thin Ethernet)

Thin Ethernet, or *ThinNet*, was similar in functionality to Thick Ethernet, except that the cable was RG-58 coaxial, about 5 millimeters in diameter, and much more flexible. For thin Ethernet (and all other Ethernet physical layer options except thick Ethernet), the MAU (transceiver) was integrated into the network interface card and no AUI cable was needed.

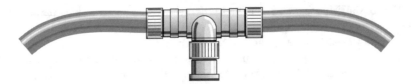

Figure 10-2 Thin Ethernet networks used T-connectors to form a single cable segment connecting up to 30 computers in a bus topology.

Thin Ethernet used Bayonet Neill-Concelman (BNC) connectors and a fitting called a *T-connector* that attaches to the network card in the PC. This connector is sometimes erroneously called a British Naval Connector or Bayonet Nut Connector. You created the network bus by running a cable to one end of the T-connector's crossbar and then using another cable on the other end of the crossbar to connect to the next system, as shown in Figure 10-2. Like thick Ethernet, a thin Ethernet network must be terminated and grounded. The two systems at the ends of the bus must have a terminator containing a 50-ohm resistor on one end of their *T*s to terminate the bus, and one end (only) should be connected to a ground.

NOTE The T-connectors on an Ethernet network had to be directly connected to the network interface cards in the computers. Using a length of cable to join the T-connector to the computer was not permitted.

Because the cable was thinner, thin Ethernet was more prone to interference and attenuation and was limited to a segment length of 185 meters and a maximum of 30 nodes. Each piece of cable forming the segment had to be at least 0.5 meters long.

Connector faults were a common occurrence on thin Ethernet networks because prefabricated cables were relatively rare (compared to twisted pair), and the BNC connectors were usually crimped onto the RG-58 cables by network administrators, which can be a tricky process. Also, some cheap connectors were prone to a condition in which an oxide layer builds up between the conductors resulting in a serious degradation in the network connectivity. These connectors were notoriously sensitive to improper treatment. An accidental tug or a person tripping over one of the two cables connected to each machine easily weakened the connection and caused intermittent transmission problems that are difficult to isolate and diagnose.

10Base-T or 100Base-T (Twisted-Pair Ethernet)

Most of the Ethernet networks today use *unshielded twisted-pair* (UTP) cable, originally known in the Ethernet world as *10Base-T,* which solved several of the problems that plague coaxial cables. Today, the differences are in the speed of transmission.

Among other things, UTP Ethernet networks are

- **Easily hidden** UTP cables can be installed inside walls, floors, and ceilings with standard wall plates providing access to the network. Only a single, thin cable has to run to the computer. Pulling too hard on a UTP cable installed in this manner damages only an easily replaceable patch cable connecting the computer to the wall plate.

- **Fault tolerant**   UTP networks use a star topology in which each computer has its own dedicated cable running to the hub. A break in a cable or a loose connection affects only the single machine to which it is connected.

- **Upgradeable**   UTP cable installation running 10 Mbps Ethernet or 100 Mbps Ethernet can be upgraded at a later time.

Unshielded twisted-pair cable consists of four pairs of wires in a single sheath, with each pair twisted together at regular intervals to protect against crosstalk and 8-pin RJ-45 connectors at both ends. Since this isn't a bus network, no termination or grounding is necessary. Both 10Base-T and 100Base-T Ethernet use only two of the four wire pairs in the cable, however: one pair for transmitting data signals (TD) and one for receiving them (RD), with one wire in each pair having a positive polarity and one a negative.

Unlike coaxial networks, 10Base-T calls for the use of a *hub*. This is a device that functions both as a wiring nexus and as a signal repeater, to which each of the nodes on the network has an individual connection (see Figure 10-3). The maximum length for each cable segment is 100 meters, but because there is nearly always an intervening hub that repeats the signals, the total distance between two nodes can be as much as 200 meters.

UTP cables are typically wired *straight through,* meaning the wire for each pin is connected to the corresponding pin at the other end of the cable. For two nodes to communicate, however, the TD signals generated by each machine must be delivered to the RD connections in the other machine. In most cases, this is accomplished by a crossover circuit within the hub. You can connect two computers directly together without a hub by using a *crossover cable,* though, which connects the TD signals at each end to the RD signals at the other end.

NOTE For more information on network cables and their installation, see Chapter 4. For more information on hubs and repeaters, see Chapter 6.

Fiber-Optic Ethernet

Fiber-optic cable is a radical departure from the copper-based, physical layer options discussed so far. Because it uses pulses of light instead of electric current, fiber optic is immune to

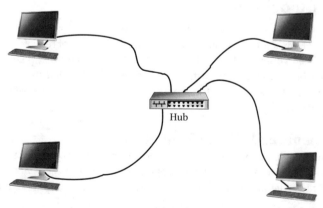

Figure 10-3   10Base-T networks used a hub to connect all the network nodes in a star topology.

electromagnetic interference and is much more resistant to attenuation than copper. As a result, fiber-optic cable can span much longer distances, and because of the electric isolation it provides, it is suitable for network links between buildings. Fiber-optic cable is an excellent medium for data communications, but installing and maintaining it is somewhat more expensive than copper, and it requires completely different tools and skills.

The medium itself on a fiber-optic Ethernet network is two strands of 62.5/125 multimode fiber cable, with one strand used to transmit signals and one to receive them.

There were two main fiber-optic standards for 10 Mbps Ethernet: the original FOIRL standard and 10Base-F, which defines three different fiber-optic configurations called 10Base-FL, 10Base-FB, and 10Base-FP. Of all these standards, 10Base-FL was always the most popular, but running fiber-optic cable at 10 Mbps is an underuse of the medium's potential that borders on the criminal. Now that 100 Mbps data link layer protocols, such as Fast Ethernet and FDDI, run on the same fiber-optic cable, there is no reason to use any of these slower solutions in a new installation.

FOIRL

The original fiber-optic standard for Ethernet from the early 1980s was called the *Fiber-Optic Inter-Repeater Link* (FOIRL). It was designed to function as a link between two repeaters up to 1,000 meters away. Intended for use in campus networks, FOIRL could join two distant networks, particularly those in adjacent buildings, using a fiber-optic cable.

10Base-FL

The 10Base-F supplement was developed by the IEEE 802.3 committee to provide a greater variety of fiber-optic alternatives for Ethernet networks. Designed with backward compatibility in mind, 10Base-FL was the IEEE counterpart to FOIRL. It increased the maximum length of a fiber-optic link to 2,000 meters and permitted connections between two repeaters, two computers, or a computer and a repeater.

As in all of the 10Base-F specifications, a computer connected to the network uses an external fiber-optic MAU (or FOMAU) and an AUI cable up to 25 meters long. The other end of the cable connects to a fiber-optic repeating hub that provides the same basic functions as a hub for copper segments.

Cabling Guidelines

In addition to the minimum and maximum segment lengths for the various types of 10Base Ethernet media, the standards imposed limits on the number of repeaters you could use in a single collision domain. This was necessary to ensure that every packet transmitted by an Ethernet node began to reach its destination before the last bit left the sender. If the distance traveled by a packet was too long, the sender was unable to detect collisions reliably, and data losses could occur.

Link Segments and Mixing Segments

When defining the limits on the number of repeaters allowed on the network, the 802.3 standard distinguishes between two types of cable segments, called *link segments* and *mixing segments*. A link segment is a length of cable that joins only two nodes, while a mixing segment joins more than two.

The 5-4-3 Rule

The Ethernet standards state that, in a single Ethernet collision domain, the route taken between any two nodes on the network can consist of no more than *five* cable segments, joined by *four* repeaters, and only *three* of the segments can be mixing segments. This is known as the *Ethernet 5-4-3 rule*. This rule is manifested in different ways, depending on the type of cable used for the network medium.

NOTE　A collision domain is defined as a network configuration on which two nodes transmitting data at the same time will cause a collision. The use of bridges, switches, or intelligent hubs, instead of standard repeaters, does not extend the collision domain and does not fall under the Ethernet 5-4-3 rule. If you have a network that has reached its maximum size because of this rule, you should consider using one of these devices to create separate collision domains. See Chapter 6 for more information.

On a coaxial network, whether it was thick or thin Ethernet, you could have five cable segments joined by four repeaters. On a coaxial network, a repeater had only two ports and did nothing but amplify the signal as it traveled over the cable. A segment is the length of cable between two repeaters, even though in the case of thin Ethernet the segment could consist of many separate lengths of cable. This rule meant that the overall length of a thick Ethernet bus (called the *maximum collision domain diameter*) could be 2,500 meters (500 × 5), while a thin Ethernet bus could be up to 925 meters (185 × 5) long.

On either of these networks, however, only three of the cable segments actually had nodes connected to them (see Figure 10-4). You can use the two link segments to join mixing segments located at some distance from each other, but you cannot populate them with computers or other devices.

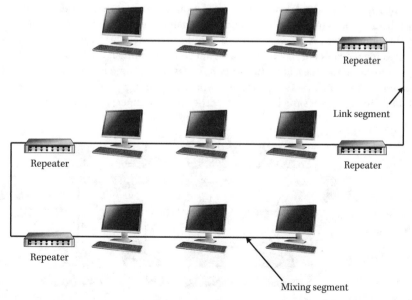

Figure 10-4　Coaxial networks consisted of up to five cable segments, with only three of the five connected to computers or other devices.

UTP Cabling

On a 10Base-T UTP network, the situation was different. Because the repeaters on this type of network were actually multiport hubs or switches, every cable segment connecting a node to the hub is a link segment. You can have four hubs in a collision domain that are connected to each other and each of which can be connected to as many nodes as the hub can support (see Figure 10-5). Because data traveling from one node to any other node passes through a maximum of only four hubs and because all the segments are link segments, the network is in compliance with the Ethernet standards.

NOTE   One potentially complicating factor to this arrangement was when you connected 10Base-T hubs using thin Ethernet coaxial cable. Some 10Base-T hubs included BNC connectors that enabled you to use a bus to chain multiple hubs together. When you did this with more than two hubs connected by a single coaxial segment, you were actually creating a mixing segment, and you had to count this toward the maximum of three mixing segments permitted on the network.

The 10Base-F specifications included some modifications to the 5-4-3 rule. When five cable segments were present on a 10Base-F network connected by four repeaters, FOIRL, 10Base-FL, and 10Base-FB segments could be no more than 500 meters long. 10Base-FP segments can be no more than 300 meters long.

Ethernet Timing Calculations

The 5-4-3 rule is a general guideline that is usually accurate enough to ensure your network will perform properly. However, it is also possible to assess the compliance of a network with the Ethernet cabling specifications more precisely by calculating two measurements: the *round-trip signal delay time* and the *interframe gap shrinkage* for the worst-case path through your network.

The round-trip signal delay time is the amount of time it takes a bit to travel between the two most distant nodes on the network and back again. The interframe gap shrinkage is the amount the normal 96-bit delay between packets is reduced by network conditions, such as the time required for repeaters to reconstruct a signal before sending it on its way.

In most cases, these calculations are unnecessary; as long as you comply with the 5-4-3 rule, your network should function properly. If you are planning to expand a complex network to the point at which it pushes the limits of the Ethernet guidelines, however, it might be a good idea to

Link segments

Figure 10-5   Twisted-pair networks use link segments to connect to the computers, making it possible to have four populated hubs.

get a precise measurement to ensure that everything functions as it should. If you end up with a severe late collision problem that requires an expensive network upgrade to remedy, your boss isn't likely to want to hear about how reliable the 5-4-3 rule usually is.

NOTE Calculating the round-trip signal delay time and the interframe gap shrinkage for your network is not part of a remedy for excessive numbers of early collisions.

Finding the Worst-Case Path

The *worst-case path* is the route data takes when traveling between the two most distant nodes on the network, both in terms of segment length and number of repeaters. On a relatively simple network, you can find the worst case path by choosing the two nodes on the two outermost network segments either that have the longest link segments connecting them to the repeater or that are at the far ends of the cable bus, as shown in Figure 10-6.

On more complex networks using various types of cable segments, you have to select several paths to test your network. In addition, you may have to account for the variations caused by having different cable segment types at the left and right ends of the path.

If your network is well documented, you should have a schematic containing the precise distances of all your cable runs. You need these figures to make your calculations. If you don't have a schematic, determining the exact distances may be the most difficult part of the whole process. The most accurate method for determining the length of a cable run is to use a multifunction cable tester, which utilizes a technique called *time domain reflectometry* (TDR). TDR is similar to radar, in that the unit transmits a test signal, precisely measures the time it takes the signal to travel to the other end of the cable and back again, and then uses this information to compute the cable's length. If you don't have a cable tester with TDR capabilities, you can measure the cable lengths manually by estimating the distances between the connectors. This can be particularly difficult when cables are installed inside walls and ceilings because there may be unseen obstacles that extend the length of the cable. If you use this method, you should err on the side of caution and include an additional distance factor to account for possible errors. Alternatively, you can simply use the maximum allowable cable distances for the various cable segments, as long as you are sure the cable runs do not exceed the Ethernet standard's maximum segment length specifications.

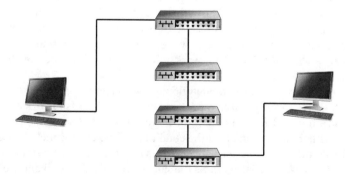

Figure 10-6 On a simple network with all 10Base-T segments, the worst-case path ran between the nodes with the longest cables on both end segments.

Once you have determined the worst-case path (or paths) you will use for your calculations, it's a good idea to create a simple diagram of each path with the cable distances involved. Each path will have left and right end segments and may have one or more middle segments. You will then perform your calculations on the individual segments and combine the results to test the entire path.

Exceeding Ethernet Cabling Specifications

The Ethernet specifications have a certain amount of leeway built into them that makes it possible to exceed the cabling limitations, within reason. If a network has an extra repeater or a cable that's a little too long, it will probably continue to function without causing the late collisions that occur when the specifications are grossly exceeded. You can see how this is so by calculating the actual amount of copper cable filled by an Ethernet signal.

Electrical signals passing through a copper cable travel at approximately 200,000,000 meters/second (2/3 of the speed of light). Ethernet transmits at 10 Mbps, or 10,000,000 bits/second. By dividing 200,000,000 by 10,000,000, you arrive at a figure of 20 meters of cable for every transmitted bit. Thus, the smallest possible Ethernet frame, which is 512 bits (64 bytes) long, occupies 10,240 meters of copper cable.

If you take the longest possible length of copper cable permitted by the Ethernet standards, a 500-meter thick Ethernet segment, you can see that the entire 500 meters would be filled by only 25 bits of data (at 20 meters/bit). Two nodes at the far ends of the segment would have a round-trip distance of 1,000 meters.

When one of the two nodes transmits, a collision can occur only if the other node also begins transmitting before the signal reaches it. If you grant that the second node begins transmitting at the last possible moment before the first transmission reaches it, then the first node can send no more than 50 bits (occupying 1,000 meters of cable, 500 down and 500 back) before it detects the collision and ceases transmitting. Obviously, this 50 bits is well below the 512-bit barrier that separates early from late collisions.

Of course, this example involves only one segment. But even if you extend a thick Ethernet network to its maximum collision domain diameter—five segments of 500 meters each, or 2,500 meters—a node would still transmit only 250 bits (occupying 5,000 meters of cable, 2,500 down and 2,500 back) before detecting a collision.

Thus, you can see that the Ethernet specifications for the round-trip signal delay time are fully twice as strict as they need to be in the case of a thick Ethernet network. For the other copper media, thin Ethernet and 10Base-T, the specifications are even more lax because the maximum segment lengths are smaller, while the signaling speed remains the same. For a full-length five-segment 10Base-T network only 500 meters long, the specification is ten times stricter than it needs to be.

This is not to say that you can safely double the maximum cable lengths on your network across the board or install a dozen repeaters (although it is possible to safely lengthen the segments on a 10Base-T network up to 150 meters if you use Category 5 UTP cable instead of Category 3). Other factors can affect the conditions on your network to bring it closer to the limits defined by the specifications. In fact, the signal timing is not as much of a restricting factor on 10 Mbps Ethernet installations as is the signal strength. The weakening of the signal due to attenuation is far more likely to cause performance problems on an overextended network than are excess signal delay times. The point here is to demonstrate that the designers of the Ethernet protocol built a safety factor into the network from the beginning, perhaps partially explaining why it continues to work so well more than 20 years later.

The Ethernet Frame

The *Ethernet frame* is the sequence of bits that begins and ends every Ethernet packet transmitted over a network. The frame consists of a header and footer that surround and encapsulate the data generated by the protocols operating at higher layers of the OSI model. The information in the header and footer specifies the addresses of the system sending the packet and the system that is to receive it and also performs several other functions that are important to the delivery of the packet.

The IEEE 802.3 Frame

The basic Ethernet frame format, as defined by the IEEE 802.3 standard, is shown in Figure 10-7. The functions of the individual fields are discussed in the following sections.

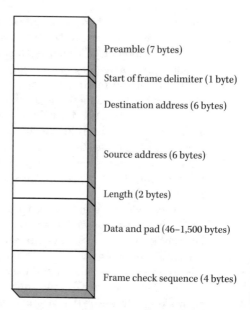

Preamble (7 bytes)

Start of frame delimiter (1 byte)

Destination address (6 bytes)

Source address (6 bytes)

Length (2 bytes)

Data and pad (46–1,500 bytes)

Frame check sequence (4 bytes)

Figure 10-7　The Ethernet frame encloses the data passed down the protocol stack from the network layer and prepares it for transmission.

Preamble and Start of Frame Delimiter

The preamble consists of 7 bytes of alternating zeros and ones, which the systems on the network use to synchronize their clocks and then discard. The Manchester encoding scheme Ethernet uses requires the clocks on communicating systems to be in sync so that they both agree on how long a bit time is. Systems in idle mode (that is, not currently transmitting and not in the process of rectifying a collision) are incapable of receiving any data until they use the signals generated by the alternating bit values of the preamble to prepare for the forthcoming data transmission.

NOTE　For more information on Manchester encoding and the signaling that occurs at the physical layer, see Chapter 2.

By the time the 7 bytes of the preamble have been transmitted, the receiving system has synchronized its clock with that of the sender, but the receiver is also unaware of how many of the 7 bytes have elapsed before it fell into sync. To signal the commencement of the actual packet transmission, the sender transmits a 1-byte start of frame delimiter, which continues the alternating zeros and ones, except for the last two bits, which are both ones. This is the signal to the receiver that any data following is part of a data packet and should be read into the network adapter's memory buffer for processing.

Destination Address and Source Address

Addressing is the most basic function of the Ethernet frame. Because the frame can be said to form an envelope for the network layer data carried inside it, it is only fitting that the envelope have an address. The addresses the Ethernet protocol uses to identify the systems on the network are 6 bytes long and hard-coded into the network interface adapters in each machine. These addresses are referred to as *hardware addresses* or *MAC addresses*. The hardware address on every Ethernet adapter made is unique. The IEEE assigns 3-byte prefixes to NIC manufacturers that it calls *organizationally unique identifiers* (OUIs), and the manufacturers supply the remaining 3 bytes. When transmitting a packet, it is the network adapter driver on the system that generates the values for the destination address and source address fields.

The destination address field identifies the system to which the packet is being sent. The address may identify the ultimate destination of the packet if it's on the local network, or the address may belong to a device that provides access to another network, such as a router. Addresses at the data link layer always identify the packet's next stop on the local network. It is up to the network layer to control end-to-end transmission and to provide the address of the packet's ultimate destination.

Every node on a shared Ethernet network reads the destination address from the header of every packet transmitted by every system on the network to determine whether the header contains its own address. A system reading the frame header and recognizing its own address then reads the entire packet into its memory buffers and processes it accordingly. A destination address of all ones signifies that the packet is a *broadcast,* meaning it is intended for all of the systems on the network. Certain addresses can also be designated as *multicast* addresses by the networking software on the system. A multicast address identifies a group of systems on the network, all of which are to receive certain messages.

The source address field contains the 6-byte MAC address of the system sending the packet. (The specifications allow for 2-byte addresses as well.)

Length

The length field in an 802.3 frame is 2 bytes long and specifies how much data is being carried as the packet's payload in bytes. This figure includes only the actual upper-layer data in the packet. It does not include the frame fields from the header or footer or any padding that might have been added to the data field to reach the minimum size for an Ethernet packet (64 bytes). The maximum size for an Ethernet packet, including the frame, is 1,518 bytes. Because the frame consists of 18 bytes, the maximum value for the length field is 1,500.

Data and Pad

The data field contains the payload of the packet—that is, the "contents" of the envelope. As passed down from the network layer protocol, the data will include an original message generated by an upper-layer application or process, plus any header information added by the protocols in the intervening layers. In addition, an 802.3 packet will contain the 3-byte logical link control header in the data field.

For example, the payload of a packet containing an Internet hostname to be resolved into an IP address by a DNS server consists of the original DNS message generated at the application layer, a header applied by the UDP protocol at the transport layer, a header applied by the IP protocol at the network layer, and the LLC header. Although these three additional headers are not part of the original message, to the Ethernet protocol they are just payload that is carried in the data field like any other information. Just as postal workers are not concerned with the contents of the envelopes they carry, the Ethernet protocol has no knowledge of the data within the frame.

The entire Ethernet packet (excluding the preamble and the start of frame delimiter) must be a minimum of 64 bytes in length for the protocol's collision detection mechanism to function.

Therefore, subtracting 18 bytes for the frame, the data field must be at least 46 bytes long. If the payload passed down from the network layer protocol is too short, the Ethernet adapter adds a string of meaningless bits to pad the data field out to the requisite length.

The maximum allowable length for an Ethernet packet is 1,518 bytes, meaning the data field can be no larger than 1,500 bytes (including the LLC header).

Frame Check Sequence

The last 4 bytes of the frame, following the data field (and the pad, if any), carry a checksum value the receiving node uses to determine whether the packet has arrived intact. Just before transmission, the network adapter at the sending node computes a cyclic redundancy check (CRC) on all of the packet's other fields (except for the preamble and the start of frame delimiter) using an algorithm called the AUTODIN II polynomial. The value of the CRC is uniquely based on the data used to compute it.

When the packet arrives at its destination, the network adapter in the receiving system reads the contents of the frame and performs the same computation. By comparing the newly computed value with the one in the FCS field, the system can verify that none of the packet's bit values has changed. If the values match, the system accepts the packet and writes it to the memory buffers for processing. If the values don't match, the system declares an *alignment error* and discards the frame. The system will also discard the frame if the number of bits in the packet is not a multiple of 8. Once a frame is discarded, it is up to the higher-layer protocols to recognize its absence and arrange for retransmission.

The Ethernet II Frame

The function of the 2-byte field following the source address was different in the frame formats of the two predominant Ethernet standards. While the 802.3 frame uses this field to specify the length of the data in the packet, the Ethernet II standard used it to specify the frame type, also called the *Ethertype*. The Ethertype specifies the memory buffer in which the frame should be stored. The location of the memory buffer specified in this field identifies the network layer protocol for which the data carried in the frame is intended.

This is a crucial element of every protocol operating in the data link, network, and transport layers of a system's networking stack. The data in the packet must be delivered not only to the proper system on the network, but also to the proper application or process on that system. Because the destination computer can be running multiple protocols at the network layer at the same time, such as IP, NetBEUI, and IPX, the Ethertype field informs the Ethernet adapter driver which of these protocols should receive the data.

When a system reads the header of an Ethernet packet, the only way to tell an Ethernet II frame from an 802.3 frame was by the value of the length/Ethertype field. Because the value of the 802.3 length field can be no higher than 1,500 (0x05DC, in hexadecimal notation), the Ethertype values assigned to the developers of the various network layer protocols are all higher than 1,500.

The Logical Link Control Sublayer

The IEEE splits the functionality of the data link layer into two sublayers: media access control and logical link control. On an Ethernet network, the MAC sublayer includes elements of the 802.3 standard: the physical layer specifications, the CSMA/CD mechanism, and the 802.3 frame. The functions of the LLC sublayer are defined in the 802.2 standard, which is also used with the other 802 MAC standards.

The LLC sublayer is capable of providing a variety of communications services to network layer protocols, including the following:

- **Unacknowledged connectionless service**   Multisource agreements (MSA) simple service that provides no flow control or error control and does not guarantee accurate delivery of data
- **Connection-oriented service**   MSA fully reliable service that guarantees accurate data delivery by establishing a connection with the destination before transmitting data and by using error and flow control mechanisms
- **Acknowledged connectionless service**   MSA midrange service that uses acknowledgment messages to provide reliable delivery but that does not establish a connection before transmitting data

On a transmitting system, the data passed down from the network layer protocol is encapsulated first by the LLC sublayer into what the standard calls a *protocol data unit* (PDU). Then the PDU is passed down to the MAC sublayer, where it is encapsulated again in a header and footer, at which point it can technically be called a *frame*. In an Ethernet packet, this means the data field of the 802.3 frame contains a 3- or 4-byte LLC header, in addition to the network layer data, thus reducing the maximum amount of data in each packet from 1,500 to 1,496 bytes.

The LLC header consists of three fields, the functions of which are described in the following sections.

DSAP and SSAP

The destination service access point (DSAP) field identifies a location in the memory buffers on the destination system where the data in the packet should be stored. The source service access point (SSAP) field does the same for the source of the packet data on the transmitting system. Both of these 1-byte fields use values assigned by the IEEE, which functions as the registrar for the protocol.

In an Ethernet SNAP packet, the value for both the DSAP and SSAP fields is 170 (or 0xAA, in hexadecimal form). This value indicates that the contents of the LLC PDU begin with a Subnetwork Access Protocol (SNAP) header. The SNAP header provides the same functionality as the Ethertype field to the 802.3 frame.

Control

The control field of the LLC header specifies the type of service needed for the data in the PDU and the function of the packet. Depending on which of the services is required, the control field can be either 1 or 2 bytes long. In an Ethernet SNAP frame, for example, the LLC uses the unacknowledged, connectionless service, which has a 1-byte control field value using what the standard calls the *unnumbered format*. The value for the control field is 3, which is defined as an *unnumbered information frame*—that is, a frame containing data. Unnumbered information frames are quite simple and signify either that the packet contains a noncritical message or that a higher-layer protocol is somehow guaranteeing delivery and providing other high-level services.

The other two types of control fields (which are 2 bytes each) are the *information format* and the *supervisory format*. The three control field formats are distinguished by their first bits, as follows:

- The information format begins with a 0 bit.
- The supervisory format begins with a 1 bit and a 0 bit.
- The unnumbered format begins with two 1 bits.

The remainder of the bits specify the precise function of the PDU. In a more complex exchange involving the connection-oriented service, unnumbered frames contain commands, such as those used to establish a connection with the other system and terminate it at the end of the transmission. The commands transmitted in unnumbered frames are as follows:

- **Unnumbered information (UI)**   Used to send data frames by the unacknowledged, connectionless service
- **Exchange identification (XID)**   Used as both a command and a response in the connection-oriented and connectionless services
- **TEST**   Used as both a command and a response when performing an LLC loopback test
- **Frame reject (FRMR)**   Used as a response when a protocol violation occurs
- **Set Asynchronous Balanced Mode Extended (SABME)**   Used to request that a connection be established
- **Unnumbered acknowledgment (UA)**   Used as the positive response to the SABME message
- **Disconnect mode (DM)**   Used as a negative response to the SABME message
- **Disconnect (DISC)**   Used to request that a connection be closed; a response of either UA or DM is expected

Information frames contain the actual data transmitted during connection-oriented and acknowledged connectionless sessions, as well as the acknowledgment messages returned by the receiving system. Only two types of messages are sent in information frames: N(S) and N(R) for the send and receive packets, respectively. Both systems track the sequence numbers of the frames they receive. An N(S) message lets the receiver know how many packets in the sequence have been sent, and an N(R) message lets the sender know what packet in the sequence it expects to receive.

Supervisory frames are used only by the connection-oriented service and provide connection maintenance in the form of flow control and error-correction services. The types of supervisory messages are as follows:

- **Receiver ready (RR)**   Used to inform the sender that the receiver is ready for the next frame and to keep a connection alive
- **Receiver not ready (RNR)**   Used to instruct the sender not to send any more packets until the receiver transmits an RR message
- **Frame reject (REJ)**   Used to inform the sender of an error and request retransmission of all frames sent after a certain point

Part III

LLC Applications

In some cases, the LLC frame plays only a minor role in the network communications process. On a network running TCP/IP along with other protocols, for example, the only function of LLC may be to enable 802.3 frames to contain a SNAP header, which specifies the network layer protocol the frame should go to, just like the Ethertype in an Ethernet II frame. In this scenario, the LLC PDUs all use the unnumbered information format. Other high-level protocols, however, require more extensive services from LLC.

The SNAP Header

Because the IEEE 802.3 frame header does not have an Ethertype field, it would normally be impossible for a receiving system to determine which network layer protocol should receive the incoming data. This would not be a problem if you ran only one network layer protocol, but with multiple protocols installed, it becomes a serious problem. 802.3 packets address this problem by using yet another protocol within the LLC PDU, called the Subnetwork Access Protocol.

The SNAP header is 5 bytes long and found directly after the LLC header in the data field of an 802.3 frame. The functions of the fields are as follows:

- **Organization code** The organization code, or vendor code, is a 3-byte field that takes the same value as the first 3 bytes of the source address in the 802.3 header.

- **Local code** The local code is a 2-byte field that is the functional equivalent of the Ethertype field in the Ethernet II header.

NOTE Many, if not all, of the registered values for the NIC hardware address prefixes, the Ethertype field, and the DSAP/SSAP fields are listed in the "Assigned Numbers" document published as a request for comments (RFC) by the Internet Engineering Task Force (IETF). Find the current version number for this document at www.ietf.org/rfc.html.

Full-Duplex Ethernet

The CSMA/CD media access control mechanism is the defining element of the Ethernet protocol, but it is also the source of many of its limitations. The fundamental shortcoming of the Ethernet protocol is that data can travel in only one direction at a time. This is known as *half-duplex* operation. With special hardware, it is also possible to run Ethernet connections in *full-duplex* mode, meaning that the device can transmit and receive data simultaneously. This effectively doubles the bandwidth of the network. Full-duplex capability for Ethernet networks was standardized in the 802.3x supplement to the 802.3 standard in 1997.

When operating in full-duplex mode, the CSMA/CD MAC mechanism is ignored. Systems do not listen to the network before transmitting; they simply send their data whenever they want. Because both of the systems in a full-duplex link can transmit and receive data at the same time, there is no possibility of collisions occurring. Because no collisions occur, the cabling restrictions intended to support the collision detection mechanism are not needed. This means you can have longer cable segments on a full-duplex network. The only limitation is the signal transmitting capability (that is, the resistance to attenuation) of the network medium itself.

This is a particularly important point on a Fast Ethernet network using fiber-optic cable because the collision detection mechanism is responsible for its relatively short maximum segment lengths. While a half-duplex 100Base-FX link between two devices can be a maximum of only 412 meters long, the same link operating in full-duplex mode can be up to 2,000 meters (2 km) long because it is restricted only by the strength of the signal. A 100Base-FX link using single-mode fiber-optic cable can span distances of 20 km or more. The signal attenuation on twisted-pair networks, however, makes 10Base-T, 100Base-TX, and 1000Base-T networks still subject to the 100-meter segment length restriction.

Full-Duplex Requirements

There are three requirements for full-duplex Ethernet operation:

- A network medium with separate transmit and receive channels

- A dedicated link between two systems

- Network interface adapters and switches that support full-duplex operation

Full-duplex Ethernet is possible only on link segments that have separate channels for the communications in each direction. This means that twisted-pair and fiber-optic networks can support full-duplex communications using regular, Fast, and Gigabit Ethernet, but coaxial cable cannot. Of the Ethernet variants using twisted-pair and fiber-optic cables, 10Base-FB and 10Base-FP did not support full-duplex (which is not a great loss, since no one used them), nor does 100Base-T4 (which is also rarely used). All of the other network types support full-duplex communications.

Full-duplex Ethernet also requires that every two computers have a dedicated link between them. This means you can't use repeating hubs on a full-duplex network because these devices operate in half-duplex mode by definition and create a shared network medium. Instead, you must use switches, also known as *switching hubs,* which effectively isolate each pair of communicating computers on its own network segment and provide the packet-buffering capabilities needed to support bidirectional communications.

Finally, each of the devices on a full-duplex Ethernet network must support full-duplex communications and be configured to use it. Switches that support full-duplex are readily available, as are Fast Ethernet NICs. Full-duplex operation is an essential component of 1000Base-T Gigabit Ethernet, and many 1000Base-X Gigabit Ethernet adapters support full-duplex as well. Ensuring that your full-duplex equipment is actually operating in full-duplex mode can sometimes be tricky. Autonegotiation is definitely the easiest way of doing this; dual-speed Fast Ethernet equipment automatically gives full-duplex operation priority over half-duplex at the same speed. However, adapters and switches that do not support multiple speeds may not include autonegotiation. For example, virtually all 100Base-TX NICs are dual speed, supporting both 10 and 100 Mbps transmissions. Autonegotiation is always supported by these NICs, which means that simply connecting the NIC to a full-duplex switch will enable full-duplex communications. Fast Ethernet NICs that use fiber-optic cables, however, are usually single-speed devices and may or may not include autonegotiation capability. You may have to manually configure the NIC before it will use full-duplex communications.

Full-Duplex Flow Control

The switching hubs on full-duplex Ethernet networks have to be able to buffer packets as they read the destination address in each one and perform the internal switching needed to send it on its way. The amount of buffer memory in a switch is, of course, finite, and as a result, it's possible for a switch to be overwhelmed by the constant input of data from freely transmitting full-duplex systems. Therefore, the 802.3x supplement defines an optional flow control mechanism that full-duplex systems can use to make the system at the other end of a link pause its transmissions temporarily, enabling the other device to catch up.

The full-duplex flow control mechanism is called the MAC Control protocol, which takes the form of a specialized frame that contains a PAUSE command and a parameter specifying the length of the pause. The MAC Control frame is a standard Ethernet frame of minimum length (64 bytes) with the hexadecimal value 8808 in the Ethertype or SNAP Local Code field. The frame is transmitted to a special multicast address (01-80-C2-00-00-01) designated for use by PAUSE frames. The data field of the MAC Control frame contains a 2-byte operational code (opcode) with a hexadecimal value of 0001, indicating that it is a PAUSE frame. At this time, this is the only valid MAC Control opcode value. A 2-byte *pause-time* parameter follows the opcode, which is an integer specifying the amount of time the receiving systems should pause their transmissions, measured in units called *quanta*, each of which is equal to 512 bit times. The range of possible values for the pause-time parameter is 0 to 65,535.

Full-Duplex Applications

Full-duplex Ethernet capabilities are most often provided in Fast Ethernet and Gigabit Ethernet adapters and switches. While full-duplex operation theoretically doubles the bandwidth of a network, the actual performance improvement that you realize depends on the nature of the communications involved. Upgrading a desktop workstation to full duplex will probably not provide a dramatic improvement in performance. This is because desktop communications typically consist of request/response transactions that are themselves half-duplex in nature, and providing a full-duplex medium won't change that. Full-duplex operation is better suited to the communications between switches on a backbone, which are continually carrying large amounts of traffic generated by computers all over the network.

CHAPTER 11

100Base Ethernet and Gigabit Ethernet

100Base Ethernet and Gigabit Ethernet are today's 100 and 1,000 Mbps variants of the Ethernet protocol, respectively. Although similar to 10Base Ethernet in many ways, the 100Base protocols have some configuration issues that you must be aware of in order to design, install, and administer the networks that use them.

100Base Ethernet

The IEEE 802.3u specification, ratified in 1995, defined what is commonly known as 100Base Ethernet, a data link layer protocol running at 100 Mbps, which is ten times the speed of the original Ethernet protocol. This is now the industry standard for many new installations, largely because it improves network performance so much while changing so little.

100Base Ethernet left two of the three defining elements of an Ethernet network unchanged. The protocol uses the same frame format as IEEE 802.3 and the same CSMA/CD media access control mechanism. The changes that enable the increase in speed are in several elements of the physical layer configuration, including the types of cable used, the length of cable segments, and the number of hubs permitted.

Physical Layer Options

The first difference between 10Base and 100Base Ethernet was that coaxial cable was no longer supported. 100Base Ethernet runs only on UTP or fiber-optic cable, although shielded twisted-pair (STP) is an option as well. Gone also was the Manchester signaling scheme, to be replaced by the 4B/5B system developed for the Fiber Distributed Data Interface (FDDI) protocol. The physical layer options defined in 802.3u were intended to provide the most flexible installation parameters possible. Virtually every aspect of the 100Base Ethernet protocol's physical layer specifications was designed to facilitate upgrades from earlier technologies and, particularly, from 10Base-T. In many cases, existing UTP networks upgraded to 100Base Ethernet without pulling new cable. The only exception to this was in cases of networks that spanned longer distances than 100Base Ethernet could support with copper cabling.

	100Base-TX	**100Base-T4**	**100Base-FX**
Maximum segment length	100 meters	100 meters	412 meters
Cable type	Category 5 UTP or Type 1 STP (two wire pairs)	Category 3 UTP (four wire pairs)	62.5/125 multimode fiber
Connector type	RJ-45	RJ-45	SC, MIC, or ST

Table 11-1   IEEE 802.3u Physical Layer Specifications

100Base Ethernet defined three physical layer specifications, as shown in Table 11-1.

In addition to the connectors shown for each of the cable types, the 802.3u standard described a *medium-independent interface* (MII) that used a 40-pin D-shell connector. Taking from the design of the original thick Ethernet standard, the MII connected to an external transceiver called a *physical layer device* (PHY), which, in turn, connected to the network medium. The MII made it possible to build devices such as hubs and computers that integrated 100Base Ethernet adapters but were not committed to a particular media type. By supplying different PHY units, you could connect the device to a 100Base Ethernet network using any supported cable type. Some PHY devices connected directly to the MII, while others used a cable not unlike the AUI cable arrangement in thick Ethernet. When this was the case, the MII cable could be no more than 0.5 meters long.

Most of the 100Base Ethernet hardware on the market today uses internal transceivers and does not need an MII connector or cable, but a few products do take advantage of this interface.

100Base-TX

Using standards for physical media developed by the American National Standards Institute (ANSI), 100Base-TX and its fiber-optic counterpart, 100Base-FX, were known collectively as 100Base-X. They provided the core physical layer guidelines for new cable installations. Like 10Base-T, 100Base-TX called for the use of unshielded twisted-pair cable segments up to 100 meters in length. The only difference from a 10Base-T segment was in the quality and capabilities of the cable itself.

100Base-TX was based on the ANSI TP-PMD specification and calls for the use of Category 5 UTP cable for all network segments. As you can see in the table, the Category 5 cable specification provided the potential for much greater bandwidth than the Category 3 cable specified for 10Base-T networks. As an alternative, using Type 1 shielded twisted-pair cable was also possible for installations where the operating environment presented a greater danger of electromagnetic interference.

For the sake of compatibility, 100Base-TX (as well as 100Base-T4) used the same type of RJ-45 connectors as 10Base-T, and the pin assignments were the same as well. The pin assignments were the one area in which the cable specifications differed from ANSI TP-PMD to maintain backward compatibility with 10Base-T networks.

100Base-T4

100Base-T4 was intended for use on networks that already had UTP cable installed, but the cable was not rated as Category 5. The 10Base-T specification allowed for the use of standard voice-grade (Category 3) cable, and there were many networks that were already wired for 10Base-T

Ethernet (or even for telephone systems). 100Base-T4 ran at 100 Mbps on Category 3 cable by using all four pairs of wires in the cable, instead of just two, as 10Base-T and 100Base-TX do.

The transmit and receive data pairs in a 100Base-T4 circuit are the same as that of 100Base-TX (and 10Base-T). The remaining four wires function as bidirectional pairs. As on a 10Base-T network, the transmit and receive pairs must be crossed over for traffic to flow. The crossover circuits in a 100Base Ethernet hub connect the transmit pair to the receive pair, as always. In a 100Base-T4 hub, the two bidirectional pairs are crossed as well so that pair 3 connects to pair 4, and vice versa.

100Base-FX

The 100Base-FX specification called for the same hardware as the 10Base-FL specification except that the maximum length of a cable segment was no more than 412 meters. As with the other 100Base Ethernet physical layer options, the medium was capable of transmitting a signal over longer distances, but the limitation was imposed to ensure the proper operation of the collision-detection mechanism. As mentioned earlier, when you eliminate the CSMA/CD MAC mechanism, like on a full-duplex Ethernet network, 100Base-FX segments can be much longer.

Cable Length Restrictions

Because the network operates at ten times the speed of 10Base Ethernet, 100Base Ethernet cable installations were more restricted. In effect, the 100Base Ethernet standard uses up a good deal of the latitude built into the original Ethernet standards to achieve greater performance levels. In 10 Mbps Ethernet, the signal timing specifications were at least twice as strict as they had to be for systems to detect early collisions properly on the network. The lengths of the network segments were dictated more by the need to maintain the signal strength than the signal timing.

On 100Base-T networks, however, signal strength is not as much of an issue as signal timing. The CSMA/CD mechanism on a 100Base Ethernet network functions exactly like that of a 10 Mbps Ethernet network, and the packets are the same size, but they travel over the medium at ten times the speed. Because the collision detection mechanism is the same, a system still must be able to detect the presence of a collision before the slot time expires (that is, before it transmits 64 bytes of data). Because the traffic is moving 100 Mbps, though, the duration of that slot time is reduced, and the maximum length of the network must be reduced as well to sense collisions accurately. For this reason, the maximum overall length of a 100Base-TX network is approximately 205 meters. This is a figure you should observe much more stringently than the 500-meter maximum for a 10Base-T network.

NOTE When you plan your network, be sure to remain conscious that the 100-meter maximum cable segment length specification in the 100Base Ethernet standard includes the entire length of cable connecting a computer to the hub. If you have an internal cable installation that terminates at wall plates at the computer site and a patch panel at the hub site, you must include the lengths of the patch cables connecting the wall plate to the computer and the patch panel to the hub in your total measurement. The specification recommends that the maximum length for an internal cable segment be 90 meters, leaving 10 meters for the patch cables.

Hub Configurations

Because the maximum length for a 100Base-TX segment is 100 meters, the same as that for 10Base-T, the restrictions on the overall length of the network are found in the configuration of the repeating hubs used to connect the segments. The 802.3u supplement described two types of hubs for all 100Base-T networks: Class I and Class II. Every 100Base Ethernet hub must have a circled Roman numeral I or II identifying its class.

Class I hubs are intended to support cable segments with different types of signaling. 100Base-TX and 100Base-FX use the same signaling type, while 100Base-T4 is different (because of the presence of the two bidirectional pairs). A Class I hub contains circuitry that translates incoming 100Base-TX, 100Base-FX, and 100Base-T4 signals to a common digital format and then translates them again to the appropriate signal for each outgoing hub port. These translation activities cause comparatively long timing delays in the hub, so you can have only one Class I hub on the path between any two nodes on the network.

Class II hubs can only support cable segments of the same signaling type. Because no translation is involved, the hub passes the incoming data rapidly to the outgoing ports. Because the timing delays are shorter, you can have up to two Class II hubs on the path between two network nodes, but all the segments must use the same signaling type. This means a Class II hub can support either 100Base-TX and 100Base-FX together or 100Base-T4 alone.

Additional segment length restrictions are also based on the combination of segments and hubs used on the network. The more complex the network configuration gets, the shorter its maximum collision domain diameter can be. Table 11-2 summarizes these restrictions.

Note that a network configuration that uses two Class II hubs actually used three lengths of cable to establish the longest connection between two nodes: two cables to connect the nodes to their respective hubs and one cable to connect the two hubs. For example, the assumption of the standard is that the additional 5 meters added to the length limit for an all-copper network will account for the cable connecting the two hubs, as shown in Figure 11-1. But in practice, the three cables can be of any length as long as their total length does not exceed 205 meters.

What these restrictions mean to 100Base-FX networks is that the only fiber segment that can be 412 meters long is one that directly connects two computers. Once you add a hub to the network, the total distance between computers drops drastically. This largely negates one of the major benefits of using fiber-optic cable. You saw earlier in this chapter that the original Ethernet standards allow for fiber-optic segments up to 2 kilometers (2,000 meters) long. The closer tolerances of the collision-detection mechanism on a 100Base Ethernet network make it impossible to duplicate the collision domain diameter of standards like 10Base-FL. Considering that other high-speed protocols such as FDDI use the same type of cable and can support distances up to 200 kilometers, 100Base Ethernet might not be the optimal fiber-optic solution, unless you use the full-duplex option to increase the segment length.

	One Class I Hub	One Class II Hub	Two Class II Hubs
All copper segments (100Base-TX or 100Base-T4)	200 meters	200 meters	205 meters
All fiber segments (100Base-FX)	272 meters	320 meters	228 meters
One 100Base-T4 segment and one 100Base-FX segment	231 meters	Not applicable	Not applicable
One 100Base-TX segment and one 100Base-FX segment	260.8 meters	308.8 meters	216.2 meters

Table 11-2   100Base Ethernet Multisegment Configuration Guidelines

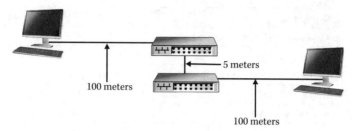

Figure 11-1   The cable segments in a network with two hubs can be of any length, as long as you observe the maximum collision domain diameter.

100Base Ethernet Timing Calculations

As with the original Ethernet standards, the cabling guidelines in the previous sections are no more than rules of thumb that provide general size limitations for a 100Base Ethernet network. Making more precise calculations to determine if your network is fully compliant with the specifications is also possible. For 100Base Ethernet, these calculations consist only of determining the round-trip delay time for the network. No interframe gap shrinkage calculation exists for 100Base Ethernet because the limited number of repeaters permitted on the network all but eliminates this as a possible problem.

Calculating the Round-Trip Delay Time   The process of calculating the round-trip delay time begins with determining the worst-case path through your network, just as in the calculations for 10Base Ethernet networks. As before, if you have different types of cable segments on your network, you may have more than one path to calculate. There is no need to perform separate calculations for each direction of a complex path, however, because the formula makes no distinction between the order of the segments.

The round-trip delay time consists of a delay per meter measurement for the specific type of cable your network uses, plus an additional delay constant for each node and repeater on the path. Table 11-3 lists the delay factors for the various network components.

To calculate the round-trip delay time for the worst-case path through your network, you multiply the lengths of your various cable segments by the delay factors listed in the table and add them together, along with the appropriate factors for the nodes and hubs and a safety buffer of 4 bit times. If the total is less than 512, the path is compliant with the 100Base Ethernet specification. Thus, the calculations for the network shown in Figure 11-2 would be as follows:

(150 meters × 1.112 bit times/meter) + 100 bit times + (2 × 92 bit times) + 4 bit times = 454.8 bit times

So, 150 meters of Category 5 cable multiplied by a delay factor of 1.112 bit times per meter yields a delay of 166.8 bit times, plus 100 bit times for two 100Base-TX nodes, two hubs at 92 bit times each, and an extra 4 for safety yields a total round-trip delay time of 454.8 bit times, which is well within the 512 limit.

NOTE As with the calculations for 10Base Ethernet networks, you may be able to avoid having to measure your cable segments by using the maximum permitted segment length in your calculations. Only if the result of this calculation exceeds the specification do you have to consider the actual lengths of your cables.

Component	Delay (in Bit Times)
Category 3 UTP cable segment	1.14 per meter
Category 4 UTP cable segment	1.14 per meter
Category 5 UTP cable segment	1.112 per meter
Category 6 UTP cable segment	1.110 per meter
STP cable segment	1.112 per meter
Fiber-optic cable segment	1.0 per meter
Two 100Base-TX/100Base-FX nodes	100
Two 100Base-T4 nodes	138
One 100Base-TX/100Base-FX node	127 and one 100Base-T4 node
Class I hub	140
Class II 100Base-TX/100Base-FX hub	92
Class II 100Base-T4 hub	67

Table 11-3   Delay Times for 100Base Ethernet Network Components

Autonegotiation

Most of today's Ethernet adapters support multiple speeds and use an *autonegotiation* system that enables a multispeed device to sense the capabilities of the network to which it is connected and to adjust its speed accordingly. The autonegotiation mechanism in 100Base Ethernet is based on *100Base link pulse* (FLP) signals, which are themselves a variation on the *normal link pulse* (NLP) signals used by the old 10Base-T and 10Base-FL networks.

Standard Ethernet networks use NLP signals to verify the integrity of a link between two devices. Most Ethernet hubs and network interface adapters have a link-pulse LED that lights when the device is connected to another active device. For example, when you take a UTP cable that is connected to a hub and plug it into a computer's NIC and turn the computer on, the LEDs on both the NIC and the hub port to which it's connected should light. This is the result of the two devices transmitting NLP signals to each other. When each device receives the NLP signals from the other device, it lights the link-pulse LED. If the network is wired incorrectly, because of a cable fault or improper use of a crossover cable or hub uplink port, the LEDs will not light. These

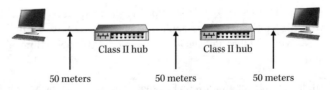

Class II hub   Class II hub

50 meters   50 meters   50 meters

Figure 11-2   This worst-case path is compliant with the round-trip delay time limitations defined in the Ethernet standard.

signals do not interfere with data communications because the devices transmit them only when the network is idle.

NOTE The link-pulse LED indicates only that the network is wired correctly, not that it's capable of carrying data. If you use the wrong cable for the protocol, you will still experience network communication problems, even though the devices passed the link integrity test.

100Base Ethernet devices capable of transmitting at multiple speeds elaborate on this technique by transmitting FLP signals instead of NLP signals. FLP signals include a 16-bit data packet within a burst of link pulses, producing what is called an *FLP burst*. The data packet contains a *link code word* (LCW) with two fields: the *selector field* and the *technology ability* field. Together, these fields identify the capabilities of the transmitting device, such as its maximum speed and whether it is capable of full-duplex communications.

Because the FLP burst has the same duration (2 nanoseconds) and interval (16.8 nanoseconds) as an NLP burst, a standard Ethernet system can simply ignore the LCW and treat the transmission as a normal link integrity test. When it responds to the sender, the multiple-speed system sets itself to operate at 10Base-T speed, using a technique called *parallel detection*. This same method applies also to 100Base Ethernet devices incapable of multiple speeds.

When two 100Base Ethernet devices capable of operating at multiple speeds autonegotiate, they determine the best performance level they have in common and configure themselves accordingly. The systems use the following list of priorities when comparing their capabilities, with full-duplex 1000Base-T providing the best performance and half-duplex 10Base-T providing the worst:

- 1000Base-T (full-duplex)
- 1000Base-T
- 100Base-TX (full-duplex)
- 100Base-T4
- 100Base-TX
- 10Base-T (full-duplex)
- 10Base-T

NOTE FLP signals account only for the capabilities of the devices generating them, not the connecting cable. If you connect a dual-speed l00Base-TX computer with a l00Base-TX hub using a Category 3 cable network, autonegotiation will still configure the devices to operate at l00 Mbps, even though the cable can't support transmissions at this speed.

The benefit of autonegotiation is that it permits administrators to upgrade a network gradually to 100Base Ethernet with a minimum of reconfiguration. If, for example, you have 10/100 dual-speed NICs in all your workstations, you can run the network at 10 Mbps using 10Base-T hubs. Later, you can simply replace the hubs with models supporting 100Base Ethernet, and the NICs will automatically reconfigure themselves to operate at the higher speed during the next system reboot. No manual configuration at the workstation is necessary.

Gigabit Ethernet

When 100 Mbps networking technologies like FDDI were first introduced, most horizontal networks used 10 Mbps Ethernet. These new protocols were used primarily on backbones. Now that 100Base and 1000Base Ethernet have taken over the horizontal network market, a 100 Mbps backbone is, in many cases, insufficient to support the connections between switches that have to accommodate multiple 100Base Ethernet networks. Gigabit Ethernet was developed to be the next generation of Ethernet network, running at 1 Gbps (1,000 Mbps), ten times the speed of 100Base Ethernet.

Gigabit Ethernet uses the same frame format, frame size, and media access control method as was standard in 10 Mbps Ethernet. 100Base Ethernet overtook FDDI as the dominant 100 Mbps solution because it prevented network administrators from having to use a different protocol on the backbone. In the same way, Gigabit Ethernet prevents administrators from having to use a different protocol for their backbones.

Connecting an ATM or FDDI network to an Ethernet network requires that the data be converted at the network layer from one frame format to another. Connecting two Ethernet networks, even when they're running at different speeds, is a data link layer operation because the frames remain unchanged. In addition, using Ethernet throughout your network eliminates the need to train administrators to work with a new protocol and purchase new testing and diagnostic equipment. The bottom line is that in most cases it is possible to upgrade a 100Base Ethernet backbone to Gigabit Ethernet without completely replacing hubs, switches, and cables. This is not to say, however, that some hardware upgrades will not be necessary. Hubs and switches will need modules supporting the protocol, and networking monitoring and testing products may also have to be upgraded to support the faster speed.

Gigabit Ethernet Architecture

Gigabit Ethernet was first defined in the 802.3z supplement to the 802.3 standard, which was published in June 1998. The 802.3z defined a network running at 1,000 Mbps in either half-duplex or full-duplex mode, over a variety of network media. The frame used to encapsulate the packets is identical to that of 802.3 Ethernet, and the protocol (in half-duplex mode) uses the same Carrier Sense Multiple Access with Collision Detection (CSMA/CD) MAC mechanism as the other Ethernet incarnations.

As with 10Base and 100Base Ethernet, the Gigabit Ethernet standard contains both physical and data link layer elements, as shown in Figure 11-3. The data link layer consists of the logical link control (LLC) and media access control (MAC) sublayers that are common to all of the IEEE 802 protocols. The LLC sublayer is identical to that used by the other Ethernet standards, as defined in the IEEE 802.2 document. The underlying concept of the MAC sublayer, the CSMA/CD mechanism, is fundamentally the same as on a standard Ethernet or 100Base Ethernet network but with a few changes in the way that it's implemented.

Media Access Control

Gigabit Ethernet is designed to support full-duplex operation as its primary signaling mode. As mentioned earlier, when systems can transmit and receive data simultaneously, there is no need for a media access control mechanism like CSMA/CD. However, some modifications are

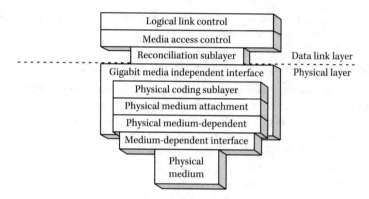

Figure 11-3   The Gigabit Ethernet protocol architecture

required for systems on a 1000Base-X network to operate in half-duplex mode. Ethernet's collision-detection mechanism works properly only when collisions are detected while a packet is still being transmitted. Once the source system finishes transmitting a packet, the data is purged from its buffers, and it is no longer possible to retransmit that packet in the event of a collision.

When the speed at which systems transmit data increases, the round-trip signal delay time during which a collision can be detected decreases. When 100Base Ethernet increased the speed of an Ethernet network by ten times, the standard compensated by reducing the maximum diameter of the network. This enabled the protocol to use the same 64-byte minimum packet size as the original Ethernet standard and still be able to detect collisions effectively.

Gigabit Ethernet increases the transmission speed another ten times, but reducing the maximum diameter of the network again was impractical because it would result in networks no longer than 20 meters or so. As a result, the 802.3z supplement increases the size of the CSMA/CD carrier signal from 64 bytes to 512 bytes. This means that while the 64-byte minimum packet size is retained, the MAC sublayer of a Gigabit Ethernet system appends a carrier extension signal to small packets that pads them out to 512 bytes. This ensures that the minimum time required to transmit each packet is sufficient for the collision-detection mechanism to operate properly, even on a network with the same diameter as 100Base Ethernet.

The carrier extension bits are added to the Ethernet frame after the frame check sequence (FCS), so that while they are a valid part of the frame for collision-detection purposes, the carrier extension bits are stripped away at the destination system before the FCS is computed, and the results are compared with the value in the packet. This padding, however, can greatly reduce the efficiency of the network. A small packet may consist of up to 448 bytes of padding (512 minus 64), the result of which is a throughput only slightly greater than 100Base Ethernet. To address this problem, 802.3z introduces a packet-bursting capability along with the carrier extension. *Packet bursting* works by transmitting several packets back to back until a 1,500-byte burst timer is reached. This compensates for the loss incurred by the carrier extension bits and brings the network back up to speed.

When Gigabit Ethernet is used for backbone networks, full-duplex connections between switches and servers are the more practical choice. The additional expenditure in equipment is

Part III

minimal, and aside from eliminating this collision-detection problem, it increases the theoretical throughput of the network to 2 Gbps.

The Gigabit Media-Independent Interface

The interface between the data link and physical layers, called the *gigabit medium-independent interface* (GMII), enables any of the physical layer standards to use the MAC and LLC sublayers. The GMII is an extension of the medium-independent interface in 100Base Ethernet, which supports transmission speeds of 10, 100, and 1,000 Mbps and has separate 8-bit transmit and receive data paths, for full-duplex communication. The GMII also includes two signals that are readable by the MAC sublayer, called *carrier sense* and *collision detect*. One of the signals specifies that a carrier is present, and the other specifies that a collision is currently occurring. These signals are carried to the data link layer by way of the *reconciliation sublayer* located between the GMII and the MAC sublayer.

The GMII is broken into three sublayers of its own, which are as follows:

- Physical coding sublayer (PCS)
- Physical medium attachment (PMA)
- Physical medium-dependent (PMD)

The following sections discuss the functions of these sublayers.

The Physical Coding Sublayer

The physical coding sublayer is responsible for encoding and decoding the signals on the way to and from the PMA. The physical layer options defined in the 802.3z document all use the 8B/10B coding system, which was adopted from the ANSI Fibre Channel standards. In this system, each 8-bit data symbol is represented by a 10-bit code. There are also codes that represent control symbols, such as those used in the MAC carrier extension mechanism. Each code is formed by breaking down the 8 data bits into two groups consisting of the 3 most significant bits (y) and the 5 remaining bits (x). The code is then named using the following notation: /Dx,y/, where x and y equal the decimal values of the two groups. The control codes are named the same way, except that the letter D is replaced by a K: /Kx,y/.

The idea behind this type of coding is to minimize the occurrence of consecutive zeros and ones, which make it difficult for systems to synchronize their clocks. To help do this, each of the code groups must be composed of one of the following:

- Five zeros and five ones
- Six zeros and four ones
- Four zeros and six ones

NOTE   The 1000Base-T physical layer option does not use the 8B/10B coding system. See "1000Base-T" later in this chapter for more information.

The PCS is also responsible for generating the carrier sense and collision-detect signals and for managing the autonegotiation process used to determine what speed the network interface card should use (10, 100, or 1,000 Mbps) and whether it should run in half-duplex or full-duplex mode.

The Physical Medium Attachment Sublayer

The physical medium attachment sublayer is responsible for converting the code groups generated by the PCS into a serialized form that can be transmitted over the network medium and for converting the serial bit stream arriving over the network into code groups for use by the upper layers.

The Physical Medium-Dependent Sublayer

The physical medium-dependent sublayer provides the interface between the coded signals generated by the PCS and the actual physical network medium. This is where the actual optical or electric signals that are transmitted over the cable are generated and passed on to the cable through the medium-dependent interface (MDI).

The Physical Layer

Collectively called 1000Base-X, there were three physical layer options for Gigabit Ethernet defined in the original 802.3z document, two for fiber-optic cable and one for copper. These three physical layer options in 802.3z were adopted from the ANSI X3T11 Fibre Channel specifications. The use of an existing standard for this crucial element of the technology has greatly accelerated the development process, both of the Gigabit Ethernet standards and of the hardware products. In general, 1000Base-X calls for the use of the same types of fiber-optic cables as FDDI and 100Base-FX but at shorter distances. The longest possible Gigabit Ethernet segment, using single-mode fiber cable, is 5 kilometers.

In the ensuing years, additions have been made to the original description, including IEEE 802 .bj, which defines a four-lane 100 Gbps standard that operates at lengths up to at least 5 meters on links consistent with copper twin-axial cables. The IEEE is also working on Gigabit Ethernet to operate over a single twisted-pair cable for industrial (and automotive) use (IEEE 802.3bp), as well as 40GBase-T (IEEE 802.3bq) for four-pair balanced twisted-pair cables with two connections over 30-meter distances. The latter standard is scheduled for implementation in early 2016.

NOTE For its multimode cable options, the 802.3z standard pioneered the use of laser light sources at high speeds. Most fiber-optic applications use lasers only with single-mode cable, while the signals on multimode cables are produced by light-emitting diodes (LEDs). The jitter effect, which was a problem with previous efforts to use lasers with multimode cable, was resolved by redefining the properties of the laser transmitters used to generate the signals.

Unlike standard and 100Base Ethernet, the fiber-optic physical layer standards for 1000Base-X were not based on the properties of specific cable types, but rather on the properties of the optical transceivers that generate the signal on the cable. Each of the fiber-optic standards supports several grades of cable, using short- or long-wavelength laser transmitters. The physical layer options for 1000Base-X are described in the following sections.

1000Base-LX

1000Base-LX was intended for use in backbones spanning relatively long distances, using long wavelength laser transmissions in the 1,270- to 1,355-nanometer range with either multimode fiber cable within a building or single-mode fiber for longer links, such as those between buildings on a campus network. Multimode fiber cable with a core diameter of 50 or 62.5 microns supports links of up to 550 meters, while 9-micron single-mode fiber supports links of up to 5,000 meters (5 km). Both fiber types use standard SC connectors.

1000Base-SX

1000Base-SX used short-wavelength laser transmissions ranging from 770 to 860 nanometers and is intended for use on shorter backbones and horizontal wiring. This option is more economical than 1000Base-LX because it uses only the relatively inexpensive multimode fiber cable, in several grades, and the lasers that produce the short wavelength transmissions are the same as those commonly used in CD and CD-ROM players. As of this writing, most of the fiber-optic Gigabit Ethernet products on the market support the 1000Base-SX standard.

1000Base-T

Although it was not included in the 802.3z standard, one of the original goals of the Gigabit Ethernet development team was for it to run on standard Category 5 UTP cable and support connections up to 100 meters long. This enables existing 100Base Ethernet networks to be upgraded to Gigabit Ethernet without pulling new cable or changing the network topology. 1000Base-T was defined in a separate document called 802.3ab.

To achieve these high speeds over copper, 1000Base-T modified the way that the protocol uses the UTP cable. While designed to use the same cable installations as 100Base-TX, 1000Base-T uses all four of the wire pairs in the cable, while 100Base-TX uses only two pairs. In addition, all four pairs can carry signals in either direction. This effectively doubles the throughput of 100Base-TX, but it still doesn't approach speeds of 1,000 Mbps. However, 1000Base-T also uses a different signaling scheme to transmit data over the cable than the other 1000Base-X standards. This makes it possible for each of the four wire pairs to carry 250 Mbps, for a total of 1,000 Mbps or 1 Gbps. This signaling scheme is called *Pulse Amplitude Modulation 5* (PAM-5).

While designed to run over standard Category 5 cable, as defined in the TIA/EIA standards, the standard recommends that 1000Base-T networks use at least Category 5e (or enhanced Category 5) cable. Category 5e cable is tested for its resistance to return loss and equal-level far-end crosstalk (ELFEXT). As with 100Base Ethernet, 1000Base-T NICs and other equipment are available that can run at multiple speeds, either 100/1000 or 10/100/1000 Mbps, to facilitate gradual upgrades to Gigabit Ethernet. Autonegotiation, optional in 100Base Ethernet, is mandatory in Gigabit Ethernet.

While networks that run Gigabit Ethernet to the desktop are not likely to be commonplace for some time, it will eventually happen, if history is any indicator.

Ethernet Troubleshooting

Troubleshooting an Ethernet network often means dealing with a problem in the physical layer, such as a faulty cable or connection or possibly a malfunctioning NIC or hub. When a network connection completely fails, you should immediately start examining the cabling and other hardware for faults. If you find that the performance of the network is degrading, however, or if a problem is affecting specific workstations, you can sometimes get an idea of what is going wrong by examining the Ethernet errors occurring on the network.

Ethernet Errors

The following are some of the errors that can occur on an Ethernet network. Some are relatively common, while others are rare. Detecting these errors usually requires special tools designed to analyze network traffic. Most software applications can detect some of these conditions, such as the number of early collisions and FCS errors. Others, such as late collisions, are much more difficult to detect and may require high-end software or hardware tools to diagnose.

- **Early collisions** Strictly speaking, an early collision is not an error because collisions occur normally on an Ethernet network. But too many collisions (more than approximately 5 percent of the total packets) is a sign that network traffic is approaching critical levels. It is a good idea to keep a record of the number of collisions occurring on the network at regular intervals (such as weekly). If you notice a marked increase in the number of collisions, you might consider trying to decrease the amount of traffic, either by splitting the network into two collision domains or by moving some of the nodes to another network.

- **Late collisions** Late collisions are always a cause for concern and are difficult to detect. They usually indicate that data is taking too long to traverse the network, either because the cable segments are too long or because there are too many repeaters. A NIC with a malfunctioning carrier sense mechanism could also be at fault. Network analyzer products that can track late collisions can be extremely expensive, but are well worth the investment for a large enterprise network. Because late collisions force lost packets to be retransmitted by higher-layer protocols, you can sometimes detect a trend of network layer retransmissions (by the IP protocol, for example) caused by late collisions, using a basic protocol analyzer such as Network Monitor.

- **Runts** A *runt* is a packet less than 64 bytes long, caused either by a malfunctioning NIC or hub port or by a node that ceases transmitting in the middle of a packet because of a detected collision. A certain number of runt packets occur naturally as a result of normal collisions, but a condition where more runts occur than collisions indicates a faulty hardware device.

- **Giants** A *giant* is a packet that is larger than the Ethernet maximum of 1,518 bytes. The problem is usually caused by a NIC that is *jabbering,* or transmitting improperly or continuously, or (less likely) by the corruption of the header's length indicator during transmission. Giants never occur normally. They are an indication of a malfunctioning hardware device or a cable fault.

- **Alignment errors** A packet that contains a *partial byte* (that is, a packet with a size in bits that is not a multiple of 8) is said to be *misaligned.* This can be the result of an error in the formation of the packet (in the originating NIC) or evidence of corruption occurring during the packet's transmission. Most misaligned packets also have CRC errors.

- **CRC errors** A packet in which the frame check sequence generated at the transmitting node does not equal the value computed at the destination is said to have experienced a CRC error. The problem can be caused by data corruption occurring during transmission (because of a faulty cable or other connecting device) or conceivably by a malfunction in the FCS computation mechanism in either the sending or receiving node.

- **Broadcast storms** When a malformed broadcast transmission causes the other nodes on the network to generate their own broadcasts for a total traffic rate of 126 packets per second or more, the result is a self-sustaining condition known as a *broadcast storm.* Because broadcast transmissions are processed before other frames, the storm effectively prevents any other data from being successfully transmitted.

Isolating the Problem

Whenever you exceed any of the Ethernet specifications (or the specifications for any protocol, for that matter), the place where you're pushing the envelope should be the first place you check when a problem arises. If you have exceeded the maximum length for a segment, for example, try to eliminate some of the excess length to see whether the problem continues. On a thin Ethernet network, this usually means cross-cabling to eliminate some of the workstations from the segment. On a UTP network, connect the same computer to the same hub port using a shorter cable run. If you have too many workstations running on a coaxial bus (thick or thin Ethernet), you can determine whether overpopulation is the problem simply by shutting down some of the machines.

Encountering excessive repeaters on a UTP network is a condition that you can test for by checking to see whether problems occur more often on paths with a larger number of hubs. You can also try to cross-cable the hubs to eliminate some of them from a particular path. This is relatively easy to do in an environment in which all the hubs are located in the same wiring closet or data center, but if the hubs are scattered all over the site, you may have to disconnect some of the hubs temporarily to reduce the size of the collision domain to perform your tests. The same is true of a coaxial network on which the primary function of the repeaters is to extend the collision domain diameter. You may have to disconnect the cable from each of the repeaters in turn (remembering to terminate the bus properly each time) to isolate the problem.

Reducing the size of the collision domain is also a good way to narrow down the location of a cable fault. In a UTP network, the star topology means that a cable break will affect only one system. On a coaxial network using a bus topology, however, a single cable fault can bring down the entire network. On a multisegment network, terminating the bus at each repeater in turn can tell you which segment has the fault.

A better, albeit more expensive, method for locating cable problems is to use a multifunction cable tester. These devices can pinpoint the exact location of many different types of cable faults.

NOTE   Once you locate a malfunctioning cable, it's a good idea to dispose of it immediately. Leaving a bad cable lying around can result in someone else trying to use it and thus the need for another troubleshooting session.

100VG-AnyLAN

100VG-AnyLAN is a 100 Mbps desktop networking protocol that is usually grouped with 100Base Ethernet because the two were created at the same time and briefly competed for the same market. However, this protocol cannot strictly be called an Ethernet variant because it does not use the CSMA/CD media access control mechanism.

100VG-AnyLAN is defined in the IEEE 802.12 specification, while all of the Ethernet variants are documented by the 802.3 working group. Originally touted by Hewlett-Packard and AT&T as a 100 Mbps UTP networking solution that is superior to 100Base Ethernet, the market has not upheld that belief. While a few 100VG products are still available, 100Base Ethernet has clearly become the dominant 100 Mbps networking technology.

As with 100Base Ethernet, the intention behind the 100VG standard is to use existing 10Base-T cable installations and to provide a clear, gradual upgrade path to the 100Base technology. Originally intended to support all the same physical layer options as 100Base

Ethernet, only the first 100VG cabling option has actually materialized, using all four wire pairs in a UTP cable rated Category 3 or better. The maximum cable segment length is 100 meters for Category 3 and 4 cables and is 200 meters for Category 5. Up to 1,024 nodes are permitted on a single-collision domain. 100VG-AnyLAN uses a technique called *quartet signaling* to use the four wire pairs in the cable.

100VG uses the same frame format as either 802.3 Ethernet or 802.5 Token Ring, making it possible for the traffic to coexist on a network with these other protocols. This is an essential point that provides a clear upgrade path from the older, slower technologies. As with 100Base Ethernet, dual-speed NICs are available to make it possible to perform upgrades gradually, one component at a time.

A 10Base-T/100VG-AnyLAN NIC, however, was a substantially more complex device than a 10/100 100Base Ethernet card. While the similarity between standard and 100Base Ethernet enables the adapter to use many of the same components for both protocols, 100VG is sufficiently different from 10Base-T to force the device to be essentially two network interface adapters on a single card, which share little else but the cable and bus connectors. This, and the relative lack of acceptance for 100VG-AnyLAN, has led the prices of the hardware to be substantially higher than those for 100Base Ethernet.

The one area in which 100VG-AnyLAN differs most substantially from Ethernet is in its media access control mechanism. 100VG networks use a technique called *demand priority,* which eliminates the normally occurring collisions from the network and also provides a means to differentiate between normal and high-priority traffic. The introduction of priority levels is intended to support applications that require consistent streams of high bandwidth, such as real-time audio and video.

The 100VG-AnyLAN specification subdivides its functionality into several sublayers. Like the other IEEE 802 standards, the LLC sublayer is at the top of a node's data link layer's functionality, followed by the MAC sublayer. On a repeater (hub), the *repeater media access control* (RMAC) sublayer is directly below the LLC. Beneath the MAC or RMAC sublayer, the specification calls for a physical medium–independent (PMI) sublayer, a medium-independent interface, and a physical medium–dependent sublayer. Finally, the medium-dependent interface provides the actual connection to the network medium. The following sections examine the activities at each of these layers.

The Logical Link Control Sublayer

The LLC sublayer functionality is defined by the IEEE 802.2 standard and is the same as that used with 802.3 (Ethernet) and 802.5 (Token Ring) networks.

The MAC and RMAC Sublayers

100VG's demand-priority mechanism replaces the CSMA/CD mechanism in Ethernet and 100Base Ethernet networks. Unlike most other MAC mechanisms, access to the medium on a demand-priority network is controlled by the hub. Each node on the network, in its default state, transmits an Idle_Up signal to its hub, indicating that it is available to receive data. When a node has data to transmit, it sends either a Request_Normal signal or a Request_High signal to the hub. The signal the node uses for each packet is determined by the upper-layer protocols, which assign priorities based on the application generating the data.

The hub continuously scans all of its ports in a round-robin fashion, waiting to receive request signals from the nodes. After each scan, the hub selects the node with the lowest port number that has a high-priority request pending and sends it the Grant signal, which is the permission for the node to transmit. After sending the Grant signal to the selected node, the hub sends the Incoming signal to all of the other ports, which informs the nodes of a possible transmission. As each node receives the incoming signal, it stops transmitting requests and awaits the incoming transmission.

When the hub receives the packet from the sending node, it reads the destination address from the frame header and sends the packet out the appropriate port. All the other ports receive the Idle_Down signal. After receiving either the data packet or the Idle_Down signal, the nodes return to their original state and begin transmitting either a request or an Idle_Up signal. The hub then processes the next high-priority request. When all the high-priority requests have been satisfied, the hub then permits the nodes to transmit normal-priority traffic, in port number order.

NOTE By default, a I00VG hub transmits incoming packets out only to the port (or ports) identified in the packet's destination address. This is known as operating in *private mode*. Configuring specific nodes to operate in promiscuous mode is possible, however, in which case they receive every packet transmitted over the network.

The processing of high-priority requests first enables applications that require timely access to the network to receive it, but a mechanism also exists to protect normal-priority traffic from excessive delays. If the time needed to process a normal-priority request exceeds a specified interval, the request is upgraded to high priority.

On a network with multiple hubs, one *root hub* always exists, to which all the others are ultimately connected. When the root hub receives a request through a port to which another hub is connected, it enables the subordinate hub to perform its own port scan and process one request from each of its own ports. In this way, permission to access the media is propagated down the network tree, and all nodes have an equal opportunity to transmit.

MAC Frame Preparation

In addition to controlling access to the network medium, the MAC sublayer assembles the packet frame for transmission across the network. Four possible types of frames exist on a 100VG-AnyLAN network:

- 802.3
- 802.5
- Void
- Link training

802.3 and 802.5 Frames   100VG-AnyLAN is capable of using either 802.3 (Ethernet) or 802.5 (Token Ring) frames so that the 100VG protocol can coexist with the other network types during a gradual deployment process. Using both frame types at once is impossible, however. You must configure all the hubs on the network to use one or the other frame type.

All 100VG frames are encapsulated within a Start of Stream field and an End of Stream field by the physical medium–independent sublayer, which informs the PMI sublayer on the receiving station when a packet is being sent and when the transmission is completed. Inside these fields, the 802.3 and 802.5 frames use the same formats defined in their respective specifications.

The MAC sublayer supplies the system's own hardware address for each packet's source address field and also performs the CRC calculations for the packet, storing them in the FCS field.

On incoming packets, the MAC sublayer performs the CRC calculations and compares the results with the contents of the FCS field. If the packet passes the frame check, the MAC sublayer strips off the two addresses and the FCS fields and passes the remaining data to the next layer.

Void Frames   *Void frames* are generated by repeaters only when a node fails to transmit a packet within a given time period after the repeater has acknowledged it.

Link Training Frames   Every time a node is restarted or reconnected to the network, it initiates a link training procedure with its hub by transmitting a series of specialized link training packets. This procedure serves several purposes, as follows:

- **Connection testing**   For a node to connect to the network, it must exchange 24 consecutive training packets with the hub without corruption or loss. This ensures that the physical connection is viable and that the NIC and hub port are functioning properly.
- **Port configuration**   The data in the training packets specifies whether the node will use 802.3 or 802.5 frames, whether it will operate in private or promiscuous mode, and whether it is an end node (computer) or a repeater (hub).
- **Address registration**   The hub reads the node's hardware address from the training packets and adds it to the table it maintains of all the connected nodes' addresses.

Training packets contain 2-byte *requested configuration* and *allowed configuration* fields that enable nodes and repeaters to negotiate the port configuration settings for the connection. The training packets the node generates contain its settings in the requested configuration field and nothing in the allowed configuration field. The repeater, on receiving the packets, adds the settings it can provide to the allowed configuration field and transmits the packets to the node.

The packets also contain between 594 and 675 bytes of padding in the data field to ensure that the connection between the node and the repeater is functioning properly and can transmit data without error.

The Physical Medium–Independent Sublayer

As the name implies, the *physical medium–independent sublayer* performs the same functions for all 100VG packets, regardless of the network medium. When the PMI sublayer receives a frame from the MAC sublayer, it prepares the data for transmission using a technique called *quartet signaling*. The quartet refers to the four pairs of wires in a UTP cable, all of which the protocol uses to transmit each packet. Quartet signaling includes four separate processes, as follows:

1. Each packet is divided into a sequence of 5-bit segments (called *quintets*) and assigned sequentially to four channels that represent the four wire pairs. Thus, the first, fifth, and ninth quintets will be transmitted over the first pair; the second, sixth, and tenth over the second pair; and so on.

Part III

2. The quintets are scrambled using a different algorithm for each channel to randomize the bit patterns for each pair and eliminate strings of bits with equal values. Scrambling the data in this way minimizes the amount of interference and crosstalk on the cable.

3. The scrambled quintets are converted to sextets (6-bit units) using a process called *5B6B encoding*, which relies on a predefined table of equivalent 5-bit and 6-bit values. Because the sextets contain an equal number of zeros and ones, the voltage on the cable remains even and errors (which take the form of more than three consecutive zeros or ones) are more easily detected. The regular voltage transitions also enable the communicating stations to synchronize their clocks more accurately.

4. Finally, the preamble, Start of Frame field, and End of Frame field are added to the encoded sextets, and, if necessary, padding is added to the data field to bring it up to the minimum length.

The Medium-Independent Interface Sublayer

The *medium-independent interface sublayer* is a logical connection between the PMI and PMD layers. As with 100Base Ethernet, the MII can also take the form of a physical hardware element that functions as a unified interface to any of the media supported by 100VG-AnyLAN.

The Physical Medium–Dependent Sublayer

The *physical medium–dependent sublayer* is responsible for generating the actual electrical signals transmitted over the network cable. This includes the following functions:

- **Link status control signal generation**   Nodes and repeaters exchange link status information using control tones transmitted over all four wire pairs in full-duplex mode (two pairs transmitting and two pairs receiving). Normal data transmissions are transmitted in half-duplex mode.

- **Data stream signal conditioning**   The PMD sublayer uses a system called *nonreturn to zero* (NRZ) encoding to generate the signals transmitted over the cable. NRZ minimizes the effects of crosstalk and external noise that can damage packets during transmission.

- **Clock recovery**   NRZ encoding transmits 1 bit of data for every clock cycle, at 30 MHz per wire pair, for a total of 120 MHz. Because the 5B6B encoding scheme uses 6 bits to carry 5 bits of data, the net transmission rate is 100 MHz.

The Medium-Dependent Interface

The *medium-dependent interface* is the actual hardware that provides access to the network medium, as realized in a network interface card or a hub.

Working with 100VG-AnyLAN

When compared to the success of 100Base Ethernet products in the marketplace, 100VG-AnyLAN obviously has not been accepted as an industry standard, but a few networks still use it. The problem is not so much one of performance, because 100VG certainly rivals 100Base Ethernet in that respect, but, instead, of marketing and support.

Despite using the same physical layer specifications and frame formats, 100VG-AnyLAN is sufficiently different from Ethernet to cause hesitation on the part of network administrators who have invested large amounts of time and money in learning to support CSMA/CD networks. Deploying a new 100VG-AnyLAN would not be a wise business decision at this point, and even trying to preserve an existing investment in this technology is a doubtful course of action.

Mixing 100VG-AnyLAN and 100Base Ethernet nodes on the same collision domain is impossible, but you can continue to use your existing 100VG segments and to add new 100Base Ethernet systems as long as you use a switch to create a separate collision domain. The most practical method for doing this is to install a modular switch into which you can plug transceivers supporting different data link layer protocols.

Part III

12 Networking Protocols

Although the vast majority of local area networks (LANs) use one of the Ethernet variants, other data link layer protocols provided their own unique advantages. Chief among these advantages was the use of media access control mechanisms (MACs) other than Carrier Sense Multiple Access with Collision Detection (CSMA/CD). Token Ring and Fiber Distributed Data Interface (FDDI) were both viable LAN protocols that approached the problem of sharing a network cable in a wholly different way.

Token Ring

Token Ring was the traditional alternative to the Ethernet protocol at the data link layer. The supporters of Token Ring were and, in many cases are, stalwart, and while it did not ever overtake Ethernet in popularity, it was far from being out of the race. Token Ring was originally developed by IBM and later standardized in the IEEE 802.5 document, so, like Ethernet, there were slightly divergent protocol standards.

The biggest difference between Token Ring and Ethernet was the media access control mechanism. To transmit its data, a workstation must be the holder of the *token,* a special packet circulated to each node on the network in turn. Only the system in possession of the token can transmit, after which it passes the token to the next system. This eliminates all possibility of collisions in a properly functioning network, as well as the need for a collision-detection mechanism.

The Token Ring Physical Layer

As the name implies, the nodes on a Token Ring network connect in a ring topology. This is, in essence, a bus with the two ends connected to each other so that systems can pass data to the next node on the network until it arrives back at its source. This is exactly how the protocol functions: The system that transmits a packet is also responsible for removing it from the network after it has traversed the ring.

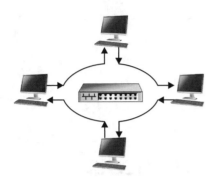

Figure 12-1   Token Ring networks appear to use a star topology, but data travels in the form of a ring.

This ring, however, is logical, not physical. That is, the network to all appearances takes the form of a star topology, with the workstations connected to a central hub called a *multistation access unit* (MAU, or sometimes MSAU). The *logical ring* (sometimes called a *collapsed ring*) is actually a function of the MAU, which accepts packets transmitted by one system and directs them out each successive port in turn, waiting for them to return over the same cable before proceeding to the next port (see Figure 12-1). In this arrangement, therefore, the transmit and receive circuits in each workstation are actually separate ports that just happen to use the same cable because the system always transmits data to the next downstream system and receives data from the next upstream system.

NOTE   The MAU is also known as a *concentrator*.

Cable Types

The original IBM Token Ring implementations used a proprietary cable system designed by IBM, which they referred to as Type 1, or the IBM Cabling System (ICS). Type 1 was a 150-ohm shielded twisted-pair (STP) cable containing two wire pairs. The ports of a Type 1 MAU use proprietary connectors called *IBM data connectors* (IDCs) or *universal data connectors* (UDCs), and the network interface cards used standard DB9 connectors. A cable with IDCs at each end, used to connect MAUs, was called a *patch cable*. A cable with one IDC and one DB9, used to connect a workstation to the MAU, was called a *lobe cable*.

The other cabling system used on Token Ring networks, called Type 3 by IBM, used standard unshielded twisted-pair (UTP) cable, with Category 5 recommended. Like Ethernet, Token Ring used only two of the wire pairs in the cable, one pair to transmit data and one to receive it. Type 3 cable systems also used standard RJ-45 connectors for both the patch cables and the lobe cables. The signaling system used by Token Ring networks at the physical layer is different from that of Ethernet, however. Token Ring uses Differential Manchester signaling, while Ethernet uses Manchester.

Type 3 UTP cabling largely supplanted Type 1 in the Token Ring world, mainly because it was much easier to install. Type 1 cable was thick and relatively inflexible when compared to Type 3, and the IDC connectors were large, making internal cable installations difficult.

NOTE   The physical layer standards for Token Ring networks were not as precisely specified as those for Ethernet. In fact, the IEEE 802.5 standard is quite a brief document that contains no physical layer specifications at all. The cable types and wiring standards for Token Ring derived from the practices used in products manufactured by IBM, the original developer and supporter of the Token Ring protocol. As a result, products made by other manufacturers differed in their recommendations for physical layer elements such as cable lengths and the maximum number of workstations allowed on a network.

Token Ring NICs

The network interface cards for Token Ring systems were similar to Ethernet NICs in appearance. Most of the cards used RJ-45 connectors for UTP cable, although DB9 connectors were also available, and the internal connectors supported all of the major system buses, including PCI and ISA. Every Token Ring adapter had a very large-scale integration (VLSI) chipset that consisted of five separate CPUs, each of which had its own separate executable code, data storage area, and memory space. Each CPU corresponded to a particular state or function of the adapter. This complexity is one of the main reasons why Token Ring NICs were substantially more expensive than Ethernet NICs.

Token Ring MAUs

To maintain the ring topology, all of the MAUs on a Token Ring network needed to be interconnected using the Ring In and Ring Out ports intended for this purpose. Figure 12-2 illustrates how the MAUs themselves were cabled in a ring that was extended by the lobe cables connecting each of the workstations. It was also possible to build a Token Ring network using a *control access unit* (CAU), which was essentially an intelligent MAU that supported a number of

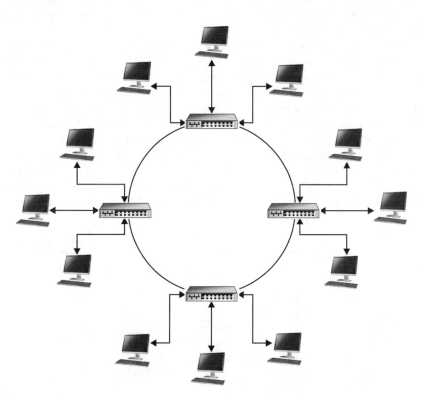

Figure 12-2   The MAUs in a Token Ring network formed the basic ring. This ring was extended with each workstation added to the network.

lobe attachment modules (LAMs). To increase the number of workstations connected to a Token Ring network without adding a new MAU, you could use lobe access units (LAUs) that enabled you to connect several workstations to a single lobe.

NOTE LAMs can support up to 20 nodes each.

Token Ring MAUs (not to be confused with an Ethernet hub, which was occasionally called a MAU, or medium access unit) were quite different from Ethernet hubs in several ways. First, the typical MAU was a *passive device,* meaning it did not function as a repeater. The cabling guidelines for Token Ring networks were based on the use of passive MAUs. There were repeating MAUs on the market, however, that enabled you to extend the network cable lengths beyond the published standards.

Second, the ports on all MAUs remained in a loopback state until they were initialized by the workstation connected to them. In the *loopback state,* the MAU passed signals it received from the previous port directly to the next port without sending them out over the lobe cable. When the workstation booted, it transmitted what was known as a *phantom voltage* to the MAU. Phantom voltage did not carry data; it just informed the MAU of the presence of the workstation, causing the MAU to add it to the ring. On older Type 1 Token Ring networks, an administrator had to manually initialize each port in the MAU with a special "key" plug before attaching a lobe cable to it. This initialization was essential in Token Ring because of the network's reliance on each workstation to send each packet it received from the MAU right back. The MAU could not send the packet to the next workstation until it received it from the previous one. If a MAU were to transmit a packet out through a port to a workstation that was turned off or nonexistent, the packet would never return, the ring would be broken, and the network would cease functioning. Because of the need for this initialization process, it was impossible to connect two Token Ring networks without a MAU, like you can with Ethernet and a crossover cable.

Finally, MAUs always had two ports for connecting to the other MAUs in the network. Ethernet systems using a star topology connected their hubs in a hierarchical star configuration (also called a *branching tree*), in which one hub could be connected to several others, each of which, in turn, was connected to other hubs, as shown in Figure 12-3. Token Ring MAUs were always connected in

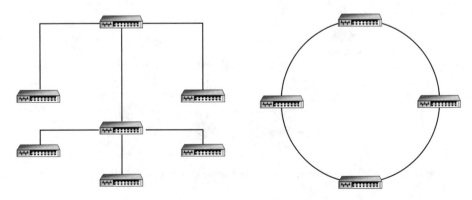

Figure 12-3 Ethernet hubs (at left) were connected using a branching tree arrangement, while Token Ring MAUs (at right) were connected in a ring.

a ring, with the Ring In port connected to the next upstream MAU and the Ring Out port connected to the next downstream MAU. Even if your network had only two MAUs, you had to connect the Ring In port on each one to the Ring Out port on the other using two patch cables.

The connections between Token Ring MAUs were redundant. That is, if a cable or connector failure caused a break between two of the MAUs, the adjacent MAUs transmitted any data reaching them back in the other direction, so the packets always reached all of the workstations connected to the network. The Token Ring standards used a specification called the *adjusted ring length* (ARL) to determine the total length of the data path in the event of this type of failure.

Calculating the ARL

To calculate the ARL for a network, you took the sum of all the patch cable lengths between wiring closets minus the length of the shortest patch cable connecting two wiring closets and made the following adjustments:

- Added 3 meters for every punchdown connection involved in the path between two MAUs
- Added 30 meters for every surge protector used on the network
- Added 16 meters for every eight-port MAU

Because MAUs were often stored in wiring closets, the standard refers to the number of wiring closets used on the network using MAUs more than 3 meters apart. Whether the MAUs were physically located in different closets is not relevant; any two MAUs connected by a cable more than 3 meters long were said to be in different wiring closets. Patch cables shorter than 3 meters were not to be included in the ARL calculations.

NOTE All of the ring lengths discussed in reference to Token Ring networks refer to passive MAU networks. Unlike an Ethernet hub, a Token Ring MAU did not usually function as a repeater. When you used active MAUs that included signal-repeating capabilities, the cables could be much longer, depending on the capabilities of the individual MAU.

Token Passing

Access to the network medium on a Token Ring network was arbitrated through the use of a 3-byte packet known as the *token*. When the network was idle, the workstations were said to be in *bit repeat mode,* awaiting an incoming transmission. The token circulated continuously around the ring, from node to node, until it reached a workstation that had data to transmit. To transmit its data, the workstation modifies a single *monitor setting bit* in the token to reflect that the network is busy and sends it to the next workstation, followed immediately by its data packet.

The packet also circulates around the ring. Each node read the destination address in the packet's frame header and either wrote the packet to its memory buffers for processing before transmitting it to the next node or just transmitted it without processing. (Compare this with Ethernet systems that simply discard packets that are not addressed to them.) In this way, the packet reaches every node on the network until it arrives at the workstation that originally sent it.

On receipt of the packet after it had traversed the ring, the sending node compared the incoming data with the data it originally transmitted to see whether any errors had occurred during transmission. If errors had occurred, the computer retransmitted the packet. If no errors occurred, the computer removed the packet from the network and discarded it and then changed the monitor setting bit back to its free state and transmitted it. The process was then repeated, with each system having an equal chance to transmit.

Although it was not part of the original standard, most 16 Mbps Token Ring systems today included a feature called *early token release* (ETR), which enabled the transmitting system to send the "free" token immediately after the data packet (instead of the "busy" token before the data packet), without waiting for the data to traverse the network. That way, the next node on the network received the data packet, captured the free token, and transmitted its own data packet, followed by another free token. This enabled multiple data packets to exist on the network simultaneously, but there was still only one token. Early token release eliminates some of the latency delays on the network that occurred while systems waited for the free token to arrive.

NOTE Early token release was possible only on 16 Mbps Token Ring networks. Systems that use ETR could coexist on the same network with systems that did not.

Because only the computer holding the token can transmit data, Token Ring networks did not experience collisions unless a serious malfunction occurred. This meant that the network could operate up to its full capacity with no degradation of performance, as can happen in an Ethernet network. The token-passing system was also deterministic, which meant that it could calculate the maximum amount of time that would elapse before a particular node could transmit.

Token Ring is not the only data link layer protocol that used token passing for its media access control method. FDDI uses token passing.

System Insertion

Before it could join the ring, a workstation had to complete a five-step insertion procedure that verified the system's capability to function on the network. The five steps were as follows:

1. **Media lobe check**   The media lobe check tested the network adapter's capability to transmit and receive data and the cable's capability to carry the data to the MAU. With the MAU looping the incoming signal for the system back out through the same cable, the workstation transmitted a series of MAC Lobe Media Test frames to the broadcast address, with the system's own address as the source. Then the system transmitted a MAC Duplication Address Test frame with its own address as both the source and the destination. To proceed to the next step, the system had to successfully transmit 2,047 MAC Lobe Media Test frames and one MAC Duplication Address Test frame. The testing sequence could be repeated only two times before the adapter was considered to have failed.

2. **Physical insertion**   During the physical insertion process, the workstation sent a phantom voltage (a low-voltage DC signal invisible to any data signals on the cable) up the lobe cable to the MAU to trigger the relay that caused the MAU to add the system into the ring. After doing this, the workstation waited for a sign that an active monitor is present on the network, in the form of either an Active Monitor Present (AMP), Standby Monitor Present (SMP), or Ring Purge frame. If the system did not receive one of these frames within 18 seconds, it initiated a monitor contention process. If the contention

process did not complete within one second or if the workstation became the active monitor (see "Token Ring Monitors" later in this chapter) and initiated a ring purge that did not complete within one second, or if the workstation received a MAC Beacon or Remove Station frame, the connection to the MAU failed to open, and the insertion was unsuccessful.

3. **Address verification**   The address verification procedure checked to see whether another workstation on the ring had the same address. Because Token Ring supported locally administered addresses (LAAs), it was possible for this to occur. The system generated a series of MAC Duplication Address Test frames like those in step 1, except that these were propagated over the entire network. If no other system was using the same address, the test frames should come back with their Address Recognized (ARI) and Frame Copied (FCI) bits set to 0, at which time the system proceeded to the next step. If the system received two test frames with the ARI and FCI bits set to 1 or if the test frames did not return within 18 seconds, the insertion failed, and the workstation was removed from the ring.

4. **Ring poll participation**   The system must successfully participate in a ring poll by receiving an AMP or SMP frame with the ARI and FCI bits set to 0, changing those bits to 1, and transmitting its own SMP frame. If the workstation did not receive an AMP or SMP frame within 18 seconds, the insertion failed, and the workstation was removed from the ring.

5. **Request initialization**   The workstation transmitted four MAC Request Initialization frames to the functional address of the network's ring parameter server. If the system received the frames with the ARI and FCI bits set to 0, indicating that there was no functioning ring parameter server, the system's network adapter used its default values, and the initialization (as well as the entire system insertion) was deemed successful. If the system received one of its frames with the ARI and FCI bits set to 1 (indicating that a ring parameter server had received the frame), it waited two seconds for a response. If there was no response, the system retried up to four times, after which the initialization failed, and the workstation was removed from the ring.

System States

During its normal functions, a Token Ring system enters three different operational states, which are as follows:

1. **Repeat**   While in the repeat state, the workstation transmitted all the data arriving at the workstation through the receive port to the next downstream node. When the workstation had a packet of its own queued for transmission, it modified the token bit in the frame's access control byte to a value of 1 and entered the transmit state. At the same time, the *token holding timer (THT)* that allows the system 8.9ms of transmission time was reset to zero.

2. **Transmit**   Once in the transmit state, the workstation transmitted a single frame onto the network and released the token. After successfully transmitting the frame, the workstation transmitted *idle fill* (a sequence of ones) until it returned to the repeat state. If the system received a Beacon, Ring Purge, or Claim Token MAC frame while it was transmitting, it interrupted the transmission and sent an Abort Delimiter frame to clear the ring.

3. **Stripping**   At the same time that a workstation's transmit port was in the transmit state, its receive port was in the stripping state. As the transmitted data returned to the workstation after traversing the ring, the system stripped it from the network so that it would not circulate endlessly. Once the system detected the end delimiter field on the receive port, it knew that the frame had been completely stripped and returned to the repeat state. If the 8.9ms THT expired before the end delimiter arrived, the system recorded a *lost frame error* for later transmission in a *Soft Error Report frame* before returning to the repeat state.

Token Ring Monitors

Every Token Ring network had a system that functioned as the *active monitor* that was responsible for ensuring the proper performance of the network. The active monitor did not have any special programming or hardware; it was simply elected to the role by a process called *monitor contention.* All of the other systems on the network then functioned as *standby monitors,* should the computer functioning as the active monitor fail. The functions of the active monitor were as follows:

- **Transmit Active Monitor Present frames**   Every seven seconds, the active monitor (AM) transmitted an Active Monitor Present MAC frame that initiated the ring polling process.

- **Monitor ring polling**   The AM had to receive either an Active Monitor Present or Standby Monitor Present frame from the node immediately upstream of it within seven seconds of initiating a ring polling procedure. If the required frame did not arrive, the AM recorded a ring polling error.

- **Provide master clocking**   The AM generated a master clock signal that the other workstations on the network used to synchronize their clocks. This ensured that all the systems on the network knew when each transmitted bit begins and ends. This also reduced network *jitter,* the small amount of phase shift that tended to occur on the network as the nodes repeated the transmitted data.

- **Provide a latency buffer**   In the case of a small ring, it was possible for a workstation to begin transmitting a token and to receive the first bits on its receive port before it had finished transmitting. The AM prevented this by introducing a propagation delay of at least 24 bits (called a *latency buffer*), which ensured that the token circulates around the network properly.

NOTE   A latency buffer is also known as *fixed latency.*

- **Monitor the token-passing process**   The active monitor had to receive a good token every 10 milliseconds, which ensured that the token-passing mechanism was functioning properly. If a workstation raised the token priority and failed to lower it or failed to completely strip its packet from the ring, the AM detected the problem and remedied it by purging the ring and generating a new token. Every node, on receiving a Ring Purge MAC frame from the AM, stopped what it was doing, reset its timers, and entered bit repeat mode in preparation for receipt of a new packet.

Ring Polling   *Ring polling* was the process by which each node on a Token Ring network identified its nearest active upstream neighbor (NAUN). The workstations used this information during the beaconing process to isolate the location of a network fault.

The ring-polling process was initiated by the active monitor when it transmitted an Active Monitor Present (AMP) MAC frame. This frame contained an Address Recognized bit and a Frame Copied bit, both of which have a value of 0. The first system downstream of the AM received the frame and changed the ARI and FCI bits to 1. The receiving system also recorded the address of the sending system as its NAUN. This is because the first station that received an AMP frame always changed the values of those two bits. Therefore, the system receiving a frame with zero-valued ARI and FCI bits knew the sender was its nearest active upstream neighbor.

Beaconing   When a station on a Token Ring network failed to detect a signal on its receive port, it assumed that there was a fault in the network and initiated a process called *beaconing*. The system broadcast MAC beacon frames to the entire network every 20 milliseconds (without capturing a token) until the receive signal commenced again. Each station transmitting beacon frames was saying, in essence, that a problem existed with its nearest active upstream neighbor because it was not receiving a signal. If the NAUN began beaconing also, this indicated that the problem was farther upstream. By noting which stations on the network were beaconing, it was possible to isolate the malfunctioning system or cable segment. There were four types of MAC beacon frames, as follows:

- **Set Recovery Mode (priority 1)**   The Set Recovery Mode frame was rarely seen because it was not transmitted by a workstation's Token Ring adapter. This frame was used only during a recovery process initiated by an attached network management product.

- **Signal Loss (priority 2)**   The Signal Loss frame was generated when a monitor contention process failed because of a timeout and the system entered the contention transmit mode because of a failure to receive any signal from the active monitor. The presence of this frame on the network usually indicated that a cable break or a hardware failure had occurred.

- **Streaming Signal, Not Claim Token (priority 3)**   The Streaming Signal, Not Claim Token frame was generated when a monitor contention process failed because of a timeout and the system had received no MAC Claim Token frames during the contention period. The system had received a clock signal from the active monitor, however, or the Signal Loss frame would have been generated instead.

- **Streaming Signal, Claim Token (priority 4)**   The Streaming Signal, Claim Token frame was generated when a monitor contention process failed because of a timeout and the system had received MAC Claim Token frames during the contention period. This frame was usually an indication of a transient problem caused by a cable that was too long or by signal interference caused by environmental noise.

When a system suspected that it may be the cause of the network problem resulting in beaconing, it removed itself from the ring to see whether the problem disappeared. If the system transmitted beacon frames for more than 26 seconds, it performed a *beacon transmit auto-removal test*.

If the system received eight consecutive beacon frames that name it as the NAUN of a beaconing system downstream, it performed a *beacon receive auto-removal test*.

Token Ring Frames

Four different types of frames were used on Token Ring networks, unlike Ethernet networks, which had one single-frame format. The data frame type was the only one that actually carried the data generated by upper-layer protocols, while the command frame type performed ring maintenance and control procedures. The token frame type was a separate construction used only to arbitrate media access, and the *abort delimiter frame* type was used only when certain types of errors occurred.

The Data Frame

Token Ring data frames carried the information generated by upper-layer protocols in a standard logical link control (LLC) protocol data unit (PDU), as defined in the IEEE 802.2 document. Table 12-1 describes the fields that made up the frame and their functions.

The Command Frame   Command frames, also called *MAC frames,* differed from data frames only in the information field and sometimes the frame control field. MAC frames did not use an LLC header; instead, they contained a PDU consisting of 2 bytes that indicated the length of the control information to follow, a 2-byte major vector ID that specified the control function of the frame, and a variable number of bytes containing the control information itself.

MAC frames performed ring maintenance and control functions only. They never carried upper-layer data, and they were never propagated to other collision domains by bridges, switches, or routers.

The Token Frame   The token frame was extremely simple, consisting of only three 1-byte fields: the start delimiter, access control, and end delimiter fields. The token bit in the access control field was always set to a value of 1, and the delimiter fields took the same form as in the data and command frames.

The Abort Delimiter Frame   The *abort delimiter frame* consisted only of the start delimiter and the end delimiter fields, using the same format as the equivalent fields in the data and command frames. This frame type was used primarily when an unusual event occurred, such as when the transmission of a packet was interrupted and ended prematurely. When this happened, the active monitor transmitted an abort delimiter frame that flushed out the ring, removing all the improperly transmitted data and preparing it for the next transmission.

Token Ring Errors

The IEEE 802.5 standard defined a number of soft error types that systems on the network could report to the workstation functioning as the *ring error monitor* using MAC frames. When a Token Ring adapter detected a soft error, it began a two-second countdown, during which it waited to see whether other errors occurred. After the two seconds, the system sent a soft error report

Frame	Function
Start Delimiter (SD), 1 byte	The start delimiter signaled the beginning of the frame by deliberately violating the rules of the Differential Manchester encoding system. The bit pattern used is JK0JK000, where the *J*s were encoding violations of the value 0 and the *K*s were encoding violations of the value 1.
Access Control (AC), 1 byte	The access control byte used the bit pattern PPPTM (*Token Meter*) RRR, where the *P*s were three *priority bits* and the *R*s were three *reservation bits* used to prioritize the data transmitted on Token Ring networks.
Frame Control (FC), 1 byte	The frame control byte used the bit pattern TT00AAAA, where the *T*s specified whether the packet contained a data or a command frame. The third and fourth bits were unused and always had a value of 0.
Destination Address (DA), 6 bytes	The destination address field identified the intended recipient of the packet, using either the hardware address coded into the network interface card or a broadcast or multicast address.
Source Address (SA), 6 bytes	The source address field identified the sender of the packet using the hardware address coded into the network interface card.
Information (INFO), variable	In a data frame, the information field contained the *protocol data unit* passed down from a network layer protocol, plus a standard LLC header consisting of DSAP, SSAP, and control fields.
Frame Check Sequence (FCS), 4 bytes	The frame check sequence field contained the 4-byte result of the CRC computation calculated from the frame control, destination address, source address, and information fields for the purpose of verifying the successful transmission of the packet.
End Delimiter (ED), 1 byte	The end delimiter field indicated the end of the packet by again violating the Differential Manchester signaling rules.
Frame Status (FS), 1 byte	The frame status field used the bit pattern AF00AF00, in which the *A* is the Address Recognized Indicator (ARI) and the *F* is the Frame Copied Indicator (FRI).

Table 12-1   Token Ring Data Frames and Their Functions

message to the address of the ring error monitor. There were several types of soft errors detectable by Token Ring systems, as shown next:

- **Burst error**   A burst error occurred when a system detected five half-bit times (that is, three transmitted bits) that lacked the clock transition in the middle of the bit called for by the Differential Manchester encoding system. This type of error was typically caused by noise on the cable resulting from faulty hardware or some other environmental influence.

- **Line error**   A line error occurred when a workstation received a frame that had an error detection bit in the end delimiter field with a value of 1, either because of a CRC error in the frame check sequence or because a bit violating the Differential Manchester encoding system was detected in any fields other than the start delimiter and end delimiter. A network with noise problems would typically have one line error for every ten burst errors.

- **Lost frame error**   A lost frame error occurred when a system transmitted a frame and failed to receive it back within the four milliseconds allotted by the *return to repeat timer* (RRT). This error could be caused by excessive noise on the network.

- **Token error**   A token error occurred when the active monitor's ten-millisecond *valid transmission timer* (VTX) expired without the receipt of a frame and the AM had to generate a new token, often caused by excessive noise on the network.

- **Internal error**   An internal error occurred when a system detected a parity error during direct memory access (DMA) between the network adapter and the computer.

- **Frequency error**   A frequency error occurred when a standby monitor system received a signal that differed from the expected frequency by more than a given amount.

- **AC error**   An AC error occurred when a system received two consecutive ring-polling frames with ARI and FCI bits set to 0, in which the first frame was an AMP or an SMP and the second frame was an SMP.

- **FC error**   A Frame Copied error occurred when a system received a unicast MAC frame with the ARI bit set to 1, indicating either a noise problem or a duplicate address on the network.

- **Abort delimiter transmitted error**   An abort delimiter transmitted error occurred when a network condition caused a workstation to stop transmitting in the middle of a frame and to generate an abort delimiter frame.

- **Receive congestion error**   A receive congestion error occurred when a system received a unicast frame but had no available buffer space to store the packet because it was being overwhelmed by incoming frames.

FDDI

Appearing first in the late 1980s and defined in standards developed by the American National Standards Institute (ANSI) X3T9.5 committee, *Fiber Distributed Data Interface* (FDDI, pronounced "fiddy") was the first 100 Mbps data link layer protocol to achieve popular use.

At the time of FDDI's introduction, 10 Mbps thick and thin Ethernet were the dominant LAN technologies, and FDDI represented a major step forward in speed. In addition, the use of fiber-optic cable provided dramatic increases in packet size, network segment length, and the number of workstations supported. FDDI packets can carry up to 4,500 bytes of data (compared to 1,500 for Ethernet), and, under certain conditions, a network can consist of up to 100km of cable, supporting up to 500 workstations. These improvements, in combination with fiber optics' complete resistance to the effects of electromagnetic interference, make it an excellent protocol for connecting distant workstations and networks, even those in different buildings. As a result, FDDI originally became known primarily as a backbone protocol, a role for which it is admirably suited. While it originally was designed to run on fiber-optic cables, FDDI can also run on copper cables using electrical signals.

Because of its use as a backbone protocol, products such as bridges and routers that connect Ethernet networks to FDDI backbones are common. FDDI is completely different from Ethernet, and the two network types can be connected only by using a device such as a router or a translation bridge that is designed to provide an interface between different networks. This protocol is reliable because FDDI networks have two counter-rotating rings that back each other up. That is, should one ring fail to function, the system provides an alternative method of sending data.

FDDI Topology

FDDI is a token-passing protocol like Token Ring that uses either a double-ring or a star topology. Unlike Token Ring, in which the ring topology is logical and not physical, the original FDDI specification called for the systems to actually be cabled in a ring topology. In this case, it is a double ring, however. The double ring (also called a *trunk ring*) consists of two separate rings, a primary and a secondary, with traffic running in opposite directions to provide fault tolerance. The circumference of the double ring can be up to 100km, and workstations can be up to 2km apart.

Workstations connected to both rings are called *dual attachment stations* (DASs). If a cable should break or a workstation should malfunction, traffic is diverted to the secondary ring that is running in the opposite direction, enabling it to access any other system on the network using the secondary path. A FDDI network operating in this state is called a *wrapped ring*. Figure 12-4 shows a properly functioning FDDI dual-ring network and a wrapped ring.

If a second cable break should occur, the network is then divided into two separate rings, and network communications are interrupted. A wrapped ring is inherently less efficient than the fully functional double ring because of the additional distance that the traffic must travel and is, therefore, meant to be a temporary measure only until the fault is repaired.

FDDI can also use a star topology in which workstations are attached to a hub, called a *dual attachment concentrator* (DAC). The hub can either stand alone or be connected to a double ring, forming what is sometimes called a *dual ring of trees*. Workstations connected to the hub are *single-attachment stations* (SASs); they are connected only to the primary ring and cannot take

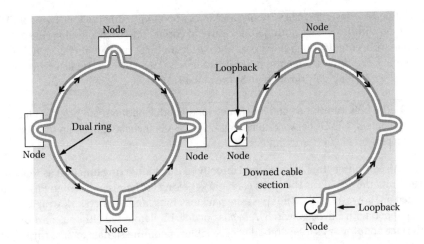

Figure 12-4   The FDDI double ring, functioning normally on the left and wrapped on the right

Module Connection	Other Device	Description
A	B	Peer connection between FDDI fiber-optic DAS and another DAS device on trunk ring
B	A	Peer connection between FDDI fiber-optic DAS and another DAS device on trunk ring
S	M	Connection between FDDI fiber-optic SAS or UTP SAS and concentrator
A	M	Connection between FDDI fiber-optic DAS and concentrator; used for dual homing
B	M	Connection between FDDI fiber-optic DAS and concentrator; used for dual homing
S	S	Connection between FDDI fiber-optic SAS or UTP SAS and another SAS station

Table 12-2   FDDI Connection Types

advantage of the secondary ring's wrapping capabilities. The FDDI specifications define four types of ports used to connect workstations to the network:

- **A** DAS connection to secondary ring
- **B** DAS connection to primary ring
- **M** DAC port for connection to an SAS
- **S** SAS connection to M port in a concentrator

Table 12-2 describes the various types of connections using the four types of FDDI ports.

DASs and DACs have both A and B ports to connect them to a double ring. Signals from the primary ring enter through the B port and exit from the A port, while the signals from the secondary ring enter through A and exit through B. An SAS has a single S port, which connects it to the primary ring only through an M port on a DAC.

NOTE The 500 workstation and 100km network-length limitations are based on the use of DAS computers. A FDDI network composed only of SAS machines can be up to 200km long and support up to 1,000 workstations.

DAS computers that are attached directly to the double ring function as repeaters; they regenerate the signals as they pass each packet along to the rest of the network. When a system is turned off, however, it does not pass the packets along, and the network wraps, unless the station is equipped with a bypass switch. A *bypass switch,* implemented either as part of the network interface adapter or as a separate device, enables incoming signals to pass through the station and on to the rest of the network, but it does not regenerate them. On a fiber-optic network, this is the equivalent of opening a window to let the sunlight into a room instead of turning on an electric light. As with any network medium, the signal has a tendency to attenuate if it is not

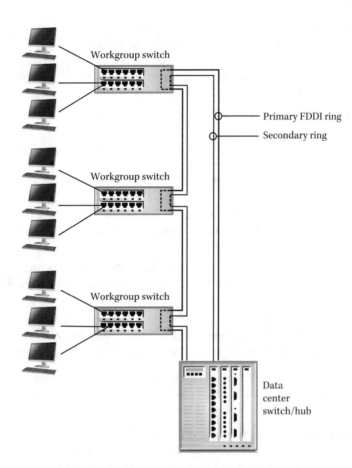

Part III

Figure 12-5   DACs connected to the double ring provide multiple SAS connections

regenerated. If too many adjacent systems are not repeating the packets, the signals can weaken to the point at which stations can't read them.

The DAC functions much like a Token Ring MAU in that it implements a logical ring while using a physical star topology. Connecting a DAC to a double ring extends the primary ring to each connected workstation and back, as shown in Figure 12-5. Notice that while the DAC is connected to both the primary and secondary rings, the M ports connect only the primary ring to the workstations. Thus, while the DAC itself takes advantage of the double ring's fault tolerance, a break in the cable connecting a workstation to the DAC severs the workstation from the network. However, the DAC is capable of dynamically removing a malfunctioning station from the ring (again, like a Token Ring MAU) so that the problem affects only the single workstation and not the entire ring.

It is sometimes possible to connect a DAS to two DAC ports to provide a standby link to the hub if the active link fails. This is called *dual homing*. However, this is different from connecting the DAS directly to the double ring because both the A and B ports on the workstation are connected to M ports on the hub. M ports are connected only to the primary ring, so a dual-homed system simply has a backup connection to the primary ring, not a connection to both rings.

Cascading hubs are permitted on a FDDI network. This means you can plug one DAC into an M port of another DAC to extend the network. There is no limit to the number of layers, as long as you observe the maximum number of workstations permitted on the ring. It is also possible to create a two-station ring by connecting the S ports on two SAS computers or by connecting an S port to either the A or B port of a DAS. Some FDDI adapters may require special configuration to do this.

FDDI Subsystems

The functionality of the FDDI protocol is broken down into four distinct layers, as follows:

- **Physical media dependent (PMD)**   Prepares data for transmission over a specific type of network medium
- **Physical (PHY)**   Encodes and decodes the packet data into a format suitable for transmission over the network medium and is responsible for maintaining the clock synchronization on the ring
- **Media access control (MAC)**   Constructs FDDI packets by applying the frame containing addressing, scheduling, and routing data, and then negotiates access to the network medium
- **Station management (SMT)**   Provides management functions for the FDDI ring, including insertion and removal of the workstation from the ring, fault detection and reconfiguration, neighbor identification, and statistics monitoring

The FDDI standards consist of separate documents for each of these layers, as well as separate specifications for some of the options at certain layers. The operations performed at each layer are discussed in the following sections.

The Physical Media Dependent Layer

The *physical media dependent* layer is responsible for the mechanics involved in transmitting data over a particular type of network medium. The FDDI standards define two physical layer options, as follows.

Fiber-Optic   The Fiber-PMD standards define the use of either single-mode or multimode fiber-optic cable, as well as the operating characteristics of the other components involved in producing the signals, including the optical power sources, photo-detectors, transceivers, and medium interface connectors. For example, the optical power sources must be able to transmit a 25-microwatt signal, while the photo detectors must be capable of reading a 2-microwatt signal.

The 2km maximum distance between FDDI stations cited earlier is for multimode fiber; with single-mode cable, runs of 40km to 60km between workstations are possible. There is also a low-cost multimode fiber cable standard, called LCF-PMD, that allows only 500 meters between workstations. All of these fiber cables use the same wavelength (1300 nm), so it's possible to mix them on the same network, as long as you adhere to the cabling guidelines of the least capable cable in use.

Twisted-Pair   The TP-PMD standard, sometimes called the Copper Distributed Data Interface (CDDI, pronounced "siddy"), calls for the use of either standard Category 5 unshielded twisted-pair or Type 1 shielded twisted-pair cable. In both cases, the maximum distance for a cable run is

100 meters. Twisted-pair cable is typically used for SAS connections to concentrators, while the backbone uses fiber optic. This makes it possible to use inexpensive copper cable for horizontal wiring to the workstations and retain the attributes of fiber optic on the backbone without the need to bridge or route between FDDI and Ethernet. CDDI never gained wide acceptance in the marketplace, probably because of the introduction of Fast Ethernet at approximately the same time.

The Physical Layer

While the PMD layer defines the characteristics of specific media types, the PHY layer is implemented in the network interface adapter's chipset and provides a media-independent interface to the MAC layer above it. In the original FDDI standards, the PHY layer is responsible for the encoding and decoding of the packets constructed by the MAC layer into the signals that are transmitted over the cable. FDDI uses a signaling scheme called *Non-Return to Zero Inverted* (NRZI) 4B/5B, which is substantially more efficient than the Manchester and Differential Manchester schemes used by Ethernet and Token Ring, respectively.

The TP-PMD standard, however, calls for a different signaling scheme, which is Multi-Level Transition (MLT-3), which uses three signal values instead of the two used by NRZI 4B/5B. Both of these schemes provide the signal needed to synchronize the clocks of the transmitting and receiving workstations.

The Media Access Control Layer

The MAC layer accepts protocol data units (PDUs) of up to 9,000 bytes from the network layer protocol and constructs packets up to 4,500 bytes in size by encapsulating the data within a FDDI frame. This layer is also responsible for negotiating access to the network medium by claiming and generating tokens.

Data Frames   Most of the packets transmitted by a FDDI station are data frames. A data frame can carry network layer protocol data, MAC data used in the token claiming and beaconing processes, or station management data.

FDDI frames contain information encoded into symbols. A symbol is a 5-bit binary string that the NRZI 4B/5B signaling scheme uses to transmit a 4-bit value. Thus, two symbols are equivalent to 1 byte. This encoding provides values for the 16 hexadecimal data symbols, 8 control symbols that are used for special functions (some of which are defined in the frame format that follows), and 8 violation symbols that FDDI does not use. Table 12-3 lists the symbols used by FDDI and the 5-bit binary sequences used to represent them.

Figure 12-6 shows the format of a FDDI data frame. The functions of the frame fields are as follows:

- **Preamble (PA), 8 bytes**   Contains a minimum of 16 symbols of idle, that is, alternating 0s and 1s, which the other systems on the network use to synchronize their clocks, after which they are discarded.

- **Starting Delimiter (SD), 1 byte**   Contains the symbols J and K, which indicate the beginning of the frame.

- **Frame Control (FC), 1 byte**   Contains two symbols that indicate what kind of data is found in the INFO field. Some of the most common values are as follows:

- **40 (Void frame)**   Contains nothing but I used to reset timers during initialization.

Symbol	5-Bit Binary Value
0 (binary 0000)	11110
1 (binary 0001)	01001
2 (binary 0010)	10100
3 (binary 0011)	10101
4 (binary 0100)	01010
5 (binary 0101)	01011
6 (binary 0110)	01110
7 (binary 0111)	01111
8 (binary 1000)	10010
9 (binary 1001)	10011
A (binary 1010)	10110
B (binary 1011)	10111
C (binary 1100)	11010
D (binary 1101)	11011
E (binary 1110)	11100
F (binary 1111)	11101
Q	00000
H	00100
I	11111
J	11000
K	10001
T	01101
R	00111
S	11001

Table 12-3   FDDI Symbol Values

- **41, 4F (Station Management [SMT] frame)**   Indicates that the INFO field contains an SMT PDU, which is composed of an SMT header and SMT information.

- **C2, C3 (MAC frame)**   Indicates that the frame is either a MAC Claim frame (C2) or a MAC Beacon frame (C3). These frames are used to recover from abnormal occurrences in the token-passing process, such as failure to receive a token or failure to receive any data at all.

- **50, 51 (LLC frame)**   Indicates that the INFO field contains a standard IEEE 802.2 LLC frame. FDDI packets carrying application data use logical link control (LLC) frames.

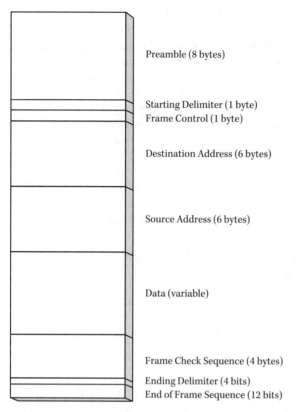

Preamble (8 bytes)

Starting Delimiter (1 byte)
Frame Control (1 byte)

Destination Address (6 bytes)

Source Address (6 bytes)

Data (variable)

Frame Check Sequence (4 bytes)

Ending Delimiter (4 bits)
End of Frame Sequence (12 bits)

Figure 12-6   The FDDI data frame

- **60 (implementer frame)**   These frames are defined by the user of the network or vendor.

- **70 (reserved frame)**   These frames are reserved for future use.

- **Destination Address (DA), 6 bytes**
  Specifies the MAC address of the system on the network that will next receive the frame or a group or broadcast address.

- **Source Address (SA), 6 bytes**   Specifies the MAC address of the system sending the packet.

- **Data (INFO), variable**   Contains network layer protocol data, an SMT header and data, or MAC data, depending on the function of the frame, as specified in the FC field.

- **Frame Check Sequence (FCS), 4 bytes**   Contains a cyclic redundancy check value, generated by the sending system, that will be recomputed at the destination and compared with this value to verify that the packet has not been damaged in transit.

- **Ending Delimiter (ED), 4 bits**   Contains a single T symbol indicating that the frame is complete.

- **End of Frame Sequence (FS), 12 bits**   Contains three indicators that can have either the value R (Reset) or the value S (Set). All three have the value R when the frame is first transmitted and may be modified by intermediate systems when they retransmit the packet. The functions of the three indicators are as follows:

  - **E (Error)**   Indicates that the system has detected an error, either in the FCS or in the frame format. Any system receiving a frame with a value of S for this indicator immediately discards the frame.

  - **A (Acknowledge)**   Indicates that the system has determined that the frame's destination address applies to itself, because the DA field contains either the MAC address of the system or a broadcast address.

  - **C (Copy)**   Indicates that the system has successfully copied the contents of the frame into its buffers. Under normal conditions, the A and C indicators are set together; a frame in which the A indicator is set and C is not indicates that the frame could not be copied to the system's buffers. This is most likely because of the systems having been overwhelmed with traffic.

Token Passing   FDDI uses token passing as its media access control mechanism, like the Token Ring protocol. A special packet called a *token* circulates around the network, and only the system in possession of the token is permitted to transmit its data. The optional feature called *early token release* on a Token Ring network, in which a system transmits a new token immediately after it finishes transmitting its last packet, is standard on a FDDI network. FDDI systems can also transmit multiple packets before releasing the token to the next station. When a packet has traversed the entire ring and returned to the system that originally created it, that system removes the token from the ring to prevent it from circulating endlessly.

Figure 12-7 shows the format of the token frame. The functions of the fields are as follows:

- **Preamble (PA), 8 bytes**   Contains a minimum of 16 symbols of idle, that is, alternating 0s and 1s, which the other systems on the network use to synchronize their clocks, after which they are discarded

- **Starting Delimiter (SD), 1 byte**   Contains the symbols J and K, which indicate the beginning of the frame

- **Frame Control (FC), 1 byte**   Contains two symbols that indicate the function of the frame, using the following hexadecimal values:
    - **80 (Nonrestricted Token)**
    - **C0 (Restricted Token)**

- **Ending Delimiter (ED), 1 byte**   Contains two T symbols indicating that the frame is complete

FDDI is a *deterministic* network protocol. By multiplying the number of systems on the network by the amount of time needed to transmit a packet, you can calculate the maximum amount of time it can take for a system to receive the token. This is called the *target token rotation time.* FDDI networks typically run in *asynchronous ring mode,* in which any computer can transmit data when it receives the token. Some FDDI products can also run in *synchronous ring mode,* which enables administrators to allocate a portion of the network's total bandwidth to a system or group of systems. All of the other computers on the network run asynchronously and contend for the remaining bandwidth in the normal manner.

The Station Management Layer

Unlike Ethernet and most other data link layer protocols, FDDI has network management and monitoring capabilities integrated into it and was designed around these capabilities. The SMT layer is responsible for ring maintenance and diagnostics operations on the network, such as the following:

- Station initialization
- Station insertion and removal
- Connection management

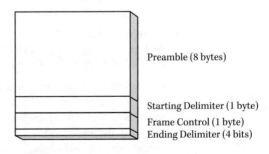

Preamble (8 bytes)

Starting Delimiter (1 byte)
Frame Control (1 byte)
Ending Delimiter (4 bits)

Figure 12-7   The FDDI token frame

- Configuration management
- Fault isolation and recovery
- Scheduling policies
- Statistics collection

A computer can contain more than one FDDI adapter, and each adapter has its own PMD, PHY, and MAC layer implementations, but there is only one SMT implementation for the entire system. SMT messages are carried within standard FDDI data frames with a value of 41 or 4F in the frame control field. In station management frames, the INFO field of the FDDI data frame contains an SMT PDU, which is composed of an SMT header and an SMT info field. Figure 12-8 shows the format of the SMT PDU. The functions of the fields are as follows:

- **Frame Class, 1 byte**   Specifies the function of the message, using the following values:
- **01 (Neighbor Information Frame [NIF])**   FDDI stations transmit periodic announcements of their MAC addresses, which enable the systems on the network to determine their *upstream neighbor addresses* (UNAs) and their *downstream neighbor addresses* (DNAs). This is known as the *Neighbor Notification Protocol.* Network monitoring products can also use these messages to create a map of the FDDI ring.
- **02 (Status Information Frame-Configuration [SIF-Cfg])**   Used to request and provide a system's configuration information for purposes of fault isolation, ring mapping, and statistics monitoring.

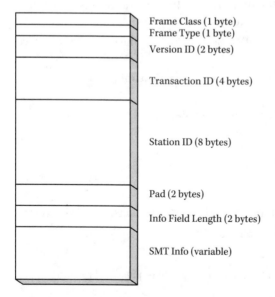

Figure 12-8   The FDDI station management layer PDU format

Frame Class (1 byte)
Frame Type (1 byte)
Version ID (2 bytes)

Transaction ID (4 bytes)

Station ID (8 bytes)

Pad (2 bytes)

Info Field Length (2 bytes)

SMT Info (variable)

- **03 (Status Information Frame-Operation [SIF-Opr])**   Used to request and provide a system's operation information for purposes of fault isolation, ring mapping, and statistics monitoring.
- **04 (Echo Frame)**   Used for SMT-to-SMT loopback testing between FDDI systems.
- **05 (Resource Allocation Frame [RAF])**   Used to implement network policies, such as the allocation of synchronous bandwidth.
- **06 (Request Denied Frame [RDF])**   Used to deny a request issued by another station because of an unsupported Version ID value or a length error.
- **07 (Status Report Frame [SRF])**   Used to report a station's status to network administrators when specific conditions occur, much like an SNMP trap. Some of these conditions are as follows:
  - **Frame Error Condition**   Indicates the occurrence of an unusually high number of frame errors

Part III

- **LER Condition** Indicates the occurrence of link errors on a port above a specified limit
- **Duplicate Address Condition** Indicates that the system or its upstream neighbor is using a duplicate address
- **Peer Wrap Condition** Indicates that a DAS is operating in wrapped mode—in other words, that it is diverting data from the primary ring to the secondary because of a cable break or other error
- **Hold Condition** Indicates that the system is in a holding-prm or holding-sec state
- **NotCopied Condition** Indicates that the system's buffers are overwhelmed and that packets are being repeated without being copied into the buffers
- **EB Error Condition** Indicates the presence of an elasticity buffer error on any port
- **MAC Path Change** Indicates that the current path has changed for any of the system's MAC addresses
- **Port Path Change** Indicates that the current path has changed for any of the system's ports
- **MAC Neighbor Change** Indicates a change in either the upstream or downstream neighbor address
- **Undesirable connection** Indicates the occurrence of an undesirable connection to the system

- **08 (Parameter Management Frame-Get [PMF-Get])** Provides the means to look at management information base (MIB) attributes on remote systems.

- **09 (Parameter Management Frame-Set [PMF-Set])** Provides the means to set values for certain MIB attributes on remote systems.

- **FF (Extended Service Frame [ESF])** Intended for use when defining new SMT services.

- **Frame Type, 1 byte** Indicates the type of message contained in the frame, using the following values:
  - **01** Announcement
  - **02** Request
  - **03** Response

- **Version ID, 2 bytes** Specifies the structure of the SMT Info field, using the following values:
  - **0001** Indicates the use of a version lower than 7.x
  - **0002** Indicates the use of version 7.x

- **Transaction ID, 4 bytes** Contains a value used to associate request and response messages.

- **Station ID, 8 bytes** Contains a unique identifier for the station, consisting of two user-definable bytes and the 6-byte MAC address of the network interface adapter.

- **Pad, 2 bytes**   Contains two bytes with a value of 00 that bring the overall size of the header to 32 bytes.

- **Info Field Length, 2 bytes**   Specifies the length of the SMT Info field.

- **SMT Info, variable**   Contains one or more parameters, each of which is composed of the following subfields:

  - **Parameter Type, 2 bytes**   Specifies the function of the parameter. The first of the two bytes indicates the parameter's class, using the following values:

    - **00**   General parameters

    - **10**   SMT parameters

    - **20**   MAC parameters

    - **32**   PATH parameters

    - **40**   PORT parameters

  - **Parameter Length, 2 bytes**   Specifies the total length of the Resource Index and Parameter Value fields.

  - **Resource Index, 4 bytes**   Identifies the MAC, PATH, or PORT object that the parameter is describing.

  - **Parameter Value, variable**   Contains the actual parameter information.

A FDDI system uses SMT messages to insert itself into the ring when it is powered up. The procedure consists of several steps, in which it initializes the ring and tests the link to the network. Then the system initiates its connection to the ring using a claim token, which determines whether a token already exists on the network. If a token frame already exists, the claim token configures it to include the newly initialized system in the token's path. If no token is detected, all of the systems on the network generate claim frames, which enable the systems to determine the value for the token rotation time and determine which system should generate the token.

Because of the SMT header's size and the number of functions performed by SMT messages, the control overhead on a FDDI network is high, relative to other protocols.

Part III

13 TCP/IP

Since its inception in the 1970s, the TCP/IP protocol suite has evolved into the industry standard for data transfer protocols at the network and transport layers of the Open Systems Interconnection (OSI) model. In addition, the suite includes myriad other protocols that operate as low as the data link layer and as high as the application layer.

Operating systems tend to simplify the appearance of the network protocol stack to make it more comprehensible to the average user. On a Windows workstation, for example, you install Transmission Control Protocol/Internet Protocol (TCP/IP) by selecting a single module called a *protocol*, but this process actually installs support for a whole family of protocols, of which TCP and IP are only two. Understanding how the individual TCP/IP protocols function and how they work together to provide communication services is an essential part of administering a TCP/IP network.

TCP/IP Attributes

There are several reasons why TCP/IP is the protocol suite of choice on the majority of data networks, not the least of which is that these are the protocols used on the Internet. TCP/IP was designed to support the fledgling Internet (then called the ARPANET) at a time before the introduction of the PC when interoperability between computing products made by different manufacturers was all but unheard of. The Internet was, and is, composed of many different types of computers, and what was needed was a suite of protocols that would be common to all of them.

The main element that sets TCP/IP apart from the other suites of protocols that provide network and transport layer services is its self-contained addressing mechanism. Every device on a TCP/IP network is assigned an IP address (or sometimes more than one) that uniquely identifies it to the other systems. Devices today use network interface adapters that have unique identifiers (MAC addresses) hard-coded into them, which makes the IP address redundant. Other types of computers have identifiers assigned by network administrators, however, and no mechanism exists to ensure that another system on a worldwide internetwork such as the Internet does not use the same identifier.

Because IP addresses are registered by a centralized body, you can be certain that no two (properly configured) machines on the Internet have the same address. Because of this addressing, the TCP/IP protocols can support virtually any hardware or software platform in use today. The IPX protocols will always be associated primarily with Novell NetWare, and NetBEUI is used almost exclusively on Microsoft Windows networks. TCP/IP, however, is truly universal in its platform interoperability, supported by all and dominated by none.

Another unique aspect of the TCP/IP protocols is the method by which their standards are designed, refined, and ratified. Rather than relying on an institutionalized standards-making body like the Institute of Electrical and Electronics Engineers (IEEE), the TCP/IP protocols are developed in a democratic manner by an ad hoc group of volunteers who communicate largely through the Internet. Anyone who is interested enough to contribute to the development of a protocol is welcome. In addition, the standards themselves are published by a body called the Internet Engineering Task Force (IETF) and are released to the public domain, making them accessible and reproducible by anyone. Standards like those published by the IEEE are available, but until very recently, you had to pay hundreds of dollars to purchase an official copy of an IEEE standard like the 802.3 document on which Ethernet is based. On the other hand, you can legally download any of the TCP/IP standards, called *request for comments* (RFCs), from the IETF's web site at www.ietf.org/ or from any number of other Internet sites.

The TCP/IP protocols are also extremely scalable. As evidence of this, consider that these protocols were designed at a time when the ARPANET was essentially an exclusive club for scientists and academics and no one in their wildest dreams imagined that the protocols they were creating would be used on a network the size of the Internet as it exists today. The main factor limiting the growth of the Internet is the 32-bit size of the IP address space itself, and a newer version of the IP protocol, called IPv6, addresses that shortcoming with a 128-bit address space. By September 30, 2014, all U.S. government agencies must update their public networks to this version.

NOTE For more information about IPv6, see Chapter 14.

TCP/IP Architecture

TCP/IP is designed to support networks of almost any practical size. As a result, TCP/IP must be able to provide the services needed by the applications using it without being overly profligate in its expenditure of network bandwidth and other resources. To accommodate the needs of specific applications and functions within those applications, TCP/IP uses multiple protocols in combination to provide the quality of service required for the task and no more.

The TCP/IP Protocol Stack

TCP/IP predates the OSI reference model, but its protocols break down into four layers that can be roughly equated to the seven-layer OSI stack, as shown in Figure 13-1.

On LANs, the link layer functionality is not defined by a TCP/IP protocol but by the standard data link layer protocols, such as Ethernet and Token

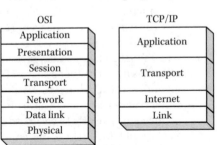

Figure 13-1 The TCP/IP protocols have their own protocol stack that contains only four layers.

Ring. To reconcile the MAC address supplied by a network interface adapter with the IP address used at the network layer, systems use a TCP/IP protocol called the *Address Resolution Protocol* (ARP). However, the TCP/IP standards do define the two protocols most commonly used to establish link layer communications using modems and other direct connections. These are the *Point-to-Point Protocol (PPP)* and the *Serial Line Internet Protocol* (SLIP).

At the Internet layer is the *Internet Protocol* (IP), which is the primary carrier for all of the protocols operating at the upper layers, and the *Internet Control Message Protocol* (ICMP), which TCP/IP systems use for diagnostics and error reporting. IP, as a general carrier protocol, is connectionless and unreliable because services such as error correction and guaranteed delivery are supplied at the transport layer when required.

Two protocols operate at the transport layer: the Transmission Control Protocol (TCP) and the User Datagram Protocol (UDP). TCP is connection-oriented and reliable, while UDP is connectionless and unreliable. An application uses one or the other, depending on its requirements and the services already provided for it at the other layers.

The transport layer can, in some ways, be said to encompass the OSI session layer as well as the transport layer in the OSI model, but not in every case. Windows systems, for example, can use TCP/IP to carry the NetBIOS messages they use for their file and printer-sharing activities, and NetBIOS still provides the same session layer functionality as when a system uses NetBEUI or IPX instead of TCP/IP. This is just one illustration of how the layers of the TCP/IP protocol stack are roughly equivalent to those of the OSI model, but not definitively so. Both of these models are pedagogical and are diagnostic tools more than they are guidelines for protocol development and deployment, and they do not hold up to strict comparisons of the various layers' functions with actual protocols.

The application layer is the most difficult to define because the protocols operating there can be fully realized, self-contained applications in themselves, such as the *File Transfer Protocol* (FTP), or mechanisms used by other applications to perform a service, such as the *Domain Name System* (DNS) and the *Simple Mail Transfer Protocol* (SMTP).

IP Versions

Currently, two versions of IP are being used. The next several sections in this chapter discuss the older version of IPv4, that is, IP version 4. Initially published in the early 1980s, this version did not anticipate the growth of the Internet nor the millions of mobile devices in use today. While such enhancements as *Classless Inter-Domain Routing* (CIDR) and *Network Address Translators* (NATs) forestalled the issue for a time, the dramatic increase in the use of smart phones, tablets, and other such devices created the demand for more IP address availability. (See the sections discussing these enhancements later in this chapter.)

In the 1990s, IPv6 was established and created 128-bit address fields in the IP packet header rather than the 32-bit addresses present in IPv4. In this manner, each time a single bit is added, the number of possible addresses doubles. However, as discussed in Chapter 14, this latest version does not solve all of the issues with IP addresses. Table 13-1 shows some of the differences between IPv4 and IPv6.

IPv4 Addressing

The IPv4 addresses used to identify systems on a TCP/IP network were the single most definitive feature of the protocol suite. The IP address is an absolute identifier of both the individual machine and the network on which it resides. Every IP datagram packet transmitted over a TCP/IP

IPv4	IPv6
32-bit addresses	128-bit addresses
Fragmentation done by both sending and forwarding routers	Fragmentation done only by sending router
Checksum field available	No checksum field available
Manual configuration (that is, static configuration) if IPv4 addresses or *Dynamic Configuration* (DHCP) is required	Autoconfiguration available
No packet flow identification	Packet flow identification available within the IPv6 header using the FlowLabel field

Table 13-1   Some Differences Between IPv4 and IPv6

network contains the IP addresses of the source system that generated it and the destination system for which it is intended in its IP header. While Ethernet and Token Ring systems have a unique hardware address coded into the network interface card, there is no inherent method to effectively route traffic to an individual system on a large network using this address.

A NIC's hardware address is composed of a prefix that identifies the manufacturer of the card and a node address that is unique among all the cards built by that manufacturer. The manufacturer prefix is useless, as far as routing traffic is concerned, because any one manufacturer's cards can be scattered around the network literally at random. To deliver network packets to a specific machine, a master list of all of the systems on the network and their hardware addresses would be needed. On a network the size of the Internet, this would obviously be impractical. By identifying the network on which a system is located, IP addresses can be routed to the proper location using a relatively manageable list of network addresses, not a list of individual system addresses.

IP addresses are 32 bits long and are notated as four 8-bit decimal numbers separated by periods, as in 192.168.2.45. This is known as *dotted decimal notation*; each of the 8-bit numbers is sometimes called an *octet* or a *quad*. (These terms were originally used because there are computers for which the more common term *byte* does not equal 8 bits.) Because each quad is the decimal equivalent of an 8-bit binary number, their possible values run from 0 to 255. Thus, the full range of possible IP addresses is 0.0.0.0 to 255.255.255.255.

IP addresses do not represent computers per se; rather, they represent network interfaces. A computer with two network interface cards has two IP addresses. A system with two or more interfaces is said to be *multihomed*. If the interfaces connect the computer to different networks and the system is configured to pass traffic between the networks, the system is said to function as a *router*.

NOTE A router can be a standard computer with two network interfaces and software that provides routing capabilities, or it can be a dedicated hardware device designed specifically for routing network traffic. At times, the TCP/IP standards refer to routers of any kind as gateways, while standard networking terminology defines a gateway as being an application layer device that forwards traffic between networks that use different protocols, as in an e-mail gateway. Do not confuse the two.

Every IP address contains bits that identify a network and bits that identify an interface (called a *host*) on that network. To reference a network, systems use just the network bits, replacing the host bits with zeros. Routers use the network bits to forward packets to another router connected to the destination network, which then transmits the data to the destination host system.

Subnet Masking

IP addresses always dedicate some of their bits to the network identifier and some to the host identifier, but the number of bits used for each purpose is not always the same. Many common addresses use 24 bits for the network and 8 for the host, but the split between the network and host bits can be anywhere in the address. To identify which bits are used for each purpose, every TCP/IP system has a subnet mask along with its IP address. A *subnet mask* is a 32-bit binary number in which the bits correspond to those of the IP address. A bit with a 1 value in the mask indicates that the corresponding bit in the IP address is part of the network identifier, while a 0 bit indicates that the corresponding address bit is part of the host identifier. As with an IP address, the subnet mask is expressed in dotted decimal notation, so although it may look something like an IP address, the mask has a completely different function.

As an example, consider a system with the following TCP/IP configuration:

```
IP address: 192.168.2.45
Subnet mask: 255.255.255.0
```

In this case, the 192.168.2 portion of the IP address identifies the network, while the 45 identifies the host. When expressed in decimal form, this may appear confusing, but the binary equivalents are as follows:

```
IP address:  11000000 10101000 00000010 00101101
Subnet mask: 11111111 11111111 11111111 00000000
```

As you can see in this example, the dividing line between the network and host bits lies between the third and fourth quads. The dividing line need not fall between quads, however. A subnet mask of 255.255.240.0 allocates 12 bits for the host address because the binary equivalent of the mask is as follows:

```
11111111 11111111 11110000 00000000
```

The dividing line between the network and host bits can fall anywhere in the 32 bits of the mask, but you never see network bits mixed up with host bits. A clear line always separates the network bits on the left from the host bits on the right.

IP Address Registration

For IP addresses to uniquely identify the systems on the network, it is essential that no two interfaces be assigned the same address. On a private network, the administrators must ensure that every address is unique. They can do this by manually tracking the addresses assigned to their networks and hosts, or they can use a service like the Dynamic Host Configuration Protocol (DHCP) to assign the addresses automatically.

On the Internet, however, this problem is considerably more complicated. With individual administrators controlling thousands of different networks, not only is it impractical to assume that they can get together and make sure that no addresses are duplicated, but no worldwide service exists that can assign addresses automatically. Instead, there must be a clearinghouse or registry for IP address assignments that ensures no addresses are duplicated.

Even this task is monumental, however, because millions of systems are connected to the Internet. In fact, such a registry exists, but instead of assigning individual host addresses to each system, it assigns network addresses to companies and organizations. The organization charged with registering network addresses for the Internet is called the *Internet Assigned Numbers Authority* (IANA). After an organization obtains a network address, the administrator is solely responsible for assigning unique host addresses to the machines on that network.

NOTE The IANA maintains a website at www.iana.org.

This two-tiered system of administration is one of the basic organizational principles of the Internet. Domain name registration works the same way. An independent domain registry registers domain names to organizations and individuals, and the individual administrators of those domains are responsible for assigning names in those domains to their hosts.

IP Address Classes

The IANA registers several different classes of network addresses, which differ in their subnet masks, that is, the number of bits used to represent the network and the host. Table 13-2 summarizes these address classes.

The idea behind the different classes was to create networks of varying sizes suitable for different organizations and applications. A company building a relatively small network can register a Class C address that, because the addresses have only 8 host bits, supports up to 254 systems, while larger organizations can use Class B or A addresses with 16 or 24 host bits and create subnets out of them. You create subnets by "borrowing" some of the host bits and using them to create subnetwork identifiers, essentially networks within a network.

The surest way to identify the class of a particular address is to look at the value of the first quad. Class A addresses always had a 0 as their first bit, which means that the binary values for the first quad range from 00000000 to 01111111, which translates into the decimal values 0 through 127. In the same way, Class B addresses always had 10 as their first two bits, providing first quad values of 10000000 to 10111111, or 128 to 191. Class C addresses had 110 as their first three bits, so the first quad can range from 11000000 to 11011111, or 192 to 223.

The IP address class determined the boundary between the host and the network addresses.

	Class A	Class B	Class C	Class D
Network	8	16	24	N/A
Host address bits	24	16	8	N/A
Subnet mask	255.0.0.0	255.255.0.0	255.255.255.0	N/A
Addresses begin with (binary)	0	10	110	1110
First byte values (decimal)	0 to 127	128 to 191	192 to 223	224 to 29
Number of networks	127	16,384	2,097,151	N/A
Number of hosts	16,777,214	65j534	254	N/A

Table 13-2 IPv4 Address Classes

In practice, network addresses are not registered with the IANA directly by the companies and organizations running the individual networks. Instead, companies in the business of providing Internet access, called *Internet service providers* (ISPs), register multiple networks and supply blocks of addresses to clients as needed.

Class D addresses are not intended for allocation in blocks like the other classes. This part of the address space is allocated for multicast addresses. *Multicast addresses* represent groups of systems that have a common attribute but that are not necessarily located in the same place or even administered by the same organization. For example, packets sent to the multicast address 224.0.0.1 are processed by all of the routers on the local subnet.

Unregistered IP Addresses

IP address registration is designed for networks connected to the Internet with computers that must be accessible from other networks. When you register a network address, no one else is permitted to use it, and the routers on the Internet have the information needed to forward packets to your network. For a private network that is not connected to the Internet, it is not necessary to register network addresses. In addition, most business networks connected to the Internet use some sort of firewall product to prevent intruders from accessing their networks from outside. In nearly all cases, there is no real need for every system on a network to be directly accessible from the Internet, and there is a genuine danger in doing so. Many firewall products, therefore, isolate the systems on the network, making registered IP addresses unnecessary.

For a network that is completely isolated from the Internet, administrators can use any IP addresses they want, as long as there are no duplicates on the same network. If any of the network's computers connect to the Internet by any means, however, there is potential for a conflict between an internal address and the system on the Internet for which the address was registered. If, for example, you happened to assign one of your network systems the same address as a Microsoft web server, a user on your network attempting to access Microsoft's site may reach the internal machine with the same address instead.

To prevent these conflicts, RFC 1918, "Address Allocation for Private Internets," specified three address ranges intended for use on unregistered networks, as shown here. These addresses were not assigned to any registered network and could, therefore, be used by any organization, public or private.

- **Class A**   10.0.0.0 through 10.255.255.255
- **Class B**   172.16.0.0 through 172.31.255.255
- **Class C**   192.168.0.0 through 192.168.255.255

Using unregistered IP addresses not only simplified the process of obtaining and assigning addresses to network systems, it also conserved the registered IP addresses for use by systems that actually needed them for direct Internet communications. As with many design decisions in the computer field, no one expected at the time of its inception that the Internet would grow to be as enormous as it is now. The 32-bit address space for the IP protocol was thought to be big enough to support all future growth (as was the original 640KB memory limitation in PCs).

Special IP Addresses

Aside from the blocks of addresses designated for use by unregistered networks, there were other addresses not allocated to registered networks because they were intended for special purposes. Table 13-3 lists these addresses.

Part IV

Address	Example	Function
All bits 0	0.0.0.0	Addressed the current host on the current network, such as during a DHCP transaction before a workstation was assigned an IP address
All bits 1	255.255.255.255	Limited broadcast; addressed all the hosts on the local network
Host bits all 0	192.168.2.0	Identified a network
Host bits all 1	192.168.2.255	Directed broadcast; addresses all the hosts on another network
Network bits all 0	0.0.0.22	Addresses a specific host on the current network
First quad 127	127.0.0.1	Internal host loopback address

Table 13-3   Special-Purpose IP Addresses

Subnetting

Theoretically, the IP addresses you assign to the systems on your network do not have to correlate exactly to the physical network segments, but in standard practice, it's a good idea if they do. Obviously, an organization that registers a Class B address does not have 65,534 nodes on a single network segment; they have an internetwork composed of many segments, joined by routers, switches, or other devices. To support a multisegment network with a single IP network address, you create subnets corresponding to the physical network segment.

A *subnet* is simply a subdivision of the network address that you create by taking some of the host identifier bits and using them as a subnet identifier. To do this, you modify the subnet mask on the machines to reflect the borrowed bits as part of the network identifier, instead of the host identifier.

For example, you can subnet a Class B network address by using the third quad, originally intended to be part of the host identifier, as a subnet identifier instead, as shown in Figure 13-2. By changing the subnet mask from 255.255.0.0 to 255.255.255.0, you divide the Class B address into 254 subnets of 254 hosts each. You then assign each of the physical segments on the network a different value for the third quad and number the individual systems using only the fourth quad. The result is that the routers on your network can use the value of the third quad to direct traffic to the appropriate segments.

NOTE The subnet identifier is purely a theoretical construction. To routers and other network systems, an IP address consists only of network and host identifiers, with the subnet bits incorporated into the network identifier.

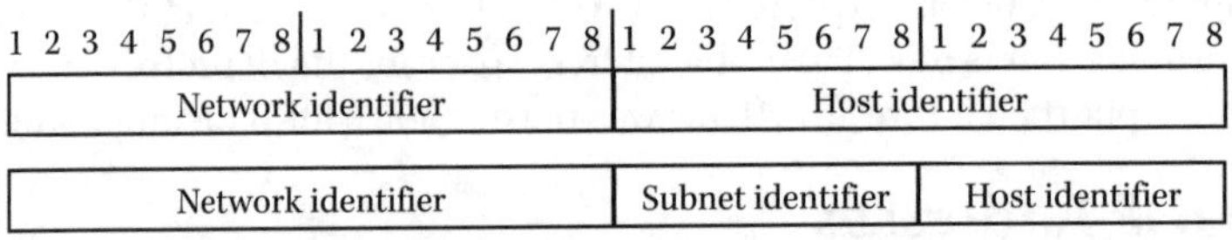

Figure 13-2   The top example shows a standard Class B address, split into 16-bit network and host identifiers. In the bottom example, the address has been subnetted by borrowing eight of the host bits for use as a subnet identifier.

The previous example demonstrates the most basic type of subnetting, in which the boundaries of the subnet identifier fall between the quads. However, you can use any number of host bits for the subnet identifier and adjust the subnet mask and IP address accordingly. This is called *variable mask subnetting*. If, for example, you have a Class B address and decide to use 4 host bits for the subnet identifier, you would use a subnet mask with the following binary value:

```
11111111 11111111 11110000 00000000
```

The first 4 bits of the third quad are changed from zeros and ones to indicate that these bits are now part of the network identifier. The decimal equivalent of this number is 255.255.240.0, which is the value you would use for the subnet mask in the system's TCP/IP configuration. By borrowing 4 bits in this way, you can create up to 14 subnets, consisting of 4,094 hosts each. The formula for determining the number of subnets and hosts is as follows:

```
2x - 2
```

where *x* equals the number of bits used for the subnet identifier. You subtract 2 to account for identifiers consisting of all zeros and all ones, which are traditionally not used, because the value 255 is used for broadcasts, and the value 0 to represent the network. For this example, therefore, you perform the following calculations:

```
24 - 2 = 14
212 - 2 = 4,094
```

NOTE Some TCP/IP implementations are capable of using 0 as a subnet identifier, but you should avoid this practice unless you are certain that all of your routers also support this feature.

To determine the IP addresses you assign to particular systems, you increment the 4 bits of the subnet identifier separately from the 12 bits of the host identifier and convert the results into decimal form. Thus, assuming a Class B network address of 172.16.0.0 with a subnet mask of 255.255.240.0, the first IP address of the first subnet will have the following binary address:

```
10101100 00010000 00010000 00000001
```

The first two quads are the binary equivalents of 172 and 16. The third quad consists of the 4-bit subnet identifier, with the value 0001, and the first 4 bits of the 12-bit host identifier. Because this is the first address on this subnet, the value for the host identifier is 000000000001.

Although these 12 bits are incremented as a single unit, when converting the binary values to decimals, you treat each quad separately. Therefore, the value of the third quad (00010000) in decimal form is 16, and the value of the fourth quad (00000001) in decimal form is 1, yielding an IP address of 172.16.16.1.

Fortunately, manually computing the values for your IP addresses isn't necessary when you subnet the network. Utilities are available that enable you to specify a network address and class and then select the number of bits to be used for the subnet identifier. The program then supplies you with the IP addresses for the machines in the individual subnets.

NOTE There are several free IPv4 and IPv6 subnet calculator utilities available. Type *free subnet calculator* in any search engine.

Part IV

Ports and Sockets

The IPv4 address makes it possible to route network traffic to a particular system, but once packets arrive at the computer and begin traveling up the protocol stack, they still must be directed to the appropriate application. This is the job of the transport layer protocol, either TCP or UDP. To identify specific processes running on the computer, TCP and UDP use port numbers that are included in every TCP and UDP header. Typically, the port number identifies the application layer protocol that generated the data carried in the packet.

The port numbers permanently assigned to specific services, which are called *well-known ports,* are standardized by the Internet Assigned Numbers Authority (IANA) and published in the "Assigned Numbers" RFC (RFC 1700). Every TCP/IP system has a file called Services that contains a list of the most common well-known port numbers and the services to which they are assigned.

For example, the IP header of a DNS query message contains the IP address of a DNS server in its Destination Address field. Once the packet has arrived at the destination, the receiving computer sees that the UDP header's Destination Port field contains the well-known port value 53. The system then knows to pass the message to the service using port number 53, which is the DNS service.

NOTE The port number assignments for the TCP and UDP protocols are separate. Although not typical, it is possible for a service to use different port numbers for TCP and UDP and for the same port number to be assigned to a different service for each protocol.

The combination of an IP address and a port number is known as a *socket.* The uniform resource locator (URL) format calls for a socket to be notated with the IP address followed by the port number, separated by a colon, as in 192.168.2.45:80.

Not all port numbers are well known. When a client connects to a well-known service, such as a web server, it uses the well-known port number for that service (which in the case of a web server is 80), but selects the port number that it will use as its Source Port value at random. This is known as an *ephemeral port number.* The web server, on receiving the packet from the client addressed to port 80, reads the Source Port value and knows to address its reply to the ephemeral port number the client has chosen. To prevent clients from selecting well-known ports for their ephemeral port numbers, all of the well-known port number assignments fall below 1,024, and all ephemeral port numbers must be over 1,024 and higher.

TCP/IP Naming

IP addresses are an efficient means of identifying networks and hosts, but when it comes to user interfaces, they are difficult to use and remember. Therefore, the Domain Name System (DNS) was devised to supply friendly names for TCP/IP systems. In a discussion of the network and transport layer TCP/IP protocols, the most important information to remember about DNS names is that they have nothing to do with the actual transmission of data across the network.

Packets are addressed to their destinations using IP addresses only. Whenever a user supplies a DNS name in an application (such as a URL in a web browser), the first thing the system does is initiate a transaction with a DNS server to resolve the name into an IP address. This occurs before the system transmits any traffic at all to the destination system. Once the system has discovered the IP address of the destination, it uses that address in the IP header to send packets to that destination; the DNS name is no longer used after that point.

NOTE The structure of DNS names and the functions of DNS servers are discussed more fully in Chapter 15.

TCP/IP Protocols

The following sections examine some of the major protocols that make up the TCP/IP suite. There are dozens of TCP/IP protocols and standards, but only a few are commonly used by the systems on a TCP/IP network.

SLIP and PPP

The Serial Line Internet Protocol (SLIP) and the Point-to-Point Protocol (PPP) are unique among the TCP/IP protocols because they provide full data link layer functionality. Systems connected to a LAN rely on one of the standard data link layer protocols, such as Ethernet and Token Ring, to control the actual connection to the network. This is because the systems are usually sharing a common medium and must have a MAC mechanism to regulate access to it.

SLIP and PPP were designed for use with direct connections in which there is no need for media access control. Because they connect only two systems, SLIP and PPP are called *point-to-point* or *end-to-end* protocols. On a system using SLIP or PPP, the TCP/IP protocols define the workings of the entire protocol stack, except for the physical layer itself, which relies on a hardware standard like that for the RS-232 serial port interface, which provides a connection to the modem.

In most cases, systems use SLIP or PPP to provide Internet or WAN connectivity, whether or not the system is connected to a LAN. Virtually every stand-alone PC that uses a modem to connect to an ISP for Internet access does so using a PPP connection, although a few system types still use SLIP. LANs also use SLIP or PPP connections in their routers to connect to an ISP to provide Internet access to the entire network or to connect to another LAN, forming a WAN connection. Although commonly associated with modem connections, other physical layer technologies can also use SLIP and PPP, including leased lines, ISDN, frame relay, and ATM connections.

SLIP and PPP are connection-oriented protocols that provide a data link between two systems in the simplest sense of the term. They encapsulate IP datagrams for transport between computers, just as Ethernet and Token Ring do, but the frame they use is far simpler. This is because the protocols are not subject to the same problems as the LAN protocols. Because the link consists only of a connection between the two computers, there is no need for a media access control mechanism like CSMA/CD or token passing. Also, there is no problem with addressing the packets to a specific destination; because only two computers are involved in the connection, the data can go to only one place.

SLIP

SLIP was created in the early 1980s to provide the simplest possible solution for transmitting data over serial connections. No official standard defined the protocol, mainly because there is nothing much to standardize and interoperability is not a problem. There is an IETF document, however, called "A Nonstandard for Transmission of IP Datagrams over Serial Lines" (RFC 1055), that defines the functionality of the protocol.

The SLIP frame is simplicity itself. A single 1-byte field with the hexadecimal value *c0* serves as an END delimiter, following every IP datagram transmitted over the link. The END character informs the receiving system that the packet currently being transmitted has ended. Some systems also precede each IP datagram with an END character. This way, if any line noise occurs between datagram transmissions, the receiving system treats it as a packet unto itself because it is delimited by two END characters. When the upper-layer protocols attempt to process the noise "packet," they interpret it as gibberish and discard it.

If a datagram contains a byte with the value *c0*, the system alters it to the 2-byte string *db dc* before transmission to avoid terminating the packet incorrectly. The *db* byte is referred to as the ESC (escape) character, which, when coupled with another character, serves a special purpose. If the datagram contains an actual ESC character as part of the data, the system substitutes the string *db dd* before transmission.

NOTE The ESC character defined by SLIP is not the equivalent of the ASCII ESC character.

SLIP Shortcomings

Because of its simplicity, SLIP was easy to implement and added little overhead to data transmissions, but it also lacked features that could make it a more useful protocol. For example, SLIP lacks the capability to supply the IP address of each system to the other, meaning that both systems had to be configured with the IP address of the other. SLIP also had no means of identifying the protocol it carried in its frame, which prevented it from multiplexing network layer protocols (such as IP and IPX) over a single connection. SLIP also had no error-detection or correction capabilities, which left these tasks to the upper-layer protocols, causing greater delays than a data link layer error-detection mechanism would.

PPP

PPP was created as an alternative to SLIP that provided greater functionality, such as the capability to multiplex different network layer protocols and support various authentication protocols. Naturally, the cost of these additional features is a larger header, but PPP still added only a maximum of 8 bytes to a packet (as compared to the 16 bytes needed for an Ethernet frame). Most of the connections to Internet service providers, whether by stand-alone systems or routers, use PPP because it enables the ISP to implement access control measures that protect their networks from intrusion by unauthorized users.

A typical PPP session consists of several connection establishment and termination procedures, using other protocols in addition to the PPP. These procedures are as follows:

- **Connection establishment**   The system initiating the connection uses the Link Control Protocol (LCP) to negotiate communication parameters that the two machines have in common.

- **Authentication**   Although not required, the system may use an authentication protocol such as the Password Authentication Protocol (PAP) or the Challenge Handshake Authentication Protocol (CHAP) to negotiate access to the other system.

- **Network layer protocol connection establishment**   For each network layer protocol that the systems use during the session, they perform a separate connection establishment procedure using a Network Control Protocol (NCP) such as the Internet Protocol Control Protocol (IPCP).

Document	Title
RFC 1661	The Point-to-Point Protocol (PPP)
RFC 1662	PPP in HDLC-like Framing
RFC 1663	PPP Reliable Transmission
RFC 1332	The PPP Internet Protocol Control Protocol (IPCP)
RFC 1552	The PPP Internetworking Packet Exchange Control Protocol (IPXCP)
RFC 1334	PPP Authentication Protocols
RFC 1994	PPP Challenge Handshake Authentication Protocol (CHAP)
RFC 1989	PPP Link Quality Monitoring

Table 13-4   PPP and Related Standards

Unlike SLIP, PPP is standardized, but the specifications are divided among several different RFCs. Table 13-4 lists the documents for each of the protocols.

The PPP Frame

RFC 1661 defined the basic frame used by the PPP protocol to encapsulate other protocols and transmit them to the destination. The frame is small, only 8 (or sometimes 10) bytes, and is illustrated in Figure 13-3.

The functions of the fields are as follows:

- **Flag (1 byte)**   Contains a hexadecimal value of *7e* and functions as a packet delimiter, like SLIP's END character.

- **Address (1 byte)**   Contains a hexadecimal value of *ff,* indicating the packet is addressed to all stations.

- **Control (1 byte)**   Contains a hexadecimal value of *03,* identifying the packet as containing an HDLC unnumbered information message.

- **Protocol (2 bytes)**   Contains a code identifying the protocol that generated the information in the data field. Code values in the *0xxx* to *3xxx* range are used to identify network layer protocols, values from *4xxx* to *7xxx* identify low-volume network layer protocols with no corresponding NCP, values from *8xxx* to *bxxx* identify network layer protocols with corresponding NCPs, and values from *cxxx* to *fxxx* identify link layer control protocols like LCP and the authentication protocols. The permitted codes, specified in the TCP/IP "Assigned Numbers" document (RFC 1700), include the following:

  - **0021**   Uncompressed IP datagram (used when Van Jacobson compression is enabled)

  - **002b**   Novell IPX datagram

  - **002d**   IP datagrams with compressed IP and TCP headers (used when Van Jacobson compression is enabled)

Flag	Address	Control	Protocol	Data	FCS	Flag

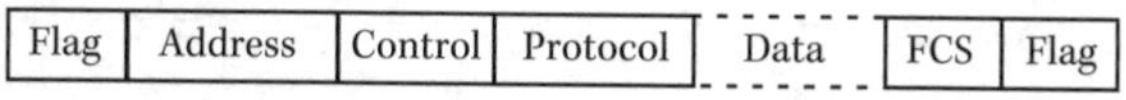

Figure 13-3   The PPP frame format

Part IV

- **002f** IP datagrams containing uncompressed TCP data (used when Van Jacobson compression is enabled)

- **8021** Internet Protocol Control Protocol (IPCP)

- **802b** Novell IPX Control Protocol (IPXIP)

- **c021** Link Control Protocol (LCP)

- **c023** Password Authentication Protocol (PAP)

- **c223** Challenge Handshake Authentication Protocol (CHAP)

- **Data and Pad (variable, up to 1,500 bytes)** Contains the payload of the packet, up to a default maximum length (called the *maximum receive unit* [*MRU*]) of 1,500 bytes. The field may contain meaningless bytes to bring its size up to the MRU.

  - **Frame Check Sequence (FCS, 2 or 4 bytes)** Contains a CRC value calculated on the entire frame, excluding the flag and frame check sequence fields, for error-detection purposes.

- **Flag (1 byte)** Contains the same value as the flag field at the beginning of the frame. When a system transmits two packets consecutively, one of the flag fields is omitted because two would be mistaken as an empty frame.

Several of the fields in the PPP frame can be modified as a result of LCP negotiations between the two systems, such as the length of the protocol and FCS fields and the MRU for the data field. The systems can agree to use a 1-byte protocol field or a 4-byte FCS field.

The LCP Frame

PPP systems use *Link Control Protocol* (LCP) to negotiate their capabilities during the connection establishment process so they can achieve the most efficient possible connection. LCP messages are carried within PPP frames and contain configuration options for the connection. Once the two systems agree on a configuration they can both support, the link establishment process continues. By specifying the parameters for the connection during the link establishment process, the systems don't have to include redundant information in the header of every data packet.

Figure 13-4 shows the LCP message format.

The functions of the individual fields are listed here:

- **Code (1 byte)** Specifies the LCP message type, using the following codes:

  - **1** Configure-Request

  - **2** Configure-Ack

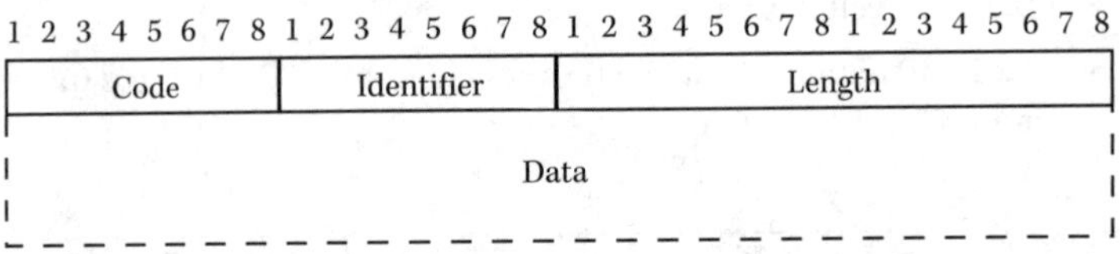

Figure 13-4 The LCP message format

- **3**   Configure-Nak
- **4**   Configure-Reject
- **5**   Terminate-Request
- **6**   Terminate-Ack
- **7**   Code-Reject
- **8**   Protocol-Reject
- **9**   Echo-Request
- **10**   Echo-Reply
- **11**   Discard-Request

- **Identifier (1 byte)**   Contains a code used to associate the request and replies of a particular LCP transaction.
- **Length (2 bytes)**   Specifies the length of the LCP message, including the code, identifier, length, and data fields.
- **Data (variable)**   Contains multiple configuration options, each of which is composed of three subfields.

Each of the options in the LCP message's data field consists of the subfields shown in Figure 13-5. The functions of the subfields are as follows:

- **Type (1 byte)**   Specifies the option to be configured, using a code from the "Assigned Numbers" RFC, as follows:
  - **0**   Vendor Specific
  - **1**   Maximum Receive Unit
  - **2**   Async Control Character Map
  - **3**   Authentication Protocol
  - **4**   Quality Protocol
  - **5**   Magic Number
  - **6**   Reserved
  - **7**   Protocol Field Compression
  - **8**   Address and Control Field Compression
  - **9**   FCS Alternatives
  - **10**   Self-Describing Pad
  - **11**   Numbered Mode

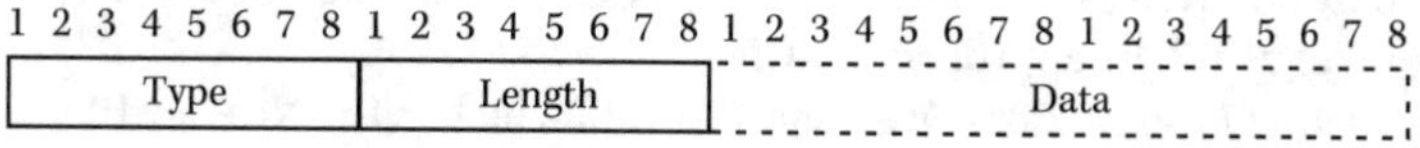

Part IV

Figure 13-5   The LCP option format

- **12**   Multilink Procedure
- **13**   Callback
- **14**   Connect Time
- **15**   Compound Frames
- **16**   Nominal Data Encapsulation
- **17**   Multilink MRRU
- **18**   Multilink Short Sequence Number Header Format
- **19**   Multilink Endpoint Discriminator
- **20**   Proprietary
- **21**   DCE Identifier

- **Length (1 byte)**   Specifies the length of the LCP message, including the code, identifier, length, and data fields.
- **Data (variable)**   Contains information pertinent to the specific LCP message type, as indicated by the code field.

The LCP protocol is also designed to be extensible. By using a code value of 0, vendors can supply their own options without standardizing them with the IANA, as documented in RFC 2153, "PPP Vendor Extensions."

Authentication Protocols

PPP connections can optionally require authentication to prevent unauthorized access, using an external protocol agreed on during the exchange of LCP configuration messages and encapsulated within PPP frames. Two of the most popular authentication protocols—PAP and CHAP—are defined by TCP/IP specifications, but systems can also use other proprietary protocols developed by individual vendors.

The PAP Frame   PAP is the inherently weaker of the two primary authentication protocols because it uses only a two-way handshake and transmits account names and passwords over the link in clear text. Systems generally use PAP only when they have no other authentication protocols in common. PAP packets have a value of *c023* in the PPP header's protocol field and use a message format that is basically the same as LCP, except for the options.

The CHAP Frame   The CHAP protocol is considerably more secure than PAP because it uses a three-way handshake and never transmits account names and passwords in clear text. CHAP packets have a value of *c223* in the PPP header's protocol field and use a message format almost identical to PAP's.

The IPCP Frame

PPP systems use Network Control Protocols (NCPs) to negotiate connections for each of the network layer protocols they will use during the session. Before a system can multiplex the traffic generated by different protocols over a single PPP connection, it must establish a connection for each protocol using the appropriate NCPs.

The *Internet Protocol Control Protocol* (IPCP), which is the NCP for IP, is a good example of the protocol structure. The message format of the NCPs is nearly identical to that of LCP, except that it supports only values 1 through 7 for the code field (the link configuration, link termination, and code reject values) and uses different options in the data field. Like LCP, the messages are carried in PPP frames, but with a value of *8021 in the PPP header's protocol field.*

The options that can be included in the data field of an IPCP message use the following values in the type field:

- **2 (IP Compression Protocol)** Specifies the protocol the system should use to compress IP headers, for which the only valid option is Van Jacobson compression.

NOTE Van Jacobson TCP/IP Header Compression is a data compression protocol described in RFC 1144, specifically designed by Van Jacobson to improve TCP/IP performance over slow serial links. This compression reduces the normal 40-byte TCP/IP packet headers down to 3 to 4 bytes for the average case by saving the state of TCP connections at both ends of a link and sending the differences only in the header fields that change. While this makes a big difference on low-speed links, it will not do anything about the processing delay inherent to most dial-up modems.

- **3 (IP Address)** Used by the transmitting system to request a particular IP address or, if the value is 0.0.0.0, to request that the receiving system supply an address (replaces the type 1 IP Addresses option, which is no longer used).

PPP Connection Establishment

Once the physical layer connection between the two systems has been established, the PPP connection establishment process begins. The two systems pass through several distinct phases during the course of the session, as illustrated in Figure 13-6 and discussed in the following sections.

Link Dead Both systems begin and end the session in the Link Dead phase, which indicates that no physical layer connection exists between the two machines. On a typical session, an application or service on one system initiates the physical layer connection. Once the hardware connection process is completed, the systems pass into the Link Establishment phase.

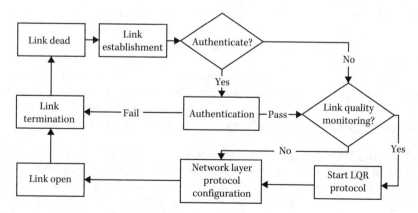

Figure 13-6 PPP connection phases

Link Establishment In the Link Establishment phase, the system initiating the connection transmits an LCP Configure Request message to the destination containing the options it would like to enable, such as the use of specific authentication, link-quality monitoring, and network layer protocols (if any), and whether the systems should modify standard features, such as the size of the FCS field or a different MRU value. If the receiving system can support all the specified options, it replies with a Configure Ack message containing the same option values, and this phase of the connection process is completed.

If the receiving system recognizes the options in the request message but cannot support the values for those options supplied by the sender (such as if the system supports authentication but not with the protocol the sender has specified), it replies with a Configure Nak message containing the options with values it cannot support. With these options, the replying system supplies all the values it does support and also may include other options it would like to see enabled. Using this information, the connecting system generates another Configure Request message containing options it knows are supported, to which the receiver replies with a Configure Ack message.

If the receiving system fails to recognize any of the options in the request, it replies with a Configure Reject message containing only the unrecognized options. The sender then generates a new Configure Request message that does not contain the rejected options, and the procedure continues as previously outlined. Eventually, the systems perform a successful request/acknowledgment exchange, and the connection process moves on to the next phase.

Authentication The Authentication phase of the connection process is optional and is triggered by the inclusion of the Authentication Protocol option in the LCP Configure Request message. During the LCP link establishment process, the two systems agree on an authentication protocol to use. Use of the PAP and CHAP protocols is common, but other proprietary protocols are available.

The message format and exchange procedures for the Authentication phase are dictated by the selected protocol. In a PAP authentication, for example, the sending system transmits an Authenticate Request message containing an account name and password, and the receiver replies with either an Authenticate Ack or Authenticate Nak message.

CHAP is inherently more secure than PAP and requires a more complex message exchange. The sending system transmits a Challenge message containing data that the receiver uses with its encryption key to compute a value it returns to the sender in a Response message. Depending on whether the value in the response matches the sender's own computations, it transmits a Success or Failure message.

A successful transaction causes the connection procedure to proceed to the next phase, but the effect of a failure is dictated by the implementation of the protocol. Some systems proceed directly to the Link Termination phase in the event of an authentication failure, while others might permit retries or limited network access to a help subsystem.

Link Quality Monitoring The use of a link quality monitoring protocol is also an optional element of the connection process, triggered by the inclusion of the Quality Protocol option in the LCP Configure Request message. Although the option enables the sending system to specify any protocol for this purpose, only one has been standardized, the Link Quality Report protocol. The negotiation process that occurs at this phase enables the systems to agree on an interval at which they should transmit messages containing link traffic and error statistics throughout the session.

Network Layer Protocol Configuration   PPP supports the multiplexing of network layer protocols over a single connection, and during this phase, the systems perform a separate network layer connection establishment procedure for each of the network layer protocols that they have agreed to use during the Link Establishment phase. Each network layer protocol has its own network control protocol (NCP) for this purpose, such as the Internet Protocol Control Protocol (IPCP) or the Internetworking Packet Exchange Control Protocol (IPXCP). The structure of an NCP message exchange is similar to that of LCP, except the options carried in the Configure Request message are unique to the requirements of the protocol. During an IPCP exchange, for example, the systems inform each other of their IP addresses and agree on whether to use Van Jacobson header compression. Other protocols have their own individual needs that the systems negotiate as needed. NCP initialization and termination procedures can also occur at any other time during the connection.

Link Open   Once the individual NCP exchanges are completed, the connection is fully established, and the systems enter the Link Open phase. Network layer protocol data can now travel over the link in either direction.

Link Termination   When one of the systems ends the session or as a result of other conditions such as a physical layer disconnection, an authentication failure, or an inactivity timeout, the systems enter the Link Termination phase. To sever the link, one system transmits an LCP Terminate Request message to which the other system replies with a Terminate Ack. Both systems then return to the Link Dead phase.

NCPs also support the Terminate Request and Terminate Ack messages, but they are intended for use while the PPP connection remains intact. In fact, the PPP connection can remain active even if all of the network layer protocol connections have been terminated. It is unnecessary for systems to terminate the network layer protocol connections before terminating the PPP connection.

ARP

The *Address Resolution Protocol* (ARP) occupies an unusual place in the TCP/IP suite because it defies all attempts at categorization. Unlike most of the other TCP/IP protocols, ARP messages are not carried within IP datagrams. A separate protocol identifier is defined in the "Assigned Numbers" document that data link layer protocols use to indicate that they contain ARP messages. Because of this, there is some difference of opinion about the layer of the protocol stack to which ARP belongs. Some say ARP is a link layer protocol because it provides a service to IP, while others associate it with the Internet layer because its messages are carried within link layer protocols.

The function of the ARP protocol, as defined in RFC 826, "An Ethernet Address Resolution Protocol," is to reconcile the IP addresses used to identify systems at the upper layers with the hardware addresses at the data link layer. When it requests network resources, a TCP/IP application supplies the destination IP address used in the IP protocol header. The system may discover the IP address using a DNS or NetBIOS name-resolution process, or it may use an address supplied by an operating system or application configuration parameter.

Data link layer protocols such as Ethernet, however, have no use for IP addresses and cannot read the contents of the IP datagram anyway. To transmit the packet to its destination, the data link layer protocol must have the hardware address coded into the destination system's network interface adapter. ARP converts IP addresses into hardware addresses by broadcasting request packets containing the IP address on the local network and waiting for the holder of that IP address to respond with a reply containing the equivalent hardware address.

NOTE ARP was originally developed for use with DIX Ethernet networks, but has been generalized to allow its use with other data link layer protocols.

The biggest difference between IP addresses and hardware addresses is that IP is responsible for the delivery of the packet to its ultimate destination, while an Ethernet implementation is concerned only with delivery to the next stop on the journey. If the packet's destination is on the same network segment as the source, the IP protocol uses ARP to resolve the IP address of the ultimate destination into a hardware address. If, however, the destination is located on another network, the IP protocol will not use ARP to resolve the ultimate destination address (that is, the destination address in the IP header). Instead, it will pass the IP address of the default gateway to the ARP protocol for address resolution.

This is because the data link protocol header must contain the hardware address of the next intermediate stop as its destination, which may well be a router. It is up to that router to forward the packet on the next leg of its journey. Thus, in the course of a single internetwork transmission, many different machines may perform ARP resolutions on the same packet with different results.

ARP Message Format

ARP messages are carried directly within data link layer frames, using *0806* as the Ethertype or SNAP Local Code value to identify the protocol being carried in the packet. There is one format for all of the ARP message types, which is illustrated in Figure 13-7.

ARP Transactions

An ARP transaction occurs when the IP protocol in a TCP/IP system is ready to transmit a datagram over the network. The system knows its own hardware and IP addresses, as well as the IP address of the packet's intended destination. All it lacks is the hardware address of the system on the local network that is to receive the packet. The ARP message exchange proceeds according to the following steps:

1. The transmitting system generates an ARP Request packet containing its own addresses in the Sender Hardware Address and Sender Protocol Address fields. The Target Protocol Address contains the IP address of the system on the local network that is to receive the

```
1 2 3 4 5 6 7 8 1 2 3 4 5 6 7 8 1 2 3 4 5 6 7 8 1 2 3 4 5 6 7 8
```

Hardware Type		Protocol Type	
Hardware Size	Protocol Size	Op Code	
Sender Hardware Address			
Sender Hardware Address (cont'd)		Sender Protocol Address	
Sender Protocol Address (cont'd)		Target Hardware Address	
Target Hardware Address (cont'd)			
Target Protocol Address			

Figure 13-7   The ARP message format

datagram, while the Target Hardware Address is left blank. Some implementations insert a broadcast address or other value into the Target Hardware Address field of the ARP Request message, but this value is ignored by the recipient because this is the address the protocol is trying to ascertain.

2. The system transmits the ARP Request message as a broadcast to the local network, asking in effect, "Who is using this IP address, and what is your hardware address?"

3. Each TCP/IP system on the local network receives the ARP Request broadcast and examines the contents of the Target Protocol Address field. If the system does not use that address on one of its network interfaces, it silently discards the packet. If the system does use the address, it generates an ARP Reply message in response. The system uses the contents of the request message's Sender Hardware Address and Sender Protocol Address fields as the values for its reply message's Target Hardware Address and Target Protocol Address fields. The system then inserts its own hardware address and IP address into the Sender Hardware Address and Sender Protocol Address fields, respectively.

4. The system using the requested IP address transmits the reply message as a unicast to the original sender. On receipt of the reply, the system that initiated the ARP exchange uses the contents of the Sender Hardware Address field as the Destination Address for the data link layer transmission of the IP datagram.

ARP Caching

Because of its reliance on broadcast transmissions, ARP can generate a significant amount of network traffic. To lessen the burden of the protocol on the network, TCP/IP systems cache the hardware addresses discovered through ARP transactions in memory for a designated period of time. This way, a system transmitting a large string of datagrams to the same host doesn't have to generate individual ARP requests for each packet.

This is particularly helpful in an internetwork environment in which systems routinely transmit the majority of their packets to destinations on other networks. When a network segment has only a single router, all IP datagrams destined for other networks are sent through that router. When systems have the hardware address for that router in the ARP cache, they can transmit the majority of their datagrams without using ARP broadcasts.

The amount of time that entries remain in the ARP cache varies with different TCP/IP implementations. Windows systems purge entries after two minutes when they are not used to transmit additional datagrams.

IP

The Internet Protocol (IP), as defined in RFC 791, is the primary carrier protocol for the TCP/IP suite. IP is essentially the envelope that carries the messages generated by most of the other TCP/IP protocols. Operating at the network layer of the OSI model, IP is a connectionless, unreliable protocol that performs several functions that are a critical part of getting packets from the source system to the destination. Among these functions are the following:

- **Addressing**   Identifying the system that will be the ultimate recipient of the packet
- **Packaging**   Encapsulating transport layer data in datagrams for transmission to the destination

- **Fragmenting**   Splitting datagrams into sections small enough for transmission over a network

- **Routing**   Determining the path of the packet through the internetwork to the destination

The following sections examine these functions in more detail.

Addressing

IP is the protocol responsible for the delivery of TCP/IP packets to their ultimate destination. It is vital to understand how this differs from the addressing performed by a data link layer protocol like Ethernet or Token Ring. Data link layer protocols are aware only of the machines on the local network segment. No matter where the packet finally ends up, the destination address in the data link layer protocol header is always that of a machine on a local network.

If the ultimate destination of the packet is a system on another network segment, the data link layer protocol address will point to a router that provides access to that segment. On receipt of the packet, the router strips off the data link layer protocol header and generates a new one containing the address of the packet's next intermediate destination, called a *hop*. Thus, throughout the packet's journey, the data link protocol header will contain a different destination address for each hop.

The destination address in the IP header, however, always points to the final destination of the packet, regardless of the network on which it's located, and it never changes throughout the journey. IP is the first protocol in the stack (working up from the bottom) to be conscious of the packet's end-to-end journey from source to destination. Most of the protocol's functions revolve around the preparation of the transport layer data for transmission across multiple networks to the destination.

Packaging

IP is also responsible for packaging transport layer protocol data into structures called *datagrams* for its journey to the destination. During the journey, routers apply a new data link layer protocol header to a datagram for each hop. Before reaching its final destination, a packet may pass through networks using several different data link layer protocols, each of which requires a different header. The IP "envelope," on the other hand, remains intact throughout the entire journey, except for a few bits that are modified along the way, just like a mailing envelope is postmarked.

As it receives data from the transport layer protocol, IP packages it into datagrams of a size suitable for transmission over the local network. A datagram (in most cases) consists of a 20-byte header plus the transport layer data. Figure 13-8 illustrates the header.

The functions of the header fields are as follows:

- **Version, 4 bits**   Specifies the version of the IP protocol in use. The value for the current implementation is 4.

- **IHL (Internet Header Length), 4 bits**   Specifies the length of the IP header, in 32-bit words. When the header contains no optional fields, the value is 5.

- **TOS (Type of Service), 1 byte**   Bits 1 through 3 and 8 are unused. Bits 4 through 7 specify the service priority desired for the datagram, using the following values:

    - **0000**   Default

    - **0001**   Minimize Monetary Cost

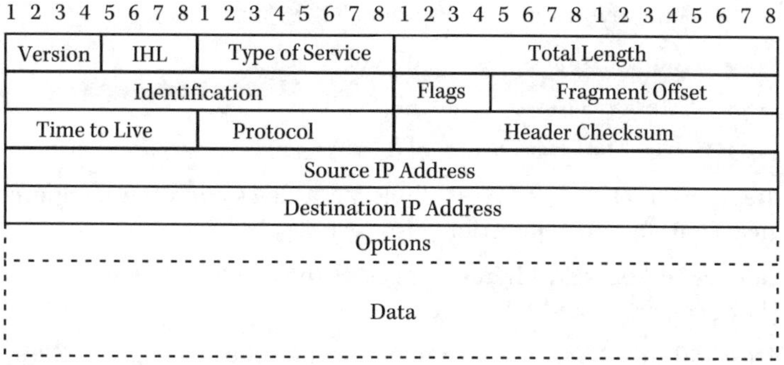

```
1 2 3 4 5 6 7 8 1 2 3 4 5 6 7 8 1 2 3 4 5 6 7 8 1 2 3 4 5 6 7 8
```

Version	IHL	Type of Service	Total Length		
Identification			Flags	Fragment Offset	
Time to Live		Protocol	Header Checksum		
Source IP Address					
Destination IP Address					
Options					
Data					

Figure 13-8   The IP header format

- **0010**   Maximize Reliability
- **0100**   Maximize Throughput
- **1000**   Minimize Delay
- **1111**   Maximize Security

- **Total Length, 2 bytes**   Specifies the length of the datagram, including all the header fields and the data.

- **Identification, 2 bytes**   Contains a unique value for each datagram, used by the destination system to reassemble fragments.

- **Flags, 3 bits**   Contains bits used during the datagram fragmentation process, with the following values:

  - **Bit 1**   Not used.

  - **Bit 2 (Don't Fragment)**   When set to a value of 1, prevents the datagram from being fragmented by any system.

  - **Bit 3 (More Fragments)**   When set to a value of 0, indicates that the last fragment of the datagram has been transmitted. When set to 1, indicates that fragments still await transmission.

- **Fragment Offset, 13 bits**   Specifies the location (in 8-byte units) of the current fragment in the datagram.

- **TTL (Time to Live), 1 byte**   Specifies the number of routers the datagram should be permitted to pass through on its way to the destination. Each router that processes the packet decrements this field by 1. Once the value reaches 0, the packet is discarded, whether or not it has reached the destination.

- **Protocol, 1 byte**   Identifies the protocol that generated the information in the data field, using values found in the "Assigned Numbers" RFC (RFC 1700) and the PROTOCOL file found on every TCP/IP system, some of which are as follows:

  - **1**   Internet Control Message Protocol (ICMP)

  - **2**   Internet Group Management Protocol (IGMP)

Part IV

- **3**   Gateway-to-Gateway Protocol (GGP)
- **6**   Transmission Control Protocol (TCP)
- **8**   Exterior Gateway Protocol (EGP)
- **17**   User Datagram Protocol (UDP)

- **Header Checksum, 2 bytes**   Contains a checksum value computer in the IP header fields only for error-detection purposes.
- **Source IP Address, 4 bytes**   Specifies the IP address of the system from which the datagram originated.
- **Destination IP Address, 4 bytes**   Specifies the IP address of the system that will be the ultimate recipient of the datagram.
- **Options (variable)**   Can contain any of 16 options defined in the "Assigned Numbers" RFC, described later in this section.
- **Data (variable, up to the MTU for the connected network)**   Contains the payload of the datagram, consisting of data passed down from a transport layer protocol.

Systems use the IP header options to carry additional information, either supplied by the sender or gathered as the packet travels to the destination. Each option is composed of the following fields:

- **Option Type (1 byte)**   Contains a value identifying the option that consists of the following three subfields:
  - **Copy Flag (1 bit)**   When set to a value of 1, indicates the option should be copied to each of the fragments that comprise the datagram.
  - **Option Class (2 bits)**   Contains a code that identifies the option's basic function, using the following values:
    - **0**   Control
    - **2**   Debugging and measurement
  - **Option Number (5 bits)**   Contains a unique identifier for the option, as specified in the "Assigned Numbers" RFC.
- **Option Length (1 byte)**   Specifies the total length of the option, including the Option Type, Option Length, and Option Data fields.
- **Option Data (Option Length minus 2)**   Contains the option-specific information being carried to the destination.

Table 13-5 lists some of the options systems can insert into IP datagrams, the values for the option subfields, and the RFCs that define the option's function. The functions of the options are as follows:

- **End of Options List**   Consisting only of an Option Type field with the value 0, this option marks the end of all the options in an IP header.
- **No Operation**   Consisting only of an Option Type field, systems can use this option to pad out the space between two other options, to force the following option to begin at the boundary between 32-bit words.

Copy Flag	Option Class	Option Number	Option Value	RFC	Option Name
0	0	1	1	RFC 791	No Operation
1	0	3	131	RFC 791	Loose Source Route
0	2	4	68	RFC 791	Time Stamp
0	0	7	7	RFC 791	Record Route
1	0	9	137	RFC 791	Strict Source Route

Table 13-5   IP Header Options

- **Loose Source Route and Strict Source Route**   Systems use the Loose Source Route and Strict Source Route options to carry the IP addresses of routers the datagram must pass through on its way to the destination. When a system uses the Loose Source Route option, the datagram can pass through other routers in addition to those listed in the option. The Strict Source Route option defines the entire path of the datagram from the source to the destination.

- **Time Stamp**   This option is designed to hold time stamps generated by one or more systems processing the packet as it travels to its destination. The sending system may supply the IP addresses of the systems that are to add time stamps to the header, enable the systems to save their IP addresses to the header along with the time stamps, or omit the IP addresses of the time-stamping systems entirely. The size of the option is variable to accommodate multiple time stamps, but must be specified when the sender creates the datagram and cannot be enlarged en route to the destination.

- **Record Route**   This option provides the receiving system with a record of all the routers through which the datagram has passed during its journey to the destination. Each router adds its address to the option as it processes the packet.

Fragmenting

The size of the IP datagrams used to transmit the transport layer data depends on the data link layer protocol in use. Ethernet networks, for example, can carry datagrams up to 1,500 bytes in size, while Token Ring networks typically support packets as large as 4,500 bytes. The system transmitting the datagram uses the *maximum transfer unit* (MTU) of the connected network, that is, the largest possible frame that can be transmitted using that data link layer protocol, as one factor in determining how large each datagram should be.

During the course of its journey from the source to the destination, packets may encounter networks with different MTUs. As long as the MTU of each network is larger than the packet, the datagram is transmitted without a problem. If a packet is larger than the MTU of a network, however, it cannot be transmitted in its current form. When this occurs, the IP protocol in the router providing access to the network is responsible for splitting the datagram into fragments smaller than the MTU. The router then transmits each fragment in a separate packet with its own IP header.

Depending on the number and nature of the networks it passes through, a datagram may be fragmented more than once before it reaches the destination. A system might split a datagram into fragments that are themselves too large for networks further along in the path. Another router, therefore, splits the fragments into still smaller fragments. Reassembly of a fragmented datagram takes place only at the destination system after it has received all of the packets containing the fragments, not at the intermediate routers.

NOTE Technically speaking, the datagram is defined as the unit of data, packaged by the source system, containing a specific value on the IP header's Identification field. When a router fragments a datagram, it uses the same Identification value for each new packet it creates, meaning the individual fragments are collectively known as a *datagram*. Referring to a single fragment as a datagram is incorrect use of the term.

When a router receives a datagram that must be fragmented, it creates a series of new packets using the same value for the IP header's Identification field as the original datagram. The other fields of the header are the same as well, with three important exceptions, which are as follows:

- The value of the Total Length field is changed to reflect the size of the fragment, instead of the size of the entire datagram.

- Bit 3 of the Flags field, the More Fragments bit, is changed to a value of 1 to indicate that further fragments are to be transmitted, except in the case of the datagram's last fragment, in which this bit is set to a value of 0.

- The value of the Fragment Offset field is changed to reflect each fragment's place in the datagram, based on the size of the fragments (which is, in turn, based on the MTU of the network across which the fragments are to be transmitted). The value for the first fragment is 0; the next is incremented by the size of the fragment, in bytes.

These changes to the IP header are needed for the fragments to be properly reassembled by the destination system. The router transmits the fragments like any other IP packets, and because IP is a connectionless protocol, the individual fragments may take different routes to the destination and arrive in a different order. The receiving system uses the More Fragments bit to determine when it should begin the reassembly process and uses the Fragment Offset field to assemble the fragments in the proper order.

Selecting the size of the fragments is left up to individual IP implementations. Typically, the size of each fragment is the MTU of the network over which it must be transmitted, minus the size of the data link and IP protocol headers, and rounded down to the nearest 8 bytes. Some systems, however, automatically create 576-byte fragments because this is the default path MTU used by many routers.

Fragmentation is not desirable, but it is a necessary evil. Obviously, because fragmenting a datagram creates many packets out of one packet, it increases the control overhead incurred by the transmission process. Also, if one fragment of a datagram is lost or damaged, the entire datagram must be retransmitted. No means of reproducing and retransmitting a single fragment exists because the source system has no knowledge of the fragmentation performed by the intermediate routers. The IP implementation on the destination system does not pass the incoming data up to the transport layer until all the fragments have arrived and been reassembled. The transport layer protocol must therefore detect the missing data and arrange for the retransmission of the datagram.

Routing

Because the IP protocol is responsible for the transmission of packets to their final destinations, IP determines the route the packets will take. A packet's route is the path it takes from one end system, the source, to another end system, the destination. The routers the packet passes through during the trip are called *intermediate systems*. The fundamental difference between end systems and intermediate systems is how high the packet data reaches in the protocol stack.

On the source computer, a request for access to a network resource begins at the application layer and wends its way down through the layers of the protocol stack, eventually arriving at the physical layer encapsulated in a packet, ready for transmission. When it reaches the destination, the reverse occurs, and the packet is passed up the stack to the application layer. On end systems, therefore, the entire protocol stack participates in the processing of the data. On intermediate systems, such as routers, the data arriving over the network is passed only as high as the network layer protocol, which, in this case, is IP (see Figure 13-9).

IP strips off the data link layer protocol header and, after determining where it should send the packet next, prepares it for packaging in a data link layer protocol frame suitable for the outgoing network. This may involve using ARP to resolve the IP address of the packet's next stop into a hardware address and then furnishing that address to the data link layer protocol.

Routing is a process that occurs one hop of a packet's journey at a time. The source system transmits the packet to its default gateway (router), and the router determines where to send the packet next. If the final destination is on a network segment to which the router is attached, it

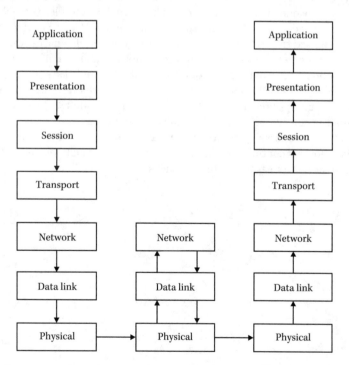

Figure 13-9 Packets passing through routers travel no higher than the network layer of the protocol stack.

sends the packet there. If the destination is on another network, the router determines which of the other routers it should send the packet to in order for it to reach its destination most efficiently. Thus, the next destination for the packet, identified by the destination address in the data link layer protocol, may not be the same system as that specified in the IP header's Destination IP Address field.

Eventually, one of the routers will have access to the network on which the packet's final destination system is located and will be able to send it directly to that machine. Using this method, the routing process is distributed among the network's routers. None of the computers involved in the process has complete knowledge of the packet's route through the network at any time. This distribution of labor makes huge networks like the Internet possible. No practical method exists for a single system to determine a viable path through the many thousands of routers on the Internet to a specific destination for each packet.

The most complex part of the routing process is the manner in which the router determines where to send each packet next. Routers have direct knowledge only of the network segments to which they are connected. They have no means of unilaterally determining the best route to a particular destination. In most cases, routers gain knowledge about other networks by communicating with other routers using specialized protocols designed for this purpose, such as the Routing Information Protocol (RIP). Each router passes information about itself to the other routers on the networks to which it is connected, those routers update their neighboring routers, and so on.

Regular updates from the neighboring routers enable each system to keep up with changing conditions on the network. If a router should go down, for example, its neighbors will detect its absence and spread the word that the router is unavailable. The other routers will adjust their behavior as needed to ensure that their packets are not sent down a dead-end street.

Routing protocols enable each router to compile a table of networks with the information needed to send packets to that network. Essentially, the table says "send traffic to network x; use interface y" where y is one of the router's own network interfaces. Administrators can also manually configure routes through the network. This is called *static routing*, as opposed to protocol-based configuration, which is called *dynamic routing*.

On complex networks, there may be several viable routes from a source to a particular destination. Routers continually rate the possible paths through the network, so they can select the shortest, fastest, or easiest route for a packet.

CHAPTER

14

Other TCP/IP Protocols

While Internet Protocol version 4 (IPv4) has been the most commonly used, there are many other parts of the Transmission Control Protocol/Internet Protocol (TCP/IP) suite of protocols. This chapter discusses other parts of the TCP/IP family as well as other groups or protocol suites encountered in today's networks.

IPv6

As mentioned in Chapter 13, no one involved in the original design and implementation of the Internet could have predicted its explosive growth. The TCP/IP protocols held up remarkably well over the decades, proving that the scalability features incorporated into them were well designed. However, the single biggest problem with the use of these protocols is the rapid consumption of the address space provided by IPv4, the current version. The last block of IPv4 addresses were allotted by the Internet Assigned Numbers Authority (IANA) in February 2011, so the free pool of IPv4 addresses is now gone.

IP addresses are no longer being used only by computers; cellular phones, tablets, global positioning systems, and other mobile devices need these addresses as well. Anticipating the eventual depletion of the 32-bit address space, work commenced on an upgraded version of IP in 1998, which has resulted in several dozen requests for comments (RFCs), including RFC 2460, "Internet Protocol, Version 6 (IPv6) Specification." IPv6 does not replace IPv4, which is still used in many applications. This version enhances and solves some of the inherent issues in IPv4.

The primary improvement in IPv6 is the expansion of the address space from 32 to 128 bits. For the near future, this should provide a sufficient number of IP addresses for all devices that can make use of them (which is probably what the designers of IPv4 said when they decided to use 32-bit addresses). In addition to the expanded address space, IPv6 includes the following enhancements:

- **Simplified header format** IPv6 removes extraneous fields from the protocol header and makes other fields optional to reduce the network traffic overhead generated by the protocol.

- **Header extensions**   IPv6 introduces the concept of extension headers, which are separate, optional headers located between the IP header and its payload. The extension headers contain information that is used only by the end system that is the packet's final destination. By moving them into extension headers, the intermediate systems don't have to expend the time and processor clock cycles needed to process them.

- **Flow labeling**   IPv6 enables applications to apply a "flow label" to specific packets in order to request a nonstandard quality of service. This is intended to enable applications that require real-time communications, such as streaming audio and video, to request priority access to the network bandwidth.

- **Security extensions**   IPv6 includes extensions that support authentication, data integrity, and data confidentiality.

IPv6 requires a number of fundamental changes to the hardware and software that make up the network infrastructure, apart from just the adaptation to 128-bit addresses. For example, the operating systems and applications that use IPv6 must also include the IPv6 version of ICMP, defined in RFC 2463. Also, networks that use IPv6 must support a maximum transfer unit value of at least 1,280 bytes. Issues like these complicated the process of transitioning the Internet from IPv4 to IPv6. RFC 1933 defined mechanisms designed to facilitate the transition process, such as support for both IPv4 and IPv6 layers in the same system and the tunneling of IPv6 datagrams within IPv4 datagrams, enabling the existing IPv4 routing infrastructure to carry IPv6 information. These are some of the differences:

- **Larger address space**   The 128-bit addresses in IPv6 allow just over 340 trillion trillion trillion addresses.

- **Datagram format**   The packet header in IPv6 enables more secure and efficient routing.

- **Improved reassembly**   The maximum transmission unit (MTU) is 1,280 bytes in IPv6.

- **Better connectivity**   Under IPv6, every system has a unique IP address and can move through the Internet without any "translators." Once it is fully implemented, each host can reach every other host directly. However, firewalls and network policies do create some limitations on this connectivity.

IPv6 Addresses

According to RFC 4291, "IP Version 6 Addressing Architecture," there are three types of identifiers for IPv6 addresses:

- **Anycast**   When using an *anycast* address, a packet is delivered to one of the interfaces identified by that address.

- **Multicast**   Packets sent to a *multicast* address in IPv6 are delivered to all interfaces identified by that address. This is the same as IPv4.

- **Unicast**   Packets sent to a *unicast* address are delivered only to that address.

Unicast Address Types

There are three types of unicast addresses in IPv6: link local, unique local, and global unicast. Each has its own configuration.

Link-Local Address   In this configuration, the autoconfigured IPv6 starts with FE80, as shown here:

1111 1110 1000 0000 (FE80 in hexadecimal)

with the next 48 bits set to 0.

These addresses are used between IPv6 hosts on a broadcast segment only and are not routable. Thus, a router never forwards the address outside the link.

Unique-Local Address   This type should be used only for local communication, even though it is globally unique. The address is divided between prefix (1111 110), local bit (1 bit only), global ID (40 bits), subnet ID (16 bits), and interface ID (64 bits). The prefix is always set to 1111 110 (as shown), with the local bit set to 1 if the address is locally assigned. At this time, the local bit has not yet been defined.

Global Unicast Address   Essentially, this is IPv4's public address. In IPv6, these addresses are globally identifiable and uniquely addressable. The most significant 48 bits are designated as the global routing prefix, and the 3 most significant bits of the prefix are always set to 001, as shown in Table 14-1.

IPv6 Address Structure

All IPv6 addresses are four times longer (128 bits instead of 32 bits) than IPv4 addresses. As discussed in Chapter 13, an IPv4 address contains four *octets* and has a decimal value between 0 and 255. A period separates each of the octets. IPv4 address must include four octets.

Normal IPv6 Addresses

IPv6 addresses have a format that looks like this:

y:y:y:y:y:y:y:y.

In this format, each *y* is called a *segment* and can be any hexadecimal value between 0 and FFFF. Normal IPv6 addresses require eight segments.

Dual IPv6 Addresses

The dual IPv6 address combines both an IPv6 and an IPv4 address and looks like this:

y:y:y:y:y:y:x.x.x.x.

The IPv6 portion is always first, and the segments are separated by colons instead of periods. It must have six segments. The IPv4 portion must contain three periods and four octets.

Global Routing Prefix	Subnet ID	Interface ID
48 bits	16 bits	64 bits

Table 14-1   The Global Unicast Address in IPv6

Other Protocols

There are other types of network protocols, some of which are discussed here. See Chapters 15 and 16 for additional information.

ICMP

The Internet Control Message Protocol (ICMP) is a network layer protocol that does not carry user data, although its messages are encapsulated in IP datagrams. ICMP fills two roles in the TCP/IP suite. It provides error-reporting functions, informing the sending system when a transmission cannot reach its destination, for example, and it carries query and response messages for diagnostic programs. The *ping* utility, for instance, which is included in every TCP/IP implementation, uses ICMP echo messages to determine whether another system on the network can receive and send data.

The ICMP protocol, as defined in RFC 792, consists of messages carried in IP datagrams, with a value of 1 in the IP header's Protocol field and 0 in the Type of Service field. Figure 14-1 illustrates the ICMP message format.

The ICMP message format consists of the following fields:

- **Type (1 byte)** Contains a code identifying the basic function of the message
- **Code (1 byte)** Contains a secondary code identifying the function of the message within a specific type
- **Checksum (2 bytes)** Contains the results of a checksum computation on the entire ICMP message, including the Type, Code, Checksum, and Data fields (with a value of 0 in the Checksum field for computation purposes)
- **Data (variable)** Contains information specific to the function of the message

The ICMP message types are listed in Table 14-2.

ICMP Error Messages

Because of the way TCP/IP networks distribute routing chores among various systems, there is no way for either of the end systems involved in a transmission to know what has happened during a packet's journey. IP is a connectionless protocol, so no acknowledgment messages are returned to the sender at that level. When using a connection-oriented protocol at the transport layer, like TCP, the destination system acknowledges transmissions, but only for the packets it receives. If something happens during the transmission process that prevents the packet from reaching the destination, there is no way for IP or TCP to inform the sender about what happened.

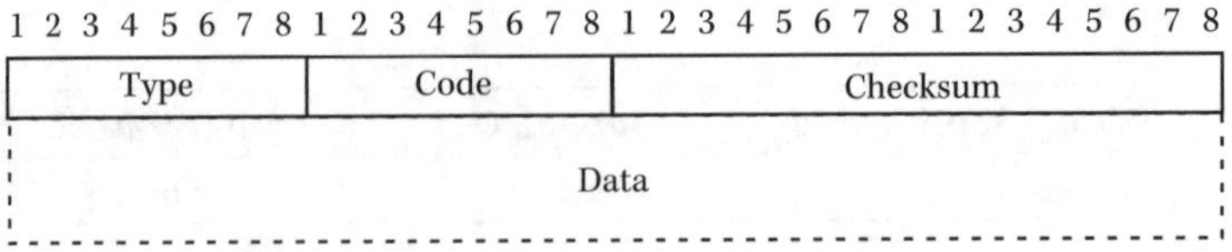

Figure 14-1 The ICMP message format

Type	Code	Query/Error	Function
0	0	Q	Echo reply
3	0	E	Net unreachable
3	1	E	Host unreachable
3	2	E	Protocol unreachable
3	3	E	Port unreachable
3	4	E	Fragmentation needed and don't fragment was set
3	5	E	Source route failed
3	6	E	Destination network unknown
3	7	E	Destination host unknown
3	8	E	Source host isolated
3	9	E	Communication with destination network is administratively prohibited
3	10	E	Communication with destination host is administratively prohibited
3	11	E	Destination network unreachable for type of service
3	12	E	Destination host unreachable for type of service
4	0	E	Source quench
5	0	E	Redirect datagram for the network (or subnet)
5	1	E	Redirect datagram for the host
5	2	E	Redirect datagram for the type of service and network
5	3	E	Redirect datagram for the type of service and host
8	0	Q	Echo request
9	0	Q	Router advertisement
10	0	Q	Router solicitation
11	0	E	Time to live exceeded in transit
11	1	E	Fragment reassembly time exceeded
12	0	E	Pointer indicates the error
12	1	E	Missing a required option
12	2	E	Bad length
13	0	Q	Time stamp
14	0	Q	Time stamp reply
15	0	Q	Information request
16	0	Q	Information reply
17	0	Q	Address mask request
18	0	Q	Address mask reply
30	0	Q	Traceroute
31	0	E	Datagram conversion error

Table 14-2   ICMP Message Types (*continued*)

Part IV

Type	Code	Query/Error	Function
32	0	E	Mobile host redirect
33	0	Q	IPv6 where-are-you
34	0	Q	IPv6 I-am-here
35	0	Q	Mobile registration request
36	0	Q	Mobile registration reply

Table 14-2   ICMP Message Types

ICMP error messages are designed to fill this void. When an intermediate system, such as a router, has trouble processing a packet, the router typically discards the packet, leaving the upper-layer protocols to detect the packet's absence and arrange for a retransmission. ICMP messages enable the router to inform the sender of the exact nature of the problem. Destination systems can also generate ICMP messages when a packet arrives successfully but cannot be processed.

The Data field of an ICMP error message always contains the IP header of the datagram the system could not process, plus the first 8 bytes of the datagram's own Data field. In most cases, these 8 bytes contain a UDP header or the beginning of a TCP header, including the source and destination ports and the sequence number (in the case of TCP). This enables the system receiving the error message to isolate the exact time the error occurred and the transmission that caused it.

However, ICMP error messages are informational only. The system receiving them does not respond nor does it necessarily take any action to correct the situation. The user or administrator may have to address the problem that is causing the failure.

In general, all TCP/IP systems are free to transmit ICMP error messages, except in certain specific situations. These exceptions are intended to prevent ICMP from generating too much traffic on the network by transmitting large numbers of identical messages. These exceptional situations are as follows:

- TCP/IP systems do not generate ICMP error messages in response to other ICMP error messages. Without this exception, it would be possible for two systems to bounce error messages back and forth between them endlessly. Systems can generate ICMP errors in response to ICMP queries, however.

- In the case of a fragmented datagram, a system generates an ICMP error message only for the first fragment.

- TCP/IP systems never generate ICMP error messages in response to broadcast or multicast transmissions, transmissions with a source IP address of 0.0.0.0, or transmissions addressed to the loopback address.

The following sections examine the most common types of ICMP error messages and their functions.

Destination Unreachable Messages   Destination unreachable messages have a value of 3 in the ICMP Type field and any one of 13 values in the Code field. As the name implies, these messages indicate that a packet or the information in a packet could not be transmitted to its destination. The various messages specify exactly which component was unreachable and, in some cases, why. This type of message can be generated by a router when it cannot forward a packet to a certain network or to the destination system on one of the router's connected networks. Destination systems themselves can also generate these messages when they cannot deliver the contents of the packet to a specific protocol or host.

In most cases, the error is a result of some type of failure, either temporary or permanent, in a computer or the network medium. These errors could also possibly occur as a result of IP options that prevent the transmission of the packet, such as when datagrams must be fragmented for transmission over a specific network and the Don't Fragment flag in the IP header is set.

Source Quench Messages   The source quench message, with a Type value of 4 and a Code value of 0, functions as an elementary form of flow control by informing a transmitting system that it is sending packets too fast. When the receiver's buffers are in danger of being overfilled, the system can transmit a source quench message to the sender, which slows down its transmission rate as a result. The sender should continue to reduce the rate until it is no longer receiving the messages from the receiver.

This is a basic form of flow control that is reasonably effective for use between systems on the same network but that generates too much additional traffic on routed networks. In most cases, this is unnecessary because TCP provides its own flow-control mechanism over additional traffic on internetworks.

Redirect Messages   Redirect messages are generated only by routers to inform hosts or other routers of better routes to a particular destination.

Because having the host send the packets intended for that destination directly to Router 2 would be more efficient, Router 1 sends a redirect datagram for the Network message (Type 5, Code 0) to the transmitting host after it forwards the original packet to Router 2. The redirect message contains the usual IP header and partial data information, as well as the IP address of the router the host should use for its future transmissions to that network.

In this example, the redirect message indicates that the host should use the other router for the packets it will transmit to all hosts on Network B in the future. The other redirect messages (with Codes 1 through 3) enable the router to specify an alternative router for transmissions to the specific host, to the specific host with the same Type of Service value, and to the entire network with the same Type of Service value.

Time Exceeded Messages   Time exceeded messages are used to inform a transmitting system that a packet has been discarded because a timeout has elapsed. The Time to Live Exceeded in Transit message (Type 11, Code 0) indicates that the Time-to-Live value in a packet's IP header has reached zero before arriving at the destination, forcing the router to discard it.

This message enables the TCP/IP traceroute program to display the route through the network that packets take to a given destination. By transmitting a series of packets with incremented values in the Time-to-Live field, each successive router on the path to the destination discards a packet and returns an ICMP time exceeded message to the source.

The Fragment Reassembly Time Exceeded message (Code 1) indicates that a destination system has not received all the fragments of a specific datagram within the time limit specified by

Part IV

the host. As a result, the system must discard all the fragments it has received and return the error message to the sender.

ICMP Query Messages

ICMP query messages are not generated in response to other activities, as are the error messages. Systems use them for self-contained request/reply transactions in which one computer requests information from another, which responds with a reply containing that information.

Because they are not associated with other IP transmissions, ICMP queries do not contain datagram information in their Data fields. The data they do carry is specific to the function of the message. The following sections examine some of the more common ICMP query messages and their functions.

Echo Requests and Replies   Echo Request and Echo Reply messages are the basis for the TCP/IP ping utility, which sends test messages to another host on the network to determine whether it is capable of receiving and responding to messages. Each ping consists of an ICMP Echo Request message (Type 8, Code 0) that, in addition to the standard ICMP Type, Code, and Checksum fields, adds Identifier and Sequence Number fields that the systems use to associate requests and replies.

If the system receiving the message is functioning normally, it reverses the Source and Destination IP Address fields in the IP header, changes the value of the ICMP Type field to 0 (Echo Reply), and recomputes the checksum before transmitting it back to the sender.

Router Solicitations and Advertisements   These messages make it possible for a host system to discover the addresses of the routers connected to the local network. Systems can use this information to configure the default gateway entry in their routing tables. When a host broadcasts or multicasts a Router Solicitation message (Type 10, Code 0), the routers on the network respond with Router Advertisement messages (Type 9, Code 0). Routers continue to advertise their availability at regular intervals (typically seven to ten minutes). A host may stop using a router as its default gateway if it fails to receive continued advertisements.

The Router Solicitation message consists only of the standard Type, Code, and Checksum fields, plus a 4-byte pad in the Data field. Figure 14-2 shows the Router Advertisement message format.

The Router Advertisement message format contains the following additional fields:

- **Number of Addresses (1 byte)**   Specifies the number of router addresses contained in the message. The format can support multiple addresses, each of which will have its own Router Address and Preference Level fields.

- **Address Entry Size (1 byte)**   Specifies the number of 4-byte words devoted to each address in the message. The value is always 2.

- **Lifetime (2 bytes)**   Specifies the time, in seconds, that can elapse between advertisements before a system assumes a router is no longer functioning. The default value is usually 1,800 seconds (30 minutes).

- **Router Address (4 bytes)**   Specifies the IP address of the router generating the advertisement message.

- **Preference Level (4 bytes)**   Contains a value specified by the network administrator that host systems can use to select one router over another.

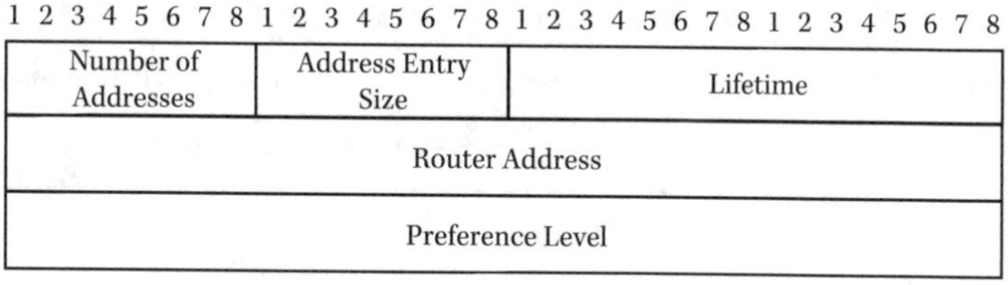

1 2 3 4 5 6 7 8	1 2 3 4 5 6 7 8	1 2 3 4 5 6 7 8 1 2 3 4 5 6 7 8
Number of Addresses	Address Entry Size	Lifetime
Router Address		
Preference Level		

Figure 14-2   The Router Advertisement message format

UDP

Two TCP/IP protocols operate at the transport layer: TCP and UDP. The *User Datagram Protocol* (UDP), defined in RFC 768, is a connectionless, unreliable protocol that provides minimal transport service to application layer protocols with a minimum of control overhead. Thus, UDP provides no packet acknowledgment or flow-control services like TCP, although it does provide end-to-end checksum verification on the contents of the packet.

Although it provides a minimum of services of its own, UDP does function as a *pass-through protocol,* meaning that it provides applications with access to network layer services, and vice versa. If, for example, a datagram containing UDP data cannot be delivered to the destination and a router returns an ICMP Destination Unreachable message, UDP always passes the ICMP message information up from the network layer to the application that generated the information in the original datagram. UDP also passes along any optional information included in IP datagrams to the application layer and, in the opposite direction, information from applications that IP will use as values for the Time-to-Live and Type of Service header fields.

The nature of the UDP protocol makes it suitable only for brief transactions in which all the data to be sent to the destination fits into a single datagram. This is because no mechanism exists in UDP for splitting a data stream into segments and reassembling them, as in TCP. This does not mean that the datagram cannot be fragmented by IP in the course of transmission, however. This process is invisible to the transport layer because the receiving system reassembles the fragments before passing the datagram up the stack.

In addition, because no packet acknowledgment exists in UDP, it is most often used for client-server transactions in which the client transmits a request and the server's reply message serves as an acknowledgment. If a system sends a request and no reply is forthcoming, the system assumes the destination system did not receive the message and retransmits. It is mostly TCP/IP support services like DNS and DHCP, services that don't carry actual user data, that use this type of transaction. Applications such as DHCP also use UDP when they have to send broadcast or multicast transmissions. Because the TCP protocol requires two systems to establish a connection before they transmit user data, it does not support broadcasts and multicasts.

The header for UDP messages (sometimes confusingly called *datagrams,* like IP messages) is small, only 8 bytes, as opposed to the 20 bytes of the TCP header. Figure 14-3 illustrates the format. The functions of the fields are as follows:

- **Source Port Number (2 bytes)**   Identifies the port number of the process in the transmitting system that generated the data carried in the UDP datagram. In some cases, this may be an ephemeral port number selected by the client for this transaction.

Part IV

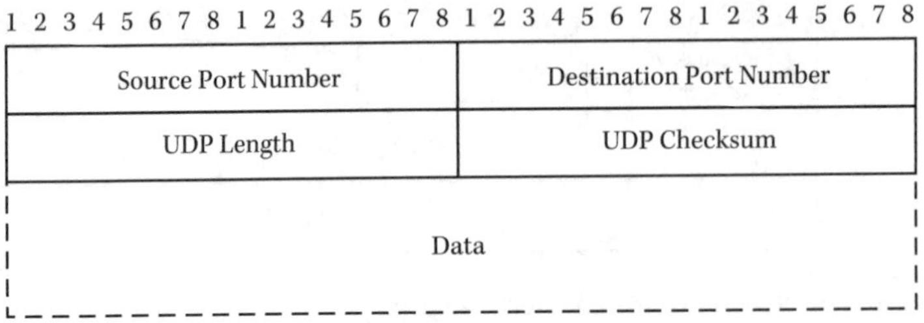

```
1 2 3 4 5 6 7 8 1 2 3 4 5 6 7 8 1 2 3 4 5 6 7 8 1 2 3 4 5 6 7 8
```

Source Port Number	Destination Port Number
UDP Length	UDP Checksum

Data

Figure 14-3   The UDP message format

- **Destination Port Number (2 bytes)**   Identifies the port number of the process on the destination system that will receive the data carried in the UDP datagram. Well-known port numbers are listed in the "Assigned Numbers" RFC and in the Services file on every TCP/IP system.

- **UDP Length (2 bytes)**   Specifies the length of the entire UDP message, including the Header and Data fields, in bytes.

- **UDP Checksum (2 bytes)**   Contains the results of a checksum computation computed from the UDP header and data, along with a pseudo-header composed of the IP header's Source IP Address, Destination IP Address, and Protocol fields, plus the UDP Length field. This pseudo-header enables the UDP protocol at the receiving system to verify that the message has been delivered to the correct protocol on the correct destination system.

- **Data (variable, up to 65,507 bytes)**   Contains the information supplied by the application layer protocol.

TCP

The Transmission Control Protocol is the connection-oriented, reliable alternative to UDP, which accounts for the majority of the user data transmitted across a TCP/IP network, as well as giving the protocol suite its name. TCP, as defined in RFC 793, provides applications with a full range of transport services, including packet acknowledgment, error detection and correction, and flow control.

TCP is intended for the transfer of relatively large amounts of data that will not fit into a single packet. The data often takes the form of complete files that must be split up into multiple datagrams for transmission. In TCP terminology, the data supplied to the transport layer is referred to as a *sequence,* and the protocol splits the sequence into *segments* for transmission across the network. As with UDP, however, the segments are packaged in IP datagrams that may end up taking different routes to the destination. TCP, therefore, assigns sequence numbers to the segments so the receiving system can reassemble them in the correct order.

Before any transfer of user data begins using TCP, the two systems exchange messages to establish a connection. This ensures that the receiver is operating and capable of receiving data. Once the connection is established and data transfer begins, the receiving system generates periodic acknowledgment messages. These messages inform the sender of lost packets and also provide the information used to control the rate of flow to the receiver.

The TCP Header

To provide these services, the header applied to TCP segments is necessarily larger than that for UDP. At 20 bytes (without options), it's the same size as the IP header.

The functions of the fields are as follows:

- **Source Port (2 bytes)**   Identifies the port number of the process in the transmitting system that generated the data carried in the TCP segments. In some cases, this may be an ephemeral port number selected by the client for this transaction.

- **Destination Port (2 bytes)**   Identifies the port number of the process on the destination system that will receive the data carried in the TCP segments. Well-known port numbers are listed in the "Assigned Numbers" RFC and in the Services file on every TCP/IP system.

- **Sequence Number (4 bytes)**   Specifies the location of the data in this segment in relation to the entire data sequence.

- **Acknowledgment Number (4 bytes)**   Specifies the sequence number of the next segment that the acknowledging system expects to receive from the sender. This is active only when the ACK bit is set.

- **Data Offset (4 bits)**   Specifies the length, in 4-byte words, of the TCP header (which may contain options expanding it to as much as 60 bytes).

- **Reserved (6 bits)**   Unused.

- **Control Bits (6 bits)**   Contains six 1-bit flags that perform the following functions:
  - **URG**   Indicates that the sequence contains urgent data and activates the Urgent Pointer field
  - **ACK**   Indicates that the message is an acknowledgment of previously transmitted data and activates the Acknowledgment Number field
  - **PSH**   Instructs the receiving system to push all the data in the current sequence to the application identified by the port number without waiting for the rest
  - **RST**   Instructs the receiving system to discard all the segments in the sequence that have been transmitted thus far and resets the TCP connection
  - **SYN**   Used during the connection establishment process to synchronize the sequence numbers in the source and destination systems
  - **FIN**   Indicates to the other system that the data transmission has been completed and the connection is to be terminated

- **Window (2 bytes)**   Implements the TCP flow-control mechanism by specifying the number of bytes the system can accept from the sender.

- **Checksum (2 bytes)**   Contains a checksum computation computed from the TCP header; data; and a pseudo-header composed of the Source IP Address, Destination IP Address, Protocol fields from the packet's IP header, and the length of the entire TCP message.

- **Urgent Pointer (2 bytes)**   Activated by the URG bit, specifies the data in the sequence that should be treated by the receiver as urgent.

Part IV

- **Options (variable)**   May contain additional configuration parameters for the TCP connection, along with padding to fill the field to the nearest 4-byte boundary. The available options are as follows:

  - **Maximum Segment Size**   Specifies the size of the largest segments the current system can receive from the connected system

  - **Window Scale Factor**   Used to double the size of the Window Size field from 2 to 4 bytes

  - **Time stamp**   Used to carry time stamps in data packets that the receiving system returns in its acknowledgments, enabling the sender to measure the round-trip time

- **Data (variable)**   May contain a segment of the information passed down from an application layer protocol. In SYN, ACK, and FIN packets, this field is left empty.

Connection Establishment

Distinguishing TCP connections from the other types of connections commonly used in data networking is important. When you log on to a network, for example, you initiate a session that remains open until you log off. During that session, you may establish other connections to individual network resources such as file servers that also remain open for extended lengths of time. TCP connections are much more transient, however, and typically remain open only for the duration of the data transmission. In addition, a system (or even a single application on that system) may open several TCP connections at once with the same destination.

As an example, consider a basic client-server transaction between a web browser and a web server. Whenever you type a URL in the browser, the program opens a TCP connection with the server to transfer the default HTML file that the browser uses to display the server's home page. The connection lasts only as long as it takes to transfer that one page. When the user clicks a hyperlink to open a new page, an entirely new TCP connection is needed. If there are any graphics on the web pages, a separate TCP connection is needed to transmit each image file.

The additional messages required for the establishment of the connection, plus the size of the header, add considerably to the control overhead incurred by a TCP connection. This is the main reason why TCP/IP has UDP as a low-overhead transport layer alternative.

The communication process between the client and the server begins when the client generates its first TCP message, beginning the three-way handshake that establishes the connection between the two machines. This message contains no application data; it simply signals to the server that the client wants to establish a connection. The SYN bit is set, and the system supplies a value in the Sequence Number field, called the *initial sequence number* (ISN), as shown in Figure 14-4.

The system uses a continuously incrementing algorithm to determine the ISN it will use for each connection. The constant cycling of the sequence numbers makes it highly unlikely that multiple connections using the same sequence numbers will occur between the same two sockets. The client system then transmits the message as a unicast to the destination system and enters the SYN-SENT state, indicating that it has transmitted its connection request and is waiting for a matching request from the destination system.

The server, at this time, is in the LISTEN state, meaning that it is waiting to receive a connection request from a client. When the server receives the message from the client, it replies with its own TCP control message. This message serves two functions: It acknowledges the receipt of

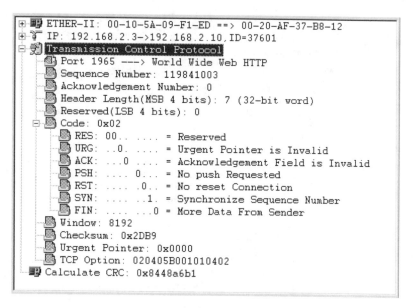

```
⊞ ▆▊ ETHER-II: 00-10-5A-09-F1-ED ==> 00-20-AF-37-B8-12
⊞ ⥷ IP: 192.168.2.3->192.168.2.10,ID=37601
⊟ ⥷ Transmission Control Protocol
      ⥷ Port 1965 ---> World Wide Web HTTP
      ⥷ Sequence Number: 119841003
      ⥷ Acknowledgement Number: 0
      ⥷ Header Length(MSB 4 bits): 7 (32-bit word)
      ⥷ Reserved(LSB 4 bits): 0
   ⊟ ⥷ Code: 0x02
        ⥷ RES: 00.. .... = Reserved
        ⥷ URG: ..0. .... = Urgent Pointer is Invalid
        ⥷ ACK: ...0 .... = Acknowledgement Field is Invalid
        ⥷ PSH: .... 0... = No push Requested
        ⥷ RST: .... .0.. = No reset Connection
        ⥷ SYN: .... ..1. = Synchronize Sequence Number
        ⥷ FIN: .... ...0 = More Data From Sender
      ⥷ Window: 8192
      ⥷ Checksum: 0x2DB9
      ⥷ Urgent Pointer: 0x0000
      ⥷ TCP Option: 020405B001010402
   ▆▊ Calculate CRC: 0x8448a6b1
```

Figure 14-4   The client's SYN message initiates the connection establishment process.

the client's message, as indicated by the ACK bit, and it initiates its own connection, as indicated by the SYN bit (see Figure 14-5). The server then enters the SYN-RECEIVED state, indicating that it has received a connection request, issued a request of its own, and is waiting for an acknowledgment from the other system. Both the ACK and SYN bits are necessary because TCP is a *full-duplex* protocol, meaning that a separate connection is actually running in each direction. Both connections must be individually established, maintained, and terminated. The server's message also contains a value in the Sequence Number field (116270), as well as a value in the Acknowledgment Number field (119841004).

Both systems maintain their own sequence numbers and are also conscious of the other system's sequence numbers. Later, when the systems actually begin to send application data, these sequence numbers enable a receiver to assemble the individual segments transmitted in separate packets into the original sequence.

Remember, although the two systems must establish a connection before they send application data, the TCP messages are still transmitted within IP datagrams and are subject to the same treatment as any other datagram. Thus, the connection is actually a virtual one, and the datagrams may take different routes to the destination and arrive in a different order from that in which they were sent.

After the client receives the server's message, it transmits its own ACK message (see Figure 14-6) acknowledging the server's SYN bit and completing the bidirectional connection establishment process. This message has a value of 119841004 as its sequence number, which is the value expected by the server, and an acknowledgment number of 116271, which is the sequence number it expects to see in the server's next transmission. Both systems now enter the ESTABLISHED state, indicating that they are ready to transmit and receive application data.

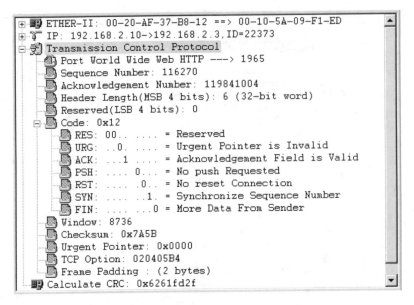

Figure 14-5 The server acknowledges the client's SYN and sends a SYN of its own.

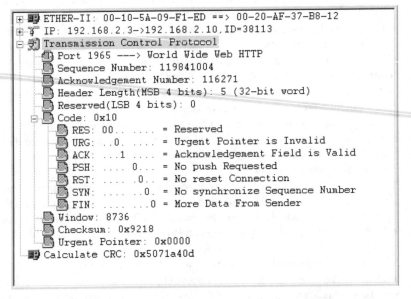

Figure 14-6 The client then acknowledges the server's SYN, and the connection is established in both directions.

Data Transfer

Once the TCP connection is established in both directions, the transmission of data can begin. The application layer protocol determines whether the client or the server initiates the next exchange. In a File Transfer Protocol (FTP) session, for example, the server sends a Ready message first. In a Hypertext Transfer Protocol (HTTP) exchange, the client begins by sending the URL of the document it wants to receive.

The data to be sent is not packaged for transmission until the connection is established. This is because the systems use the SYN messages to inform the other system of the *maximum segment size* (MSS). The MSS specifies the size of the largest segment each system is capable of receiving. The value of the MSS depends on the data link layer protocol used to connect the two systems.

Each system supplies the other with an MSS value in the TCP message's Options field. Like with the IP header, each option consists of multiple subfields, which for the Maximum Segment Size option, are as follows:

- **Kind (1 byte)**   Identifies the function of the option. For the Maximum Segment Size option, the value is 2.

- **Length (1 byte)**   Specifies the length of the entire option. For the Maximum Segment Size option, the value is 4.

- **Maximum Segment Size (2 bytes)**   Specifies the size (in bytes) of the largest data segment the system can receive.

In the client system's first TCP message, shown earlier in Figure 14-4, the value of the Options field is (in hexadecimal notation) 020405B001010402. The first 4 bytes of this value constitute the MSS option. The Kind value is 02, the Length is 04, and the MSS is 05B0, which in decimal form is 1,456 bytes. This works out to the maximum frame size for an Ethernet II network (1,500 bytes) minus 20 bytes for the IP header and 24 bytes for the TCP header (20 bytes plus 4 option bytes). The server's own SYN packet contains the same value for this option because these two computers were located on the same Ethernet network.

NOTE The remaining 4 bytes in the Options field consist of 2 bytes of padding (0101) and the Kind (04) and Length (02) fields of the SACK-Permitted option, indicating that the system is capable of processing extended information as part of acknowledgment messages.

When the two systems are located on different networks, their MSS values may also be different, and how the systems deal with this is left up to the individual TCP implementations. Some systems may just use the smaller of the two values, while others might revert to the default value of 536 bytes used when no MSS option is supplied. Windows 2000 systems use a special method of discovering the connection path's MTU (that is, the largest packet size permitted on an internetwork link between two systems). This method, as defined in RFC 1191, enables the systems to determine the packet sizes permitted on intermediate networks. Thus, even if the source and destination systems are both connected to Ethernet networks with 1,500-byte MTUs, they can detect an intermediate connection that supports only a 576-byte MTU.

Once the MSS for the connection is established, the systems can begin packaging data for transmission. In the case of an HTTP transaction, the web browser client transmits the desired URL to the server in a single packet (see Figure 14-7). Notice that the sequence number of this

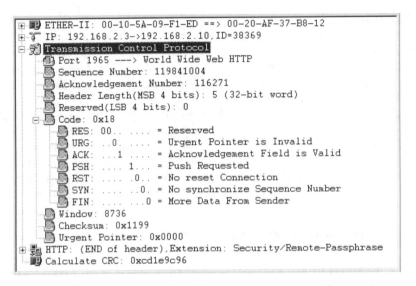

```
⊞ 🖭 ETHER-II: 00-10-5A-09-F1-ED ==> 00-20-AF-37-B8-12
⊞ 🖳 IP: 192.168.2.3->192.168.2.10,ID=38369
⊟ 🗐 Transmission Control Protocol
    ⬛ Port 1965 ---> World Wide Web HTTP
    ⬛ Sequence Number: 119841004
    ⬛ Acknowledgement Number: 116271
    ⬛ Header Length(MSB 4 bits): 5 (32-bit word)
    ⬛ Reserved(LSB 4 bits): 0
  ⊟ ⬛ Code: 0x18
      ⬛ RES: 00.. .... = Reserved
      ⬛ URG: ..0. .... = Urgent Pointer is Invalid
      ⬛ ACK: ...1 .... = Acknowledgement Field is Valid
      ⬛ PSH: .... 1... = Push Requested
      ⬛ RST: .... .0.. = No reset Connection
      ⬛ SYN: .... ..0. = No synchronize Sequence Number
      ⬛ FIN: .... ...0 = More Data From Sender
    ⬛ Window: 8736
    ⬛ Checksum: 0x1199
    ⬛ Urgent Pointer: 0x0000
  ⊞ 🖳 HTTP: (END of header),Extension: Security/Remote-Passphrase
    🖳 Calculate CRC: 0xcd1e9c96
```

Figure 14-7   The first data packet sent over the connection contains the URL requested by the web browser.

packet (119841004) is the same as that for the previous packet it sent in acknowledgment to the server's SYN message. This is because TCP messages consisting only of an acknowledgment do not increment the sequence counter. The acknowledgment number is also the same as in the previous packet because the client has not yet received the next message from the server. Note also that the PSH bit is set, indicating that the server should send the enclosed data to the application immediately.

After receiving the client's message, the server returns an acknowledgment message, as shown in Figure 14-8, that uses the sequence number expected by the client (116271) and has an acknowledgment number of 119841363. The difference between this acknowledgment number and the sequence number of the client message previously sent is 359; this is correct because the datagram the client sent to the server was 399 bytes long. Subtracting 40 bytes for the IP and TCP headers leaves 359 bytes of data. The value in the server's acknowledgment message, therefore, indicates that it has successfully received 359 bytes of data from the client. As each system sends data to the other, they increment their sequence numbers for each byte transmitted.

The next step in the process is for the server to respond to the client's request by sending it the requested HTML file. Using the MSS value, the server creates segments small enough to be transmitted over the network and transmits the first one in the message, as shown in Figure 14-9. The sequence number is again the same as the server's previous message because the previous message contained only an acknowledgment. The acknowledgment number is also the same because the server is sending a second message without any intervening communication from the client.

In addition to the acknowledgment service just described, the TCP header fields provide two more services:

- Error correction
- Flow control

The following sections examine each of these functions.

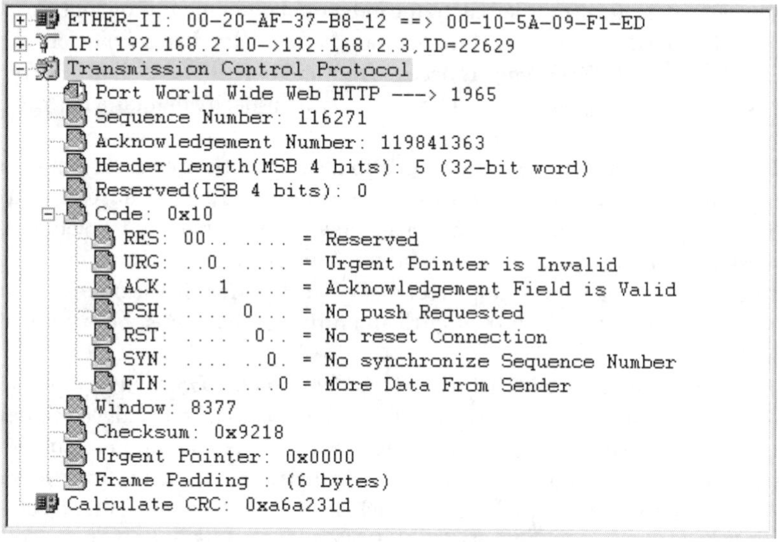

```
⊞ 📭 ETHER-II: 00-20-AF-37-B8-12 ==> 00-10-5A-09-F1-ED
⊞ 🍅 IP: 192.168.2.10->192.168.2.3,ID=22629
⊟ 🗐 Transmission Control Protocol
     🕘 Port World Wide Web HTTP ---> 1965
     🗐 Sequence Number: 116271
     🗐 Acknowledgement Number: 119841363
     🗐 Header Length(MSB 4 bits): 5 (32-bit word)
     🗐 Reserved(LSB 4 bits): 0
   ⊟ 🗐 Code: 0x10
       🗐 RES: 00.. .... = Reserved
       🗐 URG: ..0. .... = Urgent Pointer is Invalid
       🗐 ACK: ...1 .... = Acknowledgement Field is Valid
       🗐 PSH: .... 0... = No push Requested
       🗐 RST: .... .0.. = No reset Connection
       🗐 SYN: .... ..0. = No synchronize Sequence Number
       🗐 FIN: .... ...0 = More Data From Sender
     🗐 Window: 8377
     🗐 Checksum: 0x9218
     🗐 Urgent Pointer: 0x0000
     🗐 Frame Padding : (6 bytes)
   📭 Calculate CRC: 0xa6a231d
```

Figure 14-8   The server acknowledges all of the data bytes transmitted by the client.

Error Correction   You saw in the previous example how a receiving system uses the acknowledgment number in its ACK message to inform the sender that its data was received correctly. The systems also use this mechanism to indicate when an error has occurred and data is not received correctly.

TCP/IP systems use a system of *delayed acknowledgments,* meaning they do not have to send an acknowledgment message for every packet they receive. The method used to determine when

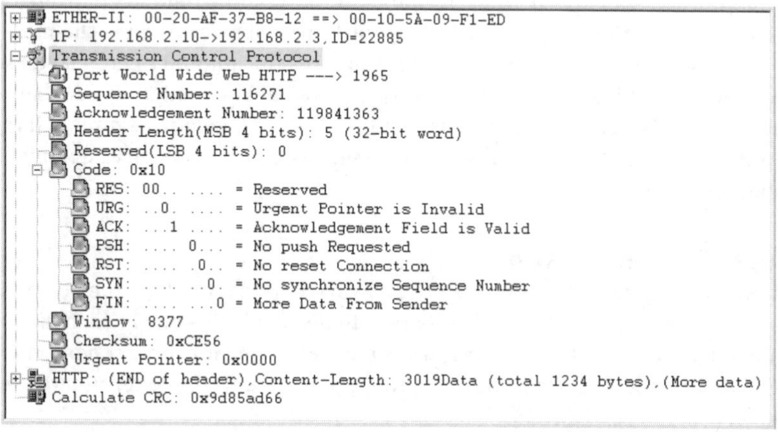

```
⊞ 📭 ETHER-II: 00-20-AF-37-B8-12 ==> 00-10-5A-09-F1-ED
⊞ 🍅 IP: 192.168.2.10->192.168.2.3,ID=22885
⊟ 🗐 Transmission Control Protocol
     🕘 Port World Wide Web HTTP ---> 1965
     🗐 Sequence Number: 116271
     🗐 Acknowledgement Number: 119841363
     🗐 Header Length(MSB 4 bits): 5 (32-bit word)
     🗐 Reserved(LSB 4 bits): 0
   ⊟ 🗐 Code: 0x10
       🗐 RES: 00.. .... = Reserved
       🗐 URG: ..0. .... = Urgent Pointer is Invalid
       🗐 ACK: ...1 .... = Acknowledgement Field is Valid
       🗐 PSH: .... 0... = No push Requested
       🗐 RST: .... .0.. = No reset Connection
       🗐 SYN: .... ..0. = No synchronize Sequence Number
       🗐 FIN: .... ...0 = More Data From Sender
     🗐 Window: 8377
     🗐 Checksum: 0xCE56
     🗐 Urgent Pointer: 0x0000
 ⊞ 🗐 HTTP: (END of header),Content-Length: 3019Data (total 1234 bytes),(More data)
   📭 Calculate CRC: 0x9d85ad66
```

Figure 14-9   In response to the client's request, the server begins to transmit the web page after splitting it into multiple segments.

acknowledgments are sent is left up to the individual implementation, but each acknowledgment specifies that the data, up to a certain point in the sequence, has been received correctly. These are called *positive acknowledgments* because they indicate that data has been received. *Negative acknowledgments* or *selective acknowledgments,* which specify that data has not been received correctly, are not possible in TCP.

What if, for example, in the course of a single connection, a server transmits five data segments to a client and the third segment must be discarded because of a checksum error? The receiving system must then send an acknowledgment back to the sender indicating that all the messages up through the second segment have been received correctly. Even though the fourth and fifth segments were also received correctly, the third segment was not. Using positive acknowledgments means that the fourth and fifth segments must be retransmitted, in addition to the third.

The mechanism used by TCP is called *positive acknowledgment with retransmission* because the sending system automatically retransmits all of the unacknowledged segments after a certain time interval. The way this works is that the sending system maintains a queue containing all of the segments it has already transmitted. As acknowledgments arrive from the receiver, the sender deletes the segments that have been acknowledged from the queue. After a certain elapsed time, the sending system retransmits all of the unacknowledged segments remaining in the queue. The systems use algorithms documented in RFC 1122 to calculate the timeout values for a connection based on the amount of time it takes for a transmission to travel from one system to the other and back again, called the *round-trip time.*

Flow Control   *Flow control* is an important element of the TCP protocol because it is designed to transmit large amounts of data. Receiving systems have a buffer in which they store incoming segments waiting to be acknowledged. If a sending system transmits too many segments too quickly, the receiver's buffer fills up and any packets arriving at the system are discarded until space in the buffer is available. TCP uses a mechanism called a *sliding window* for its flow control, which is essentially a means for the receiving system to inform the sender of how much buffer space it has available.

Each acknowledgment message generated by a system receiving TCP data specifies the amount of buffer space it has available in its Window field. As packets arrive at the receiving system, they wait in the buffer until the system generates the message that acknowledges them. The sending system computes the amount of data it can send by taking the Window value from the most recently received acknowledgment and subtracting the number of bytes it has transmitted since it received that acknowledgment. If the result of this computation is zero, the system stops transmitting until it receives acknowledgment of outstanding packets.

Connection Termination

When the exchange of data between the two systems is complete, they terminate the TCP connection. Because two connections are actually involved—one in each direction—both must be individually terminated. The process begins when one machine sends a message in which the FIN control bit is set. This indicates that the system wants to terminate the connection it has been using to send data.

Which system initiates the termination process is dependent on the application generating the traffic. In an HTML transaction, the server can include the FIN bit in the message containing the last segment of data in the sequence, or it can take the form of a separate message. The client receiving the FIN from the server sends an acknowledgment, closing the server's connection, and then sends a FIN message of its own. Note that, unlike the three-way handshake that established the connection, the termination procedure requires four transmissions because the client sends its ACK and FIN bits in separate messages. When the server transmits its acknowledgment to the client's FIN, the connection is effectively terminated.

CHAPTER

15

The Domain Name System

Computers are designed to work with numbers, while humans are more comfortable working with words. This fundamental dichotomy is the reason why the Domain Name System (DNS) came to be. Back in the dark days of the 1970s, when the Internet was the ARPANET and the entire experimental network consisted of only a few hundred systems, a need was recognized for a mechanism that would permit users to refer to the network's computers by name, rather than by address. The introduction of the Transmission Control Protocol/Internet Protocol (TCP/IP) protocols in the early 1980s led to the use of 32-bit IP addresses, which even in dotted decimal form were difficult to remember.

Host Tables

The first mechanism for assigning human-friendly names to addresses was called a *host table,* which took the form of a file called /etc/hosts on Unix systems. The host table was a simple ASCII file that contained a list of network system addresses and their equivalent hostnames. When users wanted to access resources on other network systems, they would specify a hostname in the application, and the system would resolve the name into the appropriate address by looking it up in the host table. This host table still exists on all TCP/IP systems today, usually in the form of a file called Hosts somewhere on the local disk drive. If nothing else, the host table contains the following entry, which assigns to the standard IP loopback address the hostname localhost:

```
127.0.0.1       localhost
```

Today, the Domain Name System has replaced the host table almost universally, but when TCP/IP systems attempt to resolve a hostname into an IP address, it is still possible to configure them to check the Hosts file first before using DNS. If you have a small network of TCP/IP systems that is not connected to the Internet, you can use host tables on your machines to maintain friendly hostnames for your computers. The name resolution process will be very fast because no network communications are necessary and you will not need a DNS server.

Host Table Problems

The use of host tables on TCP/IP systems caused several problems, all of which were exacerbated as the fledgling Internet grew from a small "family" of networked computers into today's gigantic network. The most fundamental problem was that each computer had to have its own host table, which listed the names and addresses of all of the other computers on the network. When you connected a new computer to the network, you could not access it until an entry for it was added to your computer's host table.

For everyone to keep their host tables updated, it was necessary to inform the administrators when a system was added to the network or a name or address change occurred. Having every administrator of an ARPANET system e-mail every other administrator each time they made a change was obviously not a practical solution, so it was necessary to designate a registrar that would maintain a master list of the systems on the network, their addresses, and their hostnames.

The task of maintaining this registry was given to the Network Information Center (NIC) at the Stanford Research Institute (SRI), in Menlo Park, California. The master list was stored in a file called Hosts.txt on a computer with the hostname SRI-NIC. Administrators of ARPANET systems would e-mail their modifications to the NIC, which would update the Hosts.txt file periodically. To keep their systems updated, the administrators would use FTP to download the latest Hosts.txt file from SRI-NIC and compile it into a new Hosts file for their systems.

Initially, this was an adequate solution, but as the network continued to grow, it became increasingly unworkable. As more systems were added to the network, the Hosts.txt file grew larger, and more people were accessing SRI-NIC to download it on a regular basis. The amount of network traffic generated by this simple maintenance task became excessive, and changes started occurring so fast that it was difficult for administrators to keep their systems updated.

Another serious problem was that there was no control over the hostnames used to represent the systems on the network. Once TCP/IP came into general use, the NIC was responsible for assigning network addresses, but administrators chose their own hostnames for the computers on their networks. The accidental use of duplicate hostnames resulted in misrouted traffic and disruption of communications. Imagine the chaos that would result today if anyone on the Internet was allowed to set up a web server and use the name microsoft.com for it. Clearly, a better solution was needed, and this led to the development of the Domain Name System.

DNS Objectives

To address the problems resulting from the use of host tables for name registration and resolution, the people responsible for the ARPANET decided to design a completely new mechanism. Their primary objectives at first seemed to be contradictory: to design a mechanism that would enable administrators to assign hostnames to their own systems without creating duplicate names and to make that hostname information globally available to other administrators without relying on a single access point that could become a traffic bottleneck and a single point of failure. In addition, the mechanism had to be able to support information about systems that use various protocols with different types of addresses, and it had to be adaptable for use by multiple applications.

The solution was the Domain Name System, designed by Paul Mockapetris and published in 1983 as two Internet Engineering Task Force (IETF) documents called request for comments (RFC): RFC 882, "Domain Names: Concepts and Facilities," and RFC 883, "Domain Names: Implementation Specification." These documents were updated in 1987, published as RFC 1034 and RFC 1035, respectively, and ratified as an IETF standard. Since that time, numerous other RFCs have updated the information in the standard to address current networking issues.

Current requests and updates to older entries can be found at rfc-editor.org.

The DNS, as designed by Mockapetris, consists of three basic elements:

- A hierarchical name space that divides the host system database into discrete elements called *domains*

- Domain name servers that contain information about the host and subdomains within a given domain

- Resolvers that generate requests for information from domain name servers

These elements are discussed in the following sections.

Domain Naming

The Domain Name System achieves the designated objectives by using a hierarchical system, both in the name space used to name the hosts and in the database that contains the hostname information. Before the DNS was developed, administrators assigned simple hostnames to the computers on their networks. The names sometimes reflected the computer's function or its location, as with SRI-NIC, but there was no policy in place that required this. At that time, there were few enough computers on the network to make this a practical solution.

To support the network as it grew larger, Mockapetris developed a hierarchical name space that made it possible for individual network administrators to name their systems, while identifying the organization that owns the systems and preventing the duplication of names on the Internet. The DNS name space is based on domains, which exist in a hierarchical structure much like the directory tree in a file system. A *domain* is the equivalent of a directory, in that it can contain either subdomains (subdirectories) or hosts (files), forming a structure called the *DNS tree* (see Figure 15-1). By delegating the responsibility for specific domains to network administrators all over the Internet, the result is a *distributed database* scattered on systems all over the network.

Part IV

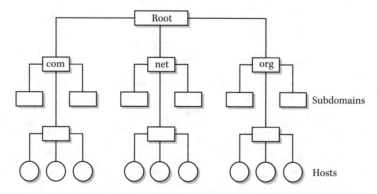

Figure 15-1   The Domain Name System uses a tree structure like that of a file system.

NOTE The term *domain* has more than one meaning in the computer industry. A domain can be a group of devices on a network administered as one unit. On the Internet, it can be an IP address, such as mcgrawhill.com in which all the devices sharing part of this address are considered part of the same domain. You may also see software that is in the *public domain,* which means the program can be used without copyright restrictions.

To assign unique IP addresses to computers all over the Internet, a two-tiered system was devised in which administrators receive the network identifiers that form the first part of the IP addresses and then assign host identifiers to individual computers themselves to form the second part of the addresses. This distributes the address assignment tasks among thousands of network administrators all over the world. The DNS name space functions in the same way: Administrators are assigned domain names and are then responsible for specifying hostnames to systems within that domain.

The result is that every computer on the Internet is uniquely identifiable by a *DNS name* that consists of a hostname plus the names of all of its parent domains, stretching up to the root of the DNS tree, separated by periods. Each of the names between the periods can be up to 63 characters long, with a total length of 255 characters for a complete DNS name, including the host and all of its parent domains. Domain and hostnames are not case sensitive and can take any value except the null value (no characters), which represents the root of the DNS tree. Domain and hostnames also cannot contain any of the following symbols:

_ : , / \ ? . @ # ! $ % ^ & * ( ) { } [ ] | ; " < > ~ `

NOTE Using a shell prompt, you can enter the IP address of a computer to look up the DNS name.

In Figure 15-2, a computer in the mycorp domain functions as a web server, and the administrator has therefore given it the hostname www. This administrator is responsible for the mycorp domain and can therefore assign systems in that domain any hostname he wants. Because mycorp is a subdomain of com, the full DNS name for that web server is www.mycorp.com. Thus, a DNS name is

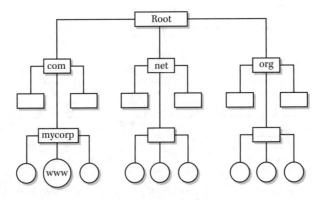

Figure 15-2   A DNS name like www.mycorp.com reflects a system's place in the domain hierarchy.

something like a postal address, in which the top-level domain is the equivalent of the state, the second-level domain is the city, and the hostname is the street address.

Because a complete DNS name traces the domain path all the way up the tree structure to the root, it should theoretically end with a period, indicating the division between the top-level domain and the root. However, this trailing period is nearly always omitted in common use, except in cases in which it serves to distinguish an absolute domain name from a relative domain name. An *absolute domain name* (also called a *fully qualified domain name* [FQDN]) does specify the path all the way to the root, while a *relative domain name* specifies only the subdomain relative to a specific domain context. For example, when working on a complex network called zacker.com that uses several levels of subdomains, you might refer to a system using a relative domain name of mail.paris without a period because it's understood by your colleagues that you're actually referring to a system with an absolute name of mail.paris.zacker.com. (with a period).

It's also important to understand that DNS names have no inherent connection to IP addresses or any other type of address. Theoretically, the host systems in a particular domain can be located on different networks, thousands of miles apart.

Top-Level Domains

In every DNS name, the first word on the right represents the domain at the highest level in the DNS tree, called a *top-level domain.* These top-level domains essentially function as registrars for the domains at the second level. For example, the administrator of zacker.com went to the com top-level domain and registered the name zacker. In return for a fee, that administrator now has exclusive use of the name zacker.com and can create any host or subdomain names in that domain that he wants. It doesn't matter that thousands of other network administrators have named their web servers www because they all have their own individual domain names. The hostname www may be duplicated anywhere, as long as the DNS name is unique.

The original DNS name space called for seven top-level domains, centered in U.S. nomenclature and dedicated to specific purposes, as follows:

- **com** Commercial organizations
- **edu** Four-year, degree-granting educational institutions in North America
- **gov** U.S. government institutions
- **int** Organizations established by international treaty
- **mil** U.S. military applications
- **net** Networking organizations
- **org** Noncommercial organizations

The edu, gov, int, and mil domains were originally reserved for use by certified organizations, but the com, org, and net domains were and are called *global domains,* because organizations anywhere in the world can register second-level domains within them. Originally, these top-level domains were managed by a company called Network Solutions (NSI, formerly known as InterNIC, the Internet Network Information Center) as a result of cooperative agreement with the U.S. government. You can still go to its web site at www.networksolutions.com/ and register names in these top-level domains.

In 1998, the agreement with the U.S. government was changed to permit other organizations to compete with NSI in providing domain registrations. An organization called the Internet Corporation for Assigned Names and Numbers (ICANN) is responsible for the accreditation of domain name registrars. Under this new policy, the procedures and fees for registering names in the com, net, and org domains may vary, but there will be no difference in the functionality of the domain names, nor will duplicate names be permitted. The complete list of registrars that have been accredited by ICANN is available at http://www.webhosting.info/registrars/.

Currently, more than 1,900 new top-level domain names have been submitted to ICANN, and during 2015, it is anticipated that each week new names will be available for open registration. While there may be conflicts, the issues will, at this time, be settled by auction or negotiation. Approval for new top-level domain names currently has three stages:

- **Sunrise stage**   During this 60-day period, legal trademark owners can "stake their claim" before registration for that name.

- **Landrush stage**   This is a preregistration period where applicants can pay a fee (which in many cases will be substantial) for a specific domain name.

- **Open registration**   During this time, anyone can register a new domain.

.com Domain Conflicts

The com top-level domain is the one most closely associated with commercial Internet interests, and names of certain types in the com domain are becoming scarce. For example, it is difficult at this time to come up with a snappy name for an Internet technology company that includes the word "net" that has not already been registered in the com domain.

There have also been conflicts between organizations that think they have a right to a particular domain name. Trademark law permits two companies to have the same name, as long as they are not directly competitive in the marketplace. However, A1 Auto Parts Company and A1 Software may both feel that they have a right to the a1.com domain, and lawsuits have arisen in some cases. In other instances, forward-thinking private individuals who registered domains using their own names have later been confronted by corporations with the same name who want to jump on the Internet bandwagon and think they have a right to that name. If a certain individual of Scottish extraction registers his domain only to find out some years later that a fast-food company (for example) is very anxious to acquire that domain name, the end result can be either a profitable settlement for the individual or a nasty court case.

This phenomenon gave rise to a particular breed of Internet bottom-feeder known as *domain name speculators.* These people register large numbers of domain names that they think some company might want someday, hoping that they can receive a large fee in return for selling them the domain name. Another unscrupulous practice is for a company in a particular business to register domains using the names of their competitors. Thus, when Internet users go to pizzaman.com, expecting to find Ray the Pizza Man's web site, they instead find themselves redirected to the site for Bob's Pizza Palace, which is located across the street from Ray's.

Cybersquatting

By definition, *cybersquatting* is the practice of registering an Internet domain name simply for the purpose of profiting by selling the name to someone else. According to the World Intellectual Property Organization (WIPO), this practice includes the following:

- Abusive registration of a domain name that is misleadingly similar or identical to an existing trademark.

- A registered domain name for which the registering party has no rights or legitimate interests.

- A domain name that is registered and used in bad faith.

ICANN created its Uniform Domain Name Resolution Policy (UDRP) to counteract cybersquatting. Since 2000, all registrants of domains such as .com, .net, and .org have been subject to this policy. In response to the new top-level domains (TLDs), in March 2013, ICANN launched the IP Trademark Clearinghouse, a centralized database of valid trademarks to protect these trademarks, especially during the time in which the new TLDs are launched.

Country-Code Domains

There are many *country-code domains* (also called *international domains*), named for specific countries using the ISO designations, such as *fr* for France and *de* for Deutschland (Germany). Many of these countries allow free registration of second-level domains to anyone, without restrictions. For the other countries, an organization must conform to some sort of local presence, tax, or trademark guidelines in order to register a second-level domain. Each of these country-code domains is managed by an organization in that country, which establishes its own domain name registration policies.

NOTE For the country codes maintained by the International Organization for Standardization (ISO), see www.iso.org/iso/country_codes.htm.

There is also a us top-level domain that is a viable alternative for organizations unable to obtain a satisfactory name in the com domain. In March 2014, the National Telecommunications and Information Administration (NTIA) arm of the U.S. Department of Commerce awarded the administrative contract to Neustar for three years. This entity registers second-level domains to businesses and individuals, as well as to government agencies, educational institutions, and other organizations. The only restriction is that all us domains must conform to a naming hierarchy that uses two-letter state abbreviations at the third level and uses local city or county names at the fourth level. Thus, an example of a valid domain name would be something like mgh.newyork.ny.us. The general format is <organization-name>.<locality>.<state>.us, where <state> is a state's two-letter postal abbreviation.

Second-Level Domains

The registrars of the top-level domains are responsible for registering second-level domain names, in return for a subscription fee. As long as an organization continues to pay the fees for its domain name, it has exclusive rights to that name. The domain registrar maintains records that identify the owner of each second-level domain and specify three contacts within the registrant's organization—an administrative contact, a billing contact, and a technical contact. In addition, the registrar must have the IP addresses of two DNS servers that function as the source for further information about the domain. This is the only information maintained by the top-level domain. The administrators of the registrant's network can create as many hosts and subdomains within the second-level domain as they want without informing the registrars at all.

To host a second-level domain, an organization must have two DNS servers. A DNS server is a software program that runs on a computer. DNS server products are available for all of the major network operating systems. The DNS servers do not have to be located on the registrant's network; many companies outsource their Internet server hosting chores and use their service provider's DNS servers. The DNS servers identified in the top-level domain's record are the *authority* for the second-level domain. This means that these servers are the ultimate source for information about that domain. When network administrators want to add a host to the network or create a new subdomain, they do so in their own DNS servers. In addition, whenever a user application somewhere on the Internet has to discover the IP address associated with a particular hostname, the request eventually ends up at one of the domain's authoritative servers.

Thus, in its simplest form, the Domain Name System works by referring requests for the address of a particular hostname to a top-level domain server, which in turn passes the request to the authoritative server for the second-level domain, which responds with the requested information. This is why the DNS is described as a *distributed database.* The information about the hosts in specific domains is stored on their authoritative servers, which can be located anywhere. There is no single list of all the hostnames on the entire Internet, which is actually a good thing because at the time that the DNS was developed, no one would have predicted that the Internet would grow as large as it has.

This distributed nature of the DNS database eliminates the traffic-congestion problem caused by the use of a host table maintained on a single computer. The top-level domain server handles millions of requests a day, but they are requests only for the DNS servers associated with second-level domains. If the top-level domains had to maintain records for every host in every second-level domain they have registered, the resulting traffic would bring the entire system to its knees.

Distributing the database in this way also splits the chores of administering the database among thousands of network administrators around the world. Domain name registrants are each responsible for their own area of the name space and can maintain it as they want with complete autonomy.

Subdomains

Many of the domains on the Internet stop at two levels, meaning that the second-level domain contains only host systems. However, it is possible for the administrators of a second-level domain to create subdomains that form additional levels. The us top-level domain, for example, requires a minimum of three levels: the country code, the state code, and the local city or county code. There is no limit on the number of levels you can create within a domain, except for those imposed by practicality and the 255-character maximum DNS name length.

In some cases, large organizations use subdomains to subdivide their networks according to geographical or organizational boundaries. A large corporation might create a third-level domain for each city or country in which it has an office, such as paris.zacker.com and newyork.zacker .com, or for each of several departments, such as sales.zacker.com and mis.zacker.com. The organizational paradigm for each domain is left completely up to its administrators.

The use of subdomains can make it easier to identify hosts on a large network, but many organizations also use them to delegate domain maintenance chores. The DNS servers for a top-level domain contain the addresses for each second-level domain's authoritative servers. In the same way, a second-level domain's servers can refer to authoritative servers for third-level administrators at each site to maintain their own DNS servers.

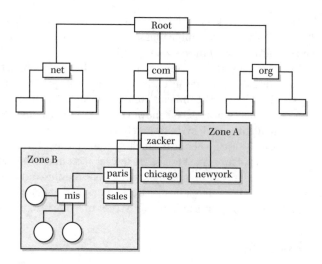

Figure 15-3   A zone is an administrative entity that contains a branch of the DNS tree.

To make this delegation possible, DNS servers can break up a domain's name space into administrative units called *zones*. A domain with only two levels consists of only a single zone, which is synonymous with the domain. A three-level domain, however, can be divided into multiple zones. A zone can be any contiguous branch of a DNS tree and can include domains on multiple levels. For example, in the diagram shown in Figure 15-3, the paris.zacker.com domain, including all of its subdomains and hosts, is one zone, represented by its own DNS servers. The rest of the zacker.com domain, including newyork.zacker.com, chicago.zacker.com, and zacker .com itself, is another zone. Thus, a *zone* can be defined as any part of a domain, including its subdomains, that is not designated as part of another zone.

Each zone must be represented by DNS servers that are the authority for that zone. A single DNS server can be authoritative for multiple zones, so you could conceivably create a separate zone for each of the third-level domains in zacker.com and still have only two sets of DNS servers.

DNS Functions

DNS servers are a ubiquitous part of most TCP/IP networks, even if you aren't aware of it. If you connect to the Internet, you use a DNS server each time you enter a server name or URL into a web browser or other application to resolve the name of the system you specified into an IP address. When a stand-alone computer connects to an Internet service provider (ISP), the ISP's server usually supplies the addresses of the DNS servers that the system will use. On a TCP/IP network, administrators or users configure clients with the addresses of the DNS servers they will use. This can be a manual process performed for each workstation or an automatic process performed using a service such as Dynamic Host Configuration Protocol (DHCP). The end user will not usually see the IP address because this is all taken care of in the background.

TCP/IP communications are based solely on IP addresses. Before one system can communicate with another, it must know its IP address. Often, the user supplies a friendly name (such as a DNS name) for a desired server to a client application. The application must then resolve that server name into an IP address before it can transmit a message to it. If the name resolution mechanism fails to function, no communication with the server is possible.

Virtually all TCP/IP networks use some form of friendly name for host systems and include a mechanism for resolving those names into the IP addresses needed to initiate communications between systems. If the network is connected to the Internet, DNS name resolution is a necessity. Private networks do not necessarily need it, however. Microsoft Windows NT networks, for example, use NetBIOS names to identify their systems and have their own mechanisms for resolving those names into IP addresses. These mechanisms include the Windows Internet Naming System (WINS) and also the transmission of broadcast messages to every system on the network. NetBIOS names and name resolution mechanisms do not replace the DNS; they are intended for use on relatively small, private networks and would not be practical on the Internet. A computer can have both a NetBIOS name and a DNS hostname and use both types of name resolution.

Resource Records

DNS servers are basically database servers that store information about the hosts and subdomain for which they are responsible in *resource records* (RRs). When you run your own DNS server, you create a resource record for each hostname that you want to be accessible by the rest of the network. There are several different types of resource records used by DNS servers, the most important of which are as follows:

- **Start of authority (SOA)**   Indicates that the server is the best authoritative source for data concerning the zone. Each zone must have an SOA record, and only one SOA record can be in a zone.

- **Name server (NS)**   Identifies a DNS server functioning as an authority for the zone. Each DNS server in the zone (whether primary, master, or slave) must be represented by an NS record.

- **Address (A)**   Provides a name-to-address mapping that supplies an IP address for a specific DNS name. This record type performs the primary function of the DNS, converting names to addresses.

- **PTR (Pointer)**   Provides an address-to-name mapping that supplies a DNS name for a specific address in the in-addr.arpa domain. This is the functional opposite of an A record, used for reverse lookups only.

- **Canonical name (CNAME)**   Creates an alias that points to the *canonical* name (that is, the "real" name) of a host identified by an A record. CNAME records are used to provide alternative names by which systems can be identified. For example, you may have a system with the name server1.zacker.com on your network that you use as a web server. Changing the hostname of the computer would confuse your users, but you want to use the traditional name of www to identify the web server in your domain. Once you create a CNAME record for the name www.zacker.com that points to server1.zacker.com, the system is addressable using either name.

- **Mail exchanger (MX)**   Identifies a system that will direct e-mail traffic sent to an address in the domain to the individual recipient, a mail gateway, or another mail server.

In addition to functioning as the authority for a small section of the DNS name space, servers process client name resolution requests by either consulting their own resource records or forwarding the request to another DNS server on the network. The process of forwarding a request is called a *referral,* and this is how all of the DNS servers on the Internet work together to provide a unified information resource for the entire domain name space.

DNS Name Resolution

All Internet applications use DNS to resolve hostnames into IP addresses. When you type a URL containing a DNS name (such as mcgrawhill.com) into the browser's Address field and press ENTER, it is while the application goes through the process of finding the site and connecting that the DNS name resolution process occurs.

From the client's perspective, the procedure that occurs during these few seconds consists of the application sending a query message to its designated DNS server that contains the name to be resolved. The server then replies with a message containing the IP address corresponding to that name. Using the supplied address, the application can then transmit a message to the intended destination. It is only when you examine the DNS server's role in the process that you see how complex the procedure really is.

Resolvers

The component in the client system that generates the DNS query is called a *resolver.* In most cases, the resolver is a simple set of library routines in the operating system that generates the queries to be sent to the DNS server, reads the response information from the server's replies, and feeds the response to the application that originally requested it. In addition, a resolver can resend a query if no reply is forthcoming after a given timeout period and can process error messages returned by the server, such as when it fails to resolve a given name.

DNS Requests

A TCP/IP client usually is configured with the addresses of two DNS servers to which it can send queries. A client can send a query to any DNS server; it does not have to use the authoritative server for the domain in which it belongs, nor does the server have to be on the local network. Using the DNS server that is closest to the client is best, however, because it minimizes the time needed for messages to travel between the two systems. A client needs access to only one DNS server, but two are usually specified to provide a backup in case one server is unavailable.

There are two types of DNS queries: recursive and iterative. When a server receives a *recursive query,* it is responsible for trying to resolve the requested name and for transmitting a reply to the requestor. Even if the server does not possess the required information itself, it must send its own queries to other DNS servers until it obtains the requested information or an error message stating why the information was unavailable and must then relay the information to the requestor. The system that generated the query, therefore, receives a reply only from the original server to which it sent the query. The resolvers in client systems nearly always send recursive queries to DNS servers.

When a server receives an *iterative query* (also called a *nonrecursive query*), it can either respond with information from its own database or refer the requestor to another DNS server. The recipient of the query responds with the best answer it currently possesses, but is not responsible for searching for the information, as with a recursive query. DNS servers processing a recursive query from a client typically use iterative queries to request information from other servers.

It is possible for a DNS server to send a recursive query to another server, thus in effect "passing the buck" and forcing the other server to search for the requested information, but this is considered bad form and is rarely done without permission.

One of the scenarios in which DNS servers do send recursive queries to other servers is when you configure a server to function as a *forwarder*. On a network running several DNS servers, you may not want all of the servers sending queries to other DNS servers on the Internet. If the network has a relatively slow connection to the Internet, for example, several servers transmitting repeated queries may use too much of the available bandwidth.

To prevent this, some DNS implementations enable you to configure one server to function as the forwarder for all Internet queries generated by the other servers on the network. Any time that a server has to resolve the DNS name of an Internet system and fails to find the needed information in its cache, it transmits a recursive query to the forwarder, which is then responsible for sending its own iterative queries over the Internet connection. Once the forwarder resolves the name, it sends a reply to the original DNS server, which relays it to the client.

This request-forwarding behavior is a function of the original server only. The forwarder simply receives standard recursive queries from the original server and processes them normally. A server can be configured to use a forwarder in either exclusive or nonexclusive mode. In *exclusive mode,* the server relies completely on the forwarder to resolve the requested name. If the forwarder's resolution attempt fails, the server relays a failure message to the client. A server that uses a forwarder in exclusive mode is called a *slave.* In *nonexclusive mode,* if the forwarder fails to resolve the name and transmits an error message to the original server, that server makes its own resolution attempt before responding to the client.

Root Name Servers

In most cases, DNS servers that do not possess the information needed to resolve a name requested by a client send their first iterative query to one of the Internet's root name servers. The *root name servers* possess information about all of the top-level domains in the DNS name space. When you first install a DNS server, the only addresses that it needs to process client requests are those of the root name servers because these servers can send a request for a name in any domain on its way to the appropriate authority.

The root name servers contain the addresses of the authoritative servers for all the top-level domains on the Internet. In fact, the root name servers are the authorities for certain top-level domains, but they can also refer queries to the appropriate server for any of the other top-level domains, including the country-code domains, which are scattered all over the world. There are currently 13 root name servers, and they process millions of requests each day. The servers are also scattered widely and connected to different network trunks, so the chances of all of them being unavailable are minimal. If this were to occur, virtually all DNS name resolution would cease, and the Internet would be crippled.

Currently, the NTIA administers authority through ICANN over these root name servers. However, in March 2014, the NTIA announced it will cede authority to another organization, which has not yet been identified.

Resolving a Domain Name

With the preceding pieces in place, you are now ready to see how the DNS servers work together to resolve the name of a server on the Internet (see Figure 15-4). The process is as follows:

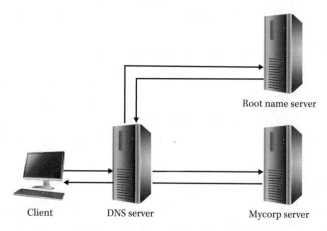

Root name server

Client   DNS server   Mycorp server

Figure 15-4   DNS servers communicate among themselves to locate the information requested by a client.

1. A user on a client system specifies the DNS name of an Internet server in an application such as a web browser or File Transfer Protocol (FTP) client.

2. The application generates an application programming interface (API) call to the resolver on the client system, and the resolver creates a DNS recursive query message containing the server name.

3. The client system transmits the recursive query message to the DNS server identified in its TCP/IP configuration.

4. The client's DNS server, after receiving the query, checks its resource records to see whether it is the authoritative source for the zone containing the requested server name. If it is the authority, it generates a reply message and transmits it to the client. If the DNS server is not the authority for the domain in which the requested server is located, it generates an iterative query and submits it to one of the root name servers.

5. The root name server examines the name requested by the original DNS server and consults its resource records to identify the authoritative servers for the name's top-level domain. Because the root name server received an iterative request, it does not send its own request to the top-level domain server. Instead, it transmits a reply to the original DNS server that contains a referral to the top-level domain server addresses.

6. The original DNS server then generates a new iterative query and transmits it to the top-level domain server. The top-level domain server examines the second-level domain in the requested name and transmits to the original server a referral containing the addresses of authoritative servers for that second-level domain.

7. The original server generates yet another iterative query and transmits it to the second-level domain server. If the requested name contains additional domain names, the second-level domain server replies with another referral to the third-level domain servers. The second-level domain server may also refer the original server to the authorities for a different zone. This process continues until the original server receives a referral

Part IV

to the domain server that is the authority for the domain or zone containing the requested host.

8. Once the authoritative server for the domain or zone containing the host receives a query from the original server, it consults its resource records to determine the IP address of the requested system and transmits it in a reply message to that original server.

9. The original server receives the reply from the authoritative server and transmits the IP address back to the resolver on the client system. The resolver relays the address to the application, which can then initiate communications with the system specified by the user.

This procedure assumes a successful completion of the name resolution procedure. If any of the authoritative DNS servers queried returns an error message to the original server stating, for example, that one of the domains in the name does not exist, this error message is relayed to the client and the name resolution process is said to have failed.

DNS Server Caching

This process may seem extremely long and complex, but in many cases, it isn't necessary for the client's DNS server to send queries to the servers for each domain specified in the requested DNS name. DNS servers are capable of retaining the information they learn about the DNS name space in the course of their name resolution procedures and storing it in a cache on the local drive.

A DNS server that receives requests from clients, for example, caches the addresses of the requested systems, as well as the addresses for particular domains' authoritative servers. The next time that a client transmits a request for a previously resolved name, the server can respond immediately with the cached information. In addition, if a client requests another name in one of the same domains, the server can send a query directly to an authoritative server for that domain, and not to a root name server. Thus, users should generally find that names in commonly accessed domains resolve more quickly because one of the servers along the line has information about the domain in its cache, while names in obscure domains take longer because the entire request/referral process is needed.

Negative Caching In addition to storing information that aids in the name resolution process, most modern DNS server implementations are capable of negative caching. *Negative caching* occurs when a DNS server retains information about names that do not exist in a domain. If, for example, a client sends a query to its DNS server containing a name in which the second-level domain does not exist, the top-level domain server will return a reply containing an error message to that effect. The client's DNS server will then retain the error message information in its cache. The next time a client requests a name in that domain, the DNS server will be able to respond immediately with its own error message, without consulting the top-level domain.

Cache Data Persistence Caching is a vital element of the DNS architecture because it reduces the number of requests sent to the root name and top-level domain servers, which, being at the top of the DNS tree, are the most likely to act as a bottleneck for the whole system. However, caches must be purged eventually, and there is a fine line between effective and ineffective caching. Because DNS servers retain resource records in their caches, it can take hours or even days for changes made in an authoritative server to be propagated around the Internet. During this period, users may receive incorrect information in response to a query. If information remains in server caches too long, the changes that administrators make to the data in their DNS servers take too long to propagate around the Internet. If caches are purged too quickly, the number of requests sent to the root name and top-level domain servers increases precipitously.

The amount of time that DNS data remains cached on a server is called its *time to live* (TTL). Unlike most data caches, the time to live is not specified by the administrator of the server where the cache is stored. Instead, the administrators of each authoritative DNS server specify how long the data for the resource records in their domains or zones should be retained in the servers where it is cached. This enables administrators to specify a time-to-live value based on the volatility of their server data. On a network where changes in IP addresses or the addition of new resource records is frequent, a lower time-to-live value increases the likelihood that clients will receive current data. On a network that rarely changes, you can use a longer time-to-live value and minimize the number of requests sent to the parent servers of your domain or zone.

DNS Load Balancing

In most cases, DNS servers maintain one IP address for each hostname. However, there are situations in which more than one IP address is required. In the case of a highly trafficked web site, for example, one server may not be sufficient to support all of the clients. To have multiple, identical servers with their own IP addresses hosting the same site, some mechanism is needed to ensure that client requests are balanced among the machines.

One way of doing this is to control how the authoritative servers for the domain on which the site is located resolve the DNS name of the web server. Some DNS server implementations enable you to create multiple resource records with different IP addresses for the same hostname. As the server responds to queries requesting resolution of that name, it uses the resource records in a rotational fashion to supply the IP address of a different machine to each client.

DNS caching tends to defeat the effectiveness of this rotational system because servers use the cached information about the site, rather than issuing a new query and possibly receiving the address for another system. As a result, it is generally recommended that you use a relatively short time-to-live value for the duplicated resource records.

Reverse Name Resolution

The Domain Name System is designed to facilitate the resolution of DNS names into IP addresses, but there are also instances in which IP addresses have to be resolved into DNS names. These instances are relatively rare. In log files, for example, some systems convert IP addresses to DNS names to make the data more readily accessible to human readers. Certain systems also use reverse name resolution in the course of authentication procedures.

The structure of the DNS name space and the method by which it's distributed among various servers is based on the domain name hierarchy. When the entire database is located on one system, such as in the case of a host table, searching for a particular address to find out its associated name is no different from searching for a name to find an address. However, locating a particular address in the DNS name space would seem to require a search of all of the Internet's DNS servers, which is obviously impractical.

Part IV

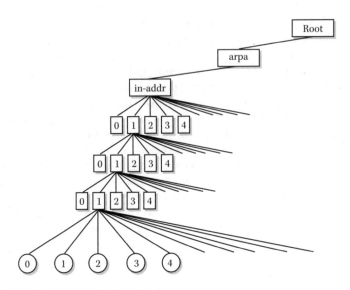

Figure 15-5   The in-addr.arpa domain hierarchy

To make reverse name resolution possible without performing a massive search across the entire Internet, the DNS tree includes a special branch that uses the dotted decimal values of IP addresses as domain names. This branch stems from a domain called in-addr.arpa, which is located just beneath the root of the DNS tree, as shown in Figure 15-5. Just beneath the in-addr domain, there are 256 subdomains named using the numbers 0 to 255 to represent the possible values of an IP address's first byte. Each of these subdomains contains another 256 subdomains representing the possible values of the second byte. The next level has another 256 domains, each of which can have up to 256 numbered hosts, which represent the third and fourth bytes of the address.

Using the in-addr.arpa domain structure, each of the hosts represented by a standard name on a DNS server also has an equivalent DNS name constructed using its IP address. Therefore, if a system with the IP address 192.168.214.23 is listed in the DNS server for the zacker.com domain with the hostname www, there is also a resource record for that system with the DNS name 23.214.168.192.in-addr.arpa, meaning that there is a host with the name 23 in a domain called 214.168.192.in-addr.arpa, as shown in Figure 15-6. This domain structure makes it possible for a system to search for the IP address of a host in a domain (or zone) without having to consult other servers in the DNS tree. In most cases, you can configure a DNS server to automatically create an equivalent resource record in the in-addr.arpa domain for every host you add to the standard domain name space.

The byte values of IP addresses are reversed in the in-addr.arpa domain because in a DNS name, the least significant word comes first, whereas in IP addresses, the least significant byte comes last. In other words, a DNS name is structured with the root of the DNS tree on the right side and the hostname on the left. In an IP address, the host identifier is on the right, and the network identifier is on the left. It would be possible to create a domain structure using the IP address bytes in their regular order, but this would complicate the administration process by making it harder to delegate maintenance tasks based on network addresses.

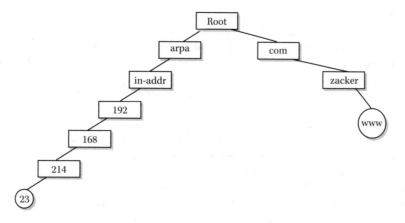

Figure 15-6   Each host in the DNS database has two resource records.

DNS Name Registration

As you have already learned, name resolution is the process by which IP address information for a hostname is extracted from the DNS database. The process by which hostnames and their addresses are added to the database is called *name registration*. Name registration refers to the process of creating new resource records on a DNS server, thus making them accessible to all of the other DNS servers on the network.

The name registration process on a traditional DNS server is decidedly low-tech. There is no mechanism by which the server can detect the systems on the network and enter their hostnames and IP addresses into resource records. In fact, a computer may not even be aware of its hostname because it receives all of its communications using IP addresses and never has to answer to its name.

To register a host in the DNS name space, an administrator has to manually create a resource record on the server. The method for creating resource records varies depending on the DNS server implementation. Unix-based servers require you to edit a text file, while Microsoft DNS Server uses a graphical interface.

Manual Name Registration

The manual name registration process is an adaptation of the host table for use on a DNS server. It is easy to see how, in the early days, administrators were able to implement DNS servers on their network by using their host tables with slight modifications. Today, however, the manual name registration process can be problematic on some networks.

If you have a large number of hosts, manually creating resource records for all of them can be a tedious affair, even with a graphical interface. However, depending on the nature of the network, it may not be necessary to register every system in the DNS. If, for example, you are running a Windows NT network using unregistered IP addresses, you may not need your own DNS server at all, except possibly to process client name resolution requests. Windows NT networks have their own NetBIOS naming system and name resolution mechanisms, and you generally don't need to refer to them using DNS names.

The exceptions to this would be systems with registered IP addresses that you use as web servers or other types of Internet servers. These must be visible to Internet users and, therefore, must have a hostname in a registered DNS domain. In most cases, the number of systems like this on a network is small, so manually creating the resource records is not much of a problem. If you have Unix systems on your network, however, you are more likely to use DNS to identify them using names, and in this case, you must create resource records for them.

Dynamic Updates

As networks grow larger and more complex, the biggest problem arising from manual name registration stems from the increasing use of DHCP servers to dynamically assign IP addresses to network workstations. The manual configuration of TCP/IP clients is another long-standing network administration chore that is gradually being phased out in favor of an automated solution. Assigning IP addresses dynamically means that workstations can have different addresses from one day to the next, and the original DNS standard has no way of keeping up with the changes.

On networks where only a few servers have to be visible to the Internet, it wasn't too great an inconvenience to configure them manually with static IP addresses and use DHCP for the unregistered systems. This situation changed with the advent of Windows 2000 and Active Directory. Windows NT networks used WINS to resolve NetBIOS names into IP addresses, but name registration was automatic with WINS. WINS automatically updated its database record for a workstation assigned a new IP address by a DHCP server so that no administrator intervention was required. Active Directory, however, relied heavily on DNS instead of WINS to resolve the names of systems on the network and to keep track of the domain controllers available for use by client workstations.

To make the use of DNS practical, members of the IETF developed a new specification, published as RFC 2136, "Dynamic Updates in the Domain Name System." This document defined a new DNS message type, called an *Update,* with which systems such as domain controllers and DHCP servers could generate and transmit to a DNS server. These Update messages modify or delete existing resource records or create new ones, based on prerequisites specified by the administrator.

Zone Transfers

Most networks use at least two DNS servers to provide fault tolerance and to give clients access to a nearby server. Because the resource records (in most cases) have to be created and updated manually by administrators, the DNS standards define a mechanism that replicates the DNS data among the servers, thus enabling administrators to make the changes only once.

The standards define two DNS server roles: the primary master and the secondary master, or slave. The *primary master* server loads its resource records and other information from the database files on the local drive. The *slave* (or *secondary master*) server receives its data from another server in a process called a *zone transfer,* which the slave performs each time it starts and periodically thereafter. The server from which the slave receives its data is called its *master server,* but it need not be the primary master. A slave can receive data from the primary master or another slave.

Zone transfers are performed for individual zones, and because a single server can be the authority for multiple zones, more than one transfer may be needed to update all of a slave server's data. In addition, the primary master and slave roles are zone specific. A server can be the primary master for one zone and the slave for another, although this practice generally should not be necessary and is likely to generate some confusion.

Although slave servers receive periodic zone transfers from their primaries, they are also able to load database files from their local drives. When a slave server receives a zone transfer, it updates the local database files. Each time the slave server starts, it loads the most current resource records it has from the database files and then checks this data with the primary master to see whether an update is needed. This prevents zone transfers from being performed needlessly.

DNS Messaging

DNS name resolution transactions use User Datagram Protocol (UDP) datagrams on port 53 for servers and on an ephemeral port number for clients. Communication between two servers uses port 53 on both machines. In cases in which the data to be transmitted does not fit in a single UDP datagram, in the case of zone transfers, the two systems establish a standard TCP connection, also using port 53 on both machines, and transmit the data using as many packets as needed.

The Domain Name System uses a single message format for all of its communications that consists of the following five sections:

- **Header**   Contains information about the nature of the message
- **Question**   Contains the information requested from the destination server
- **Answer**   Contains RRs supplying the information requested in the Question section
- **Authority**   Contains RRs pointing to an authority for the information requested in the Question section
- **Additional**   Contains RRs with additional information in response to the Question section

Every DNS message has a Header section, and the other four sections are included only if they contain data. For example, a query message contains the DNS name to be resolved in the Question section, but the Answer, Authority, and Additional sections aren't needed. When the server receiving the query constructs its reply, it makes some changes to the Header section, leaves the Question section intact, and adds entries to one or more of the remaining three sections. Each section can have multiple entries so that a server can send more than one resource record in a single message.

The DNS Header Section

The Header section of the DNS message contains codes and flags that specify the function of the message and the type of service requested from or supplied by a server. Figure 15-7 shows the format of the Header section.

The functions of the Header fields are as follows:

- **ID, 2 bytes**   Contains an identifier value used to associate queries with replies.
- **Flags, 2 bytes**   Contains flag bits used to identify the functions and properties of the message, as follows:

  - **QR, 1 bit**   Specifies whether the message is a query (value 0) or a response (value 1).

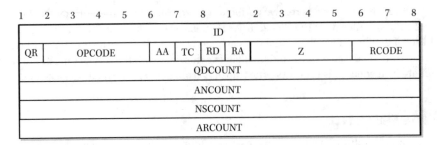

Figure 15-7   The DNS Header section format

- **OPCODE, 4 bits**   Specifies the type of query that generated the message. Response messages retain the same value for this field as the query to which they are responding. Possible values are as follows:

  - **0**   Standard query (QUERY)

  - **1**   Inverse query (IQUERY)

  - **2**   Server status request (STATUS)

  - **3–15**   Unused

- **AA (Authoritative Answer), 1 bit**   Indicates that a response message has been generated by a server that is the authority for the domain or zone in which the requested name is located.

- **TC (Truncation), 1 bit**   Indicates that the message has been truncated because the amount of data exceeds the maximum size for the current transport mechanism. In most DNS implementations, this bit functions as a signal that the message should be transmitted using a TCP connection rather than a UDP datagram.

- **RD (Recursion Desired), 1 bit**   In a query, indicates that the destination server should treat the message as a recursive query. In a response, indicates that the message is the response to a recursive query. The absence of this flag indicates that the query is iterative.

- **RA (Recursion Available), 1 bit**   Specifies whether a server is configured to process recursive queries.

- **Z, 3 bits**   Unused.

- **RCODE (Response Code), 4 bits**   Specifies the nature of a response message, indicating when an error has occurred and what type of error, using the following values:

  - **0**   No error has occurred.

  - **1 – Format Error**   Indicates that the server was unable to understand the query.

  - **2 – Server Failure**   Indicates that the server was unable to process the query.

  - **3 – Name Error**   Used by authoritative servers only to indicate that a requested name or subdomain does not exist in the domain.

- **4 – Not Implemented**   Indicates that the server does not support the type of query received.
- **5 – Refused**   Indicates that server policies (such as security policies) have prevented the processing of the query.
- **6–15**   Unused.

- **QDCOUNT, 2 bytes**   Specifies the number of entries in the Question section.
- **ANCOUNT, 2 bytes**   Specifies the number of entries in the Answer section.
- **NSCOUNT, 2 bytes**   Specifies the number of name server RRs in the Authority section.
- **ARCOUNT, 2 bytes**   Specifies the number of entries in the Additional section.

The DNS Question Section

The Question section of a DNS message contains the number of entries specified in the header's QDCOUNT field. In most cases, there is only one entry. Each entry is formatted as shown in Figure 15-8.

The functions of the fields are as follows:

- **QNAME, variable**   Contains the DNS, domain, or zone name about which information is being requested
- **QTYPE, 2 bytes**   Contains a code that specifies the type of RR the query is requesting
- **QCLASS, 2 bytes**   Contains a code that specifies the class of the RR being requested

DNS Resource Record Sections

The three remaining sections of a DNS message, the Answer, Authority, and Additional sections, each contain resource records that use the format shown in Figure 15-9. The number of resource records in each section is specified in the header's ANCOUNT, NSCOUNT, and RCOUNT fields.

The functions of the fields are as follows:

- **NAME, variable**   Contains the DNS, domain, or zone name about which information is being supplied.
- **TYPE, 2 bytes**   Contains a code that specifies the type of RR the entry contains.
- **CLASS, 2 bytes**   Contains a code that specifies the class of the RR.

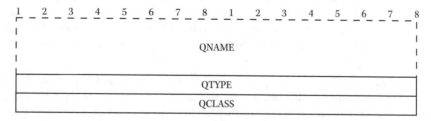

Figure 15-8   The DNS Question section format

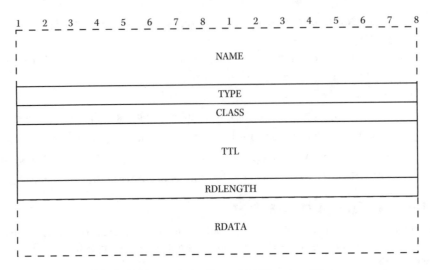

Figure 15-9   The format of the DNS Answer, Authority, and Additional sections

- **TTL, 4 bytes**   Specifies the amount of time (in seconds) that the RR should be cached in the server to which it is being supplied.

- **RDLENGTH, 2 bytes**   Specifies the length (in bytes) of the RDATA field.

- **RDATA, variable**   Contains RR data, the nature of which is dependent on its TYPE and CLASS. For an A-type record in the IN class, for example, this field contains the IP address associated with the DNS name supplied in the NAME field.

   Different types of resource records have different functions and, therefore, may contain different types of information in the RDATA field. Most resource records, such as the NS, A, PTR, and CNAME types, have only a single name or address in this field, while others have multiple subfields. The SOA resource record is the most complex in the Domain Name System. For this record, the RDATA field is broken up into seven subfields.

   The functions of the SOA resource record subfields are as follows:

- **MNAME, variable**   Specifies the DNS name of the primary master server that was the source for the information about the zone.

- **RNAME, variable**   Specifies the e-mail address of the administrator responsible for the zone data. This field has no actual purpose as far as the server is concerned; it is strictly informational. The value for this field takes the form of a DNS name. Standard practice calls for the period after the first word to be converted to the @ symbol in order to use the value as an e-mail address.

- **SERIAL, 4 bytes**   Contains a serial number that is used to track modifications to the zone data on the primary master server. The value of this field is incremented (either manually or automatically) on the primary master server each time the zone data is modified, and the slave compares its value to the one supplied by the primary master to determine whether a zone transfer is necessary.

- **REFRESH, 4 bytes** Specifies the time interval (in seconds) at which the slave should transmit an SOA query to the primary master to determine whether a zone transfer is needed.

- **RETRY, 4 bytes** Specifies the time interval (in seconds) at which the slave should make repeat attempts to connect to the primary master after its initial attempt fails.

- **EXPIRE, 4 bytes** Specifies the time interval (in seconds) after which the slave server's data should expire, in the event that it cannot contact the primary master server. Once the data has expired, the slave server stops responding to queries.

- **MINIMUM, 4 bytes** Specifies the time-to-live interval (in seconds) that the server should supply for all of the resource records in its responses to queries.

DNS Message Notation

The latter four sections of the DNS message are largely consistent in how they notate the information in their fields. DNS, domain, and zone names are all expressed in the same way, and the sections all use the same values for the resource record type and class codes. The only exceptions are a few additional codes that are used only in the Question section, called QTYPES and QCLASSES, respectively. The following sections describe how these values are expressed in the DNS message.

DNS Name Notation

Depending on the function of the message, any or all of the four sections can contain the fully qualified name of a host system, the name of a domain, or the name of a zone on a server. These names are expressed as a series of units, called *labels,* each of which represents a single word in the name. The periods between the words are not included, so to delineate the words, each label begins with a single byte that specifies the length of the word (in bytes), after which the specified number of bytes follows. This is repeated for each word in the name. After the final word of a fully qualified name, a byte with the value of 0 is included to represent the null value of the root domain.

Resource Record Types

All of the data distributed by the Domain Name System is stored in resource records. Query messages request certain resource records from servers, and the servers reply with those resource records. The QTYPE field in a Question section entry specifies the type of resource record being requested from the server, and the TYPE fields in the Answer, Authority, and Additional section entries specify the type of resource record supplied by the server in each entry. Table 15-1 contains the resource record types and the codes used to represent them in these fields. All of the values in this table are valid for both the QTYPE and TYPE fields. Table 15-2 contains four additional values that represent sets of resource records that are valid for the QTYPE field in Question section entries only.

Type	Type Code	Function
A	1	Host address
NS	2	Authoritative name server
MD	3	Mail destination (obsolete)
MF	4	Mail forwarder (obsolete)
CNAME	5	Canonical name for an alias
SOA	6	Start of a zone of authority
MB	7	Mailbox domain name (experimental)
MG	8	Mail group member (experimental)
MR	9	Mail rename domain name (experimental)
NULL	10	Null RR (experimental)
WKS	11	Well-known service description
PTR	12	Domain name pointer
HINFO	13	Host information
MINFO	14	Mailbox or mail list information
MX	15	Mail exchange
TXT	16	Text strings
SVR	33	Network server

Table 15-1   DNS Resource Record Types and Values for Use in the TYPE or QTYPE Field

Class Types

The QCLASS field in the Question section and the CLASS field in the Answer, Authority, and Additional sections specify the type of network for which information is being requested or supplied. Although they performed a valid function at one time, these fields are now essentially meaningless because virtually all DNS messages use the IN class. CSNET and CHAOS class networks are obsolete, and the Hesiod class is used for only a few experimental networks at MIT. For academic purposes only, the values for the CLASS and QCLASS values are shown in Tables 15-3 and 15-4.

QTYPE	QTYPE Code	Function
AXFR	252	Request for transfer of an entire zone
MAILB	253	Request for mailbox-related records (MB, MG, or MR)
MAILA	254	Request for mail agent RRs (obsolete)
*	255	Request for all records

Table 15-2   Additional Values Representing Sets of Resource Records for Use in the QTYPE Field Only

Class	Class Code	Function
IN	1	Internet
CS	2	CSNET
CH	3	CHAOS
HS	4	Hesiod

Table 15-3   Values for the Resource Record CLASS and QCLASS Fields

QCLASS	QCLASS Code	Function
*	255	Any Class

Table 15-4   Additional Value for the Resource Record QCLASS Field Only

Name Resolution Messages

The process of resolving a DNS name into an IP address begins with the generation of a query by the resolver on the client system. Figure 15-10 shows a query message, captured in a network monitor program, generated by a web browser trying to connect to the URL www.zacker.com/. The value of the message's OPCODE flag is 0, indicating that this is a regular query, and the RD flag has a value of 1, indicating that this is a recursive query. As a result, the DNS server receiving the query (which is called CZ1) will be responsible for resolving the DNS name and returning the

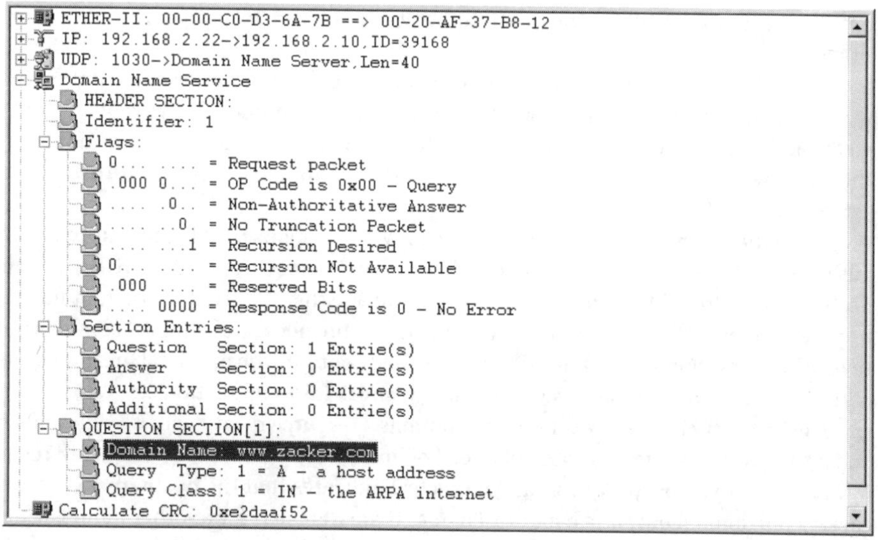

```
ETHER-II: 00-00-C0-D3-6A-7B ==> 00-20-AF-37-B8-12
IP: 192.168.2.22->192.168.2.10,ID=39168
UDP: 1030->Domain Name Server,Len=40
Domain Name Service
    HEADER SECTION:
    Identifier: 1
    Flags:
        0... .... = Request packet
        .000 0... = OP Code is 0x00 - Query
        .... .0.. = Non-Authoritative Answer
        .... ..0. = No Truncation Packet
        .... ...1 = Recursion Desired
        0... .... = Recursion Not Available
        .000 .... = Reserved Bits
        .... 0000 = Response Code is 0 - No Error
    Section Entries:
        Question   Section: 1 Entrie(s)
        Answer     Section: 0 Entrie(s)
        Authority  Section: 0 Entrie(s)
        Additional Section: 0 Entrie(s)
    QUESTION SECTION[1]:
        Domain Name: www.zacker.com
        Query  Type: 1 = A - a host address
        Query Class: 1 = IN - the ARPA internet
Calculate CRC: 0xe2daaf52
```

Figure 15-10   The name resolution query message generated by the resolver

results to the client. The QDCOUNT field indicates that there is one entry in the Question section and no entries in the three resource record sections, which is standard for a query message. The Question section specifies the DNS name to be resolved (www.zacker.com) and the type (1 = A) and class (1 = IN) of the resource record being requested.

CZ1 is not the authoritative server for the zacker.com domain, nor does it have the requested information in its cache, so it must generate its own queries. CZ1 first generates a query message and transmits it to one of the root name servers (198.41.0.4) configured into the server software. The entry in the Question section is identical to that of the client's query message. The only differences in this query are that the server has included a different value in the ID field (4114) and has changed the value of the RD flag to 0, indicating that this is an iterative query.

The response that CZ1 receives from the root name server bypasses one step of the process because this root name server is also the authoritative server for the com top-level domain. As a result, the response contains the resource record that identifies the authoritative server for the zacker.com domain. If the requested DNS name had been in a top-level domain for which the root name server was not authoritative, such as one of the country-code domains, the response would contain a resource record identifying the proper authoritative servers.

The response message from the root domain server has a QR bit that has a value of 1, indicating that this is a response message, and the same ID value as the request, enabling CZ1 to associate the two messages. The QDCOUNT field again has a value of 1 because the response retains the Question section, unmodified, from the query message. The NSCOUNT and ARCOUNT fields indicate that there are two entries each in the Authority and Additional sections. The first entry in the Authority section contains the NS resource record for one of the authoritative servers for zacker.com known to the root name/top-level domain server, and the second entry contains the NS record for the other. The type and class values are the same as those requested in the query message; the time-to-live value assigned to both records is 172,800 seconds (48 hours). The RDATA field in the first entry is 16 bytes long and contains the DNS name of the first authoritative server (ns1.secure.net). The RDATA field in the second entry is only 6 bytes long and contains only the hostname (ns2) for the other authoritative server since it's in the same domain as the first one.

These Authority section entries identify the servers that CZ1 needs to contact to resolve the www.zacker.com domain name, but it does so using DNS names. To prevent CZ1 from having to go through this whole process again to resolve ns1.secure.net and ns2.secure.net into IP addresses, there are two entries in the Additional section that contain the A resource records for these two servers, which include their IP addresses.

Using the information contained in the previous response, CZ1 transmits a query to the first authoritative server for the zacker.com domain (ns1.secure.net – 192.41.1.10). Except for the destination address, this query is identical to the one that CZ1 sent to the root name server. The response message that CZ1 receives from the ns1.secure.net server (finally) contains the information that the client originally requested. This message contains the original Question section entry and two entries each in the Answer, Authority, and Additional sections.

The first entry in the Answer section contains a resource record with a TYPE value of 5 (CNAME) and a time-to-live value of 86,400 seconds (24 hours). The inclusion of a CNAME resource record in a response to a query requesting an A record indicates that the hostname www exists in the zacker.com domain only as a canonical name (that is, an alias for another name), which is specified in the RDATA field as zacker.com. The second entry in the Answer section contains the A resource record for the name zacker.com, which specifies the IP address 192.41.15.74 in the RDATA field.

This is the IP address that the client system must use to reach the www.zacker.com web server. The entries in the Authority and Additional sections specify the names and addresses of the authoritative server for zacker.com and are identical to the equivalent entries in the response message from the root name server.

Root Name Server Discovery

Each time the DNS server starts, it loads the information stored in its database files. One of these files contains root name server hints. Actually, this file contains the names and addresses of all the root name servers, but the DNS server, instead of relying on this data, uses it to send a query to the first of the root name servers, requesting that it identify the authoritative servers for the root domain. This is to ensure that the server is using the most current information. The query is just like that for a name resolution request, except that there is no value in the NAME field.

The reply returned by the root name server contains 13 entries in both the Answer and Additional sections, corresponding to the 13 root name servers currently in operation (see Figure 15-11).

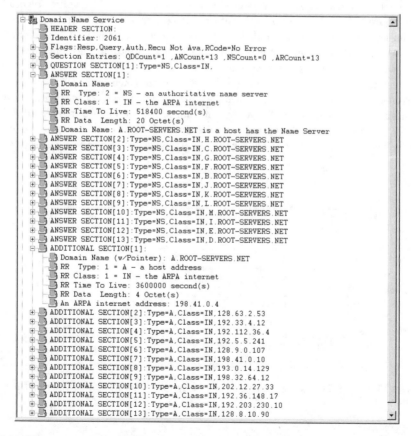

Figure 15-11   The root name server's response message, containing the RRs for all 13 root name servers

Each entry in the Answer section contains the NS resource record for one of the root name servers, which specifies its DNS name, and the corresponding entry in the Additional section contains the A record for that server, which specifies its IP address. All of these servers are located in a domain called root-server.net and have incremental hostnames from *a* to *m*. Because the information about these servers does not change often, if at all, their resource records can have a long time-to-live value: 518,400 seconds (144 hours or 6 days) for the NS records and 3,600,000 (1,000 hours or 41.67 days) for the A records.

Zone Transfer Messages

A zone transfer is initiated by a DNS server that functions as a slave for one or more zones whenever the server software is started. The process begins with an iterative query for an SOA resource record that the slave sends to the primary master to ensure that it is the best source for information about the zone (see Figure 15-12). The single Question section entry contains the name of the zone in the QNAME field and a value of 6 for the QTYPE field, indicating that the server is requesting the SOA resource record.

The primary master then replies to the slave with a response that includes the original Question section and a single Answer section containing the SOA resource record for the zone (see Figure 15-13). The slave uses the information in the response to verify the primary master's authority and to determine whether a zone transfer is needed. If the value of the SOA record's SERIAL field, as furnished by the primary master, is greater than the equivalent field on the slave server, then a zone transfer is required.

A zone transfer request is a standard DNS query message with a QTYPE value of 252, which corresponds to the AXFR type. AXFR is the abbreviation for a resource record set that consists of all of the records in the zone. However, in most cases, all of the resource records in the zone will not fit into a single UDP datagram. UDP is a connectionless, unreliable protocol in which there can be only one response message for each query because the response message functions as the

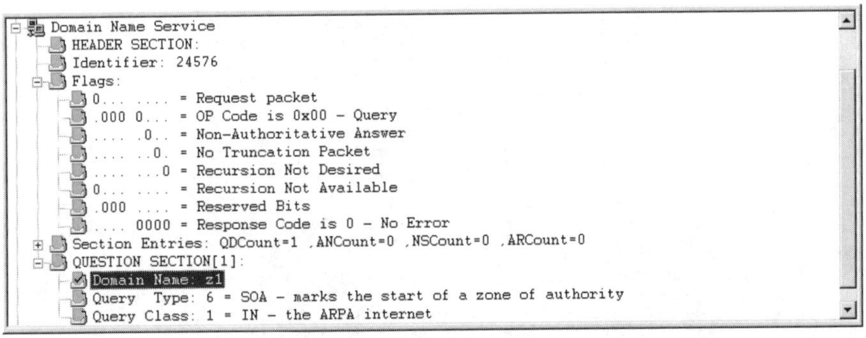

```
Domain Name Service
    HEADER SECTION:
    Identifier: 24576
    Flags:
        0... .... = Request packet
        .000 0... = OP Code is 0x00 - Query
        .... .0.. = Non-Authoritative Answer
        .... ..0. = No Truncation Packet
        .... ...0 = Recursion Not Desired
        0... .... = Recursion Not Available
        .000 .... = Reserved Bits
        .... 0000 = Response Code is 0 - No Error
    Section Entries: QDCount=1 ,ANCount=0 ,NSCount=0 ,ARCount=0
    QUESTION SECTION[1]:
        Domain Name: z1
        Query Type: 6 = SOA - marks the start of a zone of authority
        Query Class: 1 = IN - the ARPA internet
```

Figure 15-12   The SOA query message generated by a slave server to determine whether a zone transfer is warranted

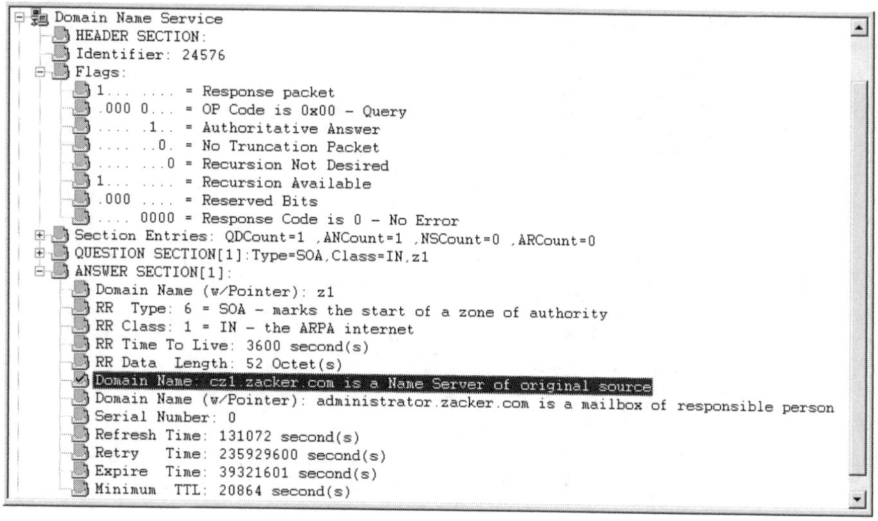

```
Domain Name Service
  HEADER SECTION:
    Identifier: 24576
  Flags:
    1... .... = Response packet
    .000 0... = OP Code is 0x00 - Query
    .... .1.. = Authoritative Answer
    .... ..0. = No Truncation Packet
    .... ...0 = Recursion Not Desired
    1... .... = Recursion Available
    .000 .... = Reserved Bits
    .... 0000 = Response Code is 0 - No Error
  Section Entries: QDCount=1 ,ANCount=1 ,NSCount=0 ,ARCount=0
  QUESTION SECTION[1]:Type=SOA,Class=IN,z1
  ANSWER SECTION[1]:
    Domain Name (w/Pointer): z1
    RR  Type: 6 = SOA - marks the start of a zone of authority
    RR Class: 1 = IN - the ARPA internet
    RR Time To Live: 3600 second(s)
    RR Data  Length: 52 Octet(s)
    Domain Name: cz1.zacker.com is a Name Server of original source
    Domain Name (w/Pointer): administrator.zacker.com is a mailbox of responsible person
    Serial Number: 0
    Refresh Time: 131072 second(s)
    Retry   Time: 235929600 second(s)
    Expire  Time: 39321601 second(s)
    Minimum  TTL: 20864 second(s)
```

Figure 15-13   The response message from the primary master server containing the SOA resource record

acknowledgment of the query. Because the primary master will almost certainly have to use multiple packets in order to send all of the resource records in the zone to the slave, a different protocol is needed. Therefore, before it transmits the zone transfer request message, the slave server initiates a TCP connection with the primary master using the standard three-way handshake. Once the connection is established, the slave transmits the AXFR query in a TCP packet using port 53 (see Figure 15-14).

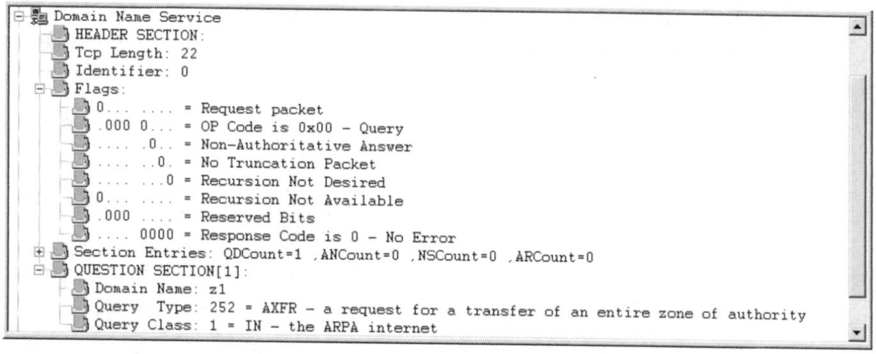

```
Domain Name Service
  HEADER SECTION:
    Tcp Length: 22
    Identifier: 0
  Flags:
    0... .... = Request packet
    .000 0... = OP Code is 0x00 - Query
    .... .0.. = Non-Authoritative Answer
    .... ..0. = No Truncation Packet
    .... ...0 = Recursion Not Desired
    0... .... = Recursion Not Available
    .000 .... = Reserved Bits
    .... 0000 = Response Code is 0 - No Error
  Section Entries: QDCount=1 ,ANCount=0 ,NSCount=0 ,ARCount=0
  QUESTION SECTION[1]:
    Domain Name: z1
    Query  Type: 252 = AXFR - a request for a transfer of an entire zone of authority
    Query Class: 1 = IN - the ARPA internet
```

Figure 15-14   The AXFR query requesting a zone transfer, transmitted to the primary master server using a TCP connection

Part IV

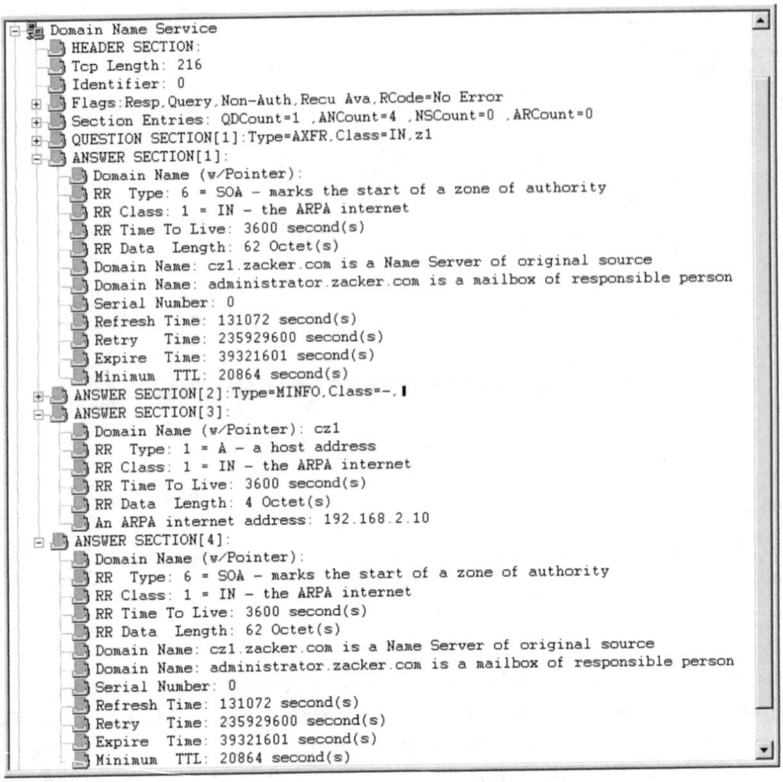

```
⊟ 🖳 Domain Name Service
  ├ 📄 HEADER SECTION:
  │  ├ 📄 Tcp Length: 216
  │  ├ 📄 Identifier: 0
  │  ├⊞📄 Flags:Resp,Query,Non-Auth,Recu Ava,RCode=No Error
  │  ├⊞📄 Section Entries: QDCount=1 ,ANCount=4 ,NSCount=0 ,ARCount=0
  │  ├⊞📄 QUESTION SECTION[1]:Type=AXFR,Class=IN,z1
  │  ⊟📄 ANSWER SECTION[1]:
  │     ├ 📄 Domain Name (w/Pointer):
  │     ├ 📄 RR Type: 6 = SOA - marks the start of a zone of authority
  │     ├ 📄 RR Class: 1 = IN - the ARPA internet
  │     ├ 📄 RR Time To Live: 3600 second(s)
  │     ├ 📄 RR Data Length: 62 Octet(s)
  │     ├ 📄 Domain Name: cz1.zacker.com is a Name Server of original source
  │     ├ 📄 Domain Name: administrator.zacker.com is a mailbox of responsible person
  │     ├ 📄 Serial Number: 0
  │     ├ 📄 Refresh Time: 131072 second(s)
  │     ├ 📄 Retry   Time: 235929600 second(s)
  │     ├ 📄 Expire  Time: 39321601 second(s)
  │     ├ 📄 Minimum TTL: 20864 second(s)
  │  ├⊞📄 ANSWER SECTION[2]:Type=MINFO,Class=-,▮
  │  ⊟📄 ANSWER SECTION[3]:
  │     ├ 📄 Domain Name (w/Pointer): cz1
  │     ├ 📄 RR Type: 1 = A - a host address
  │     ├ 📄 RR Class: 1 = IN - the ARPA internet
  │     ├ 📄 RR Time To Live: 3600 second(s)
  │     ├ 📄 RR Data Length: 4 Octet(s)
  │     ├ 📄 An ARPA internet address: 192.168.2.10
  │  ⊟📄 ANSWER SECTION[4]:
  │     ├ 📄 Domain Name (w/Pointer):
  │     ├ 📄 RR Type: 6 = SOA - marks the start of a zone of authority
  │     ├ 📄 RR Class: 1 = IN - the ARPA internet
  │     ├ 📄 RR Time To Live: 3600 second(s)
  │     ├ 📄 RR Data Length: 62 Octet(s)
  │     ├ 📄 Domain Name: cz1.zacker.com is a Name Server of original source
  │     ├ 📄 Domain Name: administrator.zacker.com is a mailbox of responsible person
  │     ├ 📄 Serial Number: 0
  │     ├ 📄 Refresh Time: 131072 second(s)
  │     ├ 📄 Retry   Time: 235929600 second(s)
  │     ├ 📄 Expire  Time: 39321601 second(s)
  │     ├ 📄 Minimum TTL: 20864 second(s)
```

Figure 15-15   One packet from a zone transfer transmitted by the primary master server

In response to the query, the primary master server transmits all of the resource records in the requested zone as entries in the Answer section, as shown in Figure 15-15. Once all of the data has been transmitted, the two systems terminate the TCP connection in the usual manner, and the zone transfer is completed.

CHAPTER

16 Internet Services

At one time, the term *server* in computer networking was nearly always used in the phrase *file server,* referring to a PC running a network operating system (NOS) that enables users to access shared files and printers. However, the rapid growth of the Internet has changed the common meaning of the term. To most Internet users, servers are the invisible systems that host web sites or that enable them to send and receive e-mail. For LAN users, servers still fill the traditional file and printer sharing roles, but also provide application-related functions, such as access to databases. Thus, people are gradually learning that a *server* is both a software as well as a hardware entity and that a single computer can actually function in multiple server roles simultaneously.

Internet servers are software products that provide traditional Internet services to clients, whether or not they are actually connected through the Internet. Web, FTP, and e-mail are all services that can be as useful on a LAN, a smart phone, or a tablet as on the Internet. This chapter examines the technology behind these services and the procedures for implementing them on your network.

Web Servers

The Web is a ubiquitous tool for business, education, and recreation. Along with the proliferation of mobile devices, a "web presence" is nearly required for most businesses. The basic building blocks of the Web are as follows:

- **Web servers**   Computers running a software program that processes resource requests from clients

- **Browsers**   Client software that generates resource requests and sends them to web servers

- **Hypertext Transfer Protocol (HTTP)**   The Transmission Control Protocol/Internet Protocol (TCP/IP) application layer protocol that servers and browsers use to communicate

- **Hypertext Markup Language (HTML)**   The markup language used to create web pages

Selecting a Web Server

A web server is actually a rather simple device. When you see complex pages full of fancy text and graphics on your monitor, you're actually seeing something that is more the product of the page designer and the browser technology than of the web server. In its simplest form, a web server is a software program that processes requests for specific files from browsers and delivers those files to the browser. The server does not read the contents of the files, nor does it participate in the rendering process that controls how a web page is displayed in the browser. The differences between web server products are in the additional features they provide and their ability to handle large numbers of requests.

Web Server Functions

A web server is a program that runs in the background on a computer and listens on a particular TCP port for incoming requests. Simply speaking, the process is as follows:

1. A computer *client* asks for a file.

2. The *server* finds the file.

3. The servers sends a response to the client, usually a header as well as the data.

4. The server closes the connection.

The standard TCP port for an HTTP server is 80, although most servers enable you to specify a different port number for a site and may use a second port number for the server's administrative interface. To access a web server using a different port, you must specify that port number as part of the URL.

Uniform Resource Locators   The format of the uniform resource locator (URL) that you type into a browser's Address field to access a particular web site is defined in RFC 1738, published by the Internet Engineering Task Force (IETF). A URL consists of four elements that identify the resource that you want to access:

- **Protocol** Specifies the application layer protocol that the browser will use to connect to the server. Some of the values defined in the URL standard are as follows (others have been defined by additional standards published since RFC 3986, which updated RFC 1738):
  - **http** Hypertext Transfer Protocol
  - **ftp** File Transfer Protocol
  - **mailto** Mail address
  - **news** Usenet news
  - **telnet** Reference to interactive sessions
  - **wais** Wide area information servers
  - **file** Host-specific filenames
- **Server name** Specifies the DNS name or IP address of the server.
- **Port number** Specifies the port number that the server is monitoring for incoming traffic.
- **Directory and file** Identifies the location of the file that the server should send to the browser.

The format of a URL is as follows:

protocol://name:port/directory/file.html

Most of the time, users do not specify the protocol, port, directory, and file in their URLs, and the browser uses its default values. When you enter just a DNS name, such as www.zacker .com, the browser assumes the use of the HTTP protocol, port 80, and the web server's home directory. Fully expanded, this URL would appear something like the following:

```
http://www.zacker.com:80/index.html
```

The only element that could vary among different servers is the filename of the default web page, here shown as index.html. The default filename is configured on each server and specifies the file that the server will send to a client when no filename is specified in the URL.

If you configure a web server to use a port other than 80 to host a site, users must specify the port number as part of the URL. The main exception to this is when the administrator wants to create a site that is hidden from the average user. Some web server products, for example, are configurable using a web browser, and the server creates a separate administrative site containing the configuration controls for the program. During the software installation, the program prompts the administrator for a port number that it should use for the administrative site. Thus, specifying the name of the server on a browser opens the default site on port 80, but specifying the server name with the selected port accesses the administrative site.

The use of a nonstandard port is not really a security measure because there are programs available that can identify the ports that a web server is using. The administrative site for a server usually has security in the form of user authentication as well; the port number is just a means of keeping the site hidden from curious users.

CGI   Much of the traffic generated by the Web travels from the web server to the browser. The upstream traffic from browser to server consists mainly of HTTP requests for specific files. However, there are mechanisms by which browsers can send other types of information to servers. The server can then feed the information to an application for processing. The Common Gateway Interface (CGI) is a widely supported mechanism of this type. In most cases, the user supplies information in a form built into a web page using standard HTML tags and then submits the form to a server. The server, upon receiving the data from the browser, executes a CGI script that defines how the information should be used. The server might feed the information as a query to a database server, use it to perform an online financial transaction, or use it for any other purpose.

Logging   Virtually all web servers have the capability to maintain logs that track all client access to the site and any errors that have occurred. The logs typically take the form of a text file, with each server access request or error appearing on a separate line. Each line contains multiple fields, separated by spaces or commas. The information logged by the server identifies who accessed the site and when, as well as the exact documents sent to the client by the server.

Most web servers enable the administrator to choose among several formats for the logs they keep. Some servers use proprietary log formats, which generally are not supported by the statistics programs, while other servers may also be able to log server information to an external database using an interface such as Open Database Connectivity (ODBC). Most servers, however, support the Common Log File format defined by the National Center for Supercomputing

Applications (NCSA). This format consists of nothing but one-line entries with fields separated by spaces. The format for each Common Log File entry and the functions of each field are as follows:

```
remotehost logname username date request status bytes
```

- **remotehost**   Specifies the IP address of the remote client system. Some servers also include a DNS reverse lookup feature that resolves the address into a DNS name for logging purposes.

- **logname**   Specifies the remote log name of the user at the client system. Most of today's browsers do not supply this information, so the field in the log is filled with a placeholder, such as a dash.

- **username**   Specifies the username with which the client was authenticated to the server.

- **date**   Specifies the date and time that the request was received by the server. Most servers use the local date and time by default, but may include a Greenwich mean time differential, such as –0500 for U.S. Eastern Standard Time.

- **request**   Specifies the text of the request received by the server.

- **status**   Contains one of the status codes defined in the HTTP standard that specifies whether the request was processed successfully and, if not, why.

- **bytes**   Specifies the size (in bytes) of the file transmitted to the client by the server in response to the request.

There is also a log file format created by the World Wide Web Consortium (W3C), called the Extended Log File format, that addresses some of the inherent problems of the Common Log File format, such as difficulties in interpreting logged data because of spaces within fields. The Extended Log File provides an extendable format with which administrators can specify the information to be logged or information that shouldn't be logged. The format for the Extended Log File consists of *fields*, as well as *entries*. Fields appear on separate lines, beginning with the # symbol, and specify information about the data contained in the log. The valid field entries are as follows:

- **#Version: *integer*.integer**   Specifies the version of the log file format. This field is required in every log file.

- **#Fields: [*specifiers*]**   Identifies the type of data carried in each field of a log entry, using abbreviations specified in the Extended Log File format specification. This field is required in every log file.

- **#Software *string***   Identifies the server software that created the log.

- **#Start-Date: *date* time**   Specifies the date and time that logging started.

- **#End-Date: *date* time**   Specifies the date and time that logging ceased.

- **#Date: *date* time**   Specifies the date and time at which a particular entry was added to the log file.

- **#Remark: *text***   Contains comment information that should be ignored by all processes.

These fields enable administrators to specify the information to be recorded in the log while making it possible for statistics programs to correctly parse the data in the log entries.

Remote Administration   All web servers need some sort of administrative interface that you can use to configure their operational parameters. Even a no-frills server lets you define a home directory that should function as the root of the site and other basic features. Some server products include a program that you can run on the computer that provides this interface, but many products have taken the opportunity to include an administrative web site with the product. With a site like this, you can configure the server from any computer using a standard web browser. This is a convenient tool for the network administrator, especially when the web server system is located in a server closet or other remote location or when one person is responsible for maintaining several servers.

The biggest problem with this form of remote administration is security, but there are mechanisms that can prevent unauthorized users from modifying the server configuration. The most basic of these mechanisms, as mentioned earlier, is the use of a nonstandard port number for the administrative site. Servers that use nonstandard ports typically require that you specify the port number during the server installation.

A second method is to include a means by which you can specify the IP addresses of the only systems that are to be permitted access to the administrative interface. IIS includes this method, and by default, the only system that can access the web-based interface is the one on which the server is installed. However, you can open up the server to remote administration and specify the addresses of other workstations to be granted access or specify the addresses of systems that are to be denied.

Virtual Directories   A web server utilizes a directory on the computer's local drive as the home directory for the web site it hosts. The server transmits the default filename in that directory to clients when they access the site using a URL that consists only of a DNS name or IP address. Subdirectories beneath that directory also appear as subdirectories on the web site. IIS, for example, uses the C:\InetPub\wwwroot directory as the default home directory for its web site. If that web server is registered in the DNS with the name www.zacker.com, the default page displayed by a browser accessing that site will be the default.htm file in the wwwroot directory. A file in the C:\InetPub\wwwroot\docs directory on the server will, therefore, appear on the site in www.zacker.com/docs.

Using this system, all the files and directories that are to appear on the web site must be located beneath the home directory. However, this is not a convenient arrangement for every site. On an intranet, for example, administrators may want to publish documents in existing directories using a web server without moving them to the home directory. To make this possible, some server products enable you to create virtual directories on the site. A *virtual directory* is a directory at another location—elsewhere on the drive, on another drive, or sometimes even on another computer's shared drive—that is published on a web site using an alias. The administrator specifies the location of the directory and the alias under which it will appear on the site. The alias functions as a subdirectory on the site that users can access in the normal manner and contains the files and subdirectories from the other drive.

NOTE See Chapters 25 and 26 for information about web and network security.

HTML

The Hypertext Markup Language is the *lingua franca* of the Web, but it actually has little to do with the functions of a web server. Web servers are programs that deliver requested files to clients. The fact that most of these files contain HTML code is immaterial because the server does not read them. The only way in which they affect the server's functions is when the client parses the HTML code and requests additional files from the server that are needed to display the web page in the browser, such as image files. Even in this case, however, the image file requests are just additional requests to the server.

HTTP

Communication between web servers and their browser clients is provided by an application layer protocol called the Hypertext Transfer Protocol. HTTP is a relatively simple protocol that takes advantage of the services provided by the TCP protocol at the transport layer to transfer files from servers to clients. When a client connects to a web server by typing a URL in a browser or clicking a hyperlink, the system generates an HTTP request message and transmits it to the server. This is an application layer process, but before it can happen, communication at the lower layers must be established.

Unless the user or the hyperlink specifies the IP address of the web server, the first step in establishing the connection between the two systems is to discover the address by sending a name resolution request to a DNS server. This address makes it possible for the IP protocol to address traffic to the server. Once the client system knows the address, it establishes a TCP connection with the server's port 80 using the standard three-way handshake process defined by that protocol.

Once the TCP connection is established, the browser and the server can exchange HTTP messages. HTTP consists of only two message types, requests and responses. Unlike the messages of most other protocols, HTTP messages take the form of ASCII text strings, not the typical headers with discrete coded fields. In fact, you can connect to a web server with a Telnet client and request a file by feeding an HTTP command directly to the server. The server will reply with the file you requested in its raw ASCII form.

Each HTTP message consists of the following elements:

- **Start line**   Contains a request command or a reply status indicator, plus a series of variables
- **Headers [optional]**   Contains a series of zero or more fields containing information about the message or the system sending it
- **Empty line**   Contains a blank line that identifies the end of the header section
- **Message body [optional]**   Contains the payload being transmitted to the other system

HTTP Requests

The start line for all HTTP requests is structured as follows:

```
RequestType RequestURI HTTPVersion
```

HTTP standards define several types of request messages, which include the following values for the *RequestType* variable:

- **GET**   Contains a request for information specified by the *RequestURI* variable. This type of request accounts for the vast majority of request messages.

- **HEAD**   Functionally identical to the GET request, except that the reply should contain only a start line and headers; no message body should be included.

- **POST**   Requests that the information included in the message body be accepted by the destination system as a new subordinate to the resource specified by the *RequestURI* variable.

- **OPTIONS**   Contains a request for information about the communication options available on the request/response chain specified by the *RequestURI* variable.

- **PUT**   Requests that the information included in the message body be stored at the destination system in the location specified by the *RequestURI* variable.

- **DELETE**   Requests that the destination system delete the resource identified by the *RequestURI* variable.

- **TRACE**   Requests that the destination system perform an application layer loopback of the incoming message and return it to the sender.

- **CONNECT**   Reserved for use with proxy servers that provide SSL tunneling.

The *RequestURI* variable contains a *uniform resource identifier* (URI), a text string that uniquely identifies a particular resource on the destination system. In most cases, this variable contains the name of a file on a web server that the client wants the server to send to it or the name of a directory from which the server should send the default file. The *HTTPVersion* variable identifies the version of the HTTP protocol that is supported by the system generating the request.

Thus, when a user types the name of a web site into a browser, the request message generated contains a start line that appears as follows:

```
GET / HTTP/1.1
```

The GET command requests that the server send a file. The use of the forward slash as the value for the *RequestURI* variable represents the root of the web site, so the server will respond by sending the default file located in the server's home directory.

HTTP Headers

Following the start line, any HTTP message can include a series of headers, which are text strings formatted in the following manner:

```
FieldName: FieldValue
```

Here, the *FieldName* variable identifies the type of information carried in the header, and the *FieldValue* variable contains the information. The various headers mostly provide information about the system sending the message and the nature of the request, which the server may or may not use when formatting the reply. The number, choice, and order of the headers included in a message are left to the client implementation, but the HTTP specification recommends that they be ordered using four basic categories.

General Header Fields   General headers apply to both request and response messages but do not apply to the entity (that is, the file or other information in the body of the message). The general header *FieldName* values are as follows:

- **Cache-Control**   Contains directives to be obeyed by caching mechanisms at the destination system
- **Connection**   Specifies options desired for the current connection, such that it be kept alive for use with multiple requests
- **Date**   Specifies the date and time that the message was generated
- **Pragma**   Specifies directives that are specific to the client or server implementation
- **Trailer**   Indicates that specific header fields are present in the trailer of a message encoded with chunked transfer-coding
- **Transfer-Encoding**   Specifies what type of transformation (if any) has been applied to the message body in order to safely transmit it to the destination
- **Upgrade**   Specifies additional communication protocols supported by the client
- **Via**   Identifies the gateway and proxy servers between the client and the server and the protocols they use
- **Warning**   Contains additional information about the status or transformation of a message

Request Header Fields   Request headers apply only to request messages and supply information about the request and the system making the request. The request header *FieldName* values are as follows:

- **Accept**   Specifies the media types that are acceptable in the response message
- **Accept-Charset**   Specifies the character sets that are acceptable in the response message
- **Accept-Encoding**   Specifies the content codings that are acceptable in the response message
- **Accept-Language**   Specifies the languages that are acceptable in the response message
- **Authorization**   Contains credentials with which the client will be authenticated to the server
- **Expect**   Specifies the behavior that the client expects from the server
- **From**   Contains an e-mail address for the user generating the request
- **Host**   Specifies the Internet hostname of the resource being requested (usually a URL), plus a port number if different from the default port (80)

- **If-Match**   Used to make a particular request conditional by matching particular entity tags

- **If-Modified-Since**   Used to make a particular request conditional by specifying the modification date of the client cache entry containing the resource, which the server compares to the actual resource and replies with either the resource or a cache referral

- **If-None-Match**   Used to make a particular request conditional by not matching particular entity tags

- **If-Range**   Requests that the server transmit the parts of an entity that the client is missing

- **If-Unmodified-Since**   Used to make a particular request conditional by specifying a date that the server should use to determine whether to supply the requested resource

- **Max-Forwards**   Limits the number of proxies or gateways that can forward the request to another server

- **Proxy-Authorization**   Contains credentials with which the client will authenticate itself to a proxy server

- **Range**   Contains one or more byte ranges representing parts of the resource specified by the *ResourceURI* variable that the client is requesting be sent by the server

- **Referer**   Specifies the resource from which the *ResourceURI* value was obtained

- **TE**   Specifies which extension transfer-codings the client can accept in the response and whether the client will accept trailer fields in a chunked transfer-coding

- **User-Agent**   Contains information about the browser generating the request

Response Header Fields   The response headers apply only to response messages and provide additional information about the message and the server generating the message. The response header *FieldName* values are as follows:

- **Accept-Ranges**   Enables a server to indicate its acceptance of range requests for a resource (used in responses only)

- **Age**   Specifies the elapsed time since a cached response was generated at a server

- **Etag**   Specifies the current value of the entity tag for the requested variant

- **Location**   Directs the destination system to a location for the requested resource other than that specified by the *RequestURI* variable

- **Proxy-Authenticate**   Specifies the authentication scheme used by a proxy server

- **Retry-After**   Specifies how long a requested resource will be unavailable to the client

- **Server**   Identifies the web server software used to process the request

- **Vary**   Specifies the header fields used to determine whether a client can use a cached response to a request without revalidation by the server

- **WWW-Authenticate**   Specifies the type of authentication required in order for the client to access the requested resource

Part IV

Entity Header Fields   The term *entity* is used to describe the data included in the message body of a response message, and the entity headers provide additional information about that data. The entity header *FieldName* values are as follows:

- **Allow**   Specifies the request types supported by a resource identified by a particular *RequestURI* value

- **Content-Encoding**   Specifies additional content-coding mechanisms (such as gzip) that have been applied to the data in the body of the message

- **Content-Language**   Specifies the language of the message body

- **Content-Length**   Specifies the length of the message body, in bytes

- **Content-Location**   Specifies the location from which the information in the message body was derived, when it is separate from the location specified by the *ResourceURI* variable

- **Content-MD5**   Contains an MD5 digest of the message body (as defined in RFC 1864) that will be used to verify its integrity at the destination

- **Content-Range**   Identifies the location of the data in the message body within the whole of the requested resource when the message contains only part of the resource

- **Content-Type**   Specifies the media type of the data in the message body

- **Expires**   Specifies the date and time after which the cached response is to be considered stale

- **Last-Modified**   Specifies the date and time at which the server believes the requested resource was last modified

- **Extension-Header**   Enables the use of additional entity header fields that must be recognized by both the client and the server

HTTP Responses

The HTTP responses generated by web servers use many of the same basic elements as the requests. The start line also consists of three elements, as follows:

```
HTTPVersion StatusCode StatusPhrase
```

The *HTTPVersion* variable specifies the standard supported by the server, using the same values listed earlier. The *StatusCode* and *StatusPhrase* variables indicate whether the request has been processed successfully by the server and, if it hasn't, why not. The code is a three-digit number, and the phrase is a text string. The code values are defined in the HTTP specification and are used consistently by all web server implementations. The first digit of the code specifies the general nature of the response, and the second two digits give more specific information. The status phrases are defined by the standard as well, but some web server products enable you to modify the text strings in order to supply more information to the client. The codes and phrases defined by the standard are listed in the following sections.

Informational Codes   Informational codes are used only in responses with no message bodies and have the numeral 1 as their first digit, as shown here:

- **100 – Continue**   Indicates that the request message has been received by the server and that the client should either send another message completing the request or continue to wait for a response. A response using this code must be followed by another response containing a code indicating completion of the request.

- **101 – Switching Protocol**   A response to an Update request by the client and indicates the server is switching as well. While not in common use, this code was created to allow migration to an incompatible protocol version.

Successful Codes   Successful codes have a 2 as their first digit and indicate that the client's request message has been successfully received, understood, and accepted. The valid codes are as follows:

- **200 – OK**   Indicates that the request has been processed successfully and that the response contains the data appropriate for the type of request.
- **201 – Created**   Indicates that the request has been processed successfully and that a new resource has been created.
- **202 – Accepted**   Indicates that the request has been accepted for processing but that the processing has not yet been completed.
- **203 – Nonauthoritative Information**   Indicates that the information in the headers is not the definitive information supplied by the server but is gathered from a local or a third-party copy.
- **204 – No Content**   Indicates that the request has been processed successfully but that the response contains no message body. It may contain header information.
- **205 – Reset Content**   Indicates that the request has been processed successfully and that the client browser user should reset the document view. This message typically means that the data from a form has been received and that the browser should reset the display by clearing the form fields.
- **206 – Partial Content**   Indicates that the request has been processed successfully and that the server has fulfilled a request that uses the Range header to specify part of a resource.

Redirection Codes   Redirection codes have a 3 as their first digit and indicate that further action from the client (either the browser or the user) is required to successfully process the request. The valid codes are as follows:

- **300 – Multiple Choices**   Indicates that the response contains a list of resources that can be used to satisfy the request, from which the user should select one.
- **301 – Moved Permanently**   Indicates that the requested resource has been assigned a new permanent URI and that all future references to this resource should use one of the new URIs supplied in the response.
- **302 – Found**   Indicates that the requested resource resides temporarily under a different URI but that the client should continue to use the same *RequestURI* value for future requests since the location may change again.
- **303 – See Other**   Indicates that the response to the request can be found under a different URI and that the client should generate another request pointing to the new URI.
- **304 – Not Modified**   Indicates that the version of the requested resource in the client cache is identical to that on the server and that retransmission of the resource is not necessary.

- **305 – Use Proxy**   Indicates that the requested resource must be accessed through the proxy specified in the Location header.

- **306 – Unused**   No longer used and is currently reserved for future use.

- **307 – Temporary Redirect**   Indicates that the requested resource resides temporarily under a different URI but that the client should continue to use the same *RequestURI* value for future requests since the location may change again.

- **308 – Permanent Redirect**   Indicates that the resource is now at another URL. While similar to the 301 response code, the exception for a 308 code is that the user agent must not change the HTTP method used.

Client Error Codes   Client error codes have a 4 as their first digit and indicate that the request could not be processed because of an error by the client. The valid codes are as follows:

- **400 – Bad Request**   Indicates that the server could not understand the request because of malformed syntax

- **401 – Unauthorized**   Indicates that the server could not process the request because user authentication is required

- **402 – Payment Required**   Reserved for future use

- **403 – Forbidden**   Indicates that the server is refusing to process the request and that it should not be repeated

- **404 – Not Found**   Indicates that the server could not locate the resource specified by the *RequestURI* variable

- **405 – Method Not Allowed**   Indicates that the request type cannot be used for the specified *RequestURI*

- **406 – Not Acceptable**   Indicates that the resource specified by the *RequestURI* variable does not conform to any of the data types specified in the request message's Accept header

- **407 – Proxy Authentication Required**   Indicates that the client must authenticate itself to a proxy server before it can access the requested resource

- **408 – Request Timeout**   Indicates that the client did not produce a request within the server's timeout period

- **409 – Conflict**   Indicates that the request could not be processed because of a conflict with the current state of the requested resource, such as when a PUT command attempts to write data to a resource that is already in use

- **410 – Gone**   Indicates that the requested resource is no longer available at the server and that the server is not aware of an alternative location

- **411 – Length Required**   Indicates that the server has refused to process a request that does not have a Content-Length header

- **412 – Precondition Failed**   Indicates that the server has failed to satisfy one of the preconditions specified in the request headers

- **413 – Request Entity Too Large** Indicates that the server is refusing to process the request because the message is too large

- **414 – RequestURI Too Long** Indicates that the server is refusing to process the request because the *RequestURI* value is longer than the server is willing to interpret

- **415 – Unsupported Media Type** Indicates that the server is refusing to process the request because the request is in a format not supported by the requested resource for the requested method

- **416 – Requested Range Not Satisfiable** Indicates that the server cannot process the request because the data specified by the Range header in the request message does not exist in the requested resource

- **417 – Expectation Failed** Indicates that the server could not satisfy the requirements specified in the request message's Expect header

Server Error Codes Server error codes have a 5 as their first digit and indicate that the request could not be processed because of an error by the server. The valid codes are as follows:

- **500 – Internal Server Error** Indicates that the server encountered an unexpected condition that prevented it from fulfilling the request

- **501 – Not Implemented** Indicates that the server does not support the functionality required to satisfy the request

- **502 – Bad Gateway** Indicates that a gateway or proxy server has received an invalid response from the upstream server it accessed while attempting to process the request

- **503 – Service Unavailable** Indicates that the server cannot process the request because of it being temporarily overloaded or under maintenance

- **504 – Gateway Timeout** Indicates that a gateway or proxy server did not receive a timely response from the upstream server specified by the URI or some other auxiliary server needed to complete the request

- **505 – HTTP Version Not Supported** Indicates that the server does not support, or refuses to support, the HTTP protocol version used in the request message

After the start line, a response message can contain a series of headers, just like those in a request, that provide information about the server and the response message. The header section concludes with a blank line, after which comes the body of the message, typically containing the contents of the file requested by the client. If the file is larger than what can fit in a single packet, the server generates additional response messages containing message bodies but no start lines or headers.

FTP Servers

The File Transfer Protocol is an application layer TCP/IP protocol that enables an authenticated client to connect to a server and transfer files to and from the other machine. FTP is not the same as sharing a drive with another system on the network. Access is limited to a few basic file management commands, and the primary function of the protocol is to copy files to your local system, not to access them in place on the server.

Part IV

Like HTTP, FTP uses the TCP protocol for its transport services and relies on ASCII text commands for its user interface. There are now many graphical FTP clients available that automate the generation and transmission of the appropriate text commands to a server.

The big difference between FTP and HTTP (as well as most other protocols) is that FTP uses two port numbers in the course of its operations. When an FTP client connects to a server, it uses port 21 to establish a control connection. This connection remains open during the life of the session; the client and server use it to exchange commands and replies. When the client requests a file transfer, the server establishes a second connection on port 20, which it uses to transfer the file and then terminates immediately afterward.

FTP Commands

An FTP client consists of a user interface, which may be text based or graphical, and a *user protocol interpreter.* The user protocol interpreter communicates with the *server protocol interpreter* using text commands that are passed over the control connection (see Figure 16-1). When the commands call for a data transfer, one of the protocol interpreters triggers a *data transfer process,* which communicates with a like process on the other machine using the data connection. The commands issued by the user protocol interpreter do not necessarily correspond to the traditional text-based user interface commands. For example, to retrieve a file from a server, the traditional user interface command is GET plus the filename, but after the user protocol interpreter receives this command, it sends an RETR command to the server with the same filename. Thus, the user interface can be modified for purposes of language localization or other reasons, but the commands used by the protocol interpreters remain consistent.

The following sections list the commands used by the FTP protocol interpreters.

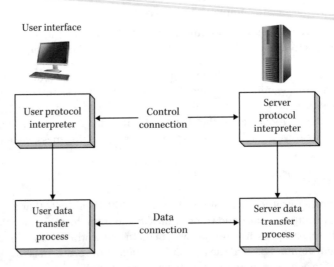

Figure 16-1   The protocol interpreters in the FTP client and server exchange control messages

Access Control Commands

FTP clients use the access control commands to log in to a server, authenticate the user, and terminate the control connection at the end of the session. These commands are as follows:

- **USER *username***   Specifies the account name used to authenticate the client to the server.

- **PASS *password***   Specifies the password associated with the previously furnished username.

- **ACCT *account***   Specifies an account used for access to specific features of the server file system. The ACCT command can be issued at any time during the session and not just during the login sequence, as with USER.

- **CWD *pathname***   Changes the working directory in the server file system to that specified by the *pathname* variable.

- **CDUP**   Shifts the working directory in the server file system one level up to the parent directory.

- **SMNT *pathname***   Mounts a different file system data structure on the server, without altering the user account authentication.

- **REIN**   Terminates the current session, leaving the control connection open and completing any data connection transfer in progress. A new USER command is expected to follow immediately.

- **QUIT**   Terminates the current session and closes the control connection after completing any data connection transfer in progress.

Transfer Parameter Commands

The transfer parameter commands prepare the systems to initiate a data connection and identify the type of file that is to be transferred. These commands are as follows:

- **PORT *host/port***   Notifies the server of the IP address and ephemeral port number that it expects a data connection to use. The *host/port* variable consists of six integers, separated by commas, representing the four bytes of the IP address and two bytes for the port number.

- **PASV**   Instructs the server to specify a port number that the client will use to establish a data connection. The reply from the server contains a *host/port* variable, like PORT.

- **TYPE *typecode***   Specifies the type of file to be transferred over a data connection. Currently used options are as follows:
  - **A**   ASCII plain-text file
  - **I**   Binary file

- **STRU *structurecode***   Specifies the structure of a file. The default setting, F (for File), indicates that the file is a contiguous byte stream. Two other options, R (for Record) and P (for Page), are no longer used.

- **MODE *modecode***   Specifies the transfer mode for a data connection. The default setting, S (for Stream), indicates that the file will be transferred as a byte stream. Two other options, B (for Block) and C (for Compressed), are no longer used.

Part IV

FTP Service Commands

The FTP service commands enable the client to manage the file system on the server and initiate file transfers. These commands are as follows:

- **RETR** *filename*   Instructs the server to transfer the specified file to the client.
- **STOR** *filename*   Instructs the server to receive the specified file from the client, overwriting an identically named file in the server directory if necessary.
- **STOU**   Instructs the server to receive the file from the client and give it a unique name in the server directory. The reply from the server must contain the unique name.
- **APPE** *pathname*   Instructs the server to receive the specified file from the client and append it to the identically named file in the server directory. If no file of that name exists, the server creates a new file.
- **ALLO** *bytes*   Allocates a specified number of bytes on the server before the client actually transmits the data.
- **REST** *marker*   Specifies the point in a file at which the file transfer should be restarted.
- **RNFR** *filename*   Specifies the name of a file to be renamed; must be followed by an RNTO command.
- **RNTO** *filename*   Specifies the new name for the file previously referenced in an RNFR command.
- **ABOR**   Aborts the command currently being processed by the server, closing any open data connections.
- **DELE** *filename*   Deletes the specified file on the server.
- **RMD** *pathname*   Deletes the specified directory on the server.
- **MKD** *pathname*   Creates the specified directory on the server.
- **PWD**   Returns the name of the server's current working directory.
- **LIST** *pathname*   Instructs the server to transmit an ASCII file containing a list of the specified directory's contents, including attributes.
- **NLST** *pathname*   Instructs the server to transmit an ASCII file containing a list of the specified directory's contents, with no attributes.
- **SITE** *string*   Carries nonstandard, implementation-specific commands to the server.
- **SYST**   Returns the name of the operating system running on the server.
- **STAT** *filename*   When used during a file transfer, returns a status indicator for the current operation. When used with a *filename* argument, returns the LIST information for the specified file.
- **HELP** *string*   Returns help information specific to the server implementation.
- **NOOP**   Instructs the server to return an OK response. This is used as a session keep-alive mechanism; the command performs no other actions.

FTP Reply Codes

An FTP server responds to each command sent by a client with a three-digit reply code and a text string. As with HTTP, these reply codes must be implemented as defined in the FTP standard on all servers so that the client can determine its next action, but some products enable you to modify the text that is delivered with the code and displayed to the user.

The first digit of the reply code indicates whether the command was completed successfully, unsuccessfully, or not at all. The possible values for this digit are as follows:

- **1## – Positive preliminary reply**   Indicates that the server is initiating the requested action and that the client should wait for another reply before sending any further commands

- **2## – Positive completion reply**   Indicates that the server has successfully completed the requested action

- **3## – Positive intermediate reply**   Indicates that the server has accepted the command but that more information is needed before it can execute it and that the client should send another command containing the required information

- **4## – Transient negative completion reply**   Indicates that the server has not accepted the command or executed the requested action due to a temporary condition and that the client should send the command again

- **5## – Permanent negative completion reply**   Indicates that the server has not accepted the command or executed the requested action and that the client is discouraged (but not forbidden) from resending the command

The second digit of the reply code provides more specific information about the nature of the message. The possible values for this digit are as follows:

- **#0# – Syntax**   Indicates that the command contains a syntax error that has prevented it from being executed

- **#1# – Information**   Indicates that the reply contains information that the command requested, such as status or help

- **#2# – Connections**   Indicates that the reply refers to the control or data connection

- **#3# – Authentication and accounting**   Indicates that the reply refers to the login process or the accounting procedure

- **#4# – Unused**   Currently unused. Is available for future use.

- **#5# – File system**   Indicates the status of the server file system as a result of the command

The error codes defined by the FTP standard are as follows:

- 110 Restart marker reply

- 120 Service ready in *nnn* minutes

- 125 Data connection already open; transfer starting

- 150 File status okay; about to open data connection
- 200 Command okay
- 202 Command not implemented, superfluous at this site
- 211 System status, or system help reply
- 212 Directory status
- 213 File status
- 214 Help message
- 215 NAME system type
- 220 Service ready for new user
- 221 Service closing control connection
- 225 Data connection open; no transfer in progress
- 226 Closing data connection
- 227 Entering Passive Mode (h1,h2,h3,h4,p1,p2)
- 230 User logged in, proceed
- 250 Requested file action okay, completed
- 257 "PATHNAME" created
- 331 Username okay, need password
- 332 Need account for login
- 350 Requested file action pending further information
- 421 Service not available; closing control connection
- 425 Can't open data connection
- 426 Connection closed; transfer aborted
- 450 Requested file action not taken
- 451 Requested action aborted; local error in processing
- 452 Requested action not taken; insufficient storage space in system
- 500 Syntax error, command unrecognized
- 501 Syntax error in parameters or arguments
- 502 Command not implemented
- 503 Bad sequence of commands
- 504 Command not implemented for that parameter
- 530 Not logged in
- 532 Need account for storing files
- 550 Requested action not taken; file unavailable (e.g., file not found, no access)
- 551 Requested action aborted; page type unknown

- 552 Requested file action aborted; exceeded storage allocation (for current directory or dataset)

- 553 Requested action not taken; filename not allowed

FTP Messaging

An FTP session begins with a client establishing a connection with a server by using either a GUI or the command line to specify the server's DNS name or IP address. The first order of business is to establish a TCP connection using the standard three-way handshake. The FTP server is listening on port 21 for incoming messages, and this new TCP connection becomes the FTP control connection that will remain open for the life of the session. The first FTP message is transmitted by the server, announcing and identifying itself, as follows:

```
220 CZ2 Microsoft FTP Service (Version 5.0)
```

As with all messages transmitted over a TCP connection, acknowledgment is required. During the course of the session, the message exchanges will be punctuated by TCP ACK packets from both systems, as needed. After it sends the initial acknowledgment, the client prompts the user for an account name and password and performs the user login sequence, as follows:

```
USER anonymous
331 Anonymous access allowed, send identity (e-mail name) as password.
PASS jdoe@zacker.com
230 Anonymous user logged in.
```

The client then informs the server of its IP address and the port that it will use for data connections on the client system, as follows:

```
PORT 192,168,2,3,7,233
200 PORT command successful.
```

The values 192, 168, 2, and 3 are the four decimal byte values of the IP address, and the 7 and 233 are the 2 bytes of the port number value, which translates as 2025. By converting these 2 port bytes to binary form (00000111 11101001) and then converting the whole 2-byte value to a decimal, you get 2025.

At this point, the client can send commands to the server requesting file transfers or file system procedures, such as the creation and deletion of directories. One typical client command is to request a listing of the files in the server's default directory, as follows:

```
NLST -l
```

In response to this command, the server informs the client that it is going to open a data connection because the list is transmitted as an ASCII file.

```
150 Opening ASCII mode data connection for /bin/ls.
```

The server then commences the establishment of the second TCP connection, using its own port 20 and the client port 2025 specified earlier in the PORT command. Once the connection is established, the server transmits the file it has created containing the listing for the directory. Depending on the number of files in the directory, the transfer may require the transmission of multiple packets and acknowledgments, after which the server immediately sends the first message in the sequence that terminates the data connection. Once the data connection is closed, the server reverts to the control connection and finishes the file transfer with the following positive completion reply message:

```
226 Transfer complete.
```

At this point, the client is ready to issue another command, such as a request for another file transfer, which repeats the entire process beginning with the PORT command or some other function that uses only the control connection. When the client is ready to terminate the session by closing the control connection, it sends a QUIT command, and the server responds with an acknowledgment like the following:

```
221
```

E-mail

While Internet services such as the Web and FTP are wildly popular, the service that is the closest to being a ubiquitous business and personal communications tool is e-mail. E-mail is a unique communications medium that combines the immediacy of the telephone with the precision of the written word, and no Internet service is more valuable to the network user. Until the mid-1990s, the e-mail systems you were likely to encounter were self-contained, proprietary solutions designed to provide an organization with internal communications. As the value of e-mail as a business tool began to be recognized by the general public, businesspeople began swapping the e-mail addresses supplied to them by specific online services. However, if you subscribed to a different service than your intended correspondent, you were out of luck. The rise of the Internet revolutionized the e-mail concept by providing a single, worldwide standard for mail communications that was independent of any single service provider. Today, e-mail addresses are almost as common as telephone numbers, and virtually every network with an Internet connection supplies its users with e-mail addresses.

E-mail Addressing

The e-mail address format soon becomes second nature to beginning e-mail users. An Internet e-mail address consists of a username and a domain name, separated by an "at" symbol (@), as in *jdoe@mydomain.com*. As in the URLs used to identify web and FTP sites, the domain name in an e-mail address (which is everything following the @ symbol) identifies the organization hosting the e-mail services for a particular user. For individual users, the domain is typically that of an ISP, which nearly always supplies one or more e-mail addresses with an Internet access account. For corporate users, the domain name is usually registered to the organization and is usually the same domain used for their web sites and other Internet services.

The username part of an e-mail address (which is everything before the @ symbol) represents the name of a mailbox that has been created on the mail server servicing the domain. The username often consists of a combination of names and/or initials identifying an individual user at the organization, but it's also common to have mailboxes for specific roles and functions in the domain. For example, most domains running a web site have a *webmaster@mydomain.com* mailbox for communications concerning the functionality of the web site.

Because Internet e-mail relies on standard domain names to identify mail servers, the Domain Name System (DNS) is an essential part of the Internet e-mail architecture. DNS servers store information in units of various types called *resource records.* The MX resource record is the one used to identify an e-mail server in a particular domain. When a mail server receives an outgoing message from an e-mail client, it reads the address of the intended recipient and performs a DNS lookup of the domain name in that address. The server generates a DNS message requesting the MX resource record for the specified domain, and the DNS server (after performing the standard iterative process that may involve relating the request to other domain servers) replies with the IP address of the e-mail server for the destination domain. The server with the outgoing message then opens a connection to the destination domain's mail server using the *Simple Mail Transfer Protocol* (SMTP). It is the destination mail server that processes the username part of the e-mail address by placing the message in the appropriate mailbox, where it waits until the client picks it up.

E-mail Clients and Servers

Like HTTP and FTP, Internet e-mail is a client-server application. However, in this case, several types of servers are involved in the e-mail communication process. SMTP servers are responsible for receiving outgoing mail from clients and transmitting the mail messages to their destination servers. The other type of server is the one that maintains the mailboxes and which the e-mail clients use to retrieve their incoming mail. The two predominant protocols for this type of server are the *Post Office Protocol, version 3* (POP3) and the *Internet Message Access Protocol* (IMAP). This is another case where it's important to understand that the term *server* refers to an application and not necessarily to a separate computer. In many cases, the SMTP and either the POP3 or IMAP server run on the same computer.

E-mail server products generally fall into two categories, those that are designed solely for Internet e-mail and those that provide more comprehensive internal e-mail services as well. The former are relatively simple applications that typically provide SMTP support and may or may not include either POP3 or IMAP as well. If not, you have to purchase and install a POP3 or IMAP server also so that your users can access their mail. One of the most common SMTP servers used on the Internet is a free Unix program called sendmail, but there are many other products, both open source and commercial, that run on a variety of computing platforms.

After installing the mail server applications, the administrator creates a mailbox for each user and registers the server's IP address in a DNS MX resource record for the domain. This enables other SMTP servers on the Internet to send mail to the users' mailboxes. Clients access the POP3 or IMAP server to download mail from their mailboxes and send outgoing messages using the SMTP server. ISPs typically use mail servers of this type because their users are strictly concerned with Internet e-mail. The server may provide other convenience services for users as well, such as web-based client access, which enables users to access their mailboxes from any web browser.

The more comprehensive e-mail servers are products that evolved from internal e-mail systems. Products like Microsoft Exchange started out as servers that a corporation would install to provide private e-mail service to users within the company, as well as other services such as calendars, personal information managers, and group scheduling. As Internet e-mail became more prevalent, these products were enhanced to include the standard Internet e-mail connectivity protocols as well. Today, a single product such as Exchange provides a wealth of communications services for private network users. On this type of e-mail product, the mail messages and other personal data are stored permanently on the mail servers, and users run a special client to access their mail. Storing the mail on the server makes it easier for administrators to back it up and enables users to access their mail from any computer. E-mail applications such as Exchange are much more expensive than Internet-only mail servers, and administering them is more complicated.

An e-mail client is any program that can access a user's mailbox on a mail server. Some e-mail client programs are designed strictly for Internet e-mail and can therefore access only SMTP, POP3, and/or IMAP servers. There are many products, both commercial and free, that perform the same basic functions. In many cases, e-mail client functionality is integrated into other programs, such as personal information managers (PIMs). Because the Internet e-mail protocols are standardized, users can run any Internet e-mail client with any SMTP/POP3/IMAP servers. Configuring an Internet e-mail client to send and retrieve mail is simply a matter of supplying the program with the IP addresses of an SMTP server (for outgoing mail) and a POP3 or IMAP server (for incoming mail), as well as the name of a mailbox on the POP3/IMAP server and its accompanying password.

The more comprehensive e-mail server products require a proprietary client to access all of their features. In the case of Exchange, the client is the Microsoft Outlook program included as part of the many Microsoft Office versions. Outlook is an unusual e-mail client in that you can configure it to operate in corporate/workgroup mode, in which the client connects to an Exchange server, or in Internet-only mode. Both modes enable you to access SMTP and POP3/IMAP services, but corporate/workgroup mode provides access to all of the Exchange features, such as group scheduling, and stores the user's mail on the server. Internet-only mode stores the mail on the computer's local drive.

Simple Mail Transfer Protocol

SMTP is an application layer protocol that is standardized in the IETF's RFC 821 document. SMTP messages can be carried by any reliable transport protocol, but on the Internet and most private networks, they are carried by the TCP protocol, using well-known port number 25 at the server. Like HTTP and FTP, SMTP messages are based on ASCII text commands, rather than the headers and fields used by the protocols at the lower layers of the protocol stack. SMTP communications can take place between e-mail clients and servers or between servers. In each case, the basic communication model is the same. One computer (called the *sender-SMTP*) initiates communication with the other (the *receiver-SMTP*) by establishing a TCP connection using the standard three-way handshake.

SMTP Commands

Once the TCP connection is established, the sender-SMTP computer begins transmitting SMTP commands to the receiver-SMTP, which responds with a reply message and a numeric code for each command it receives. The commands consist of a keyword and an argument field containing other parameters in the form of a text string, followed by a carriage return/line feed (CR/LF).

NOTE The SMTP standard uses the terms *sender-SMTP* and *receiver-SMTP* to distinguish the sender and the receiver of the SMTP messages from the sender and the receiver of an actual mail message. The two are not necessarily synonymous.

The commands used by the sender-SMTP and their functions are as follows (the parentheses contain the actual text strings transmitted by the sending computer):

- **HELLO (HELO)**   Used by the sender-SMTP to identify itself to the receiver-SMTP by transmitting its hostname as the argument. The receiver-SMTP responds by transmitting its own hostname.

- **MAIL (MAIL)**   Used to initiate a transaction in which a mail message is to be delivered to a mailbox by specifying the address of the mail sender as the argument and, optionally, a list of hosts through which the mail message has been routed (called a *source route*). The receiver-SMTP uses this list in the event it has to return a nondelivery notice to the mail sender.

- **RECIPIENT (RCPT)**   Identifies the recipient of a mail message, using the recipient's mailbox address as the argument. If the message is addressed to multiple recipients, the sender-SMTP generates a separate RCPT command for each address.

- **DATA (DATA)**   Contains the actual e-mail message data, followed by a CRLF, a period, and another CRLF (<CRLF>.<CRLF>), which indicates the end of the message string.

- **SEND (SEND)**   Used to initiate a transaction in which mail is to be delivered to a user's terminal (instead of to a mailbox). Like the MAIL command, the argument contains the sender's mailbox address and the source route.

- **SEND OR MAIL (SOML)**   Used to initiate a transaction in which a mail message is to be delivered to a user's terminal, if they are currently active and configured to receive messages, or to the user's mailbox, if they are not. The argument contains the same sender address and source route as the MAIL command.

- **SEND AND MAIL (SAML)**   Used to initiate a transaction in which a mail message is to be delivered to a user's terminal, if they are currently active and configured to receive messages, and to the user's mailbox. The argument contains the same sender address and source route as the MAIL command.

- **RESET (RSET)**   Instructs the receiver-SMTP to abort the current mail transaction and discard all sender, recipient, and mail data information from that transaction.

- **VERIFY (VRFY)**   Used by the sender-SMTP to confirm that the argument identifies a valid user. If the user exists, the receiver-SMTP responds with the user's full name and mailbox address.

- **EXPAND (EXPN)**   Used by the sender-SMTP to confirm that the argument identifies a valid mailing list. If the list exists, the receiver-SMTP responds with the full names and mailbox addresses of the list's members.

- **HELP (HELP)**   Used by the sender-SMTP (presumably a client) to request help information from the receiver-SMTP. An optional argument may specify the subject for which the sender-SMTP needs help.

- **NOOP (NOOP)**   Performs no function other than to request that the receiver-SMTP generate an OK reply.

- **QUIT (QUIT)**   Used by the sender-SMTP to request the termination of the communications channel to the receiver-SMTP. The sender-SMTP should not close the channel until it has

Part IV

received an OK reply to its QUIT command from the receiver-SMTP, and the receiver-SMTP should not close the channel until it has received and replied to a QUIT command from the sender-SMTP.

- **TURN (TURN)**   Used by the sender-SMTP to request that it and the receiver-SMTP should switch roles, with the sender-SMTP becoming the receiver-SMTP and the receiver-SMTP the sender-SMTP. The actual role switch does not occur until the receiver-SMTP returns an OK response to the TURN command.

NOTE Not all SMTP implementations include support for all of the commands listed here. The only commands that are required to be included in all SMTP implementations are HELO, MAIL, RCPT, DATA, RSET, NOOP, and QUIT.

SMTP Replies

The receiver-SMTP is required to generate a reply for each of the commands it receives from the sender-SMTP. The sender-SMTP is not permitted to send a new command until it receives a reply to the previous one. This prevents any confusion of requests and replies. The reply messages generated by the receiver-SMTP consist of a three-digit numerical value plus an explanatory text string. The number and the text string are essentially redundant; the number is intended for use by automated systems that take action based on the reply, while the text string is intended for humans. The text messages can vary from implementation to implementation, but the reply numbers must remain consistent.

The reply codes generated by the receiver-SMTP are as follows (italicized values represent variables that the receiver-SMTP replaces with an appropriate text string):

- 211 System status, or system help reply
- 214 Help message
- 220 *Domain* service ready
- 221 *Domain* service closing transmission channel
- 250 Requested mail action okay, completed
- 251 User not local; will forward to *forward-path*
- 354 Start mail input; end with <CRLF>.<CRLF>
- 421 *Domain* service not available, closing transmission channel
- 450 Requested mail action not taken: mailbox unavailable
- 451 Requested action aborted: local error in processing
- 452 Requested action not taken: insufficient system storage
- 500 Syntax error, command unrecognized
- 501 Syntax error in parameters or arguments
- 502 Command not implemented
- 503 Bad sequence of commands
- 504 Command parameter not implemented
- 550 Requested action not taken: mailbox unavailable

- 551 User not local; please try *forward-path*
- 552 Requested mail action aborted: exceeded storage allocation
- 553 Requested action not taken: mailbox name not allowed
- 554 Transaction failed

SMTP Transactions

A typical SMTP mail transaction begins (after a TCP connection is established) with the sender-SMTP transmitting a HELO command to identify itself to the receiver-SMTP by including its hostname as the command argument. If the receiver-SMTP is operational, it responds with a 250 reply. Next, the sender-SMTP initiates the mail transaction by transmitting a MAIL command. This command contains the mailbox address of the message sender as the argument on the command line. Note that this sender address refers to the person who generated the e-mail message and not necessarily to the SMTP server currently sending commands.

NOTE In the case where the SMTP transaction is between an e-mail client and an SMTP server, the sender of the e-mail and the sender-SMTP refer to the same computer, but the receiver-SMTP is not the same as the intended receiver (that is, the addressee) of the e-mail. In the case of two SMTP servers communicating, such as when a local SMTP server forwards the mail messages it has just received from clients to their destination servers, neither the sender-SMTP nor the receiver-SMTP refer to the ultimate sender and receiver of the e-mail message.

If the receiver-SMTP is ready to receive and process a mail message, it returns a 250 response to the MAIL message generated by the sender-SMTP. After receiving a positive response to its MAIL command, the sender-SMTP proceeds by sending at least one RCPT message that contains as its argument the mailbox address of the e-mail message's intended recipient. If there are multiple recipients for the message, the sender-SMTP sends a separate RCPT command for each mailbox address. The receiver-SMTP, on receiving an RCPT command, checks to see whether it has a mailbox for that address and, if so, acknowledges the command with a 250 reply. If the mailbox does not exist, the receiver-SMTP can take one of several actions, such as generating a 251 User Not Local; Will Forward response and transmitting the message to the proper server or rejecting the message with a failure response, such as 550 Requested Action Not Taken: Mailbox Unavailable or 551 User Not Local. If the sender-SMTP generates multiple RCPT messages, the receiver-SMTP must reply separately to each one before the next can be sent.

The next step in the procedure is the transmission of a DATA command by the sender-SMTP. The DATA command has no argument, and is followed simply by a CRLF. On receiving the DATA command, the receiver-SMTP returns a 354 response and assumes that all of the lines that follow are the text of the e-mail message itself. The sender-SMTP then transmits the test of the message, one line at a time, ending with a period on a separate line (in other words, a CRLF.CRLF sequence). On receipt of this final sequence, the receiver-SMTP responds with a 250 reply and proceeds to process the mail message by storing it in the proper mailbox and clearing its buffers.

Multipurpose Internet Mail Extension

SMTP is designed to carry text messages using 7-bit ASCII codes and lines no more than 1,000 characters long. This excludes foreign characters and 8-bit binary data from being carried in e-mail messages. To make it possible to send these types of data in SMTP e-mail, another standard called the *Multipurpose Internet Mail Extension* (MIME) was published in five RFC documents, numbered 2045 through 2049. MIME is essentially a method for encoding various types of data for inclusion in an e-mail message.

The typical SMTP e-mail message transmitted after the DATA command begins with a header containing the familiar elements of the message itself, such as the To, From, and Subject fields. MIME adds two additional fields to this initial header, a MIME-Version indicator that specifies which version of MIME the message is using and a Content-Type field that specifies the format of the MIME-encoded data included in the message. The Content-Type field can specify any one of several predetermined MIME formats, or it can indicate that the message consists of multiple body parts, each of which uses a different format.

For example, the header of a multipart message might appear as follows:

```
MIME-Version: 1.0
From: John Doe jdoe@anycorp.com
To: Tim Jones timj@anothercorp.com
Subject: Network diagrams
Content-Type: multipart/mixed;boundary=gc0p4Jq0M2Yt08j34c0p
```

The Content-Type field in this example indicates that the message consists of multiple parts, in different formats. The *boundary* parameter specifies a text string that is used to delimit the parts. The value specified in the boundary parameter can be any text string, just as long as it does not appear in the message text. After this header comes the separate parts of the message, each of which begins with the boundary value on a separate line and a Content-Type field that specifies the format for the data in that part of the message, as follows:

```
—gc0p4Jq0M2Yt08j34c0p
Content-Type: image/jpeg
```

The actual message content then appears, in the format specified by the Content-Type value.

The header for each part of the message can also contain any of the following fields:

- **Content-Transfer-Encoding**   Specifies the method used to encode the data in that part of the message, using values such as 7-bit, 8-bit, Base64, and Binary

- **Content-ID**   Optional field that specifies an identifier for that part of the message that can be used to reference it in other places

- **Content-Description**   Optional field that contains a description of the data in that part of the message

The most commonly recognizable elements of MIME are the content types used to describe the nature of the data included as part of an e-mail message. A MIME content type consists of a type and a subtype, separated by a forward slash, as in image/jpeg. The type indicates the general type of data, and the subtype indicates a specific format for that data type. The image type, for example, has several possible subtypes, including jpeg and gif, which are both common graphics formats. Systems interpreting the data use the MIME types to determine how they should handle the data, even if they do not recognize the format. For example, an application receiving data with the text/richtext content type might display the content to the user, even if it cannot handle the richtext format. Because the basic type is text, the application can be reasonably sure that the data will be recognizable to the user. If the application receives a message containing image/gif data, however, and is incapable of interpreting the gif format, it can be equally sure, because the message part is of the image type, that the raw, uninterpreted data would be meaningless to the user and as a result would not display it in its raw form.

The seven MIME content types are as follows:

- **Text**   Contains textual information, either unformatted (subtype: plain) or enriched by formatting commands
- **Image**   Contains image data that requires a device such as a graphical display or graphical printer to view the information
- **Audio**   Contains audio information that requires an audio output device (such as a speaker) to present the information
- **Video**   Contains video information that requires the hardware/software needed to display moving images
- **Application**   Contains uninterpreted binary data, such as a program file, or information to be processed by a particular application
- **Multipart**   Contains at least two separate entities using independent data types
- **Message**   Contains an encapsulated message, such as those defined by RFC 822, which may themselves contain multiple parts of different types

Post Office Protocol

The Post Office Protocol, version 3 (POP3) is a service designed to provide mailbox services for client computers that are themselves not capable of performing transactions with SMTP servers. For the most part, the reason for the clients requiring a mailbox service is that they may not be continuously connected to the Internet and are therefore not capable of receiving messages any time a remote SMTP server wants to send them. A POP3 server is continuously connected and is always available to receive messages for offline users. The server then retains the messages in an electronic mailbox until the user connects to the server and requests them.

POP3 is similar to SMTP in that it relies on the TCP protocol for transport services (using well-known port 110) and communicates with clients using text-based commands and responses. As with SMTP, the client transmits commands to the server, but in POP3, there are only two possible response codes, +OK, indicating the successful completion of the command, and –ERR, indicating that an error has occurred to prevent the command from being executed. In the case of POP3, the server also sends the requested e-mail message data to the client, rather than the client sending outgoing messages to the server as in SMTP.

A POP3 client-server session consists of three distinct states: the *authorization* state, the *transaction* state, and the *update* state. These states are described in the following sections.

The Authorization State

The POP3 session begins when the client establishes a TCP connection with an active server. Once the TCP three-way handshake is complete, the server transmits a greeting to the client, usually in the form of an +OK reply. At this point, the session enters the authorization state, during which the client must identify itself to the server and perform an authentication process before it can access its mailbox. The POP3 standard defines two possible authentication mechanisms. One of these utilizes the USER and PASS commands, which the client uses to transmit a mailbox name and the password associated with it to the server in clear text. Another, more secure, mechanism uses the APOP command, which performs an encrypted authentication.

While in the authorization state, the only command permitted to the client other than authentication-related commands is QUIT, to which the server responds with a +OK reply before terminating the session without entering the transaction or update states.

Once the authentication process has been completed and the client granted access to its mailbox, the session enters the transaction state.

The Transaction State

Once the session has entered the transaction state, the client can begin to transmit the commands to the server with which it retrieves the mail messages waiting in its mailbox. When the server enters the transaction state, it assigns a number to each of the messages in the client's mailbox and takes note of each message's size. The transaction state commands use these message numbers to refer to the messages in the mailbox. The commands permitted while the session is in the transaction state are as follows. With the exception of the QUIT command, all of the following commands can be used only during the transaction state.

- **STAT**   Causes the server to transmit a *drop listing* of the mailbox contents to the client. The server responds with a single line containing an +OK reply, followed on the same line by the number of messages in the mailbox and the total size of all the messages, in bytes.

- **LIST**   Causes the server to transmit a *scan listing* of the mailbox contents to the client. The server responds with a multiline reply consisting of a +OK on the first line, followed by an additional line for each message in the mailbox, containing its message number and its size, in bytes, followed by a line containing only a period, which indicates the end of the listing. A client can also issue the LIST command with a parameter specifying a particular message number, which causes the server to reply with a scan listing of that message only.

- **RETR**   Causes the server to transmit a multiline reply containing an +OK reply, followed by the full contents of the message number specified as a parameter on the RETR command line. A separate line containing only a period serves as a delimiter, indicating the end of the message.

- **DELE**   Causes the server to mark the message represented by the message number specified as a parameter on the DELE command line as deleted. Once marked, clients can no longer retrieve the message, nor does it appear in drop listings and scan listings. However, the server does not actually delete the message until it enters the update state.

- **NOOP**   Performs no function other than to cause the server to generate an +OK reply.

- **RSET**   Causes the server to unmark any messages that have been previously marked as deleted during the session.

- **QUIT**   Causes the session to enter the update state prior to the termination of the connection.

The Update State

Once the client has finished retrieving messages from the mailbox and performing other transaction state activities, it transmits the QUIT command to the server, causing the session to transition to the update state. After entering the update state, the server deletes all of the messages that have been marked for deletion and releases its exclusive hold on the client's mailbox. If the server successfully deletes all of the marked messages, it transmits a +OK reply to the client and proceeds to terminate the TCP connection.

Internet Message Access Protocol

POP3 is a relatively simple protocol that provides clients with only the most basic mailbox service. In nearly all cases, the POP3 server is used only as a temporary storage medium; e-mail clients download their messages from the POP3 server and delete them from the server immediately afterward. It is possible to configure a client not to delete the messages after downloading them, but the client must then download them again during the next session. The Internet Message Access Protocol (IMAP) is a mailbox service that is designed to improve upon POP3's capabilities.

IMAP functions similarly to POP3 in that it uses text-based commands and responses, but the IMAP server provides considerably more functions than POP3. The biggest difference between IMAP and POP3 is that IMAP is designed to store e-mail messages on the server permanently, and IMAP provides a wider selection of commands that enable clients to access and manipulate their messages. Storing the mail on the server enables users to easily access their mail from any computer or from different computers.

Take, for example, an office worker who normally downloads her e-mail messages to her work computer using a POP3 server. She can check her mail from her home computer if she wants to by accessing the POP3 server from there, but any messages that she downloads to her home computer are normally deleted from the POP3 server, meaning that she will have no record of them on her office computer, where most of her mail is stored. Using IMAP, she can access all of her mail from either her home or office computer at any time, including all of the messages she has already read at both locations.

To make the storage of clients' e-mail on the server practical, IMAP includes a number of organizational and performance features, including the following:

- Users can create folders in their mailboxes and move their e-mail messages among the folders to create an organized storage hierarchy.

- Users can display a list of the messages in their mailboxes that contains only the header information and then select the messages they want to download in their entirety.

- Users can search for messages based on the contents of the header fields, the message subject, or the body of the message.

While IMAP can be a sensible solution for a corporate e-mail system in which users might benefit from its features, it is important to realize that IMAP requires considerably more in the way of network and system resources than POP3. In addition to the disk space required to store mail on the server indefinitely, IMAP requires more processing power to execute its many commands and consumes more network bandwidth because users remain connected to the server for much longer periods of time. For these reasons, POP3 remains the mailbox server of choice for Internet service providers, the largest consumers of these server products.

Part IV

CHAPTER

17

Windows

In the years since its initial release in 1985, Microsoft's Windows operating system has become the most prevalent operating system on the market. Window's familiar interface and ease of use enabled relatively unsophisticated users to install and maintain local area networks (LANs), making LAN technology a ubiquitous part of doing business. The various versions of Windows 8 (and 8.1), the latest incarnations of the operating system, are designed for use by mobile devices, stand-alone computers, and the most powerful servers.

The Role of Windows

Windows operates on a peer-to-peer model, in which each system can function both as a client and as a server. As a result, the same familiar interface is used in all Windows computers, both clients and servers, simplifying the learning curve for users as well as the development effort for software designers.

At the time of Windows NT's introduction, installing a server was largely a manual process in which you had to modify the server's configuration files in order to load the appropriate drivers. Windows, on the other hand, had an automated installation program much like those of most applications. While the process of setting up earlier networks required considerable expertise, many people discovered that a reasonably savvy PC user could install the Windows operating system (OS) and Windows applications with little difficulty.

A major factor that contributed to Windows' rise in popularity was its adoption of Transmission Control Protocol/Internet Protocol (TCP/IP) as its default protocols. As the Internet grew, a market developed for a platform that was easier to use than Unix that would run Internet and intranet server applications, and Windows fit the bill nicely. Eventually, major database engines were running on Windows servers, and the similarity of the client and server platforms streamlined the development process.

Versions

The first version of Windows NT (which was given the version number 3.1 to conform with the then-current version of Windows) was introduced in 1993. The motivation behind it was to create a new 32-bit OS from the ground up that left all vestiges of DOS behind. Although the interface was nearly identical in appearance to that of a Windows 3.1 system, NT was a completely new OS in many fundamental ways. Backward compatibility with existing applications is a factor that has always hindered advances in operating system design, and once Microsoft decided that running legacy programs was not to be a priority with Windows NT, it was free to implement radical changes.

The various versions of Windows NT fell into three distinct generations, based on the user interface. The first generation consisted of Windows NT 3.1, 3.5, and 3.51, all three of which use the same Windows 3.1–style interface. Version 3.1 used NetBEUI as its default protocol, which immediately limited its use to relatively small networks. TCP/IP and IPX support were available, but only through the STREAMS interface.

The second generation consisted of Windows NT 4.0, which was released in 1996 as an interim upgrade leading toward the major innovation that Microsoft began promising in 1993. NT 4 used the same interface introduced in Windows 95 and positioned the OS more positively as an Internet platform with the inclusion of the Internet Explorer web browser and Internet Information Services—a combination World Wide Web, FTP, and Gopher server.

The third generation was Windows 2000, which was the long-awaited release of the operating system that was originally code-named Cairo. The Windows 2000 interface was a refined version of the NT 4/Windows 95 graphical user interface (GUI), but the biggest improvement was the inclusion of Active Directory, an enterprise directory service that represented a quantum leap over the domain-based directory service included in Windows NT. Windows XP was the next-generation operating system that brought the DOS-based world of Windows 95, 98, and ME together with the Windows NT/2000 design to form a single product line that was suitable for both home and office computers.

Since Windows XP (which was no longer automatically updated after April 2014), there have been several new systems. Windows Vista was released in 2006 and included IPv6, comprehensive wireless networking, and 64-bit support. Vista received general criticism based on several factors, such as performance, which was criticized as not being much of an improvement over Windows XP. Many users resoundingly attacked the enhancements that were supposed to create additional security such as the product activation requirements and the persistent User Account Control (UAC) security feature. (UAC in Windows Vista required approval of each application before it could be utilized.) In retrospect, Windows Vista is often considered to be one of the biggest tech failures of the early years of the 21st century.

After the failure of Windows Vista, Microsoft introduced Windows 7 in 2009. Originally designed as an incremental upgrade, this version included a revamped UAC and much better performance and intuitive interface. It offered improved performance with the multicore processors that were becoming common, support for more modern graphics cards, media features, and fast boot times, as well as support for virtual hard disks.

In 2013, Microsoft introduced Windows 8. Windows 8 was visually quite different from earlier systems and was designed to work on touch screens (such as those on mobile devices) as well as with a mouse and keyboard. By combining the mobile-friendly screens with the Windows desktop with which most were familiar, the result was a system that pleased no one. Within a few months (by Microsoft standards), Windows 8.1 was released, which kept many of the features of the "mobile" screens but made the desktop more accessible to please desktop users.

Microsoft has traditionally released its server software in conjunction with its operating systems. However, starting with Windows Server 2008 (R2), it has sometimes changed release times. The latest version, Windows Server 2012 R2, however, was released at the same time as Windows 8.1 in October of 2013.

Service Packs

Traditionally, Microsoft has released regular updates to the Windows products in the form of service packs, which contain numerous fixes and upgrades in one package, using a single installation routine. Microsoft was one of the first software companies to adopt this update release method, which was a vast improvement over dozens of small patch releases (sometimes called *hot fixes*) that addressed single, specific issues. Apart from the inconvenience of downloading and installing many small patches, this update method was a technical support nightmare because it was difficult for both the user and the technician to know exactly which patches had been installed. Service packs were designed to detect the components installed on a Windows computer and install only the updates needed by those components.

Service packs consist of a single release for all of the various editions of an operating system. Service packs often consist of more than just bug fixes. They may include upgraded versions of operating system utilities, new features, or entirely new programs. All of the components are installed at the same time by the service pack's setup program. Service packs are sometimes (but not always) cumulative, meaning that each successive service pack for a particular product contains the contents of all of the previous service packs for that product. This simplifies the process of installing Windows on a new computer or updating one that hasn't been patched in some time, but it also causes the service pack releases to grow very large. Microsoft makes its service packs available as free downloads or on CD-ROMs, for which you must pay postage, handling, and media fees.

Again, traditionally, Microsoft's policy was to produce security fixes for both the current service pack and the previous one. IT people appreciated this because this allowed plenty of time to test the new update before it was deployed across their networks. However, when the first update to Windows 8.1 was released in April 2014, this policy seems to have changed. Microsoft stated that this update was mandatory and that all future security updates would require the April update to be installed. This policy and the update may signal the end of service packs as they previously been known.

Microsoft Technical Support

For the network administrator who is heavily committed to the use of Microsoft products, Microsoft TechNet was a subscription-based CD-ROM product that was an invaluable resource for technical information and product updates that ended in 2013. The monthly releases typically included six or more CD-ROMs containing resource kits, documentation, the entire Knowledge Base for all of the Microsoft products, and a lot of other material.

Starting in 2013, Microsoft replaced this program with a number of free resources, including the TechNet Evaluation Center located at http://technet.microsoft.com/en-US/evalcenter. These new services for IT professionals include TechNet Virtual Labs for free online testing. This environment is designed to evaluate new products; the documentation states that the testing can be completed online in less than two hours, so there is no need to install evaluation copies locally. Microsoft also has paid subscriptions for access to both current and prior software versions through its MSDN and MAPS programs. Both offer IT professionals the chance to download products, ask questions, test products, and take e-learning classes on Microsoft products.

In addition, Microsoft has created a program for students called *DreamSpark*. This program allows registered students to download software for testing and study. For small business startups, a similar program called *BizSpark* is available based on certain eligibility criteria. There are additional (free) courses available through the Microsoft Virtual Academy site at www.microsoftvirtualacademy.com.

Operating System Overview

Windows systems are modular operating systems that are designed to take advantage of the advanced capabilities built into the latest processors, while leaving behind the memory and storage constraints imposed by DOS-based operating systems. Early operating systems such as DOS were *monolithic*—that is, the entire OS consisted of a single functional unit, which made it difficult to upgrade and modify. By creating an OS composed of many separate components, Microsoft made it easier to upgrade and modify parts of the operating system without affecting other elements in the overall functionality of the whole.

Kernel Mode Components

The Windows operating systems are composed of components that run in one of two modes: *kernel mode* and *user mode* (see Figure 17-1). A component running in kernel mode has full access to the system's hardware resources via the *hardware abstraction layer* (HAL), which is a virtual

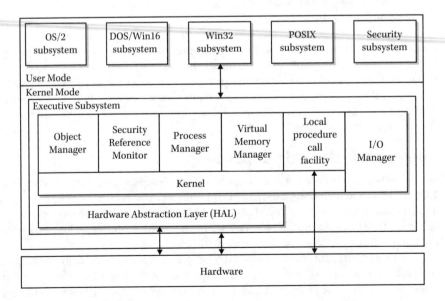

Figure 17-1   Windows architecture

interface that isolates the kernel from the computer hardware. Abstracting the kernel from the hardware makes it far easier to port the OS to different hardware platforms.

The OS kernel itself is responsible for delegating specific tasks to the system processor or processors and other hardware. Tasks consist of *processes,* broken down into *threads,* which are the smallest units that the kernel can schedule for execution by a processor. A thread is a sequence of instructions to which the kernel assigns a priority level that determines when it will be executed. When the computer has multiple processors, the kernel runs on all of them simultaneously, sharing access to specific memory areas and allocating threads to specific processors according to their priorities.

In addition to the HAL and the kernel, Windows' *executive services* run in kernel mode. These executive services consist of the following components.

Object Manager

Windows creates objects that function as abstract representations of operating system resources, such as hardware devices and file system entities. An *object* consists of information about the resource it represents and a list of *methods,* which are procedures used to access the object. A file object, for example, consists of information such as the file's name and methods describing the operations that can be performed on the file, such as open, close, and delete.

The Windows *Object Manager* maintains a hierarchical, global name space in which the objects are stored. For example, when the system loads a kernel mode device driver, it registers a device name with the Object Manager, such as \Device\CDRom0 for a CD-ROM drive or \Device\ Serial0 for a serial port. The objects themselves are stored in directories similar to those in a file system, but they are not part of any Windows file system. In addition to hardware devices, objects can reference both abstract and concrete entities, including the following:

- Files
- Directories
- Processes
- Threads
- Memory segments
- Semaphores

By using a standard format for all objects, regardless of the type of entities they represent, the Object Manager provides a unified interface for object creation, security, monitoring, and auditing. Access to objects in the name space is provided to system processes using *object handles,* which contain pointers to the objects and to access control information.

NOTE The kernel mode objects discussed here are not equivalent to the objects in the Active Directory database. They are two completely different hierarchies. Active Directory runs in user mode within the Windows security subsystem.

Usually, the only places that you see devices referred to by these object names are entries in the registry's HKEY_LOCAL_MACHINE\HARDWARE key and error messages such as those displayed in the infamous "blue screen of death." Applications typically run in the Win32

Part V

subsystem, which is a user mode component that cannot use internal Windows device names. Instead, the Win32 subsystem references devices using standard MS-DOS device names, like drive letters and port designations such as COM1. These MS-DOS names exist as objects in the Object Manager's name space, in a directory called \??, but they do not have the same properties as the original resources; they are actually only *symbolic links* to the equivalent Windows device names.

Security Reference Monitor

Every Windows object has an *access control list (ACL)* that contains *access control entries* (ACEs) that specify the *security identifiers* (SIDs) of users or groups that are to be permitted access to the object, as well as the specific actions that the user or group can perform. When a user successfully logs on to the computer, Windows creates a *security access token* (SAT) that contains the SIDs of the user and all the groups of which the user is a member. Whenever the user attempts to access an object, the *Security Reference Monitor* is responsible for comparing the SAT with the ACL to determine whether the user should be granted that access.

Process and Thread Manager

The *Process and Thread Manager* is responsible for creating and deleting the process objects that enable software to run on a Windows system. Each process (or software program) has its unique identifier, and a thread is the identifier for the part of the program that is currently running. A *process object* includes a virtual address space and a collection of resources allocated to the process, as well as threads containing the instructions that will be assigned to the system processors. When a machine has only one processor, each thread must be run by itself. After that thread has completed, the processor executes the next thread. On a machine with more than one processor, a program (application) with multiple threads can execute those multiple threads, with one thread being run on each processor.

Virtual Memory Manager

The ability to use virtual memory was one of the major PC computing advancements introduced in the Intel 80386 processor, and Windows NT and 2000 were designed around this capability. *Virtual memory* is the ability to use the computer's disk space as an extension to the physical memory installed in the machine.

Every process created on a Windows computer by the Process Manager is assigned a virtual address space that appears to be 4GB in size. The *Virtual Memory Manager* (VMM) is responsible for mapping that virtual address space to actual system memory, as needed, in 4KB units called *pages*. When there is not enough physical memory in the computer to hold all of the pages allocated by the running processes, the VMM swaps the least recently used pages to a file on the system's hard disk drive called Pagefile.sys. This swapping process is known as *memory paging*.

Local Procedure Call Facility

The environmental subsystems that run in Windows' user mode (such as the Win32 subsystem) are utilized by applications (also running in user mode) in a server-client relationship. The messages between the clients and servers are carried by the *local procedure call* (LPC) facility. Local procedure calls are essentially an internalized version of the remote procedure calls used for messaging between systems connected by a network.

When an application (functioning as a client) makes a call for a function that is provided by one of the environmental subsystems, a message containing that call is transmitted to the appropriate subsystem using LPCs. The subsystem (functioning as the server) receives the message and replies using the same type of message. The process is completely transparent to the application, which is not aware that the function is not implemented in its own code.

I/O Manager

The I/O Manager handles all of a Windows computer's input/output functions by providing a uniform environment for communication between the various drivers loaded on the machine. Using the layered architecture shown in Figure 17-2, the I/O Manager enables each driver to utilize the services of the drivers in the lower layers. For example, when an application needs to access a file on a drive, the I/O Manager passes an *I/O request packet* (IRP) generated by a file system driver down to a disk driver. Since the I/O Manager communicates with all of the drivers in the same way, the request can be satisfied without the file system having any direct knowledge of the disk device where the file is stored.

Window Manager

The Window Manager, along with the *Graphical Device Interface* (GDI), is responsible for creating the graphical user interface used by Windows applications. Applications make calls to Window Manager functions in order to create architectural elements on the screen, such as buttons and windows. In the same way, the Window Manager informs the application when the user manipulates screen elements by moving the cursor, clicking buttons, or resizing a window.

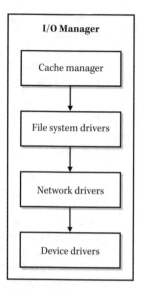

Figure 17-2   The I/O Manager provides a layered interface between Windows drivers.

User Mode Components

In addition to the kernel mode services, Windows has two types of protected subsystems that run in user mode: *environment subsystems* and *integral subsystems.* The environment subsystems enable Windows to run applications that were designed for various OS environments, such as Win32. Integral subsystems, like the security system, perform vital OS functions. User mode subsystems are isolated from each other and from the Windows executive services so that modifications to the subsystem code do not affect the fundamental operability of the OS. If a user mode component such as a subsystem or application should crash, the other subsystems and the Windows executive services are not affected.

The Win32 Subsystem

Win32 is the primary environment subsystem that provides support for all native Windows applications. All of the other environment subsystems included with Windows are optional and loaded only when a client application needs them, but Win32 is required and runs at all times. This is because it is responsible for handling the keyboard and mouse inputs and the display output for all of the other subsystems. Since they rely on Win32 API calls, the other environment subsystems can all be said to be clients of Win32.

The DOS/Win16 Subsystem

Unlike earlier versions of Windows, Windows 2000 and NT did not run a DOS kernel, and as a result, they could not shell out to a DOS session. Instead, 2000 and NT emulated DOS using a subsystem that creates *virtual DOS machines* (VDMs). Every DOS application used a separate

VDM that emulated an Intel $x86$ processor in Virtual 86 mode (even on a non-Intel system). All of the application's instructions ran natively within the VDM except for I/O functions, which were emulated using *virtual device drivers* (VDDs). VDDs converted the DOS I/O functions into standard Windows API calls and fed them to the I/O Manager, which satisfied the calls using the standard Windows device drivers.

NOTE Because of this emulation, not all DOS programs are guaranteed to run optimally.

Services

A *service* is a program or other component that Windows loads with the OS before a user logs on or sees the desktop interface. Services usually load automatically and permit no interference from the system user as they're loading. This is in contrast to other mechanisms that load programs automatically, such as the Startup program group. A user with appropriate rights can start, stop, and pause services using the Services console or the NET command and also specify whether a particular service should load when the system starts, not load at all, or require a manual startup. See Figure 17-3 for the options.

Users without administrative rights cannot control the services at all, which makes the services a useful tool for network administrators. You can, for example, configure a workstation to load a particular service at startup, and it will run whether a user logs on or not. The Server service, for example, which enables network users to access the computer's shares, loads automatically by default. Even if no one logs on to the computer, it is possible to access its shares from the network.

The Windows Networking Architecture

Networking is an integral part of Windows, and the operating systems use a modular networking architecture that provides a great deal of flexibility for the network administrator. While not perfectly analogous to the Open Systems Interconnection (OSI) reference model, the Windows networking architecture is structured in layers that provide interchangeability of modules such as network adapter drivers and protocols. Figure 17-4 shows the basic structure of the networking stack.

Windows relies on two primary interfaces to separate the basic networking functions, called the *NDIS interface* and *Transport Driver Interface* (TDI). Between these two interfaces are the protocol suites that provide transport services between computers on the network: TCP/IP, NetBEUI, and IPX. Although they have different features, these three sets of protocols are

```
C:\Users\Name>NET

The syntax of this command is:
 NET
   [ ACCOUNTS | COMPUTER | CONFIG | CONTINUE |
     FILE | GROUP | HELP | HELPMSG | LOCALGROUP |
     PAUSE | SESSION | SHARE | START | STATISTICS |
     STOP | TIME | USE | USER | VIEW ]
```

Figure 17-3   The NET command is used from the command prompt.

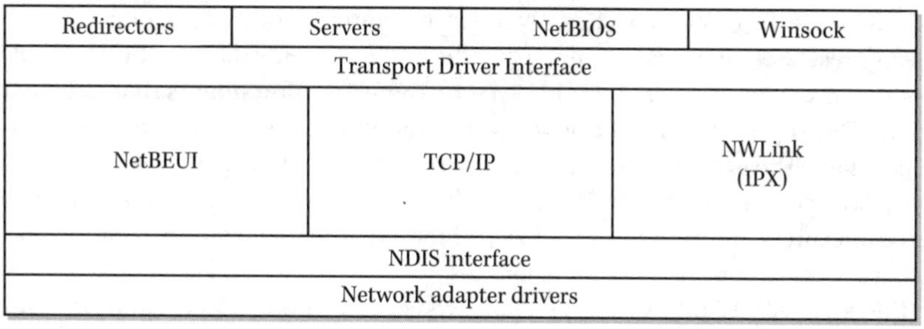

Redirectors	Servers	NetBIOS	Winsock
Transport Driver Interface			
NetBEUI	TCP/IP		NWLink (IPX)
NDIS interface			
Network adapter drivers			

Figure 17-4   The Windows networking architecture

interchangeable when it comes to basic networking services. A Windows computer can use any of these protocols or all of them simultaneously. The TDI and NDIS interfaces enable the components operating above and below them to address whichever protocol is needed to perform a particular task.

The NDIS Interface

The Network Driver Interface Specification (NDIS) is a standard developed jointly by Microsoft and 3Com that defines an interface between the network layer protocols and the media access control (MAC) sublayer of the data link layer protocol. The NDIS interface lies between the network adapter drivers and the protocol drivers. Protocols do not communicate directly with the network adapter; instead, they go through the NDIS interface. This enables a Windows computer to have any number of network adapters and any number of protocols installed, and any protocol can communicate with any adapter.

The latest version of NDIS is 6.10, which appeared in Windows Vista. NDIS 6.30 is included in Windows 8, and NDIS 6.40 with Windows 8.1. It is implemented on a Windows 8 system in two parts: the *NDIS wrapper* (Ndis.sys) and the *NDIS MAC driver*. The NDIS wrapper is not device specific; it contains common code that surrounds the MAC drivers and provides the interface between the network adapter drivers and the protocol drivers installed in the computer. This replaces the Protocol Manager (PROTMAN) used by other NDIS versions to regulate access to the network adapter.

The NDIS MAC driver is device specific and provides the code needed for the system to communicate with the network interface adapter. This includes the mechanism for selecting the hardware resources the device uses, such as the IRQ and I/O port address. All of the network interface adapters in a Windows system must have an NDIS driver, which is provided by virtually all of the manufacturers producing NICs today.

The Transport Driver Interface

The Transport Driver Interface (TDI) performs roughly the same basic function as the NDIS wrapper but higher up in the networking stack. The TDI functions as the interface between the protocol drivers and the components operating above them, such as the server and the redirectors. Traffic moving up and down the stack passes through the interface and can be directed to any of the installed protocols or other components.

Part V

Above the TDI, Windows has several more components that applications use to access network resources in various ways, using the TDI as the interface to the protocol drivers. Because Windows is a peer-to-peer operating system, there are components that handle traffic running in both directions. The most basic of these components are the *Workstation* and *Server* services, which enable the system to access network resources and provide network clients with access to local resources (respectively). Also at this layer are *application programming interfaces* (APIs), such as NetBIOS and Windows Sockets, which provide applications running on the system special access to certain network resources.

Effective with Windows 8, which has two working modes, Metro and Desktop, TDI is being phased out. (You may see a message "TDI filters and LSPs are not allowed" when working in Metro mode.) Most apps that worked in Windows 7 also work in Desktop mode, including LSP. However, Metro mode cannot use the normal Win API and instead uses WinRT, which has been developed especially for Windows 8.

> **NOTE** Layer Service Protocols is a retired Microsoft Windows service that could insert itself into the TCP/IP protocol stack and modify and intercept both inbound and outbound traffic.

The Workstation Service

When you open a file or print a document in an application, the process is the same whether the file or printer is part of the local system or on the network, as far as the user and the application are concerned. The Workstation service determines whether the requested file or printer is local or on the network and sends the request to the appropriate driver. By providing access to network resources in this way, the Workstation service is essentially the client half of Windows' client-server capability.

The Workstation service consists of two modules: Services.exe, the Service Control Manager, which functions as the user mode interface for all services; and the Windows network redirector. When an application requests access to a file, the request goes to the I/O Manager, which passes it to the appropriate file system driver. The *redirector* is also a file system driver, but instead of providing access to a local drive, the redirector transmits the request down through the protocol stack to the appropriate network resource. The I/O Manager treats a redirector no differently from any other file system drivers. Windows installs a redirector for the Microsoft Windows network by default.

The Multiple UNC Provider

In the case of a system with multiple network clients (and multiple redirectors), Windows uses one of two mechanisms for determining which redirector it should use, depending on how an application formats its requests for network resources. The multiple UNC provider (MUP) is used for applications that use Uniform Naming Convention (UNC) names to specify the desired resource, and the multiprovider router (MPR) is used for applications that use Win32 network APIs.

The UNC defines the format that Windows uses for identifying network items. UNC names take the following form:

*server**share*

The Multiprovider Router

For applications that request access to network resources using the Win32 network APIs (also known as the WNet APIs), the multiprovider router determines which redirector should process the requests. In addition to a redirector, a network client installed on a Windows computer includes a *provider DLL* that functions as an interface between the MPR and the redirector. The MPR passes the requests that it receives from applications to the appropriate provider DLLs, which pass them to the redirectors.

The Server Service

Just as the Workstation service provides network client capabilities, the Server service enables other clients on the network to access the computer's local resources. When the redirector on a client system transmits a request for access to a file on a server, the receiving system passes the request up the protocol stack to the Server service. The Server service is a file system driver (called Srv.sys) that is started by the Service Control Manager, just like the Workstation service, that operates just above the TDI. When the Server service receives a request for access to a file, it generates a read request and sends it to the appropriate local file system driver (such as the NTFS or FAT driver) through the I/O Manager. The local file system driver accesses the requested file in the usual manner and returns it to the Server service, which transmits it across the network to the client. The Server service also provides support for printer sharing, as well as remote procedure calls (RPCs) and named pipes, which are other mechanisms used by applications to communicate over the network.

APIs

Services are not the only components that interact with the TDI on a Windows system. Application programming interfaces, such as NetBIOS and Windows Sockets, also send and receive data through the TDI, enabling certain types of applications to communicate with other network systems without using the Server and Workstation services. Windows also supports other APIs that operate higher up in the stack and use the standard services to reach the TDI.

NetBIOS

NetBIOS was an integral component of Microsoft Windows networking through Windows XP because it provides the name space used to identify the domains, computers, and shares on the network. Because of its dependence on NetBIOS, Windows supports it in all of its protocols. NetBEUI is inherently designed for use with NetBIOS communications, and the NetBIOS over TCP/IP (NetBT) standards defined by the Internet Engineering Task Force (IETF) enable its use with the TCP/IP protocols. Because NetBIOS could be used to gather information about your network (and each computer), many people disable it in both Windows 7 and Windows 8.

NOTE In today's networks, NetBIOS is often used for file and print sharing on a local network. This leaves an open path for hackers. You can remove the risk in two ways. Disable NetBIOS through your network connection settings on your Ethernet adapter or disable the ports used by NetBIOS:
UDP 137, the NetBIOS name service port
UDP 138, the NetBIOS datagram service port
TCP 139, the NetBIOS session service port

Windows Sockets

The Windows Sockets specification defines one of the APIs that is most commonly used by applications because it is the accepted standard for Internet network access. Web browsers, FTP clients, and other Internet client and server applications all use Windows Sockets (Winsock) to gain access to network resources. Unlike NetBIOS, Winsock does not support all of the Windows protocols. While it can be used with NWLink (IPX), the overwhelming majority of Winsock applications use TCP/IP exclusively. As with NetBIOS, Winsock is implemented in Windows as a kernel mode emulator just above the TDI and a user mode driver, called Wsock32.dll.

File Systems

The FAT file system was a holdover from the DOS days that the developers of the original Windows NT product were seeking to transcend. While an adequate solution for a workstation, the 16-bit FAT file system used by DOS cannot support the large volumes typically required on servers, and it lacks any sort of access control mechanism.

FAT16

The traditional DOS file system divided a hard disk drive into volumes that were composed of uniformly sized clusters and used a file allocation table (FAT) to keep track of the data stored in each cluster. Each directory on the drive contained a list of the files in that directory and, in addition to the filename and other attributes, specified the entry in the FAT that represented the cluster containing the beginning of the file. That first FAT entry contained a reference to another entry that references the file's second cluster, the second entry references the third, and so on, until enough clusters are allocated to store the entire file. This is known as a *FAT chain*.

NOTE It was only with the introduction of the FAT32 file system that the traditional FAT file system came to be called FAT16. In most cases, references to a FAT drive without a numerical identifier refer to a FAT16 drive.

The other limiting factor of the FAT file system is that as clusters grow larger, more drive space is wasted because of slack. *Slack* is the fraction of a cluster left empty when the last bit of data in a file fails to completely fill the last cluster in the chain. When 3KB of data from a file is left to store, for example, a volume with 4KB clusters will contain 1KB of slack, while a volume with 64KB clusters will waste 61KB. Windows NT is designed to be a server OS as well as a workstation OS, and servers are naturally expected to have much larger drives. The amount of slack space and the 4GB limit on volume size are not acceptable for a server OS.

The other major shortcoming of the FAT file system is the amount of information about each file that is stored on the disk drive. In addition to the data itself, a FAT drive maintains the following information about each file:

- **File name**   Limited to an eight-character name plus a three-character extension
- **Attributes**   Contains four usable file attributes: Read-only, Hidden, System, and Archive
- **Date/time**   Specifies the date and time that the file was created or last modified
- **Size**   Specifies the size of the file, in bytes

FAT32

As hard disk drive capacities grew over the years, the limitations of the FAT file system became more of a problem. To address the problem, Microsoft created a file system that used 32-bit FAT entries instead of 16-bit ones. The larger entries meant that there could be more clusters on a drive. The results were that the maximum size of a FAT32 volume is 2 terabytes (or 2,048GB) instead of 2GB for a FAT16 drive, and the clusters can be much smaller, thus reducing the waste because of slack space.

The FAT32 file system was introduced in the Windows 95 OSR2 release and was also included in Windows 98, Windows ME, and Windows 2000. FAT32 supported larger volumes and smaller clusters, but it did not provide any appreciable change in performance, and it still did not have the access control capabilities needed for network servers like NTFS does.

NTFS

NTFS was the file system intended to be used through Windows 7. Without it, you cannot install Active Directory or implement the file and directory-based permissions needed to secure a drive for network use. Because it uses a completely different structure than FAT drives, you cannot create NTFS drives using the FDISK utility.

In the NTFS file system, files take the form of *objects* that consist of a number of *attributes*. Unlike DOS, in which the term *attribute* typically refers only to the Read-only, System, Hidden, and Archive flags, NTFS treats all of the information regarding the file as an attribute, including the flags, the dates, the size, the filename, and even the file data itself. NTFS also differs from FAT in that the attributes are stored with the file, instead of in a separate directory listing.

The equivalent structure to the FAT on an NTFS drive is called the *master file table* (MFT). Unlike FAT, however, the MFT contains more than just pointers to other locations on the disk. In the case of relatively small files (up to approximately 1,500 bytes), all of the attributes are included in the MFT, including the file data. When larger amounts of data need to be stored, additional disk clusters called *extents* are allocated, and pointers are included with the file's attributes in the MFT. The attributes stored in the MFT are called *resident attributes*; those stored in extents are called *nonresident attributes*.

In addition to the four standard DOS file attributes, an NTFS file includes a Compression flag; two dates/times specifying when the file was created and when it was last modified; and a security descriptor that identifies the owner of the file, lists the users and groups that are permitted to access it, and specifies what access they are to be granted.

Resilient File System

Starting with Windows Server 2012 and Windows Server 8, Microsoft has introduced Resilient File System (ReFS), an improved system that has the ability to handle much higher volumes and can share storage pools across machines. It is built on the NTFS, and one of its main advantages is the ability to detect all forms of disk corruption. Primarily designed for storage at this point, it cannot boot an operating system or be used on removable media.

The Windows Registry

The registry is the database where Windows stores nearly all of its system configuration data. As a system or network administrator, you'll be working with the registry in a variety of ways, since many of the Windows configuration tools function by modifying entries in the registry. The registry is a hierarchical database that is displayed in most registry editor applications as an expandable tree, not unlike a directory tree. At the root of the tree are five containers, called *keys,* with the following names:

- **HKEY_CLASSES_ROOT**   Contains information on file associations—that is, associations between filename extensions and applications.
- **HKEY_CURRENT_USER**   Contains configuration information specific to the user currently logged on to the system. This key is the primary component of a user profile.
- **HKEY_LOCAL_MACHINE**   Contains information on the hardware and software installed in the computer, the system configuration, and the Security Accounts Manager database. The entries in this key apply to all users of the system.
- **HKEY_USERS**   Contains information on the currently loaded user profiles, including the profile for the user who is currently logged on and the default user profile.
- **HKEY_CURRENT_CONFIG**   Contains hardware profile information used during the system boot sequence.

In most cases, you work with the entries in the HKEY_LOCAL_MACHINE and HKEY_CURRENT_USER keys (often abbreviated as the HKLM and HKCU, respectively) when you configure a Windows system, whether you are aware of it or not. When the keys are saved as files, as in the case of user profiles, they're often referred to as *hives.* When you expand one of these keys, you see a series of *subkeys,* often in several layers. The keys and subkeys function as organizational containers for the registry *entries,* which contain the actual configuration data for the system. A registry entry consists of three components: the *value name,* the *value type,* and the *value* itself.

The value name identifies the entry for which a value is specified. The value type specifies the nature of the data stored in the entry, such as whether it contains a binary value, an alphanumeric string of a given size, or multiple values. The value types found in the registry are as follows:

- **REG_SZ**   Indicates that the value consists of a string of alphanumeric characters. Many of the user-configurable values in the registry are of this type.
- **REG_DWORD**   Indicates that the value consists of a 4-byte numerical value used to specify information such as device parameters, service values, and other numeric configuration parameters.
- **REG_MULTI_SZ**   Same as the REG_SZ value type, except that the entry contains multiple string values.
- **REG_EXPAND_SZ**   Same as the REG_SZ value type, except that the entry contains a variable (such as *%SystemRoot%*) that must be replaced when the value is accessed by an application.
- **REG_BINARY**   Indicates that the value consists of raw binary data, usually used for hardware configuration information. You should not modify these entries manually unless you are familiar with the function of every binary bit in the value.
- **REG_FULL_RESOURCE_DESCRIPTOR**   Indicates that the value holds configuration data for hardware devices in the form of an information record with multiple fields.

The registry hierarchy is large and complex, and the names of its keys and entries are often cryptic. Locating the correct entry can be difficult, and the values are often less than intuitive.

When you edit the registry manually, you must be careful to supply the correct value for the correct entry or the results can be catastrophic. An incorrect registry modification can halt the computer or prevent it from booting, forcing you to reinstall Windows from scratch.

Because of the registry's sensitivity to improper handling, selecting the proper tool to modify it is crucial. The trade-off in Windows' registry editing tools is between a safe, easy-to-use interface with limited registry access and comprehensive access using a less intuitive interface. The following sections examine the various registry editing tools included with Windows.

The Control Panel

Although it isn't evident from the interface, most of the functions in the Windows Control Panel work by modifying settings in the registry. The Control Panel's graphical interface provides users with simplified access to the registry and prevents them from introducing incorrect values due to typographical errors. You can also use Windows' security mechanisms to prevent unauthorized access to certain registry settings through the Control Panel. The main disadvantage of using the Control Panel to modify the registry is that it provides user access to only a small fraction of the registry's settings.

The System Policy Editor

System policies are collections of registry settings saved in a *policy file* that you can configure a Windows computer to load whenever a user logs on to the system or the network. You can create different sets of policies for each of your network users so that when John Doe logs on to a workstation, his customized registry settings are downloaded to the computer and loaded automatically. Windows includes a tool called the System Policy Editor that you can use to create policy files; you can also use it to modify the registry directly. Like the Control Panel, the System Policy Editor uses a graphical interface to set registry values, but it is far more configurable than the Control Panel and can provide access to a great many more registry entries.

The system policies that the System Policy Editor lists in its hierarchical display are derived from a file called a *policy template*. The template is an ASCII text file with an .adm extension that uses a special format to define how each policy should appear in the System Policy Editor and which registry settings each policy should modify. Windows includes several template files that define policies for a wide range of system settings, some of which are also configurable through the Control Panel. Because creating a new system policy is simply a matter of creating a new template, software developers can include with their products template files that define application-specific system policies. You can also create your own templates to modify other registry settings.

The process of setting values for a system policy by using the System Policy Editor consists of navigating through the hierarchical display and selecting a policy. Some policies consist of a single feature that you can toggle on and off, while others have additional controls in the form of check boxes, pull-down menus, or data entry fields. To create a policy file, you select the policies you want to set, specify values for them, and then save them to a file with a .pol extension.

The System Policy Editor can also directly modify the Windows registry, however. When you select File | Open Registry, the program connects to the registry on the local machine. When you configure a policy, the program applies the necessary changes directly to the registry. In addition, when you choose File | Connect, you can select another Windows computer on the network and modify its registry from your remote location.

The use of customizable template files makes the System Policy Editor a far more comprehensive registry-editing tool than the Control Panel. You can specify values for a wider

Part V

range of registry entries, while still retaining the advantages of the graphical interface. Because the changes that the System Policy Editor makes to the registry are controlled by the policy template, the possibility of a misspelled value in a data entry field still exists, but the chances of an incorrect value damaging the system is far less than when editing the registry manually.

Group Policies

Windows group policies are the next step in the evolution of the system policies found in Windows NT and 98. Group policies include all of the registry modification capabilities found in NT system policies, plus a great deal more, such as the ability to install and update software, implement disk quotas, and redirect folders on user workstations to network shares. While NT system policies are associated with domain users and groups, Windows group policies are associated with Active Directory objects, such as sites, domains, and organizational units.

The Registry Editors

Windows includes a Registry Editor, called regedit.exe, that provides direct access to the entire registry. There are many Windows features you can configure using the Registry Editor that are not accessible by any other administrative interface. These programs are the most powerful and comprehensive means of modifying registry settings in Windows and also the most dangerous. These editors do not supply friendly names for the registry entries, and they do not use pull-down menus or check boxes to specify values. You must locate (or create) the correct entry and supply the correct value in the proper format, or the results can be wildly unpredictable. Windows installs the Registry Editor with the OS, but it does not create shortcuts for them in the Start menu or on the desktop. You must launch the Registry Editor by using the Run dialog box, by using Windows Explorer, or by creating your own shortcuts. Like the System Policy Editor, the Registry Editor enables you to connect to another Windows system on the network and access its registry.

NOTE Making registry adjustments can cause major issues with your computer. Registry editing should be done only after a complete registry backup.

Optional Windows Networking Services

In addition to its core services, Windows, particularly in the Server versions, includes a large collection of optional services that you can choose to install either with the OS or at any time afterward. Some of these services are discussed in the following sections.

Active Directory

Active Directory, the enterprise directory service included with most Windows Server products, is a hierarchical, replicated directory service designed to support networks of virtually unlimited size. For more information on Active Directory, see Chapter 18.

Microsoft DHCP Server

Unlike NetBEUI and IPX, using the TCP/IP protocols on a network requires that each computer be configured with a unique IP address, as well as other important settings. A Dynamic Host Configuration Protocol (DHCP) server is an application designed to automatically supply client systems with TCP/IP configuration settings as needed, thus eliminating a tedious manual network administration chore.

Microsoft DNS Server

The Domain Name System (DNS) facilitates the use of familiar names for computers on a TCP/IP network instead of the IP addresses they use to communicate. Designed for use on the Internet, DNS servers resolve domain names (Internet domain names, not NT domain names) into IP addresses, either by consulting their own records or by forwarding the request to another DNS server. The DNS server included with Windows has a server to function on the Internet in this capacity.

Windows Internet Naming Service

Windows Internet Naming Service (WINS) is another service that supports the use of TCP/IP on a Windows network. Windows 9x and NT identified systems using NetBIOS names, but in order to transmit a packet to a machine with a given name using TCP/IP, the sender had to first discover the IP address associated with that name. WINS is essentially a database server that stores the NetBIOS names of the systems on the network and their associated IP addresses. When a system wants to transmit, it sends a query to a WINS server containing the NetBIOS name of the destination system, and the WINS server replies with its IP address.

Part V

CHAPTER

18 Active Directory

The domain-based directory service used by Windows once came under fire for its inability to scale up to support larger networks. An enterprise network that consists of multiple domains is limited in its communication between those domains to the trust relationships that administrators must manually establish between them. In addition, because each domain must be maintained individually, the account administration process is complicated enormously. Since the original Windows NT 3.1 release in 1993, Microsoft promised to deliver a more robust directory service better suited for use on large networks, and finally Microsoft accomplished the task in Windows 2000 with Active Directory.

Active Directory (AD) is an object-oriented, hierarchical, distributed directory services database system that provides a central storehouse for information about the hardware, software, and human resources of an entire enterprise network. Based on the general principles of the X.500 global directory standards, network users are represented by objects in the Active Directory tree. Administrators can use those objects to grant users access to resources anywhere on the network, which are also represented by objects in the tree. Unlike a flat, domain-based structure for a directory, Active Directory expands the structure into multiple levels. The fundamental unit of organization in the Active Directory database is still the domain, but a group of domains can now be consolidated into a tree, and a group of trees can be consolidated into a forest. Administrators can manage multiple domains simultaneously by manipulating the tree and can manage multiple trees simultaneously by manipulating a forest.

A directory service is not only a database for the storage of information, however. It also includes the services that make that information available to users, applications, and other services. Active Directory includes a global catalog that makes it possible to search the entire directory for particular objects using the value of a particular attribute. Applications can use the directory to control access to network resources, and other directory services can interact with AD using a standardized interface and the Lightweight Directory Access Protocol (LDAP).

Active Directory Architecture

Active Directory is composed of objects, which represent the various resources on a network, such as users, user groups, servers, printers, and applications. An *object* is a collection of attributes that define the resource, give it a name, list its capabilities, and specify who should be permitted to use it. Some of an object's attributes are assigned automatically when they're created, such as the globally unique identifier (GUID) assigned to each one, while others are supplied by the network administrator. A user object, for example, has attributes that store information about the user it represents, such as an account name, password, telephone number, and e-mail address. Attributes also contain information about the other objects with which the user interacts, such as the groups of which the user is a member. There are many different types of objects, each of which has different attributes, depending on its functions.

Active Directory provides administrators and users with a global view of the network. Earlier Windows NT directory services could use multiple domains, but instead of managing the users of each domain separately, for example, as in Windows NT 4.0, AD administrators create a single object for each user and can use it to grant that user access to resources in any domain.

Each type of object is defined by an object class stored in the *directory schema*. The schema specifies the attributes that each object must have, the optional attributes it may have, the type of data associated with each attribute, and the object's place in the directory tree. The schema are themselves stored as objects in Active Directory, called *class schema objects* and *attribute schema objects*. A class schema object contains references to the attribute schema objects that together form the *object class*. This way, an attribute is defined only once, although it can be used in many different object classes.

The schema is extensible so that applications and services developed by Microsoft or third parties can create new object classes or add new attributes to existing object classes. This enables applications to use Active Directory to store information specific to their functions and provide that information to other applications as needed. For example, rather than maintain its own directory, an e-mail server application such as Microsoft Exchange can modify the Active Directory schema so that it can use AD to authenticate users and store their e-mail information.

Object Types

There are two basic types of objects in Active Directory, called *container objects* and *leaf objects*. A container object is simply an object that stores other objects, while a leaf object stands alone and cannot store other objects. Container objects essentially function as the branches of the tree, and leaf objects grow off of the branches. Active Directory uses container objects called *organizational units* (OUs) to store other objects. Containers can store other containers or leaf objects, such as users and computers. The guiding rule of directory tree design is that rights and permissions flow downward through the tree. Assigning a permission to a container object means that, by default, all of the objects in the container inherit that permission. This enables administrators to control access to network resources by assigning rights and permissions to a single container rather than to many individual users.

By default, an Active Directory tree is composed of objects that represent the users and computers on the network, the logical entities used to organize them, and the folders and printers they regularly access. These objects, their functions, and the icons used to represent them in tools such as Active Directory Users and Computers are listed in Table 18-1.

Object Type	Icon	Function
Domain		Container object that stores organizational unit objects and their contents.
Organizational unit		Container object that stores computer, user, and group objects with the tree structure.
User		Leaf object that represents a network user and stores identification and authentication data about that user.
Computer		Leaf object that represents a computer on the network, stores information about the computer, and provides the machine account needed for the system to log on to the domain.
Contact		Leaf object that represents a user outside the domain for specific purposes, such as e-mail delivery; does not enable the user to log on to the domain.
Group		Container object that represents logical groupings of users, computers, and/or other groups that are independent of the Active Directory tree structure. Group members can be located in any organizational unit or domain in the tree.

Table 18-1   Some Active Directory Object Types

Object Naming

Every object in the Active Directory database is uniquely identified by a name that can be expressed in several forms. The naming conventions are based on the Lightweight Directory Access Protocol (LDAP) standard defined in RFC 2251, published by the Internet Engineering Task Force (IETF). The *distinguished name* (DN) of an object consists of the name of the domain in which the object is located, plus the path down the domain tree through the container objects to the object itself. The part of an object's name that is stored in the object is called its *relative distinguished name* (RDN).

NOTE The Lightweight Directory Access Protocol is an adaptation of the Directory Access Protocol (DAP) designed for use by X.500 directories. Active Directory domain controllers and several other directory services use LDAP to communicate with each other.

By specifying the name of the object and the names of its parent containers up to the root of the domain, the object is uniquely identified within the domain, even if the object has the same name as another object in a different container. Thus, if you have two users, called John Doe and Jane Doe, you can use the RDN jdoe for both of them. As long as they are located in different containers, they will have different DNs.

Part V

Canonical Names

Most Active Directory applications refer to objects using their canonical names. A *canonical name* is a DN in which the domain name comes first, followed by the names of the object's parent containers working down from the root of the domain and separated by forward slashes, followed by the object's RDN, as follows:

```
mgh.com/sales/inside/jdoe
```

In this example, jdoe is a user object in the inside container, which is in the sales container, which is in the mgh.com domain.

LDAP Notation

The same DN can also be expressed in LDAP notation, which would appear as follows:

```
cn=jdoe,ou=inside,ou=sales,dc=mgh,dc=com
```

This notation reverses the order of the object names, starting with the RDN on the left and the domain name on the right. The elements are separated by commas and include the LDAP abbreviations that define each type of element. These abbreviations are as follows:

- **cn** Common name
- **ou** Organizational unit
- **dc** Domain component

In most cases, LDAP names do not include the abbreviations, and they can be omitted without altering the uniqueness or the functionality of the name. It is also possible to express an LDAP name in a URL format, as defined in RFC 1959, which appears as follows:

```
ldap://cz1.mgh.com/cn=jdoe,ou=inside,ou=sales,dc=mgh,dc=com
```

This format differs in that the name of a server hosting the directory service must appear immediately following the ldap:// identifier, followed by the same LDAP name as shown earlier. This notation enables users to access Active Directory information using a standard web browser.

Globally Unique Identifiers

In addition to its DN, every object in the tree has a *globally unique identifier* (GUID), which is a 128-bit number that is automatically assigned by the Directory System Agent when the object is created. Unlike the DN, which changes if you move the object to a different container or rename it, the GUID is permanent and serves as the ultimate identifier for an object.

User Principal Names

Distinguished names are used by applications and services when they communicate with Active Directory, but they are not easy for users to understand, type, or remember. Therefore, each user object has a *user principle name* (UPN) that consists of a username and a suffix, separated by an @ symbol, just like the standard Internet e-mail address format defined in RFC 822. This name provides users with a simplified identity on the network and insulates them from the need to know their place in the domain tree hierarchy.

In most cases, the username part of the UPN is the user object's RDN, and the suffix is the DNS name of the domain in which the user object is located. However, if your network consists of multiple domains, you can opt to use a single domain name as the suffix for all of your users' UPNs. This way, the UPN can remain unchanged even if you move the user object to a different domain.

The UPN is an internal name that is used only on the Windows 2000 network, so it doesn't have to conform to the user's Internet e-mail address. However, using your network's e-mail domain name as the suffix is a good idea so that users have to remember only one address for accessing e-mail and logging on to the network.

NOTE You can use the Active Directory Domains and Trusts console to specify alternative UPN suffixes so that all of your users can log on to the network using the same suffix.

Domains, Trees, and Forests

Windows has always based its networking paradigm on domains, and all but small networks require multiple domains to support their users. Active Directory makes it easier to manage multiple domains by combining them into larger units called *trees* and *forests*. When you create a new Active Directory database by promoting a server to domain controller, you create the first domain in the first tree of a new forest. If you create additional domains in the same tree, they all share the same schema, configuration, and global catalog server (GCS, a master list directory of Active Directory objects that provides users with an overall view of the entire directory) and are connected by transitive trust relationships.

Trust relationships are how domains interact with each other to provide a unified network directory. If Domain A trusts Domain B, the users in Domain B can access the resources in Domain A. In Windows NT domains, trust relationships operate in one direction only and must be explicitly created by network administrators. If you want to create a full network of trusts between three domains, for example, you must create six separate trust relationships so that each domain trusts every other domain. Active Directory automatically creates trust relationships between domains in the same tree. These trust relationships flow in both directions, are authenticated using the Kerberos security protocol, and are *transitive,* meaning that if Domain A trusts Domain B and Domain B trusts Domain C, then Domain A automatically trusts Domain C. A tree, therefore, is a single administrative unit that encompasses a number of domains. The administrative nightmare of manually creating trust relationships between large numbers of domains is diminished, and users are able to access resources on other domains.

The domains in a tree share a contiguous name space. Unlike a Windows NT domain, which has a single, flat name, an Active Directory domain has a hierarchical name that is based on the DNS name space, such as mycorp.com. Sharing a contiguous name space means that if the first domain in a tree is given the name mycorp.com, the subsequent domains in that tree will have names that build on the parent domain's name, such as sales.mycorp.com and mis.mycorp.com (see Figure 18-1).

The parent-child relationships in the domain hierarchy are limited solely to the sharing of a name space and the trust relationships between them. Unlike the container hierarchy within a domain, rights and permissions do not flow down the tree from domain to domain.

In most cases, a single tree is sufficient for a network of almost any size. However, it is possible to create multiple trees and join them in a unit known as a *forest*. All of the domains in a forest, including those in separate trees, share the same schema, configuration, and GCS. Every domain

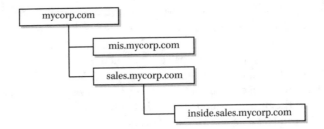

Figure 18-1 Active Directory parent and child domains

in a forest has a transitive trust relationship with the other domains, regardless of the trees they are in. The only difference between the trees in a forest is that they have separate name spaces. Each tree has its own root domain and child domains that build off of its name. The first domain created in a forest is known as the *forest root domain*.

The most common reason for having multiple trees is the merging of two organizations, both of which already have established domain names that cannot be readily assimilated into one tree. Users are able to access resources in other trees because the trust relationships between domains in different trees are the same as those within a single tree. It is also possible to create multiple forests on your network, but the need for this is rare.

Different forests do not share the same schema, configuration, and GCS, nor are trust relationships automatically created between forests. It is possible to manually create unidirectional trusts between domains in different forests, just as you would on a Windows NT network. In most cases, though, the primary reason for creating multiple forests is to completely isolate two areas of the network and prevent interaction between them.

DNS and Active Directory

Windows NT is based on NetBIOS and uses a NetBIOS name server called *Windows Internet Naming Service* (WINS) to locate computers on the network and resolve their names into IP addresses. The primary limitation of NetBIOS and WINS is that they use a flat name space, whereas Active Directory's name space is hierarchical. The AD name space is based on that of the Domain Name System (DNS), so the directory uses DNS servers instead of WINS to resolve names and locate domain controllers. You must have at least one DNS server running on your network in order for Active Directory to function properly.

The domains in Active Directory are named using standard DNS domain names, which may or may not be the same as the names your organization uses on the Internet. If, for example, you have already registered the domain name mycorp.com for use with your Internet servers, you can choose to use that same name as the parent domain in your AD tree or create a new name for internal use. The new name doesn't have to be registered for Internet use, because its use will be limited to your Windows 2000 network only.

DNS is based on resource records (RRs) that contain information about specific machines on the network. Traditionally, administrators must create these records manually, but on a Windows network, this causes problems. The task of manually creating records for hundreds of computers is long and difficult, and it is compounded by the use of the Dynamic Host Configuration Protocol (DHCP) to automatically assign IP addresses to network systems. Because the IP addresses on

DHCP-managed systems can change, there must be a way for the DNS records to be updated to reflect those changes.

The Microsoft DNS server supports dynamic DNS (DDNS), which works together with Microsoft DHCP Server to dynamically update the resource records for specific systems as their IP addresses change.

Global Catalog Server

To support large enterprise networks, Active Directory can be both partitioned and replicated, meaning that the directory can be split into sections stored on different servers, and copies of each section can be maintained on separate servers. Splitting up the directory in this way, however, makes it more difficult for applications to locate specific information. Therefore, Active Directory maintains the *global catalog,* which provides an overall picture of the directory structure. While a domain controller contains the Active Directory information for one domain only, the global catalog is a replica of the entire Active Directory, except that it includes only the essential attributes of each object, known as *binding data.*

Because the global catalog consists of a substantially smaller amount of data than the entire directory, it can be stored on a single server and accessed more quickly by users and applications. The global catalog makes it easy for applications to search for specific objects in Active Directory using any of the attributes included in the binding data.

Deploying Active Directory

All of the architectural elements of Active Directory that have been described thus far, such as domains, trees, and forests, are logical components that do not necessarily have any effect on the physical network. In most cases, network administrators create domains, trees, and forests based on the political divisions within an organization, such as workgroups and departments, although geographical elements can come into play as well. Physically, however, an Active Directory installation is manifested as a collection of domain controllers, split into subdivisions called *sites.*

Creating Domain Controllers

A *domain controller* (DC) is a system that hosts all or part of the Active Directory database and provides the services to the rest of the network through which applications access that database. When a user logs on to the network or requests access to a specific network resource, the workstation contacts a domain controller, which authenticates the user and grants access to the network.

Active Directory has only one type of domain controller. When installing a server, you have to specify whether it should be a primary domain controller (PDC), a backup domain controller (BDC), or a member server. Once a system is installed as a domain controller for a specific domain, there is no way to move it to another domain or change it back to a member server. All Windows servers start out as stand-alone or member servers; you can then promote them to domain controllers and later demote them back to member servers. Active Directory has no PDCs or BDCs; all domain controllers function as peers.

A server that is to function as a domain controller must have at least one NTFS 5.0 drive to hold the Active Directory database, log files, and the system volume, and it must have access to a DNS server that supports the SRV resource record and (optionally) dynamic updates. If the computer cannot locate a DNS server that provides these features, it offers to install and configure the Microsoft DNS Server software on the Windows system.

Directory Replication

Every domain on your network should be represented by at least two domain controllers for reasons of fault tolerance. Once your network is reliant on Active Directory for authentication and other services, inaccessible domain controllers would be a major problem. Therefore, each domain should be replicated on at least two domain controllers so that one is always available. Directory service replication is nothing new, but Active Directory replicates its domain data differently from Windows NT.

Windows NT domains are replicated using a technique called *single master replication,* in which a single PDC with read-write capabilities replicates its data to one or more BDCs that are read-only. In this method, replication traffic always travels in one direction, from the PDC to the BDCs. If the PDC fails, one of the BDCs can be promoted to PDC. The drawback of this arrangement is that changes to the directory can be made only to the PDC. When an administrator creates a new user account or modifies an existing one, for example, the User Manager for Domains utility must communicate with the PDC, even if it is located at a distant site connected by a slow WAN link.

Active Directory uses *multiple master replication,* which enables administrators to make changes on any of a domain's replicas. This is why there are no longer PDCs or BDCs. The use of multiple masters makes the replication process far more difficult, however. Instead of simply copying the directory data from one domain controller to another, the information on each domain controller must be compared with that on all of the others so that the changes made to each replica are propagated to every other replica. In addition, it's possible for two administrators to modify the same attribute of the same object on two different replicas at virtually the same time. The replication process must be able to reconcile conflicts like these and see to it that each replica contains the most up-to-date information.

Multimaster Data Synchronization

Some directory services, such as NDS, base their data synchronization algorithms on time stamps assigned to each database modification. Whichever change has the later time stamp is the one that becomes operative when the replication process is completed. The problem with this method is that the use of time stamps requires the clocks on all of the network's domain controllers to be precisely synchronized, which is difficult to arrange. The Active Directory replication process relies on time stamps in only certain situations. Instead, AD uses *update sequence numbers* (USNs), which are 64-bit values assigned to all modifications written to the directory. Whenever an attribute changes, the domain controller increments the USN and stores it with the attribute, whether the change results from direct action by an administrator or replication traffic received from another domain controller.

The only problem with this method is when the same attribute is modified on two different domain controllers. If an administrator changes the value of a specific attribute on Server B before a change made to the same attribute on Server A is fully propagated to all of the replicas, then a *collision* is said to have occurred. To resolve the collision, the domain controllers use property version numbers to determine which value should take precedence. Unlike USNs, which are a single numerical sequence maintained separately by each domain controller, there is only one property version number for each object attribute.

When a domain controller modifies an attribute as a result of direct action by a network administrator, it increments the property version number. However, when a domain controller receives an attribute modification in the replication traffic from another domain controller, it does not modify the property version number. A domain controller detects collisions by comparing the attribute values and property version numbers received during a replication event with those stored in its own database. If an attribute arriving from another domain controller has the same property version number as the local copy of that attribute but the values don't match, a collision has occurred. In this case, and only in this case, the system uses the time stamps included with each of the attributes to determine which value is newer and should take precedence over the other.

Sites

A single domain can have any number of domain controllers, all of which contain the same information, thanks to the AD replication system. In addition to providing fault tolerance, you can create additional domain controllers to provide users with local access to the directory. In an organization with offices in multiple locations connected by WAN links, it would be impractical to have only one or two domain controllers because workstations would have to communicate with the AD database over a relatively slow, expensive WAN connection. Therefore, administrators often create a domain controller at each location where there are resources in the domain.

The relatively slow speed of the average WAN connection also affects the replication process between domain controllers, and for this reason, Active Directory can break up a domain into sites. A *site* is a collection of domain controllers that are assumed to be well connected, meaning that all of the systems are connected using the same relatively high-speed LAN technology. The connections between sites are assumed to be WANs that are slower and possibly more expensive.

The actual speed of the intrasite and intersite connections is not an issue. The issue is the relative speed between the domain controllers at the same site and those at different sites. The reason for dividing a domain into logical units that reflect the physical layout of the network is to control the replication traffic that passes over the slower WAN links. Active Directory also uses sites to determine which domain controller a workstation should access when authenticating a user. Whenever possible, authentication procedures use a domain controller located on the same site.

Intrasite Replication

The replication of data between domain controllers located at the same site is completely automatic and self-regulating. A component called the Knowledge Consistency Checker (KCC) dynamically creates connections between the domain controllers as needed to create a replication topology that minimizes latency. *Latency* is the period of time during which the information stored on the domain controllers for a single domain is different—that is, the interval between the modification of an attribute on one domain controller and the propagation of that change to the other domain controllers. The KCC triggers a replication event whenever a change is made to the AD database on any of the site's replicas.

The KCC maintains at least two connections to each domain controller at the site. This way, if a controller goes offline, replication between all of the other domain controllers is still possible. The KCC may create additional connections to maintain timely contact between the remaining domain controllers while the system is unavailable and then remove them when the system comes back online. In the same way, if you add a new domain controller, the KCC modifies the replication topology to include it in the data synchronization process. As a rule, the KCC creates a replication topology in which each domain controller is no more than three hops away from any other domain controller. Because the domain controllers are all located on the same site, they are assumed to be well connected, and the KCC is willing to expend network bandwidth in the interest of replication speed. All updates are transmitted in uncompressed form because even though this requires the transmission of more data, it minimizes the amount of processing needed at each domain controller.

Replication occurs primarily within domains, but when multiple domains are located at the same site, the KCC also creates connections between the global catalog servers for each domain so that they can exchange information and create a replica of the entire Active Directory containing the subset of attributes that form the binding data.

Intersite Replication

By default, a domain consists of a single site, called Default-First-Site-Name, and any additional domains you create are placed within that site. You can, however, use the Active Directory Sites and Services console to create additional sites and move domains into them. Just as with domains in the same site, Active Directory creates a replication topology between domains in different sites, but with several key differences.

Because the WAN links between sites are assumed to be slower, Active Directory attempts to minimize the amount of replication traffic that passes between them. First, there are fewer connections between domain controllers at different sites than with a site; the three-hop rule is not observed for the intersite replication topology. Second, all replication data transmitted over intersite connections is compressed to minimize the amount of bandwidth utilized by the replication process. Finally, replication events between sites are not automatically triggered by modifications to the Active Directory database. Instead, replication can be scheduled to occur at specified times and intervals to minimize the effect on standard user traffic and to take advantage of lower bandwidth costs during off-hours.

Microsoft Management Console

Microsoft Management Console (MMC) is an application that provides a centralized administration interface for many of the services included in Windows, including those used to manage Active Directory. Windows relies on separate management applications for many of its services, such as the DHCP Manager, WINS Manager, and Disk Administrator. Windows consolidates all of these applications, and many others, into MMC. Most of the system administration tasks for the operating system are now performed through MMC.

MMC has no administrative capabilities of its own; it is, essentially, a shell for application modules called *snap-ins* that provide the administrative functions for many of Windows' applications and services. Snap-ins take the form of files with an .msc extension that you load either from the command line or interactively through the MMC menus. Windows supplies snap-in files for all of its tools, but the interface is designed so that third-party software developers can use the MMC architecture to create administration tools for their own applications.

MMC can load multiple snap-ins simultaneously using the Windows multiple-document interface (MDI). You can use this capability to create a customized management interface containing all of the snap-ins you use on a regular basis. When you run MMC (by launching the Mmc.exe file from the Run dialog box) and select Console | New, you get an empty Console Root

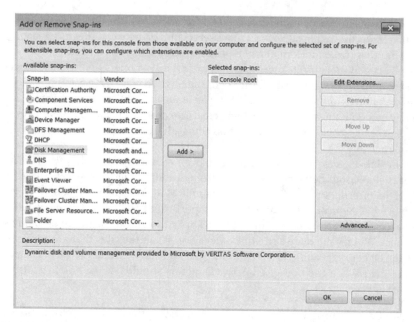

Figure 18-2   Working with snap-ins in Windows 7

window. By selecting Console | Add/Remove Snap-in, you can build a list of the installed snap-ins and load selected ones into the console. The various snap-ins appear in an expandable, Explorer-like display in the left pane of MMC's main screen, as shown in Figure 18-2.

NOTE In Windows 8 or 8.1, locate the Windows Systems app and choose Run.

Many of Window's administrative tools, such as Active Directory Sites and Services, are actually preconfigured MMC consoles. Selecting Computer Management from the Programs/ Administrative Tools group in the Start menu displays a console that contains a collection of the basic administration tools for a Windows system. By default, the Computer Management console administers the local system, but you can use all of its tools to manage a remote network system by selecting Action | Connect To Another Computer.

Creating and Configuring Sites

Splitting a network into sites has no effect on the hierarchy of domains, trees, and forests that you have created to represent your enterprise. However, sites still appear as objects in Active Directory, along with several other object types that you use to configure your network's replication topology. These objects are visible only in the Active Directory Sites and Services tool. The object called Default-First-Site-Name is created automatically when you promote the first server on your network to a domain controller, along with a server object that appears in the Servers folder beneath it. Server objects are always subordinate to site objects and represent the domain controllers operating

Part V

at that site. A site can contain server objects for domain controllers in any number of domains, located in any tree or forest. You can move server objects between sites as needed.

The other two important object types associated with sites and servers are subnet and site link objects. Subnet objects represent the particular IP subnets that you use at your various sites and are used to define the boundaries of the site. When you create a subnet object, you specify a network address and subnet mask. When you associate a site with a subnet object, server objects for any new domain controllers that you create on that subnet are automatically created in that site. You can associate multiple subnet objects with a particular site to create a complete picture of your network.

Site link objects represent the WAN links on your network that Active Directory will use to create connections between domain controllers at different sites. Active Directory supports the use of the Internet Protocol (IP) and the Simple Mail Transport Protocol (SMTP) for site links, both of which appear in the Inter-Site Transports folder in Active Directory Sites and Services. An SMTP site link can take the form of any applications you use to send e-mail using the SMTP protocol. When you create a site link object, you select the sites that are connected by the WAN link the object represents. The attributes of site link objects include various mechanisms for determining when and how often Active Directory should use the link to transmit replication traffic between sites:

- **Cost**   The cost of a site link can reflect either the monetary cost of the WAN technology involved or the cost in terms of the bandwidth needed for other purposes.

- **Schedule**   This specifies the hours of the day during each day of the week that the link can be used to carry replication traffic.

- **Replication period**   This specifies the interval between replication procedures that use this link, subject to the schedule described previously.

By default, Active Directory creates an IP site link object, DEFAULTIPSITELINK, that you can use as is or can modify to reflect the type of link used to connect your sites. If all of your sites are connected by WAN links of the same type, you don't have to create additional site link objects because a single set of scheduling attributes should be applicable for all of your intersite connections. If you use various types of WAN connections, however, you can create a separate site link object for each type and configure its attributes to reflect how you want it to be used.

There is another type of object that you can create in the Inter-Site Transports container, called a *site link bridge object*, that is designed to make it possible to route replication traffic through one remote site to others. By default, the site links you create are transitive, meaning that they are bridged together, enabling them to route replication traffic. For example, if you have a site link object connecting Site A to Site B and another one connecting Site B to Site C, then Site A can send replication traffic to Site C. If you want, you can disable the default bridging by opening the Properties dialog box for the IP folder and clearing the Bridge All Site Links check box. If you do this, you must manually create site link bridge objects in order to route replication traffic in this way. A site link bridge object generally represents a router on the network. While a site link object groups two site objects, a site link bridge object groups two site link objects, making it possible for replication traffic to be routed between them.

Once you have created objects representing the sites that form your network and the links that connect them, the KCC can create connections that form the replication topology for the entire internetwork, subject to the limitations imposed by the site link object attributes. The connections created by the KCC, both within and between sites, appear as objects in the NTDS Settings container beneath each server object. A connection object is unidirectional, representing the traffic running from the server under which the object appears to the target server specified as an attribute of the object. In most cases, there should be no need to manually create or configure connection objects, but it is possible to do so. You can customize the replication topology of your network by creating your own connections and scheduling the times during which they may be used. Manually created connection objects cannot be deleted by the KCC to accommodate changing network conditions; they remain in place until you manually remove them.

Designing an Active Directory

As with any enterprise directory service, the process of deploying Active Directory on your network involves much more than simply installing the software. The planning process is, in many cases, more complicated than the construction of the directory itself. Naturally, the larger your network, the more complicated the planning process will be. You should have a clear idea of the form that your AD structure will take and who will maintain each part of it before you actually begin to deploy domain controllers and create objects.

In many cases, the planning process will require some hands-on testing before you deploy Active Directory on your production network. You may want to set up a test network and try some forest designs before you commit yourself to any one plan. Although a test network can't fully simulate the effects of hundreds of users working at once, the time that you spend familiarizing yourself with the Active Directory tools and procedures can only help you later when you're building the live directory service.

Planning Domains, Trees, and Forests

Active Directory expands the scope of the directory service by two orders of magnitude by providing trees and forests that you can use to organize multiple domains. In addition, the domains themselves can be subdivided into smaller administrative entities called organizational units. To use these capabilities effectively, you must evaluate your network in light of both its physical layout and the needs of the organization that it serves.

Creating Multiple Trees

In most cases, a single tree with one or more domains is sufficient to support an enterprise network. The main reason for creating multiple trees is if you have two or more existing DNS name spaces that you want to reflect in Active Directory. For example, a corporation that consists of several different companies that operate independently can use multiple trees to create a separate name space for each company. Although there are transitive trust relationships between all of the domains in a tree, separate trees are connected only by trusts between their root domains.

If you have several levels of child domains in each tree, the process of accessing a resource in a different tree involves the passing of authentication traffic up from the domain containing the requesting system to the root of the tree, across to the root of the other tree, and down to the domain containing the requested resource. If the trees operate autonomously and access requests for resources in other trees are rare, this may not be much of a problem. If the trust relationships in a directory design like this do cause delays on a regular basis, you can manually create what are known as *shortcut trusts* between child domains lower down in both trees.

Just as you can create multiple trees in a forest, you can create multiple forests in the Active Directory database. Scenarios in which the use of multiple forests is necessary are even rarer than those calling for multiple trees because forests have no inherent trust relationships between them at all and use a different global catalog, making it more difficult for users even to locate resources. You may want to use a separate forest for a lab-based test network or for a project that you don't want other network users to know even exists.

CHAPTER

19 Linux

Developed as a college project by Linus Torvalds of Sweden, the Linux operating system has emerged as one of the most popular Unix variants. This chapter covers the advantages and disadvantages of Linux, Linux file systems, and how to work with Linux files.

Understanding Linux

Written in the C programming language, Linux uses GNU tools, which are freely available. Like other variants, Linux is available as a free download from the Internet in versions for most standard hardware platforms and is continually refined by an ad hoc group of programmers who communicate mainly through Internet mailing lists and newsgroups. Because of its popularity, many Linux modules and applications have been developed. Often new features and capabilities are the result of programmers adapting the existing software for their own uses and then posting their code for others to use. As the product increases in popularity, more people work on it in this way, and the development process accelerates. This activity has also led to the fragmentation of the Linux development process. Many different Linux versions are available, which are similar in their kernel functions but vary in the features they include. Some of these Linux packages are available for download on the Internet, but the growth in the popularity of the operating system (OS) has led to commercial distribution releases as well.

NOTE GNU is an operating system announced in 1993 that contains totally free software. According to www.gnu.org, GNU stands for *GNU's Not Unix*.

Linux Distributions

Many Linux variations are available free for the download, and others require some sort of payment or donation. Table 19-1 shows some of the Linux distributions (often called *distros*) available. They are listed in alphabetic order, not in order of popularity.

Today's Linux systems run on devices from tablets and cell phones to workstations and high-end servers. Since the system is *open source* (meaning that it is available for anyone),

Distro Name	Download Location	Free/Donation Requested/Paid
Arch	https://www.archlinux.org/	Free
Debian	www.debian.org/	Free
Gentoo	www.gentoo.org/	Free
Knoppix	http://knoppix.net	Free
Mandriva	www.mandriva.com/en/	Paid
Mint	www.linuxmint.com	Donation requested
OpenSUSE	www.opensuse.org	Free
PCLinuxOS	www.pclinuxos.com/	Donation requested
RedHat	www.redhat.com/	Paid
Slackware Linux	www.slackware.com	Paid
SUSE	https://www.suse.com/	Paid
Ubuntu (Kubuntu, Lubuntu, Xubuntu)	www.ubuntu.com/	Free

Table 19-1 Some Linux Distros

as problems or glitches occur, anyone worldwide can report the problem, and many people will write code to fix the issue for future users. As Linux has matured, some newer users just want to use the program, not write code. These users want a program that they can download and use right away. It is for those users that some companies have developed distributions that are guaranteed to work "out of the box." These companies require payment for Linux and offer both technical support and warranties on the downloaded program.

Advantages and Disadvantages of Linux

Besides being an open source system, Linux often requires less disk space than many other operating systems. There are other advantages as well:

- Since the system is open source, many people have contributed to its stability.
- Security flaws are often found before they become an issue.
- Its robust adaptability adjusts to many situations.
- It is easily customizable and updatable.
- Apps are usually free, and the number of apps is increasing.
- Linux is *scalable,* meaning it can be used as the operating system for small items such as wireless routers and tablets to large, multitiered systems such as storage clusters and data centers.

Open source also has some disadvantages:

- Applications may be more difficult to find and learn (although today many applications are available, and some even look like more familiar Windows programs). For example,

OpenOffice and LibreOffice both offer a set of applications including a word processor, a spreadsheet, and a presentation manager. The screens look much the same in Windows and Linux, as shown in Figure 19-1.

- There are many distributions of Linux, so it can be difficult to transfer knowledge of one distro to another.

- Linux can be confusing at first for new users.

The popularity of Linux has reached the point at which it is expanding beyond Unix's traditional market of computer professionals and technical hobbyists. In part, this is because of a backlash against Microsoft, which some people believe is close to holding a monopoly on operating systems. When you pay for a "commercial" Linux release such as Ubuntu, you download not only the OS and source code but also a variety of applications, product documentation, and technical support, which are often lacking in the free download releases. Other distributors provide similar products and services, but this does not necessarily mean that these Linux versions are binary compatible. In some cases, software written for one distribution will not run on another one.

The free Linux distributions provide much of the same functionality as the commercial ones but in a less convenient package. The downloads can be large and time consuming, and you may find yourself interrupting the installation process frequently to track down some essential piece of information or to download an additional module you didn't know you needed. One of the biggest advantages of Linux over other Unix variants is its excellent driver support. Device drivers are an integral part of any operating system, and if Unix is ever going to become a rival to Windows in the personal computer mainstream, it's going to have to run on the same computers that run Windows, using the same peripherals. Many of the other Unix variants have relatively limited device driver support. If you are trying to install a Unix product on an Intel-based computer with the latest and greatest video adapter, for example, you may not be able to find a driver that takes full advantage of its capabilities.

Device drivers, even those included with operating systems, are generally written by the device manufacturer. Not surprisingly, hardware manufacturers devote most of their driver development attention to Windows, with other systems getting only perfunctory support, if any at all. The fans of Linux are legion, however, and the OS's development model has led the operating system's supporters to develop their own drivers for many of the devices commonly found in Intel-based computers. If you are having trouble finding appropriate drivers for your hardware that run on other Unix variants, you are more likely to have success with Linux.

For example, a computer running Linux as its OS and Apache as its web server software is a powerful combination that is easily equal or superior to most of the commercial products on the market—and the software is completely free.

Figure 19-1   The OpenOffice Writer screen looks similar in both Windows and Linux.

File Systems

For the many computer users who are familiar with the Microsoft NTFS and the older FAT file system, the myriad of file systems available in open source operating systems can be daunting. Table 19-2 shows some of the file systems that are available for Linux users.

Bits and Bytes

All data in a computer is a combination of zeros and ones. Each zero or one is designated as a bit. A byte consists of 8 bits. For example, 00110111 is one byte. There are a number of other designations, indicating the amount of storage space available in each designation. Today, hard drives are measured in terabytes, while random access memory (RAM) is currently measured in gigabytes.

- A *kilobyte* is 1,024 bytes shown as 1KB.
- A *megabyte* is 1,024 kilobytes, shown as 1MB.
- A *gigabyte* is 1,024 megabytes, shown as 1GB.
- A *terabyte* is 1,024 gigabytes, shown as 1TB.
- A *petabyte* is 1,024 terabytes, shown as 1PB.
- A *exabtye* is 1,024 petabytes, shown as 1EB.

NOTE An old techie saying is that 4 bits = 1 nibble.

System Name	Maximum File Size	Maximum Partition Size	Comments
FAT16	2GB	2GB	File Allocation Table (FAT) is the original file configuration in DOS and Windows 9x versions.
FAT32	4GB	8TB	This system is still found on USB devices, memory cards, and other devices.
NTFS	2TB	256TB	While Linux cannot be installed on an NTFS system, NTFS-3g is installed by Ubuntu so that the user has read-write support.
ext2	2TB	32TB	This is a legacy Linux system.
ext3	2TB	32TB	This has been the standard Linux file since the early days of Linux.
ext4	16TB	1EB	This is the latest iteration of ext3.
XPS	8EB	8EB	This is a high-powered system created by Silicon Graphics.

Table 19-2   Linux File Systems

NOTE A *legacy system* is one that is outdated, unsupported, or obsolete. Some organizations still use older systems because of software or hardware requirements.

Linux Installation Questions

Before you install Linux on a machine, you should know the answers to the following:

- Have you read the documentation for the distribution you downloaded?
- Will this distribution work on the hardware you are using?
- How much RAM is available on this machine?
- Do you want to install just a workstation or create a Linux server? Can you download all the necessary software?
- Do you have to create a CD or DVD from the downloaded file? Normally, Linux downloads are in .iso format, and many require that you burn the downloaded file to a CD or DVD in order to perform the installation.
- Do you understand how to use an .iso file?
- Is Linux the main operating system or one of several?
- Do you need to create a new partition before you install the system?
- Since Linux expects to be on a network, what is the IP address and hostname?

Booting Linux

When you boot your Linux computer, there are several steps to the process, as shown in Figure 19-2. In text mode, once your Linux terminal displays the *login* prompt as white letters on a black background, you enter your username and password (pressing enter after each).

Logging Out of Linux

In text mode, enter the logout command and press enter.

Directory Structure

Most Linux distributions contain the directories described in Table 19-3.

Quick Commands in Linux

You can use several commands in Linux to find your way around. Table 19-4 lists several common commands and the resulting action. The command structure is as follows:

```
command option(s) argument(s)
```

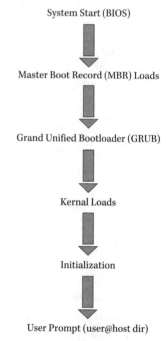

System Start (BIOS)

Master Boot Record (MBR) Loads

Grand Unified Bootloader (GRUB)

Kernal Loads

Initialization

User Prompt (user@host dir)

Figure 19-2 The boot sequence in Linux

Part V

Directory Name	Description
/bin/	This directory (file) contains installed programs that are available to all users on the system.
/boot/	This directory holds the files used during bootup.
/dev/	Because Linux lists devices such as your hard drive, DVD, or mouse as files, you find the information in this directory.
/etc/	The application files, startup, stop, and other scripts are stored here.
/home/	As each user is added to the system, a default home directory is established. This shows as /home/username. This default can be changed in /etc/. This directory contains other directories such as Desktop and Documents.
/lib/	The kernel modules as well as shared libraries (such as Python or C) are stored here.
/media/	This temporary mount directory is created for removable devices such as DVDs. It is displayed as media/dvd.
/mnt/	This is the temporary mount directory for mounting a file system, often an .iso file.
/opt/	Optional third-party applications are kept here.
/proc/	This contains information about the hardware on your system.
/root/	This is the main (default) home directory for the root user. The root directory (/) is the first or topmost directory in the system.
/sbin/	This is the storage directory for the system programs and tools.
/srv/	This contains server-specific services data.
/tmp/	This is the location for temporary files, such as installation files when installing a new program.
/usr/	This contains programs, program settings, and program resources, such as source code.
/var/	This directory contains variable files such as mail, log, and other such files.

Table 19-3   Typical Linux Directories

Command	The Result
ls	Lists files, like dir in DOS
cp	Copies files
find *filename*	Locates the named file
cd *directory*	Changes directory
rm *thatfile*	Removes the filenames
mkdir	Makes a new directory
ifconfig	Configures or obtains information on installed network devices, like ipconfig in Windows

Table 19-4   Common Linux Commands

Each would be shown from the root prompt, such as this:

```
root@username:~# command
```

Unlike other operating systems, Linux commands are case sensitive.

Working with Linux Files

For those familiar with Windows path names, this is how you would find a file:

```
C:\MyFolder\MyFinances\MyBudget.txt
```

To find the same file in Linux, you would use this pathway:

```
/MyFolder/MyFinances/MyBudget.txt
```

You may note several differences in the two. First, there is no drive name shown. Linux mounts the *root partition* when the computer first boots. Therefore, all the files and folders are found at /. Second, the slashes are forward slashes instead of the backslashes in Windows. Also, in Linux, all files and folder are case sensitive, while in Windows, case does not matter. In Linux, /School/English/essay1.txt is a different file than /School/English/Essay1.txt.

Linux file systems are often more reliable than other systems because of several factors.

Journaling

In more familiar file systems, each file is written directly to a location on the hard drive, and if the computer shuts down for any reason, the information in that file may be lost or corrupted. A file system that journals first writes information to a special file called a *journal* that is stored on another part of the hard drive. This journal contains data about both the file and location and is much easier to retrieve if there is a problem. At any given time, this system has three possible states: a saved file, a journal report that shows the file as not being saved, or a journal file that shows inconsistencies but can be rebuilt.

This system is more reliable than systems writing directly to the hard drive. Some systems write the data twice, which can prevent corruption and save after a power or software problem requires the user to reboot the system.

Editing

One of the best features of a Linux (or Unix) file is that it can be edited while it is open. Unix/Linux files are indexed by number (called a *inode*) that contains the attributes such as name, permissions, location, and so on. When a file is deleted, the inode is just unlinked from the filename. If other programs are using that file, the link to the operating system is still open and will be updated as changes are made to it.

Lack of Fragmentation

FAT and NTFS systems do not keep all the pieces of their files together in order to utilize space more efficiently. While this practice saved space in the smaller hard drives of the day, it made for difficulties when it came to performance because the processor would have to connect the parts of the files before they could be run. Starting with the ext3 system, Linux file blocks are kept together.

Part V

CHAPTER
20 Unix

Unix is a multiuser, multitasking operating system (OS) with roots that date back to the late 1960s. It was developed throughout the 1970s by researchers at AT&T's Bell Labs, finally culminating in Unix System V Release 1 in 1983. During this time, and since then, many other organizations have built their own variants on the Unix formula, and now dozens of different operating systems function using the same basic Unix components, including both Apple and Linux. This was possible because, from the beginning, Unix has been more of a collaborative research project than a commercial product. While some companies guard the source code to their operating systems, many Unix developers make their code freely available. This enables anyone with the appropriate skills to modify the OS to their own specifications.

Unix is not a user-friendly OS, nor is it commonly found on the desktop of the average personal computer user. To its detractors, Unix is an outdated OS that relies primarily on an archaic, character-based interface. To its proponents, however, Unix is the most powerful, flexible, and stable OS available. As is usually the case, both opinions are correct to some degree.

You are not going to see racks of Unix-based games and other recreational software at the computer store any time soon, nor are you likely to see offices full of employees running productivity applications, such as word processors and spreadsheets, on Unix systems. However, when you use a browser to connect to a web site, there's a good chance that the server hosting the site is running some form of Unix. Your smart phone, tablet, or Mac uses a form of Unix. In addition, many of the vertical applications designed for specific industries, such as those used when you book a hotel room or rent a car, run on Unix systems. In this instance, we are discussing the base form of Unix, aka the terminal or command line.

As a server operating system, Unix has a reputation for being stable enough to support mission-critical applications, portable enough to run on many different hardware platforms, and scalable enough to support a user base of almost any size. All Unix systems use Transmission Control Protocol/Internet Protocol (TCP/IP) as their native protocols, so they are naturally suited for use on the Internet and for networking with other operating systems. In fact, Unix systems were instrumental in the development of the Internet from an experiment in decentralized, packet-switched networking to the worldwide phenomenon it is today.

Unix Principles

More than other operating systems, Unix is based on a principle of simplicity that makes it highly adaptable to many different needs. This is not to say that Unix is simple to use because generally it isn't. Rather, it means that the OS is based on guiding principles that treat the various elements of the computer in a simple and consistent way. For example, a Unix system treats physical devices in the computer, such as the printer, the keyboard, and the display, in the same way as it treats the files and directories on its drives. You can copy a file to the display or to a printer just as you would copy it to another directory and use the devices with any other appropriate file-based tools.

Another fundamental principle of Unix is the use of small, simple tools that perform specific functions and that can easily work together with other tools to provide more complex functions. Instead of large applications with many built-in features, Unix operating systems are far more likely to utilize a small tool that provides a basic service to other tools. A good example is the *sort* command, which takes the contents of a text file, sorts it according to user-supplied parameters, and sends the results to an output device, such as the display or a printer. In addition to applying the command to an existing text file, you can use it to sort the output of other commands before displaying or printing it.

The element that lets you join tools in this way is called a *pipe* (|), which enables you to use one tool to provide input to or accept output from another tool. DOS can use pipes to redirect standard input and output in various ways, but Unix includes a much wider variety of tools and commands that can be combined to provide elaborate and powerful functions.

Thus, Unix is based on relatively simple elements, but its ability to combine those elements makes it quite complex. While a large application attempts to anticipate the needs of the user by combining its functions in various predetermined ways, Unix supplies users with the tools that provide the basic functions and lets them combine the tools to suit their own needs. The result is an OS with great flexibility and extensibility but that requires an operator with more than the average computer user's skills to take full advantage of it. However, the operator has to remember all the commands.

Because of this guiding principle, Unix is in many ways a "programmer's operating system." If a tool to perform a certain task is not included, you usually have the resources available to fashion one yourself. This is not to say that you have to be a programmer to use Unix, but many of the techniques that programmers use when writing code are instrumental to the use of multiple tools on the Unix command line.

If all of this talk of programming and command-line computing is intimidating, be assured that it is quite possible to install, maintain, and use a Unix system without a substantial investment in learning command-line syntax. Some of the Unix operating systems are being geared more and more to the average computer user, with most of the common system functions available through the graphical user interface (GUI). You can perform most of your daily computing tasks on these operating systems without ever seeing a command prompt.

The various Unix operating systems are built around basic elements that are fundamentally the same, but they include various collections of tools and programs. Depending on which variant you choose and whether it is a commercial product or a free download, you may find that the OS comes complete with modules such as web and DNS servers and other programs, or you may have to obtain these yourself. However, one of the other principles of Unix development that has endured through the years is the custom of making the source code for Unix software freely available to everyone. The result of this open source movement is a wealth of Unix tools, applications, and other software that is freely available for download from the Internet.

In some cases, programmers modify existing Unix modules for their own purposes and then release those modifications to the public domain so that they can be of help to others. Some programmers collaborate on Unix software projects as something of a hobby and release the results to the public. One of the best examples of this is the Linux operating system, which was designed from the beginning to be a free product and which has now become one of the most popular Unix variants in use today.

Unix Architecture

Because Unix is available in so many variants, Unix operating systems can run on a variety of hardware platforms. Many of the Unix variants are proprietary versions created by specific manufacturers to run on their own hardware platforms. Most of the software-only Unix solutions run on Intel-based PCs, and some are available in versions for multiple platforms.

The hardware requirements for the various Unix platforms vary greatly, depending on the functions required of the machine. You can run Linux on an old 386, for example, as long as you don't expect to use a GUI or run a server supporting a large number of users. Today, many large businesses are using Linux as a cost-saving alternative because even mid-range Unix servers can cost more than $200,000, including hardware.

No matter what hardware a Unix system uses, the basic software components are the same (see Figure 20-1). The *kernel* is the core module that insulates the programs running on the computer from the hardware. The kernel uses device drivers that interact with the specific hardware devices installed in the computer to perform basic functions such as memory management, input/output, interrupt handling, and access control.

The Unix kernel provides approximately 100 system calls that programs can use to execute certain tasks, such as opening a file, executing a program, and terminating a process. However, the system calls can vary wildly depending on the variant. These are the building blocks that programmers use to integrate hardware-related functions into their applications' more complex tasks. The system calls can vary between the different Unix versions to some extent, particularly in the way that the system internals perform the different functions.

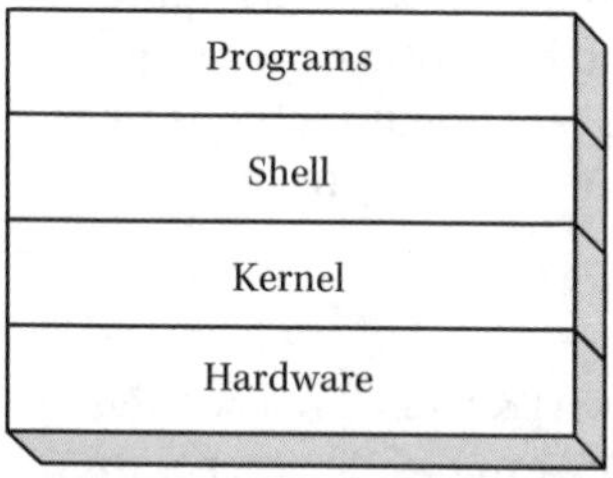

Figure 20-1 Basic components of a Unix system

Above the kernel is the shell, which provides the interface you use to issue commands and execute programs. The shell is a command interpreter, much like Command.com in DOS and Cmd.exe in Windows, which provides a character-based command prompt that you use to interact with the system. The shell also functions as a programming language you can use to create scripts, which are functionally similar to old DOS batch files but much more versatile and powerful.

Unlike Windows, which limits you to a single command interpreter, Unix traditionally has several shells you can choose from, with different capabilities. The shells that are included with particular Unix operating systems vary, and others are available as free downloads. Often, the

Part V

selection of a shell is a matter of personal preference, guided by the user's previous experience. The basic commands used for file management and other standard system tasks are the same in all of the shells. The differences become more evident when you run more complex commands and create scripts.

The original Unix shell is a program called *sh* that was created by Steve Bourne and is commonly known as the *Bourne shell*. Some of the other common shells are as follows:

- **csh**   Known as the *C shell* and originally created for use with Berkeley Software Distribution (BSD) Unix; utilizes a syntax similar to that of the C language and introduces features such as a command history list, job control, and aliases. Scripts written for the Bourne shell usually need some modification to run in the C shell.

- **ksh**   Known as the *Korn shell*; builds on the Bourne shell and adds elements of the C shell, as well as other improvements. Scripts written for the Bourne shell usually can run in the Korn shell without modification.

- **bash**   The default shell used by Linux; closely related to the Korn shell, with elements of the C shell.

Running on top of the shell are the commands that you use to perform tasks on the system. Unix includes hundreds of small programs, usually called *tools* or *commands,* which you can combine on the command line to perform complex tasks. Hundreds of other tools are available on the Internet that you can combine with those provided with the OS. Unix command-line tools are programs, but don't confuse them with the complex applications used by other operating systems, such as Windows. Unix has full-blown applications as well, but its real power lies in these small programs. Adding a new tool on a Unix system does not require an installation procedure; you simply have to specify the appropriate location of the tool in the file system in order for the shell to run it.

Unix Versions

The sheer number of Unix variants can be bewildering to anyone trying to find the appropriate operating system for a particular application. However, apart from systems intended for special purposes, virtually any Unix OS can perform well in a variety of roles, and the selection you make may be based more on economic factors, hardware platform, or personal taste than on anything else. If, for example, you decide to purchase proprietary Unix workstations, you'll be using the version of the OS intended for the machine. If you intend to run Unix on Intel-based computers, you might choose the OS based on the GUI that you feel most comfortable with, or you might be looking for the best bargain you can find and limit yourself to the versions available as free downloads. The following sections discuss some of the major Unix versions available.

Unix System V

Unix System V is the culmination of the original Unix work begun by AT&T's Bell Labs in the 1970s. Up until release 3.2, the project was wholly developed by AT&T, even while other Unix work was ongoing at the University of California at Berkeley and other places. Unix System V Release 4 (SVR4), released in the late 1980s, consolidated the benefits of the SVR operating system with those of Berkeley's BSD, Sun's SunOS, and Microsoft's Xenix. This release brought together some of the most important elements that are now indelibly associated with the name Unix, including networking elements such as the TCP/IP Internet Package from BSD, which includes file transfer, remote login, and remote program execution capabilities, and the Network File System (NFS) from SunOS.

AT&T eventually split its Unix development project off into a subsidiary called Unix System Laboratories (USL), which released System V Release 4.2. In 1993, AT&T sold USL to Novell, which released its own version of SVR4 under the name UnixWare. In light of pressure from the other companies involved in Unix development, Novell transferred the Unix trademark to a consortium called X/Open, thus enabling any manufacturer to describe its product as a Unix OS. In 1995, Novell sold all of its interest in Unix SVR4 and UnixWare to the Santa Cruz Operation (SCO), which owns it to this day. In 1997, SCO released Unix System V Release 5 (SVR5) under the name OpenServer, as well as version 7 of its UnixWare product. These are the descendants of the original AT&T products, and they are still on the market.

BSD Unix

In 1975, one of the original developers of Unix, Ken Thompson, took a sabbatical at the University of California at Berkeley, and while there, he ported his current Unix version to a PDP-11/70 system. The seed he planted took root, and Berkeley became a major developer of Unix in its own right. BSD Unix introduced several of the major features associated with most Unix versions, including the C shell and the vi text editor. Several versions of BSD Unix appeared throughout the 1970s, culminating in 3BSD. In 1979, the U.S. Department of Defense's Advanced Research Projects Agency (DARPA) funded the development of 4BSD, which coincided with the development and adoption of the TCP/IP networking protocols. For more information about BSD Unix, see Chapter 21.

Unix Networking

Unix is a peer-to-peer network operating system, in that every computer is capable of both accessing resources on other systems and sharing its own resources. These networking capabilities take three basic forms, as follows:

- The ability to open a session on another machine and execute commands on its shell
- The ability to access the file system on another machine, using a service like NFS
- The ability to run a service (called a *daemon*) on one system and access it using a client on another system

The TCP/IP protocols are an integral part of all Unix operating systems, and many of the TCP/IP programs and services that may be familiar to you from working with the Internet are also implemented on Unix networks. For example, Unix networks can use DNS servers to resolve host names into IP addresses and use BOOTP or DHCP servers to automatically configure TCP/IP clients. Standard Internet services such as File Transfer Protocol (FTP) and Telnet have long been a vital element of Unix networking, as are utilities such as Ping and Traceroute.

The following sections examine the types of network access used on Unix systems and the tools involved in implementing them.

Part V

Using Remote Commands

One form of network access that is far more commonly used on Unix than on other network operating systems is the remote console session, in which a user connects to another computer on the network and executes commands on that system. Once the connection is established, commands entered by the user at the client system are executed by the remote server, and the output is redirected over the network back to the client's display. It's important to understand that this is not the equivalent of accessing a shared network drive on a Windows computer and executing a file. In the latter case, the program runs using the client computer's processor and memory. When you execute a command on a Unix computer using a remote console session, the program actually runs on the other computer, using its resources.

Because Unix relies heavily on the command prompt, character-based remote sessions are more useful than they are in a more graphically oriented environment like that of Windows.

Berkeley Remote Commands

The Berkeley remote commands were originally part of BSD Unix and have since been adopted by virtually every other Unix OS. Sometimes known as the *r* commands, these tools are intended primarily for use on local area networks (LANs), rather than over wide area network (WAN) or Internet links. These commands enable you not only to open a session on a remote system but to perform specific tasks on a remote system without logging in and without working interactively with a shell prompt.

rlogin

The *rlogin* command establishes a connection to another system on the network and provides access to its shell. Once connected, any commands you enter are executed by the other computer using its processor, file system, and other components. To connect to another machine on the network, you use a command like the following:

```
rlogin [-l username] hostname
```

where the *hostname* variable specifies the name of the system to which you want to connect.

NOTE You can sometimes use the IP address instead of your hostname.

Authentication is required for the target system to establish the connection, which can happen using either host-level or user-level security. To use host-level security, the client system must be trusted by the server by having its hostname listed in the /etc/host.equiv file on the server. When this is the case, the client logs in without a username or password because it is automatically trusted by the server no matter who's using the system.

User-level security requires the use of a username and sometimes a password, in addition to the hostname. By default, *rlogin* supplies the name of the user currently logged in on the client system to the remote system, as well as information about the type of terminal used to connect, which is taken from the value of the TERM variable. The named user must have an account in the remote system's password database, and if the client system is not trusted by the remote system, the remote system may then prompt the client for the password associated with that username. It's also possible to log in using a different username by specifying it on the *rlogin* command line with the -*l* switch.

For the username to be authenticated by the remote system without using a password, it must be defined as an equivalent user by being listed in a .rhosts file located in the user's home directory on that system. The .rhosts file contains a list of hostnames and usernames that specify whether a user working on a specific machine should be granted immediate access to the command prompt. Depending on the security requirements for the remote system, the .rhosts files can be owned either by the remote users themselves or by the root account on the system. Adding users to your .rhosts file is a simple way of giving them access to your account on that machine without giving them the password.

NOTE The root account on a Unix computer is a built-in superuser that has full access to the entire system, much like the Administrator account in Windows but even more powerful (depending on the version of Windows).

Once you have successfully established a connection to a remote system, you can execute any command in its shell that you would on your local system, except for those that launch graphical applications. You can also use *rlogin* from the remote shell to connect to a third computer, giving you simultaneous access to all three. To terminate the connection to a remote system, you can use the *exit* command, press the CTRL-D key combination, or type a tilde followed by a period (~.).

rsh

In some instances, you may want to execute a single command on a remote system and view the resulting output without actually logging in. You can do this with the *rsh* command, using the following syntax:

```
rsh hostname command
```

where the *hostname* variable specifies the system on which you want to open a remote shell, and the *command* variable is the command to be executed on the remote system. Unlike *rlogin*, interactive authentication is not possible with *rsh*. For the command to work, the user must have either a properly configured .rhosts file on the remote system or an entry in the /etc/host.equiv file. The *rsh* command provides essentially the same command-line capabilities as *rlogin*, except that it works for only a single command and does not maintain an open session.

NOTE The *rsh* command was called *remsh* on HP-UX systems. There are many cases in which commands providing identical functions have different names on various Unix operating systems.

---

rcp

The *rcp* command is used to copy files to or from a remote system across a network without performing an interactive login. The *rcp* functions much like the *cp* command used to copy files on the local system, using the following syntax:

```
rcp [-r] sourcehost:filename desthost:filename
```

where the *sourcehost:filename* variable specifies the hostname of the source system and the name of the file to be copied, and the *desthost:filename* variable specifies the hostname of the destination system and the name that the file should be given on that system. You can also copy entire directories by adding the *-r* parameter to the command and specifying directory names instead of filenames. As with *rsh*, there is no login procedure, so to use *rcp*, either the client system must be trusted by the remote system or the user must be listed in the .rhosts file.

Secure Shell Commands

The downside of the Berkeley remote commands is that they are inherently insecure. Passwords are transmitted over the network in clear text, making it possible for intruders to intercept them. Because of this susceptibility to compromise, many administrators prohibit the use of these commands. To address this problem, there is a Secure Shell program that provides the same functions as *rlogin*, *rsh*, and *rcp*, but with greater security. The equivalent programs in the Secure Shell are called *slogin*, *ssh*, and *scp*. The primary differences in using these commands are that the connection is authenticated on both sides and all passwords and other data are transmitted in encrypted form.

DARPA Commands

The Berkeley remote commands are designed for use on like Unix systems, but the DARPA commands were designed as part of the TCP/IP protocol suite and can be used by any two systems that support TCP/IP. Virtually all Unix operating systems include both the client and server programs for Telnet, FTP, and Trivial File Transfer Protocol (TFTP) and install them by default, although some administrators may choose to disable them later.

telnet

The *telnet* command is similar in its functionality to *rlogin*, except that *telnet* does not send any information about the user on the client system to the server. You must always supply a username and password to be authenticated. As with all of the DARPA commands, you can use a Telnet client to connect to any computer running a Telnet server, even if it is running a different version of Unix or a non-Unix OS. The commands you can use while connected, however, are wholly dependent on the OS running the Telnet server. If, for example, you install a Telnet server on a Windows system, you can connect to it from a Unix client, but once connected, you can use only the commands recognized by Windows. Since Windows is not primarily a character-based OS, its command-line capabilities are relatively limited, unless you install outside programs.

ftp

The *ftp* command provides more comprehensive file transfer capabilities than *rcp* and enables a client to access the file system on any computer running an FTP server. However, instead of accessing files in place on the other system, *ftp* provides only the ability to transfer files to and from the remote system. For example, you cannot edit a file on a remote system, but you can download it to your own system, edit it there, and then upload the new version to the original location. Like with Telnet, users must authenticate themselves to an FTP server before they are granted access to the file system. Many systems running FTP, such as those on the Internet, support anonymous access, but even this requires an authentication process of sorts in which the user supplies the name "anonymous" and the server is configured to accept any password.

tftp

The *tftp* command uses the Trivial File Transfer Protocol to copy files to or from a remote system. Whereas *ftp* relies on the Transmission Control Protocol at the transport layer, *tftp* uses the User Datagram Protocol (UDP). Because UDP is a connectionless protocol, no authentication by the remote system is needed. However, this limits the command to copying only files that are publicly available on the remote system. The TFTP protocol was designed primarily for use by diskless workstations that have to download an executable operating system file from a server during the boot process.

Network File System

Sharing files is an essential part of computer networking, and Unix systems use several mechanisms to access files on other systems without first transferring them to a local drive, as with *ftp* and *rcp*. The most commonly used of these mechanisms is the Network File System (NFS), which was developed by Sun Microsystems in the 1980s and has now been standardized by the Internet Engineering Task Force (IETF) as RFC 1094 (NFS Version 2) and RFC 1813 (NFS Version 3). By allowing NFS to be published as an open standard, Sun made it possible for anyone to implement the service, and the result is that NFS support is available for virtually every OS in use today.

Practically every Unix variant available includes support for NFS, which makes it possible to share files among systems running different Unix versions. Non-Unix operating systems, such as Windows and NetWare, can also support NFS, but a separate product (marketed by either the manufacturer or a third party) is required. Since Windows and NetWare have their own internal file-sharing mechanisms, these other operating systems mostly require NFS only to integrate Unix systems into their networks.

NFS is a client-server application in which a server makes all or part of its file system available to clients (using a process called *exporting* or *sharing*), and a client accesses the remote file system by *mounting* it, which makes it appear just like part of the local file system. NFS does not communicate directly with the kernel on the local computer but rather relies on the remote procedure calls (RPC) service, also developed by Sun, to handle communications with the remote system. RPC has also been released as an open standard by Sun and published as an IETF document called RFC 1057. The data transmitted by NFS is encoded using a method called *External Data Representation* (XDR), as defined in RFC 1014. In most cases, the service uses the UDP protocol for network transport and listens on port 2049.

NFS is designed to keep the server side of the application as simple as possible. NFS servers are *stateless*, meaning they do not have to maintain information about the state of a client to function properly. In other words, the server does not maintain information about which clients have files open. In the event that a server crashes, clients simply continue to send their requests until the server responds. If a client crashes, the server continues to operate normally. There is no need for a complicated reconnection sequence. Because repeated iterations of the same activities can be the consequence of this statelessness, NFS is also designed to be as *idempotent* as possible, meaning that the repeated performance of the same task will not have a deleterious effect on the performance of the system. NFS servers also take no part in the adaptation of the exported file system to the client's requirements. The server supplies file system information in a generalized form, and it is up to the client to integrate it into its own file system so that applications can make use of it.

The communication between NFS clients and servers is based on a series of RPC procedures defined in the NFS standard and listed in Table 20-1. These basic functions enable the client to interact with the file system on the server in all of the ways expected by a typical application. An Internet-Draft released in April 2014 by IETF describes minor updates to earlier NFS versions. The goal of this revision, according to the draft, is to "improve access and good performance on the Internet, provide strong security, good cross-platform interoperability, and is designed for

Procedure Number	Procedure Name	Function
0	NULL	Does not do any work; used for server response testing and timing
1	GETATTR	Retrieves attributes for a specified file system object
2	SETATTR	Changes one or more of the attributes of a file system object on the server
3	LOOKUP	Searches a directory for a specific name and returns the file handle for the corresponding file system object
4	ACCESS	Determines the access rights that a user has with respect to a file system object
5	READLINK	Reads the data associated with a symbolic link
6	READ	Reads data from a file
7	WRITE	Writes data to a file
8	CREATE	Creates a regular file
9	MKDIR	Creates a new subdirectory
10	SYMLINK	Creates a new symbolic link
11	MKNOD	Creates a new special file
12	REMOVE	Deletes a file from a directory
13	RMDIR	Deletes a subdirectory from a directory
14	RENAME	Renames a file or directory
15	LINK	Creates a link to an object
16	READDIR	Retrieves a variable number of entries from a directory and returns the name and file identifier for each entry
17	READDIRPLUS	Retrieves a variable number of entries from a file system directory and returns complete information about each
18	FSSTAT	Retrieves volatile file system state information
19	FSINFO	Retrieves nonvolatile file system state information and general information about the NFS version 3 protocol server implementation
20	PATHCONF	Retrieves POSIX information for a file or directory
21	COMMIT	Forces or flushes data to stable storage that was previously written with a WRITE procedure call with the stable field set to UNSTABLE

Table 20-1   Some RPC Procedures in NFS Versions

protocol extensions which do not compromise backward compatibility." (See http://tools.ietf.org/ html/draft-ietf-nfsv4-rfc3530bis-33#section-1.1 for more information.)

On a system configured to function as an NFS server, you can control which parts of the file system are accessible to clients by using commands such as *share* on Solaris and SVR4 systems and *exportfs* on Linux and HP-UX. Using these commands, you specify which directories clients can access and what degree of access they are provided. You can choose to share a directory on a read-only basis, for example, or grant read-write access, and you can also designate different access permissions for specific users.

Client systems access the directories that have been shared by a server by using the *mount* command to integrate them into the local file system. The *mount* command specifies a directory shared by a server, the access that client applications should have to the remote directory (such as read-write or read-only), and the mount point for the remote files. The *mount point* is a directory on the local system in which the shared files and directories will appear. Applications and commands running on the client system can reference the remote files just as if they were located on a local drive.

Client-Server Networking

Client-server computing is the basis for networking on Unix systems, as it is on many other computing platforms. Unix is a popular application server platform largely because its relative simplicity and flexibility enable the computer to devote more of its resources toward its primary function. On a Windows server, for example, a significant amount of system resources are devoted to running the GUI and other subsystems that may have little or nothing to do with the server applications that are its primary functions. When you dedicate a computer to functioning as a web server, for example, and you want it to be able to service as many clients as possible, it makes sense to disable all extraneous functions, which is something that is far easier to do on a Unix system than in Windows.

Server applications on Unix systems typically run as *daemons,* which are background processes that run continuously, regardless of the system's other activities. There are many commercial server products available for various Unix versions and also a great many that are available free of charge. Because the TCP/IP protocols were largely developed on the Unix platform, Unix server software is available for every TCP/IP application in existence.

CHAPTER 21

Other Network Operating Systems and Networking in the Cloud

Additional operating systems have been created as computing has evolved. Today, many users are turning to the cloud for networking (and other services). As technology advances, new methods and approaches will develop.

Historical Systems

In 1977, a Unix-based operating system was developed by the University of California, Berkeley. This system was originally an extension of AT&T Research's Unix operating system. Eventually, Berkeley Software Distribution (BSD) Unix came to be the operating system (OS) that many other organizations used as the basis for their own Unix products, including Sun Microsystems' SunOS. The result is that many of the programs written for one BSD-based Unix version are binary-compatible with other versions. Once the SVR4 release consolidated the best features of BSD and several other Unix versions into one product, the BSD product became less influential and culminated in the 4.4BSD version in 1992.

Although many of the Unix variants that are popular today owe a great debt to the BSD development project, the versions of BSD that are still commonly used are public domain operating systems, such as FreeBSD, Linux, NetBSD, and Open BSD. All of these operating systems are based on Berkeley's 4.4BSD release and can be downloaded from the Internet free of charge and used for private and commercial applications at no cost.

FreeBSD

FreeBSD, available at freebsd.org/ in versions for the Intel and Alpha platforms, is based on the Berkeley 4.4BSD-Lite2 release and is binary-compatible with Linux, SCO, SVR4, and NetBSD applications. The FreeBSD development project is divided into two branches: the STABLE branch, which includes only well-tested bug fixes and incremental enhancements, and the CURRENT branch, which includes all of the latest code and is intended primarily for developers, testers, and enthusiasts. The current stable version as of January 2015 is 10.1.

NetBSD

NetBSD, available at netbsd.org/, is derived from the same sources as FreeBSD but boasts portability as one of its highest priorities. NetBSD is available in formal releases for 15 hardware platforms, ranging from Intel and Alpha to Mac, SPARC, and MIPS processors, including those designed for handheld Windows CE devices. Many other ports are in the developmental and experimental stages. NetBSD's binary compatibility enables it to support applications written for many other Unix variants, including BSD, FreeBSD, HP/UX, Linux, SVR4, Solaris, SunOS, and others. Networking capabilities supported directly by the kernel include NFS, IPv6, network address translation (NAT), and packet filtering. The latest version of NetBSD, released in September 2014 is 6.1.5.

OpenBSD

OpenBSD is available at openbsd.org/; the current version is 5.6, released in November 2014. Like the other BSD-derived operating systems, OpenBSD is binary-compatible with most of its peers, including FreeBSD, SVR4, Solaris, SunOS, and HP/UX, and it currently supports 20 hardware platforms, including Intel, Alpha, SPARC, PowerPC, and others. However, the top priorities of OpenBSD's developers are security and cryptography. Because OpenBSD is a noncommercial product, its developers feel they can take a more uncompromising stance on security issues and disclose more information about security than commercial software developers. Also, because it is developed in and distributed from Canada, OpenBSD is not subject to the American laws that prohibit the export of cryptographic software to other countries. The developers are, therefore, more likely to take a cryptographic approach to security solutions than are American-based companies.

Oracle Solaris

Sun Microsystems (sun.com) became involved in Unix development in the early 1980s, when its operating system was known as SunOS. In 1991, Sun created a subsidiary called SunSoft that began work on a new Unix version based on SVR4, which it called Solaris. Purchased by Oracle in 2010, Oracle Solaris is now a complete cloud infrastructure operating system and bills itself as the "industry's most widely deployed Unix operating system" and the "first fully virtualized operating system." See the next section to learn more about cloud computing.

Operating in the Cloud

Working "in the cloud" is not a new concept. When Vannevar Bush and J.C.R. Licklider were formulating the Advanced Research Projects Agency Network (ARPANET) in the 1960s, Licklider envisioned the "Intergalactic Computer Network." A paper written with Robert W. Taylor in 1968 entitled "The Computer as a Communication Device" predicted that computer networks would be used for communication. Although his ideas were not realized until the availability of higher bandwidths in the 1990s, much of what he described is used today. His paper is still available at several locations on the Internet, including http://memex.org/licklider.pdf.

History of the Cloud

The term *cloud computing* has been in use for several decades. While the exact origin seems to be unknown, a cloud symbol has long been used to represent the Internet when creating computer diagrams. And, the cloud itself is a networked group of servers that can be accessed over the Internet, making it possible to obtain services, resources, and storage from any world location where an Internet connection is available.

Precursors to the Cloud

In the 1950s, mainframe computers were used for communication at large companies and universities. Many were incapable of processing information but were accessible from so-called thin-client workstations. These units were quite costly, and time on them was often rented to others; therefore, "time-sharing" became a popular method of recouping the high cost of these units.

In 1960, the Dataphone was created by AT&T to convert digital computer signals to analog signals so the digital signals could be sent via AT&T's long-distance network. Online transaction processing became available over telephone lines in 1964. Created by IBM for American Airlines, telephone lines linked 65 cities to IBM computers.

The first photo-digital storage system was created by IBM in 1967 and could read and write up to a trillion bits of information. Modems appeared in 1970, and resource-sharing became commonplace thanks to ARPANET and several universities. E-mail first appeared in 1971, and the Ethernet method was created in 1973.

In 1975, Telenet became the commercial equivalent of ARPANET and linked computers in seven cities. By 1979, Usenet came into common usage and existed through the 1990s. Transmission Control Protocol/Internet Protocol (TCP/IP) was adopted in 1980, and within a few years, ARPANET was divided into two segments: MILNET for military use and ARPANET for civilian usage. This civilian segment became known as the Internet in 1995. In 1989, the first Internet service providers (ISPs) appeared in both the United States and Australia.

By 1990, Hypertext Markup Language (HTML), created by Tim Berners-Lee, made the World Wide Web possible. The specifications Berners-Lee developed made it possible for browsers to send queries to servers and view documents on linked, faraway sites. Shortly thereafter, the first commercial web browser software (Mosaic) was released for several operating systems. In 1991, Berners-Lee founded the W3 Consortium for development on the World Wide Web.

As computing power, bandwidth availability, and computers themselves gained wider usage, some telecommunication firms started offering virtual private networks (VPNs) to their larger customers. These networks made it possible for data to be processed across a public or shared network as if the network was functioning as a private network. VPNs operate in a similar manner to wide area networks and allow users to securely connect offices and personnel across widely separated geographical distances. Table 21-1 shows how the cloud has evolved from the mainframes of the 1950s.

Early Cloud Providers

Widely accepted as the beginning of cloud computing services was the Salesforce.com web site, which launched in 1999, providing business applications and other customer relationship management (CRM) products. Still in business, it offers a wide variety of sales and marketing products.

Decade	Development
1950s	Computers used for one specific task. Local, onsite infrastructure. First computer language developed (Grace Hopper developed COBOL). Transistors begin to replace vacuum tubes in computers.
1960s	Information technology services. Online transactions, such as airline reservations. Computers and peripherals work together.
1970s	Business and personal computers available to the public. Automatic teller machines. Floppy disks available for information sharing. E-mail, Ethernet, Usenet.
1980s	Personal computers, with graphical user interface and mice become available. Bulletin board systems (BBSs) flourish.
1990s	World Wide Web and first web browser (Mosaic). Virtual private networks. Dot-coms rise and fall.
2000s	Infrastructure outsourcing. Virtualization becomes widespread.
2010 and beyond	Availability of "as a service," such as infrastructure as a service, platform as a service, service as a service, and network as a service. Tablets and smart phones used as primary communication devices in the cloud.

Table 21-1   Computing Through the Decades

In 2002, Amazon unveiled its Amazon Web Services, which offered storage and computation services. It also was the first appearance of the Amazon Mechanical Turk, a service that provides businesses with workers who perform tasks that computers cannot yet accomplish. Amazon's Elastic Compute Cloud (EC2) was introduced in 2006. This service provides computer rental time to individuals and small companies on which they can run their own programs.

Google joined the cloud in 2009 when it offered, along with several other services, Google Apps, which is similar to well-known desktop software products; using Google Apps, a user can create word processing documents, spreadsheets, and presentations online. From there, users can save them to their own computer as well as access the file from any location with an Internet connection.

Benefits of the Cloud

There are many benefits for both business and individuals when working in the cloud. The following are just some of the benefits of the cloud:

- **Accessibility**   Data stored in the cloud can be accessed from anywhere. Files can be shared and updated on any device that has Internet connectivity. All services can be used on demand without outside interaction.

- **Affordability**   Applications can be used as needed, instead of investing in hardware or software that may be needed only part of the time. The cloud also eliminates long-term commitment to any specific technology.

- **Availability**   Nearly any service one needs is available for a fee from a cloud provider.

- **Competitive advantages**   Especially for smaller businesses, technical expertise can be expensive. Companies utilizing the cloud for technical services can operate at much less cost than those businesses who have in-house staff.

- **Disaster recovery**   Information stored in the cloud is available at any time. If a disaster strikes, data is still available.

- **Efficiency**   Because of the economies of scale inherent to cloud providers, costs per "transaction" are much smaller than in-house operations. Also, the load-balancing capabilities increase reliability.

- **Elasticity**   As business grows, the cloud provides scalability.

- **Theft protection**   Information stored on a laptop or tablet can be compromised if it is stolen. Were the same information stored in the cloud rather than on the mobile device, the data would not be at risk.

Disadvantages in the Cloud

As with any technology, there are disadvantages to cloud computing, covered in the following sections.

Security

The most common concern when discussing moving to the cloud is security. Malware, hackers, and unauthorized access become major concerns, and relying on a third party to ensure confidential client data or patented internal information can be a major issue.

Loss of Control

Internal data and information are no longer under your immediate control. If applications are run in another location, they may experience downtime, slow responses, or other problems that can affect daily workloads.

Dependency

If an enterprise cannot connect to the Internet, cloud computing becomes a liability instead of an asset; therefore, reliable, consistent, high-speed Internet access is critical. Also, once a company is committed to a specific cloud vendor, it can be difficult to move to another supplier.

Initial Cost

Small companies often find the initial investment can be costly. Researching exactly what a company requires and comparing those requirements to services offered by each outside service can help find the lowest cost.

Also, before committing to a specific vendor for outside cloud services, companies must ensure their equipment is compatible with an outside cloud service provider to eliminate any additional in-house equipment purchases.

Part V

Lack of Redundancy

Each service, especially those offering data storage, offers different levels of data storage protection, often with different price points. Even when all is going well, equipment can malfunction.

How the Cloud Works

Today, cloud companies are everywhere. But, how does the cloud work? The cloud works in much the same way as your office computer. However, instead of installing applications or storing data locally, your applications, your data, and even the processor are installed on a computer in another location. Figure 21-1 shows the traditional setup for an office computer with data and applications stored on a desktop (or laptop) computer within one office.

With resources, software, information, and even operating systems available in the cloud today, it is possible for businesses and individuals to bypass the onsite storage and server and have all storage, applications, and processing done via the cloud, as shown in Figure 21-2.

Front-End Cloud Architecture

The front end of the cloud architecture is the client interface, the method by which the end user connects to the Internet. It includes the way the client (end user) connects to the Internet, such as an e-mail client that uses web browsers or task-specific applications.

Back-End Cloud Architecture

At the back end are all the resources the cloud provides. This can be storage, software, platforms, and security, as shown in Figure 21-3.

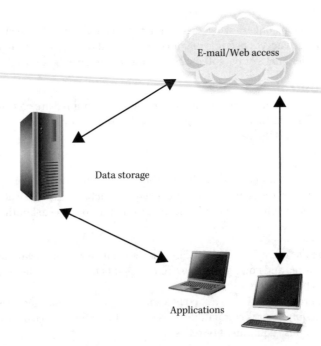

Figure 21-1 A typical office computer setup with computers, server, storage, and web access

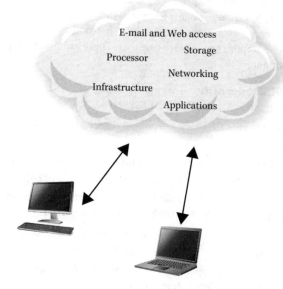

Figure 21-2   The cloud provides many services that were once handled onsite.

Figure 21-3   The architecture of cloud computing

Middleware The resources at the back end use *middleware* to support the various components. Middleware was once a term that defined the software connecting applications and networks. However, today middleware can be construed as a cloud intermediary; it's software that allows other components to work together. There are several types of middleware, some of which are shown here:

- **Content/data-centric** This method allows users to obtain specific items by a unique identifier, rather than going through servers.
- **Database** This middleware allows direct access to databases, including SQL databases.
- **Embedded** This type provides communication between other embedded applications or between embedded operating systems and external applications.
- **Message-oriented** This enables disbursement of applications over various platforms and operating systems. It is the most commonly used.
- **Portals** While portals are not always considered middleware, they create connections between the user's device and back-end services.
- **Transaction** This type, which is becoming more common, includes web application servers and transaction applications.

Components Back-end components vary from service to service but generally have three main parts:

- **Data storage** Most cloud services offer this component. Whether stored by the service itself, by a cloud application, or by the user, it is often designed to store more than one copy of each data set.
- **Application server** Each server within the service is usually designed to perform or provide only one service or function. In most cases, application servers are available for the client interface.
- **Control nodes** These task-specific computers connect to data storage or application servers by the Internet or other networks. They are the connection between the front-end architecture and servers, maintaining communication and proper data flow between the two.

Cloud Types

There are four main types of cloud services. Each has its own advantages and disadvantages.

Public Cloud

Public clouds are owned and managed by a private company that offers the service to users. The services are separate from the users, and users have no control over the structure of the company's equipment or network. There are many companies offering these services today, such as Amazon, Google, and Microsoft.

Users pay only for the services, sometimes for short-term usage to complete a time-critical project or over a longer term, such as to store data off-site. This can reduce the capital expenditures for equipment and IT support within an organization.

While such services are scalable and usually reliable, because of its public nature, public clouds are vulnerable to malware and other attacks. Moreover, some companies cannot take advantage of public cloud services because of security regulations within their industry. Also, public clouds can be slower than in-house networks.

Private Cloud

Private clouds (also called *internal clouds*) are owned and operated by one group, company, or organization. For example, the resources are used by offices in three different cities, but the equipment and other assets are kept in a fourth location. The company owns and maintains control over the entire cloud.

While the initial costs of creating such a network may be high, this method can alleviate some security concerns and give much more control than that of public offerings. Private clouds can offer the same services as public clouds, as discussed in "Cloud Service Models" later in this chapter.

Hybrid Cloud

A hybrid cloud service utilizes both public and private clouds, each of which have separate uses. For example, a company may use its internal infrastructure (that is, its own private cloud) for security, speed, or privacy and then contract with an outside data storage service.

Community Cloud

Essentially, this cloud service is designed for use by a group that wants more control than can be obtained from a public cloud service. This model can be either managed by the community or contracted with an outside service. It is usually formed to address a common issue, such as regulatory compliance or security.

Cloud Service Models

As cloud computing is becoming more widespread, there are several types of cloud services offered by today's vendors. Several of the commonly used types are discussed here.

Infrastructure as a Service

Infrastructure as a service (IaaS) replaces many of the physical assets used in computing. Users pay regular fees, often monthly or annually, to use servers, use networks, or store data on a computer at a location other than their physical office. This saves costs associated with running and maintaining hardware locally.

IaaS is often platform independent, and the users are charged for only the resources they actually use. Since the infrastructure expense is shared among all the users, hardware expense is greatly reduced. Payment for the service can be on a "pay-as-you-go" basis, where the user pays for both software and infrastructure, or "bring-your-own-license," where the business supplies its own software licenses and uses only the infrastructure in the cloud.

Most providers offer a user interface that serves as the management console for the client. Logging on with a password offers the client much the same graphic user interface (GUI) with which they are already familiar. IaaS is especially useful for businesses that are growing rapidly or have periods when the workload is especially heavy.

This service eliminates the need to upgrade hardware and provides flexibility as long as a high-speed connection to the Internet is available. Providers normally manage the servers, hard drives, networking, and storage. Some even offer database services and messaging queues. The user is still responsible for managing their applications and data. Most providers require that the user maintain middleware as well.

Benefits of IaaS

There are several benefits to using IaaS, as shown here:

- **Stretches financial resources**   When companies need to grow but currently have limited financial resources, IaaS is useful for access to enterprise-level structures without the need to invest in more hardware. This frees funds for adding personnel or enhanced marketing campaigns.
- **Flexibility**   The flexibility of using just the service a company needs, such as hardware (as a service) or storage (as a service), is another advantage to IaaS. This pay-as-you-use method can be useful.
- **Disaster recovery**   Because information is stored away from the user's facility, recovery can be much faster in the event of fire, weather-related incidents, or other catastrophes.
- **Scalability**   For businesses with temporary busy cycles, using IaaS can allow users to accommodate the schedules efficiently.

Disadvantages of IaaS

In addition to the issues of using the cloud discussed in "Disadvantages in the Cloud" earlier in this chapter, there are some specific IaaS concerns:

- **Use of mobile devices**   Because of its on-demand nature, mobile device access can cause usage to exhaust the resources available.
- **Internal requirements**   If users do not clearly define and understand their needs, IaaS may end up costing more than investing in additional equipment.
- **Minimal usage**   If the company usage is minimal, IaaS may not be the best solution.

Platform as a Service

The second layer in the cloud "stack" is platform as a service (PaaS). The National Institute of Standards and Technology (NIST) defines PaaS as follows:

> "Platform as a Service (PaaS). The capability provided to the consumer is to deploy onto the cloud infrastructure consumer-created or acquired applications created using programming languages, libraries, services, and tools supported by the provider. The consumer does not manage or control the underlying cloud infrastructure including network, servers, operating systems, or storage, but has control over the deployed applications and possibly configuration settings for the application-hosting environment."

PaaS is designed for developing and managing applications, as opposed to IaaS, which is the provision of the underlying hardware resources required in business. The cloud service provides both the lower-level infrastructure resources and the application development and deployment structure. In this way, application developers can focus on the development and management of new applications.

Benefits of PaaS

As cloud computing grows, the differences between IaaS and PaaS are blurring. Even so, the ability to create, test, assess, and deploy new software applications makes PaaS appealing for some of the following reasons:

- **No physical investment**   The ability to rent the hardware resources necessary to develop new software makes it possible for developers to focus on their applications.

- **Anyone can be a developer**   Using a web browser, even novices can create an application. Using browser-based software development tools, the developer needs only a computer with a browser and Internet connection.

- **Adaptable and flexible**   Developers have control of the features, which can be changed if necessary.

- **Connectivity**   Using the Internet, developers in different geographic locations can work on the same project at the same time to build their applications.

- **Fast testing and deploying**   Teams can assess response and performance across multiple locations, platforms, and machines. Small applications meant for a limited customer base now become more cost-effective.

Disadvantages of PaaS

Even as PaaS is being utilized in the field, there are some concerns:

- **Lack of confidence in security**   Developers of new applications or products often are concerned about the secrecy and security of that information. Skepticism about revealing their plans to someone outside the company (the cloud provider) remains high. Other clients are concerned about regulatory compliance and data retention.

- **System integration**   There is a chance of the application not working with underlying resources.

- **Workarounds**   Some users have reported the necessity of using workarounds to bypass the limitations involved on various PaaS platforms.

Software as a Service

With the advent of Office 365 and Google Docs, software as a service instead of a product to be installed and maintained on office machines is becoming mainstream. This frees users from updating their applications and investing in new hardware as new features are added to the application. Users purchase usage time rather than a license, essentially renting the application.

In some cases, the users pay nothing, like with Facebook or search engines. Revenue is generated by advertising on those sites. Instead of installing the software on an individual device, the user accesses the site via the Internet. Instead of purchasing a new computer with lots of RAM, you can access these sites from a smart phone or tablet because all of the heavy-duty technology is on the server computer.

Part V

Benefits of SaaS

In addition to the cost benefits to the user, SaaS offers the following:

- **Less user responsibility**   There is no need to upgrade, maintain, or customize software applications.
- **Anywhere availability**   Whether at a football game or in the office, documents, spreadsheets, marketing plans, and any other documents can be accessed quickly on most any device that connects with the Internet.

Disadvantages of SaaS

Despite its convenience, there are some downsides to SaaS:

- **Slowness**   An application accessed over the Internet via a browser may be slower than the same program running on a local computer.
- **Compliance**   There are concerns in some industries about data regulations and requirements. Software accessed over the Internet may not meet those regulations.
- **Third-party dependency**   Like with all cloud services, SaaS is dependent on the cloud provider. This is perhaps most concerning when using software for daily tasks.

Network as a Service

As with the other cloud services, network as a service (NaaS) delivers network services over the Internet. Instead of investing in networking hardware, software, and IT staff, a business can create a VPN or a mobile network with only one computer, an Internet connection, and a monthly or pay-per-use subscription.

PART

VI

Network Services

CHAPTER

22

Network Clients

Although network administrators frequently spend a lot of time installing and configuring servers, the primary reason for the servers' existence is the clients. The choice of applications and operating systems for your servers should be based in part on the client platforms and operating systems that have to access them. Usually it is possible for any client platform to connect to any server, one way or another, but this doesn't mean you should choose client and server platforms freely and expect them all to work well together in every combination.

For ease of administration, it's a good idea to use the same operating system on all of your client workstations wherever possible. Even today, many network installations use standard Intel-based PCs running some version of Microsoft Windows, but even if you choose to standardize on Windows, you may have some users with special needs who require a different platform. Many network administrators over the last three to four years are much more open to the fact that they have to be ready for anything and everything in their operating systems. Since the advent of iPads and iPhones and other Apple devices, many college graduates moving into the corporate world are used to working on Apple products, so younger IT administrators are already used to working with that type of system. Graphic artists, for example, are often accustomed to working on Apple systems, and other users may need Unix or Linux. When selecting server platforms, you should consider what is needed to enable users on various client platforms to access them.

When you run various server platforms along with multiple clients, the process becomes even more complicated because each workstation might require multiple clients. The impact of multiple network clients on the performance of the computer depends on exactly which clients are involved. This chapter examines the client platforms commonly used on networks today and the software used to connect them to various servers.

Windows Network Clients

Although Microsoft Windows began as a stand-alone operating system, networking soon became a ubiquitous part of Windows, and all versions now include a client that enables them to connect to any other Windows computer. Windows networking was first introduced in the Windows NT 3.1 and Windows for Workgroups releases in 1993. The Windows networking architecture is based on network adapter drivers written to the Network Device Interface Specification (NDIS) standard and, originally, on the NetBEUI protocol. Later, Transmission Control Protocol/Internet Protocol (TCP/IP) became the default networking protocol.

Windows networking is a peer-to-peer system that enables any computer on the network to access resources on any other computer, as long as the other computers are running a protocol supported by Windows. When Microsoft introduced networking into Windows, the predominant network operating system was Novell NetWare, which used the client-server model that enables clients to access server resources only. Adding peer-to-peer networking to an already popular, user-friendly operating system such as Windows led to its rapid growth in the business local area network (LAN) industry and its eventual encroachment into NetWare's market share.

Windows Networking Architecture

Windows 3.1 and 3.11 were the only major versions of the operating environment that lacked a networking stack of their own, but it was possible to use Microsoft Client 3.0 for MS-DOS to connect them to a Windows network. All of the other Windows versions have built-in networking capabilities that enable the computer to participate on a Windows network.

The basic architecture of the Windows network client is the same in all of the operating systems, although the implementations differ substantially. In its simplest form, the client functionality uses the modules shown in Figure 22-1. At the bottom of the protocol stack is an NDIS network adapter driver that provides access to the network interface card (NIC) installed in the computer. Above the network adapter driver are drivers for the individual protocols running on the system. At the top of the stack is the client itself, which takes the form of one or more services.

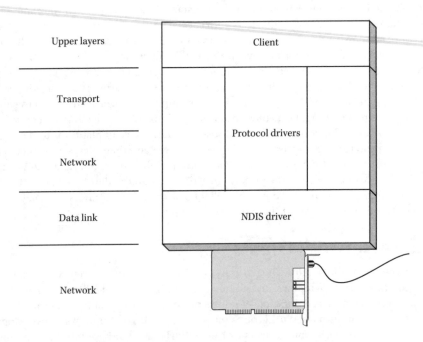

Figure 22-1   The basic Windows client architecture

These three layers form a complete protocol stack running from the application layer of the Open Systems Interconnection (OSI) model down to the physical layer. Applications generate requests for specific resources that pass through a mechanism that determines whether the resource is located on a local device or on the network. Requests for network resources are redirected down through the networking stack to the NIC, which transmits them to the appropriate devices. The following sections examine these elements in more detail.

NDIS Drivers

The Network Device Interface Specification was designed by Microsoft and 3Com to provide an interface between the data link and network layers of the OSI model that would enable a single NIC installed in a computer to carry traffic generated by multiple protocols. This interface insulates the protocol drivers and other components at the upper layers of the protocol stack so that the process of accessing network resources is always the same, no matter what NIC is installed in the machine. As long as there is an NDIS-compatible NIC driver available, the interface can pass the requests from the various protocol drivers to the card, as needed, for transmission over the network.

The various Windows network clients use different versions of NDIS for their adapter drivers, as shown in Table 22-1. NDIS 2 was the only version of the interface that runs in the Intel processor's real mode, using conventional rather than extended memory, and it used a driver file with a .dos extension. Microsoft Client 3.0 for MS-DOS relied on this version of the specification for network access, but the primary job of NDIS 2 was to function as a real-mode backup for Windows for Workgroups, Windows 95, 98, and Me. All four of these operating systems included later versions of the NDIS specification that ran in protected mode, but the real-mode driver was included for situations in which it was impossible to load the protected-mode driver.

The primary advantage of the NDIS 3 drivers included with Windows for Workgroups and the first Windows NT releases was their ability to run in protected mode, which can use both

NDIS Version	Operating Systems
2	Client 3.0 for MS-DOS; Windows 95/98 (real mode)
3	Windows NT 3.1–3.51; Windows for Workgroups 3.11
3.1	Windows 95
4	Windows NT 4.0; Windows 95 OSR2; Windows CE 3.0
5	Windows 2000; Windows 98; Windows ME
5.1	Windows XP, Server 2003, Windows CE 4.0 through 6.0
5.2	Windows Server 2003 SP2
6	Windows Vista
6.1	Windows Vista SP1, Server 2008, Windows Embedded Compact Version 7
6.20	Windows 7, Server 2008 R2
6.30	Windows 8, Windows Server 2012
6.40	Windows 8.1, Windows Server 2012 R2

Table 22-1 NDIS Versions and the Operating Systems That Use Them

Part VI

extended and virtual memory. The driver took the form of an NDIS wrapper, which is generic, and a miniport driver that is device specific. Because most of the interface code is part of the wrapper, the development of miniport drivers by individual NIC manufacturers was relatively simple.

NDIS 3.1, first used in Windows 95, introduced plug-and-play capabilities to the interface, which greatly simplified the process of installing NICs. NDIS 4 provided additional functionality, such as support for infrared and other new media and power-management capabilities. NDIS 5 added a connection-oriented service that supports the ATM protocol in its native mode, as well as its quality-of-service functions. In addition, *TCP/IP task offloading* enabled enhanced NICs to perform functions normally implemented by the transport layer protocol, such as checksum computations and data segmenting, which reduces the load on the system processor.

NDIS 6 brought improved performance for both clients and servers in addition to simplified reset handling, and it streamlined driver initialization. NDIS 6.4, the latest version, added more functions.

All of the Windows network clients ship with NDIS drivers for an assortment of the most popular NICs that are in use at the time of the product's release. This means, of course, that older clients do not include support for the latest NICs on the market, but the NIC manufacturers all supply NDIS drivers for their products.

Protocol Drivers

Since Windows 95, Windows network clients all support the use of TCP/IP. When Microsoft first added networking to Windows, NetBEUI was the default protocol because it is closely related to the NetBIOS interface that Windows uses to name the computers on the network. NetBEUI is self-adjusting and requires no configuration or maintenance at all, but its lack of routing capabilities makes it unsuitable for today's networks. This shortcoming, plus the rise in the popularity of the Internet, led to TCP/IP being adopted as the protocol of choice on most networks, despite its need for individual client configuration.

The IPX protocol suite was developed by Novell for its NetWare operating system, which was the most popular networking solution at the time that Windows networking was introduced. After the release of Windows Vista and Windows Server 2003 x645, you need to contact Novell for support on either IPX or SPX. Novell client support for Windows 7, 8, and 8.1 as well as Windows x64 can be found at https://www.novell.com/documentation/windows_client.

Client Services

The upper layers of the networking stack in a Windows client take different names and forms, depending on the operating system. A service is a program that runs continuously in the background while the operating system is loaded, the equivalent of a daemon in Unix.

In most cases, the Windows networking architecture enables you to install additional client services that can take advantage of the same protocol and adapter modules as the Windows network client. For example, to turn on the Network Client in Windows 8.1, follow these steps:

1. Hold down the Windows key and press I, and from the resulting Settings column on the right side of your window, choose Control Panel.

2. From the Control Panel, choose Network And Internet.

3. Select Network And Internet and then Network And Sharing Center.

4. From the column on the left, choose Change Adapter Settings.

5. From the choices displayed, right-click the network adapter you want to use.

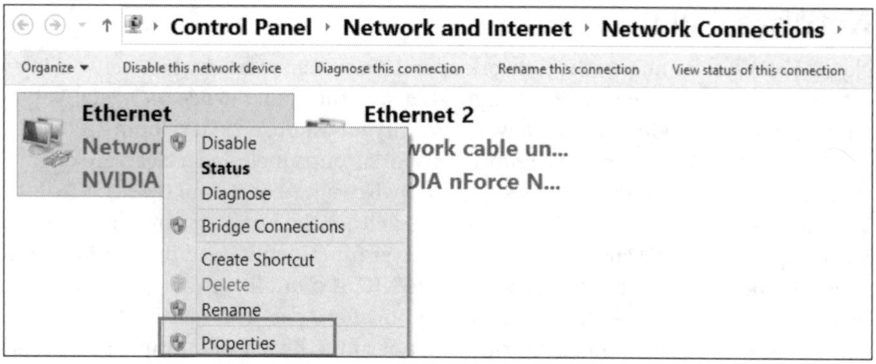

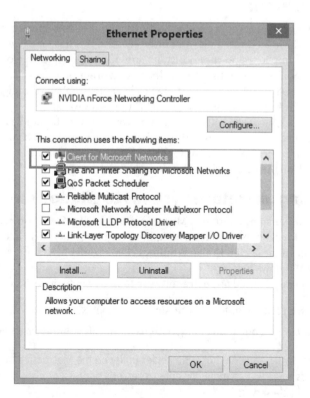

Figure 22-2 Choose Properties from the right-click menu.

6. From the resulting menu, choose Properties, as shown in Figure 22-2.

7. Ensure that the Client For Microsoft Networks list item has a check in the check box, as shown in Figure 22-3.

8. Click OK to close the dialog box and then click Control Panel to return to the Control Panel window.

Figure 22-3 The Ethernet Properties dialog has several options for each adapter.

NetWare Clients

Novell NetWare dominated the network operating system market when networking was being integrated into the Windows operating systems, so the ability to access legacy NetWare resources while running a Windows network was a priority for Microsoft's development team.

Neither Windows 3.1 nor Windows for Workgroups included a NetWare client, but both of them functioned with the clients supplied by Novell. At the time that the 16-bit versions of Windows were released, NetWare clients used either the NetWare shell (NETX) or the NetWare DOS Requestor (VLM) client for the upper-layer functionality and used either a monolithic or Open Datalink Interface (ODI) driver for the NIC. A monolithic driver is a single executable (called Ipx.com) that includes the driver support for a particular NIC, while ODI is the Novell equivalent of NDIS, a modular interface that permits the use of multiple protocols with a single network card. The combination of an ODI driver and the VLM requestor was the most advanced NetWare client available at that time.

All of these client options loaded from the DOS command line, which meant that they provided network access to DOS applications outside of Windows, but also meant that they utilized large amounts of conventional and upper memory. In fact, without a carefully configured boot sequence or an automated memory management program, it was difficult to keep enough conventional memory free to load applications.

Macintosh Clients

Many of today's networks contain workstations with different operating systems. All Macintosh systems include an integrated network interface, and this has long been touted as evidence of the platform's simplicity and superiority. In earlier times Macintosh workstations required special treatment to connect them to a network running other platforms, such as Windows or Unix. However, since OS X's initial release there has been no problem running a Mac on a Unix-based network (OS X is Unix) and few issues on a Windows network.

In most cases, however, you can configure your network to handle Macintosh clients, enabling Mac users to share files with Windows and other clients. If you select applications that are available in compatible versions for the different client platforms you're running, Mac users can even work on the same files as Windows users.

Connecting Macintosh Systems to Windows Networks

Older Windows versions contained Microsoft Services for Macintosh, which implemented the AppleTalk protocol on the Windows computer, enabling Macintosh systems to access file and printer shares on the server. Unlike Windows clients, older Mac systems did not participate as peers on the Windows network.

Today, you do not need any extra software to access network drives from your Apple machines.

1. Open a Finder window by pressing COMMAND-N.

2. Choose from one of the Shared items in the left column, as shown in Figure 22-4.

NOTE Alternatively, you can make the Finder utility on the Mac active by pressing the Finder icon. Then press COMMAND-K to manually enter a server's address, or click the Browse button to browse a list of available servers.

Figure 22-4   The Macintosh Finder window shows shared items in a network.

3. Either browse among the systems or enter the appropriate address.

4. Click Connect As to determine how you want to connect. You may sign in as a guest or with a registered username on the server to which you are trying to connect.

5. Click the Connect button in the bottom-right corner of the window when finished, as shown in Figure 22-5.

Figure 22-5   Connect to a server on the network either as a guest or with a registered username.

Microsoft Services for Macintosh

Discontinued in 2011, Microsoft Services for Macintosh made it possible for Macintosh systems to access Windows Server shares without modifying the configuration of the workstations.

Unix Clients

Three primary mechanisms provide client-server access between Unix systems. Two of these have been ported to many other computing platforms, and you can use them to access Unix systems from workstations running other operating systems. These three mechanisms are as follows:

- **Berkeley remote commands**   Designed for Unix-to-Unix networking, these commands provide functions such as remote login (*rlogin*), remote shell execution (*rsh*), and remote file copying (*rcp*).

- **DARPA commands**   Designed to provide basic remote networking tasks, such as file transfers (*ftp*) and terminal emulation (*telnet*), the DARPA commands operate independently of the operating system and have been ported to virtually every platform that supports the TCP/IP protocols.

- **Network File System (NFS)**   Designed by Sun Microsystems in the 1980s to provide transparent file sharing between network systems, NFS has since been published as RFC 1813, an informational request for comments (RFC), by the Internet Engineering Task Force (IETF). NFS is available on a wide range of computing platforms, enabling most client workstations to access the files on Unix systems.

Applications

In most cases, the TCP/IP stacks on client computers include applications providing the DARPA *ftp* and *telnet* commands. Since all Unix versions run File Transfer Protocol (FTP) and Telnet server services by default, you can use these client applications to access any Unix system available on the network. These server applications have been ported to other operating systems as well.

Earlier versions of Windows TCP/IP clients included FTP and Telnet client applications, with the exception of Microsoft Client 3.0 for MS-DOS. Installing this client provided a TCP/IP stack and the Winsock driver needed to run Internet applications, but the FTP and Telnet programs were not included. You could, however, use third-party FTP and Telnet clients to access Unix and other server systems.

Unix Access

While FTP and Telnet provide basic access to a Unix system, they are not the equivalent of full client capabilities. For example, FTP provides only basic file transfer and file management capabilities. To open a document on a Unix system using FTP, you must download the file to a local drive and use your application to open it from there. NFS, on the other hand, enables the client system to access a server volume as though it were available locally. NFS downloads only the blocks that the client application needs, instead of the whole file.

Thus, while FTP and Telnet are nearly always available at no cost, clients that need regular access to Unix file systems are better off using NFS. There are NFS products that make file system communications with Unix systems possible.

Client for Network File Systems (NFS) and Subsystem for Unix-based Applications (SUA) are available with Windows computers (through Windows 7) to access Unix volumes and to publish their drives as NFS volumes for Unix clients. The product also includes a Telnet server for Windows, as well as a password synchronization daemon for Unix systems. With the services in place, the Windows computer system can map a drive letter to an NFS volume on a Unix system or reference it using either standard Universal Naming Convention (UNC) names or the Unix *server:/export* format. Unix systems can access Windows drives just as they would any other NFS volume.

Windows 7 Interface

To install SUA in Windows 7 Ultimate or Enterprise or Windows Server 2008 R2, follow these steps:

1. From Start, click Control Panel and choose Programs.

2. Under Programs And Features, click Turn Windows Features On Or Off.

3. If the User Account Control dialog box opens, click Continue. Otherwise, proceed to the next step.

4. In the Windows Features dialog box, select the Subsystem For UNIX-based Applications check box, as shown in Figure 22-6. Click OK.

5. Click Setup to run the WinZip Self-Extractor utility, as shown in Figure 22-7.

The program appears on your Start menu, as shown in Figure 22-8. This link contains the shells and shortcuts with which you can edit Unix-based items.

Figure 22-6   Subsystem For UNIX-based Applications check box in the Windows Features dialog box

Part VI

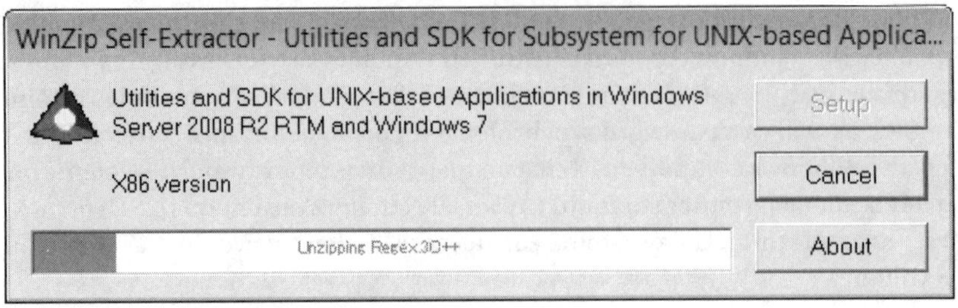

WinZip Self-Extractor - Utilities and SDK for Subsystem for UNIX-based Applica...

Utilities and SDK for UNIX-based Applications in Windows
Server 2008 R2 RTM and Windows 7

X86 version

Setup

Cancel

About

Unzipping Regex3D++

Figure 22-7   WinZip Self-Extractor utility

Windows 8 Interface

While the SUA has been deprecated in Windows 8.1 and Windows Server 2012 R2, you can still
download and install it in Windows 8 or Server 2012. Go to www.microsoft.com/en-us/download/
confirmation.aspx?id=35512 to download the program; then follow these steps:

1. Download the package that matches the architecture of the target computer.

2. After the executable program is on your computer, click Setup to open the WinZip Self-
   Extractor utility.

3. Click Setup to run the self-extractor and install the utilities and SDK for SUA.

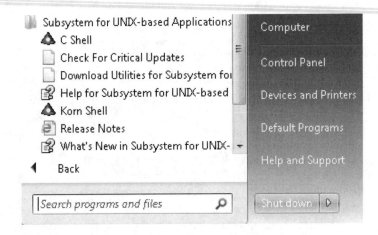

Subsystem for UNIX-based Applications
 C Shell
 Check For Critical Updates
 Download Utilities for Subsystem fo
 Help for Subsystem for UNIX-based
 Korn Shell
 Release Notes
 What's New in Subsystem for UNIX-

 Back

Search programs and files

Computer

Control Panel

Devices and Printers

Default Programs

Help and Support

Shut down

Figure 22-8   Installed SUA on the Windows 7 Start menu

CHAPTER
23

Network Security Basics

Security is an essential element of any network, and many of the daily maintenance tasks performed by the network administrator are security related. Simply put, all of the security mechanisms provided by the various components of a network are designed to protect a system's hardware, software, and data from accidental damage and unauthorized access. The goal of the security administration process is to provide users with access to all of the resources they need, while insulating them from those they don't need. This can be a fine line for the administrator to draw and a difficult one to maintain. Proper use of all the security administration tools provided by the network components is essential to maintaining a secure and productive network. There are many different security mechanisms on the average network; some are all but invisible to users and at times to administrators, while others require attention on a daily basis. This one chapter cannot hope to provide anything close to a comprehensive treatise on network security, but it does examine some of the major components you can use to protect your network and your data from unauthorized access.

Securing the File System

All of your data is stored in files on your computers, and protecting the file system is one of the most basic forms of network security. Not only does file system security prevent unauthorized access to your files, it also enables you to protect your data from being modified or deleted, either accidentally or deliberately. There are two basic forms of security that you can apply to the file system on your computers: access permissions and data encryption.

File system permissions are the most commonly used security element on network servers. All of the major server operating systems have file systems that support the use of permissions to regulate access to specific files and directories. File system permissions typically take the form of an *access control list* (ACL), which is a list of users (or groups of users), maintained by each file and directory, that have been granted a specific form of access to that file or directory. Each entry in the ACL contains a user or group name, plus a series of bits that define the specific permissions granted to that user or group.

It is standard practice for a file system to break down access permissions into individual tasks, such as read and write, and to assign them to users separately. This enables the network administrator to specify exactly what access each user should have. For example, you may want to grant certain users the read permission only, enabling them to read the contents of a file but not modify it. Manipulating permission assignments is an everyday task for the administrator of a properly protected network.

The following sections examine the file system permissions, as implemented by each of the major server operating system platforms.

The Windows Security Model

Security is an integral part of the Windows operating system design, and to fully understand the use of permissions in these operating systems (OSs), it helps to have some knowledge of the overall security model they use. The security subsystem in Windows is integrated throughout the OS and is implemented by a number of different components, as shown in Figure 23-1. Unlike other Windows environmental subsystems running in user mode, the security subsystem is known as an *integral subsystem* because it is used by the entire OS. All of the security subsystem components interact with Security Reference Monitor, the kernel mode security arbitrator that compares requests for access to a resource to that resource's ACL.

The user mode security subsystem components and their functions are as follows:

- **Logon Process**   Accepts logon information from the user and initiates the authentication process

- **Local Security Authority (LSA)**   Functions as the central clearinghouse for the security subsystem by initiating the logon process, calling the authentication package, generating access tokens, managing the local security policy, and logging audit messages

- **Security Accounts Manager (SAM)**   Database containing the user and group accounts for the local system

- **Security Policy Database**   Contains policy information on user rights, auditing, and trust relationships

- **Audit Log**   Contains a record of security-related events and changes made to security policies

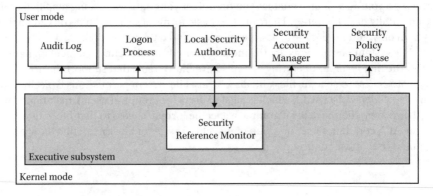

Figure 23-1   The Windows security architecture

During a typical user logon to the local machine, these components interact as follows:

1. The logon process appears in the form of the Logon dialog box produced when the user presses CTRL-ALT-DELETE after the system boots. The user then supplies a username and password.

2. The logon process calls the LSA that runs the authentication package.

3. The authentication package checks the username and password against the local SAM database.

4. When the username and password are verified, the SAM replies to the authentication package with the security IDs (SIDs) of the user and all the groups of which the user is a member.

5. The authentication package creates a logon session and returns it to the LSA with the SIDs.

6. The LSA creates a *security access token* containing the SIDs and the user rights associated with the SIDs, as well as the name of the user and the groups to which the user belongs, and sends it to the logon process, signaling a successful logon. The system will use the SIDs in this token to authenticate the user whenever he or she attempts to access any object on the system.

7. The logon session supplies the access token to the Win32 subsystem, which initiates the process of loading the user's desktop configuration.

NOTE This procedure occurs when a user logs on using an account on the local machine only, not when logging on to an Active Directory domain. Active Directory logons are more complex and are examined later in this chapter.

Much of the Windows security subsystem's work is transparent to users and administrators. The security components that are most conspicuous in day-to-day activities are the SAM database (which holds all the local Windows user, group, and computer accounts) and Active Directory. Every Windows system has a SAM database for its local accounts, a copy of which is stored on each domain controller (DC). Active Directory is a separate service that has its own security architecture, but for the purpose of assigning permissions, Active Directory objects function in the same way as accounts in the SAM database. Every object on the system that is protected by Windows security includes a security descriptor that contains an ACL. The ACL consists of *access control entries* (ACEs) that specify which users and groups are to be granted access to the object and what access they are to receive. When you specify the permissions for an object, such as a file, directory, share, or registry key, you are modifying the entries in that object's ACL. Clicking the Add button on the Security page in the Properties dialog box for a specific folder, for example (see Figure 23-2), displays a list of the users and groups in the SAM database or the objects in the Active Directory. Selecting users and granting them permission to access the share adds the users to the ACL for that share.

When you log on to an Active Directory, the system accesses an account database that is located on one of the network's domain controllers for authentication. The user, group, and computer accounts for the domain are stored in the DCs and are accessed whenever you use a utility that modifies the ACLs of system objects. During a domain session, you use the same Security page shown in Figure 23-2 to select the users and groups in the domain as you would those in the local SAM. You can also select users and groups from other domains on the network,

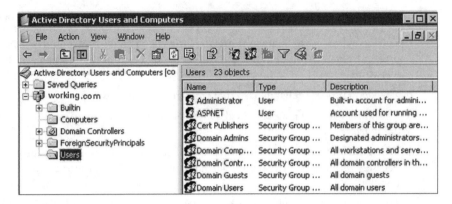

Figure 23-2   You use an Active Directory Users And Computers dialog box like this one to create ACEs for Windows objects.

as long as those other domains are trusted by the domain in which the system is currently participating.

When a Windows computer is a member of a domain, the local SAM database still exists. The Log On To Windows dialog box lets you select a domain or the local system for the current session. Note that a domain and a local SAM database can have user and group accounts with the same name. There is, for example, an Administrator account in the domain and an Administrator account for the local system, both of which are automatically created by default. These two accounts are not interchangeable. They can have different passwords and different rights and permissions. To install a network adapter driver, you must be logged on as the administrator of the local system (or an equivalent). By default, a domain administrator account does not have the rights to modify the hardware configuration on the local system.

Windows File System Permissions

Granting a user or group permissions to access a Windows resource adds them as an ACE to the resource's ACL. The degree of access that the user or group is granted depends on what permissions they are assigned. NTFS defines six standard permissions for files and folders—read, read and execute, modify, write, list folder contents, and full control—plus one extra for folders only. The standard permissions for NTFS files and folders are actually combinations of individual permissions.

The following are the functions of the standard permissions when applied to a folder:

Read   Enables a user/group to

- See the files and subfolders contained in the folder
- View the ownership, permissions, and attributes of the folder

Read and Execute   Enables a user/group to

- Navigate through restricted folders to reach other files and folders
- Perform all actions associated with the Read and List Folder Contents permissions

Modify   Enables a user/group to

- Delete the folder
- Perform all actions associated with the Write and Read and Execute permissions

Write   Enables a user/group to

- Create new files and subfolders inside the folder
- Modify the folder attributes
- View the ownership and permissions of the folder

List Folder Contents   Enables a user/group to

- View the names of the files and subfolders contained in the folder

Full Control   Enables a user/group to

- Modify the folder permissions
- Take ownership of the folder
- Delete subfolders and files contained in the folder
- Perform all actions associated with all of the other NTFS folder permissions

The following are the functions of the standard permissions when applied to a file:

Read   Enables a user/group to

- Read the contents of the file
- View the ownership, permissions, and attributes of the file

Read and Execute   Enables a user/group to

- Perform all actions associated with the Read permission
- Run applications

Modify   Enables a user/group to

- Modify the file
- Delete the file
- Perform all actions associated with the Write and Read and Execute permissions

Write   Enables a user/group to

- Overwrite the file
- Modify the file attributes
- View the ownership and permissions of the file

Full Control   Enables a user/group to

- Modify the file permissions
- Take ownership of the file
- Perform all actions associated with all of the other NTFS file permissions

The following are the individual permissions that make up each of the standard permissions:

Read Enables a user/group to

- List folder/read data
- Read attributes
- Read extended attributes
- Read permissions
- Synchronize with multithreaded, multiprocessing programs

NOTE Multithreaded programs are those that can be used by more than one user at a time without the program being loaded by each user. Each request for such use is called a thread. Synchronizing permissions allow the user (or group) to coordinate (*synchronize*) the use of such programs. Multiprocessing programs are those that can be run by two (or more) different processors on the same computer.

Read and Execute Enables a user/group to

- List folder/read data
- Read attributes
- Read extended attributes
- Read permissions
- Synchronize with multithreaded, multiprocessing programs
- Traverse folders and execute files

Modify Enables a user/group to

- Create files and write data
- Create folders and append data
- Delete files and folders
- List folders and read data
- Read attributes
- Read extended attributes
- Read permissions
- Synchronize with multithreaded, multiprocessing programs
- Write attributes
- Write extended attributes

Write Enables a user/group to

- Create files and write data
- Create folders and append data

- Read permissions
- Synchronize with multithreaded, multiprocessing programs
- Write attributes
- Write extended attributes

List Folder Contents   Enables a user/group to

- List folders and read data
- Read attributes
- Read extended attributes
- Read permissions
- Synchronize with multithreaded, multiprocessing programs
- Traverse folders and execute files

Full Control   Enables a user/group to

- Change permissions
- Create files and write data
- Create folders and append data
- Delete files and folders
- Delete subfolders and files
- List folders and read data
- Read attributes
- Read extended attributes
- Read permissions
- Synchronize with multithreaded, multiprocessing programs
- Take ownership
- Write attributes
- Write extended attributes

The functions of the individual permissions are as follows:

- **Traverse Folder/Execute File**   The Traverse Folder permission allows or denies users the ability to move through folders that they do not have permission to access, so as to reach files or folders that they do have permission to access (applies to folders only). The Execute File permission allows or denies users the ability to run program files (applies to files only).

- **List Folder/Read Data**   The List Folder permission allows or denies users the ability to view the file and subfolder names within a folder (applies to folders only). The Read Data permission allows or denies users the ability to view the contents of a file (applies to files only).

Part VI

- **Read Attributes**   Allows or denies users the ability to view the NTFS attributes of a file or folder.

- **Read Extended Attributes**   Allows or denies users the ability to view the extended attributes of a file or folder.

- **Create Files/Write Data**   The Create Files permission allows or denies users the ability to create files within the folder (applies to folders only). The Write Data permission allows or denies users the ability to modify the file and overwrite existing content (applies to files only).

- **Create Folders/Append Data**   The Create Folders permission allows or denies users the ability to create subfolders within a folder (applies to folders only). The Append Data permission allows or denies users the ability to add data to the end of the file but not to modify, delete, or overwrite existing data in the file (applies to files only).

- **Write Attributes**   Allows or denies users the ability to modify the NTFS attributes of a file or folder.

- **Write Extended Attributes**   Allows or denies users the ability to modify the extended attributes of a file or folder.

- **Delete Subfolders and Files**   Allows or denies users the ability to delete subfolders and files, even if the Delete permission has not been granted on the subfolder or file.

- **Delete**   Allows or denies users the ability to delete the file or folder.

- **Read Permissions**   Allows or denies users the ability to read the permissions for the file or folder.

- **Change Permissions**   Allows or denies users the ability to modify the permissions for the file or folder.

- **Take Ownership**   Allows or denies users the ability to take ownership of the file or folder.

- **Synchronize**   Allows or denies different threads of multithreaded, multiprocessor programs to wait on the handle for the file or folder and synchronize with another thread that may signal it.

Permissions are stored as part of the NTFS file system, not in Active Directory or the SAM database. To modify the permissions for a file or directory, you select the Security tab in the Properties dialog box of a file or folder to display controls like those shown in Figure 23-3. Here you can add users and groups from the local SAM, from the current domain, and from other trusted domains, and specify the standard permissions that each one is to be allowed or denied.

As with all file systems, the permissions that you assign to a folder are inherited by all of the files and subfolders contained in that folder. By judiciously assigning permissions throughout the file system, you can regulate user access to files and folders with great precision.

Click the Advanced button to open the Advanced Settings dialog box, as shown in Figure 23-4.

If the standard NTFS permissions do not provide you with the exact degree of access control you need, you can work directly with the individual permissions by clicking the Advanced button and then the Share tab to display the Permission Entry For Users dialog box for the file or folder,

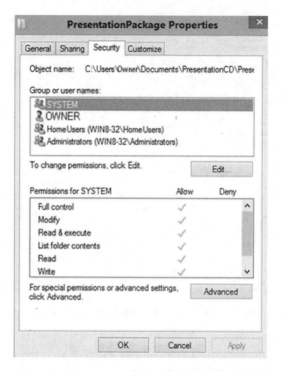

Figure 23-3   From the Properties dialog box for NTFS file system objects in Windows, use the Security tab to assign permissions.

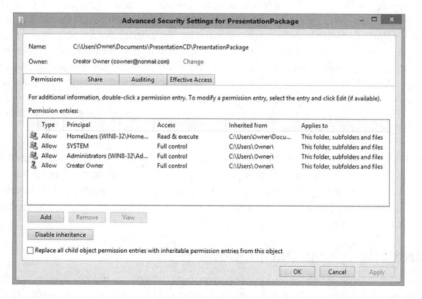

Figure 23-4   The Advanced Security Settings dialog box enables you to work with individual permissions.

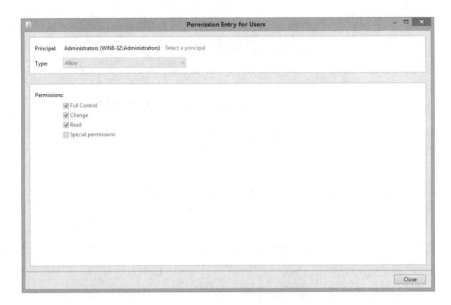

Figure 23-5   The Permission Entry For Users dialog box explains what permissions are granted for a selected user.

like the one in Figure 23-5. Select a named user and click View to see what permissions have been granted. You can modify these permissions at will to customize the user's or group's access to the file system resource.

The file and directory permissions apply to everyone who accesses the object, either on the local system or through the network. It is also possible to control network access to the file system by using *share permissions*. To make an NTFS drive or directory available for access over the network, you have to create a share out of it, and shares have access control lists just like files and directories do. To set share permissions, you open a drive's or folder's Properties dialog box, select the Sharing tab, and click the Permissions button to display a dialog box like that shown in Figure 23-5. To access the files on a share, a network user must have permissions for both the share and the files and directories in the share.

The permissions you can grant to specific users and groups for shares are different from those used for files and directories.

NOTE In Windows, it's important to understand that permissions are not the same thing as rights. Rights are rules that identify specific actions a user is allowed to perform on the local system, such as Access This Computer From The Network and Back Up Files And Directories. Many people use the term *rights* incorrectly when they mean permissions, as in "The user has the rights to access the directory."

Unix File System Permissions

Unix also uses permissions to control access to its file system, but the system is substantially different from those of Windows. In Unix, there are only three permissions: read, write, and execute.

The following are the access types provided by each permission when applied to a directory:

- **Read**   Enables a user to list the contents of the directory
- **Write**   Enables a user to create or remove files and subdirectories in the directory
- **Execute**   Enables a user to change to the directory using the *cd* command

The following are the access types provided by each permission when applied to a file:

- **Read**   Enables the user to view the contents of the file
- **Write**   Enables the user to alter the contents of the file
- **Execute**   Enables a user to run the file as a program

Each of these three permissions can be applied to three separate entities: the file's owner, the group to which the file belongs, and all other users. When you list the contents of a directory using the *ls -l* command, you see a display for each file and directory like the following:

```
-rwxr-xr--    1    csmith    sales    776    Sep 15 09:34    readme
```

The first character in the display identifies the file system element, using the following values:

- -~   File
- **d**   Directory
- **b**   Special block file
- **c**   Special character file
- **l**   Symbolic link
- **P**   Named pipe special file

The next three characters (*rwx*) indicate the permissions granted to the owner of the file (csmith). In this case, the owner has all three permissions. The next three characters indicate the permissions granted to the file's group, and the following three indicate the permissions granted to all other users. In this example, the *r-x* value indicates that the file's group (sales) has been granted the read and execute permissions only, and the *r--* value indicates that the other users have been granted only the read permission. To change the permissions, you use the *chmod* command.

This access control mechanism is common to all Unix variants, but it doesn't provide anywhere near the granularity of the NTFS and NetWare file systems. The system recognizes only three basic classes of users (users, groups, and others), making it impossible to grant permissions to several users in different groups while blocking access by everyone else. To address this shortcoming, some Unix operating systems include more advanced access control mechanisms.

Verifying Identities

User authentication is another one of the important security mechanisms on a data network. Assigning file system permissions to specific users is pointless unless the system can verify the user's identity and prevent unauthorized people from assuming that identity. Authentication is an exchange of information that occurs before a user is permitted to access secured network resources. In most cases, the authentication process consists of the user supplying an account name and an accompanying password to the system hosting the resources the user wants to access. The system receiving the name and password checks them against an account directory and, if the password supplied is the correct one for that account, grants the user access to the requested resource.

Applications and services use different types of authentication mechanisms, ranging from the simple to the extremely complex. The following sections examine some of these mechanisms.

FTP User Authentication

The File Transfer Protocol (FTP) is a basic Transmission Control Protocol/Internet Protocol (TCP/IP) service that enables users to upload files to and download them from another computer on the network, as well as to perform basic file management tasks. However, before an FTP client can do any of this, it must authenticate itself to the FTP server. FTP is an example of the simplest possible type of authentication mechanism and one of the most insecure. After the FTP client establishes a standard TCP connection with the server, it employs the *USER* and *PASS* commands to transmit an account name and password. The server checks the credentials of the user and either grants or denies access to the service.

NOTE In many cases, the authentication sequence remains invisible to the user operating the FTP client. This is because, on the Internet, access to many FTP servers is unrestricted. The server accepts any account name and password, and the tradition is to use anonymous as the account name and the user's e-mail address as the password. Many FTP client programs automatically supply this information when connecting to a server to save the user from having to supply it manually.

The FTP authentication process is inherently insecure because it transmits the user's account name and password over the network in clear text. Anyone running a protocol analyzer or other program that is capable of capturing the packets transmitted over the network and displaying their contents can view the name and password and use them to gain access to the FTP server. If the user should happen to be a network administrator who is thoughtless enough to use an account that also provides high-level access to other network resources, the security compromise could be severe.

Clearly, while FTP may be suitable for basic file transfer tasks, you should not count on its access control mechanism to secure sensitive data because it is too easy for the account passwords to be intercepted.

Kerberos

At the other end of the spectrum of authentication mechanisms is a security protocol called Kerberos, developed by MIT and originally defined in the RFC 1510 document published by the Internet Engineering Task Force (IETF). (Today's version is Version 5.) Windows Active Directory networks use Kerberos to authenticate users logging on to the network. Because Kerberos relies on the public key infrastructure when exchanging data with the clients and servers involved in the authentication process, all passwords and other sensitive information are transmitted in encrypted form instead of clear text. This ensures that even if an unauthorized individual were to capture the packets exchanged during the authentication procedure, no security compromise would result.

One of the fundamental principles of Active Directory is that it provides users with a single network logon capability, meaning that one authentication procedure can grant a user access to resources all over the network. Kerberos is a perfect solution for this type of arrangement because it is designed to function as an authentication service that is separate from the servers hosting the resources that the client needs to access. For example, during an FTP authentication, only two parties are involved, the client and the server. The server has access to the directory containing the account names and password information for authorized users, checks the credentials supplied by each connecting client, and either grants or denies access to the server on that basis. If the client wants to connect to a different FTP server, it must perform the entire authentication process all over again.

By contrast, during an Active Directory logon, the client sends its credentials to the Kerberos *Key Distribution Center* (KDC) service running on a domain controller, which in Kerberos terminology is called an *authentication server* (AS). Once the AS checks the client's credentials and completes the authentication, the client can access resources on servers all over the network, without performing additional authentications. For this reason, Kerberos is called a *trusted third-party authentication protocol.*

Public Key Infrastructure

Windows uses a *public key infrastructure* (PKI) that strengthens its protection against hacking and other forms of unauthorized access. In traditional cryptography, also called *secret key cryptography,* a single key is used to encrypt and decrypt data. For two entities to communicate, they must both possess the key, which implies the need for some previous communication during which the key is exchanged. If the key is intercepted or compromised, the entire encryption system is compromised.

The fundamental principle of a PKI is that the keys used to encrypt and decrypt data are different. Each system has a *public key* used to encrypt data and a *private key* used to decrypt it. By supplying your public key to other systems, you enable them to encrypt data before sending it to you so that you can decrypt it using your private key. However, the public key cannot decrypt the data once it has been encrypted. Thus, while intruders may intercept public keys as they are transmitted across the network, they can't access any encrypted data unless they have the private keys as well, and private keys are never transmitted over the network.

The use of a PKI makes it possible to transmit authentication data across a Windows network with greater security than clear-text authentication mechanisms like that of FTP or even other secret key cryptography mechanisms. A PKI also provides the capability to use digital signatures to positively identify the sender of a message. A *digital signature* is a method for encrypting data with a particular user's private key. Other users receiving the transmission can verify the signature with the user's public key. Changing even one bit of the data invalidates the signature. When the transmission arrives intact, the valid signature proves not only that the transmission has not been changed in any way but also that it unquestionably originated from the sending user. Today, in many locations, a digitally signed transmission can carry as much legal and ethical weight as a signed paper document.

Kerberos authentication is based on the exchange of *tickets* that contain an encrypted password that verifies a user's identity. When a user on a Windows client system logs on to

Part VI

an Active Directory domain, it transmits a logon request containing the user's account name to an AS, which is an Active Directory domain controller. The KDC service on the domain controller then issues a *ticket-granting ticket* (TGT) to the client that includes the user's SID, the network address of the client system, a time stamp that helps to prevent unauthorized access, and the session key that is used to encrypt the data. The AS encrypts the response containing the TGT using a key that is based on the password associated with the user's account (which the AS already has in its directory). When the client receives the response from the AS, it decrypts the message by prompting the user for the password, which is the decryption key. Thus, the user's identity is authenticated without the password being transmitted over the network.

The TGT is retained by the client system, to be used as a license for future authentication events. It is essentially a pass affirming that the user has been authenticated and is authorized to access network resources. Once a client has a TGT, it can use it to identify the user, eliminating the need to repeatedly supply a password when accessing various network resources.

When the user wants to access a resource on a network server, the client sends a request to a *ticket-granting service* (TGS) on the domain controller, which identifies the user and the resource server and includes a copy of the TGT. The TGS, which shares the session key for the TGT with the AS, decrypts the TGT to affirm that the user is authorized to access the requested resource. The TGS then returns a *service ticket* to the client that grants the user access to that particular resource only. The client sends an access request to the resource server that contains the user's ID and the service ticket. The resource server decrypts the service ticket and, as long as the user ID matches the ID in the ticket, grants the user access to the requested resource. A client system can retain multiple service tickets to provide future access to various network resources. This system protects both the server and the user because it provides mutual authentication; the client is authenticated to the server and the server to the client.

Digital Certificates

For the PKI to operate, computers must exchange the public keys that enable their correspondents to encrypt data before transmitting it to them over the network. However, the distribution of the public keys presents a problem. For the transmission to be truly secure, there must be some way to verify that the public keys being distributed actually came from the party they purport to identify. For example, if your employer sends you an e-mail encrypted with your public key, you can decrypt the message using your private key, sure in the knowledge that no one could have intercepted the message and read its contents. But how do you know the message did indeed come from your boss when it's possible for someone else to have obtained your public key? Also, what would stop someone from pretending to be you and distributing a public key that others can use to send encrypted information intended for you?

One answer to these questions is the use of digital certificates. A *certificate* is a digitally signed statement, issued by a third party called a *certificate authority* (CA), that binds a user, computer, or service holding a private key with its corresponding public key. Because both correspondents trust the CA, they can be assured that the certificates they issue contain valid information. A certificate typically contains the following:

- **Subject identifier information**   Name, e-mail address, or other data identifying the user or computer to which the certificate is being issued
- **Subject public key value**   The public key associated with the user or computer to which the certificate is being issued

- **Validity period**   Specifies how long the certificate will remain valid
- **Issuer identifier information**   Identifies the system issuing the certificate
- **Issuer digital signature**   Ensures the validity of the certificate by positively identifying its source

On the Internet, certificates are used primarily for software distribution. For example, when your web browser downloads a plug-in created by KoolStuff Corporation that is required to display a particular type of web page, a certificate supplied by the server verifies that the software you are downloading did actually come from KoolStuff Graphics. This prevents anyone else from modifying or replacing the software and distributing it as KoolStuff's own.

The certificates used on the Internet are typically defined by the ITU-T X.509 standard and issued by a separate company that functions as the CA. One of the most well-known public CAs is called VeriSign. It's also possible to create your own certificates for internal use in your organization. You can use certificates to authenticate users to web servers, send secure e-mail, and (optionally) authenticate users to domains. For the most part, the use of certificates is transparent to users, but administrators can manage them manually using the Certificates snap-in for the Microsoft Management Console.

Today, there are a number of certificate authentication services available. No matter which service is used, ensure you have the latest, updated version to forestall any system problems, such as those experienced during 2014 and the Heartbleed vulnerability.

Token-Based and Biometric Authentication

All of the authentication mechanisms described thus far rely on the transmission of passwords between clients and servers. Passwords are a reasonably secure method of protecting data that is somewhat sensitive, but not extremely so. When data must remain truly secret, passwords are insufficient for several reasons. Most network users have a tendency to be sloppy about the passwords they select and how they protect them. Many people choose passwords that are easy for them to remember and type, unaware that they can easily be penetrated. Names of spouses, children, or pets, as well as birthdays and other such common-knowledge information, do not provide much security. In addition, some users compromise their own passwords by writing them down in obvious places or giving them to other users for the sake of convenience. A carefully planned regimen of password length and composition requirements, rotations, and maintenance policies can help make your passwords more secure. There are also mechanisms you can use in addition to passwords that can greatly enhance the security of your network.

To address the inherent weakness of password-based authentication and provide greater security, it's possible for each user to employ a separate hardware device as part of the authentication process. *Token-based authentication* is a technique in which the user supplies a unique token for each logon, as well as a password. The token is a one-time value that is generated by an easily portable device, such as a smart card. A *smart card* is a credit card–sized device with a microprocessor in it that supplies a token each time the user runs it through a card reader connected to a computer. The idea behind the use of a token is that a password, even in encrypted form, can be captured by a protocol analyzer and "replayed" over the network to gain access to protected resources. Because a user's token changes for each logon, it can't be reused, so capturing it is pointless. Token-based authentication also requires the user to supply a personal identification number (PIN) or a password to complete the logon so that if the smart card is lost or stolen, it can't be used by itself to gain access to the network. Because this type of authentication is based on something you have (the token) and something you know (the PIN or password), the technique is also called *two-factor authentication*.

Smart cards can also contain other information about their users, including their private keys. The security of Windows PKI relies on the private encryption keys remaining private. Typically, the private key is stored on the workstation, which makes it susceptible to both physical and digital intrusion. Storing the private key on the card instead of on the computer protects it against theft or compromise and also enables the user to utilize the key on any computer.

Another tool that can be used to authenticate users is a biometric scanner. A *biometric scanner* is a device that reads a person's fingerprints, retinal patterns, or some other unique characteristic and then compares the information it gathers against a database of known values. While it may seem that we are venturing into James Bond territory, these devices do exist, and they provide excellent security since the user's "credentials" cannot easily be misplaced or stolen. The downside to this technology is its great expense, and it is used only in installations requiring extraordinary security.

Securing Network Communications

Authentication is a means for verifying users' identities to ensure that they are authorized to access specific resources. Many authentication systems use encryption to prevent passwords from being intercepted and compromised by third parties. However, authorization protocols such as Kerberos use encryption only during the authentication process. Once the user has been granted access to a resource, the participation of the authentication protocol and the encryption it provides ends. Thus, you may have data that is secured by permissions (or even by file system encryption) while it is stored on the server, but once an authorized client accesses that data, the server usually transmits it over the network in an unprotected form. Just as with the FTP passwords discussed earlier, an intruder could conceivably capture the packets while they travel over the network and view the data carried inside.

In many cases, the danger presented by unprotected network transmissions is minor. For instances when extra protection is warranted, it is possible to encrypt data as it travels over the network. The following sections examine the IP Security (IPsec) protocol and the Secure Sockets Layer (SSL) protocol, both of which are capable of encrypting data before it is transmitted over the network and decrypting it on receipt at the destination.

IPsec

Virtually all TCP/IP communication uses the Internet Protocol at the network layer to carry the data generated by the protocols operating at the upper layers. IPsec is a series of standards that define a method for securing IP communications using a variety of techniques, including authentication and encryption. Windows supports the use of IPsec, as do many Unix variants. Unlike many other TCP/IP protocols, IPsec is defined by many different documents, all published as requests for comments (RFCs) by the IETF. You can find current standards at ietf.org.

Although IPsec is usually thought of primarily as an encryption protocol, it provides several data protection services, including the following:

- **Encryption**   The IPsec standards allow for the use of various forms of encryption. For example, Windows can use the Data Encryption Standard (DES) algorithm or the Triple Data Encryption Standard (3DES) algorithm. DES uses a 56-bit key to encrypt each 64-bit block, while 3DES encrypts each block three times with a different key, for 168-bit encryption. Both DES and 3DES are *symmetrical encryption algorithms,* meaning that they use the same key to encrypt and decrypt the data.

- **Authentication**   IPsec supports a variety of authentication mechanisms, including Kerberos, Internet Key Exchange (IKE), digital certificates, and preshared keys. This enables different IPsec implementations to work together, despite using different methods of authentication.

- **Nonrepudiation**   By employing public key technology, IPsec can affix digital signatures to datagrams, enabling the recipient to be certain that the datagram was generated by the signer. The sending computer creates the digital signatures using its private key, and the receiver decrypts them using the sender's public key. Since no one but the sender has access to the private key, a message that can be decrypted using the public key must have originated with the holder of the private key. The sender, therefore, cannot deny having sent the message.

- **Replay prevention**   It is sometimes possible for an unauthorized user to capture an encrypted message and use it to gain access to protected resources without actually decrypting it, by simply replaying the message in its encrypted form. IPsec uses a technique called *cipher block chaining* (CBC) that adds a unique initialization vector to the data encryption process. The result is that each encrypted datagram is different, even when they contain exactly the same data.

- **Data integrity**   IPsec can add a *cryptographic checksum* to each datagram that is based on a key possessed only by the sending and receiving systems. This special type of signature, also called a *hash message authentication code* (HMAC), is essentially a summary of the packet's contents created using a secret, shared key, which the receiving system can compute using the same algorithm and compare to the signature supplied by the sender. If the two signatures match, the receiver can be certain that the contents of the packet have not been modified.

Encrypting network transmissions at the network layer provides several advantages over doing it at any other layer. First, network-layer encryption protects the data generated by all of the protocols operating at the upper layers of the protocol stack. Some other security protocols, such as SSL, operate at the application layer and therefore can protect only specific types of data. IPsec protects the data generated by any application or protocol that uses IP, which is virtually all of them.

Second, network layer encryption provides data security over the entire journey of the packet, from source to destination. The computer that originates the packet encrypts it, and it remains encrypted until it reaches its final destination. This not only provides excellent security but also means that the intermediate systems involved in the transmission of the packet do not have to support IPsec. A router, for example, receives packets, strips off the data link layer protocol headers, and repackages the datagrams for transmission over another network. Throughout this process, the datagram remains intact and unmodified, so there is no need to decrypt it.

IPsec is composed of two separate protocols: the *IP Authentication Header* (AH) protocol and the *IP Encapsulating Security Payload* (ESP) protocol. Together, these two protocols provide the data protection services just listed. IPsec can use the two protocols together, to provide the maximum amount of security possible, or just one of the two.

Part VI

IP Authentication Header

The IP Authentication Header protocol provides the authentication, nonrepudiation, replay prevention, and data integrity services listed earlier, in other words, all of the services IPsec provides except data encryption. This means that when AH is used alone, it is possible for unauthorized users to read the contents of the protected datagrams, but they cannot modify the data or reuse it without detection.

AH adds an extra header to each packet, immediately following the IP header and preceding the transport layer or other header encapsulated within the IP datagram. The fields of the AH header are illustrated in Figure 23-6. The functions of the fields are as follows:

- **Next Header (1 byte)**   Identifies the protocol that generated the header immediately following the AH header, using values defined in the "Assigned Numbers" RFC.

- **Payload Length (1 byte)**   Specifies the length of the AH header.

- **Reserved (2 bytes)**   Reserved for future use.

- **Security Parameters Index (4 bytes)**   Contains a value that, in combination with the IP address of the destination system and the security protocol being used (AH or ESP), forms a security association for the datagram. A *security association* is a combination of parameters (such as the encryption key and security protocols to be used) that the sending and receiving systems agree upon before they begin to exchange data. The systems use the SPI value to uniquely identify this security association among others that may exist between the same two computers.

- **Sequence Number (4 bytes)**   Implements the IPsec replay prevention service by containing a unique, incrementing value for each packet transmitted by a security association. The receiving system expects every datagram it receives in the course of a particular security association to have a different value in this field. Packets with duplicate values are discarded.

- **Authentication Data (variable)**   Contains an *integrity check value* (ICV) that the sending computer calculates for the entire AH header, including the Authentication Data field (which is set to zero for this purpose) and the encapsulated protocol header (or headers) and data that follow the AH header. The receiving system performs the same ICV calculation and compares the results to this value to verify the packet's integrity.

The IP standard dictates that the Protocol field in the IP header must identify the protocol that generated the first header found in the datagram's payload. Normally, the first header in the

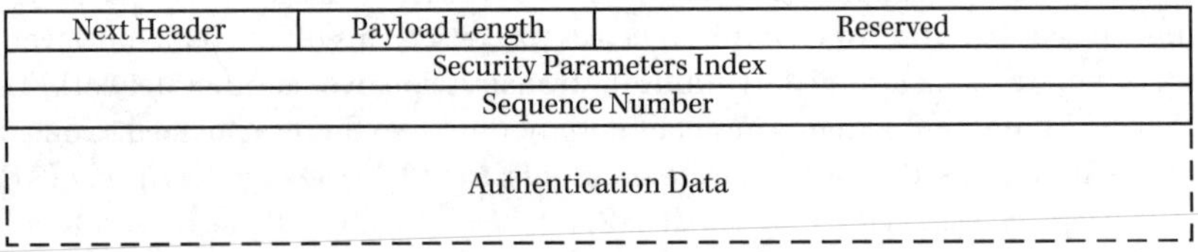

Next Header	Payload Length	Reserved
Security Parameters Index		
Sequence Number		
Authentication Data		

Figure 23-6   The Authentication Header protocol header

payload is a TCP or UDP header, so the Protocol value is 6 or 17, respectively. ICMP data can also be carried in IP datagrams, with a Protocol value of 1. When IPsec adds an AH header, it becomes the first header found in the datagram's payload, so the value of the Protocol field is changed to 51. To maintain the integrity of the protocol stack, the Next Header field in the AH header identifies the protocol that follows AH in the datagram. In the case of datagrams that use AH alone, the Next Header field contains the value for the TCP, UDP, or ICMP protocol formerly found in the IP header's Protocol field. If IPsec is using both AH and ESP, the AH Next Header field contains a value of 50, which identifies the ESP protocol, and ESP's own Next Header field identifies the TCP, UD, or ICMP protocol data encapsulated within.

IP Encapsulating Security Payload

Unlike AH, the ESP protocol completely encapsulates the payload contained in each datagram, using both header and footer fields, as shown in Figure 23-7. The functions of the ESP fields are as follows:

- **Security Parameters Index (4 bytes)**   Contains a value that, in combination with the IP address of the destination system and the security protocol being used (AH or ESP), forms a security association for the datagram. A *security association* is a combination of parameters (such as the encryption key and security protocols to be used) that the sending and receiving systems agree upon before they begin to exchange data. The systems use the SPI value to uniquely identify this security association among others that may exist between the same two computers.

- **Sequence Number (4 bytes)**   Implements the IPsec replay prevention service by containing a unique, incrementing value for each packet transmitted by a security association. The receiving system expects every datagram it receives in the course of a particular security association to have a different value in this field. Packets with duplicate values are discarded.

- **Payload Data (variable)**   Contains the original TCP, UDP, or ICMP header and data from the datagram.

- **Padding (0–255 bytes)**   Some algorithms are capable only of encrypting data in blocks of a specific length. This field contains padding to expand the size of the payload data to the boundary of the next 4-byte word.

- **Pad Length (1 byte)**   Specifies the size of the Padding field, in bytes.

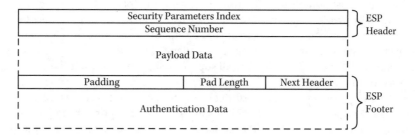

Figure 23-7   The Encapsulating Security Payload protocol frame

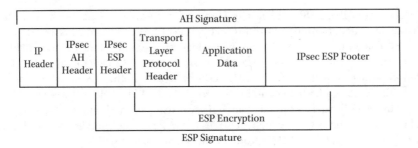

Figure 23-8   An IP datagram using both AH and ESP

- **Next Header (1 byte)**   Identifies the protocol that generated the header immediately following the ESP header, using values defined in the "Assigned Numbers" RFC.
- **Authentication Data (variable)**   Optional field that contains an ICV that the sending computer calculates for all the fields from the beginning of the ESP header to the end of the ESP trailer (excluding the original IP header and the ESP Authentication Data field itself). The receiving system performs the same ICV calculation and compares the results to this value to verify the packet's integrity.

ESP encrypts the data beginning at the end of the ESP header (that is, the end of the Sequence Number field) and proceeding to the end of the Next Header field in the ESP footer. ESP is also capable of providing its own authentication, replay prevention, and data integrity services, in addition to those of AH. The information that ESP uses to compute the integrity signature runs from the beginning of the ESP header to the end of the ESP trailer. The original IP header from the datagram is not included in the signature (although it is in the AH signature). This means that when IPsec uses ESP alone, it's possible for someone to modify the IP header contents without the changes being detected by the recipient. Avoiding this possibility is why the use of both AH and ESP is recommended for maximum protection. Figure 23-8 shows a packet using both the AH and ESP protocols and shows the signed and encrypted fields.

SSL

Secure Sockets Layer is a series of protocols providing many of the same services as IPsec but in a more specialized role. Instead of protecting all TCP/IP traffic by signing and encrypting network layer datagrams, SSL is designed to protect only the TCP traffic generated by specific applications, most notably the Hypertext Transfer Protocol (HTTP) traffic generated by web servers and browsers. In most cases, when you use a web browser to connect to a secured site (for the purpose of conducting a credit card or other transaction), the client and server open a connection that is secured by SSL, usually evidenced by an icon on the browser's status bar. The major web servers and browsers all support SSL, with the result that its use is virtually transparent to the client.

SSL consists of two primary protocols: the SSL Record Protocol (SSLRP) and the SSL Handshake Protocol (SSLHP). SSLRP is responsible for encrypting the application layer data and verifying its integrity, while SSLHP negotiates the security parameters used during an SSL session, such as the keys used to encrypt and digitally sign the data.

SSL Handshake Protocol

Clients and servers that use SSL exchange a complex series of SSLHP messages before they transmit any application data. This message exchange consists of four phases, which are as follows:

- **Establish security capabilities**   During this phase, the client and the server exchange information about the versions of SSL they use and the encryption and compression algorithms they support. The systems need this information in order to negotiate a set of parameters supported by both parties.

- **Server authentication and key exchange**   If the server needs to be authenticated, it sends its certificate to the client, along with the algorithms and keys that it will use to encrypt the application data.

- **Client authentication and key exchange**   After verifying the server's certificate as valid, the client responds with its own certificate, if the server has requested one, plus its own encryption algorithm and key information.

- **Finish**   The client and server use a special protocol called the SSL Change Cipher Spec Protocol to modify their communications to use the parameters they have agreed upon in the earlier phases. The two systems send handshake completion messages to each other using the new parameters, which completes the establishment of the secure connection between the two computers. The transmission of application data using SSLRP can now begin.

SSL Record Protocol

The process by which SSLRP prepares application layer data for transmission over the network consists of five steps, which are as follows:

1. **Fragmentation**   SSLRP splits the message generated by the application layer protocol into blocks no more than 2 kilobytes long.

2. **Compression**   Optionally, SSLRP can compress each fragment, but the current implementations do not do this.

3. **Signature**   SSLRP generates a message authentication code (MAC) for each fragment, using a secret key exchanged by the transmitting and receiving systems during the SSLHP negotiation, and appends it to the end of the fragment.

4. **Encryption**   SSLRP encrypts each fragment with any one of several algorithms using keys of various sizes. The encryption is symmetrical, with a key that is also exchanged during the SSLHP negotiation.

5. **Encapsulation**   SSLRP adds a header to each fragment before passing it down to the TCP protocol for further encapsulation.

After this entire process is completed, each SSLRP fragment consists of the following fields:

- **Content Type (1 byte)**   Identifies the application layer protocol that generated the data fragment

- **Major Version (1 byte)**   Specifies the major version of SSL in use

- **Minor Version (1 byte)**   Specifies the minor version of SSL in use
- **Compressed Length (2 bytes)**   Specifies the length of the Data field
- **Data (up to 2 kilobytes)**   Contains a fragment of (possibly compressed) application layer data
- **Message Authentication Code (0, 16, or 20 bytes)**   Contains the digital signature for the fragment, which the receiving system uses to verify its integrity

Firewalls

A *firewall* is a hardware or software entity that protects a network from intrusion by outside users by regulating the traffic that can pass through a router connecting it to another network. The term is most often used in relation to protection from unauthorized users on the Internet, but a firewall can also protect a local area network (LAN) from users on other LANs, either local or wide area networks (WANs). Without some sort of a firewall in place, outside users can access the files on your network, plant viruses, use your servers for their own purposes, or even wipe your drives entirely.

Completely isolating a network from communication with other networks is not difficult, but this is not the function of a firewall. A firewall is designed to permit certain types of traffic to pass over the router between the networks, while denying access to all other traffic. You want your client workstations to be able to send HTTP requests from their web browsers to servers on the Internet and for the servers to be able to reply, but you don't want outside users on the Internet to be able to access those clients. Firewalls use several different methods to provide varying degrees of protection to network systems. A client workstation has different protection requirements than a web server, for example.

Depending on the size of your network, the function of your computers, and the degree of risk, firewalls can take many forms. The term has come to be used to refer to any sort of protection from outside influences. In fact, a true firewall is really a set of security policies that may be implemented by several different network components that work together to regulate not only the traffic that is permitted into the network, but possibly also the traffic that is permitted out. In addition to preventing Internet users from accessing the systems on your network, you can use a firewall to prevent certain internal users from surfing the Web, while allowing them the use of Internet e-mail.

An inexpensive software router program can use network address translation (NAT) to enable client workstations on a small network to use unregistered IP addresses, and in a loose sense of the term, this is a form of a firewall. A large corporation with multiple T-1 connections to the Internet is more likely to have a system between the internal network and the Internet routers that is running software dedicated to firewall functions. Some firewall capabilities are integrated into a router, while other firewalls are separate software products that you must install on a computer.

Firewall protection can stem from either one of the following two basic policies, the choice of which is generally dependent on the security risks inherent in the network and the needs of the network users:

- Everything not specifically permitted is denied.
- Everything not specifically denied is permitted.

These two policies are essentially a reflection of seeing a glass as being either half full or half empty. You can start with a network that is completely secured in every way and open up portals permitting the passage of specific types of traffic, or you can start with a completely open network and block the types of traffic considered to be intrusive. The former method is much more secure and is generally recommended in all environments. However, it tends to emphasize security over ease of use. The latter method is less secure but makes the network easier to use. This method also forces the administrator to try to anticipate the techniques by which the firewall can be penetrated. If there is one thing that is known for certain about the digital vandals that inhabit the Internet, it is that they are endlessly inventive, and keeping up with their diabolical activities can be difficult.

Network administrators can use a variety of techniques to implement these policies and protect the different types of systems on the network. The following sections examine some of these techniques and the applications for which they're used.

Packet Filters

Packet filtering is a feature implemented on routers and firewalls that uses rules specified by the administrator to determine whether a packet should be permitted to pass through the firewall. The rules are based on the information provided in the protocol headers of each packet, including the following:

- IP source and destination addresses
- Encapsulated protocol
- Source and destination port
- ICMP message type
- Incoming and outgoing interface

By using combinations of values for these criteria, you can specify precise conditions under which packets should be admitted through the firewall. For example, you can specify the IP addresses of certain computers on the Internet that should be permitted to use the Telnet protocol to communicate with a specific machine on the local network. As a result, all packets directed to the system with the specified destination IP address and using port 23 (the well-known port for the Telnet protocol) are discarded, except for those with the source IP addresses specified in the rule. Using this rule, the network administrators can permit certain remote users (such as other administrators) to Telnet into network systems, while all others are denied access. This is known as *service-dependent filtering* because it is designed to control the traffic for a particular service, such as Telnet.

Service-independent filtering is used to prevent specific types of intrusion that are not based on a particular service. For example, a hacker may attempt to access a computer on a private network by generating packets that appear as though they originated from an internal system. This is called *spoofing*. Although the packets might have the IP address of an internal system, they arrive at the router through the interface that is connected to the Internet. A properly configured filter can associate the IP addresses of internal systems with the interface to the internal network so that packets arriving from the Internet with those source IP addresses can be detected and discarded.

Packet filtering is a feature integrated into many routers, so no extra monetary cost is involved in implementing protection in this way, and no modification to client software or procedures is required. However, creating a collection of filters that provides adequate protection for a network against most types of attack requires a detailed knowledge of the way in which the various protocols and services work, and even then the filters may not be sufficient to prevent some types of intrusion. Packet filtering also creates an additional processing burden on the router, which increases as the filters become more numerous and complex.

Network Address Translation

Network address translation is a technique that enables a LAN to use private, unregistered IP addresses to access the Internet. A NAT server or a router with NAT capabilities modifies the IP datagrams generated by clients to make them appear as though they were created by the NAT server. The NAT server (which has a registered IP address) then communicates with the Internet and relays the responses to the original client. Because the clients do not have valid Internet IP addresses, they are invisible to outside Internet users.

Proxy Servers

Proxy servers, also known as *application-level gateways,* provide a much stricter form of security than packet filters, but they are designed to regulate access only for a particular application. In essence, a proxy server functions as the middleman between the client and the server for a particular service. Packet filtering is used to deny all direct communication between the clients and servers for that service; all traffic goes to the proxy server instead.

Because the proxy server has much more detailed knowledge of the specific application and its functions, it can more precisely regulate the communications generated by that application. A firewall might run individual proxy servers for each of the applications needed by client systems.

The most common form of proxy server used today is for the Web. The client browsers on the network are configured to send all of their requests to the proxy server, instead of to the actual Internet server they want to reach. The proxy server (which does have access to the Internet) then transmits a request for the same document to the appropriate server on the Internet using its own IP address as the source of the request, receives the reply from the server, and passes the response on to the client that originally generated the request.

Because only the proxy server's address is visible to the Internet, there is no way for Internet intruders to access the client systems on the network. In addition, the server analyzes each packet arriving from the Internet. Only packets that are responses to a specific request are admitted, and the server may even examine the data itself for dangerous code or content. The proxy server is in a unique position to regulate user traffic with great precision. A typical web proxy server, for example, enables the network administrator to keep a log of users' web activities, restrict access to certain sites or certain times of day, and even cache frequently accessed sites on the proxy server itself, enabling other clients to access the same information much more quickly.

The drawbacks of proxy servers are that you need an individual server for every application, and modifications to the client program are required. A web browser, for example, must be configured with the address of the proxy server before it can use it. Traditionally, manual configuration of each client browser was needed to do this, but there are now proxy server products that can enable the browser to automatically detect a server and configure itself accordingly.

Circuit-Level Gateways

A *circuit-level gateway,* a function that is usually provided by application-level gateway products, enables trusted users on the private network to access Internet services with all the security of a proxy server but without the packet processing and filtering. The gateway creates a conduit between the interface to the private network and the Internet interface, which enables the client system to send traffic through the firewall. The gateway server still substitutes its own IP address for that of the client system so that the client is still invisible to Internet users.

Combining Firewall Technologies

There are various ways in which these firewall technologies can be combined to protect a network. For a relatively simple installation in which only client access to the Internet is required, packet filtering or NAT alone—or packet filtering in combination with a proxy server—can provide a sufficient firewall. Adding the proxy server increases the security of the network beyond what packet filtering provides because a potential intruder has to penetrate two levels of protection. However, if you run servers that must be visible to the Internet, the problem becomes more complicated.

One of the most secure firewall arrangements you can use for this type of environment is called a *screened subnet firewall.* This consists of a *demilitarized zone* (DMZ) network between the private network and the Internet. Using two routers with packet-filtering capabilities, you create a DMZ network that contains your proxy server, as well as your web, e-mail, and FTP servers, and any other machines that must be visible to the Internet.

The two routers are configured to provide systems on the private network and the Internet with a certain degree of access to certain systems on the DMZ network, but no traffic passes directly through the DMZ. Users from the Internet must then pass through three separate layers of security (router, proxy, and router) before they can access a system on the private network.

Firewalls of this type are complex mechanisms that must be configured specifically for a particular installation and can require a great deal of time, money, and expertise to implement. The prices of comprehensive firewall software products for enterprise networks can run well into five figures, and deploying them is not simply a matter of running an installation program. However, compared to the potential cost in lost data and productivity of a hacker intrusion, the effort taken to protect your network is not wasted.

24 Wireless Security

With today's proliferation of wireless appliances, it is essential that networks be protected from unauthorized access. With the many mobile devices used today, network security is more important than ever. A wireless network is one that uses high-frequency radio signals to send and receive information instead of cables that connect various appliances to each other. The devices can range from printers to laptops and from tablets to file servers.

The technology available today makes it possible for businesses to allow employee access from anyplace within their network area or from any Wi-Fi hotspot. Note that Wi-Fi has been defined in various ways, among them *wireless fidelity* or *wireless Internet*. Wi-Fi, based on the IEEE 802.11 protocol standard, is a trademarked name belonging to the Wi-Fi Alliance. This trade association formed in 1999 as a nonprofit, international group to promote the technology.

This chapter discusses the various methods of security specifically for wireless devices and networks, both at home and in business settings.

Wireless Functionality

Since Wi-Fi is based on the transmission of radio signals on a single frequency, the signals are vulnerable to interception. Both an advantage and disadvantage of wireless connectivity is that devices are potentially compatible with everything from your rack server to a game device.

Wireless Network Components

While similar to wired networks, a wireless network must have several components to function properly.

Wireless Network Adapters/Wireless Network Interface Cards

While available as stand-alone devices to be connected with Universal Serial Bus (USB) connectors, today wireless network adapters are usually included in computers or other devices to be used on a wireless network. For small networks, such as those in a home, these adapters (or network interface cards [NICs]) are often all that is needed to create a peer-to-peer or ad hoc network that allows such devices as computers, printers, tablets, and so on to talk to each other.

Wireless Router

The broadband wireless router consists of an access point, several Ethernet ports to connect to wired devices on your network such as printers, and a broadband wide area network port to connect to the Internet. (See "Wireless Access Points" later in this chapter for more information on access points.) It usually includes a built-in Dynamic Host Configuration Protocol (DHCP) server that assigns an IP address to each connected device. As the Internet gateway, each router also contains a two-way radio that both transmits and receives radio signals and comes equipped with at least one antenna to increase the range of the radio signal.) Today's wireless router usually includes Domain Name System (DNS) settings, as discussed in Chapter 15, and a firewall, and it is capable of encryption for added security.

Wireless Repeater/Range Expander/Signal Booster

To boost the signals emitted by the router, a repeater can be installed to either a router or an access point to ensure signals are being transmitted and received. This can be useful if your devices are on different floors of a building.

Wireless Router Types

Depending on the type of network with which you will be working, several IEEE 802.11 technologies are available for your wireless router, as well as other standards for different uses. See Table 24-1 for some comparisons.

Single-Band and Dual-Band Routers

The main difference between single-band and double-band routers is the range of the signal. As a rule, single-band routers, using a 2.4 GHz band, transmit weaker signals than dual-band devices. Since dual-band routers, which contain both 2.4 GHz and 5.0 GHz bands, can use more

Standard	Range	Frequency	Data Rate (Throughput)	Band (If Applicable)
802.11a	20 meters (about 65 feet)	5.25, 5.6, and 5.8 GHz	Up to 54 Mbps	
802.11b	30 meters (about 100 feet)	2.4 to 2.4835 GHz	Up to 11 Mbps	2.4 GHz single band
802.11g	30 meters (about 100 feet)	2.4 to 2.4835 GHz	Up to 54 Mbps	2.4 GHz single band
802.11n	50 meters (about 150 feet)	2.4 to 2.4835 GHz and 5.15 to 5.35 GHz	Up to 300 Mbps	Either 2.4 GHz or 5 GHz
802.11ac	802.11ac standards are currently being formalized			

Table 24-1   Router Statistics

than one signal band, their range, signal strength, and often speed can be greater. Not all wireless devices can run on the 5.0 GHz band, so there is often not as much traffic on that frequency.

Single-Band Routers   Many devices use the 2.4 GHz bandwidth found in single-band routers. Some of these are as follows:

- Cordless phones
- Microwave ovens
- Baby monitors
- Bluetooth appliances
- Wi-Fi access points
- Smart phones
- Television stations and towers
- Remote controllers for TV and cable
- Game controllers

The single-band frequency has three nonoverlapping channels with which to work, but as you can see, the many other users of this bandwidth can create quite a bottleneck for your network. This widespread usage can create interference on your connection and slow down transmissions. While it has a higher range than the 5.0 GHz frequency, the 5.0 GHz frequency allows more bandwidth through.

Dual-Band Routers   These routers have both 2.4 GHz and 5.0 GHz bands, so speed is enhanced, making this band suitable for both gaming and video streaming. Since fewer devices use the 5.0 GHz band, there is less chance for interference on this frequency; 5.0 GHz has 23 nonoverlapping channels available. If multiple devices connect to your router at the same time, consider a simultaneous dual-band router.

Dual-band routers can be either *simultaneous* or *selectable*. Simultaneous dual-band routers have the following:

- Two times the bandwidth of the single-band router
- A dedicated Wi-Fi network for high-speed transmission, such as video
- Two separate Wi-Fi networks operating at the same time

Selectable dual-band routers have the following:

- Have to select one Wi-Fi network
- Have the same bandwidth as the single-band router

Other Considerations

When deciding on a router for your wireless network, consider the age of your current hardware. Today's hardware needs higher bandwidths, so if your company and its employees have notebooks, tablets, smart phones, or other such devices, dual-band routers are important.

Also, most routers have Ethernet ports that allow connections via Ethernet cables. This connection can add speed and reliability for that device.

Wireless Transmission

The wireless network interface controller in your device converts digital data into radio waves and, in turn, sends them to your wireless router. The router then broadcasts the radio waves to the Internet. The small, wireless network formed by the NICs and the router can be accessed by anyone within range of the radio signals. Some have described the router as a small radio station, capable of both broadcasting and receiving signals.

Wireless Access Points

A wireless access point (WAP) can be part of a wireless router or a stand-alone device. Some stand-alone WAPs are used as boosters for both business and home networks. All such points are managed by a wireless LAN controller to control authentication, transmission channels, radio-frequency (RF) power, and security.

Many libraries, cafes, and other businesses offer public WAPs for their customers. These locations, called *hotspots*, mean that Internet connectivity is available at that location. While these access points provide great convenience, they also can be security risks.

WAPs are directly connected to a wired Ethernet connection and provide the link that allows several devices to be connected to this wired connection. There are several ways you can ensure that your access point suffers the least amount of interference with the highest possible Internet speed:

- **Placement**   Many obstacles to good connections are on the floor (or ground) level of your office. Consider putting your WAP higher up, perhaps on a high shelf or even the ceiling.

- **Vicinity**   If you have several devices using the same WAP, the best location for your WAP is nearest the device you use the most. The strongest signal is always the closest to your access point.

- **Line-of-sight**   The best location for your access point is in a clear line-of-sight with your primary device. Any impediment will decrease signal strength.

- **Nonreflectivity**   Reflection from windows, bright countertops, or mirrors can interfere with Wi-Fi signals. Position your access point so that the signals do not bounce off reflective surfaces.

NOTE When several devices equipped with wireless network adapters are close together, they can communicate without either a WAP or a router. This type of wireless network is known as an *ad hoc* network.

Setting Up a Wireless Access Point

WAPs come with a default IP address, some of which are assigned by DHCP and others with previously assigned addresses. The bottom of the box in which the WAP was shipped will show which method is used. Most WAPs will connect to the nearest existing network connection.

While each model is slightly different, all require at least these three steps. Keep a written note of each of these settings as you proceed. You will need the information when connecting this network to your computer.

- **Service set identifier (SSID)**   Create a name for this wireless network. This is also known as the network name.

- **Infrastructure versus ad hoc**   Choose Infrastructure.

- **Encryption**   This is a security measure. Ensure it is on, using the recommended settings on the device. See "Understanding Encryption" later in this chapter.

Some WAPs come with a CD or DVD with basic configuration instructions. Others require that you connect to the manufacturer's web site and follow the instructions on the site.

Configuring a Wireless Router

After you have physically connected your router to a broadband Internet connection with an Ethernet cable, connect at least one computer to your router with an Ethernet cable. After you have configured the router, you can disconnect this computer.

1. Locate the IP address of the router. For most routers, this address is 192.168.1.1.

2. Using the computer attached to your router, open a web browser and enter the IP address of the router in the browser's address bar. You will be prompted for your name and password, as shown here. Depending on the router model, this can be "password" and "password" or "admin" and "password." The router may show this information on an attached label or include it in the written documentation. Some web sites allow you to leave one or both fields blank.

192.168.1.1

Authentication Required   ×

The server http://192.168.1.1:80 requires a username and password. The server says: RT-N66U.

User Name:

Password:

Log In   Cancel

Part VI

3. Log on to your router, and you are taken to either the router's main menu or the status screen, as in the example of an ASUS RT-N66U shown here.

4. Enter your network name. The field is usually Name or SSID. Most routers use "default" or the brand name of the router. Ensure you have enabled SSID broadcast so your network is active.

5. Set a security/encryption method. The best choice is WPA2-PSK (Pre-shared Key Mode or Personal Mode). See "Securing a Wireless Router" later in this chapter for more information.

6. Enter a password/passphrase for your network. Make sure this includes uppercase and lowercase letters, numbers, and symbols. The best choices have at least 8 to 13 characters and contain no words found in a dictionary. Make a note of this password. (But do not put it on a sticky note on your monitor!)

7. Apply your settings. Once the router has completed its setup, you can use your wireless network.

8. Change the router username and password from the defaults that came with your router. Make a note of them both.

9. Test the network by connecting a device. As long as the new device is within range, it should see your network and ask for the password/passphrase. Once you have entered that phrase, your device will remember the network and connect automatically each time it is powered on within range of the network.

10. When everything is functioning, log out of your router.

Creating a Secure Wireless Network

The term *secure wireless network* may be a contradiction in terms. All wireless networks and the devices they connect are vulnerable to outsiders. Add this understanding to the fact that even IT professionals seldom use effective security measures, and you have the potential for widespread attacks.

Securing a Wireless Home Network

Since wireless signals can be accessed by anyone within range, including your next-door neighbor, the ramifications of unsecured home networks are great. By usurping your Internet signal, the speed by which you can connect is decreased as the signal is shared with other computers (or mobile devices). The use of your signal can also open a pathway for hackers using programs that can gain personal information from your computer or insert malware onto your system.

You can ensure your home network is protected in several ways.

Changing the Username and Password

Since most router manufacturers want to make it as easy as possible for the home user to set up a wireless network, default passwords are available on the manufacturer's web site as well as many places on the Internet. Check in any documentation that came with your router or download the documentation from the web site. To access your wireless router, follow these steps:

1. Determine the default username and password for your model router.

2. Type **192.168.1.1** into the address bar of any web browser.

3. Enter the default username and password to open your router's interface.

4. Find the administrative section that displays the username and password. The image you see will be different, depending on the router brand you are using.

5. Change both the username and the password, according to the instructions on your router. Ensure your password contains symbols, uppercase and lowercase letters, and numbers. The best ones contain at least 8 characters, and 13 is even better. Also, consider changing the password every 60 to 90 days to be more secure.

6. Save the changes.

Changing the Network Name

Changing your SSID helps in several ways. First, it makes it easy when connecting new devices to an available wireless network. Some families have one network for the parents and another for cell phone or laptop connection. Even if outside scanners find your network, they cannot join without the appropriate password.

To change the name, open the router administrative window as described earlier and find the location of your wireless name, as shown here.

Applying Media Access Control Filters

Most wireless routers provide a way with which you can add, or *whitelist,* the devices that connect to your wireless network. Consider listing the media access control (MAC) addresses of the most commonly connected devices, such as smart phones. Each device has its own address, and you can list those addresses in your router's MAC filter, as shown next.

Enabling Strong Encryption

Ensure that your router is set to Wi-Fi Protected Access 2 (WPA2) rather than the older WEP setting. See "Understanding Encryption" later in this chapter for more information.

Other Options

You have a couple other options, discussed here:

- Ensure that your router has the latest updates. Go to your manufacturer's web site and download the latest firmware.

- Use "anti Wi-Fi" paint on one of the walls. However, since this special paint has chemicals that absorb radio signals, do not paint this type of paint in the entire room.

Securing a Business Network

Wireless business networks have many of the same issues as home networks. However, there may be more tools with which to alleviate these problems because IT professionals are usually (but not always!) more aware of the issues.

When working with a small or large wireless network in a business setting, understand the process and address each concern and then follow through on a regular basis to at least lessen the threat of infiltration.

Creating a Security Policy for Wireless Networks

The first step in any policy is identifying the needs and enumerating the methods to satisfy each need. The policy should include at least the following:

- What devices are included such as both company-owned and employee-owned laptops, smart phones, tablets, and so forth

- What WAPs can be connected to the network

- What protection or settings are required on all connected or potentially connected devices

- How devices are configured, such as what devices can connect only to the Internet or which sites are on the Internet

- How the policy will be enforced

Setting Up Protection

Wired networks can be protected physically by eliminating Ethernet connectivity. In a wireless setting, access points and other devices must be protected from theft, tampering, or other physical assault. Consider using touchpad locks on all storage and wiring closets to eliminate unauthorized visits.

Passwords should be required for both internal and external use on all network devices. Set a time when all passwords must be changed, and do not allow the same password to be used more than once.

Ensure your wireless network encryption is reviewed and revised as necessary. This should be done on at least a quarterly basis. As part of this policy, ensure that wireless devices do not have administration rights access to the network.

MAC Identification Filtering

While tracking the MAC addresses of devices connected to a home wireless network can be effective, in most business environments it can be problematic. There are often too many devices, too many changes, and too much chance of incorrectly entered MAC addresses to make this a viable practice in all but very small networks.

Segmentation of Access

Best practices often limit network access by group or need. For example, some resources can be accessed only through a virtual private network (VPN), or file transfers can be blocked. This policy should be established and reviewed on a regular basis.

Using Anti-malware

As malware becomes increasingly destructive, network administrators must ensure that their systems are protected. Adware, worms, Trojans, and other potentially unwanted programs (PUPs) can infect both wireless and wired devices.

Remote Authentication Dial-In User Service

This mode of WPA2 provides greater security and requires either a hosted service or a Remote Authentication Dial-In User Service (RADIUS) server. 802.1X/RADIUS can increase security but can also be difficult for end users unless their device is preconfigured to use this level of security. Since tracking and reports are based on the name of the clients, it is easier to restrict certain users.

Maintaining Security Measure on an Ongoing Basis

No policies or procedures can survive in a vacuum. At every level, ensure the policies are followed by each employee and department. Consider using company meetings for education on current security issues and require that all new employees have copies of the policies.

Securing a Wireless Router

When setting up a wireless router, there are several ways to ensure its security:

- Disable remote administrative management. If no one outside can access the administrative tools, the likelihood of unauthorized administrative changes is lessened.
- Consider changing the default IP address of your router. Using something less common can foil *cross-site request forgery* (CSRF) attacks on your network. These attacks transmit unwanted requests in web applications and compromise user data.
- When working with the router, require everyone to actually log out.
- Ensure that AES WPA2 is turned on, and eliminate WPS. Also, change default passwords.
- As with all routers, update the firmware regularly. It is good practice to create a log to ensure all firmware and software are updated on a schedule.

Securing Mobile Devices

While the terms *mobile* and *wireless* are often used as synonyms, they are different. Mobile devices are portable, contain internal batteries and therefore need no external power, and can be taken anywhere. To exchange data, the device must be connected to a mobile network but does not need to be attached to any hardware infrastructure. The mobile network, however, must be connected at some point to a hardwired system.

Wireless does not mean portable or mobile. Wireless networks can connect devices to the Internet or each other, must be connected to an external power source, and are usually kept in one place. While wireless networks can access mobile networks, they, too, must, at some point, connect to a hardwired, broadband Internet connection. Security for mobile devices, therefore, differs from that of nonportable devices.

Although phone and tablet security is not strictly part of networking, many businesses provide these electronic devices for use by their employees. The following are some of the ways you and your employees can protect these devices and, in turn, protect your network:

- Educate your employees about phishing, malicious or unknown phone numbers, and open Wi-Fi networks. Create a written company policy about the usage of these devices.

- Enable passwords or PINs on each device. Some phones accept only a certain number of tries for the correct password and then lock the phone.

- Make sure all operating system updates are loaded on to each device.

- Install antivirus and anti-malware apps on all devices and ensure they are kept up to date.

- Install and use encryption software on each device.

- Do not download unapproved apps. Each IT department should maintain a list of approved apps for company devices.

- Turn off both Wi-Fi and Bluetooth settings when the device is not being used. In this way, unknown devices cannot connect to the network through the device.

- Periodically check each device to ensure it has not been compromised. Look for such items as the following:

  - Check for odd data patterns.

  - Check for unverifiable charges on cell phone invoices.

  - Look for unapproved apps on the device.

  - Ensure physical security of devices when not being used by the employee.

  - Each device has built-in limitations from the factory. Ensure these limitations are still in place and the device has not been "jailbroken."

What Are the Risks?

The risks in wireless technology can create havoc on your network and throughout your company. While security is important when working with a wired network, it is critical when working with a wireless network. Whether at home, in a business, or in the cloud, there are many ways in which your wireless network can be compromised.

Unsecured Home Networks

While most business networks have at least some password or passphrase protection, open wireless business networks are not common. However, home networks that connect computers, tablets, laptops, smart phones, and other devices pose security issues not only to the homeowner but to other, more protected networks, such as the business where that home network owner works. Ad hoc networks are especially vulnerable to outsiders.

Without encryption, anyone can connect to a network for both legal and illegal purposes. If a network is in *promiscuous mode*, that is, unprotected, anyone within range can use the network. If a next-door neighbor accesses an unprotected wireless network and downloads anything illegally, the action can be traced to the original IP address, and the owner of the network could be charged with the crime.

All data on such networks is transmitted in *plain text*. That is, it is legible to anyone who can access the information. With easily obtainable software, outsiders can read any data that was relayed on this network. This includes credit card or other personal information entered into a web site without an HTTPS connection.

Some hotspot access points are unencrypted, so be cautious when accessing sensitive data at your local coffee shop. The person intently studying a laptop a couple of tables away could be watching your data interchange.

The following are the possible threats for unsecured networks:

- **Password capture**   Passwords for e-mail accounts are sometimes sent in the clear, meaning anyone could access personal e-mail and take advantage of any personal information found in those e-mails.

- **Data access**   If file sharing is turned on, anyone with access to an unsecured network can read the data throughout the shared files.

- **Spam and other malware**   When an unsecured wireless network is hacked, the hacker can use the devices on that network as the source for spam and other malware.

Wireless Invasion Tools

As wireless security measures are applied, software and hardware devices are developed to overcome the measures. Some of these are discussed here.

Hidden SSID Locaters

There are some security suggestions that encourage users to hide the name or SSID of their network. When an SSID is hidden, snooping utility programs can find the network quickly. If a wireless network is suspected, simply monitoring that network will eventually reveal an attempted connection, and as part of the connection process, the name of the SSID is revealed. Devices attempt to connect to the hidden network at all times.

MAC Address Captures

When wireless packets are transmitted, the device MAC addresses are included. Hackers simply change their hardware's MAC address and log on to the network with that device.

WEP and WPA1

The encryption in WEP is vulnerable to decryption, and therefore any device still set to WEP should be updated or replaced. The first version of WPA is also vulnerable. Ensure all wireless routers are set to WPA2.

Wi-Fi Protected Setup

Some routers have a PIN with which a device can connect to your network instead of using a passphrase. Some software programs can go through all possible number connections until the router acknowledges that the right one has been found. Many security experts recommend disabling Wi-Fi Protected Setup (WPS) for this reason.

Password Vulnerabilities

With WPA2, passwords and passphrases can be between 8 and 63 characters. Dictionary attack software intercepts a router packet and runs through all possible combinations to discover the password or passphrase. Using strong passwords and passphrases with numbers, letters, and symbols is the best method.

Understanding Encryption

Encryption is a process that makes transmitted data unreadable by those not authorized to see it. When sending information on a wireless network, it is especially important to understand how and when encryption is applied. Successful encryption methods cover both static, stored information and transmitted data.

At-Rest Encryption

Information processed and stored in company servers, especially in companies that maintain financial or medical data, is regulated and protected by government regulation. However, recent events have proved that even this information is subject to attack and is vulnerable to outside sources. Encryption can be applied to individual files or to all data stored on a server or group of servers. There are several methods to protect such data.

File or Folder Encryption   At the file or folder level, no one can open the file or the folder without the appropriate encryption key. There are software programs that encrypt and decrypt the file once the appropriate key is entered. These programs offer options such as the ability to automatically encrypt specific file types, encrypt files created by particular users or applications, or encrypt all files and folders designated by the system administrator.

This method protects only the data within the files or folders. It does not protect file or folder names. Often, copying or moving these files will decrypt the data.

Full-Disk (or Whole-Disk) Encryption   Some operating systems come with utilities to encrypt an entire hard drive. Mac OS comes with FileVault encryption, Windows 8.1 includes Pervasive Device Encryption, and earlier versions of Windows included BitLocker. There are several free full-disk encryption software packages available. The only way to access the information on a protected disk is with the appropriate authorization key.

Volume and Virtual Encryption   This method encrypts only a partition on a hard drive, leaving sections of the disk open and unencrypted. The process encrypts a file, creating a *container* that can hold other files and folders. This container can be accessed only with the proper key. Encrypted containers often hold boot and system volumes on a PC, external hard drives, and USB flash drives. Since containers are portable, the contents can be copied or transferred across mediums. See Table 24-2 for a comparison of these methods.

Part VI

Method	Supported Equipment	Data Protected	Moderates Outside Threats	Moderates Inside Threats	Portable
File/folder encryption	Any user device	Individual file or folder data	Yes	Moderates but does not prevent insiders	Sometimes depending on the device
Full-disk encryption	Laptop and desktop computers	All data on the disk	Yes	No	No
Volume encryption	Laptop and desktop computers, external hard drives, and USB flash drives	All the data in the container, including system files	Yes	Moderates but does not prevent insiders	Yes

Table 24-2   At-Rest Encryption Methods

In-Transit Encryption

Data that is being transmitted is said to be *in transit*. Several types of encryption techniques can be applied to data as it moves across a network. The main focus of these techniques is to prevent unauthorized users from seeing the data.

Transport Layer Security/Secure Sockets Layer   Most web sites that require personal information use either Transport Layer Security (TLS) or the earlier Secure Sockets Layer (SSL) to protect this data. Web sites that employ this level of security are shown with the initial *https* rather than the normal *http* (which stands for Hypertext Transfer Protocol) in the address. HTTP operates in the application layer of the Internet Protocol suite.

NOTE   Originally, HTTPS stood for Hypertext Transfer Protocol with SSL. Today, it indicates that the site uses TLS.

WPA2   WPA2 is Wi-Fi Protected Access II, a program developed by the Wi-Fi Alliance to alleviate the weaknesses in WPA.

Internet Protocol Security   This method operates in the Internet layer of the Internet Protocol suite and therefore protects all data at the upper layers. It can be applied in both transport and tunnel modes:

- In tunnel mode, the entire packet is encrypted. This mode is used to create virtual private networks (see "Virtual Private Network" next), host-to-network transmissions such as remote user access connections, and private communication such as host-to-host transmissions.
- Transport mode encrypts only the message of the packet, not the header.

Virtual Private Network   This is an encrypted private "throughway" between two entities that allows information to be transmitted securely. Once established, these connections offer the following:

- Confidentiality in that any unauthorized "snooper" would see only encrypted data
- Authentication of the sender
- Message integrity
- Includes IPsec and TLS

CHAPTER

25 | Overview of Network Administration

Although business networks often run a variety of operating systems, particularly on their servers, many user workstations run some form of Windows. Whether you agree with Microsoft that the Windows interface is user friendly and intuitive, there is no question that administering a fleet of hundreds or thousands of Windows workstations is an extremely formidable task. In addition, this chapter covers network administration information on the other main operating systems in use today, Mac OS and Linux.

Nearly all software includes tools that network administrators can use to simplify the process of installing, managing, and maintaining the operating system on a large number of workstations. This chapter examines some of these tools and how you can use them to configure workstations *en masse,* rather than working on them one at a time.

One of the primary goals of any network administrator should be to create workstation configurations that are standardized and consistent so that when problems occur, the support staff is fully acquainted with the user's working environment. Failure to do this can greatly increase the time and effort needed to troubleshoot problems, thus increasing the overall cost of operating the computer. Unfortunately, users have a tendency to experiment with their computers, such as modifying the configuration settings or installing unauthorized software. This can make the system unstable and can interfere with the maintenance and troubleshooting processes. Therefore, it is advisable that administrators impose some form of restraints on network workstations to prevent this unauthorized experimentation.

Features such as user profiles and system policies are basic tools you can use to do this on most network systems, to whatever degree you judge is necessary for your users. Using these tools, you can limit the programs that a system is able to run, deny access to certain elements of the operating system, and control access to network resources. Imposing restrictive policies and limiting users' access to their workstations can be sensitive undertakings, and network administrators should carefully consider the capabilities of their users before making decisions like these. Unsophisticated computer users can benefit and may even appreciate a restricted environment that insulates them from the more confusing elements of the operating system. However, users with more experience might take offense at being limited to a small subset of the computer's features, and their productivity may even be impaired by it.

Locating Applications and Data in Windows Systems

One of the basic tasks of the network administrator is to decide where data should be stored on the network. Network workstations require access to operating system files, applications, and data, and the locations where these elements are stored is an important part of creating a safe and stable network environment. Some administrators actually exercise no control over where users store files. Fortunately, most Windows applications install themselves to a default directory located in the C:\Program Files folder on the local system, which provides a measure of consistency if nothing else. Some applications even create default data directories on the local drive, but leaving users to their own devices when it comes to storing their data files is an inherently dangerous practice. Many users have little or no knowledge of their computer's directory structure and little or no training in file management. This can result in files for different applications all being dumped into a single common directory and left unprotected from accidental damage or erasure.

Server-Based Operating Systems

In the early days of Windows, running the operating system from a server drive was a practical alternative to having individual installations on every workstation. Storing the operating system files on a server enabled the network administrator not only to prevent them from being tampered with or accidentally deleted, but also to upgrade all the workstations at once. The technique also saved disk space on the workstation's local drive. However, as the years passed, the capacity of a typical hard drive on a network workstation grew enormously, as did the size of the Windows operating system itself.

Today, the practice of installing an operating system onto a mapped server drive is not practical. A workstation running Windows must load many megabytes of files just to boot the system, and when you multiply this by hundreds of computers, the amount of network traffic created by this practice could saturate even the fastest network. In addition, disk space shortages are not a big problem now that workstations routinely ship with drives that hold anywhere from 500 GB to 1 TB or more. Installing the operating system onto the local drive is, in most cases, the obvious solution.

However, newer technologies are available today that are once again making it practical to run a Windows operating system from a server. This time, the workstations do not download the entire operating system from the server drive. Instead, the workstations function as client terminals that connect to a terminal server. The workstation operating system and applications actually run on the server, while the terminal functions solely as an input/output device. As a result, the workstations require only minimal resources because the server takes most of the burden.

Server-Based Applications

Running applications from a server drive rather than individual workstation installations is another way to provide a consistent environment for your users and minimize the network's administrative burden. At its simplest, you do this by installing an application in the usual manner and specifying a directory on a network drive instead of a local directory as the location for the program files. Windows applications are rarely simple, however, and the process is usually more complicated.

Running applications from server drives has both advantages and disadvantages. On the plus side, as with server-based operating systems, you get disk space savings on the local drives, the ability to protect the application files against damage or deletion, and the ability to upgrade and maintain a single copy of the application files rather than individual copies on each workstation. The disadvantages are that server-based applications nearly always run more slowly than local ones, generate a substantial amount of network traffic, and do not function when the server is malfunctioning or otherwise unavailable.

In the days of DOS, applications were self-contained and usually consisted of no more than a single program directory that contained all of the application's files. You could install the application to a server drive and then let other systems use it simply by running the executable file. Today's applications are much more complex, and the installation program is more than just a means of copying files. In addition to the program files, a Windows application installation may include registry settings and Windows DLLs that must be installed on the local machine, as well as a procedure for creating the Start menu entries and icons needed to launch the application.

When you want to share a server-based application with multiple workstations, you usually still have to perform a complete installation on each computer. This is to ensure that each workstation has all of the DLL files, registry settings, and icons needed to run the application. One way to implement a server-based application is to perform a complete installation of the program on each workstation, specifying the same directory on a server drive as the destination for the program files in each case. This way, each workstation receives all of the necessary files and modifications, and only one copy of the application files is stored on the server.

However, another important issue is the ability to maintain individual configuration settings for each of the computers accessing the application. When one user modifies the interface of a shared application, you don't want those modifications to affect every other user. As a result, each of the application's users must maintain their own copies of the application configuration settings. Whether this is an easy task, or even a possible one, depends on how each individual application stores its configuration settings. If, for example, the settings are stored in the registry or a Windows INI file, the installation process will create a separate configuration on each workstation. However, if the settings are stored with the program files on the server by default, you must take steps to prevent each user's changes from overwriting those of the other users.

In some cases, it is possible to configure an application to store its configuration settings in an alternative location, enabling you to redirect them to each workstation's local drive or to each user's home directory on a server. If this is not possible, the application may not be suitable for use in a shared environment. In many cases, the most practical way to run applications from a server is to select applications that have their own networking capabilities. Microsoft Office, for example, lets you create an administrative installation point on a server that you can use to install the application on your workstations. When you perform each installation, you can select whether the application files should be copied to the local drive, run from the server drive, or split between the two.

Many companies are moving toward cloud-based apps these days, which can be run on virtually any OS and any device that has an Internet connection and a web browser, eliminating the need for installing any files. These would also be considered server-based applications.

Storing Data Files

On most of today's Windows networks, both the operating system and the applications are installed on local workstation drives, but it is still up to the network administrator to decide where the data files generated and accessed by users should be stored. The two primary concerns that you must evaluate when making this decision are accessibility and security. Users must

Part VI

certainly have access to their own data files, but there are also files that have to be shared by many users. Important data files also have to be protected from modification and deletion by unauthorized personnel and have to be backed up to an alternative medium to guard against a disaster, such as a fire or disk failure.

Data files come in various types and formats that can affect the way in which you store them. Individual user documents, such as those created in word processor or spreadsheet applications, are designed for use by one person at a time, while databases can support simultaneous access by multiple users. In most cases, database files are stored on the computer running the database server application, so administrators can regulate access to them with file system permissions and protect them with regular backups. Other types of files may require additional planning.

Since many Windows operating systems are peer-to-peer network operating systems, you can allow users to store their document files on either their local drives or a server and still share them with other users on the network. However, there are several compelling reasons why it is better for all data files to be stored on servers. The first and most important reason is to protect the files from loss due to a workstation or disk failure. Servers are more likely to have protective measures in place, such as RAID arrays or mirrored drives, and are more easily backed up. Servers also make the data available at all times, while a workstation might be turned off when the user is absent.

The second reason is access control. Although Windows workstations and servers both have the same capabilities when it comes to granting access permissions to specific users, users rarely have the skills or the inclination to protect their own files effectively, and it is far easier for network administrators to manage the permissions on a single server than on many individual workstations. Another important reason for storing data on servers is that sharing the drives on every workstation can make it much more difficult to locate information on the network. To look at a Windows domain and see dozens or hundreds of computers, each with its own shares, makes the task of locating a specific file much more complicated. Limiting the shares to a relatively few servers simplifies the process.

As a result, the best strategy for most Windows networks is to install the operating system and applications on local drives and implement a strategy for storing all data files on network servers. The most common practice is to create a home directory for each user on a server, to which they have full access permissions. You should then configure all applications to store their files in that directory, by default, so that no valuable data is stored on local drives. Depending on the needs of your users, you can make the home directories private, so that only the user who owns the directory can access it, or grant all users read-only access to all of the home directories. This makes it possible for users to share files at will simply by giving another user the filename or location.

When you create a user object in the Windows Active Directory or a user account in a Windows domain, you have the option of creating a home directory for the user at the same time. By default, users are given full control over their home directories, and no one else is given any access at all. You may want to modify these permissions to grant access to the directory to the other users on the network or, at the very least, to administrators.

Setting Environment Variables in Windows

In Windows 7, open the Environment Variables dialog box. To do so, follow these steps:

1. Click Start and choose Control Panel.
2. Click User Accounts.

3. Select Change My Environment Variables from the Task pane on the left of your screen. The Environment Variables dialog box appears, as shown in Figure 25-1.

From this dialog box, you can create a new environment variable or modify an existing one. In Windows 8, it takes a few more steps.

1. Click the Desktop tile, and from the desktop, click Start.
2. Right-click the desktop folder, and from the context menu, choose File Explorer.
3. Right-click This PC at the left side of your window. From the context menu that appears, click Properties.
4. At the left pane of the System window that opens, select Advanced System Settings.
5. From the System Properties dialog box, select the Advanced tab. You will see the Environment Variables button at the bottom right of the Advanced tab.
6. Click New to add a new variable or click Edit to make changes to an existing variable. Use the Delete option to delete a variable.
7. Click OK when you have made your choices.

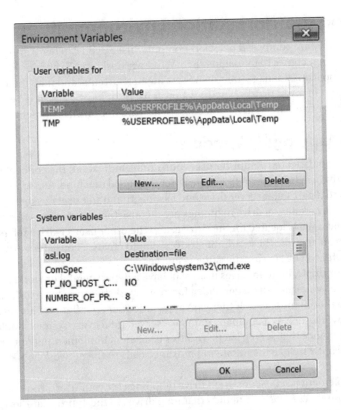

Figure 25-1   The Environment Variables dialog box in Windows 7

Setting Environment Variables in Linux

In Linux, enter the following command at a shell prompt, depending on which shell you are using:

csh/tcsh: `setenv` *variable value*
bash/ksh: `export` *variable=value*

In this case, *variable* is the name of the environment variable and *value* is the value you want to assign to this variable.

Setting Environment Variables in OS X

When you are using Mac OS X, you must first open a terminal window. If you want to run jobs from the command line, enter the following command:

`export` *variable=value*

In this example, *variable* is the name of the environment variable and *value* is the value you want to assign to this variable. You can determine any environment variables that have been set with the `env` command.

Controlling the Workstation Environment

In an organization composed of expert computer users, you can leave everyone to their own devices when it comes to managing their Windows desktops. Experienced users can create their own desktop icons, manage their own Start menu shortcuts, and map their own drive letters. However, not many networks have only power users; in most cases, it is better for the network administrator to create a viable and consistent workstation environment.

Drive Mappings in Windows

Many less sophisticated computer users don't fully understand the concept of a network and how a server drive can be mapped to a drive letter on a local machine. A user may have the drive letter F mapped to a particular server drive and assume that other users' systems are configured the same way. If workstation drive mappings are inconsistent, confusion results when one user tells another that a file is located on the F drive, and the other user's F drive refers to a different share. To avoid problems like these, administrators should create a consistent drive-mapping strategy for users who will be sharing the same resources.

As an example, in many cases users will have a departmental or workgroup server that is their "home" server, and it's a good idea for every workstation to have the same drive letter mapped to that home server. If there are application servers that provide resources to everyone on the network, such as a company database server, then every system should use the same drive letter to reference that server, if a drive letter is needed. Implementing minor policies like these can significantly reduce the number of nuisance calls to the network help desk generated by puzzled users.

To implement a set of consistent drive mappings for your users, you can create logon script files containing *NET USE* commands that map drives to the appropriate servers each time the user logs on to the network. By structuring the commands properly, you should be able to create a single logon script for multiple users. To map a drive letter to each user's own home directory, you use a command like the following:

```
NET USE X:  /home
```

where *home* is the name of the directory.

Mapping a Windows Drive in Linux

Before you can share a Windows drive, ensure that your network settings allow the connection. To do so, go to the Network and Sharing Center. In Windows 7, choose Change Advanced Sharing Settings. To access the Network Center in Windows 8, access the Network and Sharing Center through Control Panel | Network And Internet. Turn on network discovery and file and printer sharing, as shown in Figure 25-2.

Create a folder on your Windows machine to share. This example uses a folder on the desktop named LinuxShare. Right-click the new folder and click Properties to open the Properties dialog box. Click the Sharing tab and choose Advanced Sharing.

Click "Share this folder."

Click Permissions to open the Permissions dialog box. Add or remove the user accounts (on the Windows computer) and indicate the controls you want applied. Click OK to close each window. While still in the Properties dialog box, select the Security tab. Ensure the permissions showing in this tab are the same as you set in the earlier dialogs. If all is the same, click Close to close the dialog box. Your new folder is now shared and available to your Linux computer.

Your Linux computer must have either DIFS or SMBFS. The Linux kernel you are using must be configured for binary distribution. The following are the commands to install CIFS/SMBFS for Ubuntu, Debian, and Red Hat. For each, you must first open a terminal:

- In Red Hat, the command is *sudo yum install cifs-utils*.
- In Debian or Ubuntu, the command is *sudo apt-get install smbfs*.

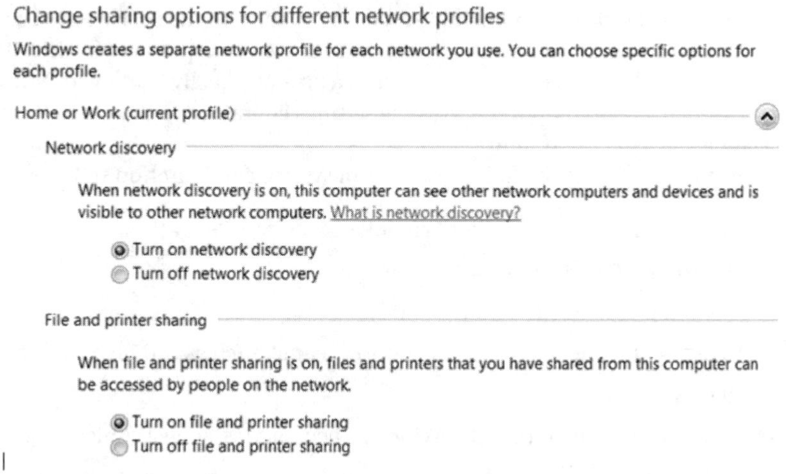

Change sharing options for different network profiles

Windows creates a separate network profile for each network you use. You can choose specific options for each profile.

Home or Work (current profile) ⌃

Network discovery

When network discovery is on, this computer can see other network computers and devices and is visible to other network computers. What is network discovery?

⦿ Turn on network discovery
◯ Turn off network discovery

File and printer sharing

When file and printer sharing is on, files and printers that you have shared from this computer can be accessed by people on the network.

⦿ Turn on file and printer sharing
◯ Turn off file and printer sharing

Figure 25-2   Change settings in Windows Network and Sharing Center to enable mapping a Linux drive.

Part VI

Then, create a directory and mount your shared folder to that directory. Use the following command:

```
mkdir ~/Desktop/Windows-LinuxShare
sudo mount.cifs //WindowsPC/Share /home/MyComputer/Desktop/Windows-
LinuxShare -o user=Bobbi
```

You may be prompted for the root password for both your Linux and Windows computers.

Mapping a Windows Drive in Apple OS X

Mac OS X contains a shortcut with which you can easily map and access network drives without any extra software.

1. Open the Finder utility.

2. Press COMMAND-SHIFT-K to open the appropriate server connections.

3. The dialog box that opens allows you to enter the appropriate network address or browse the network. Click the Connect button at the bottom right of the window when you have located the drive.

User Profiles

Creating user profiles is a method of storing the shortcuts and desktop configuration settings for individual users in a directory, where a computer can access them during the system startup sequence. By creating separate profiles for different users, each person can retrieve their own settings when they log on. When you store multiple profiles on a local machine, you make it possible for users to share the same workstation without overwriting each other's settings. When you store the profiles on a network server, users can access their settings from any network workstation; this is called a *roaming profile*. In addition, you can force users to load a specific profile each time they log on to a system and prevent them from changing it; this is called a *mandatory profile*.

The registry on a Windows computer contains two files on the local drive, called System.dat and NTUser.dat. NTUser.dat corresponds to the HKEY_CURRENT_USER key in the registry, which contains all of the environmental settings that apply to the user who is currently logged on. On a Windows operating system after Windows ME, the corresponding file is called Ntuser.dat. This file, called a *registry hive*, forms the basis of a user profile. By loading an Ntuser.dat file during the logon sequence, the computer writes the settings contained in the file to the registry, and they then become active on the system.

The user hive contains the following types of system configuration settings:

- All user-definable settings for Windows Explorer

- Persistent network drive connections

- Network printer connections

- All user-definable settings in the Control Panel, such as the Display settings

- All taskbar settings

- All user-definable settings for Windows accessories, such as Calculator, Notepad, Clock, Paint, and HyperTerminal

- All bookmarks created in the Windows Help system

In addition to the hive, a user profile can include subdirectories that contain shortcuts and other elements that form parts of the workstation environment. These subdirectories are as follows:

- **Application Data**   Contains application-specific data, such as custom dictionary files
- **Cookies**   Contains cookies used by Internet Explorer to store information about the system's interaction with specific Internet sites
- **Desktop**   Contains shortcuts to programs and files that appear on the Windows desktop
- **Favorites**   Contains shortcuts to programs, files, and URLs that appear in Internet Explorer's Favorites list
- **Local Settings**   This directory contains the following subfolders:
  - Application Data
  - History
  - Temp
  - Temporary Internet Files
- **My Documents**   Contains shortcuts to personal documents and other files
- **NetHood**   Contains shortcuts that appear in the Network Neighborhood window
- **PrintHood**   Contains shortcuts that appear in the Printers window
- **Recent**   Contains shortcuts to files that appear in the Documents folder in the Start menu
- **SendTo**   Contains shortcuts to programs and file system locations that appear in the context menu's Send To folder
- **Start Menu**   Contains folders and shortcuts to programs and files that appear in the Start menu
- **Templates**   Contains shortcuts to document templates

NOTE The NetHood, PrintHood, and Templates directories are hidden by default. To view them, you must configure Windows Explorer to display hidden files.

Between the hive and the subdirectories, the user profile configures most of a user's workstation environment—including cosmetic elements, such as screen colors and wallpaper, and operational elements, such as desktop icons and Start menu shortcuts. The more concrete elements of the system configuration, such as hardware device drivers and settings, are not included in the user profile. If, for example, you install a new piece of hardware on a system, all users will have access to it, regardless of which profile is in use.

By default, Windows creates a user profile for each different user who logs on to the machine and stores them in the Documents and Settings folder directory on the system drive. The system also creates a default user profile during the operating system installation process that functions as a template for the creation of new profiles. If there are elements that you want included in all of the new profiles created on a computer, you can make changes to the profile in the Default

User subdirectory before any of the users log on. The system will then copy the default profile to a new subdirectory each time a new user logs on. Changing the Default User subdirectory does not affect the user profiles that have already been created, however.

Creating Roaming Profiles

Windows stores user profiles on the local machine by default. You can modify this behavior by specifying a location on a network server for a particular user's profile in the same Windows Profile page or User Environment Profile dialog box in which you specified the location of the user's home directory. The profile server can be any system that is accessible by the workstation. Once you specify the location for the profile, the operating system on the workstation copies the active profile to the server drive the next time the user logs off the network.

The best way to organize user profiles on the network is to designate a single machine as a profile server and create subdirectories named for your users, in which the profiles will be stored. When you specify the location of the profile directory for each user, you can use the *%UserName%* variable as part of the path, as follows:

```
\\Ntserver\Profiles\%UserName%
```

The system then replaces the *%UserName%* variable with the user's logon name, as long as the variable appears only once in the path and the variable is the last subdirectory in the path. In other words, the path \\Ntserver\Users\ *%UserName%*\Profile would not be acceptable. However, the system does recognize an extension added to the variable, making \\Ntserver\Profiles\ *%UserName%*.man an acceptable path.

Storing user profiles on a server does not delete them from the workstation from which they originated. Once the server-based profile is created, each logon by the user triggers the following process:

1. The workstation compares the profile on the server with the profile on the workstation.

2. If the profile on the server is newer than that on the workstation, the system copies the server profile to the workstation drive and loads it from there into memory.

3. If the two profiles are identical, the workstation loads the profile on the local drive into memory without copying from the server.

4. When the user logs off, the workstation writes to both the local drive and the server any changes that have been made to the registry keys and shortcut directories that make up the profile.

Because the profile is always loaded from the workstation's local drive, even when a new version is copied from the server, it is important to consider the ramifications of making changes to the profile from another machine. If, for example, an administrator modifies a profile on the server by deleting certain shortcuts, these changes will likely have no effect because those shortcuts still exist on the workstation and copying the server profile to the workstation drive does not delete them. To modify a profile, you must make changes on both the server and workstation copies.

One of the potential drawbacks of storing user profiles on a network server is the amount of data that must be transferred on a regular basis. The registry hive and the various shortcut subdirectories are usually not a problem. But if, for example, a Windows user stores many megabytes worth of files in the My Documents directory, the time needed to copy that directory to the server and read it back again can produce a noticeable delay during the logoff and logon processes.

Creating Mandatory Profiles

When users modify elements of their Windows environment, the workstation writes those changes to their user profiles so that the next time they log on, the changes take effect. However, it's possible for a network administrator to create mandatory profiles that the users are not permitted to change so that the same workstation environment loads each time they log on, regardless of the changes they made during the last session. To prevent users from modifying their profiles when logging off the system, you simply change the name of the registry hive in the server profile directory from Ntuser.dat to Ntuser.man or from User.dat to User.man. When the workstation detects the MAN file in the profile directory, it loads that instead of the DAT file and does not write anything back to the profile directory during the logoff procedure.

> **NOTE** When creating a mandatory profile, be sure that the user is not logged on to the workstation when you change the registry hive file extension from .dat to .man. Otherwise, the hive will be written back to the profile with a .dat extension during the logoff.

Another modification you can make to enforce the use of the profile is to add a .man extension to the directory in which the profile is stored. This prevents the user from logging on to the network without loading the profile. If the server on which the profile is stored is unavailable, the user can't log on. If you choose to do this, be sure to add the .man extension both to the directory name and to the path specifying the name of the profile directory in the user object's Properties dialog box or the User Environment Profile dialog box.

It's important to note that making profiles mandatory does not prevent users from modifying their workstation environments; it just prevents them from saving those modifications back to the profile. Also, making a profile mandatory does not in itself prevent the user from manually modifying the profile by adding or deleting shortcuts or accessing the registry hive. If you want to exercise greater control over the workstation to prevent users from making any changes to the interface at all, you must use another mechanism, such as system policies, and be sure to protect the profile directories on the server using file system permissions.

Replicating Profiles

If you intend to rely on server-based user profiles to create workstation environments for your users, you should take pains to ensure that those profiles are always available to your users when they log on. This is particularly true if you intend to use mandatory profiles with .man extensions on the directory names because if the server on which the profiles are stored is malfunctioning or unavailable, the users cannot log on. One way of doing this is to create your profile directories on a domain controller and then use the Directory Replicator service in Windows to copy the profile directories to the other domain controllers on the network on a regular basis.

Once you have arranged for the profile directories to be replicated to all of your domain controllers, you can use the *%LogonServer%* variable in each user's profile path to make sure they can always access the profile when logging on, as in the following example:

```
\\%LogonServer%\users\%UserName%
```

Part VI

During the logon process, the workstation replaces the *%LogonServer%* variable with the name of the domain controller that authenticated the user. Since the profile directories have been copied to all of the domain controllers, the workstation always has access to the profile as long as it has access to a domain controller. If no domain controller is available, you have much bigger problems to worry about than user profiles.

Creating a Network Default User Profile

Windows systems have a default user profile they use as a template for the creation of new profiles. As mentioned earlier, you can modify this default profile so that all of the new profiles created on that machine have certain characteristics. It is also possible to create a default user profile on your network to provide the same service for all new profiles created on the network.

Controlling the Workstation Registry

The registry is the central repository for configuration data in most Windows systems, and exercising control over the registry is a major part of a system administrator's job. The ability to access a workstation's registry in either a remote or automated fashion enables you to control virtually any aspect of the system's functionality and also protect the registry from damage due to unauthorized modifications.

Using System Policies

Nearly all Windows operating systems include *system policies,* which enable you to exercise a great deal of control over a workstation's environment. By defining a set of policies and enforcing them, you can control what elements of the operating system your users are able to access, what applications they can run, and the appearance of the desktop. System policies are really nothing more than collections of registry settings that are packaged into a system policy file and stored on a server drive. When a user logs on to the network, the workstation downloads the system policy file from the server and applies the appropriate settings to the workstation's registry. Because workstations load the policy file automatically during the logon process, users can't evade them. This makes system policies an excellent tool for limiting users' access to the Windows interface.

Using system policies is an alternative to modifying registry keys directly and reduces the possibility of system malfunctions due to typographical or other errors. Instead of browsing through the registry tree, searching for cryptic keys and value names, and entering coded values, you create system policy files using a graphical utility called System Policy Editor (SPE). SPE displays registry settings in the form of *policies,* plain-English phrases with standard Windows dialog box elements arranged in a treelike hierarchy, such as the Local Group Policy Editor dialog as seen in Figure 25-3.

In both Windows 7 and Windows 8, you must use the Run command to open SPE. In Windows 7, type **gpedit.msc** in the search box; in Windows 8, find the Run app, type **gpedit.msc**, and click OK, as shown in Figure 25-4.

System Policy Templates

System Policy Editor is simply a tool for creating policy files; it has no control over the policies it creates. The policies themselves come from system policy templates, which are ASCII files that contain the registry keys, possible values, and explanatory text that make up the policies

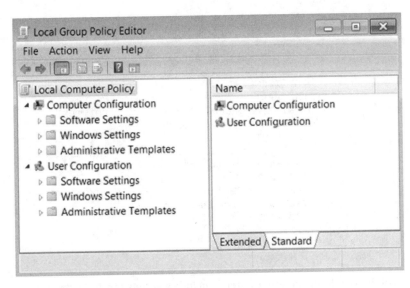

Figure 25-3   The Local Group Policy Editor dialog box

displayed in SPE. For example, the following excerpt from the Common.adm policy template creates the Remote Update policy:

```
CATEGORY !!Network
     CATEGORY !!Update
          POLICY !!RemoteUpdate
          KEYNAME System\CurrentControlSet\Control\Update
          ACTIONLISTOFF
               VALUENAME "UpdateMode"          VALUE NUMERIC 0
          END ACTIONLISTOFF
```

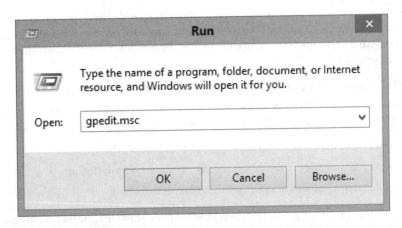

Figure 25-4   Opening the Local Group Policy Editor from the Run command or app

```
                    PART !!UpdateMode              DROPDOWNLIST REQUIRED
                    VALUENAME "UpdateMode"
                    ITEMLIST
                         NAME !!UM_Automatic       VALUE NUMERIC 1
                         NAME !!UM_Manual          VALUE NUMERIC 2
                    END ITEMLIST
                    END PART
                    PART !!UM_Manual_Path          EDITTEXT
                    VALUENAME "NetworkPath"
                    END PART
                    PART !!DisplayErrors           CHECKBOX
                    VALUENAME "Verbose"
                    END PART
                    PART !!LoadBalance             CHECKBOX
                    VALUENAME "LoadBalance"
                    END PART
               END POLICY
          END CATEGORY        ; Update
     END CATEGORY        ; Network
```

All of the Windows operating systems include a variety of administrative template files in addition to the SPE program itself. These files currently have the .admx extension, although earlier versions used .adm. Other applications, such as Microsoft Office and Internet Explorer, include their own template files containing policies specific to those applications, and you can even create your own custom templates to modify other registry settings.

By selecting Options | Policy Template, you can load the templates that SPE will use to create policy files. You can load multiple templates into SPE, and the policies in them will be combined in the program's interface. Whenever you launch SPE, it loads the templates that it was using when it was last shut down, as long as the files are still in the same locations. When you use multiple policy templates in SPE, it is possible for policies defined in two different templates to configure the same registry setting. If this type of duplication occurs, the policy closest to the bottom of the hierarchy in the object's Properties dialog box takes precedence.

System Policy Files

Using SPE, you can create policies that apply to only specific users, groups, and computers, as well as create Default User and Default Computer policies. Policies for multiple network users and computers are stored in a single file that every computer downloads from a server as it logs on to the network.

Restricting Workstation Access with System Policies

One of the primary functions of system policies is to prevent users from accessing certain elements of the operating system. There are several reasons for doing this, such as these:

- Prohibiting users from running unauthorized software
- Preventing users from adjusting cosmetic elements of the interface
- Insulating users from features they cannot use safely

By doing these things, you can prevent users from wasting time on nonproductive activities and causing workstation malfunctions through misguided experimentation that require technical support to fix. The following sections describe how you can use specific system policies to control the workstation environment.

Restricting Applications   One of the primary causes of instability on Windows workstations is the installation of incompatible applications. Most Windows software packages include dynamic link library (DLL) modules that get installed to the Windows system directories, and many times these modules overwrite existing files with new versions designed to support that application. The problem with this type of software design is that installing a new version of a particular DLL may affect other applications already installed in the system that are using the DLL.

The way to avoid problems stemming from this type of version conflict is to assemble a group of applications that supplies the users' needs and then test the applications thoroughly together. Once you have determined that the applications are compatible, you install them on your workstations and prevent users from installing other software that can introduce incompatible elements. Restricting the workstation software also prevents users from installing nonproductive applications, such as games, that can occupy large amounts of time, disk space, and even network bandwidth.

NOTE This kind of testing can take a lot of time.

Another potential source of unauthorized software is the Internet. If you are going to provide your users with access to services such as the Web, you may want to take steps to prevent them from installing downloaded software. One way of doing this, and of preventing all unauthorized software installations, is to use system policies that prevent users from running the setup program needed to install the software. Some of the policies that can help you do this are as follows:

- **Remove Run Command from Start menu**   Prevents the user from launching application installation programs by preventing access to the Run dialog box.

- **Run Only Allowed Windows Applications**   Enables the administrator to specify a list of executable files that are the only programs the user is permitted to execute. When using this policy, be sure to include executables that are needed for normal Windows operation, such as Systray.exe and Explorer.exe.

Locking Down the Interface   There are many elements of the Windows interface that unsophisticated users do not need to access, and suppressing these elements can prevent the more curious users from exploring things they don't understand and possibly damaging the system. Some of the policies you can use to do this are as follows:

- **Remove Folders from Settings on Start menu**   Suppresses the appearance of the Control Panel and Printers folders in the Start menu's Settings folder. This policy does not prevent users from accessing the Control Panel in other ways, but it makes the user far less likely to explore it out of idle curiosity. You can also suppress specific Control Panel icons on Windows systems using policies such as the following:
  - Restrict Network Control Panel
  - Restrict Printer Settings
  - Restrict Passwords Control Panel
  - Restrict System Control Panel

- **Remove Taskbar from Settings on Start menu** Prevents users from modifying the Start menu and taskbar configuration settings.

- **Remove Run Command from Start menu** Prevents users from launching programs or executing commands using the Run dialog box. This policy also provides users with additional insulation from elements such as the Control Panel and the command prompt, both of which can be accessed with Run commands.

- **Hide All Items on Desktop** Suppresses the display of all icons on the Windows desktop. If you want your users to rely on the Start menu to launch programs, you can use this policy to remove the distraction of the desktop icons.

- **Disable Registry Editing Tools** Direct access to the Windows registry should be limited to people who know what they're doing. This policy prevents users from running the registry-editing tools included with the operating system.

- **Disable Context Menus for the Taskbar** Prevents the system from displaying a context menu when you click the secondary mouse button on a taskbar icon.

You can also use system policies to secure the cosmetic elements of the interface, preventing users from wasting time adjusting the screen colors and desktop wallpaper. In addition, you can configure these items yourself to create a standardized desktop for all of your network's workstations.

As an alternative to user profiles, system policies enable you to configure with greater precision the shortcuts found on the Windows desktop and in the Start menu. Instead of accessing an entire user profile as a whole, you can specify the locations of individual shortcut directories for various elements of the interface.

Protecting the File System Limiting access to the file system is another way of protecting your workstations against user tampering. If you preconfigure the operating system and applications on your network workstations and force your users to store all of the data files on server drives, there is no compelling reason why users should have direct access to the local file system. By blocking this access with system policies, you can prevent users from moving, modifying, or deleting files that are crucial to the operation of the workstation. You can limit users' access to the network also, using policies such as the following:

- **Hide Drives in My Computer** Suppresses the display of all drive letters in the My Computer window, including both local and network drives.

- **Hide Network Neighborhood** Suppresses the display of the Network Neighborhood icon on the Windows desktop and disables UNC connectivity. For example, when this policy is enabled, users can't access network drives by opening a window with a UNC name in the Run dialog box.

- **No Entire Network in Network Neighborhood** Suppresses the Entire Network icon in the Network Neighborhood window, preventing users from browsing network resources outside the domain or workgroup.

- **No Workgroup Contents in Network Neighborhood** Suppresses the icons representing the systems in the current domain or workgroup in the Network Neighborhood window.

- **Remove Find Command from Start Menu** Suppresses the Find command, preventing users from accessing drives that may be restricted in other ways. If, for example, you use the Hidden attribute to protect the local file system, the Find command can still search the local drive and display the hidden files.

Locking down the file system is a drastic step, one that you should consider and plan for carefully. Only certain types of users will benefit from this restricted access, and others may severely resent it. In addition to system policies, you should be prepared to use file system permissions and attributes to prevent specific types of user access.

Above all, you must make sure that the system policies you use to restrict access to your workstations do not inhibit the functionality your users need to perform their jobs and that the features you plan to restrict are not accessible by other methods. For example, you might prevent access to the Control Panel by removing the folder from the Settings group in the Start menu, but users will still be able to access it from the My Computer window or the Run dialog box, unless you restrict access to those as well.

Deploying System Policies

The use of system policies by a Windows computer is itself controlled by a policy called Remote Update, which is applicable to all of the Windows operating systems. This policy has three possible settings:

- **Off**   The system does not use system policies at all.
- **Automatic**   The system checks the root directory of the Netlogon share on the authenticating domain controller for a policy file called Ntconfig.pol or Config.pol.
- **Manual**   The system checks for a policy file in a directory specified as the value of another policy called Path for Manual Update.

Using the Remote Update policy, you can configure your systems to access policy files from the default location or from any location you name. For workstations to have access to the policy files at all times, it is a good idea to replicate them to all of your domain controllers, either manually or automatically, just like you can do with user profiles.

Part VI

Network Management and Troubleshooting Tools

No matter how well designed and well constructed your network is, there are going to be times when it does not function properly. Part of the job of a network administrator is to monitor the day-to-day performance of the network and cope with any problems that arise. To do this, you must have the appropriate tools. In Chapter 2, you learned about the seven layers of the networking stack as defined in the Open Systems Interconnection (OSI) reference model. Breakdowns can occur at virtually any layer, and the tools used to diagnose problems at the various layers are quite different. Knowing what resources are available to you is a large part of the troubleshooting battle; knowing how to use them properly is another large part.

Operating System Utilities

Many administrators are unaware of the network troubleshooting capabilities that are built into their standard operating systems, and as a result, they sometimes spend money needlessly on third-party products and outside consultants. The following sections examine some of the network troubleshooting tools that are provided with the operating systems commonly used on today's networks.

Windows Utilities

The Windows operating systems include a variety of tools that you can use to manage and troubleshoot network connections. Most of these tools are included in various Windows packages, although they may take slightly different forms. To learn more about each utility, type its name followed by a space and then /?.

NOTE While Command Prompt commands look similar to old MS-DOS commands, they are not DOS commands because the current Windows configurations do not contain MS-DOS.

Accessing the Command Prompt in Windows 7

These tools are exercised at the Command Prompt line. In Windows 7, there are several ways to access the Command Prompt:

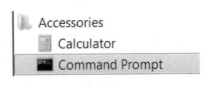

- Choose Start | All Programs | Accessories | Command Prompt, as shown in Figure 26-1.

- Type **cmd.exe** in the Start search box.

- Type **command** in the Start search box and select Command Prompt from the resulting menu.

Accessing the Command Prompt in Windows 8.1

You can quickly access the Command Prompt in Windows 8.1 in the following ways:

- Hold down the Windows key and press R. This opens the Run dialog box. Type **cmd** and click OK (or Enter), as shown in Figure 26-2.

- Hold down the Windows key and press X (or right-click the Start button) to open the Power User menu. Choose Command Prompt, as shown in Figure 26-3.

- From the Apps screen, on a touch screen, swipe to the right to find the Windows System section. Click Command Prompt. When using a mouse, drag your mouse from the right side of the screen.

Net.exe

The *NET* command is the primary command-line control for the Windows network client. You can use *NET* to perform many of the same networking functions that you can perform with graphical utilities, such as Windows Explorer in Windows 7 or File Explorer in Windows 8.

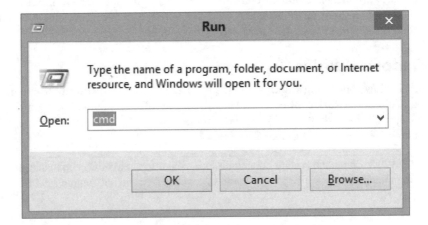

Figure 26-2   Use the Run dialog box in Windows 8.1.

Because *NET* is a command-line utility, you can include the commands in logon scripts and batch files. For example, you can use this command to log on and off of the network, map drive letters to specific network shares, start and stop services, and locate shared resources on the network.

To use the program, you execute the file from the command line with a subcommand, which may take additional parameters. These subcommands and their functions are listed in Table 26-1, with some of the key functions being examined in the following sections. The subcommands display when you type **NET** in the Command Prompt dialog, as shown in Figure 26-4.

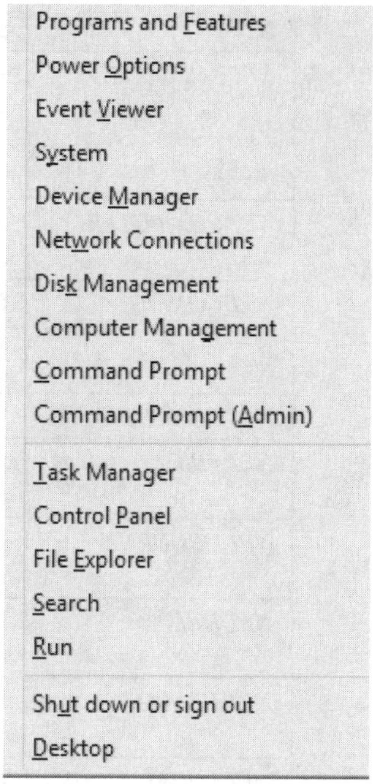

TCP/IP Utilities

Transmission Control Protocol/Internet Protocol (TCP/IP) has become the most commonly used protocol suite in the networking industry, and many network administration and troubleshooting tasks involve working with various elements of these protocols. Because virtually every computing platform supports TCP/IP, a number of basic tools have been ported to many different operating systems, some of which have also been adapted to specific needs. The following sections examine some of these tools but do so more from the perspective of their basic functionality and usefulness to the network administrator than from the operational elements of specific implementations.

Programs and Features
Power Options
Event Viewer
System
Device Manager
Network Connections
Disk Management
Computer Management
Command Prompt
Command Prompt (Admin)

Task Manager
Control Panel
File Explorer
Search
Run

Shut down or sign out
Desktop

Figure 26-3   Find Command Prompt on the Power User menu.

the network administrator than from the operational elements of specific implementations.

Ping

Ping is unquestionably the most common TCP/IP diagnostic tool and is included in virtually every implementation of the TCP/IP protocols. In most cases, Ping is a command-line utility, although some graphical or menu-driven versions are available that use a different interface to perform the same tasks. The basic function of Ping is to send a message to another TCP/IP system on the network to determine whether the protocol stack up to the network layer is functioning properly. Because the TCP/IP protocols function in the same way on all systems, you can use Ping to test the connection between any two computers, regardless of processor platform or operating system.

Ping works by transmitting a series of Echo Request messages to a specific IP address using the Internet Control Message Protocol (ICMP). When the computer using that IP address receives the messages, it generates an Echo Reply in response to each Echo Request and transmits it back to the sender. ICMP is a TCP/IP protocol that uses several dozen message types to perform various diagnostic and error-reporting functions. ICMP messages are carried directly within IP datagrams. No transport layer protocol is involved, so a successful Ping test indicates that the protocol stack is functioning properly from the network layer down. If the sending system receives no replies to its Echo Requests, something is wrong with either the sending or receiving system or the network connection between them.

Part VI

NET	Subcommand Function	Key Function(s)
NET ACCOUNTS	Configures settings and policies for all of the accounts on a particular computer or domain	Includes forced logoff time; password age minimum and maximum, and this computer's role
NET COMPUTER	Adds or removes computers from the current domain	
NET CONFIG	Displays network client information	Includes all running services that can be controlled at this computer
NET CONTINUE	Resumes a service that has been paused	
NET FILE	Displays and closes files shared with network users and removes file locks	
NET GROUP	Creates or deletes global groups and adds users to or deletes them from those groups	
NET HELP	Displays help information for specific *NET* subcommands	
NET HELPMSG	Displays additional information about a specific four-digit error code	
NET LOCALGROUP	Creates or deletes local groups and adds users to or deletes them from those groups	
NET PAUSE	Pauses a specific service without unloading it until resumed by the *NET CONTINUE* command	
NET SESSION	Displays information about and disconnects currently active sessions with other network users	
NET SHARE	Displays, creates, and deletes shares on the current system	
NET START	Starts a specific network service	
NET STATISTICS	Displays statistics for the Server or Workstation service	
NET STOP	Stops a specific network service	
NET TIME	Displays the time on the current system or synchronizes the time with another system	
NET USE	Displays information about and administers connections to shared network resources	
NET USER	Creates, modifies, and deletes user accounts	
NET VIEW	Displays available resources on the network	

Table 26-1 Windows NET Subcommands

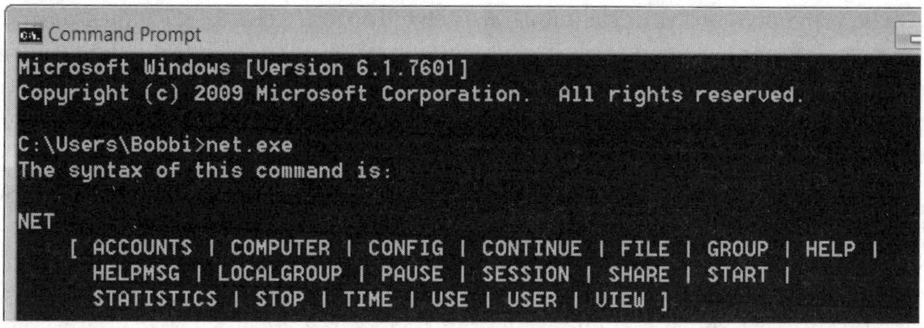

Figure 26-4   NET subcommands

When Ping is implemented as a command-line utility, you use the following syntax to perform a Ping test:

```
PING destination
```

where the *destination* variable is replaced by the name or address of another system on the network. The destination system can be identified by its IP address or by a name, assuming that an appropriate mechanism is in place for resolving the name into an IP address. This means you can use a hostname for the destination, as long as you have a DNS server or HOSTS file to resolve the name. On Windows networks, you can also use NetBIOS names, along with any of the standard mechanisms for resolving them, such as WINS servers, broadcast transmissions, or an LMHOSTS file.

The screen output produced by a *ping* command on a Windows system looks like Figure 26-5.

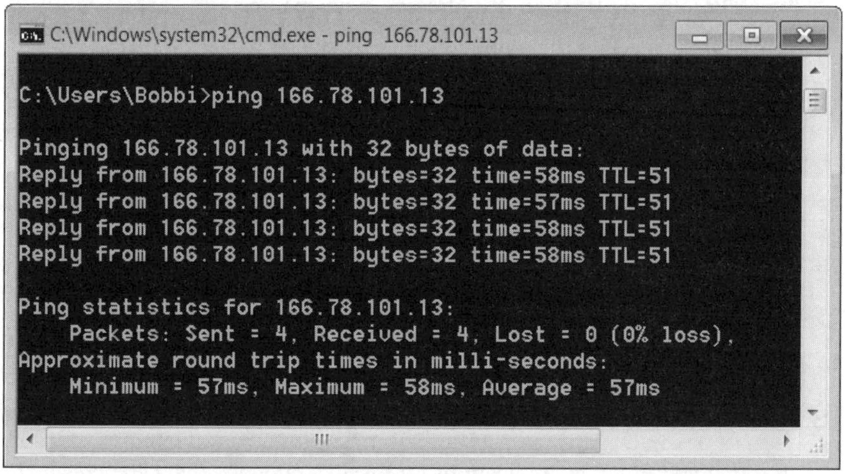

Figure 26-5   Result of using the *ping* command in a Windows 7 system

The program displays a result line for each of the four Echo Request messages it sends by default, specifying the IP address of the recipient, the number of bytes of data transmitted in each message, the amount of time elapsed between the transmission of the request and the receipt of the reply, and the target system's time to live (TTL). The TTL is the number of routers that a packet can pass through before it is discarded.

Ping has other diagnostic uses apart from simply determining whether a system is up and running. If you can successfully ping a system using its IP address but pings sent to the system's name fail, you know that a malfunction is occurring in the name resolution process. When you're trying to contact an Internet site, this indicates that there is a problem with either your workstation's DNS server configuration or the DNS server itself. If you can ping systems on the local network successfully but not systems on the Internet, you know there is a problem with either your workstation's Default Gateway setting or the connection to the Internet.

NOTE Sending a *ping* command to a system's loopback address (127.0.0.1) tests the operability of the TCP/IP protocol stack, but it is not an adequate test of the network interface because traffic sent to the loopback address travels down the protocol stack only as far as the network transport layer and is redirected back up without ever leaving the computer through the network interface.

In most Ping implementations, you can use additional command-line parameters to modify the size and number of the Echo Request messages transmitted by a single *ping* command, as well as other operational characteristics. In the Windows Ping.exe program, for example, the parameters are as follows:

```
ping [-t] [-a] [-n count] [-l size] [-f] [-i TTL] [-v TOS] [-r count]
[-s count] [[-j host-list] | [-k host-list]] [-w timeout] destination
```

- **-t** Pings the specified destination until stopped by the user (with CTRL-C)
- **-a** Resolves destination IP addresses to hostnames
- **-n** *count* Specifies the number of Echo Requests to send
- **-l** *size* Specifies the size of the Echo Request messages to send
- **-f** Sets the IP Don't Fragment flag in each Echo Request packet
- **-i** *TTL* Specifies the IP TTL value for the Echo Request packets
- **-v** *TOS* Specifies the IP Type of Service (TOS) value for the Echo Request packets
- **-r** *count* Records the IP addresses of the routers for the specified number of hops
- **-s** *count* Records the time stamp from the routers for the specified number of hops
- **-j** *host-list* Specifies a partial list of routers that the packets should use
- **-k** *host-list* Specifies a complete list of routers that the packets should use
- **-w** *timeout* Specifies the time (in milliseconds) that the system should wait for each reply

There are many different applications for these parameters that can help you manage your network and troubleshoot problems. For example, by creating larger-than-normal Echo Requests and sending large numbers of them (or sending them continuously), you can simulate user traffic on your network to test its ability to stand up under heavy use. You can also compare the performance of various routes through your network (or through the Internet) by specifying the IP addresses of the routers that the Echo Request packets must use to reach their destinations. The *-j* parameter provides *loose source routing*, in which the packets must use the routers whose IP addresses you specify but can use other routers also. The *-k* parameter provides *strict source routing*, in which you must specify the address of every router that packets will use to reach their destination.

Pathping

Combining the features of both Tracert and Ping, Pathping, designed for networks with more than one router between hosts, sends a series of packets to each router along the route to the host. Any packet loss at any link along the route is pinpointed by Pathping.

Traceroute or Tracert

Traceroute is another utility that is usually implemented as a command-line program and included in most TCP/IP protocol stacks, although it sometimes goes by a different name. On Mac, Linux, or Unix systems, the command is called *traceroute*, but Windows implements the same functions in a program called Tracert.exe. The function of this tool is to display the route that IP packets are taking to reach a particular destination system.

Each of the entries in a trace represents a router that processed the packets generated by the Traceroute program on the way to their destination. In each entry there are three numerical figures that specify the round-trip time to that router, in milliseconds, followed by the DNS name and IP address of the router. In a trace to an overseas destination, the round-trip times are relatively high and can provide you with information about the backbone networks your ISP uses and the geographical path that your traffic takes. For example, when you run a trace to a destination system on another continent, you can sometimes tell when the path crosses an ocean by a sudden increase in the round-trip times. On a private network, you can use Traceroute to determine the path through your routers that local traffic typically takes, enabling you to get an idea of how traffic is distributed around your network.

Most Traceroute implementations work by transmitting the same type of ICMP Echo Request messages used by Ping, while others use UDP packets by default. The only difference in the messages themselves is that the Traceroute program modifies the TTL field for each sequence of three packets. The TTL field is a protective mechanism that prevents IP packets from circulating endlessly around a network. Each router that processes a packet decrements the TTL value by one. If the TTL value of a packet reaches zero, the router discards it and returns an ICMP Time to Live Exceeded in Transit error message to the system that originally transmitted it.

In the first Traceroute sequence, the packets have a TTL value of 1, so that the first router receiving the packets discards them and returns error messages back to the source. By calculating the interval between a message's transmission and the arrival of the associated error, Traceroute generates the round-trip time and then uses the source IP address in the error message to identify the router. In the second sequence of messages, the TTL value is 2, so the packets reach the second router in their journey before being discarded. The third sequence of packets has a TTL value of 3, and so on, until the messages reach the destination system.

It is important to understand that although Traceroute can be a useful tool, a certain amount of imprecision is inherent in the information it provides. Just because a packet transmitted right now takes a certain path to a destination does not mean that a packet transmitted a minute from now to that same destination will take that same path. Networks (and especially those on the Internet) are mutable, and routers are designed to compensate automatically for the changes that occur. The route taken by Traceroute packets to their destination can change, even in the midst of a trace, so it is entirely possible for the sequence of routers displayed by the program to be a composite of two or more different paths to the destination because of changes that occurred in midstream. On a private network, this is less likely to be the case, but it is still possible.

Route

The routing table is a vital part of the networking stack on any TCP/IP system, even those that do not function as routers. The system uses the routing table to determine where it should transmit each packet. The Route.exe program in Windows and the *route* command included with most other versions enable you to view the routing table and add or delete entries to it. The syntax for the Windows Route.exe program is as follows:

```
ROUTE [-f] [-p] [command [destination] [MASK netmask] [gateway]
[METRIC metric] [IF interface]]
```

The *command* variable takes one of the following four values:

- **PRINT**   Displays the contents of the routing table
- **ADD**   Creates a new entry in the routing table
- **DELETE**   Deletes an entry from the routing table
- **CHANGE**   Modifies the parameters of a routing table entry

The other parameters used on the Route.exe command line are as follows:

- **–f**   Deletes all of the entries from the routing table
- **–p**   Creates a permanent entry in the routing table (called a *persistent route*) when used with the ADD command
- **destination**   Specifies the network or host address of the routing table entry being added, deleted, or changed
- **MASK** *netmask*   Specifies the subnet mask associated with the address specified by the *destination* variable
- **gateway**   Specifies the address of the router used to access the host or network address specified by the *destination* variable
- **METRIC** *metric*   Indicates the relative efficiency of the routing table entry
- **IF** *interface*   Specifies the address of the network interface adapter used to reach the router specified by the *gateway* variable

Netstat

Netstat is a command-line utility that displays network traffic statistics for the various TCP/IP protocols and, depending on the platform, may display other information as well. Nearly all operating systems support Netstat. The command-line parameters for Netstat can vary in different implementations, but one of the most basic ones is the *-s* parameter, which displays the statistics for each of the major TCP/IP protocols, as shown in Figure 26-6.

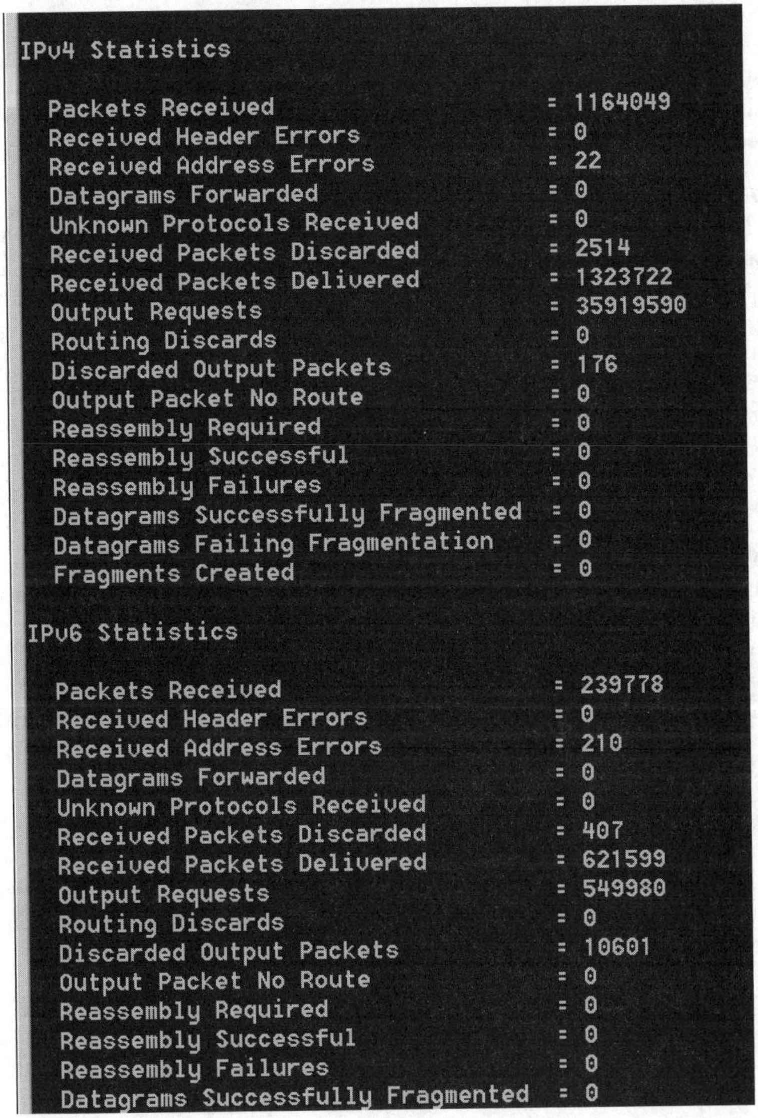

```
IPv4 Statistics

    Packets Received                         = 1164049
    Received Header Errors                   = 0
    Received Address Errors                  = 22
    Datagrams Forwarded                      = 0
    Unknown Protocols Received               = 0
    Received Packets Discarded               = 2514
    Received Packets Delivered               = 1323722
    Output Requests                          = 35919590
    Routing Discards                         = 0
    Discarded Output Packets                 = 176
    Output Packet No Route                   = 0
    Reassembly Required                      = 0
    Reassembly Successful                    = 0
    Reassembly Failures                      = 0
    Datagrams Successfully Fragmented        = 0
    Datagrams Failing Fragmentation          = 0
    Fragments Created                        = 0

IPv6 Statistics

    Packets Received                         = 239778
    Received Header Errors                   = 0
    Received Address Errors                  = 210
    Datagrams Forwarded                      = 0
    Unknown Protocols Received               = 0
    Received Packets Discarded               = 407
    Received Packets Delivered               = 621599
    Output Requests                          = 549980
    Routing Discards                         = 0
    Discarded Output Packets                 = 10601
    Output Packet No Route                   = 0
    Reassembly Required                      = 0
    Reassembly Successful                    = 0
    Reassembly Failures                      = 0
    Datagrams Successfully Fragmented        = 0
```

Figure 26-6   Netstat creates a display of IP statistics.

Apart from the total number of packets transmitted and received by each protocol, Netstat provides valuable information about error conditions and other processes that can help you troubleshoot network communication problems at various layers of the OSI model. The Windows version of Netstat also can display Ethernet statistics (using the *-e* parameter), which can help to isolate network hardware problems.

Part VI

When executed with the *-a* parameter, Netstat displays information about the TCP connections currently active on the computer and the UDP services that are listening for input. The State column indicates whether a connection is currently established or a program is listening on a particular port for messages from other computers, waiting to establish a new connection.

Nslookup

Nslookup is a utility that enables you to send queries directly to a particular DNS server in order to resolve names into IP addresses or request other information. Unlike other name resolution methods, such as using Ping, Nslookup lets you specify which server you want to receive your commands so that you can determine whether a DNS server is functioning properly and whether it is supplying the correct information. Originally designed for Unix systems, an Nslookup program is available on Mac, Linux, and Windows systems. Nslookup can run in either interactive or noninteractive mode. To transmit a single query, you can use noninteractive mode, using the following syntax from the command prompt:

```
Nslookup hostname nameserver
```

Replace the *hostname* variable with the DNS name or IP address that you want to resolve, and replace the *nameserver* variable with the name or address of the DNS server that you want to receive the query. If you omit the *nameserver* value, the program uses the system's default DNS server.

To run Nslookup in interactive mode, you execute the program from the command prompt with no parameters (to use the default DNS server) or with a hyphen in place of the *hostname* variable, followed by the DNS server name, as follows:

```
Nslookup - nameserver
```

The program produces a prompt in the form of an angle bracket (>), at which you can type the names or addresses you want to resolve, as well as a large number of commands that alter the parameters that Nslookup uses to query the name server. You can display the list of commands by typing **help** at the prompt. To exit the program, press CTRL-C.

Ipconfig

The Ipconfig program is a simple utility for displaying a system's TCP/IP configuration parameters. This is particularly useful when you are using Dynamic Host Configuration Protocol (DHCP) servers to automatically configure TCP/IP clients on your network because there is no other simple way for users to see what settings have been assigned to their workstations. Nearly all systems include the *ipconfig* command (derived from *interface configuration*).

Network Analyzers

A *network analyzer,* sometimes called a *protocol analyzer,* is a device that captures the traffic transmitted over a network and analyzes its properties in a number of different ways. The primary function of the analyzer is to decode and display the contents of the packets captured from your network. For each packet, the software displays the information found in each field of each protocol header, as well as the original application data carried in the payload of the packet. Analyzers often can provide statistics about the traffic carried by the network as well, such as the number of packets that use a particular protocol and the amount of traffic generated by each system on the network. A network analyzer is also an excellent learning tool. There is no better way to acquaint yourself with networking protocols and their functions than by seeing them in action.

There is a wide variety of network analyzer products, ranging from self-contained hardware devices costing thousands of dollars to software-only products that are relatively inexpensive or free.

A network analyzer is essentially a software application running on a computer with a network interface. This is why products can either include hardware or take the form of software only. A traveling network consultant might have a portable computer with comprehensive network analyzer software and a variety of NICs to support the different networks at various sites, while an administrator supporting a private network might be better served by a less expensive software-based analyzer that supports only the type of network running at that site.

A network analyzer typically works by switching the NIC in the computer on which it runs into *promiscuous mode.* Normally, a NIC examines the destination address in the data link layer protocol header of each packet arriving at the computer, and if the packet is not addressed to that computer, the NIC discards it. This prevents the CPU in the system from having to process thousands of extraneous packets. When the NIC is switched into promiscuous mode, however, it accepts all of the packets arriving over the network, regardless of their addresses, and passes them to the network analyzer software for processing. This enables the system to analyze not only the traffic generated by and destined for the system on which the software is running, but also the traffic exchanged by other systems on the network.

Once the application captures the traffic from the network, it stores the entire packets in a buffer from which it can access them later during the analysis. Depending on the size of your network and the amount of traffic it carries, this can be an enormous amount of data, so you can usually specify the size of the buffer to control the amount of data captured. You can also apply filters to limit the types of data the analyzer captures.

Filtering Data

Because of the sheer amount of data transmitted over most networks, controlling the amount of data captured and processed by a network analyzer is an important part of using the product. You exercise this control by applying *filters* either during the capture process or afterward. When you capture raw network data, the results can be bewildering because all the packets generated by the various applications on many network systems are mixed together in a chronological display. To help make more sense out of the vast amount of data available, you can apply filters that cause the program to display only the data you need to see.

Two types of filters are provided by most network analyzers:

- **Capture filters**   Limit the packets that the analyzer reads into its buffers
- **Display filters**   Limit the captured packets that appear in the display

Usually, both types of filters function in the same way; the only difference is in when they are applied. You can choose to filter the packets as they are being read into the analyzer's buffers or capture all of the data on the network and use filters to limit the display of that data (or both).

You can filter the data in a network analyzer in several different ways, depending on what you're trying to learn about your network. If you're concerned with the performance of a specific computer, for example, you can create a filter that captures only the packets generated by that machine, the packets destined for that machine, or both. You can also create filters based on the protocols used in the packets, making it possible to capture only the DNS traffic on your network, for example, or on pattern matches, enabling you to capture only packets containing a specific ASCII or hexadecimal string. By combining these capabilities, using Boolean operators such as AND and OR, you can create highly specific filters that display only the exact information you need.

Agents

Hardware-based network analyzers are portable and designed to connect to a network at any point. Software-based products are not as portable and often include a mechanism (sometimes called an *agent*) that enables you to capture network traffic using the NIC in a different computer. Using agents, you can install the analyzer product on one machine and use it to support your entire network. The agent is usually a driver or service that runs on a workstation elsewhere on the network. Previously, many versions of Windows included the Windows Network Monitor, a utility that provided remote capture capabilities. This application was for capturing all the traffic on your network.

In 2012, Microsoft released the Network Message Analyzer, advertised as "much more than a network sniffer or packet tracing tool." This utility, a free download, allows you to capture, display, and analyze message and traffic on your Windows network.

When you run a network analyzer on a system with a single network interface, the application captures the data arriving over that interface by default. If the system has more than one interface, you can select the interface from which you want to capture data. When the analyzer is capable of using agents, you can use the same dialog box to specify the name or address of another computer on which the agent is running. The application then connects to that computer, uses its NIC to capture network traffic, and transmits it to the buffers in the system running the analyzer. When you use an agent on another network segment, however, it's important to be aware that the transmissions from the agent to the analyzer themselves generate a significant amount of traffic.

Traffic Analysis

Some network analyzers can display statistics about the traffic on the network while it is being captured, such as the number of packets per second, broken down by workstation or protocol. Depending on the product, you may also be able to display these statistics in graphical form. You can use this information to determine how much traffic each network system or each protocol is generating.

Using these capabilities, you can determine how much of your network bandwidth is being utilized by specific applications or specific users. If, for example, you notice that user John Doe's workstation is generating a disproportionate amount of HTTP traffic, you might conclude that he is spending too much company time surfing the Web when he should be doing other things. With careful application of capture filters, you can also configure a network analyzer to alert you of specific conditions on your network. Some products can generate alarms when traffic of a particular type reaches certain levels, such as when an Ethernet network experiences too many collisions.

In addition to capturing packets from the network, some analyzers can generate them. You can use the analyzer to simulate traffic conditions at precise levels, to verify the operational status of the network, or to stress-test equipment.

Protocol Analysis

Once the analyzer has a network traffic sample in its buffers, you can examine the packets in great detail. In most cases, the packets captured during a sample period are displayed chronologically in a table that lists the most important characteristics of each one, such as the addresses of the source and destination systems and the primary protocol used to create the packet. When you select a packet from the list, you see additional panes that display the contents of the protocol headers and the packet data, usually in both raw and decoded forms.

The first application for a tool of this type is that you can see what kinds of traffic are present on your network. If, for example, you have a network that uses WAN links that are slower and more expensive than the LANs, you can use an analyzer to capture the traffic passing over the links to make sure that their bandwidth is not being squandered on unnecessary communications.

One of the features that differentiates high-end network analyzer products from the more basic ones is the protocols that the program supports. To correctly decode a packet, the analyzer must support all the protocols used to create that packet at all layers of the OSI reference model. For example, a basic analyzer will support Ethernet and possibly Token Ring at the data link layer, but if you have a network that uses FDDI or ATM, you may have to buy a more elaborate and expensive product. The same is true at the upper layers. Virtually all analyzers support the TCP/IP protocols, and many also support IPX and NetBEUI, but be sure before you make a purchase that the product you select supports all the protocols you use. You should also consider the need for upgrades to support future protocol modifications, such as IPv6.

By decoding a packet, the analyzer is able to interpret the function of each bit and display the various protocol headers in a user-friendly, hierarchical format. The analyzer has decoded the protocol headers, and the display indicates that the HTTP data is carried in a TCP segment, which in turn is carried in an IP datagram, which in turn is carried in an Ethernet frame. You can expand each protocol to view the contents of the fields in its header.

A network analyzer is a powerful tool that can just as easily be used for illicit purposes as for network troubleshooting and support. When the program decodes a packet, it displays all of its contents, including what may be sensitive information. The FTP protocol, for example, transmits user passwords in clear text that is easily visible in a network analyzer when the packets are captured. An unauthorized user running an analyzer can intercept administrative passwords and gain access to protected servers. This is one reason why the version of Network Monitor included with Windows 2000 and NT is limited to capturing the traffic sent to and from the local system.

Cable Testers

Network analyzers can help you diagnose many types of network problems, but they assume that the physical network itself is functioning properly. When there is a problem with the cable installation that forms the network, a different type of tool, called a *cable tester*, is required. Cable testers are usually handheld devices that you connect to a network in order to perform a variety of diagnostic tests on the signal-conducting capabilities of the network cable. As usual, there is a wide range of devices to choose from that vary greatly in their prices and capabilities. Simple units are available for a few hundred dollars, while top-of-the-line models can cost several thousand dollars. Some combination testers can connect to various types of network cables, such as unshielded twisted-pair (UTP), shielded twisted-pair (STP), and coaxial, while others can test only a single cable type. For completely different signaling technologies, such as fiber-optic cable, you need a separate device.

Cable testers are rated for specific cable standards, such as Category 5, so that they can determine whether a cable's performance is compliant with that standard. This is called *continuity testing*. During a cable installation, a competent technician tests each link to see whether it is functioning properly, taking into account problems that can be caused by the quality of the cable itself or by the nature of the installation. For example, a good cable tester tests for electrical noise caused by proximity to fluorescent lights or other electrical equipment; crosstalk caused by signals traveling over an adjacent wire; attenuation caused by excessively long cable segments or improperly rated cable; and kinked or stretched cables, as indicated by specific levels of capacitance.

In addition to testing the viability of an installation, cable testers are good for troubleshooting cabling problems. For example, a tester that functions as a time-delay reflectometer can detect breaks or shorts in a cable by transmitting a high-frequency signal and measuring the amount of time it takes for the signal to reflect back to the source. Using this technique, you can determine that a cable has a break or other fault a certain distance away from the tester. Knowing that the problem is 20 feet away, for example, can prevent you from having to poke your head up into the ceiling every few feet to check the cables running through there. Some testers can also help you locate the route that a cable takes through walls or ceilings, using a tone generator that sends a strong signal over the cable that can be detected by the tester unit when it is nearby.

All network problems can be solved by recognizing the signs of specific symptoms and tying those to the actual fault in a system. The speed of isolating and repairing the discrepancy is dependent on the technician's knowledge of the tools available and network architecture.

CHAPTER

27

Backing Up

One of the primary functions of a computer network is to store, manipulate, and supply data, and protecting that data against damage or loss is a crucial part of the network administrator's job description. Hard disk drives contain most of the relatively few moving parts involved in the network data storage process and are constructed to incredibly tight tolerances. As a result, they can and do fail on occasion, causing service interruptions and data loss, and server drives work the hardest of all. When you examine the inner workings of a hard drive, you may actually wonder why they don't fail more often. In addition to mechanical drive failures, data loss can occur for many other causes, including viruses, computer theft, natural disaster, or simple user error. To protect the data stored on your network, it is absolutely essential that you perform regular backups to an alternative storage medium.

When backing up information for one computer, you may use an external hard drive, a cloud destination, a CD/DVD, or even a flash drive. Many individuals simply copy information from their smart phone onto their computer and call it "good." While backing up data is an important maintenance task for all computers, it is particularly vital on a network, for several reasons. First, the data tends to be more important; a loss of crucial data can be a catastrophe for a business that results in lost time, money, business, reputation, and in some cases even lives. Second, network data is often more volatile than the data on a stand-alone computer because many different users might access and modify it on a regular basis.

Network backups differ from stand-alone computer backups in four major ways: speed, capacity, automation, and price. A business network typically has data stored on many different computers, and that, combined with the ever-increasing drive capacities in today's computers, means that a network backup solution may have to protect thousands of terabytes of data. To back up this much data, backup drives that are capable of unprecedented speeds are required.

The big advantage of backing up multiple computers that are all connected to a network is that you can use one backup drive to protect many computers, using a variety of methods to transfer the data (as shown in Figure 27-1), rather than a separate drive on each computer.

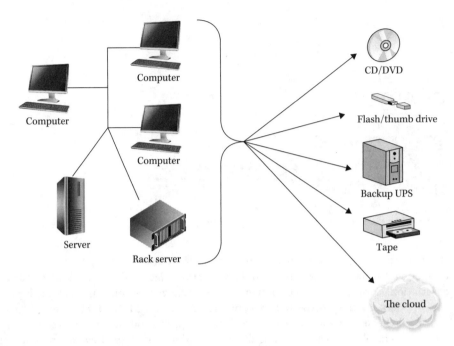

Figure 27-1   All network devices can transmit data to a variety of devices.

For this to be practical, the network administrator must be able to control the backup process for all of the computers from a central location. Without this type of automation, the administrator would have to travel to each computer to create an individual backup job. By installing the backup drive and backup software on one of the network's computers, you create a backup server that can protect all of the other computers on the network.

Automation also enables backups to occur during night or other nonworking hours, when the network is idle. Backing up remote computers naturally entails transferring large amounts of data across the network, which generates a lot of traffic that can slow down normal network operations. In addition, data files that are being used by applications are frequently locked open, meaning that no other application can gain access to them. These files are skipped during a typical backup job and are therefore not protected. Network backup software programs enable you to schedule backup jobs to occur at any time of the day or night, when the files are available for access. With appropriate hardware, the entire backup process can run completely unattended.

A network backup solution consists at the very least of a backup drive, backup media for the drive, and backup software. Depending on the amount and type of data to be backed up and the amount of time available to perform the backups, you may also need other equipment, such as multiple backup drives, an autochanger, or optional software components. Selecting appropriate hardware and software for your backup needs and learning to use them correctly are the essential elements of creating a viable network backup solution. In many cases, backup products are not cheap, but as the saying goes, you can pay now or you can pay later.

Backup Hardware

You can use virtually any type of drive that employs removable media as a backup drive. Writable CD or DVD-ROM drives are possible solutions, as are external hard drives, internal redundant array of independent (inexpensive) disks (RAID) systems, magnetic tape drives, network-attached systems (NASs), or commercial cloud backup services. However, while some of these methods are useful for single computers or small business networks, they are not as useful for large business network backups, for two main reasons: insufficient capacity and excessive media cost. One of the main objectives of a network backup solution is to avoid the need for media changes during a job so that the entire process can run unattended.

Storing backed-up data off-site is the best way to protect data. The data can be stored in the cloud, using either commercial cloud backup services or an in-house cloud location. Even if you use traditional data backup hardware, consider off-site storage for this hardware. You can house the storage devices in a different, secure location. Devices with the capability of storing information from multiple computers that has been accessed over the business network or even the Internet are the norm today. For small companies, the off-site storage can be an external hard drive housed in a bank safety-deposit box or even as basic as a designated IT person who takes the device home with them.

In addition to storage protection, you need a network backup solution to retain the history of the protected data for a given period so that it's possible to restore files that are several weeks or months old. Maintaining a backup archive like this requires a lot of storage, and the price of the medium is a major factor in the overall economy of the backup solution.

The result of this need for high media capacities and low media costs is that some combination of external hard disks, RAID systems, or magnetic tape becomes the backup medium of choice in a network environment. Magnetic tapes can hold enormous amounts of data in a small package, and the cost of the media is low. In addition, both external disks and magnetic tapes are durable and easy to store.

NOTE Many networks use data storage technologies such as RAID to increase data availability and provide fault tolerance. However, despite that these technologies can enable your network to survive a hard drive failure or similar problem, they are not a replacement for regular backups. Viruses, fires, and other catastrophes can still cause irretrievable data loss in hard drive–based storage arrays, while backups with off-site storage provide protection against these occurrences.

Backup Capacity Planning

Magnetic tape, external hard disks, and, more recently, cloud storage capabilities and network-attached storage devices are several of the methods of data backup technology, and as a result, there are many different formats and drives. In addition to the price and compatibility considerations important to every purchase, the criteria you should use to evaluate backup solutions are capacity, reliability, and media costs, plus the speed at which the drive can copy data to the medium. Together, the capacity and the transfer speed dictate whether the drive is capable of backing up your data in the time you have available. Not surprisingly, the backup drives with greater capacity and faster speeds command higher prices. Depending on your situation, you may be able to trade off some speed for increased capacity or emphasize maximum speed over capacity.

Hard Disk Drives

Hard disk drives (HDDs) have been the mainstay for many small networks, including home networks, for several years. They are available both as portable (or laptop-class) and desktop models, with the portable drives using the power from the connecting USB cable. Desktop drives often require connection to power and often come with an internal fan to prevent the overheating that can sometimes occur with the smaller, portable units.

Both types are easily attached to any device with a *Universal Serial Bus* (USB) port. Most are fairly quiet and somewhat dependable. They usually contain rotating disks, usually 2.5-inch drives in the portable units and 3.5-inch drives in the desktop models. If you are considering one of these relatively inexpensive solutions for your backup, make sure that the storage capacity is several times larger than the information you want to save or the hard drive you want to back up. Also, the speed at which the external device runs is determined by the connection speed. For example, a USB 3.0 connection will be faster than a USB 2.0 port. Consider the information in Table 27-1 when making your decision.

Solid-State Drives

With no moving parts, solid-state drives (SSDs) are more reliable, faster, and more durable. Today, most of these drives are designed to look like external HDDs; however, at this writing, they are still expensive when calculating dollars per gigabyte when compared with HDDs. HDDs work best with files that have been written with contiguous blocks, like most internal drives do today. SSDs store data on semiconductor chips instead of magnetically. The transistors (cells) are wired in series, rather than parallel as in HDDs. Solid-state drives have both advantages and disadvantages as well, as shown in Table 27-2.

Multiple Hard Drives (Multidrives)

As networks and their storage requirements grow, the third USB connection option is a RAID system with multiple disks connected to one computer. These units are usually small enclosures holding two or more hard drives that "mirror" each other. See "RAID Systems" later in this chapter for more information.

Connections

USB 2.0 (and now 3.0 and 3.1), eSATA, FireWire, and Thunderbolt are all methods by which your external drives can be connected to your computer. Each option offers various advantages and disadvantages.

Pros	Cons
Price and availability	Can be easily damaged because they are sensitive to shock
Easy to connect and use	Can back up only one device at a time
Quite transportable	Usually no built-in redundancy capabilities (see "RAID Systems" later in this chapter)
Wide variety of storage capacity	Slower than internal hard disk drives

Table 27-1   Pros and Cons of a USB-Connected HDD

Pros	Cons
No moving parts, so SSDs are more mechanically reliable	Wear out eventually because individual chips have limitations for the number of times information can be erased and overwritten
Withstand higher temperatures than HDDs	Cost per GB; while this is decreasing, the cost is still substantially more than the cost per gigabyte in HDDs
Quiet because there is no internal disk	Small capacity when compared to HDDs
Consume less power than HDDs	More expensive when compared to HDDs

Table 27-2   Pros and Cons of SDDs

USB 2.0 and 3.0   USB connections have been around since 1996, with USB 2.0 becoming the standard by 2001. USB connectors standardize connections between your computer and the many peripherals available. From keyboards to network adapters to digital cameras, the USB port has made connections quick and easy. USB has replaced the earlier serial and parallel port connections and, since it usually has its own power, has even replaced separate power appliances in some cases. Many new devices come with both USB 2.0 and USB 3.0 connections. You can determine the type of connection by the indicator on the device, as shown in Figure 27-2.

USB 2.0 and 3.0 are compatible with each other; however, the performance will default to the lower of the two connections being used.

The differences between the various connectors are shown in Table 27-3.

eSATA   *External Serial Advanced Technology Attachment* (eSATA) was often used by many because it offered faster data transfer speeds than other methods, in some cases three times that of USB 2.0 or FireWire 400. Connected directly to a SATA hard drive on a computer so that the computer's processor was dealing with only one device, the throughput transfer speed was faster than USB connections, where the processor was handling several USB devices at the same time. Connected to an internal SATA drive, eSATA connections offered SATA drive speed. With the advent of USB 3.0 devices and Thunderbolt, eSATA drives no longer have the speed advantage.

Today, in a business network environment, using eSATA can help protect your system. With the proliferation of USB devices on each workstation, the chance for accidental input of malware or the output of data is great by anyone with access to those USB ports. Some managers disable the USB ports and enable the use of external drives with eSATA.

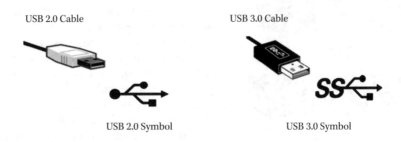

Figure 27-2   USB 2.0 and 3.0 connectors and symbols

USB 2.0	USB 3.0	USB 3.1
Advertised speed of 1.5, 12, and 480 megabits per second. However, note that field tests are often slower.	Advertised speed of up to 4.8 gigabits per second. However, note that field tests are often slower.	Advertised speed of up to 10 gigabits per second. However, note that field tests are often slower.
Standard on most electronic devices.	Adoption has been slow because many motherboards do not yet support them.	At this writing, very new.
Can deliver up to 0.5 amps of power.	Can deliver up to 0.9 amps.	Can deliver up to 5 amps.
Most USB 2.0 ports are either black or white.	In most cases, USB 3.x ports are blue.	At this writing, USB 3.x ports are blue.

Table 27-3   USB Connector Differences

For those who need to connect their computers to other media, such as TV DVRs or other media devices, the most common interface is still eSATA. eSATA makes storage for large media files efficient and quick.

To connect to an external hard drive, both that HDD and the computer must have the eSATA connector, and you must use an eSATA cable. This cable can be no longer than 2 meters (6.5 feet), so distance is an issue, and both USB and FireWire connections can be longer.

FireWire   With transfer rates of up to 400 Mbps, FireWire 400 was fast and efficient when it was introduced by Apple early in 1986 as a replacement for the parallel SCSI bus. The IEEE 1394 (FireWire) standard was originally designed for high-speed transfer, specifically for large video and audio files. FireWire can connect up to 63 devices, and it allows peer-to-peer communication without involving either the processor or the computer memory (USB requires that devices be connected to a computer in order to transfer information). FireWire is also hot-swappable (as is USB), meaning that you can remove the device without turning off the computer. FireWire 800 arrived in 2002 and was standard on Apple machines until the advent of Thunderbolt. (See "Thunderbolt" later in this chapter for more information.) FireWire 400 has either a four-pin or six-pin connection, while FireWire 800 has nine pins, as shown in Figure 27-3.

Devices equipped with six-pin FireWire can supply their own power direction from their computer connection, up to 1.5 amps at 8 to 30 volts. Devices that come with the four-pin configuration save space by omitting the two power pins. FireWire 800 with its nine-pin design offers grounding to protect the other wires. FireWire 800 is backward compatible with FireWire 400; however, transfer speed will be that of the slower FireWire 400 (see Table 27-4).

In 2007 and 2008, FireWire S1600 and S3200 were introduced to compete with USB 3.0. The development came with the same nine-pin connection as FireWire 800,

FireWire 400   FireWire 800

Figure 27-3   FireWire 400 and FireWire 800 cables and ports

FireWire 400	FireWire 800
Transfer speeds up to 400 Mbps	Transfer speeds up to 800 Mbps
Supports cable length up to 4.5 meters (about 15 feet)	Supports cable length up to 100 meters

Table 27-4   FireWire 400 and FireWire 800 Specifications

but even though the system was developed, some units were not available until 2012. Therefore, few devices other than some Sony cameras used the newer technology.

Thunderbolt   In 2011, Apple devices included a new port called Thunderbolt that had the capabilities and speed of FireWire and USB, along with external display capabilities for Video Graphics Array (VGA), High Definition Multimedia Interface (HDMI), DisplayPort, and Digital Video Interface (DVI). While not all devices had the ability to use Thunderbolt, for a time, this interface had the fastest transfer rate. Some users reported being able to transfer a 15GB HD movie in less than one minute.

While some Windows machines contain Thunderbolt connections, most devices using this technology are for the Mac. As USB 3.0 has become the standard, Thunderbolt's speedy transfer rate is often matched by the USB connection. However, for media transfers and connectivity to video devices, Thunderbolt is useful.

As USB 3.1 is being released, Thunderbolt 3 is due to be on store shelves in early 2015. This technology is tied to new Intel architecture, which is also due in early 2015.

NOTE Thunderbolt was developed by both Apple and Intel.

Wireless   While the thought of no wires can sound appealing, especially if you have a wireless (WiFi) network, backing up to a wireless external drive can be a security risk. If you use encryption on your wireless network, consider encrypting the external hard drive as well. Today, there are several types of encryption protocols to help protect both your network and your external device:

- *Wired Equivalent Privacy* (WEP) was created in the 1990s, and its name describes its main selling point, which is that it is equivalent to a wired network. As data on wireless networks is transmitted by radio waves, WEP adds some degree of security to the system by encrypting or "coding" the data being transmitted. WEP has several different levels of security, from 64-bit through 256-bit, each of which required entrance of a string of hexadecimal characters that were then translated into a secure algorithm.

- WEP has some serious security flaws, such as the following:
  - Outside devices being able to interject new data from mobile stations
  - The ability to decrypt the data from another access point
  - The ability, in some cases, to analyze the transmitted data and, after a time, decrypt it

- *Wi-Fi Protected Access* (WPA), available since 2003, was originally designed to solve some of the security issues with WEP. WPA has now been superseded by WPA2. WPA2 uses much of the same algorithms as WPA but with enhanced confidentiality.

No encryption system or mechanism is foolproof. However, running a wireless device without some system can create havoc.

Part VI

RAID Systems

The mass storage subsystems used in network servers frequently go beyond just having greater capacities and faster drives. There are also more advanced storage technologies that provide better performance, reliability, and fault tolerance. RAID is the most common of these technologies. A RAID array is a group of hard drives that function together in any one of various ways, called *levels*. There are six basic RAID levels, numbered from 0 to 5, plus several other RAID standards that are proprietary or variations on one of the other levels. The different RAID levels provide varying degrees of data protection and performance enhancement.

Originally designed for large networks to store large amounts of data at a low cost, RAID can also be a viable backup solution for smaller networks as well. Today, you may see RAID on a single computer with two hard drives connected to create more storage capacity, or with two drives, with one being used as a duplicate (clone) of the other. That way, if drive 1 fails, all the information is available on drive 2 with no interruption of service.

Using RAID

RAID can be implemented in hardware or software, in whole or in part. Third-party software products can provide other RAID levels. Generally speaking, however, the best RAID performance comes from a hardware RAID implementation.

Hardware RAID solutions can range from dedicated RAID controller cards (which you install into a server like any other PCI expansion card and connect to your hard drives) to stand-alone RAID drive arrays. A RAID controller card typically contains a coprocessor and a large memory cache. This hardware enables the controller itself to coordinate the RAID activity, unlike a software solution that utilizes the computer's own memory and processor. When you use a hardware RAID solution, the drive array appears to the computer as a single drive. All of the processing that maintains the stored data is invisible.

A RAID drive array is a unit, either separate or integrated into a server, that contains a RAID controller and slots into which you insert hard disk drives, like those shown in Figure 27-4. In some cases, the slots are merely containers for the drives, and you use standard SCSI and power cables to connect them to the RAID controller and to the computer's power supply. In higher-end arrays, the drives plug directly into a *backplane,* which connects all of the devices to the SCSI bus, supplies them with power, and eliminates the need for separate cables. In some cases, the drives are *hot-swappable*, meaning that you can replace a malfunctioning drive without powering down the whole array. Some arrays also include a hot standby drive, which is an extra drive that remains idle until one of the other drives in the array fails, at which time the standby drive immediately takes its place. Some servers are built around an array of this type, while in other cases the array is a separate unit, either standing alone or mounted in a rack. These separate drive arrays are what you use when you want to build a server cluster with shared drives.

Whether you implement RAID using software or hardware, you choose the RAID level that best suits

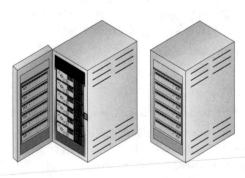

Figure 27-4   Stand-alone RAID drive arrays

your installation. Although the various RAID levels are numbered consecutively, the higher levels are not always "better" than the lower ones in every case. In some cases, for example, you are trading off speed or disk space in return for added protection, which may be warranted in one installation but not in another. The various levels of RAID are described in the following sections.

RAID 0: Disk Striping

Disk striping is a method for enhancing the performance of two or more drives by using them concurrently, rather than individually. Technically, disk striping is not RAID at all because it provides no redundancy and therefore no data protection or fault tolerance. In a striped array, the blocks of data that make up each file are written to different drives in succession. In a four-drive array like that shown in Figure 27-5, for example, the first block (A) is written to the first drive, the second block (B) is written to the second drive, and so on, through the fourth block (D). Then the fifth block (E) is written to the first drive, the sixth (F) is written to the second drive, and the pattern continues until all of the blocks have been written. Operating the drives in parallel increases the overall I/O performance of the drives during both reads and writes because while the first drive is reading or writing block A, the second drive is moving its heads into position to read or write block B. This reduces the latency period caused by the need to move the heads between each block in a single drive arrangement. To reduce the latency even further, you can use a separate controller for each drive.

As mentioned earlier, disk striping provides no additional protection to the data and indeed even adds an element of danger. If one of the drives in a RAID 0 array should fail, the entire volume is lost, and recovering the data directly from the disk platters is much more difficult, if not impossible. However, disk striping provides the greatest performance enhancement of any of the RAID levels, largely because it adds the least amount of processing overhead. RAID 0 is suitable for applications in which large amounts of data must be retrieved on a regular basis, such as video and high-resolution image editing, but you must be careful to back up your data regularly.

NOTE It's possible to stripe data across a series of hard drives either at the byte level or at the block level (one block typically equals 512 bytes). Byte-level striping is better suited to the storage of large data records because the contents of a record can be read in parallel from the stripes on different drives, thus improving the data transfer rate. Block-level striping is better suited for the storage of small data records in an environment where multiple concurrent requests are common. A single stripe is more likely to contain an entire record, which enables the various drives in the array to process individual requests independently and simultaneously.

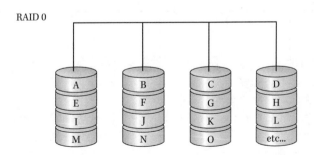

Figure 27-5   RAID level 0

RAID 1: Disk Mirroring and Duplexing

Disk mirroring and disk duplexing are the simplest arrangements that truly fit the definition of RAID. *Disk mirroring* is a technique where two identical drives are connected to the same host adapter, and all data is written to both of the drives simultaneously, as shown in Figure 27-6. This way, there is always a backup (or mirror) copy of every file immediately available. If one of the drives should fail, the other continues to operate with no interruption whatsoever. When you replace or repair the malfunctioning drive, all of the data from the mirror is copied to it, thus reestablishing the redundancy. *Disk duplexing* is an identical arrangement, except that the two drives are connected to separate controllers. This enables the array to survive a failure of one of the disks or one of the controllers.

Obviously, disk mirroring provides complete hard drive fault tolerance, and disk duplexing provides both drive and controller fault tolerance because a complete copy of every file is always available for immediate access. However, mirroring and duplexing do this with the least possible efficiency because you realize only half of the disk space that you are paying for. Two 10GB drives that are mirrored yield only a 10GB volume. As you will see, other RAID levels provide their fault tolerance with greater efficiency, as far as available disk space is concerned.

Disk mirroring and duplexing do enhance disk performance as well, but only during read operations. During write operations, the files are written to both drives simultaneously, resulting in the same speed as a single drive. When reading, however, the array can alternate between the drives, doubling the transaction rate of a single drive. In short, write operations are said to be expensive and read operations efficient. Like disk striping, mirroring and duplexing are typically implemented by software and are common features in server operating systems like Windows 2000. However, as mentioned earlier, using the system processor and memory for this purpose can degrade the performance of the server when disk I/O is heavy.

RAID 2: Hamming ECC

RAID 2 is a seldom-used arrangement where each of the disks in a drive array is dedicated to the storage either of data or of error correcting code (ECC). As the system writes files to the data disks, it also writes the ECC to drives dedicated to that purpose. When reading from the data drives, the system verifies the data as correct using the error correction information from the ECC drives. The ECC in this case is hamming code, which was the same type of ECC used on SCSI

RAID 1

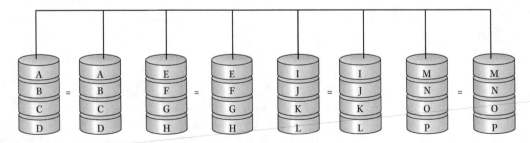

Figure 27-6   RAID level 1

hard drives that support error correction. Because all SCSI hard drives already supported ECC and because a relatively large number of ECC drives were required for the data drives, RAID 2 is an inefficient method that has almost never been implemented commercially.

RAID 3: Parallel Transfer with Shared Parity

A RAID 3 array is a combination of data striping and the storage of a type of ECC called *parity* on a separate drive. RAID 3 requires a minimum of three drives, with two or more of the drives holding data striped at the byte level and one drive dedicated to parity information. The use of striping on the data drives enhances I/O performance, just as in RAID 0, and using one drive in the array for parity information adds fault tolerance. Whenever the array performs a read operation, it uses the information on the parity drive to verify the data stored on the striped drives. Because only one of the drives holds the parity information, you realize a greater amount of usable disk space from your array than you do with RAID 2. If one of the striped drives should fail, the data it contains can be reconstructed using the parity information. However, this reconstruction takes longer than that of RAID 1 (which is immediate) and can degrade performance of the array while it is occurring.

When you hit RAID 3 and the levels above it, the resources required by the technology make them much more difficult to implement in software only. Most servers that use RAID 3 or higher use a hardware product.

RAID 4: Independent Data Disks with Shared Parity

RAID 4 is similar to RAID 3, except that the drives are striped at the block level, rather than at the byte level. There is still a single drive devoted to parity information, which enables the array to recover the data from a failed drive if needed. The performance of RAID 4 in comparison to RAID 3 is comparable during read operations, but write performance suffers because of the need to continually update the information on the parity drive. RAID 4 is also rarely used because it offers few advantages over RAID 5.

RAID 5: Independent Data Disks with Distributed Parity

RAID 5 is the same as RAID 4, except that the parity information is distributed among all of the drives in the array, instead of being stored on a drive dedicated to that purpose. Because of this arrangement, there is no parity drive to function as a bottleneck during write operations, and RAID 5 provides significantly better write performance than RAID 4, along with the same degree of fault tolerance. The rebuild process in the event of a drive failure is also made more efficient by the distributed parity information. Read performance suffers slightly in RAID 5, however, because the drive heads must skip over the parity information stored on all of the drives.

RAID 5 is the level that is usually implied when someone refers to a RAID array because it provides a good combination of performance and protection. In a four-disk array, only 25 percent of the disk space is devoted to parity information, as opposed to 50 percent in a RAID 1 array.

RAID 6: Independent Data Disks with Two-Dimensional Parity

RAID 6 is a variation on RAID 5 that provides additional fault tolerance by maintaining two independent copies of the parity information, both of which are distributed among the drives in the array. The two-dimensional parity scheme greatly increases the controller overhead since the parity calculations are doubled, and the array's write performance is also degraded because of the need to save twice as much parity information. However, a RAID 6 array can sustain multiple simultaneous drive failures without data loss and is an excellent solution for read-intensive environments working with mission-critical data.

RAID 7: Asynchronous RAID

RAID 7 is a proprietary solution marketed by Storage Computer Corporation, which consists of a striped data array and a dedicated parity drive. The difference in RAID 7 is that the storage array includes its own embedded operating system, which coordinates the asynchronous communications with each of the drives. Asynchronous communication, in this context, means that each drive in the array has its own dedicated high-speed bus and its own control and data I/O paths, as well as a separate cache. The result is increased write performance over other RAID levels and very high cache hit rates under certain conditions. The disadvantages of RAID 7 are its high cost and the danger resulting from any investment in a proprietary technology.

RAID 10: Striping of Mirrored Disks

RAID 10 is a combination of the disk striping used in RAID 0 and the disk mirroring used in RAID 1. The drives in the array are arranged in mirrored pairs, and data is striped across them, as shown in Figure 27-7. The mirroring provides complete data redundancy while the striping provides enhanced performance. The disadvantage of RAID 10 is the high cost (at least four drives are required) and the same low data storage efficiency as RAID 1.

RAID 0+1: Mirroring of Striped Disks

RAID 0+1 is the opposite of RAID 10. Instead of striping data across mirrored pairs of disks, RAID 0+1 takes an array of striped disks and mirrors it. The resulting performance is similar to that of RAID 10, but a single drive failure turns the array back to a simple RAID 0 installation.

Network-Attached Storage

Network-attached storage is a term that is generally applied to a stand-alone storage subsystem that connects to a network and contains everything needed for clients and servers to access the data stored there. An NAS device, sometimes called a *network storage appliance,* is not just a box with a power supply and an I/O bus with hard drives installed in it. The unit also has a self-contained file system and a stripped-down, proprietary operating system that is optimized for the task of serving files. The NAS appliance is essentially a stand-alone file server that can be accessed by any computer on the network. NAS appliances can reduce costs and simplify the deployment and ongoing management processes. Because the appliance is a complete turnkey solution, there is no need to integrate separate hardware and operating system products or be concerned about compatibility issues.

NAS appliances can connect to networks in different ways, and it is here that the definition of the technology becomes confusing. An NAS server is a device that can respond to file access requests generated by any other computer on the network, including clients and servers.

There are two distinct methods for deploying an NAS server, however. You can connect the appliance directly to the LAN, using a standard Ethernet connection, enabling clients and servers alike to access its file system directly, or

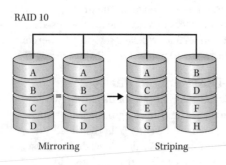

RAID 10

Mirroring   Striping

Figure 27-7   RAID level 10

you can build a dedicated storage network, using Ethernet or Fibre Channel, enabling your servers to access the NAS and share files with network clients.

The latter solution places an additional burden on the servers, but it also moves the I/O traffic from the LAN to a dedicated storage network, thus reducing network traffic congestion. Which option you choose largely depends on the type of data to be stored on the NAS server. If you use the NAS to store users' own work files, for example, it can be advantageous to connect the device to the LAN and let users access their files directly. However, if the NAS server contains databases or e-mail stores, a separate application server is required to process the data and supply it to clients. In this case, you may benefit more by creating a dedicated storage network that enables the application server to access the NAS server without flooding the client network with I/O traffic.

Magnetic Tape Drives

Unlike other mass storage devices used in computers, magnetic tape drives do not provide random access to the stored data. Hard disks and optical drives all have heads that move back and forth across a spinning medium, enabling them to place the head at any location on the disk almost instantaneously and read the data stored there. The magnetic tape drives used in computers work just like audio tape drives; the tape is pulled off of a spool and dragged across a head to read the data, as shown in Figure 27-8. This is called *linear access.* To read the data at a point near the end of a tape, the drive must unspool all of the preceding tape before accessing the desired information. Because they are linear access devices, magnetic tape drives are not mounted as volumes in the computer's file system. You can't assign a drive letter to a tape and access its files through a directory display, as you can with a CD-ROM or a floppy disk. Magnetic tape drives are used exclusively by backup software programs, which are specifically designed to access them.

Linear access devices like tape drives also cannot conveniently use a table containing information about the files they contain, as with a hard or floppy disk. When a backup system writes hard drive files to tape, it reads the information about each file from the hard drive's file allocation table (or whatever equivalent that particular drive's file system uses) and writes it to tape as a header before copying the file itself. The file is frequently followed by an error correction code that ensures the validity of the file. This way, all of the information associated with each file is found at one location on the tape. However, some tape drive technologies, such as digital audio tape (DAT) and digital linear tape (DLT), do create an index on each tape of all the files it contains, which facilitates the rapid restoration of individual files.

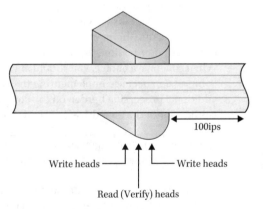

Figure 27-8   Linear access drives leave the tape in the cartridge and press it against static heads.

100ips

Write heads ———   ——— Write heads

Read (Verify) heads

Tape Drive Interfaces

To evaluate backup technologies, it's a good idea to first estimate the amount of data you have to protect and the amount of time you will have for the backup jobs to run. The object is to select a drive (or drives) that can fit all of the data you need to protect during the average backup job on a single device in the time available. Be sure to consider that it may not be necessary for you to back up all of the data on all of your computers during every backup job. Most of the files that make up a computer's operating system and applications do not change, so it isn't necessary to back them up every day. You can back these up once a week or even more seldom and still provide your computers with sufficient protection. The important files that you should back up every day are the data and system configuration files that change frequently, all of which might add up to far less data.

In addition to the capabilities of the drive, you must consider the interface that connects it to the computer that will host it. When using a tape drive, the process of writing data to a magnetic tape requires that the tape drive receive a consistent stream of data from the computer. Interruptions in the data stream force the tape drive to stop and start repeatedly, which wastes both time and tape capacity.

Magnetic Tape Capacities

The storage capacity of a magnetic tape is one of its most defining characteristics and can also be one of the most puzzling aspects of the backup process. Many users purchase tape drives with rated capacities and then are disappointed to find that the product does not store as much data on a tape as the manufacturer states. In most cases, this is not a matter of false claims on the part of the drive's maker.

There are three elements that can affect the data capacity of a magnetic tape, which are as follows:

- Compression
- Data stream
- Write errors

Compression

Magnetic tape storage capacities are often supplied by manufacturers in terms of compressed data. A reputable manufacturer will always state in its literature whether the capacities it cites are compressed or uncompressed. Most of the tape drives designed for computer backups include hardware-based compression capabilities that use standard data compression algorithms to store the maximum amount of data on a tape. In cases where the drive does not support hardware compression, the backup software might implement its own compression algorithms. When you have a choice, you should always use hardware-based compression over software compression because implementing the data compression process in the software places an additional processing burden on the computer. Hardware-based compression is performed by a processor in the tape drive itself and is inherently more efficient.

NOTE Some manufacturers express tape drive capacities using the term native. A drive's native capacity refers to its capacity without compression.

The degree to which data can be compressed, and therefore the capacity of a tape, depends on the format of the files being backed up. A file in a format that is already compressed, such as a GIF image or a ZIP archive, cannot be compressed any further by the tape drive hardware or the backup software and therefore has a compression ratio of 1:1. Other file types compress at different ratios, ranging from 2:1, which is typical for program files such as EXEs and DLLs, to 8:1 or greater, as with uncompressed image formats like BMP. It is standard practice for manufacturers to express the compressed storage capacity of a tape using a 2:1 compression ratio. However, your actual results might vary greatly, depending on the nature of your data.

Data Stream

To write data to the tape in the most efficient manner, the tape drive must receive the data from the computer in a consistent stream at an appropriate rate of speed. The rate at which the data arrives at the tape drive can be affected by many factors, including the interface used to connect the drive to the computer, the speed of the computer's processor and system bus, or the speed of the hard drive on which the data is stored. When you are backing up data from the network, you add the speed of the network itself into the equation. Even if you have a high-quality tape drive installed in a state-of-the-art server, slow network conditions caused by excessive traffic or faulty hardware can still affect the speed of the data stream reaching the tape drive. This is one of the reasons why network backups are often performed at night or during other periods when the network is not being used by other processes.

Tape drives write data to the tape in units called *frames* or sometimes *blocks,* which can vary in size depending on the drive technology and the manufacturer. The frame is the smallest unit of data that the drive can write to the tape at one time. The drive contains a buffer equal in size to the frames it uses, in which it stores the data to be backed up as it arrives from the computer. When the backup system is functioning properly, the data arrives at the tape drive, fills up the buffer, and then is written to the tape with no delay. This enables the tape drive to run continuously, drawing the tape across the heads, writing the buffered data to the tape, and then emptying the buffer for the next incoming frame's worth of data. This is called *streaming.*

NOTE The frames used by tape drives do correspond in size or construction with the data link layer protocol frames used in data networking.

When the data arrives at the tape drive too slowly, the drive has to stop the tape while it waits for the buffer to fill up with data. This process of constantly stopping and starting the tape is called *shoe-shining,* and it is one of the main signals that the drive is not running properly. The buffer has a built-in data retention timeout, after which the drive flushes the buffer and writes its contents to tape, whether it's full of data or not. If the buffer is not full when the timeout period expires, the drive pads out the frame with nonsense data to fill it up and then writes the contents of the buffer (including the padding) to the tape. The end result is that each frame written to the tape contains only a fraction of the actual data that it can hold, thus reducing the amount of usable data stored on the tape.

The way to avoid having partially filled buffers flushed to tape is to ensure that there are no bottlenecks in the path from the sources of your data to the tape drive. The path is only as fast as its slowest component, and to speed up the data transfer rate, you may have to do any of the following:

- Replace hard drives with faster models
- Install the tape drive in a faster computer
- Reduce the processing load on the computer hosting the tape drive
- Schedule backup jobs to occur during periods of low network traffic

Write Errors

Another possible reason for diminished tape capacity is an excess of recoverable write errors. A write error is considered to be recoverable when the tape drive detects a bad frame on the tape while the data is still in the buffer, making it possible for the drive to immediately write the same frame to the tape again. Drives typically detect these errors by positioning a read head right next to the write head so that the drive can read each frame immediately after writing it.

When the drive rewrites a frame, it does not overwrite the bad frame by rewinding the tape; it simply writes the same frame to the tape again, immediately following the first one. This means that one frame's worth of data is occupying two frames' worth of tape, and if there are many errors of this type, a significant amount of the tape's storage capacity can be wasted. Recoverable write errors are most often caused by dirty heads in the tape drive or bad media. Most backup software products can keep track of and display the number of recoverable write errors that occur during a particular backup job. The first thing you should do when you notice that more than a handful of recoverable write errors have occurred during a backup job is to clean the drive heads using a proper cleaning tape and then run a test job using a new, good-quality tape. If the errors continue, this might be an indication of a more serious hardware problem.

NOTE Dirty drive heads are the single most common cause of tape drive problems. The importance of regular head cleaning cannot be overemphasized.

Backup Software

For home and small business networks, there are many software products available, including the ability to back up to a server at a remote location, such as the cloud. If you decide that you must purchase a network backup software package, it's a good idea to familiarize yourself with the capabilities of the various products on the market and then compare them with your needs. In some cases, you can obtain evaluation versions of backup software products and test them on your network. This can help you identify potential problems you may encounter while backing up your network. The following sections examine some of the basic functions of a backup software package and how they apply to a typical network backup situation.

NOTE While available in earlier versions, Windows 8.1 does not contain a Backup and Restore utility.

Selecting Backup Targets

The simplest type of backup job is a full backup, in which you back up the entire contents of a computer's drives. However, full backups usually aren't necessary on a daily basis because many of the files stored on a computer do not change and because full backups can take a lot of time and use a lot of storage capacity. One of the best strategies when planning a backup solution for a network is to purchase a drive that can save all of your data files and the important system configuration files on a single media. This enables you to purchase a less expensive drive and still provide your network with complete protection.

Being selective about what you want to back up complicates the process of creating a backup job, and a good backup software program provides several different ways to select the computers, drives, directories, or files (collectively called *targets*) that you want to back up. Selecting a drive or directory for backup includes all of the files and subdirectories it contains as well. You can then deselect certain files or subdirectories that you want to exclude from the backup. Some backup software programs can also list the targets for a backup job in text form. When you're creating a large, complex job involving many computers, this format can sometimes be easier to comprehend and modify.

Using Filters

The expandable display is good for selecting backup targets based on the directory structure, but it isn't practical for other types of target selection. Many applications and operating systems create temporary files as they're running, and these files are frequently named using a specific pattern, such as a TMP extension. In most cases, you can safely exclude these files from a backup because they would only be automatically deleted at a later time anyway. However, manually deselecting all of the files with a TMP extension in a directory display would be very time consuming, and you also have no assurance that there might not be other TMP files on your drives when the backup job actually runs.

To select (or deselect) files based on characteristics such as extension, filename, date, size, and attributes, most backup software programs include filters. A filter is a mechanism that is applied to all or part of a backup target that instructs the software to include or exclude files with certain characteristics. For example, to exclude all files with a TMP extension from a backup job, you would apply an exclude filter to the drives that specified the file mask *.tmp*.

You can use filters in many ways to limit the scope of a backup job, such as the following:

- Create an include filter specifying a modification date to back up all the files that have changed since a particular day

- Create exclude filters based on file extensions to avoid backing up program files, such as EXEs and DLLs

- Create a filter based on access dates to exclude all files from a backup that haven't been accessed in the last 30 days

Incremental and Differential Backups

The most common type of filter used in backups is one that is based on the Archive attribute. This is the filter that backup software products use to perform incremental and differential backups. File attributes are single bits included with every file on a disk drive that are dedicated to particular functions. Different file systems have various attributes, but the most common ones found in almost all file systems are Read-only, Hidden, and Archive. The Read-only and Hidden attributes affect how specific files are manipulated and displayed by file management applications. Under normal conditions, a file with the Hidden attribute activated is invisible to the user, and a Read-only file can't be modified. The Archive attribute has no effect in a normal file management application, but backup programs use it to determine whether files should be backed up.

A typical backup strategy for a network consists of a full backup job that is repeated every week with daily incremental or differential jobs in between. When you configure a backup software program to perform a full backup of a drive, the software typically resets the Archive attribute on each file, meaning that it changes the value of all the Archive bits to 0. After the full backup, whenever an application or process modifies a file on the drive, the file system automatically changes its Archive bit to a value of 1. It is then possible to create a backup job that uses an attribute filter to copy to tape only the files with Archive bit values of 1, which are the files that have changed since the last full backup. The result is a backup job that uses far less tape and takes far less time than a full backup.

An *incremental backup* job is one that copies only the files that have been modified since the last backup and then resets the Archive bits of the backed-up files to 0. This means that each incremental job you perform copies only the files that have changed since the last job. If you perform your full backups on Sunday, Monday's incremental job consists of the files that have changed since Sunday's full backup. Tuesday's incremental job consists of the files that have changed since Monday's incremental, Wednesday's job consists of the files changed since Tuesday, and so forth. Files that are modified frequently might be included in each of the incremental jobs, while occasionally modified files might be backed up only once or twice a week.

The advantage of performing incremental jobs is that you use the absolute minimum amount of time and storage capacity because you never back up any files that haven't changed. The drawback of using incremental jobs is that in order to perform a complete restoration of a drive or directory, you have to restore the copy from the last full backup and then repeat the same restore job from each of the incrementals performed since that full backup, in order. This is because each of the incremental jobs may contain files that don't exist on the other incrementals and because they might contain newer versions of files on the previous incrementals. By the time you complete the restore process, you have restored all of the unique files on all of the incrementals and overwritten all of the older versions of the files with the latest ones.

If you have a lot of data to back up and want the most economical solution, performing incremental jobs is the way to go. The restore process is more complex, but performing a full restore of a drive is (ideally) a relatively rare occurrence. When you have to restore a single file, you just have to make sure that you restore the most recent copy from the appropriate full or incremental backup tape.

A *differential backup* job differs from an incremental only in that it does not reset the Archive bits of the files it backs up. This means that each differential job backs up all of the files that have changed since the last full backup. If a file is modified on Monday, the differential jobs back it up on Monday, Tuesday, Wednesday, and so on. The advantage of using differential jobs is that to perform a complete restore, you have to restore only from the last full backup and the most recent differential because each differential has all of the files that have changed since the last full backup. The disadvantage of differentials is that they require more time and tape because each job includes all of the files from the previous differential jobs. If your tape drive has sufficient capacity to store all of your modified data for a full week on a single tape, differentials are preferable to incrementals because they simplify the restoration process.

In most cases, the incremental and differential backup options are built into the software, so you don't have to use filters to manipulate the Archive attributes. The software typically provides a means of selecting from among basic backup types like the following:

- **Normal**   Performs a full backup of all selected files and resets their Archive bits
- **Copy**   Performs a full backup of all selected files and does not reset their Archive bits

- **Incremental**   Performs a backup only of the selected files that have changed and does not reset their Archive bits

- **Differential**   Performs a backup only of the selected files that have changed and resets their Archive bits

- **Daily**   Performs a backup only of the selected files that have changed today

- **Working Set**   Performs a backup only of the selected files that have been accessed in a specified number of days

NOTE Different backup software products may not provide all of these options or may provide additional options. They may also refer to these options using different names.

Backing Up Open Files

The single biggest problem you are likely to encounter while performing backups in a network environment is that of open files. When a file is being used by an application, in most cases it is locked open, meaning that another application cannot open it at the same time. When a backup program with no special open file capabilities encounters a file that is locked, it simply skips it and proceeds to the next file. The activity log kept by the backup software typically lists the files that have been skipped and may declare a backup job as having failed when files are skipped (even when the vast majority of files were backed up successfully). Obviously, skipped files are not protected against damage or loss.

Open files are one of the main reasons for performing backups during times when the network is not in use. Even during off-hours, files can be left open for a variety of reasons. For example, users may leave their computers at the end of the day with files loaded into an application. The agents included with most network backup products are capable of backing up files left open in this way. This is one of the big advantages of using an agent, rather than simply accessing files through the network.

The most critical type of open file situation involves applications and data files that are left running continuously, such as database and e-mail servers. These applications often must run around the clock, and since their data files are constantly being accessed by the application, they are always locked open. A normal backup product can back up most of an application's program files in a case like this, but the most important files, containing the databases themselves or the e-mail stores, are skipped. This is a major omission that must be addressed in order to fully protect a network.

In most cases, network backup products are capable of backing up live databases and e-mail stores, but you must purchase extra software components to do so. Network backup software products usually have optional modules for each of the major database and e-mail products, which are sold separately. The optional component may consist of an upgrade to the main backup application, a program that runs on the database or e-mail server, or both. These options generally work by creating a temporary database file or e-mail store (sometimes called a *delta file*) that can process transactions with clients and other servers while the original data files in the server are being backed up. Once the backup is complete, the transactions stored in the delta file are applied to the original database and normal processing continues.

NOTE Many cloud backup strategies back up open files on the fly when a change is made to it.

Recovering from a Disaster

Another add-on module available from many backup software manufacturers is a disaster recovery option. In this context, a disaster is defined as a catastrophic loss of data that renders a computer inoperable, such as a failure of the hard drive containing the operating system files in a server. This type of data loss can also result from a virus infection, theft, fire, or natural disaster, such as a storm or earthquake. Assuming you have been diligently performing your regular backups and storing copies off-site, your data should be safe if a disaster occurs. However, restoring the data to a new drive or a replacement server normally means that you must first reinstall the operating system and the backup software, which can be a lengthy process. A disaster recovery option is a means of expediting the restoration process in this type of scenario.

A disaster recovery option usually works by creating some form of boot medium that provides only the essential components needed to perform a restore job from a backup. In the event of a disaster, a network administrator only has to repair or replace any computer hardware that was lost or damaged, insert a CD/DVD, and boot the computer. The disaster recovery disk supplies the files needed to bring the computer to a basic operational state from which you can perform a restore, using your most recent backup.

Job Scheduling

Another important part of a network backup software product is its ability to schedule jobs to occur at particular times. Some rudimentary backup software products (such as those that come free with an external hard drive) can only execute a backup job immediately. An effective network backup solution requires that you create a series of jobs that execute at regular intervals, preferably when the network is not otherwise in use. A good backup software product can be configured to execute jobs at any time of the day or night and repeat them at specified intervals, such as daily, weekly, and monthly. More complicated scheduling options are also useful, such as the ability to execute a job on the last day of the month, the first Friday of the month, or every three weeks.

The types of jobs you create and how often you run them should depend on the amount of data you have to back up, the amount of time you have to perform the backups, the capabilities of your hardware, and the importance of your data. For example, a typical network backup scenario would call for a full backup performed once a week, and incremental or differential jobs performed on the other days, with all of the jobs running during the night.

Rotating Media

Network backup software products typically enable you to create your own backup strategy by creating and scheduling each job separately, but most also have preconfigured job scenarios that are suitable for most network configurations. These scenarios usually include a media rotation scheme, which is another part of an effective network backup strategy. A media rotation scheme is an organized pattern of device labeling and allocation that enables you to fully protect your network using the minimum possible number of devices. You can conceivably use a new drive for every backup job you run, but this can get very expensive. When you reuse drives instead, you must be careful not to overwrite a drive you may still need in the event of a disaster.

The most common media rotation scheme implemented by backup software products is called Grandfather-Father-Son. These three generations refer to monthly, weekly, and daily backup jobs, respectively. The "Son" jobs run each day and are typically incrementals or differentials. The scheme calls for several drives (depending on how many days per week you perform backups), which are reused each week. For example, you would have a drive designated for the Wednesday incremental job, which you overwrite every Wednesday. The "Father" jobs are the weekly full backups, which are overwritten each month. There will be four or five weekly jobs each month (depending on the day you perform the jobs). The drives you use for the first full backup of the month, for example, will be overwritten during the first full backup of the next month. The "Grandfather" jobs are monthly full backups, the media for which are reused once every year.

TIP The monthly drives in the media rotation are often designated for off-site storage, which is an essential part of a good backup strategy. Diligently making backups will do you and your company no good if the building burns down, taking all of your backup drives with it. Periodic full backups should be stored at a secured site, such as a fireproof vault or a bank safe deposit box. Some administrators simply bring the tapes home on a regular basis, which can be equally effective.

Backup Administration

When creating an automated network backup solution, proper planning and purchasing are the most important factors. Once the system is in place, there should be little user interaction required, except for making sure that the proper drive is connected each day. It's also important for the administrator to make sure that the backup jobs are executing as designed.

Event Logging

Network backup software products nearly always have an indicator that specifies whether each backup job has completed successfully or has failed. However, simply checking this indicator does not necessarily give an adequate picture of the job's status. The criteria used to evaluate a job's success or failure can vary from product to product. A job failure can be an indication of a major problem, such as a hardware failure that has prevented any data from being written to the external drive. With some products, a single file that is skipped because it is locked open can cause a job to be listed as having failed, even though all of the other files have been successfully written.

To check the status of the job in greater detail, you examine the event logs maintained by the software. Backup logs can contain a varying amount of detail, and many software products let you specify what information you want to be kept in the log. A full or complete log contains an exhaustive account of the backup job, including a list of all of the files copied. This type of log contains everything you could ever want to know about a backup job, including which targets were backed up and which were skipped, as well as any errors that may have occurred. The complete file listing causes a log like this to be enormous in most cases, and the average administrator is less likely to check the logs regularly when it's necessary to scroll through hundreds of pages of filenames to do so.

Maintaining a full log might be a good idea as you are learning the intricacies of your backup software, but after the first few jobs, you'll probably want to reconfigure the software to keep a summary log containing only the details that you need to examine on a regular basis, such as whether target computers were backed up or not, the names of files that were skipped, and error messages. Administrators should examine the logs frequently to make sure that the backup jobs are running as planned.

Performing Restores

Logs and success indicators are usually reliable methods of confirming that your backups are completing successfully, but they are no substitute for performing a regular series of test restores. The whole reason for running backups in the first place is so you can restore data when necessary. If you can't do this, then all of the time and money you've spent is wasted. It's entirely possible for a job to be listed as having completed successfully and for the logs to indicate that all of the targets have been backed up, only to find that it's impossible to restore any data. The reasons for this are many, but there are many horror stories told by network administrators about people who have diligently performed backups for months or years and have carefully labeled and stored the backups only to find that when they suffer a disaster, everything is blank. Performing test restores on a regular basis can prevent this sort of catastrophe.

Backup software products have a restore function that usually looks a lot like the interface you use to create backup jobs. You can browse through a directory structure to locate the files that you want to restore. When you browse in this way, you are looking at an index of all of the stored files. Without the index, the software has no way of knowing what files are where. All backup software products create an index for each backup job they complete, but where they store the index can vary.

Index

Symbols